T0213015

Lecture Notes in Computer Science   10516

Commenced Publication in 1973
Founding and Former Series Editors:
Gerhard Goos, Juris Hartmanis, and Jan van Leeuwen

More information about this series at http://www.springer.com/series/7409

Regina Bernhaupt · Girish Dalvi
Anirudha Joshi · Devanuj K. Balkrishan
Jacki O'Neill · Marco Winckler (Eds.)

Human-Computer Interaction – INTERACT 2017

16th IFIP TC 13 International Conference
Mumbai, India, September 25–29, 2017
Proceedings, Part IV

 Springer

Editors

Regina Bernhaupt
Ruwido Austria GmbH
Neumarkt am Wallersee
Austria

Girish Dalvi
Indian Institute of Technology Bombay
Mumbai
India

Anirudha Joshi
Indian Institute of Technology Bombay
Mumbai
India

Devanuj K. Balkrishan
Indian Institute of Technology Bombay
Mumbai
India

Jacki O'Neill
Microsoft Research Centre India
Bangalore
India

Marco Winckler (ID)
Université Paul Sabatier
Toulouse
France

ISSN 0302-9743   ISSN 1611-3349 (electronic)
Lecture Notes in Computer Science
ISBN 978-3-319-68058-3   ISBN 978-3-319-68059-0 (eBook)
DOI 10.1007/978-3-319-68059-0

Library of Congress Control Number: 2017954905

LNCS Sublibrary: SL3 – Information Systems and Applications, incl. Internet/Web, and HCI

Printed on acid-free paper

This Springer imprint is published by Springer Nature
The registered company is Springer International Publishing AG
The registered company address is: Gewerbestrasse 11, 6330 Cham, Switzerland

Foreword

The 16th IFIP TC13 International Conference on Human–Computer Interaction, INTERACT 2017, took place during September 25–29, 2017, in Mumbai, India. This conference was held on the beautiful campus of the Indian Institute of Technology, Bombay (IIT Bombay) and the Industrial Design Centre (IDC) was the principal host. The conference was co-sponsored by the HCI Professionals Association of India and the Computer Society of India, in cooperation with ACM and ACM SIGCHI. The financial responsibility of INTERACT 2017 was taken up by the HCI Professionals Association of India.

The International Federation for Information Processing (IFIP) was created in 1960 under the auspices of UNESCO. The Technical Committee 13 (TC13) of the IFIP aims at developing the science and technology of human–computer interaction (HCI). TC13 has representatives from 36 countries, apart from 16 expert members and observers. TC13 started the series of INTERACT conferences in 1984. These conferences have been an important showcase for researchers and practitioners in the field of HCI. Situated under the open, inclusive umbrella of the IFIP, INTERACT has been truly international in its spirit and has attracted researchers from several countries and cultures. The venues of the INTERACT conferences over the years bear a testimony to this inclusiveness.

In 2017, the venue was Mumbai. Located in western India, the city of Mumbai is the capital of the state of Maharashtra. It is the financial, entertainment, and commercial capital of the country and is the most populous city in India. *Mumbaikars* might add that it is also the most hardworking.

The theme of INTERACT 2017 was "Global Thoughts, Local Designs." The theme was designed to let HCI researchers respond to challenges emerging in the new age of global connectivity where they often design products for users who are beyond their borders belonging to distinctly different cultures. As organizers of the conference, we focused our attention on four areas: *India, developing countries, students,* and *research.*

As the first INTERACT in the subcontinent, the conference offered a distinctly Indian experience to its participants. The span of known history of India covers more than 5,000 years. Today, India is the world's largest democracy and a land of diversity. Modern technology co-exists with ancient traditions within the same city, often within the same family. Indians speak 22 official languages and hundreds of dialects. India is also a hub of the information technology industry and a living laboratory of experiments with technology for developing countries.

INTERACT 2017 made a conscious effort to lower barriers that prevent people from developing countries from participating in conferences. Thinkers and optimists believe that all regions of the world can achieve human development goals. Information and communication technologies (ICTs) can support this process and empower people to achieve their full potential. Today ICT products have many new users and many new uses, but also present new challenges and provide new opportunities. It is no surprise that HCI researchers are showing great interest in these emergent users. INTERACT 2017 provided a platform to explore these challenges and opportunities but also made it easier for people from developing countries to participate. We also introduced a new track called Field Trips, which allowed participants to directly engage with stake-holders within the context of a developing country.

Students represent the future of our community. They bring in new energy, enthusiasm, and fresh ideas. But it is often hard for students to participate in interna-tional conferences. INTERACT 2017 made special efforts to bring students to the conference. The conference had low registration costs and several volunteering opportunities. Thanks to our sponsors, we could provide several travel grants. Most importantly, INTERACT 2017 had special tracks such as Installations, a Student Design Consortium, and a Student Research Consortium that gave students the opportunity to showcase their work.

Finally, great research is the heart of a good conference. Like its predecessors, INTERACT 2017 aimed to bring together high-quality research. As a multidisciplinary field, HCI requires interaction and discussion among diverse people with different interest and background. The beginners and the experienced, theoreticians and prac-titioners, and people from diverse disciplines and different countries gathered together in Mumbai to learn from each other and to contribute to each other's growth. We thank all the authors who chose INTERACT 2017 as the venue to publish their research.

We received a total of 571 submissions distributed in two peer-reviewed tracks, five curated tracks, and seven juried tracks. Of these, the following contributions were accepted:

- 68 Full Papers (peer reviewed)
- 51 Short Papers (peer reviewed)
- 13 Case Studies (curated)
- 20 Industry Presentations (curated)
- 7 Courses (curated)
- 5 Demonstrations (curated)
- 3 Panels (curated)
- 9 Workshops (juried)
- 7 Field Trips (juried)
- 11 Interactive Posters (juried)
- 9 Installations (juried)
- 6 Doctoral Consortium (juried)
- 15 Student Research Consortium (juried)
- 6 Student Design Consortium (juried)

The acceptance rate for contributions received in the peer-reviewed tracks was 30.7% for full papers and 29.1% for short papers. In addition to full papers and short papers, the present proceedings feature contributions accepted in the form of case studies, courses, demonstrations, interactive posters, field trips, and workshops.

The final decision on acceptance or rejection of full papers was taken in a Program Committee meeting held in Paris, France, in March 2017. The full-paper chairs, the associate chairs, and the TC13 members participated in this meeting. The meeting discussed a consistent set of criteria to deal with inevitable differences among the large number of reviewers. The final decisions on other tracks were made by the corresponding track chairs and reviewers, often after additional electronic meetings and discussions.

INTERACT 2017 was made possible by the persistent efforts over several months by 49 chairs, 39 associate chairs, 55 student volunteers, and 499 reviewers. We thank them all. Finally, we wish to express a special thank you to the proceedings publication co-chairs, Marco Winckler and Devanuj Balkrishan, who did extraordinary work to put together four volumes of the main proceedings and one volume of adjunct proceedings.

September 2017

Anirudha Joshi
Girish Dalvi
Marco Winckler

IFIP TC13 (http://ifip-tc13.org/)

Established in 1989, the International Federation for Information Processing Technical Committee on Human–Computer Interaction (IFIP TC 13) is an international committee of 37 member national societies and 10 Working Groups, representing specialists of the various disciplines contributing to the field of human–computer interaction (HCI). This includes (among others) human factors, ergonomics, cognitive science, computer science, and design. INTERACT is its flagship conference of IFIP TC 13, staged biennially in different countries in the world. The first INTERACT conference was held in 1984 running triennially and became a biennial event in 1993.

IFIP TC 13 aims to develop the science, technology, and societal aspects of HCI by: encouraging empirical research; promoting the use of knowledge and methods from the human sciences in design and evaluation of computer systems; promoting better understanding of the relation between formal design methods and system usability and acceptability; developing guidelines, models, and methods by which designers may provide better human-oriented computer systems; and, cooperating with other groups, inside and outside IFIP, to promote user-orientation and humanization in system design. Thus, TC 13 seeks to improve interactions between people and computers, to encourage the growth of HCI research and its practice in industry and to disseminate these benefits worldwide.

The main focus is to place the users at the center of the development process. Areas of study include: the problems people face when interacting with computers; the impact of technology deployment on people in individual and organizational contexts; the determinants of utility, usability, acceptability, and user experience; the appropriate allocation of tasks between computers and users especially in the case of automation; modeling the user, their tasks, and the interactive system to aid better system design; and harmonizing the computer to user characteristics and needs.

While the scope is thus set wide, with a tendency toward general principles rather than particular systems, it is recognized that progress will only be achieved through both general studies to advance theoretical understanding and specific studies on practical issues (e.g., interface design standards, software system resilience, documentation, training material, appropriateness of alternative interaction technologies, guidelines, the problems of integrating multimedia systems to match system needs, and organizational practices, etc.).

In 2015, TC 13 approved the creation of a Steering Committee (SC) for the INTERACT conference. The SC is now in place, chaired by Jan Gulliksen and is responsible for:

- Promoting and maintaining the INTERACT conference as the premiere venue for researchers and practitioners interested in the topics of the conference (this requires a refinement of the aforementioned topics)
- Ensuring the highest quality for the contents of the event

- Setting up the bidding process to handle the future INTERACT conferences; decision is made up at TC 13 level
- Providing advice to the current and future chairs and organizers of the INTERACT conference
- Providing data, tools and documents about previous conferences to the future conference organizers
- Selecting the reviewing system to be used throughout the conference (as this impacts the entire set of reviewers)
- Resolving general issues involved with the INTERACT conference
- Capitalizing history (good and bad practices)

In 1999, TC 13 initiated a special IFIP Award, the Brian Shackel Award, for the most outstanding contribution in the form of a refereed paper submitted to and delivered at each INTERACT. The award draws attention to the need for a comprehensive human-centered approach in the design and use of information technology in which the human and social implications have been taken into account. In 2007, IFIP TC 13 also launched an Accessibility Award to recognize an outstanding contribution in HCI with international impact dedicated to the field of accessibility for disabled users. In 2013 IFIP TC 13 launched the Interaction Design for International Development (IDID) Award that recognizes the most outstanding contribution to the application of inter-active systems for social and economic development of people in developing countries. Since the process to decide the award takes place after papers are sent to the publisher for publication, the awards are not identified in the proceedings.

IFIP TC 13 also recognizes pioneers in the area of HCI. An IFIP TC 13 pioneer is one who, through active participation in IFIP Technical Committees or related IFIP groups, has made outstanding contributions to the educational, theoretical, technical, commercial, or professional aspects of analysis, design, construction, evaluation, and use of interactive systems. IFIP TC 13 pioneers are appointed annually and awards are handed over at the INTERACT conference.

IFIP TC 13 stimulates working events and activities through its Working Groups (WGs). Working Groups consist of HCI experts from many countries, who seek to expand knowledge and find solutions to HCI issues and concerns within their domains. The list of Working Groups and their area of interest is given here.

WG13.1 (Education in HCI and HCI Curricula) aims to improve HCI education at all levels of higher education, coordinate and unite efforts to develop HCI curricula and promote HCI teaching.

WG13.2 (Methodology for User-Centered System Design) aims to foster research, dissemination of information and good practice in the methodical application of HCI to software engineering.

WG13.3 (HCI and Disability) aims to make HCI designers aware of the needs of people with disabilities and encourage the development of information systems and tools permitting adaptation of interfaces to specific users.

WG13.4 (also WG2.7) (User Interface Engineering) investigates the nature, concepts, and construction of user interfaces for software systems, using a framework for reasoning about interactive systems and an engineering model for developing user interfaces.

WG 13.5 (Resilience, Reliability, Safety and Human Error in System Development) seeks a frame-work for studying human factors relating to systems failure, develops leading-edge techniques in hazard analysis and safety engineering of computer-based systems, and guides international accreditation activities for safety-critical systems.

WG13.6 (Human-Work Interaction Design) aims at establishing relationships between extensive empirical work-domain studies and HCI design. It promotes the use of knowledge, concepts, methods, and techniques that enable user studies to procure a better apprehension of the complex interplay between individual, social, and organizational contexts and thereby a better understanding of how and why people work in the ways that they do.

WG13.7 (Human–Computer Interaction and Visualization) aims to establish a study and research program that will combine both scientific work and practical applications in the fields of HCI and visualization. It integrates several additional aspects of further research areas, such as scientific visualization, data mining, information design, computer graphics, cognition sciences, perception theory, or psychology, into this approach.

WG13.8 (Interaction Design and International Development) is currently working to reformulate its aims and scope.

WG13.9 (Interaction Design and Children) aims to support practitioners, regulators, and researchers to develop the study of interaction design and children across international contexts.

WG13.10 (Human-Centered Technology for Sustainability) aims to promote research, design, development, evaluation, and deployment of human-centered technology to encourage sustainable use of resources in various domains.

New Working Groups are formed as areas of significance in HCI arise. Further information is available on the IFIP TC13 website at: http://ifip-tc13.org/

IFIP TC13 Members

Officers

Chair

Philippe Palanque, France

Vice-chair for Growth and Reach Out INTERACT Steering Committee Chair

Jan Gulliksen, Sweden

Vice-chair for Working Groups

Simone D.J. Barbosa, Brazil

Vice-chair for Awards

Paula Kotze, South Africa

Treasurer

Virpi Roto, Finland

Secretary

Marco Winckler, France

Webmaster

Helen Petrie, UK

Country Representatives

Australia
Henry B.L. Duh
Australian Computer Society

Austria
Geraldine Fitzpatrick
Austrian Computer Society

Brazil
Raquel Oliveira Prates
Brazilian Computer Society (SBC)

Bulgaria
Kamelia Stefanova
Bulgarian Academy of Sciences

Canada
Lu Xiao
Canadian Information Processing Society

Chile
Jaime Sánchez
Chilean Society of Computer Science

Croatia
Andrina Granic
Croatian Information Technology
  Association (CITA)

Cyprus
Panayiotis Zaphiris
Cyprus Computer Society

Czech Republic
Zdeněk Míkovec
Czech Society for Cybernetics
  and Informatics

Denmark
Torkil Clemmensen
Danish Federation for Information
  Processing

Finland
Virpi Roto
Finnish Information Processing
  Association

France
Philippe Palanque
Société informatique de France (SIF)

Germany
Tom Gross
Gesellschaft für Informatik e.V.

Hungary
Cecilia Sik Lanyi
John V. Neumann Computer Society

India
Anirudha Joshi
Computer Society of India (CSI)

Ireland
Liam J. Bannon
Irish Computer Society

Italy
Fabio Paternò
Italian Computer Society

Japan
Yoshifumi Kitamura
Information Processing Society of Japan

Korea
Gerry Kim
KIISE

The Netherlands
Vanessa Evers
Nederlands Genootschap voor
  Informatica

New Zealand
Mark Apperley
New Zealand Computer Society

Nigeria
Chris C. Nwannenna
Nigeria Computer Society

Norway
Dag Svanes
Norwegian Computer Society

Poland
Marcin Sikorski
Poland Academy of Sciences

Portugal
Pedro Campos
Associacão Portuguesa para o Desen-
volvimento da Sociedade da Informação
  (APDSI)

Singapore
Shengdong Zhao
Singapore Computer Society

Slovakia
Wanda Benešová
The Slovak Society for Computer
  Science

Slovenia
Matjaž Debevc
The Slovenian Computer Society
  INFORMATIKA

South Africa
Janet L. Wesson
The Computer Society of South Africa

Spain
Julio Abascal
Asociación de Técnicos de Informática
  (ATI)

Sweden
Jan Gulliksen
Swedish Interdisciplinary Society
  for Human–Computer Interaction
Swedish Computer Society

Switzerland
Denis Lalanne
Swiss Federation for Information
  Processing

Tunisia
Mona Laroussi
Ecole Supérieure des Communications
  De Tunis (SUP'COM)

UK
José Abdelnour Nocera
British Computer Society (BCS)

United Arab Emirates
Ghassan Al-Qaimari
UAE Computer Society

USA
Gerrit van der Veer
Association for Computing Machinery
  (ACM)

Expert Members

Dan Orwa	University of Nairobi, Kenya
David Lamas	Tallinn University, Estonia
Dorian Gorgan	Technical University of Cluj-Napoca, Romania
Eunice Sari	University of Western Australia, Australia and UX Indonesia, Indonesia
Fernando Loizides	Cardiff University, UK and Cyprus University of Technology, Cyprus
Frank Vetere	University of Melbourne, Australia
Ivan Burmistrov	Moscow State University, Russia
Joaquim Jorge	INESC-ID, Portugal
Marta Kristin Larusdottir	Reykjavik University, Iceland
Nikolaos Avouris	University of Patras, Greece
Paula Kotze	CSIR Meraka Institute, South Africa
Peter Forbrig	University of Rostock, Germany
Simone D.J. Barbosa	PUC-Rio, Brazil
Vu Nguyen	Vietnam
Zhengjie Liu	Dalian Maritime University, China

Observer

Masaaki Kurosu, Japan

Working Group Chairs

**WG 13.1 (Education in HCI
and HCI Curricula)**

Konrad Baumann, Austria

**WG 13.2 (Methodologies
for User-Centered System Design)**

Marco Winckler, France

WG 13.3 (HCI and Disability)

Helen Petrie, UK

WG 13.4/2.7 (User Interface Engineering)

José Creissac Campos, Portugal

WG 13.5 (Resilience, Reliability, Safety, and Human Error in System Development)

Chris Johnson, UK

WG 13.6 (Human-Work Interaction Design)

Pedro Campos, Portugal

WG 13.7 (HCI and Visualization)

Peter Dannenmann, Germany

WG 13.8 (Interaction Design and International Development)

José Adbelnour Nocera, UK

WG 13.9 (Interaction Design and Children)

Janet Read, UK

WG 13.10 (Human-Centered Technology for Sustainability)

Masood Masoodian, Finland

Conference Organizing Committee

General Conference Chairs

Anirudha Joshi, India
Girish Dalvi, India

Technical Program Chair

Marco Winckler, France

Full-Paper Chairs

Regina Bernhaupt, France
Jacki O'Neill, India

Short-Paper Chairs

Peter Forbrig, Germany
Sriganesh Madhvanath, USA

Case Studies Chairs

Ravi Poovaiah, India
Elizabeth Churchill, USA

Courses Chairs

Gerrit van der Veer, The Netherlands
Dhaval Vyas, Australia

Demonstrations Chairs

Takahiro Miura, Japan
Shengdong Zhao, Singapore
Manjiri Joshi, India

Doctoral Consortium Chairs

Paula Kotze, South Africa
Pedro Campos, Portugal

Field Trips Chairs

Nimmi Rangaswamy, India
José Abdelnour Nocera, UK
Debjani Roy, India

Industry Presentations Chairs

Suresh Chande, Finland
Fernando Loizides, UK

Installations Chairs

Ishneet Grover, India
Jayesh Pillai, India
Nagraj Emmadi, India

Keynotes and Invited Talks Chair

Philippe Palanque, France

Panels Chairs

Antonella De Angeli, Italy
Rosa Arriaga, USA

Posters Chairs

Girish Prabhu, India
Zhengjie Liu, China

Student Research Consortium Chairs

Indrani Medhi, India
Naveen Bagalkot, India
Janet Wesson, South Africa

Student Design Consortium Chairs

Abhishek Shrivastava, India
Prashant Sachan, India
Arnab Chakravarty, India

Workshops Chairs

Torkil Clemmensen, Denmark
Venkatesh Rajamanickam, India

Accessibility Chairs

Prachi Sakhardande, India
Sonali Joshi, India

Childcare Club Chairs

Atish Patel, India
Susmita Sharma, India

Food and Social Events Chair

Rucha Tulaskar, India

Local Organizing Chairs

Manjiri Joshi, India
Nagraj Emmadi, India

Proceedings Chairs

Marco Winckler, France
Devanuj Balkrishan, India

Sponsorship Chair

Atul Manohar, India

Student Volunteers Chairs

Rasagy Sharma, India
Jayati Bandyopadhyay, India

Venue Arrangements Chair

Sugandh Malhotra, India

Web and Social Media Chair

Naveed Ahmed, India

Program Committee

Associated Chairs

Simone Barbosa, Brazil
Nicola Bidwell, Namibia
Pernille Bjorn, Denmark
Birgit Bomsdorf, Germany
Torkil Clemmensen, Denmark
José Creissac Campos, Portugal
Peter Forbrig, Germany
Tom Gross, Germany
Jan Gulliksen, Sweden
Nathalie Henry Riche, USA
Abhijit Karnik, UK
Dave Kirk, UK
Denis Lalanne, Switzerland
Airi Lampinen, Sweden
Effie Law, UK
Eric Lecolinet, France
Zhengjie Liu, China
Fernando Loizides, UK
Célia Martinie, France
Laurence Nigay, France

Monique Noirhomme, Belgium
Philippe Palanque, France
Fabio Paterno, Italy
Helen Petrie, UK
Antonio Piccinno, Italy
Kari-Jouko Raiha, Finland
Dave Randall, Germany
Nimmi Rangaswamy, India
John Rooksby, UK
Virpi Roto, Finland
Jan Stage, Denmark
Frank Steinicke, Germany
Simone Stumpf, UK
Gerrit van der Veer, The Netherlands
Dhaval Vyas, India
Gerhard Weber, Germany
Janet Wesson, South Africa
Marco Winckler, France
Panayiotis Zaphiris, Cyprus

Reviewers

Julio Abascal, Spain
José Abdelnour Nocera, UK
Silvia Abrahão, Spain
Abiodun Afolayan Ogunyemi, Estonia
Ana Paula Afonso, Portugal
David Ahlström, Austria
Muneeb Ahmad, Australia
Deepak Akkil, Finland
Sarah Alaoui, France
Komathi Ale, Singapore
Jan Alexandersson, Germany
Dzmitry Aliakseyeu, The Netherlands
Hend S. Al-Khalifa, Saudi Arabia
Fereshteh Amini, Canada
Junia Anacleto, Brazil
Mads Schaarup Andersen, Denmark
Leonardo Angelini, Switzerland
Huckauf Anke, Germany
Craig Anslow, New Zealand
Nathalie Aquino, Paraguay
Oscar Javier Ariza Núñez, Germany
Parvin Asadzadeh, UK
Uday Athavankar, India
David Auber, France
Nikolaos Avouris, Greece
Sohaib Ayub, Pakistan
Chris Baber, UK
Cedric Bach, France
Naveen Bagalkot, India
Jan Balata, Czech Republic
Emilia Barakova, The Netherlands
Pippin Barr, Denmark
Oswald Barral, Finland
Barbara Rita Barricelli, Italy
Michel Beaudouin-Lafon, France
Astrid Beck, Germany
Jordan Beck, USA
Roman Bednarik, Finland
Ben Bedwell, UK
Marios Belk, Germany
Yacine Bellik, France
David Benyon, UK
François Bérard, France

Arne Berger, Germany
Nigel Bevan, UK
Anastasia Bezerianos, France
Sudhir Bhatia, India
Dorrit Billman, USA
Pradipta Biswas, India
Edwin Blake, South Africa
Renaud Blanch, France
Mads Bødker, Denmark
Cristian Bogdan, Sweden
Rodrigo Bonacin, Brazil
Claus Bossen, Denmark
Paolo Bottoni, Italy
Nadia Boukhelifa, France
Nina Boulus-Rødje, Denmark
Judy Bowen, New Zealand
Margot Brereton, Australia
Roberto Bresin, Sweden
Barry Brown, Sweden
Emeline Brulé, France
Nick Bryan-Kinns, UK
Sabin-Corneliu Buraga, Romania
Ineke Buskens, South Africa
Adrian Bussone, UK
Maria Claudia Buzzi, Italy
Marina Buzzi, Italy
Federico Cabitza, Italy
Diogo Cabral, Portugal
Åsa Cajander, Sweden
Eduardo Calvillo Gamez, Mexico
Erik Cambria, Singapore
Pedro Campos, Portugal
Tara Capel, Australia
Cinzia Cappiello, Italy
Stefan Carmien, Spain
Maria Beatriz Carmo, Portugal
Luis Carriço, Portugal
Stefano Carrino, Switzerland
Géry Casiez, France
Fabio Cassano, Italy
Thais Castro, Brazil
Vanessa Cesário, Portugal
Arnab Chakravarty, India

Matthew Chalmers, UK
Teresa Chambel, Portugal
Chunlei Chang, Australia
Olivier Chapuis, France
Weiqin Chen, Norway
Mauro Cherubini, Switzerland
Fanny Chevalier, France
Yoram Chisik, Portugal
Eun Kyoung Choe, USA
Mabrouka Chouchane, Tunisia
Elizabeth Churchill, USA
Gilbert Cockton, UK
Ashley Colley, Finland
Christopher Collins, Canada
Tayana Conte, Brazil
Nuno Correia, Portugal
Joelle Coutaz, France
Rui Couto, Portugal
Céline Coutrix, France
Nadine Couture, France
Lynne Coventry, UK
Benjamin Cowan, Ireland
Paul Curzon, UK
Edward Cutrell, India
Florian Daiber, Germany
Nick Dalton, UK
Girish Dalvi, India
Jose Danado, USA
Chi Tai Dang, Germany
Ticianne Darin, Brazil
Jenny Darzentas, Greece
Giorgio De Michelis, Italy
Clarisse de Souza, Brazil
Ralf de Wolf, Belgium
Andy Dearden, UK
Dmitry Dereshev, UK
Giuseppe Desolda, Italy
Heather Desurvire, USA
Amira Dhouib, Tunisia
Ines Di Loreto, Italy
Paulo Dias, Portugal
Shalaka Dighe, India
Tawanna Dillahunt, USA
Anke Dittmar, Germany
Andre Doucette, Canada
Pierre Dragicevic, France

Steven Drucker, USA
Carlos Duarte, Portugal
Julie Ducasse, France
Andreas Duenser, Australia
Bruno Dumas, Belgium
Paul Dunphy, UK
Sophie Dupuy-Chessa, France
Sourav Dutta, India
James Eagan, France
Grace Eden, Switzerland
Brian Ekdale, USA
Linda Elliott, USA
Chris Elsden, UK
Morten Esbensen, Denmark
Florian Evéquoz, Switzerland
Shamal Faily, UK
Carla Faria Leitao, Brazil
Ava Fatah gen. Schieck, UK
Camille Fayollas, France
Tom Feltwell, UK
Xavier Ferre, Spain
Pedro Ferreira, Denmark
Sebastian Feuerstack, Brazil
Patrick Tobias Fischer, Germany
Geraldine Fitzpatrick, Austria
Rowanne Fleck, UK
Daniela Fogli, Italy
Asbjørn Følstad, Norway
Manuel J. Fonseca, Portugal
Renata Fortes, Brazil
André Freire, UK
Parseihian Gaëtan, France
Radhika Gajalla, USA
Teresa Galvão, Portugal
Nestor Garay-Vitoria, Spain
Roberto García, Spain
Jose Luis Garrido, Spain
Franca Garzotto, Italy
Isabela Gasparini, Brazil
Cally Gatehouse, UK
Sven Gehring, Germany
Stuart Geiger, USA
Helene Gelderblom, South Africa
Cristina Gena, Ireland
Cristina Gena, Italy
Vivian Genaro Motti, USA

Rosella Gennari, Italy
Werner Geyer, USA
Giuseppe Ghiani, Italy
Anirban Ghosh, Canada
Sanjay Ghosh, India
Martin Gibbs, Australia
Patrick Girard, France
Victor Gonzalez, Mexico
Rohini Gosain, Ireland
Nicholas Graham, Canada
Tiago Guerreiro, Portugal
Yves Guiard, France
Nuno Guimaraes, Portugal
Tauseef Gulrez, Australia
Thilina Halloluwa, Sri Lanka
Martin Halvey, UK
Dave Harley, UK
Richard Harper, UK
Michael Harrison, UK
Heidi Hartikainen, Finland
Thomas Hartley, UK
Mariam Hassib, Germany
Ari Hautasaari, Japan
Elaine Hayashi, Brazil
Jonas Hedman, Denmark
Ruediger Heimgaertner, Germany
Tomi Heimonen, USA
Mattias Heinrich, Germany
Ingi Helgason, UK
Wilko Heuten, Germany
Uta Hinrichs, UK
Daniel Holliday, UK
Jonathan Hook, UK
Jettie Hoonhout, The Netherlands
Heiko Hornung, Brazil
Axel Hösl, Germany
Lara Houston, UK
Roberto Hoyle, USA
William Hudson, UK
Stéphane Huot, France
Christophe Hurter, France
Husniza Husni, Malaysia
Ebba Thora Hvannberg, Iceland
Aulikki Hyrskykari, Finland
Yavuz Inal, Turkey
Petra Isenberg, France

Poika Isokoski, Finland
Minna Isomursu, Denmark
Howell Istance, Finland
Kai-Mikael Jää-Aro, Sweden
Karim Jabbar, Denmark
Isa Jahnke, USA
Abhishek Jain, India
Mlynar Jakub, Switzerland
Yvonne Jansen, France
Camille Jeunet, France
Nan Jiang, UK
Radu Jianu, UK
Deepak John Mathew, India
Matt Jones, UK
Rui José, Portugal
Anirudha Joshi, India
Dhaval Joshi, China
Manjiri Joshi, India
Mike Just, UK
Eija Kaasinen, Finland
Hernisa Kacorri, USA
Sanjay Kairam, USA
Bridget Kane, Ireland
Shaun K. Kane, USA
Jari Kangas, Finland
Ann Marie Kanstrup, Denmark
Evangelos Karapanos, Cyprus
Turkka Keinonen, Finland
Pramod Khambete, India
Munwar Khan, India
NamWook Kim, USA
Yea-Seul Kim, USA
Jennifer King, USA
Reuben Kirkham, UK
Kathi Kitner, South Africa
Søren Knudsen, Denmark
Janin Koch, Finland
Lisa Koeman, The Netherlands
Uttam Kokil, USA
Christophe Kolski, France
Paula Kotze, South Africa
Dennis Krupke, Germany
Sari Kujala, Finland
David Lamas, Estonia
Eike Langbehn, Germany
Rosa Lanzilotti, Italy

Ravi Poovaiah, India
Christopher Power, UK
Girish Prabhu, India
Denise Prescher, Germany
Costin Pribeanu, Romania
Helen Purchase, UK
Xiangang Qin, Denmark
Venkatesh Rajamanickam, India
Dorina Rajanen, Finland
Rani Gadhe Rani Gadhe, India
Heli Rantavuo, Sweden
Noopur Raval, USA
Janet Read, UK
Sreedhar Reddy, India
Christian Remy, Switzerland
Karen Renaud, UK
António Nestor Ribeiro, Portugal
Michael Rietzler, Germany
Maurizio Rigamonti, Switzerland
Kerem Rızvanoğlu, Turkey
Teresa Romao, Portugal
Maki Rooksby, UK
Mark Rouncefield, UK
Gustavo Rovelo, Belgium
Debjani Roy, India
Hamed R-Tavakolli, Finland
Simon Ruffieux, Switzerland
Angel Ruiz-Zafra, UK
Katri Salminen, Finland
Antti Salovaara, Finland
Frode Eika Sandnes, Norway
Supraja Sankaran, Belgium
Vagner Santana, Brazil
Carmen Santoro, Italy
Vidya Sarangapani, UK
Sayan Sarcar, Japan
Somwrita Sarkar, Australia
Christine Satchell, Australia
Mithileysh Sathiyanarayanan, UK
Anthony Savidis, Greece
Susanne Schmidt, Germany
Kevin Schneider, Canada
Dirk Schnelle-Walka, Germany
Ronald Schroeter, Australia
Vinícius Segura, Brazil
Ajanta Sen, India

Audrey Serna, France
Marcos Serrano, France
Leslie Setlock, USA
Anshuman Sharma, India
Patrick C. Shih, USA
Shanu Shukla, India
Gulati Siddharth, Estonia
Bruno Silva, Brazil
Carlos C.L. Silva, Portugal
Milene Silveira, Brazil
Adalberto Simeone, UK
Jaana Simola, Finland
Carla Simone, Finland
Laurianne Sitbon, Australia
Ashok Sivaji, Malaysia
Keyur Sorathia, India
Alessandro Soro, Australia
Oleg Spakov, Finland
Lucio Davide Spano, Italy
Susan Squires, USA
Christian Stary, Austria
Katarzyna Stawarz, UK
Jürgen Steimle, Germany
Revi Sterling, USA
Agnis Stibe, USA
Markus Stolze, Switzerland
Selina Sutton, UK
David Swallow, UK
Aurélien Tabard, France
Marcel Taeumel, Germany
Chee-Wee Tan, Denmark
Jennyfer Taylor, Australia
Robyn Taylor, UK
Robert Teather, Canada
Luis Teixeira, Portugal
Paolo Tell, Denmark
Jakob Tholander, Sweden
Alice Thudt, Canada
Subrata Tikadar, India
Martin Tomitsch, Australia
Ilaria Torre, Italy
Noam Tractinsky, Israel
Hallvard Traetteberg, Norway
Giovanni Troiano, USA
Janice Tsai, USA
Robert Tscharn, Germany

Sponsors and Partners

Silver Sponsors

Adobe

LEAD PARTNERS

facebook

Gala Dinner Sponsor

Design Competition Sponsor

Pitney Bowes

Education Partners

Interaction Design Foundation (IDF)

Friends of INTERACT

Ruwido GmBH, Austria   Oxford University Press   Converge by CauseCode
                                                         Technologies

Exhibitors

Partners

International Federation for Information Processing

   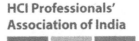

In-cooperation with ACM   In-cooperation with SIGCHI

IDC
IIT Bombay

HCI Professionals'
Association of India

Industrial Design Centre, IIT Bombay   HCI Professionals' Association of India

Computer Society of India   IIT Bombay

Contents

UX Adoption in the Organizations

Virtual Reality and Feeling of Immersion

Case Studies

Courses

Demonstrations

Field Trips

Workshops

Security and Trust

Coping with Accessibility Challenges for Security - A User Study with Blind Smartphone Users

Sylvan Lobo[(✉)], Ulemba Hirom, V. S. Shyama, Mridul Basumatori, and Pankaj Doke

Tata Consultancy Services Ltd., Mumbai, India
{sylvan.lobo,ulemba.h,shyamav.s,mridul.basumotari,
pankaj.doke}@tcs.com

Abstract. Widespread adoption of touchscreen phones among blind users seems inevitable. Blind users face significant challenges in terms of accessibility and inclusion in the smartphone environment, despite prevalence of screen-readers and assistive software. This can lead to a variety of security and privacy risks while using smartphones. This paper presents qualitative research findings of a user study about security and usability aspects of smartphone usage by 51 blind smartphone users of age 18 to 40 years in a metropolitan city of India. We discuss the challenges users face, their coping strategies, and key insights that could inform design for security and usability.

Keywords: Usable security · Blind · Smartphone · Android · iPhone

1 Introduction

Smartphones are increasingly being adopted in India [1]. As an information device, a smartphone is very personal and portable compared to desktop computers and laptops. Users tend to keep their phone with them at all times for a variety of personal information needs. It is always powered on and available on voice and data networks. This makes the smartphone attractive and vulnerable to security and privacy threats.

There is a large population of visually impaired users, who are increasingly using touchscreen-based smartphones. Visually impaired users earlier used Symbian phones which were quite accessible with their assistive features and tangible keypads. Currently we observe that market forces seem to drive users to shift to touchscreen-based smartphones, primarily Android and iPhone. There has been considerable development [2–4] in accessibility on these smartphone devices, both on iPhone and Android. Yet users still face usability challenges in certain situations where using the phone may be challenging (e.g. public transport, walking, crowded situations) [5] or simply due to unfamiliar or infrequently used interfaces. Considering the accessibility and usability challenges that visually impaired smartphone users face, we feel they are also more vulnerable with regards to privacy and security. E.g. using passwords and phone locks, or typing itself can be time consuming and error prone with currently available accessibility modes [6]. Users also perceive privacy concerns while using accessibility modes [7].

© IFIP International Federation for Information Processing 2017
Published by Springer International Publishing AG 2017. All Rights Reserved
R. Bernhaupt et al. (Eds.): INTERACT 2017, Part IV, LNCS 10516, pp. 3–22, 2017.
DOI: 10.1007/978-3-319-68059-0_1

The global visually impaired population is of a considerable size [10], with around 5 million in India alone (some report 15 million) [11, 12]. The World Health Organization (WHO) reported an estimate of 8 million people with total blindness [13] in India in 2010 [10]. Mumbai, India, is reported to have a visually impaired population of around 0.12 million [14]. We found it imperative to include visually impaired smartphone users in smartphone security studies, to help understand threats that they may be exposed to and their current practices, eventually aiding in building better usable security for smartphones. For this study, we have only considered users with total blindness [51] users (rather than users with other visual impairment. As per American Foundation ® for Blind, total blindness refers to *"an inability to see anything with either eye."* [51]. We feel blind users would face such security and privacy risks and challenges more severely than sighted users and users with other visual impairments. Investigating these challenges would hopefully help in addressing concerns other visually impaired users too.

In this paper, we present the findings of our contextual inquiry based interviews with 51 totally blind smartphone users in Mumbai, India, with regards to their security and privacy practices with smartphones (Android and iPhone), their coping strategies with security measures such as passwords and native access control measures such as PIN, pattern locks and slide locks. We first review the relevant previous research, present the method used in our study and then highlight the outcomes of the affinity analysis of the contextual inquiry discussed from the perspective of security and usability, followed by a discussion of implications for design.

2 Previous Research

There have been numerous studies with sighted users [9, 12, 13, 15, 19, 21–23, 26] as well as visually impaired users [1, 2, 4, 10, 11, 20] with smartphones, laptops and internet on various aspects of usability, privacy and security, although we have not found relevant empirical studies with visually impaired or blind users in India with regards to their security and privacy practices and behavior with smartphones.

2.1 Mobile Security Studies with Sighted Smartphone Users

Studies with sighted users suggest that users are generally concerned about privacy and security on their smartphones (even more so than on laptops). They are often signed in to multiple accounts on their phone, and use the phone to perform financial and other private transactions [9, 23]. The indispensable, personal and highly portable nature of the smartphone demands that it be well protected from threats of data loss, compromise and privacy, including threats such as loss of phone due to damage, theft or misplacing; unauthorized access through malware or physical access; and location tracking [15].

Asokan and Kuo [26], Ben-Asher et al. [27] and Jakobsson [28], all argue that security approaches for mobile phone environments need to be revisited as the environment and usage differs markedly from traditional computers. Smartphones do provide some measures to mitigate risks [22], but the decisions are often delegated to the users themselves, who may not be sufficiently prepared or have the awareness to take correct decisions [21]. However, studies suggest that users are not well informed about security and privacy decisions [22] and may often take inappropriate decisions. Users often do not find security features essential and keep them disabled [16, 21]. People also root or jailbreak their phones (Android and iPhone terminology to enable the phone for root or administrative access), leaving the phones vulnerable [21]. Users avoid regularly upgrading the operating system, missing security patches. There are many apps available from non-official sources in the market places or app stores. In order to make decisions about installing apps, users tend to rely on the price (i.e. free or very cheap) and popularity based on recommendations from friends and user reviews, rather than studying the end user license agreements, privacy policies and app permissions [15]. Users do not pay much attention nor comprehend the policies and app permissions [29]. Uses exhibit a 'click through' behavior when faced with various information prompts. Users trust the app repository with misconceptions that apps are tested for security [21].

One common means of protecting information is using authentication means like passwords or phone locks. Yet many users do not use any phone locking mechanisms such as PINs or pattern locks simply due to usability issues and a need to access the phone quickly, despite the presence of private and sensitive content on the phone [19]. Users would rather keep the phone within sight at all times, without any password protection. This form of lock-based protection on phones provides an all-or-nothing access [18], and is quite risky considering passwords saved within apps are common [19] and users are not required to key-in passwords frequently. Users report that they use simple passwords such as names or dictionary words. Users also store their passwords on their phones as contacts in plain text [19].

Users consider data such as GPS tracking, SMS, Phonebook contacts, Multimedia content (such as videos, photos and recordings), emails, documents and notes as most private, valuable and sensitive [19]. They tend to not trust keeping private data in the cloud, and prefer storing data on their computers or hard disks unless the data is shareable [19]. People do share phones among themselves for music, entertainment and making calls, but would rather have the phone in sight and depend on their relationship with the other users. Users tend to consider it a higher threat to share phones with known people rather than with strangers [19]. Photographs and messages are kept private from known people and contacts private from strangers. Unauthorized access to the phone seems fairly common [20]. Chen et al. [30] also discuss Internet security practices of users in the context of users in a developing nation. Recent work by Alsaleh et al. [31] discusses smartphone security practices of users from the dimensions of behavioral change and provide persuasive approaches for addressing unsafe practices.

2.2 Mobile Security Studies with Visually Impaired Smartphone Users

Challenges of usability and accessibility enhance the security challenges faced by visually impaired users. Touchscreens lack tangible feedback, and users mostly depend on aural feedback or assistive devices (screen readers, zoom). There are various studies on security and privacy related aspects for visually impaired users [6, 23–25] and considerable advancement [2–4] in accessibility on touchscreen. Commonly performed activities on smartphones (and computers) include reading and writing emails, browsing internet for entertainment, downloading/uploading files, education, listening to podcasts, instant messaging, and interacting on social media platforms [17]. Users also transact and bank online, but usually prefer using desktops and laptops over smartphones.

Azenkot et al. [6] found that visually impaired users are generally not aware or concerned about security, and often use their phones without password protection primarily due to inconveniences faced. For example, the phone allows passwords to be masked, i.e. the screen reader reads the characters as stars or clicks while the user types in the password. This however makes it near impossible for users to type, i.e. without text entry feedback on a touchscreen device, users are clueless about what they are typing. If the user chooses to not mask the passwords, the screen reader speaks the characters aloud, which is again not desirable for keeping the password private. Users also find password managers, password recovery mechanisms, and typing itself quite difficult [23]. Users often tend to store their password elsewhere written in Braille or in files, or save them within apps [23].

There is also a lack of sufficient feedback while browsing the Internet or using smartphones, using the assistive features available. Some users hence spend less time online [17]. For instance, browser do not highlight phishing in an easily accessible manner, and feedback about errors is poor. Often user interfaces change frequently [23], which means the user needs to learn how to use the interface again.

In terms of privacy, visually impaired users frequently face the risk of being eavesdropped, both aurally and visually, in almost all activities they perform on the phone as they are often not sure when people are in their vicinity [23]. They feel a lack of independence and have to rely on sighted users for assistance, often strangers where they need to disclose private information in various situations such as filling forms, or reading messages or letters. Some users hence prefer online transactions and online shopping over shopping in real stores, although they still have concerns of security [23]. Users have various strategies to maintain privacy like relying on close relations such as spouse, family or close friends; using assistive technology; using screen curtains to black out the display; using headphones; or using the screen reader at low volume or at a very fast talking rate where others would find it difficult to understand.

As seen in the background literature, visually impaired users as well as sighted users face quite a few security and privacy challenges with their smartphones. They risk and often fail to protect their data effectively. The lack of awareness and inconvenience due to which users do not take appropriate measures can be attributed to usability and accessibility issues in interfaces and mechanisms provided for achieving the goals of security and privacy. The security goals in themselves are not primary, although a single event of compromise of data or privacy can prove disastrous to users. The phone is shipped with security features but in the context of the user they are not usable.

2.3 Usability and Security

Usability can be defined as the: *"extent to which a system, product or service can be used by specified users to achieve specified goals with effectiveness, efficiency and satisfaction in a specified context of use."* (ISO 9241 210: 2010) [32, 33].

Products are generally created with goals of usability. There are various methods to assess usability such as Nielsen's [34] usability heuristics or Joshi's [35, 36] Usability

Goals Tool (UGT). Usability goals could include: ease of use where the conceptual model is communicated clearly so that there is a match between users' mental model and the product, without entry barriers and unnecessary tasks, minimizing user task load, and always accessible. Operation of the product should be error-free, should not induce errors and the user should be able to recover easily if and when errors do occur. The system should provide appropriate feedback, display current status and should be accessible at all times.

While security is another overarching and important goal, users might take it for granted or consider it coming in the way of their actual goals. So, when usability and security intersect there are additional considerations and methods for usability evaluation [37–39]. Saltzer proposes design principles for data protection among which the following seem relevant for when intersected with usability: *"economy of mechanism"* where the design is to be as simple and small as possible; *"fail-safe defaults"* and *"psychological acceptability"*.

Whitten defines security software as usable, through four points as follows: *"Security software is usable if the people who are expected to use it:*

1. *are reliably made aware of the security tasks they need to perform;*
2. *are able to figure out how to successfully perform those tasks;*
3. *don't make dangerous errors; and*
4. *are sufficiently comfortable with the interface to continue using it."* [39]

Whitten describes properties of security which make it difficult to get user interfaces right or usable, such as: *"unmotivated user"*, *"abstraction"*, *"lack of feedback"*, *"barn door principle"*, and *"weakest link"*. The *unmotivated user* property highlights that security is not the primary goal of the user. Instead, the user wants to achieve other tasks, and would easily not give much thought to security, assuming that they are safe. *Abstraction* refers to abstracted security rules for granting access which may not seem intuitive to most users. The *lack of feedback* property speaks about how it is difficult for security software to perform useful error checking and provide feedback that the user wants. The *barn door property* refers to leaving secrets accidently open, after which one can never be sure if any attacker might have accessed it or not. *The weakest link property* refers to security being strongest as the weakest component, which can be exploited by attackers. User interfaces for security places priority on ensuring that users understand security well enough, and they should be guided through all aspects [39].

We have considered these dimensions of usability and security as per Joshi et al. [35, 36], Whitten [38, 39] and Saltzer [37] in our analysis and discussion of our findings.

3   Method

The objective of this study was to gain insights into how total-blind [13] users used touchscreen-based smartphones, with a focus on privacy and information security issues they faced, their coping strategies and practices, and their conceptual models.

We interviewed 51 total blind smartphone users in Mumbai, India, using a Contextual Inquiry (CI) [40] approach. We chose to interview total blind and not users with other forms of visual impairments to have a homogenous group of users, assisting our analysis of responses and cause of their behavior and practices. The users were in the age group of 18 to 40 (averaging around 25 years). There were 36 male and 15 female participants. More detail about the participants is provided in the Table 1 below.

Table 1. Particpants details

	Female	Male	All
Number of participants	15	36	**51**
Average Age	25	25	**25**
18 to 20 years	3	8	**11**
21 to 25 years	6	16	**22**
26 to 30 years	4	7	**11**
31 to 35 years	2	3	**5**
36 to 40 years	0	2	**2**
Number of Android Users	12	32	**44**
Number of iPhone Users	3	4	**7**
Number of Employed participants	9	13	**22**
Students	5	22	**27**
Unemployed	1	1	**2**

A group of researchers individually visited users at their homes, colleges or workplaces, across Mumbai. The CI method recommends visiting the users in their context. The researchers first briefed the users about the study, sought consent and proceeded with the interview. The researchers simultaneously also noted observations about the user and their immediate environment. The researchers gathered basic information from the users such as their demographic details, phone models and prior experience with smartphones, and then gradually proceeded towards asking contextual questions focusing on their security practices with the smartphone. The interviews had a conversational format and the researchers played the role of an 'apprentice', where the user would demonstrate how they used certain security related features on their phones with as much detail as possible (e.g., how they set a phone lock, or how they unlocked their phone). The users were also nudged to retrospectively recite various security related situations they might have been in, and were probed to provide details. As far as possible, the researchers avoided speculative situations and relied on past situations which the user actually had been in.

The interviews primarily dwelled on the usability and security related practices and challenges blind users faced in their daily lives – i.e. beliefs, practices and challenges they faced with using the locking mechanisms, with setting locks, managing Privacy, and setting, managing and using Passwords for their online accounts and apps.

The interviews were recorded using voice recorders, and later transcribed where local language were not translated. The interviews were discussed for arriving at structured notes. The researchers read and familiarized themselves with the interview transcripts, photos and videos, and shortlisted notes that were particularly related to the focus on Smartphone Usability and Security for blind users. The notes were printed as paper chits which were shuffled around in a box. Researchers picked a chit from the box, read it out aloud or passed it around. From a discussion that ensued the researchers arrived at a consensus about a model explaining the observation in the note, and noted down the model on a Post-It™ note. The Post-It™ note was put on a table with the chit below it. The researchers continued picking up chits from the box, and arrived at more models or updated existing models on the table, till clusters and categories formed.

Once all notes were categorized, the researchers then identified key categories which had a larger number of chits and seemed highly relevant to our focus, or were novel. The researchers read through the chits one by one under that category and tried explaining it through a model which was written or sketched on Post-It™ notes on a wall. With every chit we either reclassified it with other categories on the table if appropriate or updated the model on the wall till a good understanding of observed phenomena emerged and was captured through models on the wall.

To illustrate with an example: We clustered notes with observations such as how users used Talkback at low volumes, or at very fast rates, or strategies such as touching additional 'fake' characters while entering passwords to confuse eavesdroppers. These observations led us to arrive at models such as 'Obscurity is used as a means to achieve privacy'. Such models after subsequent structuring, also developed into a primary category – 'Assistive software is used as a layer of security', which we discuss later in Sect. 4.3. In this way most of the categories and chits on the table were analyzed till we arrived at the most novel or relevant themes, in the views of the researchers, as described in the following sections. Figure 1 showcases the affinity diagramming.

Fig. 1. Affinity diagramming

4 Findings

4.1 Accessibility Challenges Lead to Predictable Passwords

Users expressed that virtual keypads were more difficult to use as compared to the Symbian based tangible keypad phones that they used earlier. Tangible keypads allowed speed and accuracy in typing as it was easy to find the correct keys. With touchscreen phones however, despite accessibility software such as Talkback or Voiceover, it is a challenge to locate keys accurately without the tangible feedback. Users often face breakdowns by accidentally pressing wrong keys or activating undesired operations. For instance, text entry usually involves three taps: one for scanning and reading out the letters on the keypad followed by a double-tap to enter the last key that was spoken out (there may be other such similar techniques). This is much slower than the tangible keypads where users could find and enter the desired keys easily, simply relying on their cognitive and muscle memory of the location of the key. With phone locks, issues are amplified as the users' desire frequent and quick access to their phones, and the lock gets in the way. Hence we found users opting out of locks or using very simple-to-type PINs and Patterns.

> *"...the screen reader speaks numbers and symbols, but at times we accidently press the small button the side which changes the language... We don't understand what's happening then, and we have to re-enter the password."* – (NJ.U4.06)[1].

Our observations led us to believe that the typing difficulty on virtual keypads led users to keep passwords that are easier to type, which are also hence predictable – those which would have minimal resistance or ease of entry. We thus observe a conscious move towards predictability to lower the entry barrier, indicating that the user goals significantly outweigh behavior towards protection interventions. E.g., User AS03 (Fig. 2) demonstrated how they entered 111111 as a PIN on her iPhone. It simply required her to first scan and locate 1 (which was easy). After that they had to double tap multiple (12) times to enter six 1's, which they did quite rapidly. We thus observe that the coping mechanisms deployed by the users significantly increases risk of compromise.

> *"It's better to keep a single digit. I've kept 1 six times."* – (AS03)

Consider an alternate example, 135743. This would require the user to scan and locate each digit followed by a double tap, which is an increase in 5 taps, slowing the user. 111111 reduces the effort required to scan, locate digits and double tap. Users may not keep PINs that require them to move all over the keypad. A similar practice was noticed with using Patterns, where they resorted to starting at edges and preferring straight lines (L's) or squares.

> *"One sleeping line goes over 3 points and one standing line goes over 2 points. I felt this is possible for blind people. I tried a lot, to at least make one sleeping line...on my phone as well on others, but I couldn't figure it out. There are just 3 sleeping lines, but it is difficult. If there was only one sleeping line, then it could help blind people."* – (SKU412)

Fig. 2. User sets a PIN using a single digit

---

[1] Note: All quotes are translated into English from Marathi and Hindi, for international readers.

It appears that users focus on ease and speed of input for passwords and locking mechanisms, rather than recallability or non-guessability, when using touchscreen devices. If users perceive access control measures as reducing productivity, they deploy weaker protection measures which are predictable based on ease of entry. A related observation about predictability of passwords, was that users kept simple and recallable passwords based on their daily personal contextual data, or rather based on their 'sign-up' information. By this we mean that passwords were combinations of details such phone numbers, account numbers, names of friends, family or places, or names of favourite movies and games, or related to religion or beliefs (such as names of gods, or lucky numbers). This is not very different from what one would expect with sighted users' passwords. The users however did demonstrate attempts to mix and combine names, numbers and characters to try keeping the passwords non-guessable.

"For Facebook, I've kept my password close to my name. In Gmail I have tweaked my phone number a little here and there. So that I don't forget." – (BBU215)

The other specific finding about password choices with blind users was that visually impaired users have a unique code for representing letters by number codes. E.g. User DTU6 encoded their passwords using this strategy, which could be a decent technique for setting a recallable password which is non-guessable at least outside the community.

*"Actually, we speak a number language, which we call 123... I had just kept my name (as password)...in Marathi – C means Cha. We call C (Cha) as 31. So, I had kept the password like 31 ** ** 12 (masked for privacy)." – (DTU614)*

Literature highlights how the keyboard layouts and small form-factor of mobiles affect influence password choices [41, 42]. Our observations suggests that accessibility of the touchscreen interfaces also affects the password choices both in case on PINs as well as Patterns.

4.2   Migration Across Locking Mechanisms – No Lock to TouchID

Figure 3 below highlights how we interpreted users' transition across various locking mechanisms, based on three dimensions – security, usability and accessibility. Users tend to start out with no phone locks when the phone is new, and might use the Swipe/Slide Lock or simply the power button to start the screen. Users commonly stated that there is nothing valuable on their phones to justify the absence of locks. They felt locks prevented hassle-free frequent access to their phones. They also feared getting locked out of their phones, in case they forgot the password. One user also believed that passwords would slow down the phone. Some users stated that they did not know how to or had not yet 'learnt' how to set the phone locks and might do so at some later point in time. Some users reported that in case of emergencies, others should be able to use and unlock their phones. They stick to the adopted mechanism (beginning with no-lock as in Fig. 3) till a trigger makes them change and adopt locks. These triggers are either from the dimension of security, usability or accessibility issues. The security trigger is usually an exposure to a risk situation where they may have lost data, faced privacy issues, etc. This prompts users to start employing a security measure, usually a PIN lock. Other reasons could be merely out of curiosity, e.g. trying out Patterns as it appears as an interesting challenge to blind users. Once they have adopted a security measure, again users would stick to it till they feel inconvenienced by usability or accessibility challenges with the mechanism, prompting them to try out other mechanisms or revert to no locks (or easier mechanisms like PINs). In case of biometric fingerprint based locks (Touch-ID on iPhones), we felt users did not revert to other mechanisms. (We did not observe users of biometric fingerprint locks on Android phones). This migration might take place till users find a good enough balance between accessibility, usability and security.

"...Once, a family member met with a bike accident. Their phone was locked completely. No one was able to call the family members as the app lock couldn't be unlocked. That's one reason (for not keeping a lock.)*" – (BBU716)*

Users seem to need a strong trigger to begin using phone locks. These are often cases of thefts, shoulder surfing and being unable to assess if anyone is watching their screens, or sensitive information/applications such as net banking installed on the phone. Similar triggers also led users to change their current PINs (or passwords). Users explored the various security phone locking options and usually settled on PINs stating that numbers are easy and less tedious compared to Passwords or Patterns. Patterns were treated as impossible to understand for blind users. iPhone users however loved the biometric fingerprint option – TouchID.

"I had a friend sitting near me, who saw me opening my phone lock. She asked me for my password. I refused, but she was insistent. Then she said she knows my password. I told her to open my phone then if she could. She unlocked it! She was partially (blind) so she could see. I immediately changed the password." – (RCU4)

Some users either preferred PINs over Patterns or Patterns over Pins due to perceptions about how they performed on speed and ease, especially during situations/context where the mechanism were difficult to use – such as being sleepy or travelling in public transport where the rides are bumpy.

"The problem with PIN was you had to double touch every time. I had kept mine (password) as 1234. So you have to type double 1, double 2 double 3, double 4 due to talkback. Talkback requires double touch. Sometimes when I'm on the road, I face difficulties. Then I changed to a Pattern. Since then my problems have reduced, because with this I can open my phone quickly." – (BBU210)

iPhone users found the fingerprint biometric authentication – Touch-ID, as a very convenient option, despite occasional issues faced in fingerprint recognition. Users who used Touch-ID would not migrate back to no locks. They felt comfort with the presence of a fallback of a PIN when fingerprint recognition failed, so they did not have the fear of getting locked out of the phone. Most other (Android) users either used PINs or reverted to the swipe lock, or no lock or interestingly used accessibility features, such as Dim-Screen as a layer of security (discussed in the next section).

"Basically I use TouchID. I also have Passcode in place. The TouchID has a good biometric sensor, it works most of the time. When it doesn't, then I use Passcode. I believe TouchID is the best, you know you need to place the thumb." – (BBU105)

Existing studies [6, 16, 43] have found that most users (sighted) use locks for security and privacy, with PINs being prevalent. For those who do not use locks, it is usually due to a lack of motivation, lack of concern or inconvenience. Users tend to start using locks when prompted to (usually by a significant other) and would then stick to using the lock, despite inconveniences faced. Users seem to face more errors with Patterns, compared to PINS. Azenkot in an earlier study with visually impaired users found all their participants avoided lock, which is not the case in our study, but those who did not use locks claimed similar reasons of not knowing about it or inconveniences faced. Similarly, the use of Screen Curtain instead of a lock was prevalent in our study too. Users in our study however claimed avoiding headphones in public, contrary to Azenkot's observation. While the studies have discussed users' motivations to use locks, their choices of pass-codes, and also compared common options such as PINS, Patterns and Biometrics, further investigation of how people choose and migrate between various forms of locks might yield interesting insights, especially concerning usability and accessibility of the interfaces with visually impaired users.

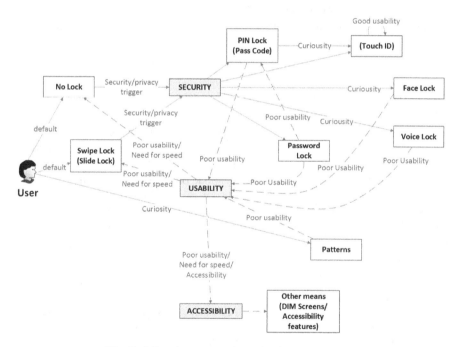

Fig. 3. Migration across phone locking mechanisms

4.3   Assistive Software as a Layer of Security

Users may not always find the existing accessibility features on their phone to effectively use the locking and security mechanisms effectively. For instance, the screen readers read the passwords aloud while entering passwords. There are settings where users can disable the screed reader from reading the passwords, but then they do not know what they are typing. This leaves them with the option of using headphones which is not suitable for frequent unlocking, and hence is a discomfort. Users also feel headphones are unsafe to use constantly as they depend on their aural senses for their activities. Users face issues of accuracy and speed with using the unlocking mechanisms as discussed in Sect. 4.1. Users tend to deal with these situations by doing away with phone locks altogether, or entering the code at low volume without headphones.

"A long time back I had tried passcode, but it used to just say dot-dot when I would enter any number. I could not know what number was pressed. That's why I never set anything for screen lock." – (ASU501)

Instead of depending on the locking mechanisms alone, users seem to also use the assistive features as an additional layer for security. For instance, when users are unable to assess if anyone is eavesdropping, then tend to obscure or hide their activity using physical means, i.e. holding the phone in a particular way or covering the screen with their hand. Another interesting way of obscuring was using the accessibility options on the phone, i.e. the Dim Screen or Screen Curtain option, or the screen reader set at a very fast speaking rate. With the Dim Screen option, the screen is totally turned off while operating so others are unable to see the screen. Hence users also went to the extent of not using a phone lock, as they felt Dim Screen was sufficient protection from snoopers.

"I use a feature present in TalkBack, called Dim Screen, so I don't need to keep any password. Nobody can see anything. Because of this feature I do not require any screen security for my phone." – (NSU215,16)

Again, the screen reader and other alternate gestures that they used when the phone is in accessibility mode were considered difficult for others, mainly sighted users. Hence they felt their phones were safe from others. They felt other users need to be skilled to use the phone with the accessibility mode on. They also kept the speech rate very high, making the speech indiscernible by others. This was another form of obscurity protecting their privacy in public. In the case where the screen readers speak the password/pin aloud, one user intentionally scanned over random keys while entering the password, thus obscuring the actual password. Although not fool proof, an untrained listener would find it difficult to understand which keys were merely scanned and which were actually entered.

"If I don't want people to know what my PIN is, I create a false PIN by touching extra numbers. If I don't release the touched numbers, they are not entered. So people do not know what PIN I entered. Generally, I keep in mind that when I enter my PIN, I hold my phone closer to me so that nobody can see anything. Even you didn't get my PIN, did you?" – (BBU108)

In some cases users felt that keeping the screen reader at a very loud is useful, especially when the phone is not on their person. This allowed them to notice if somebody started interfering with their phone.

However, it is apparent that these approaches of depending on accessibility features for obscurity for privacy and protection is limited. It only protects them from sighted and untrained users. As the phone security features are not amenable out-of-the-box to the blind users, the users have coped up by using assistive features in interesting ways. We feel that it might be interesting and useful if designers could explore this further and consider enhancing assistive features for security and privacy too. While studies have highlighted the use of Screen Curtain for privacy [6], the phenomenon and opportunity of adapting assistive software of smartphones of security and privacy would be interesting to explore further.

4.4   Patterns – a Maze

Most users felt Patterns are impossible for them to use as they cannot understand them. They face difficulty in locating the dots and connecting them by gestures (lines). Patterns are not accessible enough although there are soft buzzes when the user touches the dots. The screen reader also provides a few instructions, but are mostly not helpful enough. Some users had explored patterns but did not adopt them as were unable to use them, despite feeling that Patterns could be faster to use than PINS. We feel users found it challenging to build a mental model of Patterns. It was also a new mechanism which was not available on earlier tangible phones.

> *"It would just speak 'Pattern Area'. I would draw the wrong pattern. The phone would never unlock. I had to take somebody else's help. So, I stopped using patterns." –* (SKU409)

We found a couple of users who used patterns easily. We observed that user BBU2 had developed a strategy to locate the first dot, after which they could locate the rest and reach a speed similar to sighted users in unlocking the phone. The user held the phone in a unique way with the thumb and fingers positioned possibly to locate the first dot accurately, i.e. on the right top edge of the pattern grid (Fig. 4). However, we noticed that the few users who used Patterns appeared to use quite predictable patterns to enable accurate and quick access. The tendency was to start at edges, as they needed an anchoring point. They relied on straight paths and avoided diagonals, to avoid accidentally touching the wrong dots. This resulted in simple shapes – 'sleeping lines' or L's, and squares (a C) on the 3×3 grid. Similar to the concerns people had with PINS, users also found using Patterns accurately in certain situations where attention is difficult (e.g. sleepy or travelling).

> *"...I would want to connect four dots only. I don't want to connect more. So, I'm telling you that I would keep an L or Square." –* (BBU215)

Despite its apparent difficulty, Patterns could be widely adopted by blind users if the accessibility was improved. Example, it should be easier to locate and anchor to the starting dot in the pattern. E.g. Buzzi et al. have discussed approaches how visually challenges users can orient themselves on touchscreens more easily [44, 45]. Otherwise, for most users the Patterns is currently a maze – they need to be really motivated to attempt to understand and develop a strategy to find their way through.

Existing studies [46–48] are inconclusive about preferences of Patterns over PINs. Patterns seem to have a higher rate of errors. Yet users tend to prefer Patterns as they perceive better feedback, ease of use, efficiency and memorability. We were unable to find detailed studies discussing the use and accessibility of Patterns by visually impaired users. Users seem to need to orient themselves better on the screen to be able to use Patterns more effectively.

Fig. 4. User using a Pattern lock accurately identifying the dots

4.5   Password Backups and Fallback Users

Users frequently seek assistance from others, usually sighted users, to set up their online accounts for email, Facebook, etc. They often require assistance as they are unfamiliar with the interface, and also find CAPTCHAs challenging. They usually seek assistance from people they consider tech-savvy – e.g. trainers as blind institutions, phone vendors, or family members. While seeking assistance, they often share personal information including passwords. Some users reported that they did not change the passwords later, as they trusted the person who helped them and expected him or her to forget about it. However, some users who appeared more tech-savvy and security paranoid did change the passwords later. Some even deleted their account and set up a new account as they were now familiar with the process.

> *"I had faced a problem with my Gmail account. I had entered username properly, but when I tried to enter password, it would speak out star-star… I didn't know what to do. Then I took a sighted person's help for logging in using email id and password"* – (ASU101)

Users face similar challenges in resetting passwords, and need assistance. To prevent forgetting passwords, especially important ones, users resort to sharing passwords with a trusted person, as a backup. This trusted person is usually a family member or a close friend, who may also sometimes assist the user with operating the account. Sharing passwords is also seen in an existing study by Singh et al. [49] an emerging trend, especially among married couples, disabled users and indigenous communities. The authors [49] also highlight principles for Design considering such a phenomenon.

> *"My friend knows my password because he needs it to fill some forms for me. He is the only person who knows my password."* – (RSU412)

They also resort to keeping the password written down in a diary at home or in a password-protected file on their laptop. Users also maintained a list of passwords that they cycled through across various accounts. Other users however relied on using the "forgot password" option to reset the password instead of taking measures to remember, store or share passwords. Some used drastic measures such as creating a new account, rather than attempting recovery. Similar reactions are reported in a study with less-literate users [50].

The motivation to share or store passwords seems to stem from the difficulty faced in recalling passwords as well as in resetting their passwords. The passwords that were shared or backed up were usually those that were important and infrequently used (e.g. those related to the college/university or banking).

"My university password... I've written it in 2-3 places. It is written on my mobile, at home, and on my wall calendar as well." – (RSU714)

Table 2 provides a summary of number of notes considered supporting the themes that emerged.

Table 2. Key themes and supporting notes considered

Key themes	Supporting notes considered
Accessibility challenges lead to predictable passwords	82
Migration across locking mechanisms	97
Assistive software as a layer of security	42
Patterns – a maze	27
Password backups and fallback users	34

5 Discussion and Design Recommendations

We assessed our findings using the framework of UGT [35, 36] to define the users' usability goals and also considered usable security related aspects from Whitten [38] and Saltzer [37]. We considered the usability and security goals for blind smartphone users as (1) being able to protect their data and privacy using the security mechanisms on their phone appropriately, (2) being able to protect their online accounts with good password practices supported by the phone interfaces.

Users tend to find existing phone locking mechanisms error-prone due to lack of tangibility and ineffective feedback, affecting accuracy, speed and ease of use. Although users are often motivated to learn the locking mechanisms, apparent from how they have explored the various options, they often find it difficult to understand the mechanisms and are not comfortable with the interfaces. Users also face barriers in locating and learning the settings for setting up the locks, especially without assistance from sighted users. This activity of setting a lock is infrequent, and being unfamiliar with the interface, users tend to have a certain amount of fear to set up locks. Frequent errors while using the locks also lead to the fear of getting locked out of their own phone (*'dangerous errors'*). Tapping on areas accidentally also messes up the inter-action (*Economy of mechanism' and 'Psychological acceptability'*). Hence, users either opt to not using locks at all, or adopt very simplistic predictable passwords (*'unmo-tivated user'*). Additionally they adopt accessibility features as means to obscure and protect privacy. Accessibility concerns seem to be the key issue that affects secure adoption of phone locks by blind users. Improved accessibility and biometric approaches could improve adoption. Among the locking mechanisms available, finger print recognition seems to have the best *'economy of mechanism'* and *'psychological acceptability'*. However, it can be argued that biometric authentication still needs to evolve for better security [51]. Patterns is another promising quick approach, if accessibility could be improved. Poor accessibility also leads the user to take assistance from others – blind and sighted ('*weakest link*', '*barn door*'). They even write and sharing their passwords or accounts, leaving themselves exposed and vulnerable to attacks. Hence, improving the accessibility of especially of security features is of prime importance.

We also found that the users have an attitude of continual learning and have a close-knit community among themselves. They are informed about good practices and share tips among themselves via workshops conducted by organizations for blind or via WhatsApp and other online communities. As users seem open to technology and share information and good practices, we feel quick dissemination of security solutions and awareness is possible. Being tech savvy and explorative, alternative interfaces could be explored which might be usable and effective to visually impaired users. Researchers such as Kane, Leporini, Buzzi, Azenkot and Guerreiro have discussed novel approaches for usable and accessible interfaces on smartphones [8, 45, 52–57].

A primary challenge with visually impaired users using touchscreen smartphone interfaces is the lack of tangibility and visual cues. Sighted users usually rely on subtle or direct visual cues while interacting with user interfaces. This channel is blocked out for blind users. Instead they depend on the audio channel, which is either missing or minimal, and is usually incidental and not specifically designed for accessibility. At the most there is minimal haptic feedback through buzzes, and the screen reader but does not provide a sense of a user interface that visual cues do. In current interfaces, there seems to be little or no mapping or information redundancy between the visual and audio channels. A transfer of feedback from the visual to an aural and tangible channel is required for appropriate feedback as recommended for usability of the interfaces. Users could then subconsciously process information while interacting with the interface. Such interfaces could be translated to have a parallel aural and haptic interface. For instance a Morse-like code which vibrates privately in the hand. Vibration and aural standards could be defined as alternatives to visual interfaces, over and above screen reader which are essentially text to speech. For example, some existing studies investigate providing prosodic cues with screen readers [58, 59].

Accessible security interfaces should focus on achieving better speed and ease-of-use. Occasionally used screens such as Settings or Account creation should be accessible enough to avoid assistance from sighted users – or at least designed to allow mediation and assistance but maintaining privacy of the users wherever required.

New accessible phone locks can be explored – again focusing on ease and speed of use for visually impaired or eyes-free access. For existing phone locks, fallbacks could be introduced: e.g. Touch-ID to PIN. Instead of locking out phones after unsuccessful attempts to unlock the phones (caused by errors in input), users could be given a secondary lock interface. Anchoring points could be developed or overlaid on touch screens (as in the mark on the '5'-key on earlier phones) which could assist users to orient and anchor themselves to use visual/spatial interfaces such as PINS. There is scope for the pattern locks to be improved for accessibility. Potentially, there are a lot of cues from the earlier tangible Symbian phones, and how blind users used them, which could transition into the newer touchscreen smartphones.

Users currently use the accessibility settings for privacy, such as a rapidly speaking screen reader or dim screen. The accessibility features could be enhanced to embrace this behaviour, and designed for better obscurity, allowing privacy from blind and sighted users alike.

6 Conclusions

We believe that the area of security interventions for smartphones in the context of usability can be better aligned. Users face constant difficulties due to accessibility shortcomings. This affects their productivity and they opt out of using locking mechanisms. They cope up by appropriating the assistive features as obscurity for privacy. Improvement in the accessible phone locks, password recovery and account creation, could vastly assist them being independent and secure.

Acknowledgments. We thank all the users, volunteers, and all publication support and staff, especially the reviewers who wrote and provided helpful comments on versions of this document. We thank Interact for supporting and improving our paper through its shepherding process.

References

1. India Ericsson Mobility Report June 2016. https://www.ericsson.com/assets/local/mobility-report/documents/2016/india-ericsson-mobility-report-june-2016.pdf
2. Irvine, D., Zemke, A., Pusateri, G., Gerlach, L., Chun, R., Jay, W.M.: Tablet and smartphone accessibility features in the low vision rehabilitation. Neuro-Ophthalmol. **38**, 53 (2014)
3. Kim, H.K., Han, S.H., Park, J., Park, J.: The interaction experiences of visually impaired people with assistive technology: a case study of smartphones. Int. J. Ind. Ergon. **55**, 22–33 (2016)
4. Robinson, J.L., Avery, V.B., Chun, R., Pusateri, G., Jay, W.M.: Usage of accessibility options for the iPhone and iPad in a visually impaired population. Semin. Ophthalmol. **32**, 163–171 (2017)
5. Abdolrahmani, A., Kuber, R., Hurst, A.: An empirical investigation of the situationally-induced impairments experienced by blind mobile device users. In: Proceedings of the 13th Web for All Conference, pp. 21:1–21:8. ACM, New York (2016)
6. Azenkot, S., Rector, K., Ladner, R., Wobbrock, J.: PassChords: secure multi-touch authentication for blind people. In: Proceedings of the 14th International ACM SIGACCESS Conference on Computers and Accessibility, pp. 159–166. ACM, New York (2012)
7. Kane, S.K., Jayant, C., Wobbrock, J.O., Ladner, R.E.: Freedom to roam: a study of mobile device adoption and accessibility for people with visual and motor disabilities. In: Proceedings of the 11th International ACM SIGACCESS Conference on Computers and Accessibility, pp. 115–122. ACM (2009)
8. Chiti, S., Leporini, B.: Accessibility of android-based mobile devices: a prototype to investigate interaction with blind users. In: Miesenberger, K., Karshmer, A., Penaz, P., Zagler, W. (eds.) ICCHP 2012. LNCS, vol. 7383, pp. 607–614. Springer, Heidelberg (2012). doi:10.1007/978-3-642-31534-3_89

9. Leporini, B., Buzzi, M.C., Buzzi, M.: Interacting with mobile devices via VoiceOver: usability and accessibility issues. In: Proceedings of the 24th Australian Computer-Human Interaction Conference, pp. 339–348. ACM (2012)

10. WHO: Global Data on Visual Impairments (2010). http://www.who.int/blindness/ GLOBALDATAFINALforweb.pdf

11. Office of the Registrar General & Census Commissioner, India: CENSUS OF INDIA 2011 DATA ON DISABILITY. http://www.languageinindia.com/jan2014/disabilityinindia2011 data.pdf

12. IDA - India: Cataract Blindness Control Project. http://web.worldbank.org/WBSITE/ EXTERNAL/EXTABOUTUS/IDA/0,contentMDK:21917842 ~ menuPK: 4752068 ~ pagePK:51236175 ~ piPK:437394 ~ theSitePK:73154,00.html

13. Key Definitions of Statistical Terms - American Foundation for the Blind. http://www.afb. org/info/blindness-statistics/key-definitions-of-statistical-terms/25

14. Data on Disability, Disabled Population by type of Disability, Age and Sex - C20 Table (India & States/UTs - District Level). http://www.censusindia.gov.in/2011census/ Disability_Data/India/C_20-India.xls

15. Chin, E., Felt, A.P., Sekar, V., Wagner, D.: Measuring user confidence in smartphone security and privacy. In: Proceedings of the Eighth Symposium on Usable Privacy and Security, p. 1. ACM (2012)

16. Egelman, S., Jain, S., Portnoff, R.S., Liao, K., Consolvo, S., Wagner, D.: Are you ready to lock? In: Proceedings of the 2014 ACM SIGSAC Conference on Computer and Communications Security, pp. 750–761. ACM Press (2014)

17. Inan, F.A., Namin, A.S., Pogrund, R.L., Jones, K.S.: Internet use and cybersecurity concerns of individuals with visual impairments. J. Educ. Technol. Soc. **19**, 28–40 (2016)

18. Karlson, A.K., Brush, A.J., Schechter, S.: Can i borrow your phone?: understanding concerns when sharing mobile phones. In: Proceedings of the SIGCHI Conference on Human Factors in Computing Systems, pp. 1647–1650. ACM (2009)

19. Muslukhov, I., Boshmaf, Y., Kuo, C., Lester, J., Beznosov, K.: Understanding users' requirements for data protection in smartphones. In: 2012 IEEE 28th International Conference on Data Engineering Workshops (ICDEW), pp. 228–235. IEEE (2012)

20. Muslukhov, I., Boshmaf, Y., Kuo, C., Lester, J., Beznosov, K.: Know your enemy: the risk of unauthorized access in smartphones by insiders. In: Proceedings of the 15th International Conference on Human-Computer Interaction with Mobile Devices and Services, pp. 271–280. ACM (2013)

21. Mylonas, A., Kastania, A., Gritzalis, D.: Delegate the smartphone user? security awareness in smartphone platforms. Comput. Secur. **34**, 47–66 (2013)

22. Tchakounté, F., Dayang, P., Nlong, J., Check, N.: Understanding of the behaviour of android smartphone users in cameroon: application of the security. Open J. Inf. Secur. Appl. **2014**, 9–20 (2014)

23. Ahmed, T., Hoyle, R., Connelly, K., Crandall, D., Kapadia, A.: Privacy concerns and behaviors of people with visual impairments. In: Proceedings of the 33rd Annual ACM Conference on Human Factors in Computing Systems, pp. 3523–3532. ACM (2015)

24. Ashraf, A., Raza, A.: Usability issues of smart phone applications: for visually challenged people. World Acad. Sci. Eng. Technol. Int. J. Comput. Electr. Autom. Control Inf. Eng. **8**, 760–767 (2014)

25. Dosono, B., Hayes, J., Wang, Y.: "I'm Stuck!": a contextual inquiry of people with visual impairments in authentication. In: Eleventh Symposium on Usable Privacy and Security (SOUPS 2015), pp. 151–168 (2015)

26. Asokan, N., Kuo, C.: Usable Mobile Security. In: Ramanujam, R., Ramaswamy, S. (eds.) ICDCIT 2012. LNCS, vol. 7154, pp. 1–6. Springer, Heidelberg (2012). doi:10.1007/978-3-642-28073-3_1

27. Ben-Asher, N., Kirschnick, N., Sieger, H., Meyer, J., Ben-Oved, A., Möller, S.: On the need for different security methods on mobile phones. In: Proceedings of the 13th International Conference on Human Computer Interaction with Mobile Devices and Services, pp. 465–473. ACM (2011)

28. Jakobsson, M.: Why mobile security is not like traditional security (2011)

29. Felt, A.P., Ha, E., Egelman, S., Haney, A., Chin, E., Wagner, D.: Android permissions: user attention, comprehension, and behavior. In: Proceedings of the Eighth Symposium on Usable Privacy and Security, pp. 3:1–3:14. ACM, New York (2012)

30. Chen, J., Paik, M., McCabe, K.: Exploring internet security perceptions and practices in urban ghana. In: SOUPS, pp. 129–142 (2014)

31. Alsaleh, M., Alomar, N., Alarifi, A.: Smartphone users: Understanding how security mechanisms are perceived and new persuasive methods. PLoS ONE **12**, e0173284 (2017)

32. Bevan, N., Carter, J., Harker, S.: ISO 9241-11 revised: what have we learnt about usability Since 1998? In: Kurosu, M. (ed.) HCI 2015. LNCS, vol. 9169, pp. 143–151. Springer, Cham (2015). doi:10.1007/978-3-319-20901-2_13

33. ISO/DIS 9241-11.2(en), Ergonomics of human-system interaction — Part 11: Usability: Definitions and concepts. https://www.iso.org/obp/ui/#iso:std:iso:9241:-11:dis:ed-2:v2:en

34. 10 Heuristics for User Interface Design: Article by Jakob Nielsen. https://www.nngroup.com/articles/ten-usability-heuristics/

35. Joshi, A.: Usability goals setting tool. In: 4th Workshop on Software and Usability Engineering Cross-Pollination: Usability Evaluation of Advanced Interfaces, Uppsala (2009)

36. Joshi, A., Sarda, N.L.: Do teams achieve usability goals? evaluating goal achievement with usability goals setting tool. In: Campos, P., Graham, N., Jorge, J., Nunes, N., Palanque, P., Winckler, M. (eds.) INTERACT 2011. LNCS, vol. 6946, pp. 313–330. Springer, Heidelberg (2011). doi:10.1007/978-3-642-23774-4_26

37. Saltzer, J.H., Schroeder, M.D.: The protection of information in computer systems. Proc. IEEE **63**, 1278–1308 (1975)

38. Whitten, A.: Making security usable (2004). http://reports-archive.adm.cs.cmu.edu/anon/anon/usr/ftp/usr0/ftp/2004/CMU-CS-04-135.pdf

39. Whitten, A., Tygar, J.D.: Why johnny can't encrypt: a usability evaluation of PGP 5.0. In: Proceedings of the 8th Conference on USENIX Security Symposium, vol. 8 (1999)

40. Beyer, H., Holtzblatt, K.: Contextual Design: Defining Customer-Centered Systems. Morgan Kaufmann Publishers Inc., San Francisco (1998)

41. Genco, E., Kelley, R., Vernon, C., Aviv, A.J.: Alternative keyboard layouts for improved password entry and creation on mobile devices. Presented at the Eleventh Symposium on Usable Privacy and Security

42. von Zezschwitz, E., De Luca, A., Hussmann, H.: Honey, I shrunk the keys: influences of mobile devices on password composition and authentication performance. In: Proceedings of the 8th Nordic Conference on Human-Computer Interaction: Fun, Fast, Foundational, pp. 461–470. ACM (2014)

43. Harbach, M., De Luca, A., Egelman, S.: The anatomy of smartphone unlocking: a field study of android lock screens. In: Proceedings of the 2016 CHI Conference on Human Factors in Computing Systems, pp. 4806–4817. ACM Press (2016)

44. Buzzi, M.C., Buzzi, M., Leporini, B., Paratore, M.T.: Vibro-tactile enrichment improves blind user interaction with mobile touchscreens. In: Kotzé, P., Marsden, G., Lindgaard, G., Wesson, J., Winckler, M. (eds.) INTERACT 2013. LNCS, vol. 8117, pp. 641–648. Springer, Heidelberg (2013). doi:10.1007/978-3-642-40483-2_45

45. Buzzi, M.C., Buzzi, M., Donini, F., Leporini, B., Paratore, M.T.: Haptic reference cues to support the exploration of touchscreen mobile devices by blind users. In: Proceedings of the Biannual Conference of the Italian Chapter of SIGCHI, pp. 28:1–28:8. ACM, New York (2013)

46. Andriotis, P., Tryfonas, T., Oikonomou, G., Yildiz, C.: A pilot study on the security of pattern screen-lock methods and soft side channel attacks. In: Proceedings of the Sixth ACM Conference on Security and Privacy in Wireless and Mobile Networks, pp. 1–6. ACM (2013)

47. Loge, M., Duermuth, M., Rostad, L.: On user choice for android unlock patterns. In: Proceedings of 1st European Workshop on Usable Security (EuroUSEC) 2016 (2016)

48. von Zezschwitz, E., Dunphy, P., De Luca, A.: Patterns in the wild: a field study of the usability of pattern and pin-based authentication on mobile devices. In: Proceedings of the 15th International Conference on Human-Computer Interaction with Mobile Devices and Services, p. 261. ACM Press (2013)

49. Singh, S., Cabraal, A., Demosthenous, C., Astbrink, G., Furlong, M.: Password sharing: implications for security design based on social practice. In: Proceedings of the SIGCHI Conference on Human Factors in Computing Systems, pp. 895–904. ACM, New York (2007)

50. Doke, P., Lobo, S., Joshi, A., Aggarwal, N., Paul, V., Mevada, V., KR, A.: A user study about security practices of less-literate smartphone users. In: Basu, A., Das, S., Horain, P., Bhattacharya, S. (eds.) IHCI 2016. LNCS, vol. 10127, pp. 209–216. Springer, Cham (2017). doi:10.1007/978-3-319-52503-7_17

51. Boult, T.E., Scheirer, W.J., Woodworth, R.: Revocable fingerprint biotokens: accuracy and security analysis. In: 2007 IEEE Conference on Computer Vision and Pattern Recognition, pp. 1–8 (2007)

52. Azenkot, S., Wobbrock, J.O., Prasain, S., Ladner, R.E.: Input finger detection for nonvisual touch screen text entry in Perkinput. In: Proceedings of Graphics Interface 2012, pp. 121–129. Canadian Information Processing Society (2012)

53. Buzzi, M.C., Buzzi, M., Leporini, B., Senette, C.: Playing with geometry: a multimodal android app for blind children. In: Proceedings of the 11th Biannual Conference on Italian SIGCHI Chapter, pp. 134–137. ACM (2015)

54. Buzzi, M.C., Buzzi, M., Leporini, B., Trujillo, A.: Designing a text entry multimodal keypad for blind users of touchscreen mobile phones. In: Proceedings of the 16th International ACM SIGACCESS Conference on Computers and Accessibility, pp. 131–136. ACM (2014)

55. Guerreiro, T., Nicolau, H., Jorge, J.A.: From tapping to touching: making touch screens accessible to blind users. IEEE Multimed. 15, 48–50 (2008)

56. Kane, S.K., Bigham, J.P., Wobbrock, J.O.: Slide rule: making mobile touch screens accessible to blind people using multi-touch interaction techniques. In: Proceedings of the 10th International ACM SIGACCESS Conference on Computers and Accessibility, pp. 73–80. ACM, New York (2008)

57. Kane, S.K., Morris, M.R., Perkins, A.Z., Wigdor, D., Ladner, R.E., Wobbrock, J.O.: Access overlays: improving non-visual access to large touch screens for blind users. In: Proceedings of the 24th Annual ACM Symposium on User Interface Software and Technology, pp. 273–282. ACM, New York (2011)

58. Murphy, E., Bates, E., Fitzpatrick, D.: Designing auditory cues to enhance spoken mathematics for visually impaired users. In: Proceedings of the 12th International ACM SIGACCESS Conference on Computers and Accessibility, pp. 75–82. ACM (2010)

59. Pitt, I.J., Edwards, A.D.: Improving the usability of speech-based interfaces for blind users. In: Proceedings of the Second Annual ACM Conference on Assistive Technologies, pp. 124–130. ACM (1996)

Effects of Uncertainty and Cognitive Load on User Trust in Predictive Decision Making

Jianlong Zhou$^{(\boxtimes)}$, Syed Z. Arshad, Simon Luo, and Fang Chen

DATA61, CSIRO, 13 Garden Street, Eveleigh, NSW 2015, Australia
{jianlong.zhou, syed.arshad, simon.luo,
fang.chen}@data61.csiro.au

Abstract. Rapid increase of data in different fields has been resulting in wide applications of Machine Learning (ML) based intelligent systems in predictive decision making scenarios. Unfortunately, these systems appear like a 'black-box' to users due to their complex working mechanisms and therefore significantly affect the user's trust in human-machine interactions. This is partly due to the tightly coupled uncertainty inherent in the ML models that underlie the predictive decision making recommendations. Furthermore, when such analytics-driven intelligent systems are used in modern complex high-risk domains (such as aviation) - user decisions, in addition to trust, are also influenced by higher levels of cognitive load. This paper investigates effects of uncertainty and cognitive load on user trust in predictive decision making in order to design effective user interfaces for such ML-based intelligent systems. Our user study of 42 subjects in a repeated factorial design experiment found that both uncertainty types (risk and ambiguity) and cognitive workload levels affected user trust in predictive decision making. Uncertainty presentation leads to increased trust but only under low cognitive load conditions when users had sufficient cognitive resources to process the information. Presentation of uncertainty under high load conditions (when cognitive resources were short in supply) leads to a decrease of trust in the system and its recommendations.

Keywords: Trust · Uncertainty · Cognitive load · Predictive decision making

1 Introduction

Trust has been found to be a critical factor driving human behavior in human-machine interactions with autonomous systems [1] and more recently in modern complex high-risk domains such as aviation and military command and control [2]. It is also one of the most important factors in management and organizational behavior for all personal and business decision making as well as for efficiency and task performance [3, 4]. Trust is influenced by the types and format of information received by humans, their individual approaches to develop and determine trust, and aspects such as system capability and reliability [5].

Various definitions of trust have been used. One of the most widely cited definition of trust is from Lee and See [6], which defines trust as "the attitude that an agent will help achieve an individual's goals in a situation characterized by uncertainty and

© IFIP International Federation for Information Processing 2017
Published by Springer International Publishing AG 2017. All Rights Reserved
R. Bernhaupt et al. (Eds.): INTERACT 2017, Part IV, LNCS 10516, pp. 23–39, 2017.
DOI: 10.1007/978-3-319-68059-0_2

vulnerability". This definition shows that uncertainty is tightly coupled to trust. Uncertainty indicates it is impossible to determine whether the information available is true or not. There are many variants of uncertainty. The term could refer to statistical variability, noise in the information, nondeterministic relationship between action and consequences, or the psychological reaction to difficult problems. In human-machine interactions, uncertainty often plays an important role in hindering the sense-making process and conducting tasks: on the machine side, uncertainty builds up from the system itself; on the human side, these uncertainties often result in "lack of knowledge or trust" or "over-trust". Such human's biased interpretation can be partially resolved if we can make uncertainty transparent to users. Furthermore, system transparency is regarded as one vital aspect in maintaining human's trust in and reliance on autonomous systems [7, 8]. A user might be risking too much by completely ignoring uncertainties and having complete faith in autonomous systems. On the other hand, trivializing autonomous systems or having high uncertainty perception on autonomous systems could possibly dismiss the incredible potential of autonomous systems. Adobor [9] showed that a certain amount of uncertainty is necessary for trust to emerge. Beyond that threshold, however, increase in uncertainty can lead to a reduction in trust. This midrange proposition suggests that there may be an optimal balance between uncertainty and trust.

Moreover, Parasuraman et al. [10] showed that human cognition constructs such as Cognitive Load (CL) and trust are often invoked in considerations of function allocation and the design of automated systems. For example, in task situations of modern complex high-risk domains, users often need to make decisions in limited time. Therefore, they often make decisions under high cognitive load besides trust issues in such task situations. It was found that a higher cognitive load worsens the situation in relation to trust building [11]. However, it is still not clear how trust varies under both high cognitive load and various uncertainty conditions.

Next we look at decision making, which is now an important research topic in HCI with the fast growing use of intelligent systems [12]. Rapidly increasing data in fields such as finance, infrastructure and society has motivated users to try integrating "Big Data" and advanced analytics into business operations - in order to become more analytics-driven in their decision making. Much of machine learning (ML) research is inspired by such expectations. As a result, we continuously find ourselves coming across ML-based appealing viewgraphs and other predictions that seem to work (or have worked) surprisingly well in practical scenarios (e.g. AlphaGO's beating with professional GO players in 2016 and 2017). So far these machine learning success stories originate from ML technical experts or computing professionals (e.g. Google DeepMind). For many of non-ML users, ML-based predictive analytics software is like a "black box", to which they simply provide their source data and (after selecting some menu options on screen) colorful viewgraphs and/or recommendations are displayed as output. The "black box" approach has obvious drawbacks: it is difficult for the user to understand the complicated ML models [13, 14]. It is neither clear nor well understood that how trustworthy is this output, or how uncertainties are handled by underlying algorithmic procedures. As a result, the user is more or less unconfident in the ML model output when making decisions based on the ML model output and thus also unconfident in the ML models themselves.

From this perspective, Winkler [15] emphasized the importance of communicating uncertainties in predictions (as imprecision and uncertainty are unavoidable in predictive analytics). He believed that the consideration of uncertainty is greatly necessary in making rational decisions. It was also found that the presentation of automation uncertainty information helped the automation system receive higher trust ratings and increase acceptance of the system [16]. This display might improve the acceptance of fallible systems and further enhances human–automation cooperation. However, it remains unclear whether different types of uncertainty (e.g. risk and ambiguity) affect trust building, and if yes how they affect trust building, especially in predictive decision making. Here risk refers to situations with a known distribution of possible outcomes, and ambiguity is the situation where outcomes have unknown probabilities.

This paper aims to investigate the effects of uncertainty on user trust under various cognitive load levels in predictive decision making. Two uncertainty types of risk and ambiguity are presented with predictive model results in a decision making scenario. This follows the user method and approach to design cognitive systems, as reviewed by Candello [17], and used in [18]. This user study was deployed as a simulation (derived from the case study) of water pipe failure history analysis for future pipe failure prediction. It shows that both uncertainty presentation and cognitive load levels affect user trust in predictive decision making. The investigation results can be used to design effective user interfaces for ML-based intelligent systems and improve the acceptability of ML techniques by users.

2 Related Work

The research in human-machine trust and similar cognitive engineering constructs has a rich history [10]. Several of the efforts in this area can be traced back to Rouse's [19] ideas about adaptive aiding, that later, among other things evolved into more advanced HCI techniques. Also that psychophysiology was proposed for adaptive automation [20] and then trust and self-confidence argued into adaptive automation [21].

Winkler [15] demonstrated, with the help of several effective examples (from different fields), that probabilities are needed to understand the risk associated with potential decisions as well as to determine measures such as expected payoffs and expected utilities. LeClerc and Joslyn [22] successfully demonstrated that adding a probabilistic uncertainty estimate in public weather forecasts improved both decision quality and compliance (to evacuation instructions in cases of severe weather threats). Uggirala et al. [23] studied humans using systems that include uncertainties by having the users rate their trust at each level through questionnaires. Their study showed that trust relates to competence and an inverse relation to uncertainty, meaning that an increase in uncertainty decreases trust in the systems.

Allen et al. [24] investigated the effects of communicating uncertainty information with users using different representations on cognitive tasks. Uncertainty information is typically presented to users visually, most commonly in graphical format [24, 25]. Edwards et al. [26] compared different graphical methods from presenting quantitative uncertainty in decision making tasks. The representation of uncertainty can have significant impact on human performance. It was shown that when the representation of uncertainty for a spatial task better matches the expert's preferred representation of the problem even a non-expert can show expert-like performance [27]. This is actually a very good motivation for trying to figure out the preferred representation of uncertainty by different user groups.

Decision making under uncertainty is widely investigated in decision theory [28], where uncertainty is usually considered as probabilities in utility functions. de Visser and Parasuraman [29] conducted two experiments to examine the effects of automation reliability and adaptive automation on human-system performance with different levels of task load by using a high-fidelity multi-UV (uninhabited vehicles) simulation involving both air and ground vehicles. User trust and self-confidence were higher and workload was lower for adaptive automation compared with the other conditions. It was found that human-robot teams can benefit from imperfect static automation even in high task load conditions and that adaptive automation can provide additional benefits in trust and workload.

However, little research has been done on the effects of uncertainty, especially different types of uncertainty such as risk and ambiguity uncertainty, on user trust in predictive decision making under various cognitive load levels. With the use of a case study of predictive decision making for the water pipe failure budget planning, this paper investigates user trust changes under variations of both uncertainty types and cognitive load levels. Two types of uncertainty presentations (risk and ambiguous) and four cognitive load levels are introduced in the study to learn their effects on user trust in predictive decision making.

3 Experiment

3.1 Experiment Data

This research used water pipe failure prediction as a case study for predictive decision making (replicated in lab environment). Water supply networks constitute one of the most crucial and valuable urban assets. The combination of growing populations and aging pipe networks requires water utilities to develop advanced risk management strategies in order to maintain their distribution systems in a financially viable way [30]. Pipes are characterized by different attributes, referred to as features, such as laid year, material, diameter size, etc. If pipe failure historical data is provided, future water pipe failure rate is predictable with respect to the inspected length of the water pipe network [30]. Such models are used by utility companies for budget planning and pipe maintenance. However, different models with various uncertainty conditions may be achievable resulting in different possible budget plans. The experiment is then set up to determine what uncertainty conditions may influence the user's trust during the decision process. The prediction models were simulated following the models such as Weibull and Hierarchical Beta Process (HBP) [30].

3.2   Experimental Data

In this study, models are simulated and based on different pipe features (e.g. size or laid year). The model performance curve was presented to let the participants evaluate different models. The model performance is the functional relationship between the inspected length of the network and the percentage of failures detected by the model. Figure 1 shows the performances of two sample models, where the "blue model" outperforms the "red model", because the former detects more failures than the latter for a given pipe length.

ML models are usually imperfect abstractions of reality. As a result, imprecision can occur in the prediction through model uncertainty. Model uncertainty here refers to an interval within which the true value of a measured quantity would lie. For example, in Fig. 2(a), in order to inspect 20% of the pipes in length, the uncertainty interval of the failure rate is [46%, 60%] for the blue model, and about [15%, 25%] for the red model: the red model is said to have less uncertainty in prediction than the blue model because the red model has smaller uncertainty interval than the blue model.

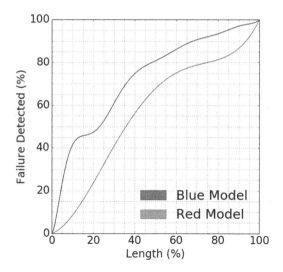

Fig. 1. Performance curves of ML models. (Color figure online)

Model uncertainty usually spans as a band in the model performance diagram as shown in Fig. 2. By considering model uncertainty, the relationship between two models may have two cases as shown in Fig. 2: non-overlapping models (see Fig. 2a), and overlapping models (see Fig. 2b). In Fig. 2b, the interval of the model with lower uncertainty is subsumed in the interval of the model with higher uncertainty, whereas in Fig. 2a, the two bands are disjoint.

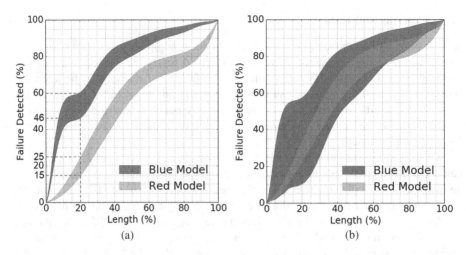

Fig. 2. Predictive models with uncertainty: (a) non-overlapping models, and (b) overlapping models. (Color figure online)

3.3 Task Design

According to the water pipe failure prediction framework, we investigated the decisions made by users under varied conditions. Each user was asked to make a budget plan, i.e. a budget in terms of network length to be inspected, using the failure prediction models learned from the historical pipe failure records. Two ML models were provided for each estimation task. Participants were required to make decisions by selecting one of two presented ML models and then making a budget estimate based on the selected ML model. The budget estimate needs to meet the following requirements:

- To inspect as short length of pipes as possible (low cost);
- To be as precise in budget estimate as possible (higher accuracy would reflect greater confidence in estimation).

In this study, a module named Automatic Predictive Assistant (APA) is introduced to the user as a new module 'under testing' phase. The APA is a simulated module which reads in the information provided by the ML models, and then recommends a typical decision (of average accuracy) for the participant. Users can choose to trust, modify or totally ignore the recommendations of APA. The participant needs to evaluate whether she trusts the estimation recommended by the APA. If she does not trust the APA, she is asked to provide her own estimation. Figure 3 shows the screenshot of a task performed in the study.

The actions a participant needed to do during a task session include answering questions to validate understanding of machine learning performance and uncertainty, and to validate cognitive load levels introduced, as well as making decisions according to information presented. In summary, each task is divided into following major steps:

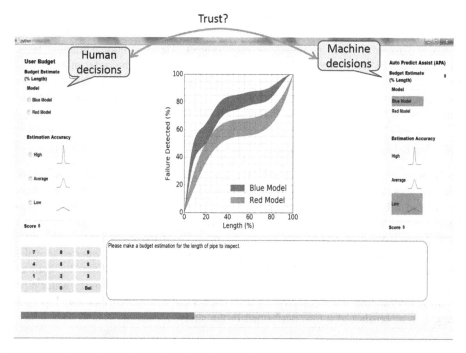

Fig. 3. Screenshot of a task performed in the study. (Color figure online)

(1) The participant is firstly asked to study the ML performance diagram (in the middle of the screenshot in Fig. 3) and answer questions on model performance and uncertainty to validate her understanding of the information presented.

(2) Next, the APA recommendations (at the right side of the screenshot in Fig. 3) are displayed and again the user understanding validated.

(3) Finally, the participant is required to estimate the budget by selecting an ML model and its estimation accuracy. If he/she does not trust the recommendations from the APA, he/she is required to provide his/her own estimations (at the left side of the screenshot in Fig. 3) based on the ML performance displayed at the first step. Subjective trust ratings are obtained immediately after this step.

Participants were encouraged to reach the best budget estimates they could as quick as possible.

In this study, cognitive load was introduced by asking participants to remember a random number digit sequence for the duration of task time and reciting it after the task. This dual-task load inducing technique is quite popular in decision making scenarios [31]. The cognitive load level was determined based on the number of digits being remembered. Four cognitive load levels were applied in this study – from low to high, the number of random digits to be remembered ranged from three, five, seven and nine. Three-digit number is for lowest load condition and nine-digit is for the highest load.

There were three different uncertainty visualizations (no uncertainty, non-overlapping uncertainty, and overlapping uncertainty). Each condition was performed under four different cognitive load levels. Each task was performed for three rounds. All together 36 estimation tasks (3 uncertainty conditions × 4 cognitive load levels × 3 rounds) were conducted by each subject. Three additional training tasks were also conducted by each subject before the formal tasks. The order of tasks was randomized during the experiment to avoid any bias. Slides-based instructions on the concepts of predictive models and uncertainty as well as predictive decision making were presented to each participant before the task time.

3.4   Participants and Apparatus

Forty-two participants were recruited from three groups with different background, with the ages ranging from 20 to 57 years: Fourteen participants were ML researchers (experts in ML or data mining research), nineteen were non-ML researchers (participants who were researchers but not in ML or data mining), and nine administrative staff. These three user groups constituted the majority of the users for this particular type of predictive decision making scenario we considered. All were requested to make predictive decisions (using historical data visualized on screen) about the optimal length of pipe (thus budget estimation) to be checked in order to minimize water pipe failures. Information was presented on a 21-inch Dell widescreen monitor. Figure 3 presents a screenshot of a task performed in the study.

3.5   Data Collection

After each decision making task, participants were asked to rate their trust in APA recommendations and also confidence in their own decisions (using a 9-point Likert scale where 1 = least trust, and 9 = most trust). Besides trust subjective ratings, cognitive load rankings for each task from subjects were also collected using a 9-point Likert scale (1 = least mental effort, and 9 = most mental effort) for load validation purposes.

4   Results

Figures 4 and 5 depict the summary visualization of trust measured via subjective responses of all 42 subjects. Trust values were normalized with respect to each subject to minimize individual differences in rating behavior. Since we had more than two dependent samples, we first performed Friedman test and then followed it up with post-hoc analysis using Wilcoxon signed-rank tests (with a Bonferroni correction) to analyze differences in participant responses of trust for various conditions.

Trust and Uncertainty: Figure 4 shows normalized trust values over the uncertainty treatments. *Control task* had only point prediction lines (refer to Fig. 1) and no uncertainty was presented. *Risk* uncertainty was presented by models with non-overlapping uncertainty (see Fig. 2a) and *ambiguity* by overlapping uncertainty models (see Fig. 2b).

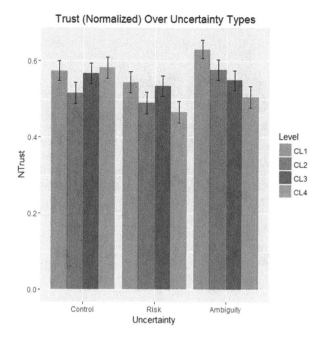

Fig. 4. Trust over uncertainty presented; control (No Uncertainty), risk (Non-Overlapping Uncertainty) and ambiguity (Overlapping Uncertainty).

When participants experienced uncertainty type ambiguity (rightmost group of columns in Fig. 4), Friedman test for cognitive load level conditions showed a statistically significant difference in trust among four CL levels, $\chi^2(3) = 12.363$, $p < .006$. Then post-hoc Wilcoxon tests (with a Bonferroni correction under a significance level set at $p < .013$) was applied to find pair-wise differences between levels in trust. The adjusted significance alpha level of .013 was calculated by dividing the original alpha of .05 by 4, based on the fact that we had four load level conditions to test.

The post-hoc tests found that for uncertainty condition of ambiguity, participants had significantly lower trust under high cognitive load (CL4), with $p < .001$, compared to that of low load (CL1). More details of this result and its implications for subject groups appear in discussion ahead.

Trust and Cognitive Load: Figure 5 shows normalized trust values over cognitive load levels. Here we are interested only in the extreme load levels administered, namely CL1 (the lowest) and CL4 (the highest), as they are the most relevant for automated cognitive load management [32]. Friedman's test of cognitive load level conditions of the lowest (CL1) and highest (CL4) both gave statistically significant differences in trust among three uncertainty conditions, $\chi^2(2) = 11.227$, $p < .004$ and $\chi^2(2) = 10.356$, $p < .006$ respectively. Then post-hoc Wilcoxon tests (with a Bonferroni correction under a significance level set at $p < .017$) was applied to find pair-wise differences between uncertainty conditions. The adjusted significance alpha

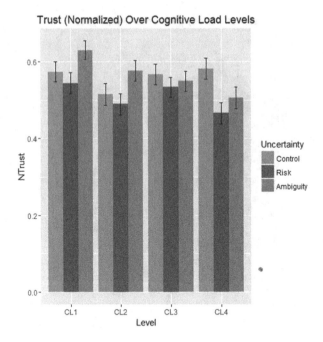

Fig. 5. Trust over cognitive load levels.

level of .017 was calculated by dividing the original alpha of .05 by 3, based on the fact that we had three uncertainty conditions to test.

The post-hoc tests found that for low cognitive load condition (CL1), trust in the condition of ambiguity was significantly higher ($p < .006$) than that of risk condition (Fig. 5, leftmost group of three columns). Whereas, for high cognitive load (CL4) condition, trust in risk condition was significantly lower ($p < .003$) than control condition. More details of this result and its implications for subject groups appear in discussion ahead.

5 Discussion

As discussed in earlier sections, trust is a challenging concept to study and investigate in, therefore, we opted to study human-machine trust in a specialized predictive decision making scenario. Predictive decision making support and automated aids have become quite popular with the advent of new machine learning based intelligent applications. Now that machines are becoming more intelligent – human-computer interaction must also evolve accordingly. Only by working together as a trusted team can humans and machines improve efficiency and productivity.

Trust and Uncertainty: Generally, in an automated predictive decision making scenario, humans are required to make future oriented decisions based on the information or recommendation presented on the screen by a machine learning (and data crunching) model/algorithm that mostly works on historical data behind the scenes (appearing like a black box to user). Since these decisions are about the future, there can be no absolutely correct answers - but only better and more appropriate ones based on a more precise understanding of the underlying data presented during the decision making process. Therefore, better presentation and adequate communication of uncertainty inherent in the underlying ML process can improve the trust of the user in the system and lead to better and effective decisions. In our case, we experimented with visualizing and communicating two forms of uncertainty, namely, risk and ambiguity. Risk is a form of uncertainty where all probabilities related to outcomes are known. The user, with the help of these known probabilities, can be expected to make better and well-informed decisions quickly. Such risk type uncertainty was represented by non-overlapping models (see Fig. 2a). The other type of uncertainty we experimented with was ambiguity, which was represented by overlapping models (see Fig. 2b) and where probabilities of outcomes were either unknown or not clearly stated. The control condition was the case where models were presented without any uncertainty component.

Looking at the overall results (Fig. 4), no clear trends can be observed for risk type uncertainty condition, but a clear trend of falling trust can be seen for uncertainty of type ambiguity as cognitive load level increases. It can be said that under low cognitive load (implying greater availability of cognitive resources), users felt more confident analyzing and interpreting the ambiguity type of uncertainty and therefore appear to trust the judgement/recommendation of the automated predictive assistant as it made more sense to them. However, under high cognitive load, the users might find themselves almost at the edge of their working memory capacity. Limited cognitive resources would result in lesser understanding of the ambiguity type of visual. This in turn is indicated by reduced trust in the system and its recommendations. This phenomenon seems to be in line with findings that the better the person understands the system and it's working the greater the person is willing to trust it [27].

Further drilling down deeper into this trust (over ambiguity type uncertainty) phenomenon into subject groups (administration, machine learning experts and non-machine learning experts) also leads to an interesting insight (see Fig. 6). Clearly the level of trust for ambiguity type uncertainty presentation appears to drop for all subject groups as cognitive load increases. High cognitive load appears to impact the trust same for all administrative staff and experts (whether they be machine learning or non-machine learning).

Important lessons here for improved trust can be to either avoid ambiguity type of uncertainty representation altogether or present it only when condition of low cognitive load. Also another direction could be to look for alternate ways of visualizing ambiguity type of uncertainty.

Trust and Cognitive Load: It is well known that human performance can be significantly affected by high cognitive or mental workload [33]. Cognitive workload is the load on working memory that the user experiences when engaged in a cognitive problem. In our case, the trust in decision making is influenced by a cognitive phase where user tries to make sense of the model data/visuals presented. Since the decision making task was soft time bound, the user must make efficient use of available cognitive resources in order to complete the task. Here we look at the two extreme

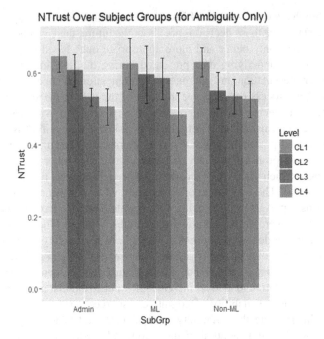

Fig. 6. Trust for ambiguity type uncertainty.

conditions where most cognitive resources were expected to be available (CL1) and where least cognitive resources were expected to be available (CL4). As stated earlier in the results section, Friedman test for both these extreme conditions (CL1 & CL4) turned out to be significant.

In low load condition (CL1), trust for ambiguity type uncertainty was significantly higher than risk type uncertainty (see leftmost group of columns in Fig. 5). The trend seems to be the same for all subject subgroups (see Fig. 7). Trust, under low load conditions, seems to be consistently higher for all groups whenever uncertainty of ambiguity type is presented. However, on further testing, only non-ML group (right-most group of columns in Fig. 7) yielded significantly ($p < .006$) higher trust level uncertainty types ambiguity to that of risk. A limitation here could be the lower number of subjects in groups other than non-ML experts. These findings go on to support the idea discussed earlier that uncertainty of type ambiguity can be readily processed by users only under low cognitive load conditions.

Likewise in high load condition (CL4), trust for risk type uncertainty was signifi-cantly lower than control condition of no uncertainty presentation (see rightmost group of columns in Fig. 5). The trend seems to be similar for all subject subgroups (see Fig. 8). Trust, for both uncertainty conditions, seems to be consistently lower for all groups with respect to control condition. On further testing, only non-ML group (rightmost group of columns in Fig. 8) yielded significantly ($p < .003$) lower trust level uncertainty type risk to that of control. A limitation here could be the lower number of subjects in other groups than non-machine learning experts. Of the total 42, there were 9 administrative staff, 14 machine learning experts and 19 non-machine learning experts.

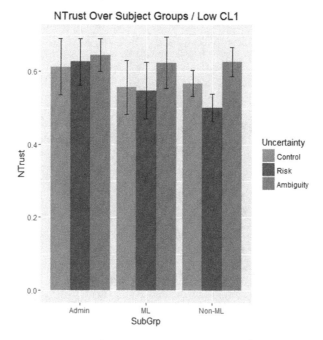

Fig. 7. Trust over subject groups (Low CL).

These findings go on to support the idea that people trust less what they have not had time to understand. Visuals presented in control condition are straightforward with no complication – however, they are simple, but only at the cost of hiding away the uncertainty inherent in the ML models. Once attempts are made to communicate the uncertainty – the trust seems to increase from control to risk and ambiguity uncertainty only under conditions of low cognitive load (see Fig. 7) and decrease under conditions of high cognitive load (see Fig. 8).

User Groups: The three user groups of administrative staff, ML experts and Non-ML experts constitute the majority of the users of such predictive decision making interfaces [18]. Of the people involved in predictive decision making, administrative staff is expected to be least knowledgeable of statistical probability and its representations. Non-ML experts may or may not be knowledgeable of statistical probability but they can be expected to be familiar with model representations. Finally the ML experts are expected to be the most knowledgeable of statistical probability and also of uncertainty inherent in ML models. In our case, from the total of 42, there were 9 administrative staff, 14 machine learning experts and 19 non-machine learning experts. The administrative group by itself is too small in number for any meaningful inference. ML-experts were reasonably good in number but nothing significant would be inferred. Only the Non-ML group appears to significant results in certain conditions as discussed above.

Overall, we can say that uncertainty presentation can lead to increased trust but only under low cognitive load conditions when user has sufficient cognitive resources to process the information. Presentation of uncertainty under high load conditions,

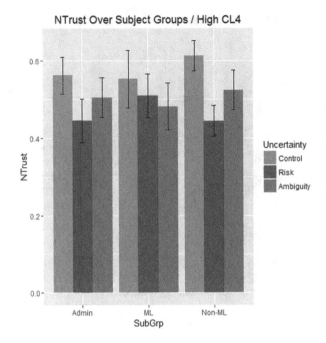

Fig. 8. Trust over subject groups (High CL).

when cognitive resources are short in supply can lead to lowering of trust in the system and its recommendations.

In order to incorporate these findings in HCI and real-world applications, the user interface for an ML-based intelligent system needs to include the following components:

- Components which show uncertainty of ML models. This could help users increase trust in their decisions;
- Feedback on user trust and load levels that allow users interfaces to adapt accordingly.

These components may be incorporated into the framework of adaptive measureable decision making proposed in [34], thereby introducing trust levels into an adaptive decision making process and allowing for efficient and informed decisions. Therefore, besides decision quality as demonstrated in [35], the revealing of user trust levels in predictive decision making also benefits the evaluation of ML models. From this perspective, this study made "black-box" ML models transparent through revealing user responses to ML models, but not directly explain how ML algorithms process data to get outputs with visualizations or feature contributions [36–38], where domain users still have difficulty to understand those complex visualizations and abstract numbers. The revealing of user trust in a predictive decision making scenario is more meaningful for both ML researchers and domain experts, and therefore help improve the acceptance of ML solutions by users.

In summary, this study showed that uncertainty and cognitive load played significant roles in affecting user trust in predictive decision making. Furthermore, various uncertainty types had different effects on user trust perceptions. These findings have at least two benefits in real-world applications: (1) to design intelligent user interface of predictive decision related applications in HCI. The user interface, which shows user trust in decision making in real-time, would help users make informed decisions effectively; (2) to evaluate ML models in ML research areas by measuring what is the user trust level in decision making based on ML output.

6   Conclusions and Future Work

This paper investigated the effects of uncertainty of ML models and cognitive load on user trust in predictive decision making in order to design effective user interfaces for ML-based intelligent systems. A user study found that both uncertainty types, as well as the cognitive load levels affected user trust in decision making. Furthermore, various user groups showed different trust perceptions under both uncertainty and cognitive load conditions.

Our future work will focus on analyzing physiological signals, such as Galvanic Skin Response (GSR) and Blood Volume Pulse (BVP) signals, as well as behavioral signals (mouse movement) of participants for indexing user trust levels during ML-based decision making. The relationship between the trust and the task performance will also be analyzed. Our ultimate goal is to set up a framework of measurable trust in decision making in order to dynamically adjust trust levels in ML-based intelligent systems.

Acknowledgements. Authors thank all volunteer participants for the experiment. This work was supported in part by the Asian Office of Aerospace Research & Development (AOARD) under grant No. FA2386-14-1-0022 AOARD 134131.

References

1. Hoff, K.A., Bashir, M.: Trust in automation integrating empirical evidence on factors that influence trust. Hum. Factors J. Hum. Factors Ergon. Soc. **57**, 407–434 (2015). doi:10.1177/0018720814547570
2. Marusich, L.R., Bakdash, J.Z., Onal, E., et al.: Effects of information availability on command-and-control decision making performance, trust, and situation awareness. Hum. Factors J. Hum. Factors Ergon. Soc. **58**, 301–321 (2016). doi:10.1177/0018720815619515
3. Mayer, R.C., Davis, J.H., Schoorman, F.D.: An integrative model of organizational trust. Acad. Manage. Rev. **20**, 709–734 (1995). doi:10.5465/AMR.1995.9508080335
4. Schoorman, F.D., Mayer, R.C., Davis, J.H.: An integrative model of organizational trust: past, present, and future. Acad. Manage. Rev. **32**, 344–354 (2007). doi:10.5465/AMR.2007.24348410
5. Wheeler, S.: Trusted Autonomy: Concept Development in Technology Foresight. Defense Technical Information Center, Defense Science & Technology Group, Australia (2015)

6. Lee, J.D., See, K.A.: Trust in automation: designing for appropriate reliance. Hum. Factors **46**, 50–80 (2004)

7. Mercado, J.E., Rupp, M.A., Chen, J.Y.C., et al.: Intelligent agent transparency in human-agent teaming for Multi-UxV management. Hum. Factors **58**, 401–415 (2016)

8. Ososky, S., Sanders, T., Jentsch, F., et al.: Determinants of system transparency and its influence on trust in and reliance on unmanned robotic systems. In: Karlsen, R.E., Gage, D. W., Shoemaker, C.M., Gerhart, G.R. (eds.), p. 90840E (2014)

9. Adobor, H.: Optimal trust? Uncertainty as a determinant and limit to trust in inter-firm alliances. Leadersh. Org Dev. J. **27**, 537–553 (2006). doi:10.1108/01437730610692407

10. Parasuraman, R., Sheridan, T.B., Wickens, D.C.: Situation awareness, mental workload, and trust in automation: viable, empirically supported cognitive engineering constructs. J. Cogn. Eng. Decis. Making **2**, 140–160 (2008)

11. Khawaji, A., Chen, F., Zhou, J., Marcus, N.: Trust and cognitive load in the text-chat environment: the role of mouse movement. In: Proceedings of the 26th Australian Computer-Human Interaction Conference on Designing Futures: The Future of Design, pp. 324–327 (2014)

12. Smith, P.J., Geddes, N.D., Beatty, R.: Human-centered design of decision-support systems. In: Human-Computer Interaction: Design Issues, Solutions, and Applications (2009)

13. Zhou, J., Li, Z., Wang, Y., Chen, F.: Transparent machine learning — revealing internal states of machine learning. In: Proceedings of IUI 2013 Workshop on Interactive Machine Learning (2013)

14. Zhou, J., Khawaja, M.A., Li, Z., et al.: Making machine learning useable by revealing internal states update — a transparent approach. Int. J. Comput. Sci. Eng. **13**, 378–389 (2016)

15. Winkler, R.L.: The importance of communicating uncertainties in forecasts: overestimating the risks from winter storm Juno. Risk Anal. **35**, 349–353 (2015)

16. Beller, J., Heesen, M., Vollrath, M.: Improving the driver-automation interaction an approach using automation uncertainty. Hum. Factors J. Hum. Factors Ergon. Soc. **55**, 1130–1141 (2013). doi:10.1177/0018720813482327

17. Candello, H.: User methods and approaches to design cognitive systems. In: Marcus, A. (ed.) DUXU 2016, Part I. LNCS, vol. 9746, pp. 231–242. Springer, Cham (2016). doi:10.1007/978-3-319-40409-7_23

18. Arshad, S.Z., Zhou, J., Bridon, C., et al.: Investigating user confidence for uncertainty presentation in predictive decision making. In: Proceedings of the Annual Meeting of the Australian Special Interest Group for Computer Human Interaction, pp. 352–360. ACM, New York (2015)

19. Rouse, W.B.: Adaptive aiding for human/computer control. Hum. Factors J. Hum. Factors Ergon. Soc. **30**, 431–443 (1988). doi:10.1177/001872088803000405

20. Byrne, E.A., Parasuraman, R.: Psychophysiology and adaptive automation. Biol. Psychol. **42**, 249–268 (1996)

21. Moray, N., Inagaki, T., Itoh, M.: Adaptive automation, trust, and self-confidence in fault management of time-critical tasks. J. Exp. Psychol. Appl. **6**, 44–58 (2000)

22. LeClerc, J., Joslyn, S.: The cry wolf effect and weather-related decision making. Risk Anal. **35**, 385–395 (2015). doi:10.1111/risa.12336

23. Uggirala, A., Gramopadhye, A.K., Melloy, B.J., Toler, J.E.: Measurement of trust in complex and dynamic systems using a quantitative approach. Int. J. Ind. Ergon. **34**, 175–186 (2004)

24. Allen, P.M., Edwards, J.A., Snyder, F.J., et al.: The effect of cognitive load on decision making with graphically displayed uncertainty information. Risk Anal. **34**, 1495–1505 (2014)

25. Ibrekk, H., Morgan, M.G.: Graphical communication of uncertain quantities to nontechnical people. Risk Anal. **7**, 519–529 (1987)
26. Edwards, J.A., Snyder, F.J., Allen, P.M., et al.: Decision making for risk management: a comparison of graphical methods for presenting quantitative uncertainty. Risk Anal. **32**, 2055–2070 (2012). doi:10.1111/j.1539-6924.2012.01839.x
27. Kirschenbaum, S.S., Trafton, J.G., Schunn, C.D., Trickett, S.B.: Visualizing Uncertainty The Impact on Performance. Hum. Factors J. Hum. Factors Ergon. Soc. **56**, 509–520 (2014). doi:10.1177/0018720813498093
28. Damghani, K.K., Taghavifard, M.T., Moghaddam, R.T.: Decision Making Under Uncertain and Risky Situations. Enterprise Risk Management Symposium Monograph Society of Actuaries-Schaumburg, Illinois, vol. 15 (2009)
29. de Visser, E., Parasuraman, R.: Adaptive aiding of human-robot teaming effects of imperfect automation on performance, trust, and workload. J. Cogn. Eng. Decis. Making **5**, 209–231 (2011). doi:10.1177/1555343411410160
30. Li, Z., Zhang, B., Wang, Y., et al.: Water pipe condition assessment: a hierarchical beta process approach for sparse incident data. Mach. Learn. **95**, 11–26 (2014)
31. Deck, C., Jahedi, S.: The effect of cognitive load on economic decision making: a survey and new experiments. Eur. Econ. Rev. **78**, 97–119 (2015)
32. Arshad, S.Z., Wang, Y., Chen, F.: Interactive mouse stream as real-time indicator of user's cognitive load. In: Proceedings of the 33rd Annual ACM Conference Extended Abstracts on Human Factors in Computing Systems, pp. 1025–1030. ACM, New York (2015)
33. Chen, F., Zhou, J., Wang, Y., et al.: Robust Multimodal Cognitive Load Measurement. Springer International Publishing, Cham (2016)
34. Zhou, J., Sun, J., Chen, F., et al.: Measurable decision making with GSR and pupillary analysis for intelligent user interface. ACM Trans. Comput. Hum. Interact. **21**, 33 (2015)
35. Helgee, E.A.: Improving Drug Discovery Decision Making using Machine Learning and Graph Theory in QSAR Modeling. Ph.D. thesis, University of Gothenburg (2010)
36. Štrumbelj, E., Kononenko, I.: Explaining prediction models and individual predictions with feature contributions. Knowl. Inf. Syst., **41**, 647–665 (2014)
37. Zhou, J., Chen, F.: Making machine learning useable. Int. J. Intell. Syst. Technol. Appl. **14**, 91 (2015). doi:10.1504/IJISTA.2015.074069
38. Krause, J., Perer, A., Ng, K.: Interacting with predictions: visual inspection of black-box machine learning models. In: Proceedings of the 2016 CHI Conference on Human Factors in Computing Systems, New York, USA, pp. 5686–5697 (2016)

Modelling Trust: An Empirical Assessment

Siddharth Gulati[✉], Sonia Sousa, and David Lamas

School of Digital Technologies, Tallinn University,
Narva mnt 29, 10120 Tallinn, Estonia
{sid,scs,drl}@tlu.ee

Abstract. Trust has shown to be a key factor influencing user uptake and acceptance of technologies. Despite the increase in interest in trust research and its stated importance in HCI, prior research has mainly focused on understanding its role in human to human interactions mediated through technology. The ongoing and rapid technological developments have made it necessary to move beyond studying trust relationships between people mediated by information technology (IT) and focus on studying the relationship of the user with the IT artifact itself. We recognize that HCI discipline lacks a focused body of knowledge on trust and there is a lack of theoretically grounded and robust psychometric instruments for quantifying trust. With this in mind, this article is aimed at empirically evaluating a socio-technical model of trust so as to assess its feasibility in user technology interactions. Using prior established measures and theories, we identify seven trust attributes and test the proposed model using partial least square structural equation modelling (PLS-SEM). Our study contributes to the literature by advancing the discussion of trust in human-artefact relationship.

Keywords: Trust in technology · Theory development · PLS-SEM

1 Introduction

The field of Human computer interaction (HCI) has witnessed tremendous growth over the past decade. The place that information technology has in people's lives has drastically changed as technology has now become seamlessly integrated and diffused into every aspect of a person's life. People are getting more engaged, involved and reliant on technology for their day to day tasks. Considering the kind of technology being developed and the rate at which it is being developed, it is safe to say that computing is at one its most exciting moments, playing an essential role in supporting human activities, facilitated by growing availability of services, devices and interaction modalities, all associated with tangible consequences [67]. This is also supported by Häkkinen [24] who recognize the seamless integration of technology into modern life and call for theoretically sound and empirically grounded research to explore such a wide swath of technological applications (p. 1).

R. Bernhaupt et al. (Eds.): INTERACT 2017, Part IV, LNCS 10516, pp. 40–61, 2017.
DOI: 10.1007/978-3-319-68059-0_3

In light of such exciting developments, uncertainties and increasing dependency on technologies, there has been a greater call among scholars to understand and research trust within HCI [5,37,64]. The main reason for this can be attributed to the fact that trust has shown to be a key factor in technology adoption and user satisfaction with technology [32,63] and its absence could lead to a user proceeding more cautiously when using the technology and taking unnecessary time to think through their actions, which will ultimately lead to dissatisfaction, failure to continue using the system and the user not being able to fully realize the potential which the technology has to offer [9]. However, despite the benefits of studying trust in technology, the HCI community is lacking a coherent & focused body of knowledge on trust that can be referred to for developing systems which would foster trust [34]. There is also a lack of theoretically grounded and robust psychometric instruments for quantifying trust [64]. Finally, the HCI discipline needs deepening of understanding the role of trust in a user-artefact relationship [4,37,63,69].

With this in mind, the main aim of the present article is twofold: (1) First, we address the need for a dedicated model to quantify trust in the HCI domain. To advance this discussion, we wish to refine and empirically assess the suitability of socio-technical model (STM) of human computer trust proposed by Sousa et al. [67] in user technology interactions and (2) secondly, we advance the discussion on understanding the role of trust with technological artefacts and suggest directions for future research on the topic.

1.1 Research Questions

As explained earlier, the present study is aimed at empirically assessing and refining the human-computer trust model [67]. The research questions associated with achieving this goal are as follows:

RQ1: How well do the proposed attributes of STM predict trust levels of a user with a system? In other words, is there a statistically significant relationship between these attributes and trust?

RQ2: Which attributes of the STM hold true in case of user technology interactions?

2 Background

One of the earliest scholarly works that addressed trust between humans and technology is that of Muir [48] who developed a trust model for studying human-machine relationships. This model by Muir was based on a prior model developed by Rempel et al. [56], which focused on understanding the role of trust in interpersonal relationships. Interestingly, in both these works, the notion of predictability was of prime importance. In the case of Muir [48], the amount of trust that a human has on a machine would be estimated based on the predictability of the machine's behavior. On similar lines, the study by Rempel et al. [56] found out that couples who can predict how their partners would behave with them in certain situations decides how much they will trust them in a given situation. This work by Muir [48] was further extended by Lee and Moray [38,39] who in their studies to understand trust levels of machine operators with regards to automating their tasks pointed out that when machine operators are able to predict how the machine would behave in different circumstances, trust levels would be higher. However, they also observed that most of the times, the operators were reluctant to switch to automation because of the complexity of the machines. Due to this inherent complexity, the willingness of the operators to trust how the machine would act if given control was low.

Although research on trust was slowly progressing at this stage, Mayer et al. [43] pointed out certain deficiencies with these researches. Specifically, they pointed out three issues which were (1) Lack of understanding in the literature regarding how trustful relationships are developed between trustor(s) and trustee(s), (2) Confusion between trust and its antecedents and outcomes and (3) Problems with regards to defining trust. To address these concerns, Mayer et al. [43] proposed a model of trust and its antecedents and outcomes which was formed as a result of aggregation of research from multiple disciplines. Their model incorporated ability, benevolence and integrity as main antecedents of trust. This model was further extended by McKnight et al. [46] who proposed a theory of initial trust formation by bringing together dispositional, situational and interpersonal constructs to explain trust formation from four divergent research streams.

Researching role and effect of trust in technology gained prominence soon afterwards with plethora of scholarly research emerging on the topic in several disciplines such as group collaboration [7], e-commerce [45], e-Government [3] and social networks [36]. The increased interest in trust research is also in line with the seminal work of Luhman [41] who envisioned that "one should expect trust to be increasingly in demand as a means of enduring the complexity of a future which technology will generate" (p. 16).

2.1 Relevance of Trust in HCI

Before discussing the relevance of trust in HCI, it is important to understand the different school of thoughts regarding trust. Is trust really relevant in HCI? Should researchers even worry about trust? The issues of whether to study the role of trust with IT artifacts is an ongoing and a vivid discussion in our field [63]. The first view is that of Friedman et al. [16] who opine "people trust people, not technology" (p. 36). They argue that unlike humans, technology does not possess moral agency and the ability to do right or wrong and hence it should be viewed as being a participant in a trust-distrust relationship between a user and the person who programmed the technology. This view is also held by Olson and Olson [55] who argue that when people interact through technology, it is not the technology that needs to be trustworthy. Instead, the trust-distrust relationship is between two humans independent of whatever technology they would use. Similarly, Shneiderman [62] also claims that "if users rely on a computer and *it fails, they may get frustrated or vent their anger by smashing a keyboard, but there is no relationship of trust with a computer*" (p. 58). Essentially, these views can be distilled to the following two points, which are:

- People cannot enter into a relationship with technology, and
- The question of people trusting the technology does not arise as people cannot develop a trusting relationship with technology because it lacks volition and moral agency.

However, both these views are extremely narrow and can easily be refuted. Firstly, research has demonstrated that computers can act as social actors and people can enter into relationships with and respond to them in a way comparable to responding to other people [4,53]. Studies have shown that people assign personalities [51], gender [52] and readily form team relationships with computers and consider them as teammates [50]. In their work on understanding anthropomorphism of technology, Waytz et al. [72] defended the notion of people having a human like relationship with a computer by putting forth "*Anthropomorphizing a nonhuman does not simply involve attributing superficial human characteristics (e.g., a humanlike face or body) to it, but rather attributing essential human characteristics to the agent (namely a humanlike mind, capable of thinking and feeling)*" (p. 113). Essentially, it is possible to associate human like characteristics to technology such as benevolence, competence, integrity etc. and perceive it as a social actor [4].

Similarly, users can enter into trusting relationships with a technological artifact. A study by McKnight et al. [44] showed that people can and do develop a trusting relationship with an IT artifact such as Microsoft access or excel. The authors recognize the fact that trust in technology helps in shaping people's belief and behavior towards the technology. A similar assertion is also made by Lankton et al. [37], who empirically demonstrated that not only can people develop trust with technological artifacts but they also associate technology as having human like characteristics. Human computer trust becomes even more important when considering the increasingly non-deterministic and distributed nature of computing [33]. The latter has led to an increase in interest in trust research within the IS and the HCI community as scholars get engaged in identifying technological attributes that would make it more trustworthy [36,63,69]. Therefore, not only do people perceive technology to have human characteristics, but they also form trusting relationships with technological artifacts.

Concerning the role of trust within HCI, it has shown to be a key factor in reducing risk and uncertainty associated with a technological interaction, creating positive and meaningful experiences with technology and is crucial in helping a user adopt and maintain a gradual and steady relationship with the system [37,44,63].

2.2   Research Gap

Despite the relevance and the crucial role that trust plays in HCI, there exists a strong emphasis in the literature on understanding its role in human to human interactions mediated through technology, and neglecting technology's social presence and social affordances and also ignoring its effectiveness as a communication medium [37]. This view is supported by Söllner et al. [63] who put forth that as technology matures, it is necessary to move beyond studying trust relationships between people mediated by IT and focus on studying the relationship of the user with the IT artifact itself. As has already been pointed out that people form trusting relationships with computers and assign them human characteristics. In light of this, a comprehensive socio-technical approach taking into account user's interaction with technology is needed as this would help us determine what exactly it is about technology which makes it trustworthy [44]. Therefore, HCI discipline needs deepening of understanding the role of trust in a user-artefact relationship where the artefact is considered as a trustee and not merely a mediator of information [4,37,63,69].

One of the factors underpinning the research problem is the challenge in defining and measuring trust due to its multi-dimensional nature [40]. This view is supported by Knowles et al. [34] who put forth that HCI discipline still lacks a focused body of knowledge on trust which can be referred to for developing systems which would foster trust. There is also a lack of theoretically grounded and robust psychometric instruments for quantifying trust [64]. One of the earliest works towards a psychometric instrument to measure trust in HCI is that of Madsen and Gregor [42] who developed a human computer trust scale but there is no full validation which has been reported on this and the empirical validity of the scale is questionable because of its low sample size. Another recent attempt at quantifying trust in HCI is that of Rieser et al. [59], who built on prior work by Mayer et al. [43] and McKnight et al. [45] and proposed a semantic differential scale to measure trust but such scales are difficult to analyze, require more cognitive effort on the part of the respondent and therefore can be harder to respond to when compared to likert scales [66]. There have been other empirical attempts to come up with statistical models and scales to measure trust [18,36,45]. However, these are proposed within a particular context such as e-commerce or social networking and the results are difficult to generalize. These limitations are also recognized by the authors themselves but there has been little attempt made within the literature to move beyond them. In their review on empirical nature of trust in technology research, Söllner and Leimeister [64] criticized empirical and methodological rigor of trust models which exist in the literature and call for future research in terms of developing trust models and scales. Finally, Riegelsberger and Sasse [57] have also proposed ten principles that can be used to develop systems that foster trust but their work is conceptual and is not empirically validated.

The present state of trust research can be regarded as being incoherent and there is a need to unify the existing body of literature so as to develop a systematic and a sound theoretical framework which would help identify the core elements of trust [11]. As Li [40] rightly puts forth *"we do not have a generally accepted framework or model to integrate the core elements that constitute the contextual components across diverse disciplines in social studies"* (p. 83). From a HCI stand point, this holds true as there have been calls to come up with a dedicated and robust model and scales for trust and advance theoretical and empirical research on trust [58,63].

With new ICT's, there is a need to develop new frameworks and models to explain trust formation and maintenance which would complement the existing ones [29]. Therefore, a careful approach would not be to refute the existence of these prior models but to extend the existing body of knowledge on trust and come up with new research ideas on conceptualizing trust to have a sound theoretical base to understand trust in technology. This becomes even more important when we consider the ongoing and rapid technological developments in HCI, in light of which there is a need to re-examine, strengthen and extend current theories to ascertain how these can be epistemologically revised [13].

3   Hypothesis Development

Before discussing hypothesis formulation, it is important to point out why we are interested in refining the human computer trust model. This model was proposed by Sousa et al. [67] to study the role of trust in technology mediated interactions and was developed as a result of participatory design sessions with users, extensive literature review on trust and was based on the combination of unification of Davis [10] and Venkatesh et al. [70] technology acceptance models. However, the trust attributes proposed in this model had not been empirically assessed in terms of how much they explain trust. The main aim of our research was to assess which aspects of this model hold true in human technology interactions and contribute towards developing an instrument for trust measurement in HCI. In this section, we further refine, explain and define the different components of the model (as shown in Fig. 1), along with associated hypothesis that can be empirically tested.

3.1   Motivation

We define Motivation as the degree to which an individual believes (even under conditions of vulnerability and dependence) in themselves to carry out certain technologically oriented tasks. We explain this through the concept of self-efficacy, a notion grounded in the social cognitive theory (SCT), which acts as a theoretical framework for analyzing human motivation, thought and action and at its very core the theory holds the view that humans acquire and maintain certain behavioral patterns which are determined by a dynamic interaction between people and environments and central to this interaction is the concept of self-efficacy [2]. According to Bandura [2], *"people's self-efficacy beliefs determine their level of motivation, as reflected in how much effort they will exert in an endeavor and how long they will persevere in the face of obstacles"* (p. 1176).

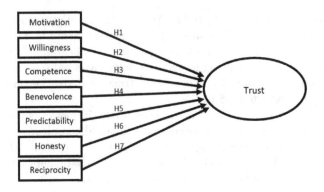

Fig. 1. Model under investigation

Essentially, the stronger the belief an individual has in their abilities, the more motivated they would be to carry out a certain task and their efforts would be more persistent. Studies have shown that self-efficacy has a direct affect (positive or negative) and acts as a precursor to understanding levels of motivation of an individual when performing a task. For instance, people with high level of self-efficacy are more likely to complete a task and persist longer in their efforts to complete the task. Similarly, people with low self-efficacy have less motivation to carry out a task and tend to avoid performing these tasks [2,61]. Since self-efficacy is domain specific [2], we are specifically interested in Computer self-efficacy (CSE). CSE is an individual's inherent belief in themselves in whether or not they feel that they can execute a technologically oriented task [8]. Prior research [30] done on CSE has shown that a user would engage in an activity or attempt to use a system if they feel it is worthwhile and if they have the belief and the motivation that they would be successful. In essence, these scholarly works present self-efficacy as an important determinant of motivation of a user to use a system.

Correlating this notion of motivation (as explained through self-efficacy) and trust, if we refer to the definition of trust put forth by Mayer et al. [43], they define it as *"the willingness of a party to be vulnerable to the actions of another party based on the expectation that the other will perform a particular action important to the trustor, irrespective of the ability to monitor or control that other party"* (p. 712). During a user's interaction with a technological artifact, the user is both vulnerable and cannot monitor how the system would behave, but if they feel that (a) using the system would fulfill a certain purpose and (b) that they themselves have the inner capability to complete a certain task, this would lead to an interaction with the technical artifact. Therefore, we opine that higher the CSE of an individual, the higher the trust they would place in the system and as a consequence, they would feel less vulnerable. Consequently, we hypothesize that:

H1. User self-efficacy has a positive effect on their trust towards using technology.

3.2 Willingness

We define willingness as an individual's reflection of positive or negative feelings, evaluating pros and cons and considering risk and incentives associated with performing a given action when using a system. Psychological research has also demonstrated that human behavior is goal directed [17]. Study of such a goal directed behavior can be explained using Theory of planned behavior (TPB) [1]. The underlying principle of this theory is that intention of an individual is the best predictor of their behavior. This intention is in turn determined by three constructs namely attitude, subjective norm and perceived behavioral control. Essentially, a person will perform behaviors if:

- Advantages of success outweigh the disadvantages of failure (behavioral attitude).
- Other people with whom they are or interact think they should perform the behavior (subjective norm).
- Have sufficient control over factors which influence success or ability to perform the behavior [perceived behavioral control (PBC)].

Prior research by Belanche et al. [3] on understanding user trust in public e-services found out that evaluation of outcome expectations, both from the service (performance expectations) and what an individual would achieve using an e-service (individual expectations) play an important role in fostering trust. Outcome expectations are also an important pre-cursor for technology usage and acceptance [8]. Studies have also shown trust to be a key factor in deciding whether users will continue to interact with and use the system [18,44]. Therefore, we assert that after evaluating pros and cons and considering risk and incentives associated with their interaction, if a user feels that their interaction will have a positive outcome, their trust with regards to the technology that they are interacting with would be well placed. Therefore, we hypothesize that:

H2. The higher the willingness or outcome expectations associated with performing an action, the greater the trust towards the technology.

3.3 Competence

We define competence as the ease of use associated with the use of a system in that it is perceived to perform its tasks accurately and correctly. While trying to understand the degree to which human operators would trust automated control of systems, Muir and Moray [49] came up with the concept of competence and defined it as the extent to which the technology performs its functions properly. On similar lines, Constantine [9] note that competence means that the system is capable of doing what the user needs it to do, performs reliably and delivers accurate results. He also states that in order for the system to be competent or in order for the user to perceive the system as being competent, it must perform with sufficient speed and meet user's needs with respect to timeliness.

The competence of a system can be explained through the technology acceptance model (TAM) [10], specifically the perceived ease of use determinant of TAM. According to Davis [10], a user would interact with and accept the technology when they perceive technology to be useful, easy to use and performing as it says. When the user perceives that technology is easy to use, their PBC, according to theory of planned behavior [1], would also be higher which means that it is likely that they will use and interact with technology and higher the competence that a user would assign to a system, greater would be the trust of the user with that system [4,45]. Therefore, this leads to our third hypothesis:

H3. The higher the competence associated with the use of a system, the greater the trust of the user with that system.

3.4 Benevolence

In a conventional sense, benevolence has been understood as the perceived level of courtesy and positive attitude a trustee displays towards the trustor [43]. It is also viewed as the trustee being genuinely interested in the trustor's welfare without any ulterior motives and is motivated to seek joint gain [12]. We define benevolence as a user's perception that a particular system will act in their best interest and that most people using the system share similar social behaviors and values.

It can be further understood through the lens of social response theory [47]. According to this theory, when people interact with technology, they view it as a social actor and their relationship with it is governed by same social rules which would govern an interpersonal relationship. Hence, people look for cues to associate their interaction with technology. They expect certain human like behavior from technology i.e. the technology would act in their best interest and not try to deceive them [37,47]. When individual's perceive that technology would help them and act in their best interest, there is a likelihood of higher continued use and fostering a higher level of trust with that technology [4,36]. Synthesizing these arguments, we hypothesize:

H4. There exists a positive relationship between perceived benevolence of a technological artifact and trust.

3.5 Predictability

We define predictability as the belief of an individual that systems actions (whether good or bad) are consistent enough that one can forecast them and it will help the user to perform a desired action in accordance with what is expected. This can be understood based on Expectation confirmation theory which posits that every action is associated with certain expectations and when these expectations are met, it leads to satisfaction [54]. Though the theory was initially proposed in a marketing context, it has been adopted in a technological context to study user adoption and continual use of technology [27]. If a user can predict the use of a system, then it is likely that they would use it and if the use of the system matches their expectations, they would not only be satisfied but also perceive the system to be trustworthy [19]. This leads us to our fifth hypothesis:

H5. The greater the predictability of a technological artifact, the higher the level of the trust associated with it.

3.6   Honesty

Honesty can be defined as a secure belief of an individual that the other person makes good faith agreements, tells the truth, and fulfils promises [6]. Since people can enter into relationships with technology, they expect it to work towards their good, adhere to a certain set of standards and not betray them. If a user is confident that the technological artifact they are dealing with exhibits a certain level of sincerity and is genuine, then it is perceived to be honest which will affect user trust. For instance, while using electronic payment services such as PayPal for sending or receiving money, a user can be rest assured that their money is being channeled through a trustworthy, reliable source that is sincere and genuine (which basically means that PayPal as an organizations exists and is not just a spoof) and in case, there are issues with regards to money transfer, it would be well taken care of by the customer services team of PayPal.

Thus, there exists a positive relationship between user perception of honesty with regards to technology/software and subsequent trust manifestation. Honesty can be best understood through the Source credibility theory, according to which people are more likely to be persuaded and follow a course of actions if the source is credible [28], which in this example was PayPal. Through this lens, if a user perceives an application or a software to not be trustworthy, it is highly unlikely that they would act on the advice or information provided by that software. This leads us to the following hypothesis:

H6. The higher the level of perceived honesty of a technological artifact, the higher the level of trust associated with it.

3.7   Reciprocity

In his seminal work, Gouldner [21] put forth that reciprocity involves a give and take relationship and asserted that people are helpful and kind to those who are helpful and kind to them. We build on this work and define reciprocity as the degree to which an individual sees oneself as a part of a group. It is built on the principle of mutual benefit, feeling a sense of belonging and feeling connected. Psychological research has demonstrated that if people feel helped, they respond in kind [26]. Within the context of HCI, research has demonstrated that people have a friendlier attitude towards a system when they have received some help from it. If people feel that a system has been helpful towards them, they respond in kind by deciding to adopt and continually use it and develop a symbiotic relationship with that system [14, 47]. This leads us to our final hypothesis:

H7. The higher the level of perceived reciprocity associated with a technological artifact, higher would be the level of trust associated with it.

4   Method

A semi-structured questionnaire was chosen to measure user trust levels with the Estonian I-voting service. The main reason behind choosing this artefact was that despite Estonia being a digitally advanced and a tech savvy EU member state and the rate of technology uptake and new technology diffusion being higher in the country when compared to other EU countries [60], trust levels of the citizens with the I-voting service are low [65]. Despite its first use in parliamentary elections in 2005, there have been issues with regards to the design of the I-voting system and questions raised as to whether it should be implemented or not [68]. A report published by Heiberg et al. [25] has identified several inconsistencies, software bugs and audit deficiencies with the electronic voting service.

The aforementioned issues, along with the fact that trust plays an important role in maximizing voter turnout in an electronic environment, and that the next set of elections in Estonia are to be held in 2017 [65], it is important that any underlying trust issues with the I-Voting system be systematically analyzed. From a technological standpoint I-voting is also labelled as an emerging technology which will continue to develop in the years to come. Several countries such as Germany, Austria, Norway etc. have expressed a desire to use Internet voting but have rejected its adoption, primarily due to trust issues [20]. Therefore, trust issues with an I-voting service need an in-depth exploration. To the best of our knowledge, this is one of the first studies to analyze user trust levels with the Estonian I-voting service.

4.1   Participants

The data for the survey was collected with the help of Republic of Estonia's Information Systems Authority[1], a government body coordinating development and administration of the information systems of Estonia from April 2016-January 2017. We also enlisted help of local Estonian public universities and professional organizations to disseminate our research. We used LimeSurvey as a tool for making our questionnaire and collecting data. The questionnaire was constructed in both English and Estonian.

A total of 227 responses were obtained out of which 207 had used the Estonian i-voting service before. Hence, these respondents were chosen for our analysis since we were interested in understanding user trust levels with the Estonian i-voting service of people who have used it before. Totally, 122 females

---

[1] https://www.ria.ee/en/.

(53.74%) and 105 males (46.26%) took part in the survey. Most of the respondents (35.68%) were between the age of 18 and 27 years. This was followed by 32.60% and 22.47% for age groups 28–37 and 38–47 respectively.

4.2 Apparatus

All the survey measures were adopted from well-established prior studies. Scales measuring motivation and willingness were adapted from Compeau and Higgins [8]. Competence, benevolence and honesty were derived from McKnight et al. [45]. The work of Gefen and Straub [19] was referred to for adapting predictability. Each of the two measures for reciprocity were derived from Wasko and Faraj [71] and Kankanhalli et al. [31]. To collect data using these scales, we used 5 point likert scales in our questionnaire, where 1 indicates strongly disagree and 5 indicates strongly agree.

4.3 Procedure

The data obtained was analyzed using PLS-SEM and the main reason behind choosing this technique was because our main goal is theory development rather than theory testing, for which other covariance based SEM approaches are more appropriate [22]. Secondly, the objective of our study was to empirically assess the suitability of the human computer trust model [67] in a HCI context and assess whether the exogenous variables in the model explain the endogenous latent variable of interest which is trust. Such an approach is predictive in nature since we wish to empirically explain the variance in trust by identifying its driver constructs. Thus, the predictive nature of the study coupled with the main goal being theory development justify use of PLS-SEM for data analysis [23].

5 Results

It has been rightly pointed out by Hair et al. [23] that hypothesis testing involving structural relationships among constructs will only be as reliable or valid as the measurement model which is explaining these constructs (p. 45). Within the trust literature, Söllner and Leimeister [64] have pointed out measurement model mis-specifications wherein researchers have modelled reflective constructs as being formative and formative as being reflective. They further argue for a more systematic modelling approach to trust based on sound theory. In line with this, we use prior research done on trust by Lankton and McKnight [36] and McKnight et al. [44] and model trust as being a reflective endogenous construct conceptualized through 7 exogenous constructs.

PLS-SEM involves assessment of the outer measurement model that explains relationships between the exogenous latent variables and their indicators and an inner structural model which explains relationships between the endogenous variable of interest with its exogenous constructs. These are explained as follows:

5.1   Evaluation of the Measurement Model

An initial analysis in SmartPLS revealed certain outer loadings of the exogenous constructs to be below 0.7. We retained only those indicators that had outer loadings above 0.6 and removed all below 0.4 [23]. Finally, 20 measures were dropped and final instrument had 22 measures in total across exogenous and endogenous constructs. The evaluation of measurement model involves assessment of internal consistency [Cronbach's alpha (CA), composite reliability (CR)], convergent validity [indicator reliability, average variance extracted (AVE)] and discriminant validity [23]. Regarding internal consistency, both CA & CR values should be between 0.60 and 0.90 [22]. Barring willingness for which the CA value was 0.574, all other latent variables were between 0.60–0.90. According to Hair et al. [23], such a low value can be attributed to the fact that CA values are sensitive to the number of items in the scale and generally tend to underestimate the internal consistency reliability (p. 111). Even though our value is not considerably below the 0.60 threshold, one should generally not rely on CA values alone and also report CR values [22]. As can be seen from Fig. 2, the CR values for all latent variable well exceeded the recommended threshold of 0.80 [23]. Since both the CR & CA values exceed the threshold, this establishes internal consistency reliability of the measures used in our study.

Latent Variable	Indicators	Convergent Validity			Internal Consistency Reliability	
		Loadings	Indicator Reliability	AVE	Composite Reliability	Cronbach's Alpha
		>0.70	>0.50	>0.50	0.60-0.90	0.60-0.90
MOT	MOT 1	0.864	0.746	0.741	0.851	0.650
	MOT 2	0.858	0.736			
WIL	WIL 1	0.620	0.384	0.574	0.842	0.751
	WIL 2	0.767	0.588			
	WIL 3	0.804	0.646			
	WIL 4	0.823	0.677			
COM	COM 1	0.825	0.680	0.665	0.856	0.748
	COM 2	0.832	0.692			
	COM 3	0.789	0.623			
REC	REC 1	0.819	0.671	0.689	0.815	0.548
	REC 2	0.840	0.706			
PRED	PRED 1	0.858	0.736	0.749	0.857	0.665
	PRED 2	0.873	0.762			
BEN	BEN 1	0.809	0.654	0.631	0.837	0.707
	BEN 2	0.781	0.610			
	BEN 3	0.792	0.627			
HON	HON 1	0.854	0.729	0.713	0.882	0.799
	HON 2	0.857	0.734			
	HON 3	0.822	0.676			
TRU	TRU 1	0.813	0.661	0.702	0.876	0.788
	TRU 2	0.850	0.722			
	TRU 3	0.850	0.722			

Fig. 2. Results summary for reflective measurement of trust

Concerning convergent validity, indicator reliability and AVE values need to be greater than 0.50 [23]. As can be observed from Fig. 2, only one indicator namely WIL1 for willingness which asks the respondent to rate their agreement with the statement *"If I use i-voting, it will help me be more efficient and organized during the voting season"* has an outer loading of 0.620 and an indicator reliability of 0.384, but based on guidelines set by Hair et al. [23], this was not dropped as from a theoretical perspective, its inclusion is justified based on the premise that the Estonian i-voting service was designed and implemented not just to ease the overall voting processes in the country but to also make it easy for Estonians to vote from anywhere in the world making it more efficient for them to be involved with the democratic process of the country [65]. Further, if we observe the AVE values for Willingness, it exceeds the threshold of 0.50. The AVE values for all latent variables are above 0.50, thus establishing convergent validity for the study.

Concerning discriminant validity, which is the extent to which a construct is distinct from other constructs by empirical standards, two approaches, namely the Fornell-Lacker criterion and cross-loadings approach are to be reported [23]. For adequate discriminant validity, the Fornell-Larcker criterion requires the square root of each construct's AVE to be greater than its correlation with each of the remaining constructs [15]. If we observe the square root of these values in Table 1 as shown by the bold values in the diagonal, our results meet this requirement. Secondly, regarding cross-loadings, discriminant validity is established when an indicators cross-loading on an assigned construct is higher than all of its cross-loadings with other constructs [23]. If we observe Fig. 3, all the cross loadings values are highlighted and satisfies this requirement as well. Therefore, our instrument satisfies requirement for internal consistency reliability and convergent and discriminant validity.

Indicators	Benevolence	Competence	Honesty	Motivation	Predictability	Reciprocity	Willingness	Trust
BEN01	0.809	0.662	0.612	0.559	0.580	0.502	0.426	0.612
BEN02	0.781	0.606	0.480	0.568	0.547	0.411	0.291	0.565
BEN03	0.792	0.542	0.523	0.489	0.456	0.455	0.275	0.604
COM01	0.628	0.825	0.638	0.533	0.627	0.561	0.420	0.673
COM02	0.662	0.832	0.627	0.611	0.612	0.523	0.428	0.657
COM03	0.567	0.789	0.603	0.533	0.577	0.465	0.381	0.636
HON01	0.556	0.627	0.854	0.577	0.608	0.439	0.421	0.700
HON02	0.633	0.688	0.857	0.593	0.602	0.513	0.480	0.695
HON03	0.532	0.619	0.822	0.558	0.572	0.455	0.376	0.664
MOT01	0.577	0.561	0.570	0.864	0.542	0.498	0.304	0.601
MOT02	0.590	0.620	0.604	0.858	0.645	0.511	0.468	0.588
PRED01	0.516	0.628	0.576	0.580	0.858	0.459	0.373	0.602
PRED02	0.630	0.657	0.641	0.612	0.873	0.461	0.367	0.635
RECO1	0.411	0.496	0.448	0.441	0.445	0.819	0.275	0.476
RECO2	0.541	0.555	0.473	0.530	0.438	0.840	0.351	0.504
WIL01	0.227	0.295	0.350	0.194	0.228	0.227	0.620	0.256
WIL02	0.326	0.380	0.420	0.303	0.309	0.267	0.767	0.348
WIL03	0.347	0.402	0.395	0.382	0.365	0.362	0.804	0.398
WIL04	0.350	0.430	0.376	0.432	0.370	0.280	0.823	0.415
TRUST01	0.619	0.637	0.591	0.538	0.567	0.512	0.342	0.813
TRUST02	0.640	0.686	0.695	0.591	0.616	0.500	0.429	0.850
TRUST03	0.623	0.695	0.749	0.603	0.611	0.478	0.419	0.850

Fig. 3. Cross loadings of indicators with corresponding constructs

Table 1. Latent construct correlations and square root of AVEs.

	BEN	COM	HON	MOT	PRED	REC	TRU	WIL
BEN	**0.794**							
COM	0.760	**0.816**						
HON	0.680	0.764	**0.844**					
MOT	0.678	0.686	0.682	**0.861**				
PRED	0.664	0.742	0.704	0.689	**0.861**			
REC	0.576	0.634	0.556	0.586	0.532	**0.830**		
TRU	0.749	0.804	0.813	0.691	0.715	0.591	**0.838**	
WIL	0.418	0.502	0.505	0.447	0.427	0.378	0.475	**0.758**

5.2   Evaluation of the Structural Model

Addressing the issue of collinearity i.e. to examine if the predictor variables are correlated to each other is important when evaluating the structural model [22]. This is done by examining the variance inflation factor (VIF) values. Upon examination, the VIF values for benevolence, competence, honesty, motivation, predictability, reciprocity and willingness were 2.765, 3.950, 2.976, 2.589, 2.734, 1.831 and 1.420 respectively, which are below the threshold of 5 [23]. Therefore, there is no issue of multi-collinearity in our model. Secondly, we use coefficient of determination R^2 to assess model explanatory power. The R^2 is interpreted in the same way as it would be in a conventional regression analysis [23]. In our study, both the R^2 and the R^2 adjusted values are 0.768 and 0.760 respectively. Generally, values of R^2 above 0.7 are substantial or strong [22,23]. Thus, based on this, our model has a good predictive power, which essentially means that the exogenous variables predict the endogenous variable (trust) with a high degree of accuracy.

To test our proposed hypotheses and analyze the statistical significance of the path coefficients, we performed nonparametric bootstrapping with 5000 subsamples and 207 cases (the sample size of the current study) at a significance level of 0.05 [23]. As can be seen from Table 2, the only hypothesis which are statistically supported are H3 (Competence→Trust), H4 (Benevolence→Trust) and H6 (Honesty→Trust). To further assess empirical validity of the results, we used the blindfolding method and report the Q^2 value, which is a measure of predictive relevance [22]. According to Hair et al. [23], blindfolding procedure is a re-sampling technique that systematically deletes and predicts every data point of the indicators in the reflective measurement model of endogenous constructs (p. 222). Using the cross validated redundancy approach, the Q^2 value which we obtained for trust was 0.502. Q-square values above zero suggest that the model has predictive relevance for a certain endogenous construct [23].

Table 2. Significance testing results of structural model path coefficients

Hypothesis	Path coefficients	t values	p values	Sig (p < 0.0.5)
H1	0.056	0.909	0.363	No
H2	0.009	0.207	0.836	No
H3	0.248	2.951	0.003	Yes
H4	0.189	2.775	0.006	Yes
H5	0.078	1.223	0.221	No
H6	0.376	5.369	0.000	Yes
H7	0.039	0.739	0.460	No

Therefore, not only do we provide bootstrapping measures, but we also go one step further in reporting the predictive relevance through the blindfolding approach. Based on our results, we can state that the constructs which are associated with the significant hypothesis in our model accurately predict trust.

6 Discussion

This study has explored the role of trust in HCI using Estonian I-voting service as the artefact. To the best of our knowledge, this is the first study to systematically analyze user trust levels when they interact with this online voting service. The data from this study has helped us evaluate certain aspects of the socio-technical model of trust, while certain hypotheses were not statistically significant.

As can be observed from Table 2, the relationship between motivation (operationalized through technology self-efficacy) and trust is statistically not significant. Even though self-efficacy predicts motivation [61] and we hypothesized that higher levels of self-efficacy are associated with higher levels of trust, this was not the case in our research. This does not mean necessarily that there exists no relationship between these constructs in general. We argue that such a limitation may only be specific to our study. Since the current study was carried out with the Estonian I-voting service within Estonia, which is not just one of the most tech savvy countries in Europe but the technology diffusion and the reliance of people on technology to carry out tasks is much higher when compared to other European countries. For instance, the number of National Digital IDs, a mandatory national card used by the citizens of the country to access Estonia's e-services has exceeded one million and nearly 95% of the Estonian population is used to declaring their taxes online [65]. The Estonian population is used to using the internet for various purposes and people's use of e-services offered by the government is considerably high. With such high technological diffusion and everyday reliance on technology, the statistically non-significant relationship between motivation (operationalized through self-efficacy) and trust is not surprising. If we recall, self-efficacy is an individual's inherent belief in themselves in whether or not they feel that they can execute a technologically oriented task [8]. If people are used to using technology on a daily basis, then immaterial of their trust levels with the technology, their innate capacity to overcome challenges using such technology would be high, which is why there is a negative relationship between motivation and trust.

The statistically non-significant relationship between Willingness and Trust (H2) and predictability and trust (H5) can also be explained on similar lines. H2 was operationalized based on how willing a user is to interact with and place trust on an artefact based on the consequences of their interaction [8]. Essentially, if a user feels that there can be positive outcomes associated with the interaction, their trust levels would be high. Similarly, H5 was concerned with assessing user's certainty or their belief of how they expect a system to behave and whether or not they can foresee or predict the actions of the system. The common denominator in how both these hypothesis were operationalized was that the user should either be able to foresee and predict tangible consequences associated with interacting with an artefact or assess if the technological artefact is performing a desired action in accordance with what is expected. The results of the study indicated that such an operationalization does not hold true in the Estonian context since citizens are used to interacting with numerous e-services on a daily basis and whether or not they can expect the outcome beforehand or predict how the service would operate is not related to how much they would trust the service. Since the technology uptake and reliance on technology on a daily basis is much higher in Estonia when compared to other EU countries, future research could benefit from using alternative ways to conceptualize willingness and predictability and see if these indicators are relevant in a user technology interaction.

Finally, the relationship between reciprocity and trust (H7) was also statistically non-significant. To our knowledge, the existing literature on conceptualizing reciprocity has done so using social capital theory. Since social capital is fundamentally how people interact with each other, it has been adopted to explain technology mediated interactions [31,71]. In the current context, the results of the study demonstrated that such a conceptualization does not hold true as social capital theory cannot be used to explain user interaction with the Estonian I-voting service since it is an example of user technology interaction and not technology mediated interactions. This result was expected since the human computer trust model was proposed to study human to human interaction mediated through technology and not user technology interactions. Hence, based on the results of the current study, the current conceptualization of reciprocity cannot be used to study human-technology interactions and future studies involving the use of the current model should take this into consideration.

Our results demonstrate that it is not so much the social aspects of a user interaction but the focus on technological attributes which tell whether or not the Estonian I-voting system is perceived as trustworthy. For instance, our results demonstrate that what was important to the users was how competent and efficient is the I-voting service (competence), if the I-voting service was designed with the user's best interest in mind and will always operate in such a way (benevolence) and finally if the online voting service is honest in its interaction with the user. This also answers research question two which was aimed at understanding which attributes of the model hold true in case of user technology interactions. It would be interesting to see if these results could be generalized to other e-services which are used in Estonia and see if they still hold fit.

6.1 Study Limitations

Our study is not without its own limitations which can be directions for future research. As has been rightly put forth by Kyriakoullis and Zaphiris [35] that it is important to pay attention to cultural aspects when studying a user interaction with technology. They further put forth that *"understanding cultural values is essential for the design of successful and widely accepted user interfaces"*. In our study, we did not take into consideration the impact of culture on trust and user acceptance of the I-voting service. However, future research involving the use of this model could take into account such cultural and ethnic considerations keeping in mind that these differences impact user trust and their desire to continually use technology in different ways [69]. These studies can either be intercultural wherein trust levels of people within a particular culture are studied and compared or cross-cultural wherein trust levels within different cultures are examined simultaneously.

Secondly, our research was situated in Estonia, a tech-savvy EU member state. Since trust research is contextual and results can vary depending on the context in which the research is situated [11,40], future research should take into account other contexts in which citizens of the countries are not used to using technology on a regular basis and then see if there exists a positive correlation between attributes such as self-efficacy, willingness and predictability with trust.

Finally, we did not control for citizens trust with the government and the impact which that might have with their use of I-voting service. Future research can benefit by including citizen government relationship as an attribute to measure user trust with the I-voting service or e-services in general.

7   Conclusions

Based on well-established social psychological theories, this study has empirically assessed and refined human computer trust model [67]. Since the model was initially proposed to study trust in technologically mediated interactions, the data from this study has helped us evaluate certain aspects of this model and we empirically demonstrated which attributes of the model hold fit in the case of user technology interactions. Even though the proposed indicators explain a significant amount of variance of our dependent variable trust in our structural model, future research should work on identifying more reflective indicators and test whether or not they enrich our model and can be used to extend and refine it. There have been recent attempts made by Söllner et al. [63] and Lankton and

Mcknight [37] to propose more trust in technology attributes but they also call for more research on the topic.

As technology becomes more autonomous, ubiquitous and its nature becomes increasingly non-deterministic and stochastic, it becomes more important to study trust since it is crucial for ensuring its acceptance and continual use [37,63,72]. It would be important to see how the current model can be used in different contexts to study user interactions with artefacts that fit this criteria. Future research should therefore focus on identifying more trust in technology attributes and developing robust psychometric instruments to measure trust as this will have enormous implications for both research and practice.

Appendix:

Further details regarding Data, Measures used for the survey research and questionnaire are available online at: https://goo.gl/PTQBEj

References

1. Ajzen, I.: From intentions to actions: a theory of planned behavior. In: Kuhl, J., Beckmann, J. (eds.) Action Control, pp. 11–39. Springer, Heidelberg (1985)
2. Bandura, A.: Human agency in social cognitive theory. Am. Psychol. **44**(9), 1175 (1989)
3. Belanche, D., Casaló, L.V., Flavián, C., Schepers, J.: Trust transfer in the continued usage of public e-services. Inf. Manage. **51**(6), 627–640 (2014)
4. Benbasat, I., Wang, W.: Trust in and adoption of online recommendation agents. J. Assoc. Inf. Syst. **6**(3), 72–101 (2005)
5. Biel, B., Grill, T., Gruhn, V.: Patterns of trust in ubiquitous environments. In: Proceedings of the 6th International Conference on Advances in Mobile Computing and Multimedia, pp. 391–396. ACM (2008)
6. Bromiley, P., Cummings, L.L.: Transactions costs in organizations with trust. Res. Negot. Organ. **5**, 219–250 (1995)
7. Cheng, X., Macaulay, L.: Investigating individual trust for collaboration using spider diagram. In: Proceedings of the 15th European Conference on Cognitive Ergonomics: the Ergonomics of Cool Interaction, p. 24. ACM (2008)
8. Compeau, D.R., Higgins, C.A.: Computer self-efficacy: development of a measure and initial test. MIS Q. 189–211 (1995)
9. Constantine, L.L.: Trusted interaction: user control and system responsibilities in interaction design for information systems. In: Dubois, E., Pohl, K. (eds.) CAiSE 2006. LNCS, vol. 4001, pp. 20–30. Springer, Heidelberg (2006). doi:10.1007/11767138_3
10. Davis, F.D.: Perceived usefulness, perceived ease of use, and user acceptance of information technology. MIS Q. 319–340 (1989)
11. Dietz, G.: Going back to the source: why do people trust each other? J. Trust Res. **1**(2), 215–222 (2011)
12. Doney, P.M., Cannon, J.P.: An examination of the nature of trust in buyer-seller relationships. J. Mark. **61**(2), 35–51 (1997)

13. Farooq, U., Grudin, J.: Human-computer integration. Interactions **23**(6), 26–32 (2016)
14. Fogg, B.J.: Persuasive technology: using computers to change what we think and do. In: Ubiquity 2002 (December), Article no. 5 (2002)
15. Fornell, C., Larcker, D.F.: Evaluating structural equation models with unobservable variables and measurement error. J. Mark. Res. **18**, 39–50 (1981)
16. Friedman, B., Khan Jr, P.H., Howe, D.C.: Trust online. Commun. ACM **43**(12), 34–40 (2000)
17. Fritz, H., et al.: The psychology of interpersonal relations. J. Mark. **56**, 322 (1958)
18. Gefen, D., Karahanna, E., Straub, D.W.: Trust and tam in online shopping: an integrated model. MIS Q. **27**(1), 51–90 (2003)
19. Gefen, D., Straub, D.W.: Consumer trust in B2C e-commerce and the importance of social presence: experiments in e-products and e-services. Omega **32**(6), 407–424 (2004)
20. Gibson, J.P., Krimmer, R., Teague, V., Pomares, J.: A review of e-voting: the past, present and future. Ann. Telecommun. **71**(7–8), 279–286 (2016)
21. Gouldner, A.W.: The norm of reciprocity: a preliminary statement. Am. Sociol. Rev. **25**, 161–178 (1960)
22. Hair, J.F., Ringle, C.M., Sarstedt, M.: PLS-SEM: indeed a silver bullet. J. Mark. Theory Pract. **19**(2), 139–152 (2011)
23. Hair Jr., J.F., Hult, G.T.M., Ringle, C., Sarstedt, M.: A Primer on Partial Least Squares Structural Equation Modeling (PLS-SEM). Sage Publications, Thousand Oaks (2016)
24. Häkkinen, P.: Evolving technologies for a variety of human practices. Hum. Technol. Interdisc. J. Hum. ICT Environ. **9**(1), 1–3 (2013)
25. Heiberg, S., Parsovs, A., Willemson, J.: Log analysis of Estonian internet voting 2013–2014. In: International Conference on E-Voting and Identity, pp. 19–34. Springer, Heidelberg (2015)
26. Hill, C.T., Stull, D.E.: Disclosure reciprocity: conceptual and measurement issues. Soc. Psychol. Q. **45**, 238–244 (1982)
27. Hossain, M.A., Quaddus, M.: Expectation-confirmation theory in information system research: a review and analysis. In: Dwivedi, Y., Wade, M., Schneberger, S. (eds.) Information Systems Theory, pp. 441–469. Springer, Heidelberg (2012)
28. Hovland, C.I., Weiss, W.: The influence of source credibility on communication effectiveness. Public Opin. Q. **15**(4), 635–650 (1951)
29. Hung, Y.T., Dennis, A.R., Robert, L.: Trust in virtual teams: towards an integrative model of trust formation. In: Proceedings of the 37th Annual Hawaii International Conference on System Sciences, pp. 1–11. IEEE (2004)
30. Johnson, R.D.: An empirical investigation of sources of application-specific computer-self-efficacy and mediators of the efficacy-performance relationship. Int. J. Hum. Comput. Stud. **62**(6), 737–758 (2005)
31. Kankanhalli, A., Tan, B.C., Wei, K.K.: Contributing knowledge to electronic knowledge repositories: an empirical investigation. MIS Q. **29**(1), 113–143 (2005)
32. Kassim, E.S., Jailani, S.F.A.K., Hairuddin, H., Zamzuri, N.H.: Information system acceptance and user satisfaction: the mediating role of trust. Procedia Soc. Behav. Sci. **57**, 412–418 (2012)
33. Kiran, A.H., Verbeek, P.P.: Trusting our selves to technology. Knowl. Technol. Policy **23**(3–4), 409–427 (2010)

34. Knowles, B., Rouncefield, M., Harding, M., Davies, N., Blair, L., Hannon, J., Walden, J., Wang, D.: Models and patterns of trust. In: Proceedings of the 18th ACM Conference on Computer Supported Cooperative Work & Social Computing, pp. 328–338. ACM (2015)
35. Kyriakoullis, L., Zaphiris, P.: Culture and HCI: a review of recent cultural studies in HCI and social networks. Univ. Access Inf. Soc. **15**(4), 629–642 (2016)
36. Lankton, N.K., McKnight, D.H.: What does it mean to trust Facebook? Examining technology and interpersonal trust beliefs. ACM SiGMiS Database **42**(2), 32–54 (2011)
37. Lankton, N.K., McKnight, D.H., Tripp, J.: Technology, humanness, and trust: rethinking trust in technology. J. Assoc. Inf. Syst. **16**(10), 880 (2015)
38. Lee, J., Moray, N.: Trust, control strategies and allocation of function in human-machine systems. Ergonomics **35**(10), 1243–1270 (1992)
39. Lee, J.D., Moray, N.: Trust, self-confidence, and operators' adaptation to automation. Int. J. Hum. Comput. Stud. **40**(1), 153–184 (1994)
40. Li, P.P.: A tentative typology of context for trust research and beyond. J. Trust Res. **4**(2), 83–89 (2014)
41. Luhmann, N.: Trust and Power. Willey, New York (1979)
42. Madsen, M., Gregor, S.: Measuring human-computer trust. In: 11th Australasian Conference on Information Systems, vol. 53, pp. 6–8. Citeseer (2000)
43. Mayer, R.C., Davis, J.H., Schoorman, F.D.: An integrative model of organizational trust. Acad. Manage. Rev. **20**(3), 709–734 (1995)
44. Mcknight, D.H., Carter, M., Thatcher, J.B., Clay, P.F.: Trust in a specific technology: an investigation of its components and measures. ACM Trans. Manage. Inf. Syst. (TMIS) **2**(2), 12 (2011)
45. McKnight, D.H., Choudhury, V., Kacmar, C.: Developing and validating trust measures for e-commerce: an integrative typology. Inf. Syst. Res. **13**(3), 334–359 (2002)
46. McKnight, D.H., Cummings, L.L., Chervany, N.L.: Initial trust formation in new organizational relationships. Acad. Manage. Rev. **23**(3), 473–490 (1998)
47. Moon, Y.: Intimate exchanges: using computers to elicit self-disclosure from consumers. J. Consum. Res. **26**(4), 323–339 (2000)
48. Muir, B.M.: Trust between humans and machines, and the design of decision aids. Int. J. Man Mach. Stud. **27**(5–6), 527–539 (1987)
49. Muir, B.M., Moray, N.: Trust in automation. Part ii. Experimental studies of trust and human intervention in a process control simulation. Ergonomics **39**(3), 429–460 (1996)
50. Nass, C., Fogg, B., Moon, Y.: Can computers be teammates? Int. J. Hum. Comput. Stud. **45**(6), 669–678 (1996)
51. Nass, C., Moon, Y., Fogg, B., Reeves, B., Dryer, D.: Can computer personalities be human personalities? Int. J. Hum. Comput. Stud. **43**(2), 223–239 (1995)
52. Nass, C., Moon, Y., Green, N.: Are machines gender neutral? Gender-stereotypic responses to computers with voices. J. Appl. Soc. Psychol. **27**(10), 864–876 (1997)
53. Nass, C., Steuer, J., Tauber, E.R.: Computers are social actors. In: Proceedings of the SIGCHI Conference on Human Factors in Computing Systems, pp. 72–78. ACM (1994)
54. Oliver, R.L.: A cognitive model of the antecedents and consequences of satisfaction decisions. J. Mark. Res. **17**, 460–469 (1980)
55. Olson, J.S., Olson, G.M.: i2i trust in e-commerce. Commun. ACM **43**(12), 41–44 (2000)

56. Rempel, J.K., Holmes, J.G., Zanna, M.P.: Trust in close relationships. J. Person. Soc. Psychol. **49**(1), 95–112 (1985)

57. Riegelsberger, J., Sasse, M.A.: Ignore these at your peril: ten principles for trust design. In: Proceedings of the 3rd International Conference on Trust and Trustworthy Computing (2010)

58. Riegelsberger, J., Vasalou, A.: Trust 2.1: advancing the trust debate. In: CHI 2007 Extended Abstracts on Human Factors in Computing Systems, CHI EA 2007, pp. 2137–2140 (2007)

59. Rieser, D.C., Bernhard, O.: Measuring trust: the simpler the better?. In: Proceedings of the 2016 CHI Conference Extended Abstracts on Human Factors in Computing Systems, pp. 2940–2946. ACM (2016)

60. Särav, S., Kerikmäe, T.: E-residency: a cyberdream embodied in a digital identity card? In: Kerikmäe, T., Rull, A. (eds.) The Future of Law and eTechnologies, pp. 57–79. Springer, Cham (2016). doi:10.1007/978-3-319-26896-5_4

61. Schunk, D.H.: Goal setting and self-efficacy during self-regulated learning. Educ. Psychol. **25**(1), 71–86 (1990)

62. Shneiderman, B.: Designing trust into online experiences. Commun. ACM **43**(12), 57–59 (2000)

63. Söllner, M., Hoffmann, A., Hoffmann, H., Wacker, A., Leimeister, J.M.: Understanding the formation of trust in it artifacts. In: Proceedings of the International Conference on Information Systems (ICIS). Association for Information Systems (2012)

64. Söllner, M., Leimeister, J.M.: What We Really Know about Antecedents of Trust: A Critical Review of the Empirical Information Systems Literature on Trust. Nova Science Publishers (2013)

65. Solvak, M., Vassil, K.: E-voting in Estonia: technological diffusion and other developments over ten years (2005–2015). The Johan Skytte Institute of Political Studies, University of Tartu, Tartu (2016)

66. Sommer, B., Sommer, R.: A Practical Guide to Behavioral Research: Tools and Techniques. Oxford University Press, Oxford (1991)

67. Sousa, S., Lamas, D., Dias, P.: A model for human-computer trust. In: Zaphiris, P., Ioannou, A. (eds.) International Conference on Learning and Collaboration Technologies, pp. 128–137. Springer, Heidelberg (2014)

68. Springall, D., Finkenauer, T., Durumeric, Z., Kitcat, J., Hursti, H., MacAlpine, M., Halderman, J.A.: Security analysis of the estonian internet voting system. In: Proceedings of the 2014 ACM SIGSAC Conference on Computer and Communications Security, pp. 703–715. ACM (2014)

69. Vance, A., Elie-Dit-Cosaque, C., Straub, D.W.: Examining trust in information technology artifacts: the effects of system quality and culture. J. Manage. Inf. Syst. **24**(4), 73–100 (2008)

70. Venkatesh, V., Morris, M.G., Davis, G.B., Davis, F.D.: User acceptance of information technology: toward a unified view. MIS Q. 425–478 (2003)

71. Wasko, M.M., Faraj, S.: Why should i share? Examining social capital and knowledge contribution in electronic networks of practice. MIS Q. **29**(1), 35–57 (2005)

72. Waytz, A., Heafner, J., Epley, N.: The mind in the machine: Anthropomorphism increases trust in an autonomous vehicle. J. Exper. Soc. Psychol. **52**, 113–117 (2014)

Towards Understanding the Influence of Personality on Mobile App Permission Settings

Frederic Raber$^{(\boxtimes)}$ and Antonio Krueger$^{(\boxtimes)}$

DFKI, Saarland Informatics Campus, 66123 Saarbrücken, Germany
{frederic.raber,krueger}@dfki.de

Abstract. In this paper we investigate the question whether users' personalities are good predictors for privacy-related permissions they would grant to apps installed on their mobile devices. We report on results of a large online study (n = 100) which reveals a significant correlation between the user's personality according to the big five personality scores, or the IUIPC questionnaire, and the app permission settings they have chosen. We used machine learning techniques to predict user privacy settings based on their personalities and consequently introduce a novel strategy that simplifies the process of granting permissions to apps.

Keywords: Usable privacy · Mobile privacy · App privacy · Machine learning

1 Introduction

In earlier days of smartphones, users had no ability to choose the permissions each app received. Every app had a fixed set of permissions, which the user had to accept prior to installing the app. If she did not agree with even one of the requested permissions, she had no other choice than to not install the app.

This changed with Android 4.3 ("Jellybean"), where a hidden permission manager called *AppOps* for the first time gave the users the ability to change the individual permissions of an app. Since Android OS 6.0, the permission manager is integrated and visible to the user by default. For each of the permissions an app requests, the user is given a switch to either allow or deny the permission. On average, an average user has 95 apps [25] with five permissions on average [26] for each of them, resulting in a massive amount of 475 permission settings in total. According to earlier work, many users are unaware of, or at least uncomfortable with, permissions they granted to their apps [9,11,13,18].

Even worse, apps request more permissions than they need for operation [6]. Despite this fact, the average smartphone user is not aware of the risks that remain in relation to this. App stores, and also the community ratings, which are the basis for app decisions of most users, do not indicate these privacy risks at all [6].

R. Bernhaupt et al. (Eds.): INTERACT 2017, Part IV, LNCS 10516, pp. 62–82, 2017.
DOI: 10.1007/978-3-319-68059-0_4

Felt et al. [10,11] and Kelley et al. [17] have shown that the current way of displaying permissions is not clear to users and ineffective in informing them about potential risks.

Apart from better visualizing permissions and the associated privacy risks and still letting the user decide on each permission, other researchers explored the possibilities of automatically predicting and setting the app permissions using different techniques. Liu et al. successfully trained a machine learning prediction using the settings of the four million users of the *LBE Privacy Guard app* [22], or in another approach the purpose of each permission [21], to derive a set of user profiles and assign each user the permission profile she needs.

There is evidence that a user's personality, captured by the big five personality measures [7], correlates with privacy and posting behavior, for example, on Facebook [1]: *Extraverted* users have more friends, and post more statuses and likes on Facebook. Similar results could be observed for *openness*. In contrast, more conscentious subjects are less likely to "like" a post or be a member in a large number of groups. There is also a correlation of the personality and mobile apps that are chosen by the users, and vice versa it is possible to derive the personality of a user given the installed apps on her smartphone [31]. Although it is known that personality corresponds to the usage pattern and privacy behavior on online social networks, there has not been a deeper look into the effect of personality and privacy attitudes on the choice of permission settings, and how such a correlation can be facilitated to generate an individual permission settings profile for each user.

In this paper, we try to shed light on this question and explore the influence of personality and privacy on the choice of permission settings on mobile apps, using the big five personal inventory and the IUIPC[1] questionnaire. This paper does not advance machine learning or AI, nor does it test a fully working prototype, but it bridges the gap between those two. The core contribution is the feasability analysis of the application of these techniques to mobile app privacy/security; and the derivation of design guidelines for future user interfaces in that research area. In detail we try to solve the following research questions:

1. Is there a correlation between the **general** personality measures (e.g. Big Five) and the app permission choice? ·
2. Is there a correlation between the **privacy attitude** (e.g. IUIPC) and the app permission choice?
3. Are there correlations inside the permission settings?
4. Are the correlations big enough to be facilitated within a machine learning prediction?
5. How could a system look like that uses machine-learning based prediction to support the user during his privacy setting process?

We conducted a user study to capture the privacy attitudes of 100 users, together with their desired app permission settings. The results have been used as training data for a *privacy wizard*, that automatically sets the individual app permissions

---

[1] Internet Users' Information Privacy Concerns.

based on machine learning. In addition to this static approach, we examined a *Dynamic Permission Settings Prediction*, which observes the user as she adapts the Permission Settings of an app, and proposes additional changes based on the user's input on the fly. The results show that both the static as well as the dynamic setting prediction perform better than the current standard.

These two approaches allow us to support two different use-cases that capture the typical privacy setting behavior of most smartphone users: The static approach supports a use-case where a user just bought a new smartphone, and wants to set all permissions togehter. In contrast to this the dynamic approach targets for the group of users that already own a smartphone, and supports them in adapting the settings of the apps from time to time.

2   Related Work

Privacy and Personality Questionnaires. There exist several approaches for measuring a person's privacy attitude within different domains. One of the earliest publications in this field is Alan Westin's work on consumer privacy indices, which was later summarized by Kumaraguru and Cranor [19]. Westin proposed three different categories of users to express their privacy attitudes: The *Unconcerned* hardly care about their privacy and tend to publish all information to the entire audience of a network. *Fundamentalists* in contrast try to disclose as little information as possible in order to preserve their privacy. The third group of persons, the *Pragmatists*, attempt to keep a balance between privacy and usability: Pragmatists believe that privacy is an important aspect, but on the other hand accept the necessity to share information in order to benefit, for example, from an additional app feature.

Although the Westin Categories have been widely used in research, the concept has several design flaws, as Woodruff and Pihur discovered recently [30]. The members of the different categories do not behave significantly differently in their actions regarding privacy. Especially the coarse-grained categorization into three categories makes it hard to predict the user's reactions to hypothetical scenarios or permission settings. The authors critisize the questionnaire as too unspecific to capture any significant effects.

The PCS[2] questionnaire [3] is more detailed and consists of 28 questions in four categories: General Caution, Technical Protection and Privacy Concern. Although more detailed, the questionnaire still adresses the general privacy attitude of a person, and not the specific context of app privacy and privacy in the context of online companies.

In contrast, the CFIP[3] [29] and the IUIPC [24] questionnaire based on it, were designed explicitly to measure the privacy of internet users, especially in the context of online shopping companies and their data collection. The authors found that the privacy attitude regarding online companies can be well expressed using three privacy measures: The *control* measure, which determines how far a

---

[2] Privacy Concern Scale.
[3] Scale of Concern For Information Privacy.

subject desires to have control over the disclosure and transfer of her personal information, the desired *awareness* on how and to whom the personal information is disclosed, and *collection* describing how important it is for the subject to know which personal data is collected. As the IUIPC is the privacy questionnaire which best fits the goals of our paper, we used it in the survey of our main study.

The big five personal inventory, first created by Costa and McCrae [7], is currently the most widely accepted questionnaire to capture a person's personality. Although most reviews are very positive [7,15], there are also some critical voices [2]. Nevertheless, it is established as the standard personal inventory questionnaire. The big five is a questionnaire (also called the NEO-PI-R) in its newer form consisting of 240 items, resulting in five personality measures: *Openness to experience*, denoting general appreciation for art, emotion, adventure etc.; *Conscientiousness*, meaning the tendency to show self-discipline; *Extraversion* meaning higher or lower social engagement; *Agreeableness* in terms of cooperation with other people and *Neuroticism* as the tendency to experience negative emotions. The questionnaire in its original version is very long and requires up to 30 to 40 min for completion, making it unsuitable in most scenarios. Our scenario also requires a shorter solution, as we cannot prompt a user to fill in a 40-minute questionnaire before the first use of a permission recommendation app. Gosling et al. developed a shorter version to capture the big five personality traits, consisting of only ten questions [12]. Although the precision of this so-called Ten Item Personality Measure (TIPI) is not as good as with the NEO-PI-R, the results can still precisely describe the personality of a subject. The "big five" of personality can also be extracted out of written text, e.g. blog or social network entries [5]. The user burden for gathering the big five personality measures can therefore be reduced to a minimum. As stated in the introduction, there is evidence that personality correlates with the Facebook sharing behavior. We also expect some effects on the permission settings of mobile apps, and therefore included the TIPI questionnaire in our study.

Permission Prediction Techniques. Privacy settings prediction has been a popular topic in several domains, among others online social networks. Fang and LeFevre [8] proposed a semi-supervised machine learning technique to infer privacy settings of a user's social network (SN) friends: The user is asked to label several of her friends on the SN with privacy privileges. The decision on how many and which friends have to be labeled is made by their algorithm. After this annotation phase, the software predicts the privacy privileges for the remaining, unlabeled friends.

Ravichandran et al. [28] propose the use of privacy templates for each user, in the context of location sharing with mobile apps. They observed 30 users using a mobile phone app and asked them to annotate their privacy desires towards location sharing (share location/do not share location) whenever they changed their context, e.g. when they came home from work. The app recorded the time when a context change appeared, as well as the corresponding privacy desires. Using decision trees and clustering techniques, they created several privacy profile templates. Their experiment has shown that with only three templates, the preferences of a user are matched with 90% accuracy.

There are several publications describing the prediction of mobile application settings using different data sources for the prediction. Other approaches use machine learning to predict the settings [20–22]. Ismail et al. [14] describe an approach which facilitates crowdsourcing in order to find an optimal tradeoff between denied permissions and usability of the app, tailored to an individual user. Liu et al. [22] use a large online database of the LBE Privacy Guard app, containing the app settings of 4.8 million users, as training data for their prediction using a linear support vector machine. 90% of the user records are used for training, 10% for testing the accuracy of the prediction. When it comes to prediction, the system uses 20% of the app settings of a user to predict the remaining 80% of settings. They used only permissions, the user and the app id for the prediction to achieve a precision score of 64.28% to 87.8%, depending on the features used. Privacy or personality attitudes were not taken into account. A similar work [21] used feedback to suggest the permission settings: For each critical permission, the system gives the user an overview on other apps and their usage frequency of the questionable permission. The user is then asked whether she feels comfortable with the previous usage or not. Based on this feedback, permission settings are recommended for the app. In total, 78.7% of the recommendations were accepted. Nevertheless, the approach needs the knowledge about the permission usage frequency of the already installed apps, and can therefore not be applied if a user just started using a new smartphone (known as the *cold start problem*). The last related work to be mentioned here [20] uses static code analysis to reconstruct the purpose of each app permission. Privacy preferences that reflect people's comfort with a permission's purpose are used to cluster the settings and to gather a finite set of privacy profiles. These profiles can later be used to assign the appropriate set of permissions for each individual user.

To conclude the related work on permission prediction, there have been several approaches using crowdsourcing or machine learning techniques like clustering, based on the permission settings themselves or using comfort with the purpose of a permission. The effect of personality on the choice of permissions has to the best of our knowledge not been explored so far. In the next sections, we will describe a system which predicts the app permission settings using the privacy attitude or personality of a user. Unlike other related work [21], our approach does not need any knowledge about previous smartphone usage behavior, and can therefore be seen as a first step towards solving the cold start problem in this scenario.

3   User Study

We conducted an online user study to discover correlations between the personality or privacy attitudes of a person, and her app permission settings. The focus was hereby on discovering *whether* there are correlations that can be used for a prediction, rather than measuring how strong the correlation could be with a large training set. To avoid side-effects, we decided to record the personality and privacy measures directly using a questionnaire rather than trying to infer the data from online social network behavior. As discussed in the last section, broader questionnaires like Westin's categories or the CFIP lead to suboptimal results. Therefore we used the more specific IUIPC questionnaire in order to capture the privacy wishes of the subjects. The personality was captured using the big five personality measure [7], more specifically the abbreviated Ten Item Personality score (TIPI) [12], which is a compressed version of the big five scale using only ten questions in total. Although possible, we did not extract the personality measures but used the TIPI for this study, to reduce any possible side-effects caused by the derivation of the measures.

In addition to these two questionnaires, we posed two additional questions regarding privacy and privacy invasion (see Table 1). In detail, we asked the subjects how recently they have been a target of a privacy invasion (five point ordinal scale from very frequently to never), and how often they enter wrong information on purpose on online websites (percentage as a numeric scale). The next subchapter describes the participants, procedure and parts of the survey in greater detail.

Table 1. Question text and label of the additional question set.

Label	Question
Falsify	Some websites ask you for personal information. When asked for such information, what percent of the time would you falsify the information?
Invasion	Have you ever been the target of a privacy invasion (e.g. your data was misused or shared without your knowledge)?

3.1 Methodology

The study was conducted as an online survey using the software LimeSurvey[4]. 100 participants were recruited using Prolific Academic,[5] which allows us to select only active Android smartphone users with at least three of their own apps installed. Users had to conduct the study at a PC or Laptop at home. Studies in the past have shown that participants who are recruited via online services, like in our case, lead to a similar quality of the results, like participants recruited at a university [4]. The participants were paid a compensation of 2£ upon successful participation. To motivate the subjects to fill out the questionnaire honestly, the compensation was only paid after the submitted data was checked for plausibility by us.

---

[4] https://www.limesurvey.org, last accessed 09-05-2016.
[5] https://www.prolific.ac/, last accessed 09-05-2016.

If the result of a subject was rejected, for example if she failed to answer the control questions correctly, a new participant has been recruited to fill in the gap. Therefore we have exactly 100 viable results.

The age of the participants ranged from 18 to 61 years (average 30.13, SD 8.53). The recruited audience was very diverse: We recruited students, self-employed workers, employees, and also homemakers.

The survey can be divided into two parts: In the first part, we asked the subjects to fill out the above described privacy and personality questionnaires. In the second phase, we asked them to look up the permissions of their *up to ten* most frequently used apps, and let them enter them into the survey form (see upper right of Fig. 1). Next to each of the permissions, just like in the Andoid OS 6.0 interface where permissions are allowed per default, we asked them to state whether they would reject the permission if they could. The second column ("I would revoke the permission") is only active for permissions that are marked as "owned by the app" in the first column. According to previous work [13], users hardly know which permissions are requested and how they can determine which ones are used. Therefore the subjects were given simple step-by-step instructions including screenshots of every step (see lower right of Fig. 1), in order to make sure they are able to retrieve the permissions for their apps correctly. To make sure users can conduct the task correctly, the questionnaire asked to enter the permissions of a specific app (namely google maps). Only if the task was done correctly, participants were allowed to continue. Different app versions or different android os versions can request a different set of permissions, therefore we only checked whether different subjects entered a different permission set for the same application, if the version was the same. In our study, this was not the case.

The survey ended with a short feedback question in free-text style.

3.2   Results

The 100 participants entered in total the settings of 876 apps into the system. On average each user filled in the details of three to ten apps, 8.65 on average. Figure 2 shows a detailed graph on the number of settings with a specific amount of denied permissions. In most cases (447 out of the 876 settings), no permission was denied. The answers to the different items of the IUIPC and TIPI questionnaires have been reversed if needed, and combined to the according three (IUIPC) or five (TIPI) personality measures, as described in literature [12,24]. We only used these combined measures for the machine learning, as well as for the statistical analysis.

Table 2 shows how often each of the permissions was denied throughout the study.

For each participant and app permission, we computed a *permission coefficient*, that denotes how often the permission is denied by this user. The permission coefficient $comb$ is computed as $comb = \frac{|rejected|}{|used|}$, where $|used|$ denotes how many of his four to ten apps used the permission, and $|rejected|$ how often the

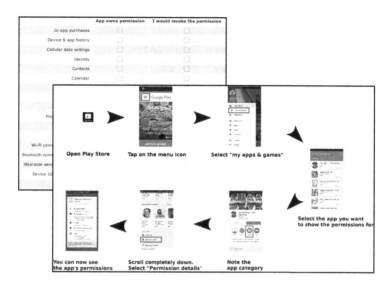

Fig. 1. Step-by-step instructions for permission retrieval given to the subjects (lower right) and one of the ten questionnaire pages for capturing the app permissions and settings preference (allow/reject) in the upper left.

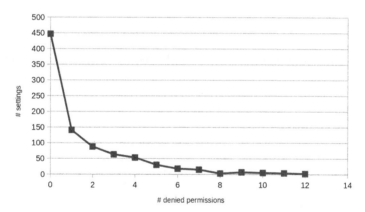

Fig. 2. Number of settings with a specific number of denied permissions.

permission has been rejected. For each participant, we thereby have 17 *permission coefficients*, one for each permission, that give us the normalized likelihood of a permission to be denied. These coefficient values range continuously from 0 (never denied) to 1 (always denied) and are independent between participants. In the next step, we wanted to find out whether the questionnaire answers correlate with the *permission coefficients*. According to the shape of our data (independent, mostly ordinal values, not necessarily normal-distributed), we decided to use a non-parametric test, and therefore performed a Spearman correlation ("Spearman's Rho") on the results of the questionnaire and the permission coefficients.

Table 2. Percentages of denies for each app permission.

Permission	% denied
Purchase	18.4
History	17.6
Cellular	9.5
Identity	26.6
Contacts	36.3
Calendar	16.7
Location	34.6
SMS	37.2
Phone	28.6
Photos	30.9
Camera	28.9
Microphone	25.1
Wifi	12.8
Bluetooth	5.0
ID	31.0
Other	17.9

The results are shown in Tables 3 and 4. The measures of the privacy and personality questionnaires are on the rows, whereas the app permission coefficients are plotted as the columns of the table. Significant and highly significant correlations are marked with one or two asterisks, and colored in gray or dark gray, respectively. Note that for our purpose, the correlation coefficient is more important than the significance, as it denotes the ascent of the regression line between the data points. The higher the value, the easier it is to forecast a *permission coefficient* given the questionnaire answers. The measures of the specialized IUIPC privacy questionnaire (collection, control, awareness) received the best correlation scores, the collection measure yields high correlation coefficients which are mostly (highly) significant for most of the permissions. Control and awareness both correlate on *some* of the permissions.

The general privacy questionnaires (TIPI) received lower but still useful correlation scores. The *open to experiences* of the subjects correlates with two of the app permissions and is, together with *conscientousness* and *emotional stability* (one significant correlation each) the most expressive personality measure. Although only four personality - permission pair lead to significant correlations, the *correlation coefficients* still remain medium high for several other combinations, making it a promising candidate for machine-learning based prediction. The additional questions on the other hand, received only small correlation scores. We therefore dropped the additional questionnaires for the machine learning and the evaluation.

In addition to the correlations between privacy, personality and the permission settings, we also observed the pairwise correlations between the permission settings. In contrast to the correlation between questionnaire and permissions, not only some but the whole lot of pairwise correlations are highly significant with correlation coefficients reaching from 0.217 (Phone - Wifi) up to 0.859. The highest correlations can be achieved with the permission pairs *cellular information - identity* ($r = 0.859$), *cellular information - purchase* ($r = 0.81$) and *cellular information - history* ($r = 0.778$).

		purchase _comb	history _comb	cellular _comb	identity _comb	contacts _comb	calendar _comb	location _comb	sms _comb
control	Correlation Coefficient	,218	-,004	,098	-,006	,202	-,017	,236	,050
	Sig. (2-tailed)	,038	,971	,587	,959	,040	,895	,015	,655
	N	91	82	33	89	104	62	105	84
awareness	Correlation Coefficient	,169	,170	,309	,064	,267	,112	,178	,108
	Sig. (2-tailed)	,109	,127	,080	,554	,006	,387	,069	,326
	N	91	82	33	89	104	62	105	84
collection	Correlation Coefficient	,314	,203	,370	,314	,344	,324	,297	,209
	Sig. (2-tailed)	,002	,067	,034	,003	,000	,010	,002	,056
	N	91	82	33	89	104	62	105	84
Extraversion	Correlation Coefficient	-,043	,155	,148	,062	-,017	,121	-,124	,082
	Sig. (2-tailed)	,688	,163	,412	,562	,862	,349	,209	,460
	N	91	82	33	89	104	62	105	84
Agreeableness	Correlation Coefficient	,193	-,060	-,208	,020	-,032	,108	,117	-,012
	Sig. (2-tailed)	,066	,595	,245	,852	,744	,402	,235	,911
	N	91	82	33	89	104	62	105	84
Conscientousness	Correlation Coefficient	,097	-,088	-,106	-,047	,020	,009	,087	,036
	Sig. (2-tailed)	,360	,432	,557	,665	,842	,942	,375	,745
	N	91	82	33	89	104	62	105	84
Emotional_Stability	Correlation Coefficient	,161	,050	-,165	,014	,005	,115	,059	-,005
	Sig. (2-tailed)	,128	,656	,350	,896	,957	,374	,552	,966
	N	91	82	33	89	104	62	105	84
OpenExperiences	Correlation Coefficient	-,023	-,094	-,233	-,093	-,144	-,171	,259	-,229
	Sig. (2-tailed)	,832	,400	,191	,386	,145	,184	,008	,036
	N	91	82	33	89	104	62	105	84
invasionfrequency	Correlation Coefficient	-,012	,076	,158	,158	,084	,160	,110	,126
	Sig. (2-tailed)	,918	,536	,433	,179	,438	,258	,310	,298
	N	81	68	27	74	87	52	87	70
falsify	Correlation Coefficient	,077	-,065	-,060	,028	,096	,181	,095	,065
	Sig. (2-tailed)	,495	,596	,766	,815	,377	,199	,383	,591
	N	81	68	27	74	87	52	87	70

Fig. 3. Correlations between the privacy/personality questions and app permission settings.

4   Permission Wizard

Based on the results of the user study, we decided to use the results as training data to predict the privacy settings of a user's apps, based on her personality and privacy attitudes. The current Android interface allows all permissions, therefore the interesting cases are the ones where at least one permission is denied. We followed the example of earlier work [21,22] and concentrated on these harder cases for our evaluation, and took only them into account for the prediction and evaluation.

Similar publications [22] used a simple SVM algorithm for their prediction. We also tried out SVM and several other classification methods, and achieved the best results with a KNeighbors implementation with two as the number of neighbors.

		phone _comb	photos _comb.	camera _comb	micro _comb	wifi _comb	bluetooth _comb	wearables _comb	id _comb	other _comb
control	Correlation Coefficient	,085	,163	,167	,039	,017	,148	-,128	,050	-,020
	Sig. (2-tailed)	,468	,106	,101	,707	,871	,282	,624	,647	,852
	N	75	100	98	95	98	55	17	88	94
awareness	Correlation Coefficient	,106	,198	,027	,126	,116	,129	-,182	,171	-,068
	Sig. (2-tailed)	,365	,049	,792	,225	,257	,349	,485	,112	,517
	N	75	100	98	95	98	55	17	88	94
collection	Correlation Coefficient	,163	,333	,254	,220	,246	,135	-,026	,333	,083
	Sig. (2-tailed)	,161	,001	,012	,032	,015	,324	,922	,002	,427
	N	75	100	98	95	98	55	17	88	94
Extraversion	Correlation Coefficient	,040	-,088	-,022	,115	,078	,062	,077	,071	,141
	Sig. (2-tailed)	,733	,385	,829	,268	,446	,652	,768	,509	,175
	N	75	100	98	95	98	55	17	88	94
Agreeableness	Correlation Coefficient	,018	,108	,103	-,074	,015	,067	,181	-,083	,017
	Sig. (2-tailed)	,880	,286	,313	,475	,884	,629	,486	,441	,874
	N	75	100	98	95	98	55	17	88	94
Conscientousness	Correlation Coefficient	,012	,025	-,072	-,018	-,123	,079	-,104	-,067	-,20
	Sig. (2-tailed)	,919	,806	,481	,863	,228	,568	,692	,536	,048
	N	75	100	98	95	98	55	17	88	94
Emotional_Stability	Correlation Coefficient	,006	,024	-,135	,022	,026	,351	,130	,005	-,130
	Sig. (2-tailed)	,962	,813	,186	,835	,800	,009	,619	,965	,212
	N	75	100	98	95	98	55	17	88	94
OpenExperiences	Correlation Coefficient	-,201	-,039	-,162	-,116	,005	,029	,206	-,168	,031
	Sig. (2-tailed)	,084	,697	,112	,265	,957	,836	,427	,119	,764
	N	75	100	98	95	98	55	17	88	94
Invasionfrequency	Correlation Coefficient	,118	,173	,002	,091	,035	-,058	,000	,045	-,055
	Sig. (2-tailed)	,364	,116	,989	,421	,759	,710	1,000	,708	,633
	N	61	84	83	81	80	43	13	71	79
falsify	Correlation Coefficient	,195	,148	,094	,000	,008	,022	-,428	,078	-,014
	Sig. (2-tailed)	,132	,180	,397	,999	,945	,888	,144	,517	,901
	N	61	84	83	81	80	43	13	71	79

Fig. 4. Correlations between the privacy/personality questions and app permission settings continued.

As we only have $2^9 = 512$ combinations of input features, we were able to determine the optimum set of features by using a brute-force procedure of training and selecting the features according to the precision of each of the combinations one after another. We followed the usual way for training, adjusting parameters, and validating the prediction of a machine learning algorithm. We used a ten-fold cross validation to prevent a biasing of the data. In this validation method, the data is split into ten parts of the same size, and the validation procedure is performed ten times: In each of the ten runs, the data set is split into two basic parts: The first part is called the *training set*, and is composed of 90% of the data set. It is used to train, to calibrate the prediction algorithm and select the optimal features. The second and remaining part is called the *test set*, and is **not** used for training and fitting, it remains untouched. It is used for the evaluation of the results later. We used 80% of the *training set* (**not** the test set, as this remains untouched until the evaluation in the next chapter) to fit the algorithm, and 20% to find the optimal set of features using the above-mentioned brute-force method. After each run, another of the ten splits is used as the *test set*, and the remaining splits for the *training set*. After the ten distinct runs, we used the average precision of all runs for selecting the best set of features. Table 3 shows the features selected for the prediction using the IUIPC or the big five personality measures as input features.

The selected features correspond to the measures with the highest correlation in Tables 3 and 4, supporting the correctness of the selection method.

Table 3. Selected features for each of the two feature sets IUIPC and personality.

Feature set	Selected features
IUIPC	Collection, Control
Personality	Extraversion, OpenExperiences

Evaluation. We evaluated the results of the prediction following a similar approach as for the selection of input features using ten-fold cross validation: First the prediction is trained with the *training set* consisting of 90% of the data. This time, we used a static set of input features as described in Table 3, that was not changed throughout the evaluation procedure. Afterwards, the feature values from the *test set* are used to predict the permission settings, and compared with the actual permission settings of the *test set*. Again this procedure was repeated ten times, and the results were averaged.

In order to get an impression of the quality of the results, we implemented a naive approach to predict the settings, which will later be called the *baseline* or *random* condition. We started with a simple random method, which randomly predicts "allow" or "deny" for each of the permissions, giving a 50% accuracy. Since the percentage of allow and deny differs from permission to permission and is rarely at 50% for both (see Table 2), we enhanced the random approach by a probabilistic component: We first use the *training set* to calculate the probability of getting allowed or denied for each permission respectively. Based on these probabilities, we then predict the permission settings on the *test set*. If for example a setting for *Contacts* permission has to be chosen, the prediction will decide to "allow" with a probability of 63.7%, and to "deny" in 36.3% of all cases.

As before, ten runs have been conducted to evaluate the probabilistic random method, and the results have been averaged.

The percentage of correct predictions of this probabilistic *Random* approach, as well as the correctness using only the IUIPC or the personality metrics as features, is shown in Table 4. The columns denote the feature sets, whereas the rows contain the different app permissions. The topmost row ("all") denotes the average percentage over all permissions.

Although the probabilistic approach achieves significantly better results ($M = 59, 64$) than a pure random method, the machine learning-based prediction can still outperform it with both feature sets ($M_{IUIPC} = 70.92$, $M_{Personality} = 69.37$). Best results can be achieved for the bluetooth ($M_{IUIPC} = 96.66$, $M_{Personality} = 93.33$) and cellular info permissions ($M_{IUIPC} = 92.5$, $M_{Personality} = 91.25$). The location permission was hardest to predict ($M_{IUIPC} = 53.33$, $M_{Personality} = 58.48$). Overall, the machine learning approach outperformed the random probabilistic method by more than 10%.

Table 4. Prediction accuracy (in percent of correct predictions) for the prediction with the Random Probabilistic Model (Random), and prediction using the IUIPC questionnaire or the Big Five Personality test.

Permission	Random	IUIPC	Personality
All	59.64	70.92	69.37
Purchase	59.37	78.13	67.50
History	65.88	72.94	78.82
Cellular	78.75	92.50	91.25
Identity	51.87	68.44	60.62
Contacts	48.88	55.18	64.44
Calendar	70.00	80.00	81.11
Location	45.15	53.33	58.48
SMS	54.37	50.00	57.50
Phone	53.33	67.33	58.66
Photos	47.31	63.65	62.44
Camera	53.92	60.00	61.07
Microphone	52.50	74.00	69.00
Wifi	68.82	86.47	78.82
Bluetooth	84.44	96.66	93.33
ID	56.08	64.78	58.70
Other	63.55	71.33	68.22

4.1 Dynamic Setting Prediction

Besides the prediction of all settings at once using the personality and privacy measures, we discovered techniques for how the pairwise correlation between the permission settings can be used to actively support the smartphone user during her decision process, while setting the permission settings. Given that the permission settings are displayed as a scrollable list as on Android OS, we assume that most smartphone users traverse the list from the top to the bottom, and change the permissions they want to set to "deny". As soon as a change is made, we can take this change as well as the permission settings above this entry, as an input to predict the remaining settings below. This technique will later be called *dynamic setting prediction*. In detail, we trained estimators for all possible combinations of selected permissions, and serialized them to a file which is loaded into a cache at startup of the application. As soon as the user interacts with the settings, the estimator corresponding to the selected settings is retrieved from the cache and used for the prediction.

We used the study data to simulate the subject's behavior when setting the permission settings of all of her apps, either without support, or with the support of the *dynamic setting prediction*. We observed the prediction accuracy using only the already-set permissions, as well as the set permissions in addition to the IUIPC, personality, and all together. The distribution of study data to training and test set is the same as described in the last chapter: 90% for training, and 10% as the *test set* for validating the correctness of the prediction.

The procedure for the validation works as follows: Initially, the predicted setting allows all permissions. Then we traverse each permission of the setting to be evaluated, one after another, and check whether the prediction meets the actual permission setting. If not, the predicted setting is adjusted, and the remaining permissions below are predicted based on the permissions above. Whenever this occurs, a user interaction (later called a *click*) is recorded. The validation in pseudo-code is described below.

```
# traverse all the user settings
for each user_settg in testset:

    # initially, all settings are
    # set to "allow"
    pred=allow_all

    for each perm in user_settg:
        if user_settg[perm]!=pred[perm]:

            # prediction was wrong,
            # user had to change the setting
            # -> predict remaining settings

            pred[perm]=user_settg[perm]
            predict_settings_below()
```

We compared the number of *clicks* needed when using the *dynamic setting prediction* to a case where the user simply clicks on all permissions she wants to deny, without any support, as it is currently implemented on Android. As our prediction technique requires a user input, e.g. setting at least one permission to "deny", we used only app settings for the evaluation where one or more permissions were denied.

Table 5 shows the results of the evaluation procedure. For each of the input sets described above, we compared the average clicks needed for each app setting with ("Clicks (supported)") and without ("Clicks (unsupported)") the support of the Dynamic Setting Prediction. Columns one to three describe the percentage of cases where the user needed fewer clicks ("won"), the same amount of clicks ("draw"), or more clicks ("lost") with the prediction than without any support.

The prediction works best when using all features, e.g. the previously set permissions, IUIPC, Personality and Additional questions as described in Table 3. In that case, the rate of needed clicks for the *dynamic setting prediction* drops to an average of 1.58 per setting, compared to 2.00 for the unsupported case. 91.89% of the settings require at maximum the same amount of clicks, 24.66% even less clicks than the unsupported version. Only in 8.11% of the cases did

Table 5. Results of the dynamic settings prediction, using only the previously selected permissions, or the permissions in addition to the IUIPC questionnaire, the Big Five Personality Score, our additional questionnaire or all previously mentioned questionnaires together.

Input	Won %	Draw %	Lost %	Clicks(supp.)	Clicks(unsupp.)
Only permissions	23.49	59.40	17.15	1.91	2.22
IUIPC	25.76	60.60	13.63	1.83	2.21
Personality	26.58	59.30	14.12	1.70	2.10
All	24.66	67.23	8.11	1.58	2.00

the user need more interactions with the prediction enabled. The ratio of needed clicks and the win/lose ratio slightly decreases with a decreasing feature set. Using only the previous permissions as the prediction input, the *dynamic setting prediction* needed on average 1.91 clicks for each setting, compared to 2.22 clicks without the prediction. In 82.89% of the cases, the prediction needed the same or fewer clicks, whereas in 17.15% of the settings, the unsupported version required less user interaction.

5   Discussion and Limitations

We were able to prove significant correlations both between the general personality (captured by the TIPI questionnaire) as well as the privacy attitude and the app permission choice. Furthermore, the correlations are powerful enough to train a machine learning algorithm, that is able to predict these settings based on the personality, with a precision of more than 70%. The machine learning can be used in two different use-cases, first in a traditional privacy wizard, and second in a *dynamic* approach that supports the user on the fly while she is doing her settings, as described below. Nevertheless, there are still some points which can be improved, as discussed in the following subsections.

5.1   Possible Implementations of the Approaches

The two techniques presented in the former chapters can be used to implement two different use-cases: In the first use-case, a smartphone user buys a new smartphone, and has to enter his app permission settings for the first time. This is also the case, if the older smartphone was running an Android version below 6.0, where app permissions are not supported. As mentioned in the related work section, users are either overchallenged by the technicality and complexity of the app permissions, or fear the burden of setting every single permission for each app they use. A privacy wizard based our machine learning estimators reduce this problem: An implementation of our approach offers the user to either answer the twelve questions of the IUIPC questionnaire, or to connect to facebook/twitter to read in the user's posts and to extract the big five personality measures out of her written text [5]. Afterwards the wizard suggests a complete set of permission settings, that can be reviewed by the user. Especially lay users profit from the questionnaire, as it contains only non-technical questions that are easy to answer. Furthermore, both user groups save a lot of time by answering only twelve IUIPC questions (or by just connecting to facebook) instead of on average 475 distinct app permission settings.

The second use-case considers a user which has a running smartphone, who wants to individually set the permission settings rather than to trust a permission wizard. In this case, the dynamic settings prediction could be integrated into Android's permission setting dialogue. When the users traverses the list of app permissions from top to the bottom (which can sometimes take a while), Android recognizes when a permission is set to deny, and denies also other permissions further below, which might also be denied according to our dynamic privacy prediction. Changes are marked in orange, so that the user can see which changes have been made automatically, and review them. According to the study results, this technique should save the user a significant amount of interaction (clicks) and save time which should also lead to a smaller frustration.

5.2 Different Precision for Different Questionnaires

Both the IUIPC, as well as the personality questionnaire performed well in the validation study, giving an average precision of 70% and 69% of correct predictions. Although the personality measures can be automatically extracted in contrast to the IUIPC, we do not recommend to stick only to that questionnaire: Having a closer look at Table 4 reveals that both the IUIPC and the personality questionnaire complement each other: Permissions which are hard to predict in the additional questionnaire (like Contacts, Location, SMS, History) can be better predicted using the personality measures, and vice versa. If the best questionnaire is selected for each permission, a precision of 72.80% can be achieved within our test data. Whether that assumption holds for larger data sets has to be proven in future work.

5.3 Limited Size of the Training Data Set and Precision of the Prediction

The results in Figs. 3 and 4 indicate there is a strong correlation between the answers to the personality and privacy questionnaires, and the permission settings of the apps. We were also able to predict these settings using machine learning. The proposed approach predicted about ten percent more of the permission settings correctly compared to the naive approach. Compared to related work like Liu et al. [20, 22], we did not have the possibility to draw on a large online database, containing millions of datasets. As we need the personality measures in addition to the permission settings, we had to gather the training data in an online survey, and therefore have, compared to the mentioned work, a relatively small dataset. Thus the performance of our personality-based prediction cannot directly be compared to these approaches. As usual with a machine learning approach, we expect the prediction precision to increase with an increasing data set size. We would like to explore how our approach performs with a large training database in the future, and compare it to other systems that base their prediction on the permissions of similar users [20], or the purpose of the permission [22].

5.4   Control of Context Factors

Each experiment faces the problem of contextual factors that cannot be controlled, we designed the experiment in a way to decrease these factors to a minimum. By using prescreening, our survey could only be edited using a laptop or computer, and not "on the go" using a mobile phone. We further required the participants to be at home. We were therefore able to assure the same location/occasion for each participant. There are still some context factors left, like general distrust towards app producers, that cannot be controlled. Similar work also discovered that the purpose of the permission has an impact on the decision [20], which we would also like to add in a future version. To avoid personality biasing, we compared the results of the personality questionnaire with the mean values that have been recorded in earlier research. With our final data set, we could not prove any significant difference with one of the five personality traits.

5.5   Number of Denied Permissions per Setting and Dynamic Prediction Accuracy

The dynamic prediction of permission settings often has the same amount of clicks as the unsupported permission setting procedure, ranging from 59.4% without additional features up to 67.23% with all features enabled. The dynamic prediction clearly profits from user interaction; the more permissions the user sets to deny, the more input features are available for the prediction. Having a look at Fig. 2, we can see that about one third of the permissions that have at least one denied permission, have *exactly* one denied permission. In these 33% of all cases, the dynamic prediction does not give any advantage, as it starts predicting only after the first user interaction. To the contrary, it is even possible that the algorithm predicts one of the following permissions as "deny", leading to more clicks than without the prediction. An additional 20% have only two denied permissions, which are also hard for the approach to predict. Despite these difficulties, the prediction still needs fewer clicks on average than the unsupported approach.

5.6   Prediction Precision for the Different Permissions

The prediction accuracy greatly differs between the different permissions that Android offers to the apps. Comparing Tables 2 and 4, we can see that these differences negatively correlate with the percentage of denial of a permission. When a permission is often allowed, the prediction accuracy, especially for the probabilistic model, is also high. Therefore the *location information*, as well as the *SMS* and *contacts* permissions are hardest to predict with the probabilistic model. On the other hand, these are the categories where the prediction outperforms the random probabilistic model the most.

5.7   Future Work

We took a first step towards an automatic permission settings prediction using personality and privacy attitude as input features. We could prove a significant correlation between those two, and were able to design a static, as well as an on-the-fly prediction for the permissions. Nevertheless, the evaluation was done only theoretically, using the study data. In future work, we would like to implement the described approach as a mobile app, and conduct a lab study on the effects of the prediction support. We are especially interested in how far the dynamic prediction will be accepted. Although in our theoretical study, the approach works as well as or better than a standard android permission manager in more than 91% of the cases, we would like to confirm our results in an applied scenario, where people interact with concrete examples rather than hypothetical ones.

In a second step, an in-the wild study would be desirable where a prototypical app is released to the app store. Having a larger user base and additional training data would hopefully help to improve the prediction accuracy, and make it possible to compare the prediction to related work with a similar user base [20, 22].

The decision for location privacy settings in Social Networks depends also on context factors like the current location of the user, the occasion, or the purpose for a location retrieval [23, 27]. The context a permission is given might also have an effect on the choice of mobile app permission settings, for example if a user wants to grant the web browser access to the internal storage only to store e-ticket receipts. The domain of app permissions further has several contexts which require a temporary or one-time permission grant, for instance when an app needs access to the SMS permission for sending a registration SMS once [16]. Context information could be easily integrated into our prediction system as an additional feature.

6   Conclusion

The Android permission system is powerful, but the maintenance of each of the apps' permissions is very cumbersome and time-consuming. Related work already elaborated on the prediction of these settings using large online permission setting databases, crowdsourcing approaches or privacy profiles based on the permission purpose. We conducted an online user study with 100 participants to discover the effects of personality and privacy attitude on the permission settings. We found strong correlations between personality, privacy attitudes and the settings. We evaluated two approaches for supporting the user during her decision process. The first uses the personality and privacy measures to directly predict all app settings, whereas the second supports the user while doing the permission settings, taking the user's interaction as an input to predict the settings not done so far. Although the training set is very small compared to related work, we were able to outperform the current standard with both approaches.

References

1. Bachrach, Y., Kosinski, M., Graepel, T., Kohli, P., Stillwell, D.: Personality and patterns of Facebook usage. In: Proceedings of the 4th Annual ACM Web Science Conference, WebSci 2012, NY, USA, pp. 24–32 (2012). http://doi.acm.org/10.1145/2380718.2380722
2. Block, J.: A contrarian view of the five-factor approach to personality description. Psychol. Bull. **117**, 187–215 (1995)
3. Buchanan, T., Paine, C., Joinson, A.N., Reips, U.D.: Development of measures of online privacy concern and protection for use on the internet. J. Am. Soc. Inf. Sci. Technol. **58**(2), 157–165 (2007). http://dx.doi.org/10.1002/asi.20459
4. Buhrmester, M., Kwang, T., Gosling, S.: Amazon's mechanical turk: a new source of inexpensive, yet high-quality, data? Perspect. Psychol. Sci. **6**(1), 3–5 (2011)
5. Chen, J., Haber, E., Kang, R., Hsieh, G., Mahmud, J.: Making use of derived personality: the case of social media ad targeting. In: International AAAI Conference on Web and Social Media (2015). http://www.aaai.org/ocs/index.php/ICWSM/ICWSM15/paper/view/10508
6. Chia, P.H., Yamamoto, Y., Asokan, N.: Is this app. safe?: a large scale study on application permissions and risk signals. In: Proceedings of the 21st International Conference on World Wide Web, WWW 2012, NY, USA, pp. 311–320 (2012). http://doi.acm.org/10.1145/2187836.2187879
7. Costa, P., McCrae, R., Psychological Assessment Resources, I.: Revised NEO Personality Inventory (NEO PI-R) and NEO Five-Factor Inventory (NEO-FFI). Psychological Assessment Resources (1992). https://books.google.co.in/books?id=mp3zNwAACAAJ
8. Fang, L., LeFevre, K.: Privacy wizards for social networking sites. In: Proceedings of the 19th International Conference on World Wide Web, WWW 2010, NY, USA, pp. 351–360 (2010). http://doi.acm.org/10.1145/1772690.1772727
9. Felt, A.P., Chin, E., Hanna, S., Song, D., Wagner, D.: Android permissions demystified. In: Proceedings of the 18th ACM Conference on Computer and Communications Security, CCS 2011, NY, USA, pp. 627–638 (2011). http://doi.acm.org/10.1145/2046707.2046779
10. Felt, A.P., Greenwood, K., Wagner, D.: The effectiveness of application permissions. In: Proceedings of the 2nd USENIX Conference on Web Application Development, WebApps 2011, p. 7. USENIX Association, Berkeley, CA, USA (2011). http://dl.acm.org/citation.cfm?id=2002168.2002175
11. Felt, A.P., Ha, E., Egelman, S., Haney, A., Chin, E., Wagner, D.: Android permissions: user attention, comprehension, and behavior. In: Proceedings of the Eighth Symposium on Usable Privacy and Security, SOUPS 2012, NY, USA, pp. 3:1–3:14 (2012). http://doi.acm.org/10.1145/2335356.2335360
12. Gosling, S.D., Rentfrow, P.J., Swann, W.B.: A very brief measure of the big-five personality domains. J. Res. Pers. **37**(6), 504–528 (2003). http://dx.doi.org/10.1016/S0092-6566(03)00046-1

13. Harbach, M., Hettig, M., Weber, S., Smith, M.: Using personal examples to improve risk communication for security & privacy decisions. In: Proceedings of the 32rd Annual ACM Conference on Human Factors in Computing Systems, CHI 2014, NY, USA, pp. 2647–2656 (2014). http://doi.acm.org/10.1145/2556288.2556978

14. Ismail, Q., Ahmed, T., Kapadia, A., Reiter, M.K.: Crowdsourced exploration of security configurations. In: Proceedings of the 33rd Annual ACM Conference on Human Factors in Computing Systems, CHI 2015, NY, USA, pp. 467–476 (2015). http://doi.acm.org/10.1145/2702123.2702370

15. John, O.P., Srivastava, S.: The big five trait taxonomy: history, measurement, and theoretical perspectives. In: Pervin, L.A., John, O.P. (eds.) Handbook of Personality: Theory and Research, 2nd edn. pp. 102–138. Guilford Press, New York (1999). http://darkwing.uoregon.edu/~sanjay/pubs/bigfive.pdf

16. Jung, J., Han, S., Wetherall, D.: Short paper: enhancing mobile application permissions with runtime feedback and constraints. In: Proceedings of the Second ACM Workshop on Security and Privacy in Smartphones and Mobile Devices, SPSM 2012, NY, USA, pp. 45–50 (2012). http://doi.acm.org/10.1145/2381934.2381944

17. Kelley, P.G., Consolvo, S., Cranor, L.F., Jung, J., Sadeh, N., Wetherall, D.: A conundrum of permissions: installing applications on an android smartphone. In: Blyth, J., Dietrich, S., Camp, L.J. (eds.) FC 2012. LNCS, vol. 7398, pp. 68–79. Springer, Heidelberg (2012). doi:10.1007/978-3-642-34638-5_6

18. Kelley, P.G., Cranor, L.F., Sadeh, N.: Privacy as part of the app. decision-making process. In: Proceedings of the SIGCHI Conference on Human Factors in Computing Systems, CHI 2013, NY, USA, pp. 3393–3402 (2013). http://doi.acm.org/10.1145/2470654.2466466

19. Kumaraguru, P., Cranor, L.F.: Privacy indexes: a survey of westin's studies. ISRI Technical report (2005)

20. Lin, J., Liu, B., Sadeh, N., Hong, J.I.: Modeling users' mobile app. privacy preferences: restoring usability in a sea of permission settings. In: Symposium On Usable Privacy and Security (SOUPS 2014), pp. 199–212. USENIX Association, Menlo Park, CA, July 2014. https://www.usenix.org/conference/soups2014/proceedings/presentation/lin

21. Liu, B., Andersen, M.S., Schaub, F., Almuhimedi, H., Zhang, S.A., Sadeh, N., Agarwal, Y., Acquisti, A.: Follow my recommendations: a personalized privacy assistant for mobile app. permissions. In: Twelfth Symposium on Usable Privacy and Security (SOUPS 2016), pp. 27–41. USENIX Association, Denver, CO, June 2016. https://www.usenix.org/conference/soups2016/technical-sessions/presentation/liu

22. Liu, B., Lin, J., Sadeh, N.: Reconciling mobile app. privacy and usability on smartphones: could user privacy profiles help? In: Proceedings of the 23rd International Conference on World Wide Web, WWW 2014, NY, USA, pp. 201–212 (2014). http://doi.acm.org/10.1145/2566486.2568035

23. Lugano, G., Saariluoma, P.: To share or not to share: supporting the user decision in mobile social software applications. In: Conati, C., McCoy, K., Paliouras, G. (eds.) UM 2007. LNCS, vol. 4511, pp. 440–444. Springer, Heidelberg (2007). doi:10.1007/978-3-540-73078-1_61

24. Malhotra, N.K., Kim, S.S., Agarwal, J.: Internet users' information privacy concerns (IUIPC): the construct, the scale, and a causal model. Info. Sys. Research 15(4), 336–355 (2004). http://dx.doi.org/10.1287/isre.1040.0032

25. Olmstead, K., Atkinson, M.: The next web. Android users have an average of 95 apps installed on their phones, according to yahoo aviate data (2015). http://www.pewinternet.org/2015/11/10/an-analysis-of-android-app-permissions/. Accessed 01 Feb 2016

26. Olmstead, K., Atkinson, M.: Pew research center. An analysis of android app. Permissions (2015). http://www.pewinternet.org/2015/11/10/an-analysis-of-android-app-permissions/. Accessed 01 Feb 2016

27. Patil, S., Le Gall, Y., Lee, A.J., Kapadia, A.: My privacy policy: exploring end-user specification of free-form location access rules. In: Blyth, J., Dietrich, S., Camp, L.J. (eds.) FC 2012. LNCS, vol. 7398, pp. 86–97. Springer, Heidelberg (2012). doi:10.1007/978-3-642-34638-5_8

28. Ravichandran, R., Benisch, M., Kelley, P.G., Sadeh, N.: Capturing social networking privacy preferences: can default policies help alleviate tradeoffs between expressiveness and user burden? In: Proceedings of the 5th Symposium on Usable Privacy and Security, SOUPS 2009, NY, USA, p. 47:1 (2009). http://doi.acm.org/10.1145/1572532.1572587

29. Smith, H.J., Milberg, S.J.: Information privacy: measuring individuals' concerns about organizational practices. MIS Q. **20**(2), 167–196 (1996). http://dx.doi.org/10.2307/249477

30. Woodruff, A., Pihur, V., Acquisti, A., Consolvo, S., Schmidt, L., Brandimarte, L.: Would a privacy fundamentalist sell their DNA for $1000.. if nothing bad happened thereafter? a study of the westin categories, behavior intentions, and consequences. In: Proceedings of the Tenth Symposium on Usable Privacy and Security (SOUPS). ACM, NY (2014). iApp SOUPS Privacy Award Winner. https://www.usenix.org/conference/soups2014/proceedings/presentation/woodruff

31. Xu, R., Frey, R.M., Vuckovac, D., Ilic, A.: Towards understanding the impact of personality traits on mobile app adoption - a scalable approach. In: Becker, J., vom Brocke, J., de Marco, M. (eds.) ECIS (2015). http://dblp.uni-trier.de/db/conf/ecis/ecis2015.html#XuFVI15

Social Media and Design Innovation

10 Design Themes for Creating 3D Printed Physical Representations of Physical Activity Data

Rohit Ashok Khot[1(✉)], Simon Stusak[2], Andreas Butz[2], and Florian 'Floyd' Mueller[1]

[1] Exertion Games Lab, RMIT University, Melbourne, Australia
{rohit,floyd}@exertiongameslab.org
[2] University of Munich (LMU), Munich, Germany
{simon.stusak,butz}@ifi.lmu.de

Abstract. Self-monitoring technologies (such as heart rate monitors and activity trackers) that sense and collect physical activity data are becoming increasingly common and readily available. These devices typically represent the captured data using numbers and graphs that primarily appear on digital screens. More recently, representing data in a physical form such as 3D printed physical artifacts is gaining currency within HCI, owing to the engagement opportunities that come with physical representations. However, there exists a limited understanding of how to design such physical representations of personal data. To contribute to this understanding, we present a set of ten design themes, developed from the analysis of two independently designed systems that construct 3D printed physical artifacts from physical activity data. Each design theme describes a unique design feature that designers could incorporate in their design to make physical representations more engaging and playful. We envisage that our work would encourage and guide designers to think about different ways of supporting physical activity experiences.

Keywords: Physical exercise · Personal informatics · Quantified self · 3D printing · Digital fabrication · Physical visualization · Self-monitoring

1 Introduction

In recent years, there has been a significant surge in the sale of wearable self-monitoring devices and smartphone-based apps that track data about an individual's active life [5, 49]. Prominent amongst them are heart rate monitors [44] and pedometers [11] that enable tracking of heart rate and steps respectively. These devices predominantly use numbers, graphs and charts to represent tracked data on an accompanying smartphone screen. Individuals use this information to gain a better understanding of their active self and to utilize this gained knowledge towards making actionable changes in their lifestyle. To this end, self-monitoring is perceived as an eudaimonic pursuit [22], where the self-monitored data serves as a motivational tool for improving athletic performance [5, 33].

© IFIP International Federation for Information Processing 2017
Published by Springer International Publishing AG 2017. All Rights Reserved
R. Bernhaupt et al. (Eds.): INTERACT 2017, Part IV, LNCS 10516, pp. 85–105, 2017.
DOI: 10.1007/978-3-319-68059-0_5

However, in line with recent studies [5, 9, 10, 29, 47] we believe that self-monitored data can offer much more than just rational self-analysis. Quantification is good for bringing awareness and discipline to exercise, but this "*number crunching*" [17] activity can also make exercise feel like work. For instance, people may take more steps, or try to be more active for a while but they may not enjoy this experience for a long time [10]. This lack of engagement is evident from multiple reports that indicate abandonment of self-monitoring devices within six months of use [53]. Secondly, as Rooksby et al. [47] note, not everyone approaches self-monitoring for the sole purpose of changing one's behavior. People take interest in self-monitoring for a variety of reasons, for instance, for collecting rewards, knowing more about oneself and with an interest in exploring new technology. For such users, quantified data and its in-depth analysis may offer very little value over time. Secondly, the data-centric view of representing data visually on a screen can also miss out on other opportunities of engagement that can potentially come with multisensorial representations of data, as Lupton notes [35] "*numbers and graphs as a source of knowledge serve to represent bodies and selves in a very limited impoverished ways. Compare these flat forms of data materialization with the complexities of the affective embodied knowledge that is a response to a scent, taste, or the touch of skin*".

Embracing the possibility of greater pleasurable interactions with one's own data, we put forward a complementary perspective on representing physical activity data through physical artifacts. We construct these physical representations using a digital fabrication process like 3D printing, that allows for an easy transformation of digital information into a physical form [1, 38]. To this end, our perspective involves a "*physical – digital – physical*" mode of interaction where the physical energy of an individual is first invested to generate digital data such as heart rate. This data is then converted back into a physical form to make a re-entry into the physical world. This circular process is interesting to us because we believe closing this loop could illustrate new ways of engaging or sustaining an interest in one's data representations.

Our interest in creating physical representations also stems from the rich tactile appeal of physical artifacts [20, 23]. For instance, unlike digital representations, the three dimensional nature of physical artifacts allows embedded data to be "*touched, explored, carried and even possessed*" [51]. Researchers argue that the tangible nature of physical artifacts offer possibilities to convey meaning beyond the data, which in turn might encourage people to reflect on their behavior in new and different ways, thereby yielding a more engaging experience.

Furthermore, existing literature [24, 37, 52] also signifies the human fascination towards collecting and making artifacts. According to Miller [37], people also like to express themselves with physical artifacts that embody their lives, personalities, emotions and achievements. For example, photographs of trips and events are often printed, framed and displayed in a physical form despite the fact that they could just as well be seen on a screen. Such an arrangement of artifacts can spatially denote the identity of an individual and trigger reminiscence of good moments at a later point in time [52]. Sports in particular capitalize on such opportunities by rewarding individuals with physical trophies and medals. We believe that such physical instantiations of someone's achievements could further benefit from embedding data in them, which is now possible with the use of digital fabrication processes like 3D printing that allows creation of physical artifacts from digital designs. Consequently, design and HCI researchers are increasingly investigating the role of digital fabrication in HCI [36, 39, 40], particularly towards creating meaningful manifestations of personal data [27, 30, 42]. In this regard, investigating the opportunity of digital fabrication for supporting physical activity is also timely.

Although physical representations can provide many opportunities to enrich the self-monitoring experience, there is only limited understanding of how to design such representations of physical activity data. Designers for instance, can face multiple challenges starting from how the representations should look, to what they should convey and what processes to follow in order to construct them. Prior works on ambient and physical visualizations [43, 50, 57] primarily focus on improving users' understanding of data through the tactile experience of handling data presented in physical form. These works however do not reveal how to apply these tactics to represent personal data generated from one's physical activity. Therefore to contribute to this understanding, we have taken a research through design [58] approach where we have independently designed and studied two systems: *SweatAtoms* [25] and *Activity Sculptures* [48] that construct 3D printed physical representations of physical activity data. *SweatAtoms* utilizes heart rate data of physical activity to create five physical artifacts, namely, *Graph*, *Flower*, *Frog*, *Dice* and *Ring*. *Activity Sculptures*, on the other hand, uses running data to create four physical artifacts, namely, *Necklace*, *Robot*, *Lamp* and *Jar*.

We utilized the insights gained from the respective study of *SweatAtoms* and *Activity Sculptures*, and supplemented them with the knowledge from the literature and our personal experiences in designing these systems, to develop a set of 10 design themes. Through these design themes, we unfold a rich design space [32, 34] for creating physical representations from personal data coming from self-monitoring. Our aim is to inform designers about not only the visualization benefits of physical artifacts but also about the polyvalent values that these artifacts can offer within our everyday life. As such, we look at physical visualizations not just for visualizations but also as substances to enrich our interaction with materials and artifacts. With each theme, we articulate important design features and opportunities to create engaging physical representations. We however note that these design themes do not represent a complete set and also limited by the use of one particular technology, 3D printing to create these representations. Despite this, these themes serve as important starting pointers to inspire future investigations. Before moving to each individual theme, we describe the two systems.

2 SweatAtoms

SweatAtoms [23] utilizes heart rate data of physical activity for creating five 3D printed physical artifacts. Each representation reflects a different aspect of physical activity as follows (Fig. 1):

Graph: The first representation is *Graph*, where recorded heartbeat per minute is mapped to a traditional 2D graph. We then extruded the result along z-axis to create a 3D graph.

Frog: The second representation is *Frog*, where the size of the *Frog* denotes the amount of physical activity done in a day. As a result, a bigger *Frog* means more physical activity was done in a day. We calculate the amount of physical activity based on the concept of 'active time'. An active time is the amount of time an individual spent exercising, where the heart rate was above the resting zone.

Flower: The third representation is *Flower*, which describes only the significant changes in the heart rate i.e. when the heart rate elevates or decreases by 20 beats per minute. We record these significant changes and map them to the length of petals, resulting in a floral patterned jewelry.

Dice: The fourth representation is *Dice* where six faces of the *Dice* describe the amount of time spent in each of the six zones of heart rate data. Each face of the *Dice* has a center circle, which grows in size as the user spends more time in that particular heart rate zone. By looking at the size of the central circle, one can compare time spent in each zone.

Ring: The final representation is *Ring*, which is a wearable ring with circles of different diameter on its periphery. The number and the diameter of each circle define the number and duration of active hours in a day. To this end, more circles mean more active hours and a circle of bigger diameter means more activity in that hour.

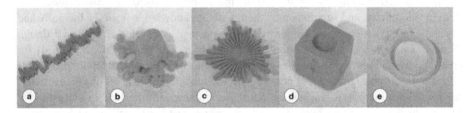

Fig. 1. SweatAtoms translates heart rate data into five 3D physical representations: (a) Graph; (b) Frog; (c) Flower; (d) Dice; (e) Ring.

We conducted a field study of *SweatAtoms* system with 7 participants in 6 households to understand the impact of these representations on the behavior and experience of the participants. We installed our system along with the 3D printer in every household and asked participants to use the system every day for a period of two weeks. On each day of the study, participants wore the heart rate monitor and recorded their heart rate data for 6–7 h during the day. In the evening, participants then 3D printed all five representations of their entire day's activity. To gain insights into the underlying experiences, we also asked participants to maintain a daily diary. Finally, we interviewed them in person on the first and last day of the study to gather subjective data on their experiences with the *SweatAtoms* system.

3 Activity Sculptures

Activity Sculptures [48] transforms running activity data into individual 3D printed pieces of four modular sculptures. The final four representations varied between just being decorative to having a practical purpose (see Fig. 2):

Necklace: The first representation is *Necklace* that contains an arbitrary number of beads, each representing one run. The size of a bead indicates the duration of the run while the shape describes distance and average running speed.

Robot: The second representation is *Robot*. It has eight body parts, each representing one run. Their size and shape are based on the duration, distance, calories burned as well as the average running speed.

Lamp: The third representation *Lamp* has ten pillars, where the difference in elevation associated with a running session is represented by the progression of a pillar. Thickness and shape are influenced by the average speed, distance, and duration.

Jar: The final representation is *Jar*, which is composed of an arbitrary number of round layers. The diameter of the layer is based on the duration of a running session, while the shape is influenced by the average speed and distance.

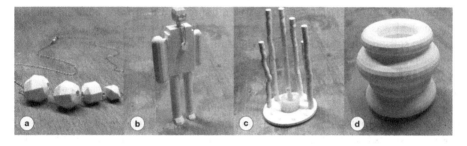

Fig. 2. Activity *Sculptures* are created from running data and they embed four forms: (a) *Necklace*; (b) *Robot*; (c) *Lamp*; (d) *Jar*.

We evaluated *Activity Sculptures* system through a three-week field study with 14 participants. The participants used a mobile application to track their running data. In addition, participants chose the type of *Activity Sculptures* and the kind of delivery (personal handover or postal delivery). To gain insights on the impact of these representations, we conducted semi-structured interviews and asked the participants to fill out a questionnaire at the beginning and end of the study (Table 1).

Table 1. A comparison between *SweatAtoms* and *Activity Sculptures*

Study aspects	*SweatAtoms*	*Activity sculptures*
Physical activity data	Heart rate	Running data
Tracking method	Heart rate monitor	Smartphone based tracking
Tracking duration	Entire day (6–8 h)	Exercise session
Representations	Graph, Frog, Flower, Dice and Ring	Necklace, Robot, Lamp and Jar
3D printing process	Printing at home	Via manual handover or mail
Field study	In households	In workplace
Number of participants	7	14
Study duration	2 weeks	3 weeks
Data collection method	Diaries and interviews	Questionnaire and interviews

3.1 Design Process

The foundations for this work were laid during an intensive collocated collaboration of the first two authors for three months. The core strategy that is used to build these themes was to compare and contrast findings from the two studies [25, 48]. We used inductive thematic analysis [3] to analyse the transcribed data from both the studies. This method was considered appropriate, as designing 3D printed physical representations is still an emerging topic, for which limited relevant theory exists. The data contained transcriptions of audio recordings of 21 participants (7 from the *SweatAtoms*, 14 from the *Activity Sculptures*). First and second author independently read all transcripts a number of times to generate an initial set of codes. The codes were written on index cards along with descriptions and exemplary participants' quote. These codes were examined, cross-referenced, sorted and further analysed for overarching themes in close discussions between the first two authors. We repeatedly reviewed and refined the themes in order to maximize internal homogeneity and external heterogeneity. We combined similar themes into overarching themes and also drew coherent links or distinctions between them. These themes were further discussed and refined in a face-to-face meeting with the remaining two authors and narrowed down to a final set of 10 themes. We next invited 7 participants (4 male) from the surrounding research community to a focus group discussion, where our aim was to collect feedback on the wording, structure, and usability of the themes. Based on their feedback, we rephrased titles for some of the themes. For example, the theme 'self-expression' was initially titled as 'identity', which participants found ambiguous and they were worried that it might carry different meaning to different people. During the discussions, participants also brought up related topics such as 'shape-changing interfaces' to resolve questions raised in theme 'attachment', which we incorporated in the writing. The final set of 10 design themes is presented next.

4 Design Themes

We present 10 themes that describe key qualities of physical representations that designers might benefit from considering in their designs. These themes also highlight the tradeoffs and tensions in making any such decisions related to the design as identified through the field study of *SweatAtoms* and *Activity Sculptures*.

There is no predefined order in which a designer should make use of the design themes. Rather, we offer designers flexibility to start with any theme and work their way through all the themes. It is also not mandatory that the final design for the physical representation should include all the themes. We however recommend that designers should at least discuss each theme before they embark on the development stage. Designers can also utilize them to analyze their existing design choices and to identify if they satisfy the intended objectives. Table 2 describes the 10 design themes at a glance but in no particular order.

Table 2. Ten design themes for creating 3D printed physical representations

#	Design themes	Theme description
1	Purpose	Intended purpose for creating physical representations
2	Data	Aspects related to the data used to create physical representations such as its type and quantity
3	Physical properties	Physical properties used for representing data, e.g. size, texture
4	Information mapping	Internal mapping between data and physical representations
5	Practical purposes	Additional utility value of physical representations
6	Self-expression	Expressive qualities of physical representation to support one's identity
7	Fabrication process	Method used to create physical representation
8	Timing	Point in time when physical representations are created
9	Context	Contextual settings that affect interactions with physical representations
10	Attachment	Level of engagement with physical representations

4.1 Purpose

The first design theme focuses on the objective behind creating physical representations. For example, the objective can be to help people start or maintain a physically active lifestyle. However, this rather broad purpose can be fulfilled in various ways based on the individual user's needs [19, 41]. For instance, users who want to change their behavior but do not commit to taking action could benefit from rewards as incentives [33, 41]. On the other hand, users who are already physically active on a regular basis are perhaps more interested in keeping track of their progress [5, 31]. To this end, we discuss four possible ways of supporting *Purpose* by: eliciting richer reflections on data, rewarding activity, keeping track of progress and giving testimony to invested efforts.

The purpose behind creating *SweatAtoms*, for example, was to elicit richer reflections on data. As a result, *SweatAtoms* were created from the heart rate data of an entire day's activity and not just from a one physical activity session. Secondly, each of the chosen five representations convey a different piece of information about physical activity as understood from the gathered data. *Activity Sculptures* on the other hand relied more on the rewarding component where the aim was to influence and motivate running activity by rewarding each run with an individual piece of the modular physical representation. Studies of the two systems revealed that users liked and approached these representations as rewards or external push. For instance, participants of the *Activity Sculptures* study mentioned that the urge to receive all the pieces of the modular design served as a motivational factor for them to run more. In *SweatAtoms*, four participants also did more exercise to get a bigger *Frog* as a reward. However, intrinsically motivated participants were more interested in keeping track of their progress, hence their focus was on the information aspects of the representations. For instance, In *SweatAtoms*, by stacking different sized *Frog*s, or comparing printed *Graphs* from different days, participants were able to track their progress over time (see Fig. 3), which they liked. Besides *Frog*, participants also admired the *Graph* and *Flower* as they offered insights into one's activity at a snapshot.

Fig. 3. Participants treasured getting physical artifacts as rewards to their efforts. Secondly by stacking them next to each other, participants were able to track their progress.

We also found that participants treasured receiving a physical reward as a testimony to their invested physical efforts. Inline with earlier study findings, physical rewards felt more satisfying than its virtual counterparts [41]. Although these physical rewards provided more of an extrinsic motivation, they in a way supplemented the pre-existing intrinsic motivations of several of the users. For five participants of *SweatAtoms*, physical rewards contributed to an increase in physical activity. Participants appreciated getting a bigger *Frog* although printing a bigger *Frog* also required more printing time. To this end, the perceived value of the physical representation also increased over time as participants eagerly waited for them to be printed. In future, it could be interesting to examine the relationship between printing time and size of the reward.

4.2 Data Types

The second design theme draws designers' attention to selecting the right type of data for creating physical representations.

Let us start by looking into the data type. Physical activity typically can be measured in terms of physiological outputs (e.g., heart rate data) or movement based data (e.g., distance, speed). Our studies suggest that the selection between the two is important, as it could affect how individuals would perceive the constructed artifacts. For instance, *SweatAtoms* used physiological data in the form of heart rate to construct physical representations. In contrast, *Activity Sculptures* used several movement data variables such as duration, distance and average speed of a running session for creating physical representations. There are however, concerns with using heart rate data to represent one's physical activity level. Heart rate is not always a true representative of one's physical performance. An individual's heart rate might also increase in response to stress, anxiety and shock [55]. However, to obtain this level of detailed analysis would require more explicit interventions in one's life and greater logging commitments from participants. Movement based data in comparison is less ambiguous and more specific to physical activity.

The accompanying study of *SweatAtoms* revealed that the use of heart rate generated empathy towards the constructed physical representations as users could relate to these representations as *"tokens of their heart"*. Participants showcased self-esteem and pride in showing them around. *Activity Sculptures*, which are constructed from the running data, on the other hand, did not gather a similar appeal amongst participants. Rather, these artifacts were looked at primarily for analytical purposes.

The selection of the data type can also be based on the comfort and convenience of the tracking method [2]. Physiological data requires the use of a monitoring device such as chest worn heart rate monitor, which can be awkward with a burden of carrying an additional device around. In contrast, *Activity Sculptures* study used the smartphones that participants already own to track the running data. Wrist worn smart watches that could now detect physiological signals could offer less awkward way of measuring physiological data.

Finally, designers should also consider ways to normalize data and prepare it into a form that is suitable for visualization [4, 18, 23]. In *SweatAtoms*, the raw heart rate data was classified into six heart rate zones, which was then used to define the shape of different representations. Similarly, in the *Activity Sculptures* system, the elevation gain data was normalized for 3D printing because of its large variances. Similarly, granularity of data can also be explored through the printing of interlocked physical artifacts, where each artifact can carry a different data set. Unlike screen-based systems, physical artifacts can afford distributed interactions with other artifacts in a large space [21]. Users can thus join, interlock, and mix physical artifacts to generate additional meaning [27].

4.3 Physical Properties

This design theme looks into the physical properties of the material when designing physical representations. According to Zhao et al. [57], physical properties of a material can be split into four dimensions: (1) Geometrical dimension: e.g. volume, shape or texture (2) Physical-chemical dimension: e.g. color, weight, temperature, hardness or moisture (3) Emotional dimension: e.g. comfort, elegance (4) Associative dimension: subjective comparison to existing things of the perceiver's experience, e.g. tangible qualities such as feather-like or silky touch.

While designing physical representations, it is important that designers pay attention to the above-mentioned dimensions to support self-expression and information mapping (discussed as subsequent themes). In *SweatAtoms* and *Activity Sculptures*, we used recyclable ABS and bio-gradable PLA as printing materials. In terms of the associative dimension, both ABS and PLA have a rigid and firm feel when touched. Participants however preferred the use of PLA to ABS as PLA is more sustainable and does not cause a striking unpleasant smell like ABS during printing. In terms of geometric dimension such as volume, both systems followed a simple mapping where the size of an artifact increased based on the amount of activity. Participants appreciated this kind of mapping. For instance, a participant from the *SweatAtoms* study said after receiving a *Frog* printed from her data, "*It is like burning your body fats and putting them onto the frog.*" In terms of physical-chemical dimension, *Activity Sculptures* system used only white filament for all the representations, whereas *SweatAtoms* gave users the option to choose plastic filaments from a set of colors (red, green, blue, yellow and white). Participants liked the option of changing filaments as it helped them to segregate and categorize artifacts from different days.

Our choices for geometrical and physical-chemical dimensions were also restricted by the available technology. The state-of-the-art 3D printers, for example, cannot control variables such as temperature or moisture. Printing with more than one type of material at a time is also a challenge. However, with increased interest of both academic and industrial communities into digital fabrication [40], we expect that most of these challenges will be resolved in the near future. The ongoing research in shape-changing interfaces [46] and 3D printing [39] might also unveil new ways to incorporate physical properties into the design.

4.4   Information Mapping

The fourth design theme describes the importance of internal mapping between the data and the physical representation. Finding a suitable mapping the digital data to a physical representation can be challenging, as a standard encoding process is still an area of ongoing research [23].

Drawing from our study insights, we put an emphasis on creating physical representations that are simple and easy to interpret. Common methods of representing data such as using numbers or graphs are often difficult to interpret with increase in data points as most users lack statistical skills [7, 9, 13]. Instead designers can think of using metaphors for representing data in an easy-to-interpret form. Additionally, metaphors might also offer an advantage that users might develop an empathy with them [32]. However, while choosing metaphors, designers must consider the metaphorical distance [6] between a chosen metaphor and the underlying data, as it can affect interpretive qualities of the representation.

In our systems, we used known metaphors such as flower, lamp and frog and kept the mapping simple. In the majority of the selected representations, an increase of physical activity resulted in a bigger physical artifact. However, in the *Activity Sculptures* project, the various data dimensions were further used to influence the shape of the physical representation, whereas in *SweatAtoms*, some of the representations were selected to emphasize and map different aspects of the heart rate and its corresponding zones. For example, *Ring* and *Dice* described the active and sedentary time based on heart rate zones.

The study results reflect that participants were happy with the choice of metaphors that offer abstract information about their activity in an aesthetically pleasing way. The fact that these representation required personal knowledge to be interpreted seemed to have fostered reflection on data. It led participants to engage with the artifacts, by observing them, testing their limits or comparing them. It also meant that participants could display them freely without feeling as if they were over-exposing themselves. For example, *Frog* from *SweatAtoms* was the favorite of all representations despite the fact that it contains very little information about physical activity (see Fig. 4). It was readily displayed in people's surroundings and facilitated healthy competition among participants in order to get a bigger *Frog*. More informative models like *Graph* and *Dice* did not become a part of people's home ambience. This suggests to us that while mapping the data, paying attention to the aesthetics of the physical representations is important, although the embodied information can be as brief as "*I did more physical activity than yesterday.*"

Fig. 4. Participants were happy with the choice of metaphors such as *Frog* that summarizes the amount of physical activity done in a day but in an aesthetically pleasing way.

Secondly, the mapping is also dependent on the quantity of the data [4]. *SweatAtoms* used only one type of data, i.e., heart rate, which participants found relatively easy to map and understand. However, *Activity Sculptures* had a variety of data about individual's movement embedded within the artifacts. Some participants struggled to understand all bits of captured information (particularly in the beginning of the study) and how different shapes represent different pieces of information. However, these difficulties diminished as participants received more representations of a similar shape (see Fig. 3).

Participants also devised their own ways of inferring and keeping track of the communicated information. In *Activity Sculptures* one participant wrote the number of the runs at the bottom of each piece of the *Lamp* figure to allow him to track the order. While another participant spelled out a strategy on how to arrange the beads of her *Necklace* by putting the biggest piece in the middle and the others around it.

As such, the physical nature of the artifacts made it easier for participants to discover meaning through handling and playful exploration. However, embedding too much information within artifacts can make them less readable. Instead, designers could focus on representing a summary or only key bits of information using easy to interpret metaphors, in line with earlier study on self-monitoring devices [29]. To this end, a designer should utilise an information mapping that brings out the intended purpose of the representation. For example, a representation with the purpose to track progress should choose a mapping that makes it easy to compare different instances and encode those data variables that a user wants to improve on.

4.5   Practical Purposes

This theme is concerned with additional utility value of the physical representation, going beyond its main purpose. The advantage of physical representations over its digital counterparts is that they can also fulfill other practical purposes in everyday life [51]. While creating physical representations, designers could think about possible uses for these representations but users can also bring their creativity and imagination into play to devise new ways of using the representations in their life.

While designing these two systems, we had several practical purposes in mind for some of the selected representations. For example, we designed the *Robot* and *Frog* to serve as a decorative object, while we designed the *Necklace*, the *Ring* and the *Flower* as jewelry. The *Lamp* and *Jar* also have practical value in domestic life (see Fig. 5). These prescribed uses helped participants in finding the appropriate place to keep and interact with the artifacts. For example, the *Frog* and *Flower* were placed near the desk. *Necklace* and *Flower* were worn by participants. Representations that had little practical utility, however, gathered less interest from participants, for instance *Graph*.

Fig. 5. Activity *Sculptures* were embedded in everyday life: (a) '*Necklace*' worn by a participant; (b) '*Robot*' placed on an office desk; (c) '*Lamp*' placed on a nightstand; (d) unintended use of the '*Jar*' as a *Lamp*.

Participants were discovering new utility values for the physical representations. For example, one of the participants from the *SweatAtoms* study suggested using the *Flower* model as a floating candleholder on water. One participant stacked his *Dice* models like a skyscraper. To this end, in both systems, personalization was an important aspect and participants loved to style and utilize the physical artifacts according to their needs and creative abilities.

Designers should therefore consider how users could find additional utility for the physical representations in everyday life. The user may not necessarily utilize the artifact in accordance with the use intended by the designer. However, having these additional uses prescribed in the design could increase user's interaction with the artifacts and thus supporting the main purpose and overall engagement with the physical representations.

4.6 Self-expression

This theme looks at expressive qualities of physical representations, synonymous with the individual's understanding of his or her self [14, 35]. Since the physical representation is an external manifestation of an individual's data, its relation with the individual can be dependent on how reflective the representation is of an individual's identity.

To support such reflection, in the *SweatAtoms* study, we used the fact that bodily responses to physical activity, such as heart rate values, are not only different for each individual, but also vary based on different types of physical activity. The *Flower* artifact as such was designed to signify these unique aspects of the individual's heart rate. Significant increases or decreases in the heart rate were mapped to an evolving floral pattern. Since these shifts in heart rate differed from person to person and also from one day to another, the resulting floral pattern in the *Flower* artifact was different for different days for each participant, creating a unique representation of individual's heart rate data (see Fig. 6a).

To this end, when users first encountered these artifacts, they experienced emotional responses such as intrigue, joy, disappointment and satisfaction. As Desmet [8] argued, these responses were based on not only the visceral, but also the behavioral and reflective components of individual's cognition. They appreciated them because these artifacts embodied their personal data and represented past activities, something that cannot be "*bought at a shop*". In *Activity Sculptures*, participants liked *Necklace* because it can be worn on the body and therefore easily be seen and shown to others. They often discussed with their families and visitors how these representations made sense in their life. The aesthetic properties of physical representations also gave users opportunities to be self-expressive, drawing from Goffman's theory [14] that any physical artifact, if put on display, becomes the public representation of the self and craftsmanship. Both systems thus highlight a design quality: uniqueness that goes beyond the traditional design strategies for digital representations. Designers should try to incorporate individual's traits in the data in order to increase appeal for these artifacts.

Most participants in both studies were vocal and enthusiast about designing representations for themselves. Participants also altered the way in which they printed and used their representation, not only to improve their understanding but also to reflect their personality. In the *SweatAtoms* study, some participants also chose material filaments from the given pool of material filaments to match their favorite color. Three participants wanted to change the filaments color every day so that there is a distinctive feel and order to the representation once assembled together. In the *Activity Sculptures*

Fig. 6. (a) The visible differences in *Flower* pattern offered insights into how heart rate changed on different days. (b) Participants were also creating in using physical artifacts: one participant from the *SweatAtoms* study created a clock from his 3D printed artifacts.

study, one participant thought about personalizing his *Robot* sculpture by dressing it in a shirt with a name or number while another participant from the *SweatAtoms* study created a clock with all artifacts from the study (Fig. 6b). Therefore, involving users in the design process might unveil new ways of supporting self-expression.

4.7   Fabrication Process

This theme is concerned with aspects related to the physical creation of the artifacts. Although we currently limit our discussion to one of the digital fabrication processes – 3D printing – the theme described here might also be relevant to other fabrication techniques such as laser cutting.

As Jansen et al. [23] have argued, the assembly and manufacturing features of physical representations can play an influential part in engaging participants with their data along with the design goals and the aesthetic features. Unlike screen based representations, creating physical representations using processes such as 3D printing takes time. Therefore, it becomes an important decision whether individuals should be involved in the printing process. In *SweatAtoms*, participants printed the artifacts in their home whereas in *Activity Sculptures*, we did printing at our side and then handed over the printed artifacts to the participants. Both these approaches had reasonable success. In *SweatAtoms*, although participants liked printing artifacts at home, their interest in the printing process faded with time, mainly because of the noise and the unpleasant smell of plastic during printing.

Despite this shortcoming, involving users in the creation process of physical representations was found advantageous as this gave users more time to anticipate and reflect on their data, thereby possibly increasing the potential value of these representations. This happened because users felt more ownership and responsibility, as they were able to see directly how their physical representations are produced from their own data [12]. Earlier research [24, 52] highlights that physical artifacts become mementos by virtue of the time and emotion invested in them by their owner.

Creating an artifact can be an enjoyable experience, giving individuals the feeling of wonder, agency and satisfaction [12]. Thus, it is not usually the physical characteristic of the artifacts that make them biographical, but the meaning imputed to them by users as their significant personal possession.

Involving the user in the creation process however requires that the user has access to a 3D printer and suitable materials at home, as well as the time and necessary skills to 3D print these artifacts. Effort is needed on behalf of the designer to ensure that the process is user-friendly and less prone to error. Although there is rapid progress in the advancements of 3D printers, the printing time, noise and printing costs are still limiting factors, which should be kept in mind. Similarly, it is important to realize the limitations and capabilities of 3D printers and understand what kinds of physical representations are printable. Both projects, for example, used rather simple shaped and small objects for 3D printing to keep time and costs reasonable.

4.8 Timing

This theme talks about how often and when the physical representation should be printed or received. Physical representations can be printed during or after a physical activity.

If the 3D printing takes place 'during' the physical activity, then the user can directly influence the final shape of physical representation by changing the course of the activity. For example, a user can intentionally control the heart rate responses to influence the design of *Flower*. However, this would assume that the physical activity takes place near the fabrication process such as 3D printing, which is not always suitable as dynamic updates to 3D printed models in runtime is challenging and would also require technical expertise to avoid runtime printing errors. As a result this option is less viable.

Feedback "after physical activity" allows for the possibility for users to think and reflect on their physical activity performance and make different choices next time they partake same activity. Supporting this, both *SweatAtoms* and *Activity Sculptures* chose the final option and offered delayed feedback on physical activity.

In the *SweatAtoms* study, users printed artifacts of their data in the evening whereas in the *Activity Sculptures* study, participants received the artifact via mail or through a personal handover on the next day. Giving feedback in a delayed manner kept participants anticipating, unlike normal smartphone based apps where the continuous stream of data is just a glance away [15]. This process thus allowed them to concentrate more on the activities at hand and somewhat altered their habit of frequently checking their phone for feedback on the data. In *SweatAtoms*, participants wanted to get a bigger *Frog*. Since there was uncertainty in accurately predicting whether they had done enough activity to receive better looking physical representations, participants continued to remain active throughout the day and unknowingly did more exercise. Participants in the *Activity Sculptures* study stated that a delay between the run and the reward was beneficial, as it leaves room to speculate how the run would be reflected in the physical representation and furthermore act as an additional reward for the run. The timing also depends on the printing process itself. Participants in the *SweatAtoms* study had to print the physical representations manually and could choose the timing of the printing process on their own, which they liked.

Following the work on slow technology [16], we emphasize the need for thinking about reflection and contemplation in opposition to efficiency and performance while designing physical representations. Interestingly, recovering and gaining personal health is also a slow and steady process, which demands time and consistency in the effort from the user [56]. For example, the result of burning body fat through exercise is only visible after the user has followed the exercise regularly and for a sufficient amount of time. Apparently, the 3D printing process is also quite slow at this moment. Efforts were being made to tackling the slowness of 3D printing and make the digital fabrication process more efficient [39]. In contrast, we suggest designers to embrace the slowness as a useful design resource to support a delayed feedback on physical activity data.

4.9 Context

This theme identifies the role of physical representations in the external schema of things, based on the context and their association with other artifacts and people. Borrowing Goffman's [14] analogy of public and private stage, there is a clear distinction in terms of how an individual presents himself to others in a public setting and in a personal private setting. A physical representation similarly has a different role to play in a public and private context. For example, placing a physical representation in a home ambience has to satisfy and cater to existing aesthetic details and surroundings, while an object that is worn on the skin should match the body types, comfort and dressing styles. It is therefore essential to customize and design such representations that can cater to a particular context of use.

The context is also crucial to understand and determine the level of abstraction required while mapping data to the representation. For example, an individual might desire more abstraction and privacy in a public setting whereas the same individual might appreciate a more detailed mapping between the data and physical representation to enable an in-depth understanding about him/herself in a private setting. Within our studies, we found that participants liked the idea of having a physical object, which cannot be identified as being easily related to their physical activity levels and therefore its significance is only revealed if the user wants to. As a result, they were happy to share it with others. For instance, one participant from the *Activity Sculptures* study said that she normally did not like to share her running data, e.g. by posting a run on Facebook, however she liked to show her *Necklace* as it is abstract form of self-expression, without revealing too much of her running data.

Verbeek [54] also brings forward the tendency of artifacts to adjust to and act according to the environment in which they were put in. Latour [28] suggests that artifacts work in a close relationship with people and other artifacts, creating networks that shape each other. Therefore, while designing physical representations designer should also identify and analyze how a physical representation would pair with other artifacts as well as the people who would interact with it.

The findings of the *SweatAtoms* study revealed that one of the reasons why participants appreciated the *Frog* and the *Flower* over other representations was that participants found immediate applications and places where they can place these representations. For example, the *Frog* was placed on top of computer screen and the *Flower* was used as a coaster on the dining table. Similarly, public visibility of the artifacts in *Activity Sculptures* made it possible that others easily notice the data and serve as a conversation starter. These artifacts generated a sense of curiosity and sparked conversations among the visitors who did not know what the design actually meant. Participants were enthusiastic to explain the meaning to them. Some participants also gave these artifacts to their loved ones as a gift. Although, most of the physical representations from the studies worked as standalone artifacts, participants suggested to us that they would love having artifacts that can easily pair with things that they already have. In the future, it would be interesting to create artifacts that represent data from multiple people and see how it would facilitate social interactions and shared understanding of each other's data.

4.10   Attachment

The last theme points to the longevity of an individual's relationship with the physical representations. Previous literature on archiving suggests that physical artifacts have a longer life and value in people's life than its digital counterparts [24, 52]. However, with physical artifacts there is always a burden to keep them, moreover creating and destroying them is not as easy as a digital object as argued by Kirk and Sellen [24]. As a result, designers should focus on how these representations could be able to sustain a user's interest over a longer period.

To answer this question, designers must look into the frequency of users' interactions with physical artifacts. A digital representation on a smartphone, for example, affords multiple moments of engagement at any moment in time as most users carry such devices with them and frequently interact with them on regular basis. An individual's interaction with physical artifacts is often ad-hoc, as these artifacts have a tendency to disappear in the surrounding [37]. However once noticed, these interactions with physical artifacts seem to last for a relatively longer duration. To this end, the location and the practical utility of the physical artifacts play a crucial role in determining the frequency of interaction and thus the level of one's attachment with these artifacts.

With physical representation also comes the issue of environmental sustainability, where producing plastic artifacts increase the amount of products in the environment. One of the main benefits of using digital media for representations lies in its dynamic properties: most data visualizations work supports runtime updates to visualizations whenever new data comes in. These visualizations also allow users to manipulate the view to match their interest. Physical representations are different in that they are extremely static and hard to update once they have been printed. To this end, one must print a new representation whenever new data is generated. Besides, mobile activity tracking, remote data storage and processing also consume great deals of energy.

To overcome this concern, physical representations should use biodegradable materials like PLA and allow the recycling and reuse of 3D prints. Selective printing is also an option. For example, designer can chose one type of physical representation for a specified goal and once user achieves this goal, another representation can be unlocked, following well-known gamification principles, e.g. unlocking new levels or badges after attaining specific achievements. Other interesting directions to resolve this issue would be to allow people to repurpose these representations, or use perishable materials like food to represent data [26]. Designers can also look into creating dynamic physical representations that augment themselves over time rather than printing new artifacts each time. For example, using shape-changing interfaces [46] that can update its shape in accordance with the changes on the personal data.

5 Conclusion and Future Work

This work contributes to the emerging research field of physical representations by unfolding a rich design space outlined across 10 design themes. The proposed design themes could inspire designers to think about different ways of creating representations to offer greater reflection on data. These themes not only have applications in the context of physical activity and self-monitoring, but also in other areas where personal data is of central interest e.g. recommendation systems and personalizing sports experience [27]. The presented design themes can be utilized during the ideation phase in order to come up with new design possibilities, as well as in the iteration phase where the themes could help designers in refining initial designs. Designers can use the proposed themes in any particular order and it is also not mandatory to include all the themes in one design. In order to understand how designers would make use of these themes, we are planning to conduct workshops centered on different design context such as sports and exertion games.

We also make a note that these themes were created from the design and study of two systems that construct 3D printing artifacts for physical activity data. To this end, the themes are primarily focused around digital fabrication process such as 3D printing to create physical representations. We invite future research towards extending these themes to other contexts and by discussing other methods (e.g., CNC milling, laser cutting) of creating physical representations. Furthermore, by including reflections from other physical representation systems, such as *Patina Engraver* [30], *EdiPulse* [26] would broaden the scope of this work.

To conclude, we invite designers and researchers - both in academia and industry alike - to challenge their notion of representing physical activity data to users on screen. As technology evolves, it is important that we as designers harness and explore the exciting opportunities that emerging new technologies like 3D printing can offer. By presenting the design and study of two systems that utilizes 3D printing, a technology, we imagined a possible design future, where individuals can create artifacts of their choice at home with their own data. To this end, we would argue that the proposed themes not only embarks the first conceptualized approach to the design, but also paves the way for future explorations in this context.

References

1. Anderson, C.: The new industrial revolution. Wired Mag. **18**, 2 (2010)
2. Benson, R., Connolly, D.: Heart rate training. Human Kinetics (2011)
3. Braun, V., Clarke, V.: Using thematic analysis in psychology. Qual. Res. Psychol. **3**(2), 77–101 (2006)

4. Card, S., Mackinlay, J., Schneiderman, B.: Readings in Information Visualisation. Kaufmann, San Francisco (1999)
5. Choe, E.K., Lee, N.B., Lee, B., Pratt, W., Kientz, J.A.: Understanding quantified-selfers' practices in collecting and exploring personal data. In: Proceedings of the SIGCHI Conference on Human Factors in Computing Systems (CHI 2014), pp. 1143–1152. ACM (2014). http://dx.doi.org/10.1145/2556288.2557372
6. Clevenger, T., Edwards, R.: Semantic distance as a predictor of metaphor selection. J. Psycholinguist. Res. 17(3), 211–226 (1988)
7. Consolvo, S., McDonald, D.W., Landay, J.: Theory- driven design strategies for technologies that support behavior change in everyday life. In: Proceedings of the SIGCHI Conference on Human Factors in Computing Systems (CHI 2009), pp. 405–414. ACM (2009)
8. Desmet, P.: Measuring emotion: development and application of an instrument to measure emotional responses to products. In: Blythe, M.A., Overbeeke, K., Monk, A.F., Wright, P.C. (eds.) Funology, pp. 111–123. Springer Netherlands (2003)
9. Elsden, C., Kirk, D.S., Durrant, A.C.: A quantified past: towards design for remembering with personal informatics. Hum. Comput. Interact. 31(6), 518–557 (2015)
10. Etkin, J.: The hidden cost of personal quantification. J. Consum. Res. 42, 967–984 (2016)
11. Fitbit. http://fitbit.com
12. Gauntlett, D.: Making is Connecting. Wiley, New York (2013)
13. Galesic, M., Garcia-Retamero, R.: Graph literacy: a crosscultural comparison. Med. Decis. Making 31, 444–457 (2011)
14. Goffman, E.: The Presentation of Self in Everyday Life. Penguin Books (1959)
15. Gouveia, R., Pereira, F., Karapanos, E., Munson, S.A., Hassenzahl, M.: Exploring the design space of glanceable feedback for physical activity trackers. In: Proceedings of the 2016 ACM International Joint Conference on Pervasive and Ubiquitous Computing (UbiComp 2016), pp. 144–155. ACM (2016)
16. Hallnas, L., Redström, J.: Slow technology; designing for reflection. J. Personal Ubiquit. Comput. 5(3), 201–212 (2001)
17. Hassenzahl, M., Laschke, M., Praest, J.: On the stories activity trackers tell. In: Proceedings of the 2016 ACM International Joint Conference on Pervasive and Ubiquitous Computing: Adjunct (UbiComp 2016), pp. 582–587. ACM (2016)
18. Huang, D., Tory, M., Aseniero, B.A., Bartram, L., Bateman, S., Carpendale, S., Tang, A., Woodbury, R.: Personal visualization and personal visual analytics. IEEE Trans. Visual. Comput. Graph. 21(3), 420–433 (2015)
19. Hermsen, S., Frost, J., Renes, R.J., Kerkhof, P.: Using feedback through digital technology to disrupt and change habitual behavior: a critical review of current literature. Comput. Hum. Behav. 57, 61–74 (2016)
20. Hogan, T., Hornecker, E.: Towards a design space for multisensory data representation. Interacting with Computers (2016)
21. Hornecker, E.: A design theme for tangible interaction: embodied facilitation. In: Gellersen, H., Schmidt, K., Beaudouin-Lafon, M., Mackay, W. (eds.) ECSCW 2005, pp. 23–43. Springer, Netherlands (2005)
22. Huta, V.: Pursuing eudaimonia versus hedonia: distinctions, similarities, and relationships. In: Waterman, A. (ed.) The Best within Us: Positive Psychology Perspectives on Eudaimonic Functioning. APA Book, Washington, DC (2013)
23. Jansen, Y., Dragicevic, P., Isenberg, P., Alexander, J., Karnik, A., Kildal, J., Subramanian, S., Hornbæk, K.: Opportunities and challenges for data physicalization. In: Proceedings of the SIGCHI Conference on Human Factors in Computing Systems (CHI 2015), pp. 3227–3236 ACM (2015)

24. Kirk, D.S., Sellen, A.: On human remains: Values and practice in the home archiving of cherished objects. ACM Trans. Comput. Hum. Interact. **17**(3), 1–43 (2010)
25. Khot, R.A., Hjorth, L., Mueller, F.: Understanding physical activity through 3D printed material artifacts. In: Proceedings of the SIGCHI Conference on Human Factors in Computing Systems (CHI 2014), pp. 3835–3844. ACM (2014)
26. Khot, R.A., Pennings, R., Mueller, F.: EdiPulse: supporting physical activity with chocolate printed messages. In: Proceedings of the 33rd Annual ACM Conference Extended Abstracts on Human Factors in Computing Systems (CHI EA 2015), pp. 1391–1396. ACM (2015)
27. Khot, R.A., Andres, J., Lai, J., von Kaenel, J., Mueller, F.F.: Fantibles: capturing cricket Fan's story in 3D. In: Proceedings of the 2016 ACM Conference on Designing Interactive Systems (DIS 2016), pp. 883–894. ACM, June 2016
28. Latour, B.: Pandora's Hope. Essays on the Reality of Science Studies. Harvard University Press, Cambridge (1999)
29. Lazar, A., Koehler, C., Tanenbaum, J., Nguyen, D.H.: Why we use and abandon smart devices. In: Proceedings of the 2015 ACM International Joint Conference on Pervasive and Ubiquitous Computing (UbiComp 2015), pp. 635–646. ACM (2015)
30. Lee, M., Cha, S., Nam, T.: Patina engraver: visualizing activity logs as patina in fashionable trackers. In: Proceedings of the 33rd Annual ACM Conference on Human Factors in Computing Systems (CHI 2015), pp. 1173–1182. ACM (2015)
31. Li, I., Dey, A., Forlizzi, J.: Understanding my data, myself: supporting self-reflection with ubicomp technologies. In: Proceedings of the 2011 ACM International Joint Conference on Pervasive and Ubiquitous Computing (UbiComp 2011), pp. 405–414. ACM (2011)
32. Lin, J.L., Mamykina, L., Lindtner, S., Delajoux, G., Strub, H.B.: Fish'n'Steps: encouraging physical activity with an interactive computer game. In: Proceedings of the 2006 ACM International Joint Conference on Pervasive and Ubiquitous Computing (UbiComp 2006), pp. 261–278. Springer (2006)
33. Locke, E., Latham, G.: A Theory of Goal Setting and Task Performance. Prentice Hall, Englewood Cliff (1990)
34. Löwgren, J.: Annotated portfolios and other forms of intermediate-level knowledge. Interactions **20**(1), 30–34 (2013)
35. Lupton, D.: The Quantified Self: A Sociology of Self-Tracking, Polity (2016)
36. Mellis, D., Follmer, S., Hartmann, B., Buechley, L., Gross, M.D.: FAB at CHI: digital fabrication tools, design, and community. In: Proceedings of the 31st Annual ACM Conference Extended Abstracts on Human Factors in Computing Systems (CHI EA 2013), pp. 3307–3310. ACM (2013)
37. Miller, D.: Stuff. Polity Press, Cambridge (2010)
38. Mota, C.: The rise of personal fabrication. In: Proceedings of Creativity and Cognition (CandC 2011), pp. 279–288. ACM (2011)
39. Mueller, S., Mohr, T., Guenther, K., Frohnhofen, J., Baudisch, P.: faBrickation: fast 3D printing of functional objects by integrating construction kit building blocks. In: Proceedings of the SIGCHI Conference on Human Factors in Computing Systems (CHI 2014), pp. 3827–3834. ACM (2014)
40. Mueller, S., Devendorf, L., Coros, S., Ochiai, Y., Gannon, M., Baudisch, P.: CrossFAB: bridging the gap between personal fabrication research in HCI, computer graphics, robotics, art, architecture, and material science. In: Proceedings of the 2016 CHI Conference Extended Abstracts on Human Factors in Computing Systems, pp. 3431–3437. ACM (2016)
41. Munson, S.A., Consolvo, S.: Exploring goal-setting, rewards, self-monitoring, and sharing to motivate physical activity. In: Pervasive Health 2012, pp. 25–32 (2012)

42. Nissen, B., Bowers, J.: Data-things: digital fabrication situated within participatory data translation activities. In: Proceedings of the SIGCHI Conference on Human Factors in Computing Systems (CHI 2015), pp. 2467–2476. ACM (2015)
43. Pousman, Z., Stasko, J.: A taxonomy of ambient information systems: four patterns of design. In: Proceedings of the Working Conference on Advanced Visual Interfaces (AVI 2006), pp. 67–74. ACM (2006)
44. Polar Heart rate monitors. http://www.polar.com/products/H7_heart_rate_sensor
45. Prochaska, J., Velicer, W.: The transtheoretical model of health behavior change. Am. J. Health Promotion 12(1), 38–48 (1997)
46. Rasmussen, M.K., Pedersen, E.W., Petersen, M.G., Hornbæk, K.: Shape-changing interfaces: a review of the design space and open research questions. In: Proceedings of the SIGCHI Conference on Human Factors in Computing Systems (CHI 2012), pp. 1163–1172. ACM Press (2012)
47. Rooksby, J., Rost, M., Morrison, A., Chalmers, M.: Personal tracking as lived informatics. In: Proceedings of the SIGCHI Conference on Human Factors in Computing Systems (CHI 2014), pp. 1163–1172. ACM (2014)
48. Stusak, S., Tabard, A., Sauka, F., Khot, R., Butz, A.: Activity sculptures: exploring the impact of physical visualizations on running activity. TVCG 20(12), 2201–2210 (2014)
49. Swan, M.: Sensor mania! The internet of things, wearable computing, objective metrics, and the quantified self 2.0. J. Sens. Actuator Netw. 1, 217–253 (2012)
50. Tomitsch, M., Kappel, K., Lehner, A., Grechenig, T.: Towards a Taxonomy for ambient information systems. In: Ambient Information Systems (2007)
51. Vande Moere, A.: Beyond the tyranny of the pixel: exploring the physicality of information visualization. In: Proceedings of IV 2008 (2008)
52. Van den Hoven, E.: Graspable Cues for Everyday Recollecting. Ph.D. thesis, Technische Universiteit Eindhoven, The Netherlands (2004)
53. Velayanikal, M.: Can a fitness tracker, which rewards users solve the problem of wearable tech? (2014). https://www.techinasia.com/mymo-fitness-tracker-gives-rewards-to-users/. Accessed 17 July 2015
54. Verbeek, P.P.: What Things Do - Philosophical Reflections on Technology, Agency and Design. The Pennsylvania State Press, University Park (2005)
55. Vermeulen, J., Lindsay, M., Johannes, S., Russell, B., Sheelagh, C.: Heartefacts: augmenting mobile video sharing using wrist-worn heart rate sensors. In: Proceedings of the 2016 ACM Conference on Designing Interactive Systems (DIS 2016), pp. 712–723. ACM (2016)
56. Weinberg, R.S., Gould, D.: Foundations of Sport and Exercise Psychology. Human Kinetics, Champaign (2006)
57. Zhao, J., Vande Moere, A.: Embodiment in data sculpture: a model of the physical visualization of information. In: Proceedings of the 3rd International Conference on Digital Interactive Media in Entertainment and Arts, pp. 343–350. ACM (2008)
58. Zimmerman, J., Forlizzi, J., Evenson, S.: Research through design as a methods for interaction design research in HCI. In: Proceedings of the SIGCHI Conference on Human Factors in Computing Systems (CHI 2007), pp. 493–502. ACM (2007)

Breathing Friend: Tackling Stress Through Portable Tangible Breathing Artifact

Miroslav Macik[1]([✉]), Katerina Prazakova[2], Anna Kutikova[2], Zdenek Mikovec[1], Jindrich Adolf[1], Jan Havlik[1], and Ivana Jilekova[1]

[1] Faculty of Electrical Engineering, Czech Technical University in Prague,
Prague, Czech Republic
`macikmir@fel.cvut.cz`
[2] Faculty of Architecture, Czech Technical University in Prague,
Prague, Czech Republic

Abstract. We present Breathing Friend – a portable and tangible device that uses haptic interaction to unobtrusively stimulate mindful breathing as efficient stress coping method. Its design is optimized for holding in user's hands. By changing its shape, it sends haptic signals to the user. Several studies were conducted where we explored and verified the form factors of the artifact, interaction methods, therapeutic effect, fitting to everyday life, and influence on the breathing pattern.

Keywords: Stress · Industrial design · Mindful breathing · Tactile device

1 Introduction

Long-term stress becomes a serious issue. It negatively influences the cognitive, emotional and physical well-being of many individuals. Stress can increase the probability of health problems like various cardiovascular diseases [12], hypertension, obesity, and depression [8]. An individual can deal with a stressful situation at any time and any place [13].

Traditional ways to tackle stress without medication include meditation, deep breathing, and relaxation. From the variety of breathing techniques, we selected the mindful breathing meditation that is used as a stress coping method [10]. It requires sophisticated training to tackle stress, or it is conducted with the help of a therapist.

Feijs et al. in [4] describe the relationship between stress, heart rate variability (HRV), and breathing. Breathing affects the heart rate through an effect called respiratory sinus arrhythmia. Training of breathing pattern can increase the HRV which lowers the stress level. Authors also suggest employing a portable device as it offers an opportunity to find a quiet place for relaxation. They recommend that such a device should not resemble computer or other ICT used for stressful work activities.

© IFIP International Federation for Information Processing 2017
Published by Springer International Publishing AG 2017. All Rights Reserved
R. Bernhaupt et al. (Eds.): INTERACT 2017, Part IV, LNCS 10516, pp. 106–115, 2017.
DOI: 10.1007/978-3-319-68059-0_6

In our research, we investigate a possibility to design such alternative device that would efficiently stimulate mindful breathing. We introduce Breathing Friend (*Bf*) – a portable and tangible device that does not resemble ICT. Instead of already overloaded visual or auditory modality, it uses haptic interaction to discreetly and unobtrusively stimulate mindful breathing.

2   Related Work

We focus on approaches aiming at controlling the breathing patterns. Particular attention is put to solutions exploiting haptic interaction modality.

Applications exist that help individuals with mindful breathing, e.g. Breathe App for Apple Watch [7], Spire [14]. However, those applications require the use of complex ICT devices which are identified as an inherent source of stress stimuli [5].

In [1], Rhawi et al. introduce a personalized biofeedback game that trains subjects to relax while playing a game. The game difficulty increases if the subject's breathing rate differs from a prescribed target rate. Validation on small group suggests that the game helps to acquire deep breathing skill and reducing arousal in following stress-inducing tasks.

Stahl et al. in [15] present a somaesthetic approach to support meditative bodily introspection by using light and heat modalities. Subjects report on an increased awareness of their breathing. Sato et al. [11] propose a music presentation system that uses listener's respiration information to change replay speed to minimize the difference between the target of and observed (listener?s) respiration phase. Paro [17] is a therapeutic robot resembling baby seal equipped with touch sensors allowing physical interaction. However, it is not intended to support mindful breathing.

Alonso et al. in [2] present *Wigo*, an embedded tangible device that aims to contribute to stress reduction. While under stress, people tend to make irrelevant gestures with physical objects (i.e. a pen), the intensity of such an activity increases when individuals are given a mentally demanding task. The stress-coping method is based on detection of stress by measuring irrelevant gesture activity – wiggling and making the movement increasingly more difficult. In [3], they present three devices (including *Wigo*) that show various kinds of haptic feedback to support stress reduction. The other two methods employed following activities: rolling over acrylic marbles (*Marmoro*) and squeezing (*Squeeze-it*).

Analysis of the related work indicates that tackling stress by stimulating mindful breathing can be successful [1,4,11]. Other research [2,3,15] shows that tactile stimulation of hands can be used for stimulating mindful breathing.

3   Design

During the design, we had in mind that the final form should be visually and haptically pleasing [18], not inducing stigmatization [9], and providing efficient haptic signals to stimulate breathing.

Fig. 1. Evolution of coating: knitted from wool (left), sewed from an elastic material (middle), easily exchangeable pattern sewed from an elastic material (right).

Form factors. The design process started by molding several shape prototypes from clay and consequently from plaster (for fine surface finishing). The final shape resembles an embryo evoking something alive that supports positive affect for users without elimination of public use. We conducted an informal study focused on the perception of the *Bf* form. The most promising embryonic shape resembled a small animal like a hamster or a tiny bird. The final prototype was created from silicone which has similar tactile properties as human skin and provides enough flexibility for breath-like motion. It is hollow to allow insertion of an electro-mechanical engine to provide tactile sensation of breathing.

Surface and personalization. Silicone is flexible but sticky. Therefore a coating was introduced. The first version was knitted from wool (see Fig. 1 left). The evaluation showed that it is too warm and fluffy, and can discourage some participants (see 4.1). Next version was made from an elastic material and had happy and bright colors (see Fig. 1 middle). The final version used a similar material, but more decent colors and different pattern (see Fig. 1 right). We also made the coating exchange easier for the user to support personalization.

Interaction and breathing pattern. The interaction with *Bf* starts by its activation via motion detection. The electro-mechanical engine in *Bf* starts cyclic inflation and deflation phases. The inflation phase is faster than the deflation phase. As therapist suggest (see 4.2) breathing rate gradually slows down from 15 brpm (breath rate per minute) to 6 brpm. The electro-mechanical engine is placed in a silicone enclosure to provide distinct and smooth mechanical movement. Figure 2 shows individual development versions of the engine.

Implementation. An off-the-shelf high torque servo mechanism was used as an actuator spreading out two hemispheres. We developed three versions with gradually increasing servo mechanism torque and reliability as depicted in Fig. 2. Since version 2, we used a custom electronic board with a microcontroller (ATmega328), servo-control, voltage booster, Li-Po charging, accelerometer, real-time clock, 8M flash memory, and FTDI USB serial interface. Most components are 3D-printed to simplify manufacturing and assembly.

Fig. 2. Evolution of *Bf* electro-mechanical engine: the original handcrafted prototype (left), 3D printed + linear movement (center), 3D printed + strong servo (right).

4   Evaluation

We conducted several formative evaluations focused on various aspects of human interaction with the device and its effect on the stress: first impression, the way of holding the device; therapeutic effect; how it fits into everyday life. We also investigated the existence of an effect on the breathing pattern.

4.1   Form Factors Evaluation

In this qualitative evaluation, we focused on the subjective perception of the final shape and wool coating (see Fig. 1 left). Based on the consultation with therapists and the study [6], in this evaluation, we focused on women returning to work after maternity leave as they are highly endangered by stress.

Participants. We recruited five female with kids and full/part time jobs (3 full-time, 2 part-time), average age 39.8 ($MIN = 36$, $MAX = 43$, $SD = 2.6$).

Procedure. We conducted five semi-structured interviews (about 45 min each), which took place in an informal, non-lab setting. First, we asked participants about their stress coping strategies. Second, we provided the participants with the *Bf* prototype and observed their reactions.

Results. All participants acknowledged that stress is a non-trivial thing and that it should be prevented or handled. Two said that prevention is the best form of the stress coping strategy (P4, P5). One of them had serious health problems caused by stress in the past (P4).

Two participants stated they would not feel to be ashamed while tackling stress by *Bf* (P4, P5); however, they indicated that *Bf* should be discreet (P4, P5). Three participants stated that it is not acceptable to be in stress in public (P1 – P3) and that they feel sorry for their family members, who sometimes have to deal with a stressed out person (P2, P3).

All participants identified some animal form in the *Bf* (mouse, little hedge-hog, mole, kitty). Some commented on the shape (bean, potato, sausage, kidney) and live-like movements (breathing child, snoring guy). Except for P5, all participants expressed positive attitude. P1 stated that it feels like *"somebody is holding her hand"*. Participants used their dominant hand or both hands to hold it. Some were careful and gentle (P1, P2, P4) while others were trying to squeeze the *Bf* (P3, P5). Some participants stated that the *Bf* is too big to be handled discreetly; however, they did not experience difficulties in handling it. The movement reminded them of heart beating (P3 – P5), slow flow of fluid (P1), breathing (P5). Most found the movement pleasant (P1 – P4), one unpleasant (P5). They mentioned that they would prefer more cheerful and bright colors. They described the fuzzy appearance as *"suitable for the winter months"*, most would prefer something *"not so warm"*.

This evaluation led to the design of more appropriate coating (see Fig. 1) and more reliable electro-mechanical engine to provide stronger movement sensation.

4.2   Potential Therapeutic Effect

In this study, we focused on the potential of *Bf* to serve as a therapeutic aid. We interviewed therapists to gain insight into the usage of breathing in their praxis and to estimate the usefulness of the *Bf* for their clients.

Participants. Six therapists were inquired. Their specialization varied from a medical doctor, psychologist to yoga lecturer. All use therapeutic breathing for the training of self-awareness, and stress prevention and management.

Procedure. A semi-structured interview focused on their profession and characteristics of their patients was followed by presentation of the *Bf* device. They were asked to try it and express their opinions and suggestions. Afterward, they were asked to comment on the breathing pattern of the *Bf*.

Results. Therapists described the *Bf* as very calming, useful for sensing mindful breathing, better focusing on breathing itself, and for a faster education of breathing patterns. Their methods spring from both research and ancient meditation techniques. Therapists teach patients to slow down their breathing to a particular frequency. P3 stated: *"Tactile input is a promising method how to educate mindful breathing faster and perform it without direct contact with a therapist"*. This finding is in correlation with our subsequent literature overview. E.g. Vaucelle et al. [16] states: *"Touch is fundamental to our emotional well-being. Medical science is starting to understand and develop touch-based therapies for autism spectrum, mood, anxiety, and borderline disorders"*.

They suggested potential use also as a tool for rehabilitation. P4 suggested: *"It could be utilized after intubation of children"*. Most therapists suggested decreasing breathing frequency. Based on these results, we configured the electro-mechanical engine to provide tactile sensation with a gradually decreasing rate from 15 down to a preset value of 6 brpm.

4.3   Fitting into Everyday Life

We explored how the *Bf* fits into everyday life activities of potential users.

Participants. We recruited four participants (three female), average age 36.75 ($MIN = 34$, $MAX = 39$, $SD = 2,22$) without previous experience with the *Bf*.

P1 works as a project manager; P2 as babysitter coordinator; P3 as manager in a small restaurant; P4 as a waiter in a teahouse.

Procedure. We conducted a fourteen-day diary study. Each participant was provided with a *Bf* device, a charging cable and a paper diary with a short questionnaire for each event of use. Improved version 3 of electro-mechanical engine was used for P3–4 (see Fig. 2). They were instructed to fill the diary at least daily and to charge the *Bf* overnight. In the end, we conducted semi-structured post-test interviews.

Results. The first impressions were diverse. P1 described the *Bf* as *"...something for a massage?"*; P2 as a bean-shaped object with a movement that reminds her of heart contractions; P3 described the *Bf* as an animal and highlighted its cuteness; P4 as a pink kidney.

For P1, the study was limited to one week due to a technical issue. She used the *Bf* seven times. She preferred to use it at work or home; *"I used it when I feel to have time for myself,"* she mentioned. In the post-test interview, she highlighted the irregular movement caused by the technical issue.

For P2, twelve usages were recorded. She did not use it at work but at home when falling asleep (*"I liked that I fell asleep."*). She mentioned that it is not comfortable for her to breathe synchronously with it.

P3 used the *Bf* ten times, always at home in the evening for around 10 min. She mentioned the lack of free time as the reason for not using it. The most common positive comments in the diary were the movement of inflation, regularity of the motion, surface, moment to myself, contribution to relaxation. The negative comments were the whirring sound (*"Once I wanted to use it in a tram but, because of the whirr I could not."*), fast battery discharging (*"I would like to use it longer while watching a movie, but the battery discharged after 10 min."*) and difficult synchronization of breath with Bf (*"It is difficult for me to synchronize my breathing, it is not clear when to breathe in."*).

For P4, only four usages were recorded. He used the *Bf* at home or in the teahouse, where he works. He mentioned serious work problems as the reason for not using it for the second week of the study. The negative comments were problems with charging, a bad response to the on/off switch, and the sound: *"At the beginning I disliked the sound, but later I got used to it. In the end, I used it just while listening without touching. It makes the breathing pattern more clear than the movement"*.

Participants used *Bf* mostly once a day. There were positive outcomes; P2 used *Bf* for calming before sleep, P2, P3 described the use as *"I like the time for myself."*. All of them liked the surface material. P2 described that the pre-set breathing rate was too fast. Technical issues reported (discharging, unwanted activation) had an adverse impact on the use. However, only P2 contacted us to get technical help.

4.4   Effect on the Breathing Frequency

To evaluate the effect of *Bf* on breathing pattern we conducted a quantitative study.

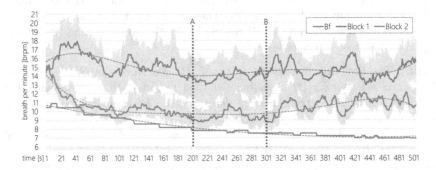

Fig. 3. Breath frequency and 95% confidence intervals of quantitative evaluation. The blue curve represents values from Block 1, orange curve values from Block 2, and green curve *Bf* frequencies (quantization error is caused by the 1 s accuracy of RTC chip).

Participants. We recruited 16 participants (5 female), average age 28.5 ($SD = 9.4$, $MIN = 22$, $MAX = 61$).

Apparatus. The experiment was conducted in usability lab decorated to support relaxation. It was equipped with a comfortable chair, footstool, and TV set, where an unintrusive movie clip was played in a loop. A prototype of *Bf* device was at disposal. There was a standard camera directed on the upper part of the participant's body. *Bf* device recorded its breathing frequency using internal memory and an RTC chip.

Experiment design. The experiment was one factor (two levels) within-subject design. The independent variable was the way of interaction with the *Bf*. Main measures were breathing frequency of participant and the *Bf* (brpm). For statistical evaluation, we used 95% confidence intervals.

Procedure. Participants were comfortably seated and the *Bf* was introduced as a device for tackling stress. Before the experiment started, they were sitting for at least 5 min. The experiment was divided into two blocks where the brpm was measured. In the Block 1 we instructed the participants to relax avoiding any instruction regarding the breathing. Participants were left alone in the room for approximately 10 min. After the first block, the subjective evaluation (at least 5 min) by means of a questionnaire (Likert scale 1–5) was performed. Then the Block 2 was started. Before the start, the participants were instructed to relax again and try to follow the simulated breathing of the *Bf* device. After the second block, the subjective evaluation was performed.

Results. The breath frequency was calculated from the video signal by application of a set of filters and an autocorrelation function. The average values with 95% confidence intervals are depicted in Fig. 3. In the Block 2, participants breath frequency was much closer to *Bf* than in Block 1. This is clearly visible in the first 200 seconds (indicated by red vertical dashed line A). Then the frequency stagnated and from 300th second (indicated by red vertical dashed line B) it even started to increase. The results show that during the Block 1 the breath frequency almost did not change, oscillating around 15–16 brpm. This is in contrast to values in Block 2, where the frequency clearly dropped down from 14.1 brpm to below 9.6 brpm.

The subjective evaluation (Fig. 4) shows that more participants tried to voluntarily breathe in Block 2. However, the feeling of relaxation was much lower during Block 2 (39% not relaxed vs. 0% in Block 1). This can be explained by the inability to breathe as slowly as the *Bf*, as eight participants reported problems with adaption to low frequencies of *Bf*. The surface of *Bf* was perceived as pleasant (83%) and 94% agreed on the comprehensibility of *Bf* use. The noise of the electro-mechanical engine was disturbing for 69% of participants.

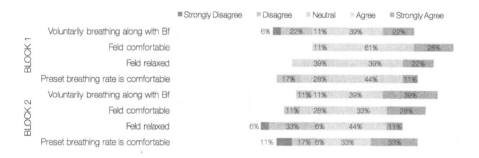

Fig. 4. Subjective evaluation of *Bf*. Likert scale scores for both Blocks usage of *Bf*.

5   Conclusion and Future Work

We successfully designed a portable, tangible artifact that shows the ability to stimulate mindful breathing as a stress coping method. Evaluations indicate that it is possible to rely on haptic interaction only while avoiding the necessity to employ ICT like devices and audio-visual interaction.

Our evaluations showed the need for personalization of breathing pattern. Gradual adjustment of target breathing rate could eliminate discomfort during the attempt to slow down the breathing rate. The electro-mechanical engine should be as silent and as fluent as possible as the sensitivity of users to these aspects is very high. The user acceptance of the artifact can be significantly increased by introducing customization of the surface; thus the variability and ease of exchange of the coating are essential.

The future research should focus on finding an optimal course of breathing rate adjustment to reduce personal discomfort while preserving target rates suggested by therapists. Other research direction can focus on the usage of such artifact within the therapy session. Yohanan and MacLean in [18] leverage touch as an important part of emotional communication. Further research can focus on emotional communication potential of devices like *Bf*.

Acknowledgments. This research has been supported by the TACR research program TE01020415, by internal CTU grants SGS16/236/OHK3/3T/13 and SGS17/183/OHK3/3T/13.

References

1. Al Rihawi, R.G., Ahmed, B., Gutierrez-Osuna, R.: Dodging stress with a personalized biofeedback game. In: Proceedings of the first ACM SIGCHI annual symposium on Computer-human interaction in play, pp. 399–400. ACM (2014)
2. Alonso, M.B., Keyson, D.V., Hummels, C.: Squeeze, rock, and roll; can tangible interaction with affective products support stress reduction?. In: Proceedings of the 2nd international conference on Tangible and embedded interaction, pp. 105–108. ACM (2008)
3. Alonso, M.B., Varkevisser, M., Keyson, D.V.: Expressive stress relievers. In: Proceedings of the 7th Nordic Conference on Human-Computer Interaction: Making Sense Through Design, pp. 761–764. ACM (2012)
4. Feijs, L., Langereis, G., Van Boxtel, G.: Designing for heart rate and breathing movements. Design and semantics of form and movement, 57 (2010)
5. Fuglseth, A.M., Sorebo, O.: The effects of technostress within the context of employee use of ICT. Comput. Hum. Behav. **40**, 161–170 (2014)
6. Houston, D.M., Marks, G.: The role of planning and workplace support in returning to work after maternity leave. Br. J. Ind. Relat. **41**(2), 197–214 (2003)
7. Ingber, J.: The Apple Worldwide Developers Conference 2016: What's coming this fall. In: AccessWorldMagazine, vol. 17(6) (2016)
8. McEwen, B.S., Seeman, T.: Stress and affect: applicability of the concepts of allostasis and allostatic load. In: Handbook of Affective Sciences, pp. 1117–1137 (2003)
9. Parette, P., Scherer, M.: Assistive technology use and stigma. Educ. Training Dev. Disabil. **39**(3), 217–226 (2004)
10. Paul, G., Elam, B., Verhulst, S.J.: A longitudinal study of students' perceptions of using deep breathing meditation to reduce testing stresses. Teach. Learn. Med. **19**(3), 287–292 (2007)
11. Sato, T.G., Kamamoto, Y., Harada, N., Moriya, T.: A playback system that synchronizes the musical phrases with listener's respiration phases. In: CHI 2013 Extended Abstracts on Human Factors in Computing Systems, pp. 1035–1040. ACM (2013)
12. Schnall, P.L., Landsbergis, P.A., Baker, D.: Job strain and cardiovascular disease. Annu. Rev. Public Health **15**(1), 381–411 (1994)
13. Spector, P.E.: Employee control and occupational stress. Curr. Dir. Psychol. Sci. **11**(4), 133–136 (2002)
14. Spire. 2017. Spire Breath and activity tracker. Accessed: June 2017 (2017). https://www.spire.io/

15. Ståhl, A., Jonsson, M., Mercurio, J., Karlsson, A., Höök, K., Johnson, E.-C.B.: The Soma Mat and Breathing Light. In: Proceedings of the 2016 CHI Conference Extended Abstracts on Human Factors in Computing Systems, pp. 305–308. ACM (2016)
16. Vaucelle, C., Bonanni, L., Ishii, H.: Design of haptic interfaces for therapy. In: Proceedings of the SIGCHI Conference on Human Factors in Computing Systems, pp. 467–470. ACM (2009)
17. Wada, K., Shibata, T., Saito, T., Tanie, K.: Effects of robot-assisted activity for elderly people and nurses at a day service center. Proc. IEEE **92**(11), 1780–1788 (2004)
18. Yohanan, S., MacLean, K.E.: A tool to study affective touch. In: CHI 2009 Extended Abstracts on Human Factors in Computing Systems, pp. 4153–4158. ACM (2009)

Citizen Tagger: Exploring Social Tagging
of Conversational Audio

Delvin Varghese$^{(\boxtimes)}$, Patrick Olivier, and Madeline Balaam

Open Lab, Newcastle University, Newcastle upon Tyne, UK
{d.varghese2, patrick.olivier,
madeline.balaam}@newcastle.ac.uk

Abstract. This paper discusses Citizen Tagger (CT), a mobile application for tagging audio-based chat-show content. The application allows users to create audio and text tags (annotations). Through an iterative design process, CT was designed and deployed with 16 members of a faith-based community who tagged a panel discussion about 'faith and vocation'. Based on usage statistics, analysis of created tags, and other qualitative data, the user experiences of tag creation were assessed. Questions around how to configure tagging-related parameters were investigated, and diverse user motivations for creating tags were also explored. Tagging was discovered to be a subjective experience, with participants expressing a desire to customise their tagging setup. Furthermore, despite being instructed to tag for content organisation and retrieval, users utilised tagging as a tool for self-reflection.

Keywords: Social tagging · Multimodal interaction · Audio annotations · Assisted note-taking · Speech modality

1 Introduction

Human interaction with the world is inherently multimodal [20]. Schaffer et al. [18] looked at the state of the art in speech interfaces and found that despite Voice User Interfaces (VUIs) being part of many smartphones and navigational systems (and often saving interaction steps or time), Graphical User Interfaces (GUIs) are still the more common input modality. However, providing alternate input modalities accommodate a wider range of users, tasks, and environmental conditions [15]. While audio as an input modality has received much attention in the HCI literature [2, 18, 20], relatively little work has looked at it within the context of audio annotation or tagging of audio files. Anguera [1] presented a tagging application to annotate digital photos using speech input, which showed that such interfaces can harness this under-used input modality in everyday tasks. Cherubini et al. [4] have previously compared the differences between text and audio tags in the context of a mobile-based photo annotation and retrieval task. They found that participants took longer to tag text and in general, participants preferred voice-based tagging.

Social tagging [11] is defined as a community of users applying free-form tags to digital objects [23]. When applied to chat show content, which is conversational and unscripted in nature, serves as a way of giving voice to the (otherwise passive) users

R. Bernhaupt et al. (Eds.): INTERACT 2017, Part IV, LNCS 10516, pp. 116–125, 2017.
DOI: 10.1007/978-3-319-68059-0_7

who are part of radio shows, giving them a role in knowledge production [7, 11]. CT was designed to assess the feasibility of such a concept i.e. investigating the complexities of tagging resources such as conversational audio. This mobile application enables a user to add audio and text tags as they are listening to a piece of audio content. This technology was deployed with 16 members of a UK Christian community, and the application usage statistics and feedback that was received through post-usage surveys and interviews was analyzed. The primary contribution of this piece of work is to assess (i) the concept of audio and text-based tagging of audio content, and (ii) user experiences of audio-based tagging.

1.1 Note-Taking During Meetings

Chiu et al. have done previous work on capturing meetings and assisting note taking by using digital video and ink in a physical conference room. They augmented the meeting recording process by enabling tools to support indexing, accessing and browsing the captured meeting [5]. By noting various changes in the meeting room e.g. timestamp of user note creation, presentation slide changes etc. multimedia systems can support users in indexing and annotating interesting areas in the content [6]. Similarly, other work has explored the indexing of notes in an automated meeting capture environment [12, 14], where the index in the notes is populated with the relevant multimedia content i.e. presentation slide for which the notes are taken [12].

1.2 Social Tagging and Folksonomies

When tagging is studied in the literature, it is taken to refer to tagging of entire resources and not within resources i.e. music is tagged but tagging of indices or segments within music files (i.e. *intra*-content tagging) [21] is an under-researched area. Sack et al. [16] state that current tagging systems "produce a hit list that contains entire resources, although the tags describing these resources might refer to specific parts of those resources". SoundCloud (soundcloud.com), a technology that is a well-known social audio platform that utilizes timed comments within audio content, is an interesting technology to look at in relation to this work as it provides a framework for user-generated text-based comments (or tags) that are visible during playback. Text-based applications are common, and Singh et al. have commented how speech has been under-utilized as an input modality for tagging [19]. They utilized a narrative structure to help reconcile the technological challenges of speech-based applications and the challenges arising from unmet user expectations and needs.

2 Initial Design of CT

In our initial design iterations, it was considered important to ensure that a tagging user was not unduly influenced by the tags created by another user. A *blind tagging* system (where a tagging user cannot view tags assigned to the same resource by other users while tagging) was thus used to assist the tagging process [13]. Another key design consideration was to encourage free-form tagging, where the users are given the ability

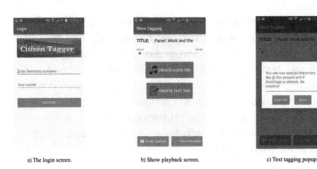

a) The login screen.   b) Show playback screen.   c) Text tagging popup.   d) Audio tagging popup.

Fig. 1. Citizen Tagger app screenshots

to express their tags in any keyword(s) as deemed relevant by them [22]. To ensure that tags are created on a regular basis, a timer was built into the application which displayed tagging popups. The popups prompted the user to create an audio tag by giving a brief instruction followed by a 'Record' button (seen in Fig. 1). Users could dismiss the tag if they did not want to create a tag at that moment. The frequency of the prompts can be configured in the *Config* menu tab, where other options such as logging out, clearing previous tags, changing the live show settings etc. are also available. Users were also able to add text and audio tags manually at their discretion.

The show is stored on the web server and can either be streamed by the user or downloaded for offline listening and tagging. The ability to pause/rewind/fast-forward playback was also present. It was important to not disrupt the flow of the audio playback when users were creating a tag. To ensure this, when time-sensitive input was required from the users, pop-up dialog boxes were used [8]. Additionally, they performed as a cue to prompt the user to tag. When the text or audio tagging popups appear, the phone provides haptic feedback to alert the user, who then has the option to either create and post a tag or to touch an area of the screen not used by the popup to hide the tag-creation popup. The system uses two kinds of popups: (1) text tagging popup features a box where users can type their text and then submit it, and (2) audio tagging popup shows a timer (that signals how long they have to record an audio tag), a Record button, and an instruction on tagging. A text tag contains the typed text, the author of the tag and a timestamp. The audio tag is similar except the content of the tag is an audio clip. The tags are automatically synced to the server when the user has finished tagging. The user can also access all their tags in the 'History' area of the app.

2.1 Tagging Frequency and Audio-Tag Length

One aim of this research was to explore how to configure the tagging frequency and audio-tag length for the tagging user. A number of frequencies were used to understand the effect of different time intervals on user perceptions of tagging. Over a four-week period, the initial application was designed and tested iteratively. Each test consisted of a group of five postgraduate students and researchers, who were asked to tag a radio show discussion. Through initial testing, values of 1 min and 2 min intervals emerged as ideal tagging frequencies, and these needed to be tested with other users. The application assigned the tagging popup frequency/audio-tag length for the user. This was achieved by creating a set of configurations on the server, and when the application connects to the server, the server shuffles through the configurations set and sends the next configuration on the list to the user. Three tagging configurations were designed by the author to test the ideal set of audio-tag length and prompting frequency (how often the application asked them to create a tag) for the study. These parameters were chosen based on feedback received during the design phase, where 1 min (High Frequency, HF) and 2-minute (Low Frequency, LF) tagging frequencies were tested. A third frequency, in between, of 90 s (Medium Frequency, MF) was also used. As the frequency was decreased, the tag-length was increased proportionally to reflect the extra time that was being afforded to the user to reflect on their tag (HF: 5 s, MF: 10 s, LF: 15 s).

3 Deployment

The next phase involved testing CT with a community who would engage with audio content and would potentially be interested in the audio tagging concept. The author used an opportunistic sampling approach [17] to contact 35 individuals from 3 different Christian communities in the UK. 16 individuals opted to take part in the study (9 males and 7 females; aged between 20 and 32; $M = 23.13$, $SD = 3.07$, Response rate = 45.7%). Individuals in the communities are already encouraged to consume and engage with audio content, particularly in the form of sermons and panel discussions, and thus readily expressed interest in taking part in this study. The deployment was conducted over a two-week period, and a between-subjects study design was used. The participants were informed that their tags would be used by other listeners of the show in the future to find summaries of different sections of the show. This was done based on previous feedback in the design informing workshops, where several attendees stated that knowing how their tags would be used would motivate them to create the tags. The participants were entered into a raffle to win one of ten £20 vouchers for taking part in the study.

Participants were asked to listen to and tag a Christian audio show using the CT application, around the theme of Christian Vocation, lasting 45 min. The show was titled 'Redefining Work Panel Discussion' from the TGC13 Faith at Work Post-Conference [9]. The panel had 5 speakers who were having an unstructured free-form conversation about the concept of 'calling' or vocation, and how that impacts the way Christians work. The speakers were topic experts, but the conversational style of the discussion was informal.

After using the application, the participants were asked to fill in an online survey. The survey contained 4 sections: (1) general questions about their current audio listening habits, (2) questions about the tagging prompts and tag lengths, and how they would configure that experience, (3) general usability questions about the CT application itself, and (4) concluding questions about their likes/dislikes about the application and other comments. Semi-structured interviews were conducted with the participants to ask them about their experience. The interviews were audio-recorded, transcribed and thematically analyzed [3].

4 Findings

16 participants used CT to listen and tag the aforementioned show. 202 tags were generated in total using the application (152 audio tags, 50 text tags). Based on the usage statistics, post-usage survey, and interviews that were held, the themes that emerged are presented below.

4.1 Tagging-Prompt Frequencies and Tag Creation

The data from the participants shows that those in the HF tagging group created many more tags than those in the LF tagging group. An individual in the HF group created on average 4.67 audio tags manually and 8.17 tags through the tagging-prompts issued by the application every minute. The MF tagging group individuals however, still created 4.67 manual audio tags per person but the tags recorded as a response to application prompts fell to 5.17 tags on average, per person (39.24% of prompts shown were responded to). Furthermore, the LF tagging group's prompted tagging rate was similarly low at 2.75 tags per person.

In the survey, participants expressed mixed opinions about the tagging frequencies assigned to them. 3 out of the 6 HF participants felt, that the application prompted them too frequently to keep up. The other 3 felt that the frequency was appropriate. Similar results were received from the 6 MF participants: 3 of them felt the prompts were too frequent, 2 of them felt it was appropriate, and another was undecided. Participants were also asked whether they would prefer to be prompted to create tags, or would they rather create tags themselves without external prompts. Five out of the six HF taggers expressed a preference for manual tagging. In the MF tagging group, 4 participants wanted to only create manual tags, while one wanted to be prompted, while yet another wanted both types of tagging to be present. Finally, in the LF tagging group, 3 persons desired both kinds of tagging-creation to be present while one participant opined that they preferred manual tagging.

Those that expressed a desire for prompted-tagging justified it by saying that "*its easier and I won't forget to tag*" (Alan). While others who did not want automated prompting said, "*being prompted is quite distracting and disrupts my train of thought*" (Sam). By contrast, those eager for both mechanisms to be present opined, "*I like to be prompted in case I have lost concentration, but like the opportunity to create my own tags so that I can make extra notes*" (Nicola). Interestingly, one user who found the tagging prompts quite disconcerting (and quit the tagging process partly through because '*it drove me nuts*'), stated that they would only want manual tagging because "*it would make it more listenable, but then I'd probably never tag*" (Colin).

It was interesting to note that no single person was fully satisfied with the parameters of tagging set in CT. Regardless of the tagging group assigned to them, a lot of the users would have preferred a longer tag length. This was expressed by all but seven of the participants. Three users (one from the HF tagging group, and two from the MF group) expressed a desire for an "unlimited" tag length, so as to "*be concise when I need to be, but also not be restricted by an arbitrary time limit*" (Aisha). Others were a bit more cautious, and stipulated that a tag "*shouldn't be longer than 25–30 s region else it becomes an audio show in itself*" (Sam)". Another feature that was requested in the post-show discussions, was the ability to pause a show while recording a tag. The application was built with the idea of continuous playback while tagging, which was meant to encourage rapid tag-creation as slowness in the process penalized the user by making them miss part of the show, which would be playing at a reduced volume in the background as they recorded a tag.

4.2   Text Tags vs Audio Tags

There was a diversity of opinion among the participants regarding their choice for text or audio. 5 users did 60% or more of their tags using text, while 9 users did 60% or more of their tagging via audio. Text tagging was not very popular, with only 50 of the 202 tags created using the system being in written format. A significant portion of these 50 text tags were done by a few individuals (68% of text tags were done by 3 individuals).

Furthermore, the tags were analyzed to see how the tag format affected the verbosity of the tags. To enable this comparison, all 152 audio tags were transcribed. The results of the comparison between audio and text tags is shown in the number of words used in the audio tags outnumbers the number of words used in the text tags. The transcribed tags were thematically analyzed, which resulted in a qualitative understanding of the tag contents. While most of the tags were descriptive tags that summarized current conversation, they were not succinct. An example audio tag that matches this description is given here (emphasis has been added to indicate words that are not necessary): "*the guy says about language plays such a big part for him*". (Anita). Some utilized tagging as more of a personal reflection and note-taking tool. Only 2% of the tags were self-reflective in nature. One user's tag contained: "need to teach people to love and interpret other people's actions as love instead of a negative way **and I personally might need to change my personality and working habits when dealing with customers or others**." (Andrea, emphasis added).

4.3   Tagging Motivations

An interesting theme that was uncovered lay around the tension between the perceived benefits and drawbacks of the experience of using CT. Many enjoyed the content of the show they listened to using the application, others stated that they didn't enjoy it as much and that this contributed to their tagging motivation being lower. Many tried to maintain a balance between the extra effort that they felt was required by them to create tags while listening, and the ability to reflect which they felt they received as a result. One participant stated they would have been more proactive in making tags '*if it was a topic I was a bit more personally interested in*' (Amit). Another person added that despite liking the quality of the show, their dislike of discussion panels in general meant they '*lost interest as the podcast went on*' (Alex).

Occasionally, participants were motivated despite their non-favorable perception of the content. Omar, for instance, created 8 audio tags (5 manually created, 3 when prompted to by the application). Conversely, Colin had a poor tagging experience and said that though he wanted to listen to the entire clip, "*the constant interruptions drove me nuts so I had to quit*". Furthermore, he added that the concept of tagging is not very useful for someone like him who can '*only think about doing one thing at a time*'.

This, he explained, meant that tagging was '*not very good if you actually want to enjoy the listening experience*'. In one sense, this was backed up by Judith, the most prolific tagger (author of 29 tags), who stated in an interview that she didn't feel like she '*listened to a full show*' because '*it was broken down a lot*' by the prompts.

The survey results suggest that many participants felt that tagging required extra effort, as opposed to just passive listening. When asked the question, 'Did the process of creating tags require extra effort on your part?', one participant responded that it did require more effort than merely listening to the audio since '*tagging is an active process*'. They added: '*getting used to the new system also took a bit of time and effort.*' (Aisha). Others praised the positive side of this tagging demand from the application, stating that it helped them '*stop and think about what I was hearing*' (Sofia). Alan quipped that the tagging prompts '*presented an opportunity to articulate and summarize the subject matter*' and tagging '*enhanced the experience rather than having a negative effect*'.

5   Discussion

The results highlight that many participants felt that CT prompted them to tag too often, and that given the choice they would reduce the frequency of tagging prompts. Through content analysis of the audio and text tags, it was apparent that many tags that had timestamps near each other, were similar in terms of the gist of their tag, even if the wording of the tags varied. Building on Chiu et al.'s work [6], more work should be done to explore how context-aware content tagging can be done. For example, the tagging prompts could be based on cues in the audio e.g. pauses, change of speaker, advertisement breaks etc. The timer-based prompts, while appreciated by some users, were not preferred by others. This raises the question of whether more should be done to train users to increase their tolerance for 'still-evolving' speech-based mobile applications, as recommended by Singh et al. [19].

Another design consideration that has arisen from this study is the need to spread the content tagging across the tagging users, for example, by distributing different sections of the chat-show to different users to tag. Doing this would allow users to listen to most of the show without feeling obliged to tag, until their tagging contributions are required. On the other hand, cues in the audio could also be used to divide the content into separate sections. Tagging distribution could be particularly relevant if a third type of tagger (besides the audio and text-based ones) is utilized: a *section tagger*. This could be a tagging role which involves marking the start and end of segments (or points in the show when new themes/topic are introduced). The role would be appropriate for those who want to tag but are unsure where to start, or do not feel confident creating text/audio tags. This role can be deployed either during the real-time show listening stage, or during the post-show content playback stage. Once this tagger has adequately segmented the show into distinct sections, the system could simply ask for one tag from an audio or text-based tagger that best summarizes the content within. This would allow the app to prepare the user adequately in advance for when they need to be ready for interruptions, possibly increasing tagging usability.

5.1 The Purpose of Tagging

Despite the fact that participants were instructed to tag for content organization and ease of information retrieval, they started using the tagging feature in novel ways. Many saw CT as a tool to create personal notes and annotations for audio content. As stated in the literature, user motivations and incentives '*may influence the resultant tags*' [13]. This might be a reason why some chose to create long, self-reflective tags. This was also apparent in the post-usage feedback from some participants, where the positives of the system were framed against how they benefitted from it and then negative feedback was around what they wished the system would be able to do for them. Thus, only a few of the incentives and motivations for tagging mentioned in the literature [10, 11], were observed in the participants. This might be due to previous work focusing on the tagging of entire content (particularly music) and often conducted in non-blind tagging scenarios (i.e. user can see tags created by other users and may use tags as a way of social signaling). Future work needs to look at the possibility of training CT users, as it might be beneficial to undergo some tagging exercises to familiarize them with the system so that user expectations are matched with system capabilities. Frameworks such as Kustanowitz et al.'s annotation framework [10] need to be used to try different annotation technologies to lower the effort-barrier for users who found tagging difficult and to encourage them 'to spend time adding rich metadata'.

The design implications proposed in the literature, that when designing for mobile tagging applications, multiple modalities (i.e. both text and audio) should be presented to the user [4], still hold true. The design, content and community of a platform can influence the motivations of a user and affect the tags that are created [23]. In future studies, further comparisons need to be done on how each of these favors the annotation of audio content.

6 Conclusion

In this paper, a mobile application (CT) was designed, developed and deployed to assess experiences of audio and text-based social tagging of chat-show audio. The findings suggest that there is still much work to be done to refine the tagging experience for the user. Although plenty of rich, descriptive tags were generated using the CT application, majority of the participants saw tagging as a subjective experience and wanted to customize one or more of the tagging parameters like tag length, tagging frequency etc. Further work needs to be explored to identify the design principles for a generalizable audio-tagging interaction that also intelligently prompts the user for tag contributions, as the findings presented here are preliminary in nature due to the small sample size and exploratory study design.

References

1. Anguera, X., Xu, J., Oliver, N.: Multimodal photo annotation and retrieval on a mobile phone. In: Proceeding of the 1st ACM international conference on Multimedia information retrieval – MIR 2008, p. 188 (2008). https://doi.org/10.1145/1460096.1460127
2. Azenkot, S., Lee, N.B.: Exploring the use of speech input by blind people on mobile devices. In: Proceedings of the 15th International ACM SIGACCESS Conference on Computers and Accessibility – ASSETS 2013, pp. 1–8 (2013). https://doi.org/10.1145/2513383.2513440
3. Braun, V., Clarke, V.: Using thematic analysis in psychology. Qual. Res. Psychol. 3(2), 77–101 (2006)
4. Cherubini, M., Anguera, X., Oliver, N., De Oliveira, R.: Text versus speech : a comparison of tagging input modalities for camera phones. In: Proceedings of the 11th International Conference on Human-Computer Interaction with Mobile Devices and Services, pp. 1:1–1:10 (2009). https://doi.org/10.1145/1613858.1613860
5. Chiu, P., Kapuskar, A., Reitmeier, S., Wilcox, L.: Room with a rear view. Comput.-Support. Coop. Work Room 7, 48–54 (2000)
6. Chiu, P., Kapuskar, A., Wilcox, L., Reitmeier, S.: Meeting capture in a media enriched conference room. In: International Workshop on Cooperative Buildings, pp. 79–88 (1999)
7. Font, F., Serrà, J., Serra, X.: Audio clip classification using social tags and the effect of tag expansion. AES 53rd International Conference on Semantic Audio, pp. 1–9 (2014)
8. Jedrzejczyk, L., Price, B.A., Bandara, A.K., Nuseibeh, B.: On the impact of real-time feedback on users' behaviour in mobile location-sharing applications. Computer 38(12), 14:1–14:12 (2010). https://doi.org/10.1145/1837110.1837129
9. Keller, T., Doll, B., Alsdorf, K.L., Kiersznowski, D., Forster, G.: Redefining Work (Panel) (2013). http://resources.thegospelcoalition.org/library/redefining-work-panel-discussion-tim-keller-bob-doll-katherine-leary-alsdorf-greg-forster-dave-kiersznowski. Accessed 18 Aug 2016
10. Kustanowitz, J., Shneiderman, B.: Motivating annotation for digital photographs: lowering barriers while raising incentives. HCIL-2004-18 (2004)
11. Lamere, P.: Social tagging and music information retrieval. J. New Music Res. 37(2), 101–114 (2008). https://doi.org/10.1080/09298210802479284
12. Lee, D., Hull, J.J., Erol, B., Graham, J.: MinuteAid : multimedia note-taking in an intelligent meeting room. In: IEEE International Conference on Multimedia and Expo (ICME) (2004)
13. Marlow, C., Naaman, M., Boyd, D., Davis, M.: HT06, tagging paper, taxonomy, Flickr, academic article, to read. In: Proceedings of the Seventeenth Conference on Hypertext and Hypermedia, pp. 31–40 (2006)
14. Moran, T.P., Palen, L., Harrison, S., Chiu, P., Kimber, D., Minneman, S., Van Melle, W., Zellweger, P.: "I' ll Get That Off the Audio": a case study of salvaging multimedia meeting records. In: Conference on Human Factors in Computing Systems, pp. 202–209 (1997)
15. Oviatt, S., Cohen, P.: Perceptual user interfaces: multimodal interfaces that process what comes naturally. Commun. ACM 43(3), 45–53 (2000). doi:10.1145/330534.330538
16. Sack, H., Waitelonis, J.: Integrating social tagging and document annotation for content-based search in multimedia data. In: CEUR Workshop Proceedings p. 209 (2006)
17. Sada, A.N., Maldonado, A.: Research methods in education. Sixth Edition - by Louis Cohen, Lawrence Manion and Keith Morrison. Br. J. Educ. Stud. 55(4), 469–470 (2007). https://doi.org/10.1111/j.1467-8527.2007.00388_4.x
18. Schaffer, S., Schleicher, R., Möller, S.: Modeling input modality choice in mobile graphical and speech interfaces. Int. J. Hum. Comput. Stud. 75, 21–34 (2015). doi:10.1016/j.ijhcs.2014.11.004

19. Singh, A., Larson, M.: Narrative-driven multimedia tagging and retrieval: investigating design and practice for speech-based mobile applications. In: SLAM@ INTERSPEECH, pp. 90–95 (2013)
20. Turk, M.: Multimodal interaction: a review. Pattern Recogn. Lett. **36**(1), 189–195 (2014). https://doi.org/10.1016/j.patrec.2013.07.003
21. Yadati, K., Chandrasekaran Ayyanathan, P.S.N., Larson, M.: Crowdsorting timed comments about music: foundations for a new crowdsourcing task. In: CEUR Workshop Proceedings, p. 1263 (2014)
22. Yew, J., Gibson, F.P., Teasley, S.: Learning by tagging: the role of social tagging in group knowledge formation1. CEUR Workshop Proceedings, vol. 312, pp. 48–62 (2007)
23. Zollers, A.: Emerging motivations for tagging: expression, performance, and activism. WWW (2007). https://doi.org/10.1.1.118.7409

Exploring Offline Context and Consciousness in Everyday Social Media Use

Yubo Kou[(⊠)]

Purdue University, West Lafayette, IN, USA
Kou2@purdue.edu

Abstract. Much social media research has been done to understand interactions and communication on social media, while less attention has been paid to the offline contexts of social media use. How do offline contexts influence everyday social media use? This paper presents an interview study with a focus on Chinese citizens' use of social media in everyday activities. The study found that informants' use of social media and attention on social media was intricately related to their offline social and physical contexts, as well as their varying levels of consciousness. The work draws on activity theory to analyze the interplay between informants' consciousness, everyday social media use, and offline contexts. Implications for design and social media research are provided.

Keywords: Consciousness · social media · Activity theory · Offline context

1 Introduction

Social media data such as likes on Facebook and retweets on Twitter are widely used as basic unit of analysis in the examination of human behavior. However, seemingly similar social media data generated by different human behaviors might carry different meanings, values, and intentions. Palen and Anderson warned that critical distinctions between human behaviors might be ignored in the analysis of large volumes of social media data [1]. Wulf et al. argued that investigations of online materials can be complemented by on-the-ground studies that looked into local conditions that interact with people's use of social media [2]. Therefore, it becomes important to understand the relationship between social media behavior and offline contexts in everyday life.

This paper presents an interview study where 32 regular social media users from mainland China described their experience and rationale behind social media use in a variety of everyday activities. Drawing from activity theory, the paper analyzes the complicated interplay between informants' everyday social media use, consciousness, and offline social and physical circumstances. Consciousness refers to "a phenomenon that unifies attention, intention, memory, reasoning, and speech" [3]. Informants often used social media with attention to their social and physical surroundings. Informants' consciousness for social media changed when they needed to attend to offline contexts. The contributions include a detailed analysis of how offline contexts influence people's interaction with social media; in-depth discussion of people's relatively low consciousness for social media when social media is not the major artifact that people interact with; and implications for social media design and social media research.

© IFIP International Federation for Information Processing 2017
Published by Springer International Publishing AG 2017. All Rights Reserved
R. Bernhaupt et al. (Eds.): INTERACT 2017, Part IV, LNCS 10516, pp. 126–135, 2017.
DOI: 10.1007/978-3-319-68059-0_8

2   Related Work

2.1   Social Media Activity and Online Contexts

In the last few years, a surging body of research examines individuals' high-level consciousness in making sophisticated, deliberate decisions of social media use. For instance, there are studies demonstrating how people coordinate diverse social media platforms. Through an interview study Zhao et al. revealed how people considered both content and audience simultaneously as they decided which platform to use. They also showed how each individual contrasted their own "communication ecosystem" [4], indicating careful consideration of platforms' advantages and disadvantages. Semaan et al. conducted a qualitative study of social media use for political deliberation and found that their participants purposefully used multiple platforms to obtain diverse political information and engage in respectful and reasoned discussions with different people [5]. Some research revolves around information curation where individual citizens carefully aggregate and disseminate information to large numbers of people. Monroy-Hernández et al. reported that a group of Mexican curators developed complicated views of other curators and their audience in curating information about the Mexican Drug War [6].

Much research has been done to reveal people's careful choices and nuanced practices on and around social media, yielding insights into conscious use of social media and deriving design implications to facilitate such use. However, little attention has been paid to the offline, local contexts within which people use social media.

2.2   Activity Theory

Activity theory (AT) is a descriptive framework mostly developed by Soviet psychologists Lev Vygotsky [7] and Alexei Leont'ev [8]. AT is widely adopted in the human-computer interaction literature to contextualize people's interactions with artifacts [9–12]. AT seeks to understand the relationship between the human mind and activity as socially and culturally situated phenomenon, and attempts to integrate three perspectives: the objective, the ecological, and the sociocultural [13]. AT posits that activity connects human and their external environments and plays a central role in development of human mind [14]. The objective of AT is the unity of consciousness and activity, where consciousness treats the human mind as a whole and activity refers to human interactions with the objective reality [13]. AT developed a hierarchy of activity, where an activity is composed of actions, and an action is made up of operations (see Fig. 1).

An activity is governed by motive(s), which is not necessarily conscious but may become conscious. Actions are governed by goals and are conscious. Operations are governed by conditions, and are conscious during learning but can become unconscious or automatic in routine [15, 16]. An example is driving a car from place A to place B. The activity is that the subject drives the car with the motive of reaching place B. The subject is conscious of their tool (a car) and destination. The activity contains many actions such as waiting at an intersection, merging onto a highway, and turning left/right. Actions like these have clear goals where the subject knows what they want

Fig. 1. The Hierarchy of Activity.

to achieve. An action includes operations such as controlling the steering wheel, observing the traffic, and pushing the gas pedal or the brake pedal. For an experienced driver, these operations are often accomplished unconsciously and sometimes simultaneously.

The hierarchy is also dynamic in that activity, action, and operation can become one another as conditions change. For example, a novice driver might pay careful attention to the steering wheel in order to keep the car moving in a straight line. In this case, controlling the steering wheel is an activity. However, such activity might transform into an operation while the driver becomes more experienced through learning. An operation may become an action or an activity as well. For example, even an experienced driver may pay more attention to how they press the brake pedal when the braking system produces unusual noise.

From the perspective of activity theory, much research on the use of social media concerns the *activity* level in *online contexts*, where people are driven by a variety of clear motivations. For instance, previous work has examined information needs and networking [17, 18], or use of social media for particular purposes such as to advocate for racial equality [19], to show support and solidarity [20], to seek diverse political information [5], and to learn [21].

3 Methodology

32 semi-structured, open-ended interviews were conducted with mainland Chinese citizens between April 2014 and January 2016. Informants included 19 males and 13 females between the ages of 18 and 46, with an average of 29. They had varying occupations including student, government employee, editor, journalist, programmer, and engineer. All of them had lived in mainland China by the time of this study.

Informants reported using social media on a regular basis. The social media services they frequented included, but were not limited to, WeChat, a mobile instant messenger, Weibo, China's largest microblogging service, and Tianya, one of the most popular Chinese online forums. They had at least two years of experience using social media for communication with friends and family, entertainment, or news consumption.

The informants were selected randomly and recruited through direct contact on Weibo. There was no monetary compensation for informants. Interviews were conducted in Mandarin Chinese and mostly lasted between 30 min and one hour. The author, a native Chinese speaker, conducted and transcribed the interviews and translated them into English.

The interviews were started with general questions such as whether they owned a smartphone or a personal computer, when they first used social media, what platform they first used, what they expected to obtain from social media, and whether they thought they benefited from social media use. Next, informants were asked to list scenarios in which they usually used social media, and their motives and rationales behind such use. The interviewer also asked them if other artifacts were used while they interacted with social media.

The author used the initial understanding to code the data through an open coding process [22]. The initial codes generated concerned activities that informants performed with the use of social media. From there, the author sorted the codes based on the offline contexts of social media use in relation to these activities. The author then used an axial coding process [22] to refine codes that mapped social media use operation, action, and activity. The paper only reports social media use at the levels of **operations** and **actions**, where informants paid considerable attention to their offline contexts. The study did not found strong evidence in which informants' accounts of their **activities** on social media were related to their offline contexts.

Because of informants' diverse backgrounds, they have different habits and usage with social media. The oldest informant at the age of 46, for instance, rarely used social media as operation or action. He usually accessed social media on his laptop and stayed concentrated on reading social media updates. However, this paper focuses on the commondalities among informants' use of social media that was related to offline contexts.

4   Findings

4.1   Routinized Social Media Use as Operation

This study found many accounts where informants treated their use of social media as peripheral to their primary concern or attention. Social media use thus appeared to be operations or actions. For example, informants reported that reading social media was a habit that was often coupled with other primary activities. For instance, Lei, a 21-year-old male college student, said that "*I often check news on Weibo [China's largest micro-blogging service], particularly when I eat meals alone at those canteens on campus, with a pair of chopsticks in my right hand and my phone in the left hand. I only needed my left thumb to swipe to read more news.*" In this example, Lei's social media use became an operation situated in an offline context where Lei managed his meal, his chopsticks, as well as other elements.

While Lei's social media use was combined with the main activity of eating meals, Yuan, a 32-year-old female news editor, described another offline context where social media use was secondary to her main activity of working on her laptop. She told us that

"*I put my iPhone aside my laptop while I am working. The phone faces up so that I get to know the latest information.*" In her account, Yuan described an online physical context, highlighting several key elements including the physical proximity between her phone and laptop, as well as the specific way she placed her phone (to face up).

Similar to Lei and Yuan, a few more informants described scenarios where they interacted with social media while engaging in other major activities situated in offline contexts that required their immense attention such as watching television shows or even driving a car.

Their interaction with social media was not planned with a clear, clearly defined purpose, but in a spontaneous way. For example, Lei explained that "*I browse through hundreds of Weibo news of all sorts, ranging from military to politics to entertainment. It feels more like a habit now. If I don't do it, I feel I have missed something. But I'm not really looking for any specific information. I can't remember most of what I have read either.*" Here Lei's description of how he "browses" on Weibo matches the definition of operation where such interaction is automatic, routinized, and unconscious.

Yuan's explanation echoed Lei's response. She said that "*My phone's screen turns on when new information comes in, such as a private message from my friend. I will notice it when I'm working on my laptop. I see what my friend says. But sometimes I'm too busy to react to it immediately, and totally forget it later.*" In Yuan's account, her work was an activity in which social media use was an operation. Social media was part of her working conditions and habits, and social media use was subject to the working context. If Yuan was absorbed in work, she would have little attention on social media.

Informants also mentioned how their own physiological conditions influenced their social media use and turned conscious use of social media into unconscious operations. Rong, a 31-year-old female designer, explained, "*Some days I was so tired especially after working overtime. After I was off from work, when I was sitting in a bus I still tried to read things on forums. But I was between falling asleep and seeing the words without comprehending them.*" Here Rong indicated a state of declined consciousness as she was tired and exhausted. Physically she was still able to hold her phone and use her eyes to see social media content. However, mentally she was unable to concentrate on comprehending words.

In the stories of Lei, Yuan, and Rong, reading social media in particular offline contexts was highly habitual to the point that such social media use became automatic and unconscious and routinized as operations. It is important to note that social media design, and together with smartphone design, was intended to minimize the effort of humans to interact with technology. In Lei's case, one left thumb was sufficient to operate on his smartphone for more content. In Yuan's case, her phone automatically turns up with minimum human effort. In Rong's example, operating on her phone to load online forums also required little mental effort.

The routinization of these basic interactions gradually took place as informants became familiar with social media platforms. The routinization also allows they to distribute more mental effort to their offline context.

4.2   Arranged Social Media Use as Action

This study found instances where the use of social media had clear goals but were not their primary activity. such use was considered as action. Informants talked about how certain offline contexts demanded their conscious use of social media to be combined with other actions to satisfy a need. For instance, Rong told us that "*I have followed many great graphic designers and photographers. I enjoy reading their microblogs to kill time while I'm commuting in a bus between home and work...I can't pay full attention to my phone. The bus is often crowded and I need to prevent my purse from being snatched. I'll also need to stay alert of unoccupied seats.*" For Rong, reading social media is part of the activity of commuting. The goal is to "kill time" but she also pays attention to physical surroundings such as empty seats.

Many informants also mentioned how social media use was situated in their social activities. Wan, a 31-year-old male engineer, shared with us a situation where he used social media while paying attention to his offline social context. He told us that "*When friends and I dine out, many of us are staring at our phones while waiting for the food to be served. I like reading posts on Tianya and Zhihu. Because it feels awkward if we do not have much to say and just stare at each other. But we do chat with each other and sometimes show each other interesting stuff we come across on social media.*" Tianya is a popular online forum in China, while Zhihu is a Chinese Q&A website. Similar to Wan, Ling, a 26-year-old male graduate student, said that "*My friends and I use WeChat a lot when we play board games. We send pictures of cards in hands to allies to 'cheat'. Of course others know. Sometimes we take pictures of interesting combinations of cards and share these pictures in WeChat's group chat and laugh together.*" Wan and Ling's stories point to offline social contexts in which they gathered with friends with the motive of socializing and having fun together. Their action of using social media was an essential component of the social contexts to avoid certain social awkwardness, to stimulate conversations around newfound content, and to communicate.

Another informant shared an experience where social media use incompatible with offline social contexts caused problems. Zhe, a 37-year-old male writer, told us, "*My wife likes to take pictures of food and share them on WeChat before I can eat. Usually I'm okay with it. But there was one time she changed too many angles only to shoot the best photos and I became really impatient. We ended up having an argument.*" In Zhe's account, the action of taking pictures of food has been established by him and his wife a component of the social activity of having meals. But such action might become inappropriate when his wife focused all her attention onto taking a satisfactory picture, ignoring other social factors such as her waiting husband.

Social media actions were part of larger activities such as the commuting activity of Rong, the socializing activities of Wan and Ling, and the eating activities of Zhe's wife. In these instances, social media use was not at the center of those larger activities, but played a meaningful role nonetheless.

5 Discussion

In this paper, social media use was analyzed at the two basic levels of activity, each indicating a distinct degree of consciousness involved in knowing social media and making decisions about how to use social media in certain offline contexts. The study shows that many types of social media use might take place while people pay more attention to their offline contexts. Next the paper discusses situated social media use and derives implications for social media design.

5.1 Situated Social Media Use

The findings included many instances in which informants used social media during a variety of activities where the major motives were neither consuming social media content nor creating content on social media. To understand such social media inter-action, it is important to pay attention to the specific context in which social media use is enacted. For instance, a person's physical surroundings might be a dominant factor if he or she is reading social media updates while commuting in a crowded bus. The social context matters if a person uses social media when collocated with friends and family. Local cultural factors such as etiquettes might also impact certain social media behaviors. Similarly, Mark et al. showed how the Iraqi culture might influence local citizens' trust and information seeking through social media [23]. When a person interacts with a rich context where physical conditions, norms, social relationships come into play, social media is not the core artifact that demands attention. The findings echo Skatova et al's study [24] of office workers whose use of technology mediated their breaks during their working time. Social media research might attend to these different contexts by incorporating external data sources and triangulating heterogeneous types of data. For example, it might be useful to know through what device people are using social media. Compared to laptops, mobile devices such as tablet and smartphone are more likely to indicate lower consciousness in social media, because people often need to pay attention to other physical conditions. As a result, their interactions with social media, such as liking or re-tweeting, might be less cal-culated and more improvisational.

Informants often mentioned whether they paid attention to their social media, and how much. Attention is a limited resource that users consciously spend in interpretation of their context and corresponding behavior. Attention also bubbles up or trickles down according to users' shifting conditions and reaction to their context. Rong, for instance, could be either tired or not, which deeply influenced how much attention she had on social media, and how meaningful her social media interaction was to herself. Exist-ing HCI research has concerned multi-tasking at workplace [25]. Similarly in social media research, it is worth attention that even for the same person, his or her social media use might contain varied meanings at different times and locations. Future social media research might pay more attention to individual social media users' behavioral patterns, instead of treating the social media population as a homogeneous one.

5.2   Implications for Social Media Design

This study shows that offline contexts, user consciousness, and social media design are intricately related, and sometimes at odds. On the one hand, guided by usability principles, the goal of design is to make interactions on social media simple and easy to use. Driven by a commercial agenda, design is inclined to prolong user stickiness, and encourage user participation. Consequently, the goal of design seems to be weakening users' consciousness, making the behavior of creating clicks, likes, and posts on social media faster and more automatic, and in doing so engaging users in the online contexts. On the other hand, users often have to attend to their offline social and physical contexts. Social media use becomes part of their social or cultural practices to the point that users do not need reasoning processes to carry out certain interactions with social media.

Offline contexts can be leveraged in social media design to create more contextualized experiences, such as contextualized social media updates. For example, if users are browsing social media updates as an operation while engaging in other major activities, they are less likely to have sufficient attention or cognitive capacity for comprehending complicated ideas such as an academic argument, compared to news. Social media might automatically balance the volume of different types of content, attending to users' focus and attention.

6   Conclusion

The paper reported a small-scale interview study of how offline context factors into social media use. Although activity has three levels, this paper only reported the two basic levels, *operations* and *actions*. The study found that informants' accounts of social media use at these two levels sufficiently illustrates the relationship between offline context and social media use. Social media might not be the central artifact in these activities as people consciously reacted to their offline social and physical context. Future social media research needs to pay attention to the influence of offline contexts while analyzing large-scale social media data. Finally implications for social media design were discussed.

References

1. Palen, L., Anderson, K.M.: Crisis informatics—New data for extraordinary times (2016)
2. Wulf, V., Misaki, K., Atam, M., Randall, D., Rohde, M.: "On the ground" in Sidi Bouzid: investigating social media use during the tunisian revolution. In: Proceedings of the 2013 Conference on Computer Supported Cooperative Work - CSCW 2013, pp. 1409–1418. ACM Press, New York (2013)
3. Nardi, B.A.: Activity theory and human-computer interaction. In: Context and Consciousness: Activity Theory and Human-Computer Interaction. MIT Press, Cambridge (1996)
4. Zhao, X., Lampe, C., Ellison, N.B.: The social media ecology. In: Proceedings of the 2016 CHI Conference on Human Factors in Computing Systems - CHI 2016, pp. 89–100. ACM Press, New York, (2016)

5. Semaan, B., Robertson, S., Douglas, S., Maruyama, M.: Social media supporting political deliberation across multiple public spheres: towards depolarization. In: Proceedings of the 17th ACM Conference On Computer Supported Cooperative Work & Social Computing - CSCW 2014, pp. 1409–1421. ACM Press, New York (2014)
6. Monroy-Hernández, A., Boyd, D., Kiciman, E., De Choudhury, M., Counts, S.: The new war correspondents: the rise of civic media curation in urban warfare. In: Proceedings of the 2013 Conference on Computer Supported Cooperative Work - CSCW 2013, pp. 1443–1452. ACM Press, New York (2013)
7. Vygotsky, L.: Mind in Society : The Development of Higher Psychological Processes. Harvard University Press, Cambridge (1978)
8. Leont'ev, A.: Activity, Consciousness, and Personality. Prentice-Hall, Englewood Cliffs (1978)
9. Bødker, S.: Applying activity theory to video analysis: how to make sense of video data in human-computer interaction. In: Context and consciousness, pp. 147–174. MIT Press, Cambridge (1996)
10. Schoenebeck, S.Y.: Giving up Twitter for Lent: how and why we take breaks from social media. In: Proceedings of the 32nd Annual ACM Conference on Human Factors in Computing Systems - CHI 2014, pp. 773–782. ACM Press, New York (2014)
11. Cassens, J.: User aspects of explanation aware CBR systems. In: IFIP Conference on Human-Computer Interaction - INTERACT 2005, pp. 1087–1090 (2005)
12. Lindgren, H., Nilsson, I.: Designing systems for health promotion and autonomy in older adults. In: IFIP Conference on Human-Computer Interaction – INTERACT 2009, pp. 700–703 (2009)
13. Kaptelinin, V.: Activity theory: implications for human-computer interaction. In: Context and Consciousness: Activity Theory and Human-computer Interaction, pp. 103–116. MIT Press, Cambridge (1996)
14. Kaptelinin, V., Nardi, B.A.: Acting with Technology: Activity Theory and Interaction Design. The MIT Press, Cambridge (2006)
15. Bertelsen, O.W., Bødker, S.: Activity theory. In: HCI Models, Theories, and Frameworks: Towards an Interdisciplinary Science, pp. 291–324. Morgan Kauffman Publishers, San Francisco (2003)
16. Karanasios, S.: Framing ICT4D research using activity theory: a match between the ICT4D field and theory? Inf. Technol. Int. Dev. **10**, 1–18 (2014)
17. Ames, M., Naaman, M.: Why we tag: motivations for annotation in mobile and online media. In: Proceedings of the SIGCHI Conference on Human factors in Computing Systems - CHI 2007, pp. 971–980. ACM Press, New York (2007)
18. DiMicco, J., Millen, D.R., Geyer, W., Dugan, C., Brownholtz, B., Muller, M.: Motivations for social networking at work. In: Proceedings of the ACM 2008 Conference on Computer Supported Cooperative Work - CSCW 2008, pp. 711–720. ACM Press, New York (2008)
19. De Choudhury, M., Jhaver, S., Sugar, B., Weber, I.: Social media participation in an activist movement for racial equality. In: ICWSM, pp. 92–101 (2016)
20. Starbird, K., Palen, L.: (How) will the revolution be retweeted? information diffusion and the 2011 Egyptian uprising. In: Proceedings of the ACM 2012 Conference on Computer Supported Cooperative Work - CSCW 2012, pp. 7–16. ACM Press, New York (2012)
21. Claros, I., Cobos, R.: Social Media Learning: An approach for composition of multimedia interactive object in a collaborative learning environment. In: Proceedings of the 2013 IEEE 17th International Conference on Computer Supported Cooperative Work in Design (CSCWD), pp. 570–575. IEEE (2013)
22. Corbin, J., Strauss, A.: Basics of Qualitative Research: Techniques and Procedures for Developing Grounded Theory. SAGE Publications, Thousand Oaks (2007)

23. Mark, G.J., Al-Ani, B., Semaan, B.: Resilience through technology adoption: merging the old and the new in Iraq. In: Proceedings of the 27th International Conference on Human Factors in Computing Systems - CHI 2009, pp. 689–698. ACM Press, New York, (2009)
24. Skatova, A., Bedwell, B., Shipp, V., Huang, Y., Young, A., Rodden, T., Bertenshaw, E.: The role of ICT in office work breaks. In: Proceedings of the 2016 CHI Conference on Human Factors in Computing Systems - CHI 2016, pp. 3049–3060. ACM Press, New York (2016)
25. Su, N.M., Mark, G.: Communication chains and multitasking. In: Proceedings of the Twenty-sixth Annual CHI Conference on Human Factors in Computing Systems - CHI 2008, pp. 83–92. ACM Press, New York (2008)

Special *Digital* Monies: The Design of Alipay and WeChat Wallet for Mobile Payment Practices in China

Yong Ming Kow[1(✉)], Xinning Gui[2], and Waikuen Cheng[1]

[1] School of Creative Media, City University of Hong Kong,
Kowloon Tong, Hong Kong
yongmkow@cityu.edu.hk, wikncheng@gmail.com
[2] Department of Informatics, University of California, Irvine,
Irvine CA 92697-3440, USA
guix@uci.edu

Abstract. While research studies of digital and mobile payment systems in HCI have pointed out design opportunities situated within *informal and nuanced mobile contexts*, we have not yet understood how we can design digital monies to allow users to use monies more easily in these contexts. In this study, we examined the design of Alipay and WeChat Wallet, two successful mobile payment apps in China, which have been used by Chinese users for purposes such as playing, gifting, and ceremonial practices. Through semi-structured interviews with 24 Chinese users and grounded theory coding, we identified five contexts in which the flexibility and extensive functions of these payment apps have allowed these users to adaptively use digital monies in highly flexible ways. Finally, our analysis arrived at our conceptual frame—*special digital monies*—to highlight how digital monies, by allowing users to alter and define their transactional rules and pathways, could vastly expand the potential of digital monies to support users beyond standard retail contexts.

Keywords: Mobile payment · China · Money · Qualitative study · Special monies

1 Introduction

Many digital and mobile payment systems have focused on fulfilling a small set of design needs, chiefly to increase transaction speed, and reduce cost of use [1–8]. But monies contain much more *informal and nuanced uses* (e.g., between friends, and with microenterprises [8]. These uses could alter the interactions the users would expect of digital monies), such as who should send the money, who the money is for, what the money is for, when the money should be sent, and on what condition the money should be sent. For example, if a group of co-workers is sharing a retirement gift for a colleague, these co-workers would need to split the cost evenly—not a straightforward interaction that we could easily perform with most digital monies. While research studies in HCI have pointed out design opportunities situated within these informal and

R. Bernhaupt et al. (Eds.): INTERACT 2017, Part IV, LNCS 10516, pp. 136–155, 2017.
DOI: 10.1007/978-3-319-68059-0_9

nuanced mobile contexts [1–8], we have not yet understood how we can design digital monies to allow users to use monies more easily in these contexts.

In this paper, we address the research gap by identifying design principles guiding the design of digital monies so that they fit more readily into informal and nuanced mobile contexts. In order to identify these design principles, we conducted an exploratory study, examining the design of two successful *digital* payment apps, *Alipay* and *WeChat Wallet*, with specific attention to whether and how they serve nuanced activities. With the Chinese mobile payment market poised to hit nine trillion yuan (1.4 trillion USD) in 2016, these two mobile payment apps are currently dominating this market [9–11]. Numerous Chinese retailers, municipal services, peer-exchange services such as *Didi Taxi* (similar to *Uber* but used in China), and even instant messaging apps, are relying on these apps for payment. Thus, we ask the research question: What are the design principles of Alipay and WeChat Wallet that mediated the use of these apps to support nuanced practices?

We conducted 24 semi-structured formal interviews with mobile payment app users in Beijing, Hong Kong, and California. All these users were Chinese nationals. From March 27 to April 2, 2016, we also visited Beijing to conduct first-hand observations and additional informal interviews with mobile payment users such as restaurant owners and taxi drivers. Apart from examining the design of mobile payment apps supporting nuanced monetary activities, this case study is valuable to the HCI field in two other ways. First, while there were previous studies examining mobile payment technologies used in urban areas, most of this past research documented the ways in which entrenched retail payment practices (e.g., the use of credit cards) tend to stifle mobile payment innovations [5, 12]. As far as we are aware, Alipay and WeChat Wallet are the first cases of mobile payment technologies being successfully introduced to a major urban city. These apps also fulfilled many previously unmet needs such as those of microenterprises and instant messaging users in the city.

Through grounded theory coding and analysis of our data, we identified the design principles of Alipay and WeChat that mediated the use of these apps to support nuanced practices. We arrived at the term *special digital monies (special purpose monies)*, a term coined by the anthropologist Zelizer [13] which suggests that the attributes and meaning of a monetary transaction could change according to the specific social context. Presenting our findings through the special digital monies lens, we aim to highlight the ways in which designers need to identify the principles of designing digital monies for these *special* purposes. We have structured our paper by first discussing related work on *special monies* and design studies of mobile payment systems. We then introduce features of Alipay and WeChat Wallet to our readers. In the Findings section, we present five examples of *special digital monies* cases to illustrate how these mobile payment apps serve each specific activity. Finally, we provide concrete design implications for mobile tools supporting *special digital monies* activities.

2 Related Work

In her paper, "The Social Meaning of Money: Special Monies," Viviana Zelizer [13, 14] discusses a social property of money—of changing meanings according to by whom and for what purposes it is being used. According to Zelizer [15]:

> [W]hile the economic model assumes that all monies are the same in the modern world, the "special monies" model assumes that there is a plurality of different kinds of monies, each "special money" shaped by a particular set of cultural and social factors and is thus qualitatively distinct.

Zelizer [13, 14] used the concept *special monies* to challenge the more narrowly construed economic definitions of money, often taken for granted by institutions that assume the artifact can be universally defined using attributes of trades and exchanges [13, 16, 17]. Instead, Zelizer [13, 14] argues that users—in a myriad of social contexts—view and use money in vastly different ways beyond simple economic definitions (e.g., faster and cheaper). For example, Zelizer [13] examined "domestic money" in the early twentieth century, and analyzed the differences between "women's household money" and "husband's allowances." In her study, she found that "women's household money" was to be spent prudently, unlike the money of men. Household money were obtained from the husbands, who were at times unwilling and had to be coaxed to part with the money; and the money had to be used only for specific purposes [15]. Furthermore, in her analysis of manipulation and contest in "domestic money" within American households, she argues that gender role in this context changes the properties of money, including (1) "allocation"—who gives who money and why, (2) "timing"—when the money is allocated, (3) "uses"—what the purposes of the allocated money are, and (4) "quantity"—how much money is allocated.

The concept of *special monies* can be useful to inform HCI researchers and designers to pay attention to how users see and use monies, which can be very different from the perspectives of considering money as homogeneous, neutral medium of exchange. This concept may be even more important as digital devices are offering new forms of payment options which may allow us to use money quite differently from the traditional cash and banking models [18]. Currently, research studies in HCI have already pointed out examples of how social practices could detract from a narrower set of digital payment design features, which commonly include transaction speed, and cost of use. Specifically, these features—transaction speed, and cost of use—have arisen from economic rationalization, an idea emerging from the work of Weber and Simmel [19]. And economic rationalization is already clearly seen in the design of monetary artifacts such as credit cards and credit ratings, which, while bringing some users certain convenience, also introduced uniformity to payment processes. The uniformity may sidestep nuanced ways in which users may like to use these monies [18, 19]. Olsen, et al. [8], who interviewed a variety of mobile payment users, argue that "evaluation criteria [for mobile payment] have to be expanded beyond 'functionality, completeness, consistency, accuracy, performance, reliability, usability, fit with the organization, and other relevant quality attributes' that are used within current design work."

One design feature often accompanying new designs of digital monies is that of increasing monetary transaction speed. Many studies have examined associated emerging technologies such as the contactless smart cards and credit cards [1–4]. For example, in the studies of stored value contactless smart-cards in congested cities, researchers focused on the ways these financial technologies offer crisp transactions for fast-moving urban dwellers [2, 3]. However, unexpected social situations may diminish the effectiveness of these monies. For example, Ferreira et al. [20] found that users' need for fast payment seems to become less prominent in less populated towns and cities [20]. And in an investigation of smart card uses in cities like London, Pritchard et al. [4] caution that these technologies introduced unexpected issues, such as diminishing social engagements between drivers and passengers, and suggest that designers consider social complexities of monetary uses more carefully.

The second design feature, seen in technologies such as the SMS-based payment platform M-Pesa, has been the lowering cost of using and setting up such systems in developing regions [6, 7]. The argument is that these mobile payment systems allow users in developing regions with low-cost cell phones to send money home and to save money securely [6]. However, Gannamaneni et al. [5] have found that the same design features have had no success in the urban cities. For example, an SMS-based payment system introduced in Switzerland in 2005 offered the system free of charge to consumers, and charged the same costs as credit cards to businesses, but the system failed to take off [5].

Some studies have shown that money in different social contexts (e.g., different cultures) could be attached to different social meanings and used in different ways [8, 14, 21]. In the study of virtual currencies in Chinese online games, Wang and Mainwaring [21] have illustrated how these Chinese players have tended to use virtual currencies creatively to reinforce their social cohesion and group values [21]. These Chinese game players often generously share virtual gold and gaming accounts with their friends, a practice rarely observed among Western gamers [21]. However, these researchers have also yet to discuss general design implications which can be applied to support special money uses.

Importantly, Zelizer [13] argues that the ways money is being passed along from one user to another needs deeper examination:

> No money, including market money, escapes such extraeconomic influences. For instance, at the turn of the century, not only the domestic dollar but other kinds of monies created different yet equally significant cultural and social dilemmas for American society. "Charitable money" raised questions about the proper uses and allocation of money as a gift among strangers or between kin, whether in the form of charity, wills, "ritual" gifts (for weddings, birthdays, bar mitzvahs, and Christmas), or even tippings, while "sacred money" provoked discussions about the moral quality of money… we must then explain the sources and patterns of variation among special monies, exploring how various structures of social relations and cultural values shape and constrain the qualitative life of different monies.

If we consider the ways that different context may require users to transmit money differently from one person to another, then digital monies may also need to account for social rules governing how, when, to whom it is transmitted.

Lastly, to the best of our knowledge, there had not been any case of *mobile* payment technologies being successfully introduced to users in major urban cities.

While previous studies borrowing economic design factors (e.g., speed, cost, or ease of use) have attributed this to emerging payment technologies encountering insurmountable challenges competing with entrenched technologies like the credit cards [5], the success of Alipay and WeChat Wallet directly raised the possibility that there may be design features of digital monies that could support a great variety of social situations among urban users. Thus, this study is poised to have significant impact on how HCI should conceptualize future modes of digital monies and payment systems, in order to serve the myriad ways which users have to deal with monies.

Thus, the main contribution of the study of Alipay and WeChat Wallet is that we will examine special purposes of digital monies within a selected sample of the Chinese context, and identify general design features of special digital monies.

3 Background

3.1 Alipay

Alipay is a third-party online payment platform launched by *Alibaba Group* on October 18, 2003 [22]. Initially, Alipay was designed as an online payment platform for *Taobao* (taobao.com), which is an online shopping website like *Amazon* and *eBay*. On May 26, 2011, Alipay obtained the first Payment Business Permit issued by the People's Bank of China, which allows its users to make payments to their friends, to mobile phone companies, prepaid cards, and municipal services [22]. By April, 2015, Alipay's mobile app had more than 270 million active users, who use it to make payments both online and in offline retail stores [23]. Today, more than 200,000 offline retail stores in China accept Alipay [22].

Alipay supports many money-related functions (see Fig. 1), such as money transfer between end users, quick pay though Quick Response Codes (QR codes), mobile top up, paying utilities, and in-app payment through third-party apps using Alipay SDK. For consumers, Alipay is free to use and does not charge a transaction fee. For most merchants, Alipay charges a fee of 0.6% per transaction. For merchants belonging to specific industries, such as gaming, computing, and lottery, Alipay charges a fee of 1.2% per transaction. Alipay allows both consumers and merchants to withdraw money from their Alipay accounts to designated bank accounts free of charge.

3.2 WeChat Wallet

WeChat is a mobile instant messaging app launched in 2011 by *Tencent Group* in China. As of December 2015, it was also the most popular IM in China, with more than 679 million monthly active users [24]. WeChat provides services similar to other IMs, such as voice chat, group chat, video call, location sharing, and message broadcast to multiple users at once; but beyond typical IM functions, the app also includes features seen on social networking sites (e.g., Facebook), such as status update, and online games.

In 2014, following Alipay's success in mobile payment, *WeChat* launched *WeChat Wallet*, a mobile payment system integrated into its IM platform. WeChat Wallet

Fig. 1. The diagram shows the many money-related services provided by Alipay.

supports payment media similar to those of Alipay, including a "Quick Pay" feature via QR codes, and in-app payment through third-party apps using WeChat Wallet SDK. Like Alipay, WeChat Wallet has also included money-related services similar to those in Alipay, such as mobile phone bill and municipal service payments. As of the first quarter of 2015, WeChat Wallet had 400 million users [25].

Like Alipay, WeChat Wallet charges no fee for consumers to transfer money to anyone. But for most merchants, WeChat Wallet charges a fee of 0.60% per transaction (same as Alipay), except for merchants of specific industries like online gaming, which pay up to 2% fee per transaction [26].

WeChat Wallet used to charge no withdrawal fees, like Alipay; but since March 1, 2016, Tencent modified its terms of use, and only allows users (both consumers and merchants) to freely transfer money from their WeChat Wallet to a designated bank up to a cumulative amount of 1,000 yuan, beyond which the users will have to pay a 0.1% withdrawal fee (with a minimum fee of 10 cents).

4   Method

Between February 22 and May 5, 2016, we conducted 24 in-depth and semi-structured formal interviews with Alipay and WeChat Wallet users, of which 16 were residents of Beijing, five of Hong Kong, and three of California. We first conducted five interviews in Hong Kong as a preliminary step to understand Alipay and WeChat uses and commonly used features. These interviews were conducted in person. We recruited these participants from a one-year media art postgraduate program. They were citizens of mainland China, and were frequent users of Alipay and WeChat Wallet.

From March 27 to April 2, 2016, we visited Beijing, where we conducted 16 additional interviews with local users. Our second author is a Chinese living in California who has been using Alipay and WeChat Wallet frequently. First, our second author recruited three friends and residents in Beijing to be our initial interviewees. Second, we snowballed this sample and eventually found another 13 interviewees. Although we used the snowball sampling method, we paid special attention to diversifying our interviewees in terms of their occupation, educational background, and gender. Among these 16 interviews in Beijing, 14 were conducted in person, and two were conducted on the phone. In order to examine possible variation in practices by overseas Chinese (e.g., expatriates and foreign students), our second author further recruited three friends who were residents of California. We intentionally snowballed our samples to the US because through the course of our interviews, we realized that when senders and receivers live in different locations, they could conceive alternative ways to use these apps, which may not otherwise manifest when they live in the same country and could meet more readily.

Among the 24 participants, 15 were females and 9 were males. Their ages ranged from 20 to 33 years old; 13 were postgraduate students, two were undergraduate students, and nine were working adults. All of our participants in Beijing and California were regular users of both Alipay and WeChat Wallet apps. The purpose of our study was not to identify an exhaustive list of practices around the two apps (which is impossible for a study consisting only 24 participants), but to uncover sufficient variations in order to identify useful design principles. We asked our participants questions including reasons for using these apps, and how they had used them as they were conducting activities with their friends, family members, and colleagues. This approach follows the qualitative user research tradition of asking users descriptive questions, thus probing their day-to-day practices around the two apps, in order to for us to gather the data which we analyzed to uncover meanings and design implications [27–30]. All interviews were audio-recorded and transcribed. We retained original orthography and punctuation in interview quotes. We use pseudonyms to anonymize and protect our participants' identity.

While we were in Beijing, we also conducted participant observation and informal interviews in person with merchants such as taxi drivers, food peddlers, and restaurant owners regarding their experience with Alipay and WeChat Wallet. We took photos of Alipay and WeChat Wallet being used by these merchants.

We performed memoing and theoretical sampling during and after each interview [31] from the time we started our interviews in Hong Kong. We paid attention to how features of these two apps served the Chinese users in different social contexts. For example, we identified early on in Hong Kong that while there were common uses of Alipay and WeChat for online shopping across a large section of the user population, those who live in mainland China may have other uses such as paying bills. Thus, we realized the importance of interviewing users who live in mainland China. While in Beijing, we were informed by student interviewees of other forms of gifting and play practices among office workers and distant friends, and we thus interviewed office users and Chinese who reside in the US. We utilized the grounded-theory method of axial coding [31] to identify how these mobile app features integrated into various social settings, social norms, and hidden rules inhabiting these contexts. First, we identified several activities mediated by different uses of the apps. Second, in each of these activities, we identified the ways in which different actors and contexts change meanings and interactions with the apps. Third, we identified how the apps' designs allow these users to choose how the payment apps behave and interact with them in order to fit into these different activities. Finally, our analysis led us to identifying theories and concepts to explain how these apps were supporting informal and nuanced mobile payment activities, and arrived at *special monies* and *special digital monies* as our theoretical frame, as well as the codes presented in the Findings and Discussion sections.

5 Findings

Alipay and WeChat Wallet have facilitated use of digital monies in new mobile payment contexts in China, which contributed to our participants using them frequently. Note that the concept of special monies does not assume that money used in commerce is "ordinary." In fact, Zelizer [13] wrote that "Market money does not escape extraeconomic influences but is in fact one type of special money" (p. 351). That is, even in market contexts, there are social and cultural nuances influencing money use (e.g., [13]). Our Findings section reflects this idea by including "mobile and placeless money" as a special money context—which serves to highlight special monies' transcending definition. In our coding, we identified five examples including "mobile and placeless money," "ceremonial money," "play money," "dining money," and "gift money." These are only a subset of what may encompass *special digital monies*, particularly in a country as diverse and populous as China; but these activities illustrate how digital monies uses vary in attributes and design needs in a myriad of contexts, which helps set up the stage for our later discussion on design implications.

5.1 Providing Interfaces for "Mobile and Placeless Money"

We use the phrase "mobile and placeless" to refer to actors' monetary activities which are on the move, or for other reasons, disconnected from retail infrastructure. For example, retailers in malls have access to telephone lines and sales counters to install standard point-of-sales systems. However, mobile and placeless microenterprises, such as taxi drivers in China, often do not have this luxury or the resources to install the equipment.

Alipay and WeChat Wallet facilitated the digitization of "mobile and placeless money" by bringing in sole proprietors and students, whose monetary activities had previously mostly comprised cash transactions.

One way in which Alipay and WeChat Wallet ease the way Chinese taxi drivers receive digital payments from customers is through printed QR codes (see Fig. 2), which facilitate payments in mobile contexts.

Figure 2 shows how a Chinese taxi driver was able to neatly tuck away the card in a card slot in his taxi. In Beijing, every taxi driver we met (more than 10 of them) had accepted both Alipay and WeChat Wallet as payment options; but they preferred Alipay as it did not charge any withdrawal fee.

These printed and self-service QR codes also worked for sole proprietors receiving payments in amounts too small or too frequent to be feasible for credit card transactions. For example, we had seen food peddlers accepting Alipay and WeChat Wallet payment through printed QR codes, prominently displayed at their stall front, to avoid handling loose change with their hands. One participant—Yunqing, an undergraduate student from Beijing—had used Alipay for small purchases throughout the campus. She said:

Fig. 2. A WeChat Wallet QR code card (left), tidily tucked away in a card slot when not in use (right), was used by a taxi driver to collect customer's payment.

> There are many food stalls and peddlers in the campus, selling pancakes and street food. And they have supported Alipay. Now, for example, for one or two yuan [worth of goods], it is troublesome for them to receive your money, or to return you any change. But Alipay is convenient.

Without using their hands to handle money, these peddlers could focus on food preparation, which eased their work processes. These sole proprietors and their customers had saved a lot of effort and time by conducting their exchanges in more efficient ways.

Another example of "mobile and placeless money" comes from that of ad-hoc labor required by Peking University's student clubs, associations, and student projects. Within the university, many student associations and research groups regularly distribute survey questionnaires to Peking's student population. And it was becoming commonplace that the token reimbursements to respondents were paid through WeChat Wallet to their IM accounts. For example, Keli, another undergraduate student from Beijing, told us:

> Many students need to distribute questionnaires, like you [are conducting this interview]. They have certain requests or some tasks [for the respondents], but each questionnaire will take one or five minutes. And there is no way to know if the respondent filled in the questionnaire. If they did, they are helping you, but you will never know. But if you [send the questionnaire] along with a payment [in WeChat], you will make the respondent feels like he owes you a favor, and he will become more inclined to fill in the questionnaire.

This way, students conducting voluntary work have used digital payments to tokenize favors (i.e., digital money as a request for help) in order to encourage participation.

In these cases, sole proprietors and students benefitted from ubiquitous mobile payment options presented as QR codes displayed in physical forms (see Fig. 2), or through IMs (e.g., for student activities). These payment options met "mobile and placeless money" needs in three ways: (1) the QR Code cards can be installed in convenient locations in taxis and peddler carts; (2) the merchants do not have to receive payments with their hands, thus smoothing work processes for these microenterprises; and (3) workers without access to retail infrastructure (e.g., students) can use digital payment options.

5.2   Bringing *Hongbao* "Ceremonial Money" to Digital Spaces

A cultural artifact in China, known as *hongbao* (literally "red envelope" or "red packet"), has deep significance as a mediator of relationships between family members, friends, and colleagues. A *hongbao*, containing a token sum of money, can be given by one Chinese to another for many reasons, including childbirth, Chinese New Year, marriage, birthday, promotion, and other ceremonial occasions.

Both Alipay and WeChat Wallet digitized hongbao within their payment apps (see Fig. 3), thus bringing the use of "ceremonial money" to online and digital spaces.

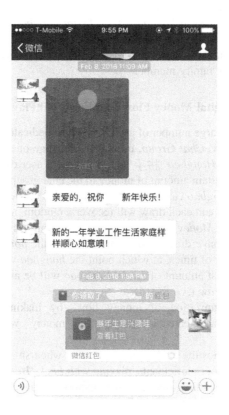

Fig. 3. A *Happy Chinese New Year Hongbao* in the WeChat conversation.

In modern-day China, *hongbao* giving is increasingly difficult for young Chinese who had left their hometowns to work in the cities. This changing social structure of family members needing to maintain traditional ties across distance diminishes the effectiveness of paper *hongbao*. For this reason, the giving of *digital hongbao* is becoming popular among distant relatives. For example, Meilin, a writer and journalist, who lives about 500 miles away from her hometown, explained:

> We always send *hongbao* [back home] during festivals. For example, during [the last] Chinese New Year, I sent a *hongbao* to my niece (through WeChat Wallet). We could not meet since we live in in different cities. If we could meet face to face, I would rather give her traditional [paper] *hongbao* instead.

The giving of *digital hongbao* embodies lower cultural value when compared with traditional paper *hongbao*, but its digital forms are acceptable when the giver and recipient cannot meet in person.

As seen in Fig. 3, a *digital hongbao* imitates a physical *hongbao* in appearance (a red envelope), while also allowing users to send text messages along with it. In mainland China, it is customary for hongbao givers to write congratulatory or auspicious messages on the physical *hongbao*. This *digital hongbao* feature meets Chinese "ceremonial money" needs by allowing users to express cultural meanings through a digitized monetary artifact. In other words, users can send symbols of love and blessing —with money—to their family members.

5.3   Reorganizing Digital Money Flow as a Form of "Play Money"

The WeChat IM allows large number of users to create a dedicated chat room known as a *WeChat Group*. In a *WeChat Group*, users can exchange one form of digital *hongbao*, known as a *Lucky Hongbao* (拼手气红包). First, a user can contribute a Lucky Hongbao containing a certain amount of money to the chat group; she then specifies the number of times this *hongbao* can be drawn on. Members of the group then take turns to draw on the *hongbao*, and each draw will recover a random, non-average, amount of money (known as *Lucky Money*); everyone within the group can see how much Lucky Money other members have drawn; this continues until the *hongbao* has been drawn for the indicated number of times, at which point the *hongbao* will be fully spent. The one who drew the highest amount of *Lucky Hongbao* will be assigned a crown badge representing *Luckiest Draw* (see Fig. 4).

Through this reorganization of money flow—by making receiving amounts random—Lucky Hongbao created a form of "play money" within the instant messaging environment.

Lucky Hongbao carries the quality of playfulness when small quantities are gifted to friends. According to our participants, playing with *Lucky Hongbao* is a good way to kill time and promote bonding among family members, friends, and colleagues. For instance, Xiaoyu, a master's student in Beijing, told us:

> We treated this as a game. Let's say someone contributed a *hongbao*, and see who may draw the largest amount, say I divide the *hongbao* into 10 piles. Whoever gets the largest amount will contribute the next *hongbao*. This is how we played. But this is just for fun, you cannot earn or lose much out of it. But it helps killing boredom, and we can play with it together.

According to Xiaoyu, this person who won the Luckiest Draw will also become the next player to contribute a Lucky Hongbao. In this game, digital *hongbao* becomes a gaming artifact to spice up social relations (聯絡感情). Another participant described such games as not so much containing notions of gifting, as the amount involved is usually small (e.g., 50 yuan), but more akin to "sharing snacks" in offices (分享零食).

Fig. 4. A list of Lucky Money gained by people within a WeChat Group from a Lucky Hongbao. The list shows who had the Luckiest Draw.

Interestingly, senior management in Chinese organizations and workplaces are also beginning to use *Lucky Hongbao* as an alternative to *digital hongbao*, shifting traditional gifting practices in these places. When senior staff gives traditional paper *hongbao* to junior staff, the act contains connotations of goodwill and gratitude for the staff's services. Traditionally, this gifting practice happens during Chinese New Year, and other celebrative occasions. Staff will usually receive a certain amount of money but sealed in a red packet, so that no one will know how much the other person has received. But today, in some offices, especially those in which colleagues have set up a WeChat Group, managers have at times opted to give *Lucky Hongbao* to their subordinates instead—to add an element of fun and loosen the rigidity of traditional hongbao practice. When the amount each person receives is different and visible to everyone, this activity gives rise to a new play activity, which we translate as "Hongbao Rush" (搶红包), a light-hearted contest among employees to see who can draw the largest hongbao. Qinzi, an editor who works in a publishing company, explained:

> There are also WeChat Groups for my company. Our superiors give us physical *hongbao* during Chinese New Year. Each group has about 20 to 30 people. This *hongbao* is meant to add fun into the [office] atmosphere... with WeChat Wallet, they also give us more frequently [but each time] in smaller amounts for fun.

For Qinzi and her colleagues, with the giving of Lucky Hongbao being so easy and casual, her superiors can perform this gifting practice more often and casually, thus altering its ceremonial meanings.

In this context, *Lucky Hongbao* meets "play money" needs by reorganizing money flow from a standard "one person to one person format," into a "one to many format, but with a condition that each person will receive a random amount." As in previous cases, while the economic value of the *hongbao* money remains the same, these design attributes change the connotation of hongbao giving to include a playful tone.

5.4 Deciding Who Pays the "Dining Money"

In China, it is commonplace for family members, friends, and colleagues to pay for purchases and meals of their counterparts. For example, a colleague could offer to pay for a meal, or a family member could pay for the purchases of loved ones (similar to gift registry practice, in which the form of gift is determined by the recipient). *And* Chinese users have used Alipay and WeChat Wallet to support "dining money" practices, by intentionally blocking or altering transactions between payers and payees to determine who will foot the bill in the particular dining contexts.

In the Chinese dining tradition, it is often considered impolite for a group of diners to even contemplate the idea of splitting bills, or "go dutch." Someone, by social norms, has to offer to pay for everyone else, and this person is usually a hierarchically senior person. For example, Linhui, a master's student in Beijing, told us:

> [Splitting bills] hurts our relationship. If it becomes too much [for someone to pay all the time], I will pay this time, and you will pay next time... but we will never split the bill in half. Splitting bills is very weird in our culture.

However, in modern China, friends and colleagues dine together very often, and the practice of paying for someone else has thus become less meaningful—even unfair if someone has been paying too often for others. With the use of Alipay, users have found a way to sidestep this unfairness; because while the splitting of the bill in a restaurant is still considered socially and culturally awkward, the repaying of a bill on the digital platform is not, as Xiangdong, another master's student, explained:

> If someone [fights] to foot the [dining] bill, and we [feel it is] unfair to him, the rest of us will transfer our share of the bill to him. Due to Alipay's design, he cannot reject our transaction to him on Alipay.

Alipay does not allow the payee to refuse payment, therefore relieving the payer of any guilt over not making an effort to pay for others. This approach of splitting dining bills, however, is not available on WeChat, which allows the payee to refuse a payment. Therefore, our participants have tended to prefer Alipay to WeChat Wallet for sharing dining expenses.

In this context, Alipay met "dining money" needs by allowing payers to turn down repayment, thus halting the flow of money to manage complex practices of "dining money."

5.5 Getting Someone to Pay "Gift Money"

Lastly, Alipay and WeChat Wallet have made it possible for good friends and loved ones to pay for each other's purchases—with a symbolic meaning of "gift money"—even when they are a distance apart. Both Alipay and Wechat Wallet include a *Get Someone To Pay* feature (see Fig. 5). After a user is done shopping, he can indicate a

等待付款

-713.00

:

| 1 找人代付 | 2 立即付款 |

Fig. 5. "Get Someone to Pay" feature on Alipay (1. Get Someone to Pay; 2. Pay Instantly)

payer within his friends list and send out a *Get Someone to Pay* request. For instance, Yuxin, a PhD student who lived in California, told us:

> Last year, I went back to China for several days. However, one of my best friends could not meet me as she was traveling. She wanted to express her love to me. Thus, she asked me to place a coffee order online at a Coffee Shop and send out a "get someone to pay" request to her on Alipay. In this way, she instantly bought a cup of coffee for me, although she was hundreds of kilometers away. I was so touched.

This feature makes it easier for our informants to show concerns for friends and families whom they do not see often.

In this context, the *Get Someone to Pay* feature met "gift money" needs by allowing buyers to direct the payment to a third person, altering the flow of money so as to symbolize a form of cultural expression in gifting practices.

Alipay and WeChat Wallet have served our participants in many *special monies* activities—from everyday commuting to dining, shopping, and socializing. They served not only economic purposes, but were also integrated into contexts of "mobile and placeless money," "ceremonial money," "play money," "dining money," and "gift money." To the extent that these covered significant aspects of daily uses, Alipay and WeChat Wallet are thus becoming ubiquitous in large cities like Beijing. In fact, many of our informants, having used these apps so much, reported the experience of not even aware if they carried any cash at all in their physical wallets. For instance, when we asked one participant how much cash he had in his wallet. he pondered for a moment, then picked up his wallet, looked into it, and drew from it the only 100 yuan note he had. He paused to think where it came from, and quickly recalled that one of his colleagues had repaid him for an earlier purchase. "I don't know why he paid me in cash," he candidly said; "Alipay would have been better."

6 Discussion

We have reported the ways in which Alipay and WeChat Wallet are remarkable in their ability to support mobile and nuanced monetary activities, and for our informants to nearly eliminate traditional cash payments on a day-to-day basis. Our informants have used these apps to utilize money for microenterprises and student activities, maintaining family relationships, facilitating play, and supporting dining and gifting protocols. In order to support these activities, the apps have provided features which alter transactional processes, such as to graphically depict money as a *hongbao* gift, or as a gaming token (i.e., in Lucky Money). Based on this data, we identified *special monies* as our lens to emphasize our need to design digital money by benchmarking it against purposes beyond that of straightforward retail exchanges (i.e., faster and cheaper transactions with money flowing from consumer to merchant) [2, 3, 32, 33], and to pay attention to situated actions which influence the flow, timing, rules, and participants of monetary uses. And *special digital monies* can be considered new forms of *special monies* for digital artifacts—much more malleable and appropriable than cash money as originally examined by Zelizer (e.g., sending digital monies in virtual contexts like an IM chatroom). For example, while the Chinese food peddlers had to handle paper money in the past, they can rely on QR codes to receive these payments today. Therefore, *special digital monies* have additional potential to improve traditional special monies activities.

We analyzed our findings to uncover general design principles which can support special monies activities, and we identified two principles: (1) a multimodal on-screen representation of money and its different uses to befit varying meanings of payment in digital spaces (e.g., within an IM), and (2) a physical and customizable payment media design that can be embedded on user-defined real world artifacts. We will discuss these two principles in this section, and end our discussion by addressing additional concerns about designing for *special digital monies*.

6.1 Multimodal UI on-Screen Representations to Support Varying Meanings of Payment in Digital Spaces

Alipay and WeChat Wallet provide users with flexible and multimodal on-screen representations of money and its possible behaviors; that is, money is fittingly represented as a direct digital payment, digital hongbao, Lucky Hongbao, and Get Someone to Pay. These multimodal on-screen designs allow users to use money in appropriate ways to express specific cultural connotations—even to create new meanings (e.g., in "play money" in an office)—beyond treating money as utilitarian instruments for impersonal exchanges.

Applications supporting *special monies* activities have to afford sufficient flexibility so that users can select appropriate money behaviors befitting a specific context. For example, when digital money is represented on-screen as a *Lucky Hongbao* within lines of an online discourse, it changes that discourse with additional meanings of luck, fun, and excitement. Our study of Alipay and WeChat Wallet shows that through design of on-screen payment media which are adaptable, digital money could even create new values by enabling new forms of social interactions within these exchanges. In the Chinese cultural context, money can take the form of an economic exchange medium, a gift, an expression of goodwill or gratitude, or an embodiment of blessing. For instance, money, in the Chinese forms of *hongbao*, is a mediator of social relationships at home, with friends, or in offices. But at other times (e.g., as payment to survey respondents), money may yet demand its economic qualities as an efficient medium of exchange. These varying meanings could be represented on-screen—as a favor for survey respondents, a gift for loved ones, gaming artifacts to kill time, or a forceful but culturally admissible mode of repaying dining bills.

In order to assist designers to consider ways in which software could support *digital monies*, we provide the following set of *transactional attributes* derived from our findings:

1. ***Actors***: Who are the payers, and who are the payees? There can be multiple payers and payees in a transaction.
2. ***Context***: Where is this transaction going to take place? For example, within instant messaging, online forums, a mobile app, or other digital spaces.
3. ***Representation***: How should money be graphically represented? For example, money can be represented as numbers on screen, or as graphical representations of digital artifacts, such as *hongbao*.
4. ***Quantity***: How much money will each payer give, and each payee receive?
5. ***Flow***: How will the money flow from one actor to another? The money may flow from one actor to another, one to many, many to one, many to many, or in a combination of these processes. Certain money flow may also be forbidden.
6. ***Timing***: When and under what conditions will the above transaction rules be activated? For example, *Lucky Money* is spent when it has been drawn the defined number of times.

Compared with Zelizer's original analysis of how gender role and context influence "timing," "allocation," "uses," and "quantity" of cash money [13], our transactional attributes are more focused on technical features and new potentials of a digital payment system. We contributed "representation" to reflect how digital devices can change how digital monies look on a user interface, unlike traditional forms of cash currencies. In Zelizer's [13] study, her notion of "allocation" implies that a housewife could obtain money as her regular allowance, or she could ask for it from her husband; and the notion of "uses" suggests limited purposes for which she could spend the money (e.g., to buy her children clothes). Our attribute "flow," which focuses on the division of money and possibility of complex movements between multiple senders and receivers, combines both Zelizer's notions of "allocation" and "uses" [13]. By having the freedom to choose between different "flow" of money, users can fulfill both digital money "allocation" and "uses" at the same time.

In the following, we further elaborate how these *transactional attributes* were derived from our Findings, and how they can be used. We picked "Mobile and Placeless Money" and "Play Money" as examples because they are different in most attributes. And we listed each specific design feature right next to each attribute in Table 1.

From these two examples in Table 1, each of these attributes can be altered to conform to intended meaning of money in a particular payment context. For example, the *Get Someone to Pay* feature adds a third-party payee (who is not the consumer or the merchant) into the transaction, and adds a form of "gift money" connotation into that purchase.

6.2   Customizable Media Designs to Embed on Physical Artifacts

Alipay and WeChat Wallet provide a physical and customizable payment medium—the QR codes—which can be printed out, enlarged, and be displayed on cards, tables,

Table 1. Identifying transactional attributes from the examples of "Mobile and Placeless Money" and "Play Money"

Mobile and placeless money

Transactional attributes	Usability issues	Design features
Actors: Microenterprise and consumer		
Context	No access to credit card terminals	The QR Code cards can be installed in convenient locations in taxis and peddler carts; workers without access to retail infrastructure (e.g., students) can use digital payment options
Representation	Some merchants find it cumbersome to handle cash or receive payment on mobile phone	Consumers can pay directly to QR codes, thus smoothing work processes for these microenterprises
Quantity	Small quantity of money in each transaction	Low transaction fee

Play money

Transactional attributes	Usability issues	Design feature
Actors: Family members/friends/colleagues		
Context	The Lucky Hongbao game is played in a chatroom	WeChat supported money transactions in the chatroom interface
Representation	The tone of payment is fun and play	WeChat Wallet supported Lucky Hongbao through fun representations (e.g., crown badge)
Quantity	Small quantity of money in each transaction	Low transaction fee
Flow	The game requires money to flow in a one player to many players format; each receiver will receive random and non-average amount	WeChat allows the sender to specify the number of times a pool of money can be drawn on; each draw will allocate a random amount from the pool to be sent
Timing	Each receiver determines when she wants to draw from the pool of money	Each receiver initiates the draw herself

storefront, and any other convenient physical artifacts so as to blend into the physical exchange context.

Despite money today being pervasively transacted in digital forms, we still saw contexts relying on physical monetary artifacts to support transactions, and these contexts (in our study) typically happened with mobile and microenterprises. On the other hand, physical spaces seem to have more limited uses for family and friends, who are more likely to transact over digital spaces. In these physical spaces, merchants have chosen to display the payment medium on artifacts most convenient to them and their customers.

Taking food peddlers as an example, their hands are too busy and it would be considered unhygienic to handle smartphone apps. Since their customers often clutter prominently in front of their stall, a large printed QR code can be appropriately displayed in front of their crowded stall for these customers to see. Since the payment medium is detached from the mobile app, other sole proprietors can display them on any physical artifacts suited to their environments.

We also took note of QR code uses within peer-exchange economies in China [34]. An example of such economies includes the peer-exchange car sharing network *Didi Taxi*. In the US, while companies offering money-mediated peer exchanges tend to build digital payments into their apps [35], many peer-exchange service apps in China have opted for QR codes and other payment interfaces offered by Alipay and WeChat Wallet. Thus, the relationship between mobile payment technologies and smartphone based peer-exchange economies should be examined more closely.

Importantly, the customizable payment media features in these Chinese mobile payment apps are simple yet novel to HCI. To our knowledge, most mobile payment designs had offered a fixed on-screen or physical payment medium without variability —for example, contactless smartcards, SMS, or a standard payment gateway [3, 7, 21]. Similarly, Google has offered payment through Gmail, while Facebook offers payment through its IM Messenger; but even these offer no alternative options. Also, new classes of financial technologies such as the *Apple Pay* are even restrictive in their uses to specific smartphone models. This is interesting since end-user customization and appropriation, a staple topic in HCI [36–38], appears to have not yet informed the design of digital money. We question the need to rigidly couple payment platforms and media designs, which seems counterintuitive to the adaptive potentials of software artifacts. In this sense, one of the strengths of the design of Alipay and WeChat Wallet is providing a range of transactional media and features which allow users to mix and match themselves; and through user appropriation, users become the agent which makes the money "special."

7   Conclusion

Special monies are changing meanings of money according to the social contexts in which they are being used [13]. In this study, we examined how two mobile payment apps, *Alipay* and *WeChat Wallet*, serve *special digital monies* activities of Chinese residing in Beijing, Hong Kong, and California. Through our interviews with participants, as well as fieldwork in Beijing, we found that *Alipay* and *WeChat Wallet* are successfully used in many nuanced transactional contexts due to their multimodal and customizable payment media designs. In terms of multimodal design, the designers have created several different on-screen representations of money which can be used flexibly to support Chinese monetary activities *online*. Thus, we argue that designers could support other forms of *special digital monies* by providing payment media designs which users could easily customize and appropriate for myriad intents and purposes.

Acknowledgements. We thank the participants of this research. We also thank the reviewers for their suggestions to improve the paper. The work described in this paper was partially supported by grants from City University of Hong Kong (Project No. 6000535).

References

1. Kaye, J.J., Mccuistion, M., Gulotta, R., Shamma, D.A.: Money talks: tracking personal finances. In: Proceedings of 32nd Annual ACM Conference on Human Factors in Computing Systems, CHI 2014, pp. 521–530 (2014). doi:10.1145/2556288.2556975
2. Chau, P.Y.K., Poon, S.: Octopus: an e-cash payment system success story. Commun. ACM **46**, 129 (2003). doi:10.1145/903893.903927
3. Mainwaring, S.D., March, W., Maurer, B.: From meiwaku to tokushita! lessons for digital money design from Japan. In: Proceedings of SIGCHI Conference on Human Factors in Computing Systems, pp. 21–24 (2008). doi:10.1145/1357054.1357058
4. Pritchard, G., Vines, J., Olivier, P.: Your money's no good here: the elimination of cash payment on London buses. In: Proceedings of 33rd Annual ACM Conference on Human Factors in Computing Systems, CHI 2015, pp. 907–916. ACM Press, New York (2015)
5. Gannamaneni, A., Ondrus, J., Lyytinen, K.: A post-failure analysis of mobile payment platforms. In: 2015 48th Hawaii International Conference on System Sciences, pp. 1159–1168. IEEE (2015)
6. Kuriyan, R., Nafus, D., Mainwaring, S.: Consumption, technology, and development: the "Poor" as "Consumer". Inf. Technol. Int. Dev. **8**, 1–12 (2012)
7. Wyche, S.P., Oreglia, E., Ames, M.G., et al.: Learning from marginalized users: reciprocity in HCI4D. In: Proceedings of ACM 2012 Conference on Computer-Supported Cooperative Work Companion, CSCW 2012, p. 27. ACM Press, New York (2012)
8. Olsen, M., Hedman, J., Vatrapu, R.: Designing digital payment artifacts. In: Proceedings of 14th Annual International Conference on Electronic Commerce, pp. 161–168 (2012). doi:10.1145/2346536.2346568
9. FinTech Asia: Alipay vs WeChat: War of Chinese Payments. FinTech Asia (2015)
10. Mobile Ecosystem Forum: China market focus: mobile payments. Mobile Ecosystem Forum (2016)
11. Weinland, D.: Can the state take China's mobile payments market in 2016? Experts think not. South China Morning Post (2016)
12. Evans, D.S., Schmalensee, R.: Paying with Plastic: The Digital Revolution in Buying and Borrowing. The MIT Press, Cambridge (2004)
13. Zelizer, V.A.: The social meaning of money: "Special Monies". Am. J. Sociol. **95**, 342–377 (1989)
14. Zelizer, V.A.: How do we know whether a monetary transaction is a gift, an entitlement, or compensation? In: Ben-Ner, A., Putterman, L. (eds.) Economic Values, Organ, pp. 329–333. Cambridge University Press (1999)
15. Zelizer, V.A.: Economic Lives: How Culture Shapes the Economy, pp. 1–478 (2011). doi:10.2307/j.ctt7rgdv
16. Marx, K.: Early Writings. Penguin, London (1992)
17. Simmel, G.: The Philosophy of Money. Routledge, New York (2011)
18. Rogoff, K.S.: The Curse of Cash. Princeton University Press, Princeton (2016)
19. Ritzer, G.: Expressing America: A Critique of the Global Credit Card Society. SAGE Publications, Thousand Oaks (1995)

20. Ferreira, J., Perry, M., Subramanian, S.: Spending time with money: from shared values to social connectivity. In: Proceedings of 18th ACM Conference on Computer Supported Cooperative Work and Social Computing, CSCW 2015, pp. 1222–1234. ACM Press, New York (2015)

21. Wang, Y., Mainwaring, S.D.: Human-currency interaction: learning from virtual currency use in China. In: Proceedings of ACM CHI 2008 Conference on Human Factors in Computing Systems, pp. 25–28 (2008)

22. Alipay: About Alipay alipay.com (2014). https://ab.alipay.com/i/jieshao.htm. Accessed 29 Apr 2017

23. Sina Technology: Alipay has surpassed 270 million active users, exceeded 80% of mobile payment market 支付宝钱包活跃用户数2.7亿 移动支付份额超80% (2015). tech. sina.com.cn

24. TechWeb: Wechat surpassed 700million users; Tencent: Fees will be charged for Wechat Wallet withdrawal 微信用户已达7亿 腾讯：零钱提现 必须收费 (2016). techweb. com

25. Sohu: New data: WeChat has 549 million monthly active users, and WeChat Wallet has 400 million users! 微信最新数据：月活跃5.49亿, 支付 用户达4亿！(2016). sohu.com

26. Tencent Customer Service: Rates and settlement cycles for different kinds of merchants 商户类目对应资质、费率、结算周期 kf.qq.com (2017). https://kf.qq.com/faq/140225MveaUz1501077rEfqI.html. Accessed 29 Apr 2017

27. Spradley, J.P.: Ethnographic Interview. Harcourt Brace Jovanovich, San Diego (1988)

28. Fine, G.A.: Ten lies of ethnography: moral dilemmas of field research. J Contemp Ethnogr 22, 267–294 (1993). doi:10.1177/089124193022003001

29. Geertz, C.: Deep play: notes on the Balinese cockfight. Daedalus 134, 56–86 (2005). doi:10.1162/001152605774431563

30. Grudin, J., Grinter, R.E.: Ethnography and design. Comput. Support. Coop. Work 3, 55–59 (1994). doi:10.1007/BF01305846

31. Strauss, A.L., Corbin, J.M., Strauss, A.L.: Basics of Qualitative Research. SAGE Publications, Thousand Oaks (2014)

32. Weisner, S.: Quantum Money. Commun. ACM 55, 84–92 (2012). doi:10.1145/2240236.2240258

33. Panurach, P.: Money in electronic commerce: digital cash, electronic fund transfer, and Ecash. Commun. ACM 39, 45–50 (1996). doi:10.1145/228503.228512

34. Carroll, J.M., Bellotti, V.: Creating value together: the emerging design space of peer-to-peer currency and exchange. In: Proceedings of ACM 2015 Computer Supported Cooperative Work and Social Computing, CSCW 2015 (2015). doi:10.1145/2675133.2675270

35. Ikkala, T., Lampinen, A.: Monetizing network hospitality: hospitality and sociability in the context of Airbnb. In: Proceedings of ACM 2014 Conference on Computer-Supported Cooperative Work, CSCW 2014 (2014). doi:10.1145/2675133.2675274

36. Nardi, B.A.: A small matter of programming: perspectives on end user computing. SIGCHI Bull. (1993). doi:10.1145/191642.1047947

37. Dourish, P.: The appropriation of interactive technologies: some lessons from placeless documents. Comput. Support. Coop. Work CSCW Int. J. 12, 465–490 (2003). doi:10.1023/A:1026149119426

38. March, W., Jacobs, M., Salvador, T.: Designing technology for community appropriation. In: Proceedings of SIGCHI Conference on Human Factors in Computing Systems, CHI 2005, pp. 2126–2127 (2005)

UX Adoption in the Organizations

Active Involvement of Software Developers in Usability Engineering: Two Small-Scale Case Studies

Nis Bornoe[(⊠)] and Jan Stage

Aalborg University, Aalborg, Denmark
{nis, jans}@cs.aau.dk

Abstract. The essence of usability evaluations is to produce feedback that supports the downstream utility so the interaction design can be improved and problems can be fixed. In practice, software development organizations experience several obstacles for conducting usability engineering. One suggested approach is to train and involve developers in all phases of usability activities from evaluations, to problem reporting, and making redesign proposals. Only limited work has previously investigated the impact of actively involving developers in usability engineering. In this paper, we present two small-scale case studies in which we investigate the developers' experience of conducting usability evaluations and participating in a redesign workshop. In both case studies developers actively engaged in both activities. Per the developers, this approach supported problem understanding, severity ratings, and problem fixing. At the organizational level, we found that the attitude towards and understanding of the role of usability engineering improved.

Keywords: Usability engineering · Redesign · Case study

1 Introduction

Usability evaluations are widely accepted and used during iterative software development for measuring usability and identifying flaws in the interaction design of IT systems [7]. One form of evaluation is the formative approach often conducted with a think-aloud evaluation [27]. Such evaluations are used to get feedback about users' behavior, and the flows, concepts, and designs used. Evaluations provide new and more detailed insights about the state of a given interaction design not already known to the developers [16]. Insights that can be used to improve and develop an application [32]. Several obstacles to deploying usability engineering into organizations have been found. This includes resource requirements, recruiting participants [5, 23, 24], lack of knowledge and competencies [1, 33], establishing credibility [9, 13, 22], and developers neglecting usability perspectives [1, 22]. On top, integration with software engineering processes is challenging [29], and organizational factors have an influence [13, 20], for example, often a decision about who has the responsibility of usability is missing [8]. In a study Vukelja and colleagues found that developers commonly develop user interfaces by themselves without the involvement of designers, they lack

© IFIP International Federation for Information Processing 2017
Published by Springer International Publishing AG 2017. All Rights Reserved
R. Bernhaupt et al. (Eds.): INTERACT 2017, Part IV, LNCS 10516, pp. 159–168, 2017.
DOI: 10.1007/978-3-319-68059-0_10

relevant knowledge, do not effectively include users in the design process, and if they conduct an evaluation, it rarely has a substantial impact [33]. In addition, problem priority and severity assessment [14], fixing problems, and reevaluating systems are also commonly overlooked challenging activities [22, 31, 32]. Because fixing usability problems is an essential [14, 22, 35] non-trivial complex part of usability engineering [31, 32], concentrated focus and planning are required [12, 31].

To overcome some of these obstacles it has been suggested to involve and train the developers in usability engineering because this can increase interest and support for usability engineering [18, 21]. This approach is reported to be relevant for both organizations without usability competences and the ability to hire consultants [5, 11], and to improve cross-disciplinary collaboration in organizations employing both designers and developers [21, 26]. A study report that having developers observe evaluations resulted in increased empathy towards the users, and a comprehensive understanding of the severity and context of problems [15]. A study about involving developers in field studies report increased knowledge of the context of use, and a better understanding of user perspectives [11]. A study about training novices in think-aloud evaluations concludes that conducting the evaluation and creating user tasks went well, but the identification and description of usability problems were flawed in comparison to experts [30]. Involving developers in the process of creating redesign suggestions have also shown to be beneficial because they possess domain knowledge [12].

It has been pointed out that insights about the impact of usability engineering in real world projects are needed [22, 32] along with focusing research on concepts that can be implemented into practical settings [11, 17, 25]. We here present two small-scale case studies building upon previous work focused on providing developers with basic skills in usability engineering [3, 4, 6].

Our research question is: *"What are the experiences of actively involving the developers in usability engineering?"*

2   Method

We designed an interpretive case study and collected qualitative data. We chose this research design because software development projects are complex and dynamic and therefore challenging to study in isolation. A case study is a relevant research approach when investigating phenomena in the context of practical circumstances of real-world development projects where it is difficult to maintain fixed parameters, and the data collection process can be unpredictable [28].

Walsham points out that making generalizations based on case studies has been widely debated, but argue that the description of phenomena grounded in interpretation of empirical data can turn out to be beneficial for other organizations or contexts. For example, case studies can support generalizing the generation of theory or drawing of specific implications. He emphasizes that the outcome of case studies should be considered tendencies rather that a precise forecasting [34].

In the following, we will present the two case organizations, outline the activities they were involved in, and describe the data collection and analysis.

2.1   Cases

Both case organizations are relatively small. They employ about 20 developers each, and follow the agile development approach Scrum. They had no competencies and practical experience with conducting systematic usability engineering and interaction design. A few developers had limited knowledge about human-computer interaction and interaction design gained during their studies. Both organizations participated in similar usability evaluation training [6] and redesign activities [3, 4]. The purpose was to introduce usability engineering into the organizations and provide the development teams with basic competencies applicable in their day-to-day development practices. The idea was to provide a starting point from where the organizations would be able to evolve their usability engineering competencies further and conduct the activities on their own or request facilitation when needed. Below we outline the two activities.

- **Usability evaluation training.** The two organizations received training following the barefoot usability evaluation learning approach focused on providing elemental evaluation skills [6]. During a mini course, lasting about 30 h, they were taught how to conduct a think-allowed evaluation (TA), video analysis [27], and Instant Data Analysis (IDA), an approach used to analyze data from TA evaluations rapidly [19]. The usability mini course consisted of a mix of lectures and exercises, for example, they were asked to plan, conduct, and analyze an evaluation on their own under the supervision of usability specialists [6].
- **Redesign workshop participation.** The developers participated in redesign workshops facilitated by usability specialists [3, 4]. By facilitating problem fixing through a collaborative workshop actively involving the developers, the aim was to unite usability and domain knowledge, and by working in small groups, the developers can produce several alternative redesign suggestions. The workshop was not only about fixing the identified problems but also progressing the design. Firstly, they received a basic introduction to interaction design principles (only C2). Secondly, they discussed the problem list and picked a subset of problems. Thirdly, groups of three developers participated in focused discussions internally, and together with a usability specialist to outline redesign suggestions. Finally, in plenum, the groups presented and discussed their redesign suggestions.

Case organization 1 (C1). They develop self-service solutions and administrative forms for the public sector. This includes the frontend system for the users, and backend system for the administrative staff. Initially, they produced paper-based forms and had a portfolio of about 300. Interactive PDF documents replaced these forms, and finally, the interactive PDF documents were transformed into web-based services available through a self-service citizen portal. As it became a requirement for citizens to use the self-service solutions, usability became part of the system specifications. At this point the developers designed interaction designs haphazardly.

- **The system:** The system is an interactive PDF document used by citizens and companies when applying for a permit or submitting a notification required for construction of new buildings or certain types of renovations. Essentially the system is an interactive version of a paper-based form. This application was chosen because it was relevant to many citizens, and reasonably complicated to fill out.

- **Usability evaluation:** Four usability specialists conducted a TA usability evaluation with 10 participants. The participants had previous experience with public citizen services, but no experience with this system. The developers observed the evaluation. The result was a problem list consisting of 75 usability problems [4].
- **Redesign workshop:** Divided into three groups five developers including two programmers, two project managers, and a head of development participated in the redesign workshop along with four usability specialists. 25 out of the 75 problems were selected to make the workshop more focused and manageable. The outcome of the workshop was three suggestions for redesign suggestions [4].

Case organization 2 (C2). They develop audio equipment for the music industry. One product line is guitar and bass pedals, which are effects units used for altering audio source sounds. Recent years, they have increased the production of software extending the functionality of the pedals. The development team initially decided to increase the focus on interaction design and usability because of two main reasons: (1) users reporting difficulties to understand and use the advanced options in the interactive user interface, and (2) many decisions about interaction design were often based on the "gut feeling" of individuals. Instead, they wanted a methodical approach as the basis for making informed decisions. They wanted more of the team to get knowledge and understanding of the importance of having a methodical approach. In addition, they wanted to acquire or modify approaches practical in terms of their scrum-rhythm.

- **The system:** The organization has developed an application used to customize the settings of the guitar effect pedals they produce.
- **Usability evaluation:** The developers conducted a TA evaluation with four hobby musicians as participants. The evaluation resulted in a list of 19 usability problems. For each problem, the following was given: a short description, a severity rating in the form: minor, moderate and severe, a list of all evaluators identifying the problem, a short redesign suggestion, a complexity rating (1–8) decided by two programmers, and a business value rating (1–8) decided by two product managers. This rating was used to determinate which problems to prioritize and focus on [3].
- **Redesign workshop:** Divided into two groups six developers including two software developers, one hardware developer, two product managers, and one software quality assurance manager participated in the redesign workshop along with two usability specialists. The conclusion of the redesign workshop is that the developers participating were able to reconsider the existing design based on a top-down approach constructively and outlined new ideas for the use flow [3].

2.2 Data Collection and Analysis

We conducted semi-structured interviews because this allowed dynamic conversations, covered our set of questions, and made the answers comparable. From C1 we conducted an interview with the head of development (HoD). From C2 we conducted an interview with, a developer, and a product manager (PM). All three had participated in both the usability training and the redesign workshop. Additionally, we had some observation notes, and collected archival data in the form of usability problem lists, presentations, and sketches. For the interpretive analysis of the qualitative data, we followed the principles suggested by Elliott and colleagues [10].

3   Findings

We here present the findings divided into the impact of involvement in the usability evaluation, the redesign workshop, and what impact this had on the organization.

3.1   Impact of Involvement and Training in Usability Evaluations

Problem discovery and insights. The developers' involvement in the evaluations provided both insights about problems, but also underlined users' perception and actual use of the system. *"...the developers could see that there really were some major problems and could see people desperately get stuck with a solution they had developed."* (HoD, C1) In addition to getting aware of new problems, they found it useful to get confirmation or disconfirmation of problems they were already suspecting. They got a more detailed understanding of the problems, and their fuzzy ideas were concretized and extended. *"Maybe we had the feeling that it could be done better, but it was not made completely clear and formulated explicitly."* (PM, C2) For example, C2 found that the flow of operations on a particular screen was not in line with the flow of operations found logic by the users, and how the users wanted to interact with the application. Getting direct insights into this design flaw was by the PM in C2 characterized as *"...a big eye opener..."*, and the developer added: *"We had not thought of the flow as a major problem. It is not certain that the order of elements would be different had we not conducted a user test."* (Developer, C2) In summary, these direct insights increased an understanding of the users, as also reported by an earlier study [15]. This understanding from interacting with, and seeing users in action made fuzzy ideas of problems specific, more detailed and inspired and motivated the developers to make changes. One challenge was the thoroughness of problem identification and severity ratings [6].

Prioritizing and rating problems. Being part of the usability evaluation supported the prioritization process, and forced the organizations to actively reconsider their current strategy. *"When you are used to making systems in a certain way, you just keep doing the same."* (HoD, C1) During the compilation of the list, both organizations provided a classic severity rating in the form 'minor,' 'moderate,' and 'severe.' A study of the training of C1 found that the developers had success conducting and creating user tasks, but the thoroughness of the problem identification and severity rating was less successful [6]. To partly overcome this obstacle, C2 experimented with two additional ratings. The interviewed programmer and a colleague would give a complexity rating (1–8). This rating is the estimated technical complexity of fixing the problem. The interviewed project manager and colleague would give a business value rating (1–8). This rating is the estimated importance related to the functionality of the application.

Both are also related to the resource requirement estimation for fixing a given problem. The three ratings (severity, complexity, and business value) were then used to decide which problems to prioritize. Through this prioritizing process, the development team could understand and analyze the problems from more angles. This also served to make the fixing of usability problems more specific and goal oriented. The developer noted that: *"The problem list had much greater influence than was intended when we made it."* (Developer, C2) In summary, being part of all steps of the evaluation made the identified problems relevant and creditable to the developers. Instead of simply adding problems to the backlog, there were some clear thoughts behind what problems to prioritize.

3.2   Impact of Participation in the Redesign Workshop

Intermediate design phase. The redesign workshop acted as an intermediate phase with a dedicated and concentrated focus outlining specific problems and what could be done to solve the problems. For both organizations, the redesign workshop was a major brainstorming session. As also reported in a recent study [12], they could use their extensive domain knowledge and produce several redesign suggestions or ideas with a short time span, while receiving guidance from a usability specialist. They did not generate implementable designs but used this session to dig into the specific problems. The division into groups and the afterward discussion provided insights from different angles and redesign proposals. Inspiration was brought back home for further refinement *"...we had something concrete to bring back home."* (HoD, C1) *"...after we participated in the workshop we had a list of things you could change, things that could be interesting..."* (PM, C2).

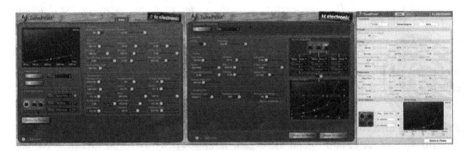

Fig. 1. The interface redesign by C2. From left: initial design, first revision, and final version.

In the immediate period following the redesign workshop, C1 engaged in an iterative design process and had discussions with the usability specialists and showcased prototypes to get feedback. C2 also wanted to make technical changes to the system and decided to merge two systems into one. During this process, they returned to the inspiration from the workshop. *"We had these things on a list that we looked over and prioritized in relation to what we thought was the most important and relative to what was comparatively affordable."* (PM, C2).

Of criticism, it was mentioned that a stricter frame for the part of the workshop concerned with actually making redesigns was wanted. For example, specific design exercises, and a better way of collecting and comparing the ideas generated.

Design changes. Both organizations redesigned and released new systems. During the redesign workshop, C1 decided on a wizard approach as the overall design pattern. Over a couple of months, they redesigned and implemented a new solution. They changed the form into a wizard approach with questions for each step. The essence of the approach was *"...to reformulate [the form] into something people can decide on."* (HoD, C1) This approach was used to derive the information needed and to guide the user through the application instead of requiring the users to figure out which fields are relevant and what and how to fill in the requested information. When evaluating the redesigned application, it was found that the handling of an application by a caseworker had decreased from an average of 53 min to 18½ min [2]. This indicates that a lot fewer applications with errors were submitted. The intention was to develop some principles based on this case that could be used in the other solutions.

C2 released the second revision of their app two years later. During the redesign process, a couple of significant design changes were made. The flow of operations and order of options on a screen was found to be problematic, something they noticed during the evaluation. While this was not a specific usability problem, the development team decided to work on this problem during the redesign workshop. During the initial design of the application, they wanted to make the application 'flashy.' *"[This element] is a fine smart impressive graph, an eye catcher, therefore we had probably kept it as a prominent element [in the top]."* (Developer, C2) During the workshop, they instead created redesign proposals based on the insights from the evaluation and the basic interaction design principles introduced. Afterward, they further evolved these proposals into a specific deign and implemented it (see Fig. 1).

3.3   Impact on the Organization

The developer effect. There was skepticism about usability engineering and its importance among serval developers, an obstacle reported by several other studies [1, 22]. The original believe in C1 about improving the usability of the building permit form was that: *"It is the user that has to obtain knowledge about how to fill in these forms, that it is not our problem."* (HoD, C1) The focus shifted from purely focusing on technical aspects to also considering usability as a quality factor for good software development. *"It means a lot [when] you deliver a system and receives positive feedback about the solution."* (HoD, C1) C2 also acknowledged that they had not prioritized usability *"You tend to neglect such things."* (PM, C2) *"The user evaluation [of our application] highlighted how big the problems were. We would probably not have realized that if we did not make that evaluation."* (Developer, C2).

Prime mover. Because usability engineering was not the primary concern or skill of any developers involved in the project, it was essential to have a prime mover, a person acting as the primary driving force and spearhead. Someone needed to take responsibility, and promote, manage, and prioritize these activities. In C1 the head of development took this role, and in C2 a developer that have completed several university level courses, and an interest in usability took this role. *"...to have someone on the team that is the prime mover that this is one of the important things to make it cool, ensuring it's done right and that someone considers this. If it is me, then it will just be a priority in many priorities."* (PM, C2) C2 has since hired a dedicated UX specialist to act as the prime mover.

Towards integrating user-centered design. After participation, both organizations have on their own conducted evaluations of other products and experimented with user-centered activities. However, the activities in C1 later stopped because of a change in management, and several key people left the organization. Opposite, C2 has experimented with future technology workshops and contextual inquiry and design. This is still at an early stage, and they have yet to figure out exactly how to proceed and use the output of such activities. *"We held a workshop...[where]...we focused on what could make sense for users in terms of integrating [our products] with the Internet and social media."* (Developer, C2) In another project, they wanted early feedback from users. *"'Here's an app and pedal, they are connected in one way or another. Try to solve this problem or how will you do this?' We observed if they could figure it out or not. Based on that, we changed it along the way as there were some things they were having troubles with."* (PM, C2).

4   Conclusion

Based on two small-scale case studies, we have presented developers' experiences of engaging in an evaluation and redesign process. Both organizations had previously learned the basics of conducting a TA evaluation and how to organize a redesign workshop to come up with different redesign proposals. In response to the usability activities, they have afterward come up with proposed fixes for several identified usability problems and, perhaps more importantly, made some fundamental design changes. We learned and will advocate that by being a continuous part of the process, developers get a better understanding of the roots to underlying usability areas not necessarily explicit identified as specific usability problems. This knowledge is hard to get by only reading a usability report, but is valuable to make systems better and to change the mindset of an entire organization by explicating specific problems and showing specific design changes.

While both organizations are positive and believe they have gained new strategic knowledge, the caveat is that maintaining the skills require work by the involved parties. To avoid that the skills do not fade away but progress it is essential to have this acknowledged and prioritized by management as well as a prime mover taking the lead and acting as the spearhead. The two introduction activities only provide a basic entrance to usability engineering and do not make them experts [6]. This integration is a long-term commitment. The training and involvement only acted as a starting point from which the organizations need to evolve skills further.

References

1. Bak, J.O., et al.: Obstacles to usability evaluation in practice: a survey of software development organizations. In: Proceedings of the 5th Nordic Conference on Human-Computer Interaction: Building Bridges, pp. 23–32. ACM, New York (2008)
2. Billestrup, J., et al.: UX requirements to public systems for all: formalisation or innovation. In: INTERACT 2015 Adjunct Proceedings: 15th IFIP TC. 13 International Conference on Human-Computer Interaction, Bamberg, Germany, p. 2015407, 14–18 September 2015
3. Bornoe, N., et al.: Redesign workshop: involving software developers actively in usability engineering. In: Proceedings of the 8th Nordic Conference on Human-Computer Interaction Fun, Fast, Foundational - NordiCHI 2014, pp. 1113–1118. ACM, New York (2014)
4. Bruun, A., Jensen, J.J., Skov, M.B., Stage, J.: Active collaborative learning: supporting software developers in creating redesign proposals. In: Sauer, S., Bogdan, C., Forbrig, P., Bernhaupt, R., Winckler, M. (eds.) HCSE 2014. LNCS, vol. 8742, pp. 1–18. Springer, Heidelberg (2014). doi:10.1007/978-3-662-44811-3_1
5. Bruun, A.: Training software developers in usability engineering: a literature review. In: Proceedings of the 6th Nordic Conference on Human-Computer Interaction: Extending Boundaries, pp. 82–91. ACM, New York (2010)
6. Bruun, A., Stage, J.: Barefoot usability evaluations. Behav. Inf. Technol. 33(11), 1148–1167 (2014)
7. Bygstad, B., et al.: Software development methods and usability: perspectives from a survey in the software industry in Norway. Interact. Comput. 20(3), 375–385 (2008)
8. Cajander, Å., Larusdottir, M., Gulliksen, J.: Existing but not explicit - the user perspective in scrum projects in practice. In: Kotzé, P., Marsden, G., Lindgaard, G., Wesson, J., Winckler, M. (eds.) INTERACT 2013, Part III. LNCS, vol. 8119, pp. 762–779. Springer, Heidelberg (2013). doi:10.1007/978-3-642-40477-1_52
9. Chilana, P.K., et al.: Understanding usability practices in complex domains. In: Proceedings of the SIGCHI Conference on Human Factors in Computing Systems, pp. 2337–2346. ACM, New York (2010)
10. Elliott, R., et al.: Descriptive and interpretive approaches to qualitative research. Handb. Res. Methods Clin. Heal. Psychol. 1, 147–159 (2005)
11. Eriksson, E., Cajander, Å., Gulliksen, J.: Hello world! – experiencing usability methods without usability expertise. In: Gross, T., Gulliksen, J., Kotzé, P., Oestreicher, L., Palanque, P., Prates, R.O., Winckler, M. (eds.) INTERACT 2009. LNCS, vol. 5727, pp. 550–565. Springer, Heidelberg (2009). doi:10.1007/978-3-642-03658-3_60
12. Garnik, I., et al.: Creative sprints: an unplanned broad agile evaluation and redesign process. In: Proceedings of the 8th Nordic Conference on Human-Computer Interaction: Fun, Fast, Foundational, pp. 1125–1130. ACM, New York (2014)
13. Gulliksen, J., et al.: Usability professionals—current practices and future development. Interact. Comput. 18(4), 568–600 (2006)
14. Hertzum, M.: Problem prioritization in usability evaluation: from severity assessments toward impact on design. Int. J. Hum. Comput. Interact. 21(2), 125–146 (2006)
15. Høegh, R.T., et al.: The impact of usability reports and user test observations on developers' understanding of usability data: an exploratory study. Int. J. Hum. Comput. Interact. 21(2), 173–196 (2006)
16. Høegh, R.T., Jensen, J.J.: A case study of three software projects: can software developers anticipate the usability problems in their software? Behav. Inf. Technol. 27(4), 307–312 (2008)
17. Juristo, N., et al.: Analysing the impact of usability on software design. J. Syst. Softw. 80(9), 1506–1516 (2007)

18. Karat, J., Dayton, T.: Practical education for improving software usability. In: Proceedings of the SIGCHI Conference on Human Factors in Computing Systems, pp. 162–169. ACM Press/Addison-Wesley Publishing Co., New York (1995)

19. Kjeldskov, J., et al.: Instant data analysis: conducting usability evaluations in a day. In: Proceedings of the Third Nordic Conference on Human-Computer Interaction, pp. 233–240. ACM, New York (2004)

20. Kuusinen, K., Mikkonen, T., Pakarinen, S.: Agile user experience development in a large software organization: good expertise but limited impact. In: Winckler, M., Forbrig, P., Bernhaupt, R. (eds.) HCSE 2012. LNCS, vol. 7623, pp. 94–111. Springer, Heidelberg (2012). doi:10.1007/978-3-642-34347-6_6

21. Latzina, M., Rummel, B.: Soft (ware) skills in context: corporate usability training aiming at cross-disciplinary collaboration. In: Proceedings of the 16th Conference on Software Engineering Education and Training (CSEE&T 2003), pp. 52–57 (2003)

22. Law, E.L.-C.: Evaluating the downstream utility of user tests and examining the developer effect: a case study. Int. J. Hum. Comput. Interact. 21(2), 147–172 (2006)

23. Lizano, F., et al.: Is usability evaluation important: the perspective of novice software developers. In: The 27th International BCS Human Computer Interaction Conference (HCI 2013) (2013)

24. Monahan, K., et al.: An investigation into the use of field methods in the design and evaluation of interactive systems. In: Proceedings of the 22nd British HCI Group Annual Conference on People and Computers: Culture, Creativity, Interaction, vol. 1, pp. 99–108. British Computer Society, Swinton (2008)

25. Nørgaard, M., Hornbæk, K.: What do usability evaluators do in practice?: an explorative study of think-aloud testing. In: Proceedings of the 6th Conference on Designing Interactive Systems, pp. 209–218. ACM, New York (2006)

26. Øvad, T., et al.: Teaching software developers to perform UX tasks. In: Proceedings of the Annual Meeting of the Australian Special Interest Group for Computer Human Interaction on - OzCHI 2015, pp. 397–406. ACM (2015)

27. Rubin, J., Chisnell, D.: Handbook of Usability Testing [Electronic Resource]: How to Plan, Design, and Conduct Effective Tests, 2nd edn. John Wiley & Sons (2008)

28. Runeson, P., Höst, M.: Guidelines for conducting and reporting case study research in software engineering. Empir. Softw. Eng. 14(2), 131 (2009)

29. Salah, D., et al.: A systematic literature review for agile development processes and user centred design integration. In: Proceedings of the 18th International Conference on Evaluation and Assessment in Software Engineering, pp. 5:1–5:10. ACM, New York (2014)

30. Skov, M.B., Stage, J.: Training software developers and designers to conduct usability evaluations. Behav. Inf. Technol. 31(4), 425–435 (2012)

31. Smith, A., Dunckley, L.: Prototype evaluation and redesign: structuring the design space through contextual techniques. Interact. Comput. 14(6), 821–843 (2002)

32. Uldall-Espersen, T., et al.: Tracing impact in a usability improvement process. Interact. Comput. 20(1), 48–63 (2008)

33. Vukelja, L., Müller, L., Opwis, K.: Are engineers condemned to design? A survey on software engineering and UI design in Switzerland. In: Baranauskas, C., Palanque, P., Abascal, J., Barbosa, S.D.J. (eds.) INTERACT 2007, Part II. LNCS, vol. 4663, pp. 555–568. Springer, Heidelberg (2007). doi:10.1007/978-3-540-74800-7_50

34. Walsham, G.: Interpretive case studies in IS research: nature and method. Eur. J. Inf. Syst. 4(2), 74–81 (1995)

35. Wixon, D.: Evaluating usability methods: why the current literature fails the practitioner. Interactions 10(4), 28–34 (2003)

Adoption of UX Evaluation in Practice: An Action Research Study in a Software Organization

Kristine Bang[1], Martin Akto Kanstrup[2], Adam Kjems[3],
and Jan Stage[4(✉)]

[1] Nykredit IT, Fredrik Bajers Vej 1, 9220 Aalborg East, Denmark
bang.kristine@gmail.com
[2] BAE Systems Applied Intelligence,
Bouet Møllevej 3-5, 9400 Nørresundby, Denmark
martin.kanstrup@baesystems.com
[3] Lego Koncernen, Aastvej 1, 7190 Billund, Denmark
adam.kjems@lego.com
[4] Department of Computer Science, Aalborg University,
Selma Lagerlöfs Vej 300, 9220 Aalborg East, Denmark
jans@cs.aau.dk

Abstract. This paper describes an action research study focusing on adoption of UX and UX evaluation methods in a software organisation. The aim of adopting UX was to exceed a traditional approach to design of banking applications. The action research study involved collaboration over several months between the researchers and a group of developers with no prior knowledge of UX. The study demonstrates how UX methods can be introduced in an IT organisation and how UX decisions can be prioritised in the software industry. Focusing on understanding, supporting and improving the practice of the development team, we employed several adoption activities of UX evaluation methods by presenting these in a visual form (video records) and a practical form (workshops). Our results show that specific UX materials have been adopted in the development process of the IT department. Based on the study, we present our experience with adopting UX in an IT organisation with focus on the collaboration process, working with the UX definition, and the obstacles that occurred during the collaboration.

Keywords: User experience · UX · Evaluation methods · Action research · Method adoption

1 Introduction

User Experience (UX) is a term that is appearing more and more frequently in the IT industry [1, 21]. Today, the preceding concept of usability, which emphasizes mainly pragmatic aspects of IT products, is to a large extent being taken for granted by contemporary users. To offer more, IT companies have started to focus on products that are both practical tools and deliver interesting experiences for the users [21].

R. Bernhaupt et al. (Eds.): INTERACT 2017, Part IV, LNCS 10516, pp. 169–188, 2017.
DOI: 10.1007/978-3-319-68059-0_11

Introducing UX work in the software industry turns the attention towards the user's thoughts and feelings before, during and after using a product. Thus design and evaluation of UX is about capturing and predicting these thoughts and feelings, including the study of e.g. emotions, preferences, brand image, functionality, attitudes, and context of use [10].

An increasing number of researchers create new UX design and evaluation methods and evaluate qualities of existing methods. Some of these researchers depart from the UX challenges that the IT industry is facing. Unfortunately, only few of them also conduct research on adoption and use of UX methods in that industry [1, 5, 15, 18]. Accordingly, it is exceedingly difficult for IT companies to move from being inspired by UX methods to adoption of these methods in their development practices.

Although the IT industry is turning its focus towards UX, it is far from all IT development companies that have already adopted UX work, and some of those that have, have not embraced it as intended by UX research [1]. Many IT companies are motivated to adopt UX work in their development processes, in order to enhance the user experience of their products and make them more appealing, but they are missing guidance on strategies for carrying UX adoption through.

This paper describes an action research study focusing on adoption of UX and UX evaluation methods in an IT company. The aim of adopting UX in the company was to exceed a traditional approach to design of banking applications. The action research study deals with a specific project in the company where UX was introduced to stimulate design of more interesting services in a banking system to manage loans with a smartphone. The study involved collaboration over several months between the researchers and a group of developers with no prior knowledge of UX. The study demonstrates how UX methods can be introduced in an IT organisation and how UX decisions can be prioritised in the software industry.

The following section presents related work, including existing qualitative research about UX and usability in the IT industry. Then the framework of our empirical study is presented, followed by the description of method of the study. Next, the findings from the study are presented, followed by a discussion that compares our results to existing studies of UX in industry. Finally, we provide our conclusion on the study.

2   Related Work

Research investigations of UX work, including UX evaluation in companies are limited. Only few articles have made qualitative research about the adoption of UX in companies [1, 5, 18]. This section outlines some of the inquiries, and because of their limited number, also a study of usability work in industry. In the description, we emphasize the setup and methods of the investigations.

2.1   Study of Usability Evaluation in Industry

Since UX can be seen as related to usability, studies about usability in industry can be used as inspiration to conducting UX studies in industry. A good example of a qualitative process-oriented study about usability in industry is Nørgaard and Hornbæk

[16]. They conducted an explorative study of 14 think-aloud sessions in order to investigate what usability evaluators do in practice. The researchers used observations to investigate seven companies and their use of test sessions in a usability evaluation. The study resulted in an overall picture of how companies are working with usability test sessions as they did not investigate one company in depth.

2.2 Definitions of UX

There is still no agreed upon definition of UX [11], but various academic papers have been given their take on how to define UX. Hassenzahl [6] describe that people perceive interactive products along two different dimensions: Pragmatic quality, referring to the functional usefulness of the product, and hedonic quality, referring to the feelings associated with the product. This definition has been developed to: "A consequence of a user's internal state, the characteristics of the designed system and the context (or the environment) within which the interaction occurs" [7].

Law et al. [12] took a different approach and conducted a survey with 275 researchers and practitioners in search of a common UX definition. The general understanding was that UX is "dynamic, context-dependent, and subjective, stemming from a broad range of potential benefits users may derive from a product." Later, it was added that UX is dynamic over time, and that feelings towards a product may be different during and after the interaction with it [20].

ISO 9240-2010 [10] aims to provide a common definition with a main definition and three notes with descriptions of the different dimensions of UX: "Person's perceptions and responses resulting from the use and/or anticipated use of a product, system or service". The notes add that UX is about emotions, psychological responses, behaviors, brand image, the user's prior experiences, context of use, and that UX occurs before, during, and after use.

2.3 Study of Adoption of UX in Industry

In order to investigate the existing qualitative research about UX in industry, an experimental study was conducted in 2014 with a collaboration between researchers and software companies [1]. The purpose was to investigate how to adopt UX in practice and several research methods were used, including an explorative study with one company. In the explorative study, several activities were carried out, e.g. team meetings, observations, interviews, and heuristic inspections. The study suggests using empirical research to reduce the gap between the research and industry use of UX. They found collaboration studies with researchers and practitioners instrumental in showing practitioners why to improve their development processes and how to do so.

An exploratory case study from 2015 had the goal of investigating how UX knowledge can be obtained and shared within a company [5]. Three case studies were conducted with three companies, who already had integrated UX in their development process. These studies included six interviews with the designers from the companies. Different methods to spread UX knowledge within a company were analysed and these methods were centred on UX competence flow between individual UX designers and the company in which they worked.

Another case study from 2012 investigated Microsoft and their practice behind UX management [18]. The study was conducted in situ at Microsoft where several interviews were conducted with seven managers from research and development departments. Since Microsoft has already integrated UX in their development process, this study describes a successful UX integration in a company.

The above mentioned papers about UX describe qualitative studies of integration of UX in industry, but they do not work specifically with UX evaluation, are based on interviews with other actors, provide only general and short descriptions of the different cases, and two of them investigate companies where UX is already integrated and do not address how UX can be adopted.

3 Framework

The theoretical framework of our action research study is adopted from Mathiassen [13] as our purpose was to "understand, support, and improve practice as part of the ongoing professional development". The concept of UX used in this study is ISO's definition (see Sect. 2.2).

We selected methods for our study based on the following criteria: they should be easy to use for practitioners with little to no prior UX experience, the materials and equipment required should be minimal, they should represent different approaches to evaluation of UX, they should include both expert and user based evaluation, and they should facilitate collection of both quantitative and qualitative data. A previous study identified 96 UX evaluation methods [21]. Based on this survey and our criteria, we chose the following UX evaluation methods: SUXES [19], Product Reaction Cards [4], AttrakDiff [22] and UX Heuristic Inspection [17].

4 Method

The purpose of our empirical study was to study support of adoption of UX work in an IT organisation. We decided to base it on an action research (AR) approach. Action research was pioneered by Lewin [18] who used it in his study of field theory in the social sciences. Action research has often been used in information system research to study changes in an organisation. Thus it may be used to study adoption of new concepts in a social setting. However, in HCI this research approach is rarely used and only few guidelines and cases for inspiration are available [10]. In the following, we present the method of our AR study.

4.1 Research Approach

AR studies are a duality of action and research; practice and theory. They are working towards producing new knowledge through the creation of solutions and/or improvements to "real-life" practical problems [14]. AR has been used previously in HCI [8] but is more prevalent in information systems research [9].

We have used [14], where AR is described as "two, interlinked cycles", one of practical problem solving and the other with production of scientific knowledge (see Fig. 1). The Problem Solving cycle aims to help our collaborating company in regards to using UX and UX evaluation in their IT-system development, and the Research cycle aims to investigate how UX evaluation can be adopted in the IT-industry.

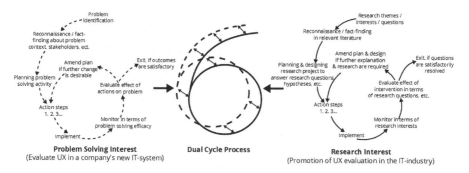

Fig. 1. The AR of this paper viewed as a dual cycle process. Consist of both a problem solving interest cycle and a research interest cycle. Adapted from McKay and Marshall [14].

In AR the cycle continues with no definite ending point, but the goal is to enable the company to maintain the positive changes that have been made, once the researchers leave the company [5]. In our case, the exit points from both cycles in Fig. 1 were based on a predefined deadline.

The limited time influenced our criterion of success. Ultimately, the adoption process is successful if the methods adopted are used competently and effectively. However, we did not expect that to be realistic because of the limited amount of time allocated to the study. Instead, we saw the adoption as successful if the participants could use the techniques we introduced and intended to keep using them in the future.

4.2   Research Practice

The AR study was carried out in cooperation with IT developers from the IT department of a Danish bank. The IT department had recently shifted their development method to a user focused approach.

The company requested us to support them in adopting methods and techniques that were relevant to their new focus. We offered to conduct an AR study where we supported adoption of UX methods that could enhance their user focus and help them develop more interesting services. The purpose was to help them solve the challenges they were experiencing with selection and adoption of relevant UX methods. This was accepted by the company.

In cooperation with the company, we chose a new project where the purpose was to develop a banking system to manage loans with a smartphone.

The development team of 10, which we have been working with, consisted of UX designers, a method expert, a product manager, bank domain experts, business architects and software developers. In the collaboration, we were mostly in contact with the following key development team members: P1; our contact person in the company who also had the role of method consultant and UX specialist, P2; Project manager, P3; the chief specialist who worked with the design of the new system including UX, P4; senior specialist who worked with both the design and technical aspects of the system.

Table 1. Action Research in regards to the key steps in Problem Solving Interests Cycle. Showing the activities conducted in a project in the IT-department of a Danish bank company.

Activities		Action Research in regards to the key steps in 'problem solving interests cycle' (Key: p1-4 = company employees, pa = all the member of the team, r = the authors)				
		Problem identification + company info	Planning problem solving activity	Action steps - planning	Action steps - implement	Action steps - evaluation
1.	Initiating meeting (15/12/14)	Info about the new development method, the company and the new project (p1,r)				
2.	First team meeting (12/3/15)	Presentation of the team members, the new project, our plan for the action study & presentation of the UX term (pa,r)				
3.	Second team meeting (20/3/15)		Planning of the action research study + status of the project (p1,p2,r)			
4.	Third team meeting (27/3/15)		Status of the project + planning of the action research study (p3,p4,r)			
5.	Workshop - early UX evaluation (27/3/15)			Planning of the workshop (r)	Facilitation of the workshop (pa,r)	Knowledge about UX before the workshop + lessons learned in the workshop (pa,r)
6.	Fourth team meeting (17/4/15)			Planning of UX evaluations + status of the project (p2-4,r)		Lessons learned in the workshop (p2-4, r)
7.	Fifth team meeting (24/4/15)			Presentation of design sketches (p3-4,r)		
8.	Sixth team meeting (30/4/15)			Planning of UX evaluations + functional prototypes (p1, p3-4, r)		
9.	UX evaluations (6/5/15-11/5/15)			Planning of UX evaluations (r)	Conducting UX evaluations (r)	
10.	Seventh team meeting (12/5/15)				Presentation of UX evaluation results (p1, p3-4, r)	Feedback on the results (p1,p3-4,r))
11.	Workshop - presentation of UX test results (19/5/15)				Presentation of UX evaluation results (pa)	Feedback on the results (pa)
12.	Last team meeting (29/5/15)					Feedback on the action research study (p1-4,r)

The AR study lasted 6 months, using 98 company employee hours. During this period, idea creation and the construction and evaluation of prototypes were done. Table 1 provides a timetable of relevant AR activities conducted in regards to the Problem Solving Interests Cycle. Not included in Table 1 are the weekly design workshops the development team held. We did not attend these meetings but the findings were reported back to us.

Initiating meeting (activity 1). The first meeting with the company was held at the end of 2014. The meeting was conducted with P1. The purpose of the meeting was to gain information about the new HCI software development method, created by P1, as well as getting information about the new project in the company. Furthermore, we identified the main problems in regards to the adoption and work with UX evaluations, and discussed how we could contribute to the company's new project. We also collected information about the company's expectations from our collaboration. Team meetings (activities 2, 3, 4, 6, 7, 8, 10, 12).

Throughout the collaboration with the company, we participated in team video meetings consisting primarily of the key members (P1, P2, P3, P4). The meetings lasted between 20 min to 1 h and took place three to four times per month. In each meeting, the team members presented the status of the project. We then presented our suggestions for current and future UX integration and used these meetings to educate team members on UX topics. These topics consisted of presentation of the UX term in regards to the ISO definition as well as when, how, and why the company could benefit from UX evaluation methods. In the later stages of the collaboration, the meetings functioned as a means to evaluate the effect of our UX adoption.

Workshop - early UX evaluation (activity 5). In this workshop we were invited as UX consultants and our role was to educate the whole team about UX as well as how they could evaluate UX in the concept design phase. The presented evaluation methods were modified so they could function as developer tests, meaning that the developers could evaluate their own system. The workshop lasted one day and was divided into several activities, designed to expose the team to UX methods.

The agenda for the workshop was: The workshop started with a 10 min presentation of UX. We then asked the team members to brainstorm potential UX strengths and weaknesses of the new system. The same activity was conducted at the end of the workshop and functioned as an evaluation of our influence on their UX knowledge.

After the brainstorm, the team members were divided into two groups (5 each). Each group was presented with a UX evaluation method (SUXES [19] or Product Reaction Cards [4]). None of the team members were familiar with the presented evaluation methods prior to the workshop. Both methods were modified to be a 'design brainstorming tool' and an evaluation method that they could try on their own product. They were modified on the different UX parameters being measured (such as fun, effective, complex, and sophisticated). We wanted to make sure that the methods presented relevant parameters to measure for the new banking system. SUXES provides little information on which UX parameters should be measured, while Product Reaction Card provides 118 different UX related words, which we reduced.

The SUXES method and the parameters were also first used as a 'design brainstorming tool' by the SUXES team, where they first chose which parameters (out of a selection of 20 words, e.g. fun, sophisticated) they wanted their new banking system to represent. Afterwards in a scale from 1–7 (as the SUXES method also suggest), they decided what they expected the different parameters to score. After a sketching session with the parameters in mind, the Product Reaction Card team used the SUXES methods to evaluate the design from the SUXES group.

After the method presentations, each group used their method as a tool for choosing which UX dimensions will be focused on in the new project. Afterwards they brainstormed ideas based on the chosen UX dimensions and lastly one group member from each team was used as a test person and conducted a UX evaluation based on the other group's method.

The workshop ended with the development team evaluating the workshop and the methods they had been presented.

UX evaluations (activities 9, 10, 11). As a way to show the team which kind of results you can get from an UX evaluation, we conducted both expert evaluations (UX Heuristic Inspection [17]) with HCI experts, and user evaluations (AttrakDiff [22]) with potential end-users. The evaluations were conducted in a lab and were videotaped for the development team to see how the evaluations were conducted, how the test moderator controlled the evaluations, and to hear participants' comments. To show the diversity of UX evaluation methods, we evaluated both a paper prototype and a functional prototype on a smartphone. The prototypes were a result of the previous workshops conducted in the development team (e.g. activity 5) and were modeled to fit the size of a smartphone. This was to explore how and what one can gain from evaluating UX of different stage of development. Since the company was making a prototype which should function on a smartphone, we designed a wooden smartphone-mockup to make the evaluation of the paper prototype more realistic (Fig. 2). This made it possible to evaluate the actual screen size elements, to use the swipe function, and to change between different screenshots.

Fig. 2. The wooden smartphone prototype designed to test paper prototypes.

The results from the evaluations were analyzed and presented to three of the team members (P1, P3, P4) in a video meeting where results were discussed as well as how possible design changes could address the negative comments from the experts and users in the UX evaluations. Lastly, we gave comments about the potential future uses of the UX evaluations in the company.

Last team meeting (activity 12). The last team meeting was conducted as a final evaluation of our collaboration. Here, two of the key members of the development team (P3, P4) evaluated our adoption of UX and UX evaluation methods as well as giving a report on which promoted material has been adopted in the company so far. Since not all key members were able to participate in the meeting, we also conducted a survey, which all employees in the development team answered.

4.3   Data Collection and Analysis

Throughout the AR study, we collected data from the different meetings with the company through both audio records (in total = 5 h 33 min.) and notes taken during the meetings (36 p.). Furthermore, we used three surveys throughout the collaboration:

- Survey 1: Conducted before activity 5 to collect information about the development team's knowledge about UX.
- Survey 2: Conducted the day after activity 5 to collect information about the changes in the development team's knowledge about UX and opinion about the workshop.
- Survey 3: Conducted before activity 12 in order to gather information from the development team about the overall opinion on the collaboration, the adopted UX material, as well as the status on the adoption of the material.

Since the development team was anonymous in the surveys, we have used the term "anonymous" after the citations from the surveys.

To analyze the statements of the development team, we used a modified version of the Conventional Analysis Method [19], where we generated names for categories from the collected data. Using this method, we first read all the collected data to get an overview of it and were then analyzed word by word in order to derive codes. Afterwards, notes about our impression and initial analysis of the data were made, and codes were sorted into categories where some were combined in order to create new ones.

5   Findings

The analysis of the statements from the development team resulted in 8 topics that are presented below. The results consist of the following categories: Process (P), obstacles (O), and definition (D).

5.1   (P1) From No UX Consensus to a Comprehensive Understanding

In the beginning of the collaboration with the IT-development team, all the members had different understandings and definitions of UX:

> "There are not many (of the team members) that have knowledge about UX. We are not experts in the field of UX and when we are discussing it, it is clear that we have different views on it." – Anonymous

These multiple views may have been due to the company not establishing a companywide definition. This concern was expressed by P1 during one of the first meetings.

To investigate the development team's understanding of UX further, survey 1 was conducted (see Table 2). Results showed that there was disagreement about the definition of UX and the dimensions of UX. Furthermore, the results indicated that most team members saw UX as consisting mostly of dimensions related to usability such as functionality, effectiveness, cognitive load, ease of learning. Dimensions as brand

Table 2. Results from survey 1 (n = 7) and 2 (n = 8) showing a selection of the UX dimensions and how many agree that these are a part of UX.

	Select UX dimensions	Survey 1 (before workshop)	Survey 2 (after workshop)
Usability	Functionality	5	7
	Effectiveness	5	7
	Easy to learn	4	8
	Cognitive load	4	6
UX	Brand image	2	4
	Social aspect	1	3
	Emotions	3	7
	Context	4	8
	Trust	3	6

image and the social aspects were not seen as part of UX. Even though 7 out of 8 said they knew about UX, the results indicated that it was limited.

The aim of activity 5 was to make the development team understand that UX is more than usability. The UX term was presented based on the ISO definition, and all team members worked with UX and UX evaluation. An analysis of the results of a follow-up survey showed that the team developed a uniform understanding of UX dimensions, and they saw UX as broad and consisting of different dimensions. Furthermore they saw UX as more than usability (see Table 2).

5.2   (P2) UX Adoption or No Changes in UX Focus

During activity 12, when the collaboration with the development team and our promotion of UX were evaluated, the designers seemed happy to be introduced to UX and new UX evaluation tools. They also expressed that they had learned something new about working with UX that has already had an impact on how they work in their system development process:

> "If you haven't been here so we could get the knowledge from you this early (in the process), we would not have been where we are now. I have no doubt about that… It is also good to shake the heavy company culture up a bit and it has succeeded for you. Changes have been made." - P4

In regards to the changes and definite use of the adopted UX and UX evaluation methods, the key members of the development team, expressed a concern. They were positive towards UX and UX evaluation methods and wanted to use the methods we presented, but were concerned about how other employees in the company would accept them. When presenting the UX topics to members of other development teams, they were more interested in the outcome than the process:

> "It didn't seem that they were very interested in the process. They all just wanted to see the prototype and to be able to interact with it… it's a little sad." - P4

That it is difficult to promote UX to employees in a company were a problem which both P1, P3 and P4 were struggling with. However, they saw the UX workshop as a very positive way to promote UX, since people are then able to work with the presented UX tools and through this a greater possibility of seeing the value behind the methods. That other than designers and UX experts were part of the workshop, was expressed as positive, since the designers felt that the team now had a shared understanding of UX. It was also seen as being positive since the "non-designers" were able to get an understanding of the UX-workers' tasks and decisions.

> "Using workshops is the best thing you can do in a company (when adopting new methods and techniques). You can send us lots of material, but half of the people will not read it, and the other half will read it and not use it. Participating in a workshop is the way to get things changed in a company." - P4

> "When you have a workshop, people are quickly committed. As soon as you feed them with what they should do, they quickly start working with the methods and tools." - P3

Whether the company is going to use the UX methods and tools provided is uncertain. However in the development team, small changes have already been adopted and the team is motivated towards continuing working with UX and UX evaluation, both in regards to this project and others.

5.3   (P3) Opinion and Adoption of UX Evaluation Methods

From the beginning of the collaboration with the company, P1 expressed that they had already decided to conduct user evaluations with the thinking aloud technique, but had not found a method for evaluating UX yet. When presenting the possibility of conducting UX on paper prototypes, it was clear that they did not have a method for that and P2 seemed surprised that you are able to conduct these kinds of evaluations. P2 was therefore very interested in a presentation of these kinds of evaluation methods. P1 also expressed a wish to work with both low-fi and hi-fi prototypes with the possibility of conducting user evaluations on these.

As a result of this, the two UX evaluation methods 'Attrakdiff' and 'UX Heuristic Inspection' were presented. Since the key members of the development team expressed a wish to learn about the methods, but did not have the time to conduct the evaluations, we decided to conduct them through activity 9.

After presenting the methods and results of the evaluations, the key members of the development team expressed enthusiasm in regards to the Attrakdiff user test. They found it a good evaluation tool which provided a clear overview of UX dimensions measured in the evaluation and were motivated towards conducting more, using the Attrakdiff method. They saw the method as being simple and straightforward, and were interested in the tools used to conduct the evaluation.

The two designers (P3, P4) were on the other hand a bit skeptical in regards to letting experts evaluate their system in the later steps of the process, since they saw them as being "fake users". However, they saw a potential use of expert evaluations in the early stages of their future system's development process as a way to find early problems and a way to get inspiration for new solutions. It was therefore seen as being an evaluation tool to test prototypes. From one of the later team meetings, it was however clear that the designers began to see the benefits of conducting evaluations, especially after reading the results from our conducted expert evaluations.

In regards to conducting evaluations on paper prototypes versus functional prototypes, they expressed that they were able to use the results from both evaluations, and were especially motivated in conducting tests with paper prototypes to catch early problems in the design phase.

When evaluating the strengths of the presented UX evaluation methods, most of the members of the development team were positive about these and wanted to continue using them:

"We have moved from having a gut feeling about the quality (of the system) to have actual knowledge." – Anonymous

"By working with and evaluating UX with real users and experts which doesn't have the background knowledge that we have, we are able to get closer to the best result." – Anonymous

This indicates that the development team is open towards adopting UX evaluation methods in their development process.

5.4   (D1) UX Dimensions of Fun and Enjoyment

Since the goal for the development team was to create a bank application, one would expect that popular UX dimensions such as enjoyment and fun would not be taken into consideration. The bank industry may be seen as conservative and boring, but being part of the development team for four months demonstrates that they were open towards all sorts of UX dimensions. They e.g. included words such as interesting, fun and different when describing which product they wanted to create in activity 5:

"We have an opportunity to make it a little more fun today... I think it is possible to make it interesting." - P4

Even though they did not end up working with these kinds of UX dimensions later on, they were open towards using them in the initial idea generation phase. This shows that they are interested in creating a different experience for future users of their bank system and express that they wanted to move away from their boring image.

In addition, after presenting the UX term for the development team, their view of UX widened, making them understand that UX is more than making systems fun to use, but is about giving the user an overall good experience in regards to the system (see Table 2). However it is important to clarify that even though the development team see UX as being broad it does not indicate if they are going to work with UX broadly in practice.

5.5   (D2) More Than One Meaning Per UX Dimension

Especially during activity 5, it became clear that different UX dimensions were interpreted differently among the team members, which resulted in many discussions:

"We spent a long time on creating a shared understanding of these (UX dimensions). When we evaluated the system with one from the other team (in the workshop), the person did not have the same understanding of the words." - P4

However, during activity 5 the team created a shared understanding of the different meanings of the UX dimensions (see Table 2). During defining the UX dimensions, new ideas also arose in regards to the new system. Most of the development team therefore saw the time used to make a shared understanding of the dimensions as being useful:

"Now we use these words (UX dimensions) and we have this understanding of them. We have then established the conceptual universe of this project and can use the same words." - Anonymous

Especially the presented UX evaluation method 'Product Reaction Cards' were seen as being a good discussion tool, since it presents various UX dimensions.

5.6   (O1) A Skepticism Towards UX Work

Even though the development team seemed excited about working with UX in their new development process, it was clear that they had some concerns in regards to the project. In one of the first meetings with the key members of the development team, P3 expressed a concern in regards to the new UX development method:

"We are all novices. None of us have tried to work like this before... so it will probably take a little longer (to work with UX). When we know the process, things will go faster. In the next project we will know the method and therefore be more confident with it." - P3

"What worries me is that I think there is an expectation from the board of managers that this is something we just do... and I do not think that. You have to practice and we are going to have a hard time prioritizing what should be made and what should not be made." - P3

Not only did P3 have skepticism towards working with a more human-centered and UX focused development method, the people working with the design of the system also expressed concerns towards this new shift in focus:

"It has previously been very uphill for this company to use the time and energy on these things (design and UX) and I am concerned that it will also be uphill in this project. I do not think so, but it is not a Google Labs business we're in. It is about finding a balance, cause we could easily use 100 million (DKK) on this." - P4

In regards to working with UX early in the development phase, concerns were expressed by the two designers, and it appeared to be a consensus that UX is something one work with in later phases of a design process:

"UX work first appears later on in the process when we test the sketches... then we begin to take UX into consideration." - P4

"I am a little nervous about becoming lost in the detail elements, when we first start to work with UX." - P3

The skepticism towards working with UX early and fear of not challenging the team in regards to UX was a motivation for us to make the team work with early UX evaluation methods in activity 5.

5.7   (O2) Working with Creatures of Habit in a UX Workshop

In a meeting with key members of the development team, before the UX workshop, the designers (P3, P4) were skeptical in regards to adopting new UX tools and UX thinking to the development team:

> "We are creatures of habits. Many quickly fall back into the old way of doing things… the old way of thinking. One of the major challenges is to challenge the status quo." - P4

However, they expressed that they were interested in learning new methods and techniques to bring them out of their comfort zone. Especially methods for bringing up UX early in the design process, which also functioned as a motivation for the UX workshop, facilitated by us:

> "It is always great to work with UX, unfortunately I see a lack of understanding of what UX is among my colleagues and often we discuss details that are unnecessary at this stage of the process (the concept phase). I wish we could take it (UX) in earlier in the process." - Anonymous

In the workshop, this concern became reality. Even though they were given the task of thinking about which UX dimensions they wanted their system to represent, they began talking about technical aspects and future goals of the project, neglecting their future users and UX aspect.

However, after we presented the task again for the teams, emphasizing the different aspects of UX, they began working towards UX goals, using more UX dimensions in their conversation. By doing this, a more creative idea generating process began to emerge and it was clear, that they were thinking more about what the future users might want in regards to the system.

Comparing the activity in the beginning and the activity in the end of the workshop, some changes in the team members' way of thinking were observed. From being much focused on technical aspects, and the current way of doing things in their concept brainstorming phase, they began being more open towards thinking out-of-the-box. The workshop also resulted in the team members being more focused on specific goals for the project, including UX dimensions they wanted to focus on. Further, several team members expressed that the workshop exercises about making the developer evaluate the design ideas early in the concept creating phase were useful. However, they mostly saw the concept UX evaluation methods as a design tool for specifying key UX dimensions in regards to the new system, rather than an evaluation tool:

> "I think the methods (UX evaluation methods) are good to bring up discussions in the group, but I do not like to use the method to evaluate with." - Anonymous

> "I think the many concepts (UX dimensions) are a good way to get the ideas flowing and simultaneously narrow the focus on the essentials." - Anonymous

The key team members of the development team were expressing that they were happy to introduce new ways of thinking to the other members of the development team and liked that the workshop resulted in a shared understanding of UX. However, P4 expressed a concern in regards to a permanent change in the team:

"(The method) introduced the colleagues to other ways of doing things. The question is whether it can be kept alive or whether we fall back into old habits." - P4

To investigate this concern, activity 6 was held three weeks after the workshop. It was here expressed that they had integrated aspects of the tools from the UX workshop, and that the UX dimension cards from SUXES and Product Reactions Cards were already integrated in their weekly workshops:

"It (the UX dimensions cards) is one of our bibles... we have decided to hang them on our whiteboards." - P2

Further, P1 also expressed that he had already planned to use the SUXES method in an evaluation of another system in the company, and that the two designers (P3, P4) wanted to integrate the method in their project: "It shows that you have had an effect on us. SUXES has already been integrated" - P1

5.8   (O3) A Need for UX Evaluation Method Modification

When presenting the UX evaluation methods from the research literature to the development team, these methods were often modified to fit the development team's wishes and available resources. Sometimes these modifications were made by us, but the development team also made their own modifications to the methods.

SUXES and Product Reaction Cards both use cards with prespecified UX dimensions. In activity 5, however, both teams found some of the dimensions irrelevant in regards to the goal of their new system, which resulted in both removals of cards as well as creation of new cards with UX dimensions.

From activity 5, it was also clear that the development team did not see the methods as fixed. Many of the team members talked about different techniques and parts of the methods which could be combined into one that would suit their development process better. They e.g. saw the Product Reaction Cards as being more useful as a brainstorming tool among the developers instead of being a user evaluation tool.

When presenting the Attrakdiff method to the designers of the development team (P3, P4), they also discussed possible modifications to the tool, e.g. combining the notation of 'acceptable' and 'desirable' levels of the UX dimensions from SUXES into the Attrakdiff method. The reason for this was that the company was focused on prioritizing the different goals for the new system to match team resources.

P4 further expressed that the words used in the Attrakdiff method were too academic and talked about substituting these with ones that are more interesting for the company to measure on:

"Attrakdiff uses a lot of words that are not used in the danish language anymore. Its academia and we cannot use it, but we can drag the things out which make sense to use and throw out the rest." - P4

The development team was therefore positive towards the academic methods, but did not see them as methods that can be used without modifications in the company, since they saw parts of the methods as being too academic for practical use.

"Everything has to be modified to fit our culture." - P3

6 Discussion

In this section, we discuss the lessons learned in this AR study.

6.1 Do Not Just Talk About the Methods, Show the Procedures and Results

Since the development team expressed that they had not worked with UX evaluation methods before and were skeptical in regards to the outcome of these, we decided to conduct the evaluations ourselves and video record the whole procedure as well as making an analysis of the results in a document form. The feedback from the key members of the development team was very positive, since they were able to see both the outcome of the evaluations methods as well as the procedure of the different methods. The videos gave a more realistic view on the methods as well as easy guidelines for conducting the evaluations.

An adoption technique of UX evaluation methods similar to ours has been used in the experimental study by Ardito et al. [1]. Here the researchers conducted heuristic evaluations by themselves to show the company they collaborated with, that these kinds of methods require limited resources and little training of company employees.

To adopt UX evaluation methods, it can therefore be beneficial to not only present the methods, but show the company the results you can get from them when evaluating the company's own products, as well as showing them the procedure behind the methods. This is seen as being very important in companies, since companies tend to be very results-focused and want to know the procedure behind the methods in order to calculate the resources needed to use these.

6.2 Joint UX Workshops Results in Shared Knowledge

As an adoption strategy in our AR study, we facilitated a UX workshop with the development team, to teach all the members UX and UX evaluation methods. Conducting workshops in a development team is already used in Microsoft, and is described by Szóstek [18] as a way to promote UX within the company. She highlights the effects of joint UX workshops: "It is the most effective way to show others the value of UX". In our case, we also learned that employees are very keen on using workshops to learn about new things. The designers of the development team expressed that they liked that the workshop created a shared knowledge about UX, and that non-designers now have both an understanding of UX work and why the designers want to work with it. As in the Microsoft case study, it was also expressed by the employees, that workshops are an effective way of adopting UX, since the employees are able to work with the term in practice instead of just listening to what others claim UX is.

When adopting UX in a company, it is therefore important to educate more than just the designers of a development team. Since UX and UX evaluation are often seen by non-designers as being messy and difficult to understand, they have difficulties understanding why designers are working with UX and what they can benefit from this. By educating the entire development team and making them used it in practice; it is our experience that the designers work with UX is more appreciated.

6.3   Towards UX Adoption

Even though the company we collaborated with was positive towards both our adoption strategies and the evaluation methods presented, we do not know if it is going to incorporate and use them in the long run, since our study lasted only four months.

Looking at other experimental studies of UX however shows that these are also conducted in a limited time period, making it difficult to talk about an actual UX adoption. The study by Ardito et al. [1] lasted only three months and speculations towards the effects of their adoption of UX in a company were therefore dimmed. However, their study mentioned that the company they collaborated with was positive towards the presented UX material and in the end of their study; some small elements of the adopted UX were already incorporated in the company's development process.

In our case, we are also not capable of talking about permanent UX adoption of our UX evaluation methods. However, just as Ardito et al. [1] were able to see some indications of UX adoption, we also witnessed parts of our UX evaluation methods being integrated in the development process by the end of the study.

Since we were not able to find investigations of long term adoption of UX techniques and methods we cannot say whether the adoption strategies actually work in the long run. In addition, the concept of UX that we employed [10] is very vague and difficult to measure. It would be interesting for a software organisation to employ a concept of UX that is simpler or even possible to measure.

6.4   Academic Evaluation Methods Need Changes

In our AR study we promoted UX and UX evaluation methods from research literature. With all the presented UX evaluation methods, both we and the development team saw a need to modify these in order to make them fit the development method and the goals of the company in regards to the new system. The development team expressed that some of the methods were using words that were too academic and wanted to make their own modifications on them in order to make them useful for the purpose of their projects.

Looking at the Ardito et al. study [1], this also resulted in modifications of the material from scientific articles in order to use it in a more practical context. They concluded that researchers have to be "more careful in transferring academic work into practical value for industry" [1] and describe that "it is the responsibility of academics to translate scientific articles, which formally describe evaluation methods, into something that makes sense for companies and is ready to be applied." [1].

From our experience in regards to this AR study, we also believe that modifications have to be made in order to make the scientific methods useful in a more practical oriented situation. The reason for this is that scientific papers often have another purpose and goal for methods, e.g. finding if certain UX dimensions are measureable and testing certain conditions, whereas the practical use of the methods is not studied often. It would also be useful if the prerequisites for applying specific UX methods were available. In our case, the company had a very low level or no UX maturity, and we did not know what level of maturity was required for the methods we selected.

6.5 The Usefulness of AR in Studies of UX Adoption

In this study, we have worked with AR in regards to UX research. In HCI, some AR studies have already been made and researchers are trying to promote the usefulness of this research approach in order to increase their use. Hayes [8] investigated the relationship between AR in HCI. She explained that some researchers do not see AR as providing scientific rigor, since it only investigates few cases that cannot be generalized. However, she states that: "AR provides a rigorous framework for generating and sharing sufficient knowledge about a solution that it may potentially be transferred to other contexts." [8].

The purpose behind AR is therefore not to be able to construct one solution that can be used by others, but to focus on local solutions to local problems, which may be reused in other cases. Further, since studies about adoption of UX evaluation methods in companies are sparse in the literature, investigations are needed to explore this. Such an investigation requires testing different techniques. Baskerville [3] describes AR as an opportunity to study social processes by "introducing changes into these processes and observing the effects of these changes." [3].

7 Conclusion

We have presented an action research study with an IT development team of a Danish bank, investigating how UX and UX evaluation can be adopted in industry. We used different adoption strategies with the development team. Our results indicate that changes have already been made and part of the material has been adopted by the company.

In the process of adopting UX and UX evaluation, demonstrations and workshops are effective strategies. The employees have different meanings of the different UX dimensions, so it is important for employees to create a shared understanding and definition of UX dimensions in order to work towards the same goal. It is difficult to use UX evaluation methods from research literature without modifying these to fit the individual company.

Our study is limited in regards to the period being studied. In addition, we have only conducted one action research study. Since the purpose of action research is to construct local solutions to local problems which may potentially be used in other cases, it is possible to build upon our study and results in order to investigate how UX evaluation can be adopted in practice.

Acknowledgments. We are grateful to the company that provided an interesting setting for our action research study and the team members who participated in a very constructive and positive manner.

References

1. Ardito, C., Buono, P., Caivano, D., Costabile, M.F., Lanzilotti, R.: Investigating and promoting UX practice in industry: An experimental study. Int. J. Hum Comput Stud. **72**(6), 542–551 (2014)
2. Bang, K., Kanstrup, M.A., Kjems, A.: What area they measuring: A Literature Review of Empirical Studies of UX Evaluation Methods (2015)
3. Baskerville, R.L.: Investigating information systems with action research. Commun. AIS **2** (3es), 4 (1999)
4. Benedek, J., Miner, T.: Measuring desirability: new methods for evaluating desirability in a usability lab setting. In: Proceedings of Usability Professionals Association, pp. 8–12 (2002)
5. Gray, C.M., Toombs, A., Gross, S.: Flow of competence in UX design practice. In: CHI 2015 (2015)
6. Hassenzahl, M.: The thing and I: understanding the relationship between user and product. Funology: from usability to enjoyment, pp. 31–42 (2003)
7. Hassenzahl, M., Tractinsky, N.: User experience – a research agenda. Behav. Inf. Technol. **25**(2), 91–97 (2006)
8. Hayes, G.R.: The relationship of action research to human-computer interaction. ACM Trans. Comput. Hum. Interact. (TOCHI) **18**(3), 15 (2011)
9. Iversen, J.H., Mathiassen, L., Nielsen, P.A.: Managing risk in software process improvement: an action research approach. Mis Q. 395–433 (2004)
10. ISO DIS 9241-210:2010. Ergonomics of human system interaction - Part 210: Human-centred design for interactive systems (formerly known as 13407). International Organization for Standardization (ISO), Switzerland (2010)
11. Law, E., Roto, V., Vermeeren, A., Kort, J., Hassenzahl, M.: Towards a shared definition for user experience. In: Special Interest Group in CHI 2008, Proceedings of Human Factors in Computing Systems, pp. 2395–2398 (2008)
12. Law, E.L.-C., Roto, V., Hassenzahl, M., Vermeeren, A.P.OS., Kort, J.: Understanding, scoping and defining user experience: a survey approach. In: Proceedings of the SIGCHI Conference on Human Factors in Computing Systems (CHI 2009). ACM, New York, pp. 719–728 (2009)
13. Mathiassen, L.: Collaborative practice research. Inf. Technol. People **15**(4), 321–345 (2002)
14. McKay, J., Marshall, P.: The dual imperatives of action research. Inf. Technol. People **14**(1), 46–59 (2001)
15. Norman, D., Miller, J., Henderson, A.: What you see, some of what's in the future, and how we go about doing it: HI at Apple Computer. In: Conference Companion on Human Factors in Computing Systems, p. 155. ACM (1995)
16. Nørgaard, M., Hornbæk, K.: What do usability evaluators do in practice? An explorative study of think-aloud testing. In: Proceedings of the 6th Conference on Designing Interactive Systems, pp. 209–218. ACM (2006)
17. Roto, V., Rantavuo, H., Väänänen-Vainio-Mattila, K.: Evaluating user experience of early product concepts. In: Proceedings of DPPI, vol. 9, pp. 199–208 (2009)
18. Szóstek, A.A.: A look into some practices behind Microsoft UX management. In: CHI 2012 Extended Abstracts on Human Factors in Computing Systems, pp. 605–618. ACM (2012)
19. Turunen, M., Hakulinen, J., Melto, A., Heimonen, T., Laivo, T., Hella, J.: SUXES-user experience evaluation method for spoken and multimodal interaction. In: 10th Annual Conference of the International Speech Communication Association, INTERSPEECH 2009, Brighton, UK, 6–10 September 2009, pp. 2567–2570 (2009)

20. Vermeeren, A.P.O.S., Roto, V., Law, E.L-C., Obrist, M., Hoonhout, J., Väänänen-Vainio-Mattila, K.: User experience evaluation methods: current state and development needs. In: Proceedings of NordiCHI 2010, pp. 521–530. ACM, New York (2010)
21. Väänänen-Vainio-Mattila, K., Roto, V., Hassenzahl, M.: Now let's do it in practice: user experience evaluation methods in product development. In: CHI 2008 Extended Abstracts on Human Factors in Computing Systems, pp. 3961–3964. ACM (2008)
22. Wetzlinger, W., Auinger, A., Dörflinger, M.: Comparing effectiveness, efficiency, ease of use, usability and user experience when using tablets and laptops. In: Marcus, A. (ed.) DUXU 2014. LNCS, vol. 8517, pp. 402–412. Springer, Cham (2014). doi:10.1007/978-3-319-07668-3_39

Empowering Project Managers in Enterprises - A Design Thinking Approach to Manage Commercial Projects

Aparna Kongot[(⊠)] and Monisha Pattanaik[(⊠)]

SAP Labs India Private Limited, Bangalore, India
{aparna.kongot,monisha.pattanaik}@sap.com

Abstract. Lack of insights into potential issues in enterprise projects is a major problem that leads to cost and revenue targets being missed. This not only lowers project margins but also adversely affects customer relationship and future businesses for the organization. Many oversights occur during the project execution phase, especially for large scale enterprise projects, where the project manager spends a lot of time in proactively ensuring various deadlines are met. Commercial Project Management is an Enterprise solution from SAP that provides Project Managers an overview of the potential issues along with insights into their impact on margin, statuses and several key performance indicators. This allows Project Managers to ensure smooth delivery while meeting project targets, thereby gaining time to hone skills needed increase profit for their organizations. This paper explains how SAP adopted the Design Thinking methodology to build this product that addresses their varied customer's needs from diverse industries.

Keywords: User experience · Project management · Design thinking · Enterprise software · Formative usability testing · SAP fiori user experience

1 Introduction

Project managers are often in firefighting mode as they lack insights into upcoming issues that could impact deadlines and thereby the overall project deliverable. They run the risk missing the revenue targets and end up being answerable for the consequences to senior management and customers. Hence, their biggest need is to stay up-to-date and gain insights into potential issues so that they can be proactively handled [1]. In the Project Management Lifecycle, the project manager is involved in Project Bidding, Planning, Executing and Monitoring [2]. During the execution and monitoring phase, he sometimes misses generating a Debit Memo Request to inform the Account Manager to bill the customer according to the terms of the contract. He can also overlook pending invoices for a customer leading to aggregating debts. Payment collection could be one time or recurring. In either case, missing a deadline could have a negative impact on the Revenue. Likewise, Project Managers need to keep a track on the delivery of Purchase order items. A delay or reversal of goods or services could mean that the project cannot start on time or there is an immediate need for alternate solutions.

© IFIP International Federation for Information Processing 2017
Published by Springer International Publishing AG 2017. All Rights Reserved
R. Bernhaupt et al. (Eds.): INTERACT 2017, Part IV, LNCS 10516, pp. 189–197, 2017.
DOI: 10.1007/978-3-319-68059-0_12

This can lead to unplanned increase in costs. In the existing Commercial Project Management (CPM) [3] Enterprise solution, all the information about Purchase orders, Billing, Cost and Revenue are available in different modules and the process of manually searching for each of this information is very time consuming for the project manager. There was an imminent need to help Project Managers with timely information that can help them meet targets. This would also give them enough time to focus on bringing value and business to the organization. To address this challenge, we adopted the Design Thinking Methodology[1] (DT) [4] with our customers illustrated in Fig. 1. We conducted Co-innovation Workshops and remote sessions with customers and all stakeholders to understand user needs and define concepts. The final prototype was tested in the annual Americas' SAP Users' Group (ASUG) in a Formative Usability Testing environment. Feedback from the test results were incorporated into the product that was finally implemented and released to the customers.

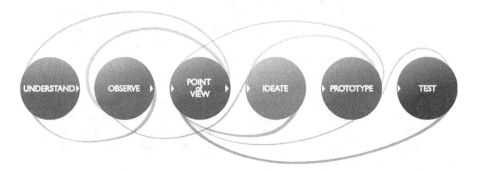

Fig. 1. Design thinking process; adapted from [4]

2   Design Thinking Journey

Since the past 5 years, SAP has adopted DT methodology [5, 6] to co-innovate with their customers during the product development lifecycle. DT is a flexible framework that allows people with diverse skills and professional backgrounds tackle complex problems and arrive at a set of ideas that can be prototyped and tested with customers prior to development. Human nature is to immediately try and solve a problem that presents itself. DT emphasizes to spend time in understand the problem from multiple perspectives and narrowing down to the core issues before proceeding to solve them. This not only get the whole product development team aligned on the product goals but also ensures that the correct problem gets solved. This is possible because End Users and their perspective is key to DT. The process kick starts in 2-day workshop with customers and the engagement continues throughout the product lifecycle through calls

---

[1] Design Thinking Methodology is a problem-solving methodology that was originally used to solve Business problems by David Kelley, founder and chairman of the global design and innovation company IDEO.

until several weeks where ideas and prototypes get validated. However, there are some challenges in executing this methodology in the world of cross located enterprises.

- Access to End users is not always easy especially in Large enterprises. Many times, in the world of on premise applications, the IT team of customers is the direct point of contact and it takes some effort convince them to include the end users into the discussion by letting them take some time off from their regular tasks.
- The DT tools and techniques need a certain amount of time to be carried out. Customer's time is precious and often there is a need to improvise on the techniques and come up with a proposal that works given the time and audience.
- Existing customer may also see this an opportunity to engage with us to address their current concerns, sometimes technical. While this is important, the focus should not be lost. There is a constant effort to channel the discussions in the right direction while ensuring customer concerns are also addressed.

Some learnings from conducting Design Thinking workshops, that could be applied to other products adopting this methodology is the importance to be flexible with the process and improvise. It is also important to manage customer expectations without losing focus. Sometimes, customer may need to see early design concepts as a proof of our commitment and knowledge in the domain. Though starting with solutions is against the design thinking philosophy, it helps in triggering discussions and getting customers to open up with their requirements. As time is always a constraint, planning ahead for research based on user profiles helps arranging meetings, calls efficiently.

3 Understand and Research

We conducted two Co-innovation DT workshops with our customers in the Services industry who were amongst the top 5 firms in Data Warehousing and Auditing in the United States of America (USA). Prior to the workshop at customer's location, we had a few calls with them to understand their problems and expectations. This helped us identify the need for a DT workshop to get to the core problem. Based on this, we prepared high level designs. Though it is not theoretically recommended to enter a DT workshop with a solution, in enterprises this approach often helps in motivating our customers to spend their time giving us valuable insights. The high-level designs also helped to kick start the discussions and paved way for an in-depth discussion of the product ecosystem, persona[2] [7], challenges and goals.

Each DT workshop had around 20 participants from the customer's end with diverse expertise like Project Managers, Business users and the IT experts. From SAP, we were a team of 7 comprising of roles like Solution Owner, Product Owner, User Experience Designer, Technical Architect, Lead Developer and SAP Consultants. The diverse set of experts helped us look at the product holistically from all perspectives like business needs, end user needs and high level technical challenges. While the plan

---

[2] Persona is a fictional character derived from user interviews to determine the user type for a product which helps understanding user goals, environment, needs, pain points to achieve certain tasks. This helps in guiding the solution to meet the user expectations.

was to have one to one end user interviews, we altered it to focus group [8] discussions to make the best use of everyone's time and knowledge. This helped us empathize with the key user of our product – the Project Manager who handled multiple projects, travelled often to meet their customers, had to balance budget, time and quality of the project. Research also helped us understand the severity of the issue. To help their project managers meet their goals, one of our customers had invested time and money in hiring a team of support staff who assisted project managers in data entry. They also built an in-house complex excel based solution that fetched information from various modules of SAP's software and showcased them in a unified screen. However, this not only added to the company's costs but also left room for delay and errors.

4   Synthesis

After both the workshops, the SAP team had a lot of research data from customers who managed their projects very differently and had stark contrasts in terms of the number of projects handled by a manager and the typical duration of each project. A main takeaway was how 'one size fits all' approach would not work for all our customers. While at a high level our customers had similar needs, the product also needed to be flexible enough to allow a lot of customization that would cater to the business of SAP's diverse customer portfolio. Currently, the project managers found the software very demanding in terms of usability and the time taken to access information. They had to proactively look for information and status updates thereby not having access to real time data upfront. Many times, they would perform the same action on a group of projects like updating status or changing the key contact person. Currently the product required them to manually update these for one project at a time. This was again causing a lot of frustration for project managers.

5   Ideation

After spending an extensive effort in creating design concepts, the designs underwent a series of design checks on SAP standard FIORI design guidelines [9]. During our brainstorming sessions to come up with ideas, it also became clear that we were looking at a suite of applications that can be accessed from a Fiori launch pad. These apps needed to be linked with each other as well. We proposed a unified dashboard view containing the list of all projects a manager is responsible for along with certain KPIs for each that would give insights into potential issues. We included customization capabilities. Personalization of filters was provided, ex: Projects belonging to a certain customer from a certain geography. There was also a solution provided to take bulk actions on a group of projects. From the Dashboard view, based on the insights the manager received he could investigate in detail by navigating into a dedicated Project View that provided a 360-degree perspective of the project and its performance. The dashboard informed the project manager about the debt and receivables, open purchase orders and requisitions that can potentially impact project margins. We came up with a

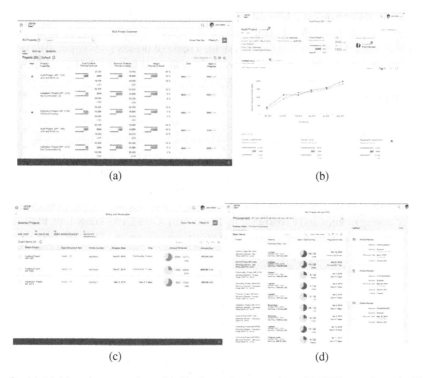

Fig. 2. (a) Multi-project overview; (b) Single project overview; (c) Billing and receivables; (d) Procurement overview.

set of four applications - Multi Project Overview, Single Project Overview, Billing and Receivables, Procurement Overview as shown in Fig. 2a, b, c, d.

6 Usability Evaluation

A usability study was conducted at ASUG on May 2016 at Orlando, Florida, USA. It involved users being asked to perform tasks to evaluate the product's ease of use, discoverability of the features and user's perception on the overall experience of the product.

6.1 Set up and Procedure

Each usability test was conducted by a moderator and a note taker for 90 min. The test began with an introduction that explained to the participants the nature of the test and the method of thinking aloud [10]. The users were given clickable prototypes on a laptop for the test. Each session was recorded using Camtasia 2 software on an Apple MacBook Pro laptop. Real-time screen recording and video/audio recording helped in capturing user's feedback and emotions. The test started with few background questions to deep dive into user's persona and his daily work environment. The users were then asked to complete various tasks. Moderators noted the level of assists that users needed to perform the task. User also rated each task on a scale of 0(Easy) – 5(Difficult). Post-test each user was asked to fill a post-test survey where the user had to rate the task on a scale of 0–7 on various measuring parameters like the ease of use, usefulness, consistency, terminology, recommending to others.

6.2   Participants

The usability test was conducted with a sample size of 11 users. Recruitment of users was done as part of the event. 11 out of 12 registered users attended the test. 5 of them were project managers, 4 were project directors, and 2 were independent project management consultants. The set of users who signed up for the testing were diverse in terms of demographics and experience in the domain. On a CPM know how basis 3 had CPM experience as they were CPM's co- innovation customers. Most of them had 10+ years expertise in the industry. 3 of them wanted early peek of the product to be able to sell it to the client.

6.3   Tasks Undertaken, Results and Recommendation

Finding the project with highest Cost Deviation using charts. Task intent was the user should consider the "Cost till current month "column in the table of multi project overview app as shown in Fig. 2a and find out maximum delta in a project from the list. Test result showed 10 out of 11 users could complete this task with an average of 2 assists. Average task rating was 4.3 out of 5.

Recommendation. Retain the use of charts with semantic colors as the graphical charts with semantic coloring helped users to identify good or bad situations in a project. Severity of this issue was recorded as low.

Adding additional columns to the table and save a variant of the table. Task intent was the user should trigger the settings button to open the view settings dialog as shown in Fig. 3 where he can add more columns to the table. He can save the displayed table as a variant from the table toolbar. Test result showed all 11 users could complete this task with an average of 4 assists. Average task rating was 2.6 out of 5.

Recommendation. Addition of save button on view settings dialog. The users could identify the settings icon but were struggling to find a save button on the dialog to save a variant for the table. Since there was no save button dialog the task could be completed only with assists. Severity of this issue was recorded as high.

Mass editing and editing content in a table. Task intent was the user should navigate to third tab called 'General' and mass edit the contact person. After that he should add a comment for a status under status tab as shown in Fig. 4a. Test result showed all 11 users could complete this task with an average of 3.5 assists. Average task rating was 3 out of 5.

Fig. 3. View settings dialog

Fig. 4. (a) Mass updating of project statuses and sub-statuses; (b) For selected projects view data.

Recommendation. Design evaluation required to make mass editing more intuitive. The users felt there were too many steps to do a mass update for a contact person. Severity of this issue was recorded as medium.

Navigating to other application by selecting few projects from the list. Task intent was the user should select few projects and click on "Open Selected In" button as shown in Fig. 4b to view list of other applications where he can further drill down. Test result showed 10 out of 11 users could complete this task with an average of 4 assists. Average task rating was 3 out of 5.

Recommendation. Usage of terminology for the button "Open In" needs to be changed. The terminology used for button "Open In" was found misleading for users resulting in increased level of assistance during the task. Severity of the issue was recorded as high.

Navigating to Procurement application from Multi Project Overview application and view Purchase order details. Task intent was the user should select few projects and click on 'Open Selected In' button as shown in Fig. 4b to view list of other applications where he can further drill down to Procurement application. Then user should click on one purchase order from the list to view details. Test Result showed 3 out of 11 users could complete this task with an average of 2 assists. Average task rating was 3.3 out of 5.

Recommendation. Usage of terminology for the button "Open In" needs to be changed. After knowing the technique of navigating to other apps from task 4, users could relate to this task and hence required lower level of assistance. Severity of this issue was recorded as high.

Navigating to detail page of a project from the list of projects. Task intent was the user clicks on the chevron icon placed at each row of the list of projects as shown in Fig. 2a to navigate detail page for each project. Test Results showed all 11 users could complete this task with an average of 1 assist. Average task rating was 4 out of 5.

Recommendation. No further recommendations as this task was very easily performed by each user. Severity of this issue was recorded as low.

6.4   Overall Results

The result from the usability tests indicates that the participants were impressed with the possibilities the application offers the aggregated unified view of all key Performance indicators (KPIs) in a single screen and ability to navigate to multiple transactional applications. The users felt the applications were easy to use once they were made aware about the functionalities for the first-time use. The users could not follow many terminologies used in the application. The chart plotted below Fig. 5 shows the post-test survey result based on various parameters.

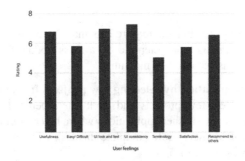

Fig. 5. Post usability test result of the applications as rated by users.

7   Conclusion

We designed, developed and released a Suite of SAP Fiori Enterprise Design applications to our customers by adopting the Design Thinking Methodology. Customers have started using these applications in their day to day life. Their project managers are benefitting from the real time KPI driven data that is pushed upfront to them and it helps them to take timely decisions. Usability tests revealed that customers are likely to recommend it to other companies as well.

Acknowledgements. The CPM Product Team helped us with domain knowledge and feedback on designs. Customers who shared time to co-innovate and validate the designs. Michelle Clary, from SAP Labs, Palo Alto, helped us in organizing the usability test and recruiting users for the test.

References

1. Bisk: Project Cost Management Strategies. Villanova University. https://www.villanovau. com/resources/project-management/project-cost-management-strategies/#.WPWubBKGPdc
2. Keith, H.: The Roles & Responsibilities of a Commercial Project Manager. Chron. http:// work.chron.com/roles-responsibilities-commercial-project-manager-27885.html
3. SE, S.: SAP Commercial Project Management. SAP SE (2017). https://www.sap.com/ product/plm/commercial-project-management.html. Accessed Mar 2017
4. SE, S.: Introduction to Design Thinking. SAP (2017). https://experience.sap.com/skillup/ introduction-to-design-thinking/
5. Hiremath, M., Sathiyam, V.: Fast train to DT: a practical guide to coach design thinking in software industry. In: Kotzé, P., Marsden, G., Lindgaard, G., Wesson, J., Winckler, M. (eds.) INTERACT 2013. LNCS, vol. 8119, pp. 780–787. Springer, Heidelberg (2013). doi:10. 1007/978-3-642-40477-1_53
6. Sathiyam, V., Hiremath, M.: Design re-thinking for the bottom of the pyramid: a case study based on designing business software for SMEs in India. In: CHI, Austin, Texas USA (2012)
7. Goodwin, K.: Designing for the Digital Age. Wiley Publishing Inc, New York (2009). ISBN 978-0-470-22910-1
8. Nielsen, J.: Usability Engineering. Morgan Kaufmann, Burlington (1993)
9. SAP, S.: SAP Fiori, 3 February 2015. https://www.sap.com/india/product/technology-platform/fiori.html
10. Clayton, L., Rieman, J.: Task-Centered User Interface Design: A Practical Introduction, Boulder, USA (1994). http://hcibib.org/tcuid/tcuid.pdf

Learning HCI Across Institutions, Disciplines and Countries: A Field Study of Cognitive Styles in Analytical and Creative Tasks

José Abdelnour-Nocera[1,2(✉)], Torkil Clemmensen[3],
and Tatiane G. Guimaraes[4]

[1] IT University of Copenhagen, Copenhagen, Denmark
josa@itu.dk
[2] Madeira Interactive Technologies Institute, Funchal, Portugal
[3] Copenhagen Business School, Frederiksberg, Denmark
tc.itm@cbs.dk
[4] Universidade Federal de Minas Gerais, Belo Horizonte, Brazil
tatiguimaraes@dcc.ufmg.br

Abstract. Human-computer interaction (HCI) is increasingly becoming a subject taught in universities around the world. However, little is known of the interactions of the HCI curriculum with students in different types of institutions and disciplines internationally. In order to explore these interactions, we studied the performance of HCI students in design, technology and business faculties in universities in UK, India, Namibia, Mexico and China who participated in a common set of design and evaluation tasks. We obtained participants' cognitive style profiles based on Allinson and Hayes scale in order to gain further insights into their learning styles and explore any relation between these and performance. We found participants' cognitive style preferences to be predominantly in the adaptive range, i.e. with combined analytical and intuitive traits, compared to normative data for software engineering, psychology and design professionals. We further identified significant relations between students' cognitive styles and performance in analytical and creative tasks of a HCI professional individual. We discuss the findings in the context of the distinct backgrounds of the students and universities that participated in this study and the value of research that explores and promotes diversity in HCI education.

Keywords: HCI education · Cognitive styles · Culture · Design · Evaluation

1 Introduction

The field of Human-Computer Interaction (HCI) is diverse in terms of institutions, disciplines, countries and the people who are or are becoming HCI researchers and practitioners. HCI focuses on the human users with their goals and tasks, needs and requirements, tools and contexts. This is not always be the case for other related disciplines [1]. Learning to do a HCI professional's work requires learning a specific skillset and qualifications. This knowledge is different from the one required by other

R. Bernhaupt et al. (Eds.): INTERACT 2017, Part IV, LNCS 10516, pp. 198–217, 2017.
DOI: 10.1007/978-3-319-68059-0_13

designers such as software engineers [2] and system developers [1], and which may even vary across countries [3].

HCI communities vary across the globe. While some countries are small and have only one HCI community, other countries are large and multicultural countries with several different HCI communities with distinct approaches, see e.g. [4]. HCI research and education should thus recognize the cross-cultural nature of the field [3]. It is quite likely that in the future HCI will further grow and get rather more diverse, and so will HCI education with respect to both contents and formats of teaching [1], and with regard to the diversity among students.

Diversity in students thinking and learning styles is important, as cognitive style can predict students' achievement in design and technology studies [5, 6]. Therefore, it is important to understand how likely students of HCI are to succeed in developing the required HCI skills. The research reported in this paper seeks to contribute to this understanding by exploring the interaction of aspects of the HCI curriculum with students across different institutions, disciplines and countries.

Previous research in higher education of computer science and information technology has established that academic performance is influenced by the cognitive styles of students [7] and by their culture [8]. However, HCI is a growing field increasingly taught in different cultural and professional contexts, not only in computer science but also in design and business, which lends itself to attract students with different cognitive styles. HCI students' cognitive styles may thus be diverse, and perhaps different from the cognitive styles of traditional computer science and engineering students. There is no universal standard or unified view on HCI education. The idea of a global unified curriculum has been deemed as implausible by a multinational survey [9]. Therefore, the lack of consideration of multicultural aspects in the HCI curriculum presents a challenge for promoting diversity in a field inherently aimed at satisfying human needs and goals [10].

This is why in this paper we try to address the question of cognitive styles and learning HCI in diverse contexts. We report how undergraduate HCI students engaged and performed in equal evaluation and design tasks in workshops conducted in institutions in China, Namibia, India, Mexico and the United Kingdom. This paper develops from a previous one where we reported preliminary findings about cognitive styles and cultural attitudes [11]. In this paper, we report the analysis of the complete dataset with extended findings and discuss implications for the study and promotion of diversity in HCI education through the construct of cognitive styles.

The paper first presents on overview of related work in HCI education and diversity and a review of cognitive style theory as a construct to study learning and cultural diversity. This is then followed by a presentation of the methodological design, the empirical settings, and the workshop structure. Findings related to the cognitive style profiles of HCI students, and how they performed in analytical and creative tasks are presented next. We then move on to a discussion of these findings in terms of related work in diversity in HCI and in terms of the different institutional, disciplinary and cultural contexts where the workshops took place. The paper concludes with a set of recommendations for HCI educators and paves the way for further research reflecting on the limitations and experiences of this project.

2 Studies of HCI Education, Disciplines and Countries

There are many studies regarding HCI Education around the world [12]. Some of them focus on specific contexts, such as how HCI has been taught in different countries or regions like Asia-Pacific [13], Brazil [14–16], China [17], Costa Rica [18], India [19], Mexico [20], Namibia [21], New Zealand [22], Romania [23], South Africa [24], and Sweden [25].

Each of these regions has their own challenges when it comes to HCI education, some of which are reported by the above-mentioned authors. For example, Pribenau and Chisăliţă [23] mention how politics, especially the communist period, has influenced the development of higher education in Romania, and the development of HCI as a field being integrated in different universities. In developing countries in the Asia-Pacific region such as Indonesia, Malaysia and Sri Lanka, HCI is not yet considered an essential subject, but an 'extra' [13]. This is also the reality in South Africa, where HCI is not considered part of the core of the curriculum for computing [24]. However, in some countries in the Asia-Pacific region, such as Singapore and Australia the opposite is the case. Sari and Wadhwa [13] also note that the promotion of HCI communities is essential to the growth of the field, using Indonesia as an example.

We can see this also in Brazil: one of the challenges faced by HCI was the lack of books in Portuguese to teach [15]. Results from a survey in this country six years later show how books produced by the Brazilian HCI community have been adopted in most undergraduate courses, showing the empowerment that comes from supporting national or regional communities [14].

In a survey about HCI education with New Zealand students and academics it is possible to see the differences on their interests regarding different topics – while students' most interested subject was Voice Telephony Interaction, this was the least important topic for academics [22]. This is an example of how communities formed by different groups – i.e., academics, students and practitioners – could increase the exchange of knowledge within a region.

Oestreicher and Gulliksen [25] report on the discussions of a national workshop on HCI education focused on curricula and course differences in Sweden. It is possible to see that even within the same country there is a great variety of courses that range from 3 weeks to 1 year of duration, from 6 to 175 students in class. More important than that, the report shows how this exchange and discussions are important for the community members and invaluable for further developing HCI education further in the country.

More recently, a report from the SIGCHI Education Project including several countries shows how important is for the HCI community to have a place where they can share this knowledge, which led to a proposal to develop a living curriculum [9]. This will be a space where members of the HCI community around the world can interact and share their perspectives and resources. The SIGCHI Education Project found that regional and contextual differences should be taken into consideration in the HCI curriculum. Hence, the curriculum should be flexible and diverse, offering locally relevant content to the students.

While the SIGCHI Education project as well as some of the work from authors referred to in this section point towards a clear need for HCI education and its curriculum to be flexible and sensitive to diverse needs, cultures and perspectives, more empirical research on student experience is needed. For instance, Calderon [18] reports her experiences in Costa Rica providing information not only on the HCI courses being taught, but also on the students that took these courses. Students fell in two categories: on one hand, undergraduate students, mostly full-time, not proficient in English, who know their classmates, enjoy working in groups, and do not generate discussions in class; and on the other hand, postgraduate students, part-time, who work during the day, with good in English due to their work, not very familiar with any of their classmates but who enjoy in-class discussions. This knowledge was then applied to the course design and delivery to make the students feel more comfortable and learn the same topics but in different ways – i.e. while the topics of both courses were very similar, the classes' format and evaluation were different for both classes. The overall results indicate students were satisfied with nearly 70% feeling they have met the learning outcomes comfortably. However, both cohorts indicated the need for more exposure to the practical elements of usability evaluation and interface design. On a similar approach, Day and Foley [26] report on how changing teaching methods by increasing online lectures to allow more co-located hands-on learning activities had a positive effect in the success rates for an HCI course.

We need more studies like that of Calderon's [18] or Day and Foley's [26] reporting on student experience and performance. Our research adds to this body of knowledge in HCI education by analyzing students' performance, taking their cognitive styles and diverse contexts into consideration. In the next section, we introduce the concept of cognitive style and the motivations for using it as construct to study cultural and learning diversity.

3 Relevant Cognitive Style Research

3.1 Culture and Cognitive Styles

The relation between culture, learning and cognitive styles has been well established by [27, 28]. These authors demonstrate how cultural positions influence holistic and analytic reasoning. Holistic reasoning indicates an orientation to the context or field as a whole, and analytical reasoning indicates a tendency to detach the object from its context in the search of causal relations. Using Hofstede's four dimensions of Power Distance, Uncertainty Avoidance, Individualism-Collectivism and Masculinity-Femininity [29], and the Theorist/Pragmatist scores of Honey and Mumford's Learning Style Questionnaire [30], Hayes and Allinson [28] identified two dimensions of learning style, Analysis and Action. Further research in this area led to Allinson and Hayes' Cognitive Style Index (CSI) [31], a compact questionnaire which is designed to test whether individuals tend more towards an intuitivist (right brain dominant) or analyst (left brain dominant) approach. Table 1 below indicates the score range for CSI.

In recent years the validity of measuring cognitive styles as a single analytical-intuitive dimension has been put to question [32], e.g., for studies of technology adoption and use [33]. Nevertheless, CSI as a construct remains as one of the most widely used measures of academic research in management and education [34, 35].

Table 1. CSI Scores Ranges

CSI score ranges for the five cognitive styles Style	Score range
Intuitive	0–28
Quasi-Intuitive	29–38
Adaptive	39–45
Quasi-Analytic	46–52
Analytic	53–76

In response to critiques, Alison and Hayes [36] have demonstrated the validity of their scale through independent tests. Thus, there is already a body of cognitive and learning styles research in higher education developed by an active community of academics [34, 37, 38].

3.2   Cognitive Styles in HCI Tasks

HCI may require different skills and thinking styles for different ends of the HCI professionals' work continuum between user studies/evaluations and sketching/prototyping/persona creation. Bishop-Clark [39] established early that within computer programming certain cognitive styles and personality dimensions affect some phases but not others. Capretz and co-authors have studied the relations between personality and software engineering for years [6, 40, 41]. In their attempt to map job requirements and skills to personality characteristics, they found that the analysis phase aims to establish users' needs, clients' requirements, system features and to provide abstract models of the to-be-designed application. These tasks and the related requirements for 'soft' people skills go well with personality traits such as being extrovert (likeable, expressive, talkative) and feeling–oriented (emotion-oriented, warm-hearted and have strong interpersonal skills). In contrast, the design phase aims to prototype, elaborate processing functions, and define input and output; these tasks and the related requirements for strong problem solving and innovative skills go well with strong thinking and intuitive personality traits. Further along the system development phase model, system testers need to pay attention to details and should display strong tendencies to be sensing and judging personalities. For HCI, the takeaway is not the precise correlation between the system development phases that may be defined and how they correlate with specific personality traits, but the idea is that predominantly analytical HCI tasks vs creative tasks may require different thinking styles among HCI professionals. So, if diversity among professionals is good in society, problem solving and in software engineering, it should also be good in HCI.

For analytic HCI evaluation tasks - such as usability evaluation tasks - we know that cognitive style has an impact and may be different across cultures. Clemmensen et al. [42] used the literature on cultural cognition, e.g. [43], to argue that classical think aloud usability evaluation assumes that humans are analytic thinkers who tend to separate different subtasks and states of information processing, but that in real life many users and evaluators - and in particular in Asia - tend to think more holistically.

For creative design tasks – such as creating a persona – there are indications from research with other software professionals, e.g. programmers, that designers have increased tendencies toward introversion and intuition preferences [6].

3.3 Normative CSI Data and Where HCI Should Sit

There is a body of research providing CSI normative data for different domains, compiled by Allison and Hayes [36] and shown in Table 2. This data places computing professionals and graduate psychology students as mainly adaptive with mean scores ranging from 43.34 to 38.01. There is no normative data that specifically relates to designers, but some normative data is provided for employees in the creative arts, who have a mean CSI score of 35.13 [44]. The sample size of this study was comparatively small (38 participants), but this score is substantially lower than the profile of the computing professionals and the psychology students presented in Table 2, suggesting a more intuitive approach.

Table 2. CSI Normative Data

Source	Sample	n	Mean	SD	CSI Style
Moore, O'Maiden & McElligott (2003) [7]	Irish computer systems students	145	43.34	11.43	Adaptive
Papavero (2005) [45]	Chinese software engineers	314	42.84	9.60	Adaptive
Allinson & Hayes (1996) [31]	Teachers	74	42.54	13.47	Adaptive
Frampton et al. (2006) [46]	Australian IT architects	40+	41.85	10.30	Adaptive
Park & Black (2007) [37]	US psychology grad students	31	41.77	10.74	Adaptive
Papavero (2005) [45]	US software engineers	158	40.45	11.5	Adaptive
Armstrong, Allinson & Hayes (1997) [38]	University lecturers	11	39.64	9.10	Adaptive
Allinson & Hayes (1996) [31]	IT managers	40	38.28	12.09	Quasi-Intuitive
Corbett (2007) [47]	US technology professionals	380	38.01	12.80	Quasi-Intuitive
Allinson & Hayes (1996) [31]	University lecturers	19	37.68	12.84	Quasi-Intuitive
Bennett (2010) [44]	Employees in the creative arts	38	35.13		Quasi-Intuitive

There is no data supplied specifically for HCI students, but as the subject of HCI generally has some psychology content, it would not be unreasonable to expect some similarity in the profile of HCI students on computing based courses with psychology students and computing professionals. This means that the expectation is that HCI students would tend to show a predominantly adaptive type of cognitive style.

4 Methodology

4.1 Why Explore the Relation Between CSI and HCI Student Performance

The body of research in HCI education we have presented above provides good descriptions of how HCI teaching occurs in different locations. It is reasonable to infer from this literature that HCI education and learning experiences differ because of local academic and professional cultures. However, it is challenging to visualize the cultural and learning preferences of students and how they shape their performance in learning tasks because their work is usually more private and inaccessible. Our research contributes toward addressing that visibility gap. In addition, there is no systematic research mapping the cognitive styles of HCI students with those of other disciplines and professions. Allinson and Hayes's CSI provides a parsimonious method to profile cultural and learning diversity in HCI students, as well as a substantial empirical work base based on this construct.

4.2 Methodological Design and Workshop Description

The study included visits to five different groups of undergraduate students in UK, India, Namibia, Mexico and China. They represent a broad set of demographics, economy and cultural conditions [12]. Furthermore, cultural usability research done in these countries suggest that while HCI research, practice, and education are growing everywhere, each country faces some unique HCI problems (e.g., Chinese Input Method Improvement [17], Indian design for low literacy [19], United Mexican States' need for unique state websites [20], or websites that can maintain cross-border connections) [48] and have different traditions for HCI research, practice and education (e.g., Chinese engineering psychology [17], Indian design schools [19], Mexican computer science [20]). However, none of the research so far has formally looked at correlating cultural and psychological profiles to learning performance in HCI education across a set of countries, universities, and disciplines.

The participant universities were Namibian University of Science and Technology (NUST), the Instituto Tecnológico Autónomo de México (ITAM), the Indian Institute of Technology Guwahati (IITG), the Dalian Maritime University in China (DMU), and University of West London (UWL). All 5 institutions are well known within their country. Within these institutions, HCI was a core subject in NUST and UWL, an option in ITAM, embedded within the whole curriculum in IITG and a core subject in the last semesters in DMU's Computer Science course. The visit also included meetings with lecturers and staff in charge of curriculum design in which we were able to have an understanding of the educational programs and the local context. The educational programs were also different across the surveyed institutions: digital design in IITG, software engineering in UWL and NUST, business engineering and management in ITAM and computer science in DMU. The groups of students who completed the survey were nationals of the same country, except in Namibia where we had two Angolans and one South African, and the UK, where 10 different nationalities or cultural backgrounds were represented, reflecting the cosmopolitan character of the university.

In each university, between 18 and 22 undergraduate HCI students were asked to complete the CSI survey [31] and engage in a workshop, which included HCI analytic and creative tasks for a science education portal. All participants had a similar level of instruction in HCI, and none had taken similar subjects in previous semesters. The activity given to students contained elements focusing on analytical and holistic thinking, i.e. heuristic evaluation as stimulating analytic thinking and persona creation as stimulating intuitive thinking. The performance of students in the workshop was analyzed and correlated in terms of their cognitive styles and task outputs.

The format of the workshop and data collection was planned in consultation with lead tutors in the five participant universities. The authors and partners in each country made sure the content and activities of workshop were of learning value to all participants. The workshop activities and materials were based on those of a real usability evaluation project in which one of the authors of this paper participated. This was done to secure validity, relevance and comparability with HCI industrial practice. The workshop materials and CSI questionnaires were sent to each course leader a week in advance of each visit. The course leader identified a suitable class and scheduled the workshop at a convenient time. In all cases, students completed the CSI questionnaire before the workshop took place.

As mentioned in Sect. 3.1, the CSI survey is a compact questionnaire to identify peoples' approach when thinking about problems. It includes a set of statements the students should mark as true, false or uncertain about themselves. This way, for each statement the student should choose answer closest to their own opinion. Examples of statements in the survey are: *"I am most effective when my work involves a clear sequence of tasks to be performed"*, and *"I make decisions and get on with things rather than analyse every last detail"*. The results CSI survey [3] were used to situate each student in an analytical-intuitive scale.

The workshop was structured according to the following stages: (a) briefing, explanation of heuristics and personas (45 min); (b) introduction to SEED portal and relevant scenarios; individual heuristic Instrument and persona creation tasks for 'school teacher' and 'student' (45 min); and (c) debriefing (up to 30 min).

After the briefing (stage a), the students were introduced to a learning node in a science education portal sponsored by Schlumberger Excellence in Education Development (SEED) program and relevant use scenarios. The target audience of this portal was schoolchildren aged between 10 and 18. HCI students participating in our study were required to conduct their tasks by considering this context. The SEED portal supported several language options, allowing students to use their preferred language option and concentrate on the task in question. The following is an example of one of the scenarios used:

"Mary, a 14-year-old girl, is ready to complete their science activity on Porosity. She is sitting together with her teacher who is guiding her on the objectives of this activity, which must be completed in the portal. The particular task she needs to do is to experiment with the Porosity Explorer and then to read the two accompanying pages, Hands-on Porosity Explorer and Porosity Explorer: How we built it and why it behaves the way it does. The teacher guides her to the start point of the task within the portal and then lets her complete the task. Once the activity is completed, Mary and her teacher should feel satisfied that the learning objectives have been accomplished and that the usability of the portal has supported this process fully

leading to a positive user experience. As a usability consultant in India you should look at this task in the portal and evaluate the extent to which this portal will be usable by local students and teachers attracting a positive user experience."

With scenarios like this in mind, each HCI student conducted a heuristic evaluation and created personas [49] individually.

In the heuristic evaluation task, the student should consider a set of five heuristics: Visibility of system status; Match between system and the real world; Consistency and standards; Help users recognize, diagnose and recover from errors; and Recognition rather than recall. For each heuristic, they should mark it as Violated, Not violated or Can't be assessed. In addition, they should explain their reasoning behind their answer, provide examples, and indicate recommendations for redesign if the heuristic was violated. The richness of observations in each student's heuristic assessment varied, and that was taken into consideration in our analysis. We quantified this richness according to the scale on Table 3. This way, we labeled with a three an answer such as *"Missing error messages when the user tries to fill without the beaker. The volume setting works but fill button doesn't. Either all should be enabled or none"*; and with a one an answer such as *"Error messages absent. No guidance if student not able to understand what is to be done".*

Table 3. Scale used to code the level of richness for each heuristic assessment done by students

Richness	Criteria
3	Clear example reference to a concrete aspect of the design of Planetseed.
2	Reference to the website but only a general comment, description is provided. It is not possible to identify reference to a concrete aspect of the site.
1	General comment about the heuristic without clearly referring to website.
0	No meaningful comment or no comment provided but a Yes, NO or NA was recorded for each question about the design.

In the persona task, each student was asked to produce a persona for a 'teacher' using the portal to support their students, and a persona for a 'student' using the portal in the school. Both the 'teacher' and the 'student' were introduced to the HCI students through the scenarios included in the workshop materials, such as the one presented above. In a similar way to the heuristic evaluation task, the persona descriptions varied in depth. For the persona creation, the number of features added to each persona per students was quantified. The features counted were categorized into physical, skills, context and psychological. For example, a student persona was described as *"Has many friends. Good in maths, science. Goes to school in class 8. Watches TV. Plays football."*. The text shows one skill feature and four context features, with a total of five features.

The performance of students in the workshop was analyzed and correlated with the findings for CSI profiles. The analysis centered on the distribution of CSI scores across the five groups. These values would then be used to compare with normative CSI data for related professions, and to explore if there is any correlation between CSI and performance in both tasks. The performance of each group was also compared to test for any difference with an analysis of variance (ANOVA). The next section presents the findings from running these analyses.

5   Results

5.1   CSI Score Profiles and Distribution

A total of one hundred HCI students surveyed across the five institutions completed the CSI survey. The total mean for all students was 42.51 falling clearly in the adaptive band (Table 4). This score falls between normative data for students of psychology and computer science provided in Table 2, which meets our expectations for HCI students as discussed in Sect. 2.

Table 4. CSI Mean Scores

Country Group	Mean Score	N	Std. Deviation
China (DMU)	44.2500	20	9.83482
India (IITG)	42.1429	21	7.08721
Mexico (ITAM)	42.6818	22	9.30124
Namibia (NUST)	37.6667	18	10.49930
UK (UWL)	45.4737	19	7.74861
Total	42.5100	100	9.13810

CSI mean scores for all groups indicate a predominant adaptive cognitive style, except NUST's, which sits in the upper end of the quasi-intuitive range. An ANOVA test was performed in order to establish if statistically significant differences exist between the country groups' means. The resulting test shows that variances across all groups can be compared and no significant difference between CSI profiles for each group was found [$F(4,95) = 2.037$, $p = .095$].

While no statistical difference in the means can be found, the percentage distribution of CSI profiles for each country group shows the IITG student group differing from the rest. China, Mexico, Namibia and UK have 70%, 73%, 78% and 79% respectively falling in the categories of quasi-intuitive, adaptive and quasi analyst; however, in the case of the Indian students, 95% fell into this range (Table 5). Possible reasons for this will be discussed in the next section when looking at the context of each student group in more detail.

Table 5. CSI Profile Count and Percentage Distribution

CSI Profile	China		India		Mexico		Namibia		UK		Total
	n	%	n	%	n	%	n	%	n	%	%
Analyst	5	25,00	1	4,76	4	18,18	1	5,56	4	21,05	15,00
Quasi analyst	4	20,00	7	33,33	5	22,73	4	22,22	6	31,58	26,00
Adaptive	4	20,00	5	23,81	6	27,27	5	27,78	5	26,32	25,00
Quasi intuitive	6	30,00	8	38,10	5	22,73	5	27,78	4	21,05	28,00
Intuitive	1	5,00	0	0,00	2	9,09	3	16,67	0	0,00	6,00
Total	**20**	**100,00**	**21**	**100,00**	**22**	**100,00**	**18**	**100,00**	**19**	**100,00**	**100,00**

5.2   Heuristic Evaluation Performance Analysis

Out of the hundred students surveyed, sixty-one attempted and completed the heuristic evaluation and persona creation tasks. It was not always possible for the students who completed the survey to attend the workshop due to scheduling and personal reasons. From all the students who participated on the workshop, the group with the highest relative participation was China with 32.8% (20 students), followed by India with 23% (14 students), Namibia with 21.3% (13 students), UK with 13.1% (8 students) and Mexico with 9.8% (6 students).

Considering the performance of all groups, CSI scores correlate positively with performance in the heuristics evaluation task $[r = 0.281, n = 61, p = 0.028]$. This means the higher the analytical cognitive profile for a student, the more likely this student will provide a richer analysis. A similar correlation test was applied to performance in the persona creation task but no significant correlation was found $[r = 0.190, n = 53, p = 0.890]$.

Comparing heuristic evaluation performance for each institution some differences can be observed (Table 6). The Indian country group displayed the richest set of heuristic evaluations.

Table 6. Heuristic Task Performance Means per Country Group

Country Group	N	Mean	SD
India (IITG)	14	2.5286	.44795
Namibia (NUST)	13	1.9577	.56673
UK (UWL)	8	1.8500	.48697
China (DMU)	20	2.2300	.48677
Mexico (ITAM)	6	2.3667	.44572
Total	**61**	**2.2041**	**.53317**

An ANOVA reveals a statistically significant difference between group means $[F(4,56) = 3.535, p = .012]$. The Tukey post hoc test (Table 7) shows the performance of India (IITG) to be significantly different from those of UK(UWL) and Namibia (NUST).

5.3   Persona Creation Performance Analysis

There was a fall in the number of completed persona creation tasks (53) with respect to the heuristic evaluation task (61) because some Indian students ran out of time or had to leave the workshop earlier. As with the heuristic evaluation task, country group differences, between performance means in completing this task were also observed. Table 8 shows students from DMU in China with the highest mean for persona richness.

An ANOVA reveals a statistically significant difference between group means $[F(4,48) = 4.901, p = .002]$.. The Tukey post hoc test shows this difference lies mainly between the best and worst performers in the task, namely China (DMU) and Namibia (NUST) (Table 9).

Table 7. Tukey HSD Multiple Comparisons Post Hoc Test

(I) Country	(J) Country	Mean Difference (I-J)	Std. Error	Sig.	95% Confidence Interval	
					Lower Bound	Upper Bound
India (IITG)	Namibia	.57088*	.18994	.031	.0355	1.1062
	UK	.67857*	.21856	.024	.0625	1.2946
	China	.29857	.17184	.420	-.1858	.7829
	Mexico	.16190	.24062	.961	-.5163	.8401
Namibia (NUST)	India	-.57088*	.18994	.031	-1.1062	-.0355
	UK	.10769	.22159	.988	-.5169	.7323
	China	-.27231	.17569	.535	-.7675	.2229
	Mexico	-.40897	.24339	.454	-1.0950	.2770
UK (UWL)	India	-.67857*	.21856	.024	-1.2946	-.0625
	Namibia	-.10769	.22159	.988	-.7323	.5169
	China	-.38000	.20629	.360	-.9615	.2015
	Mexico	-.51667	.26632	.309	-1.2673	.2340
China (DMU)	India	-.29857	.17184	.420	-.7829	.1858
	Namibia	.27231	.17569	.535	-.2229	.7675
	UK	.38000	.20629	.360	-.2015	.9615
	Mexico	-.13667	.22954	.975	-.7837	.5103
Mexico (ITAM)	India	-.16190	.24062	.961	-.8401	.5163
	Namibia	.40897	.24339	.454	-.2770	1.0950
	UK	.51667	.26632	.309	-.2340	1.2673
	China	.13667	.22954	.975	-.5103	.7837

*. The mean difference is significant at the 0.05 level.

Table 8. Persona Creation Performance Means per Country Group

Country Group	N	Mean	SD
India (IITG)	6	17.3333	9.91295
Namibia (NUST)	13	13.0769	5.69300
UK (UWL)	8	15.8750	6.55608
China (DMU)	20	22.6500	5.43163
Mexico (ITAM)	6	20.0000	6.69328
Total	**53**	**18.3774**	**7.29654**

Table 9. Analysis of Variance for Persona Creation Task Performance

(I) Country	(J) Country	Mean Difference (I-J)	Std. Error	Sig.
Namibia (NUST)	India	-4.25641	3.15839	.663
	Uk	-2.79808	2.87560	.866
	China	-9.57308*	2.27985	.001
	Mexico	-6.92308	3.15839	.200

6 Discussion

Our findings merit discussion in relation to the diverse contexts in which the studies took place. There are implications for the nature of HCI as a distinct field in the context of related disciplines, and implications for the study of cognitive styles in the learning of HCI.

6.1 HCI Cognitive Styles: Between Arts and Computer Science

The overall CSI mean distribution for all students surveyed is 42.51 (SD = 9.13), which falls clearly in the adaptive band. This mean falls below scores for students in computer science, software engineering and psychology, and is more analytical than students of arts courses, as reported in Table 2. This reinforces our expectations that HCI professionals need to be able to draw on a balance of intuitive and analytical skills to perform the best possible solutions for users within a good understanding of the affordances and constraints provided by technological systems. Furthermore, these findings are also in line with ongoing cognitive style research on more than 300 HCI professionals (practitioners, educators and those who are both) where 66% of practitioners are clustered in and around the adaptive bands [50]. This study also reports HCI educators to be more analytical and those who have both roles to be the most intuitive of the three professional groups studied.

Our findings on the cognitive styles of HCI students resonate with those of the above mentioned studies on HCI professionals [50] and students [18, 26]: there is a clear need to develop more skills natural to the adaptive-intuitive range of cognitive styles, which are needed to support situated and creative design practice.

6.2 Cognitive Style Congruence with Analytical and Creative Tasks

We found a positive correlation between CSI scores and the performance of the heuristic evaluation, which is fundamentally an analytical task. This echoes findings by Moore [7] when comparing computer science students' cognitive styles with their academic performance. This finding indicates that analytical HCI tasks can be sensitive to students with congruent cognitive styles. However, when correlating the persona creation task with student performance we did not find the expected negative correlation where students with lower CSI scores, i.e. more intuitive, would be more likely to produce richer personas. In retrospective, in the schools participating in our research with educational programs with a strong analytical orientation and where the relation between tutor and students is very hierarchical, our assessment of the persona creation task might not necessarily have measured HCI students' level of empathy with the user types presented in the scenarios, but measured the compliance with the tutors' instructions on the analytic and systematic application of the persona method. This was the case with DMU students as discussed below.

While these correlations are mainly indicative and cognitive styles only explain a percentage of the overall variance between students in their learning, e.g. [51], our results pave the way for more systematic studies of HCI curriculum adoption and development sensitive to diverse cognitive and learning styles.

6.3   Supporting the Case for Quasi-Intuitive and Adaptive Styles When Comparing Task Performance

We consider the following facts in discussing the differences between Namibia (NUST) and China (DMU) found in the ANOVA for the persona creation task. The Namibian group has the lowest CSI mean score, in the upper end of the quasi-intuitive band, and is the only group not in the adaptive band (Table 4), though close to it. This group produced the lowest number of features in the personas they created. In contrast, the Chinese group were the most analytical group, with a CSI score in the upper range of adaptive, and the best performers in the persona creation tasks, i.e. they added more features to their personas. Therefore, following the reflection from the previous section about the nature of the persona creation task, we could see how the group with the more intuitive profile, i.e. the lowest CSI score, might not explicitly include as many features to the persona descriptions due to the high-context nature of the group, which corresponds with the generally collectivistic cultural traits for sub-Saharan Africans documented in cultural [52] as well as HCI research for that region [53–55]

In discussing differences in the performance of the HCI heuristic evaluation task, there is also an interesting observation. As indicated in Table 6, 95% of students from India (IITG) were situated in the three central bands (quasi-analytic, adaptive, quasi-intuitive) of the CSI scale, with a mean CSI of 42.14 and the lowest standard deviation (SD = 7.08) of all the groups. One possible reason for the high concentration of profiles around the adaptive band could be due to the unique nature of their educational program. IITG has both a Department of Computer Science and Engineering and a Department of Design. The students who took part in these workshops were design students, but were admitted thorough a competitive process consisting of an admission test based on maths and algorithms. This filter is likely to admit analytical students with an aptitude for design, which in CSI terms means adaptive students. Interestingly, the highest score for heuristic evaluation richness belongs to this group. This theoretically suggests adaptive students are better prepared to engage in usability evaluations with a balance of analytic and intuitive skills.

As an additional validity check we compared the CSI profile count distribution for only those students who completed the design and evaluation tasks and the same proportions were maintained: the Indian group showed the highest concentration in the central bands (quasi-intuitive, adaptive and quasi analytical) with 92.9%; the Namibian was group was the lowest cluster of CSI scores with 46.2% in the intuitive and quasi-intuitive bands; the Chinese group retained the highest concentration of students with CSI scores in the top bands (quasi-analytical and analytical) with 45%.

6.4   Institutional Cultures and the Perceived Value of HCI in the Curriculum

Institutional cultures not only influenced student performance in the workshops, but also their level of participation. China (DMU) and India (IITG) had the highest workshop attendance and completion rate where almost all students who filled the CSI survey attempted and finished the tasks. In these institutions students carefully followed instructions from their tutors and the process of booking classrooms and fitting the workshops into their timetable went smoothly. Organizing the workshops in ITAM was more challenging. ITAM is a highly ranked private technological university in Mexico. Their institutional discourse takes pride in a tradition of forming elites that will manage and lead the country reinforcing a culture of individualism, independence and competitiveness, giving students more control of their study time and choices. This made it difficult to timetable and run the workshops in the same space and time slots, which translated into lower participation when compared to the other country groups. UK (UWL) was also challenging as students are also seen as more independent, with those taking the HCI module were coming from different educational programs, each of which had different patterns of attendance.

The role of HCI as a subject in the curriculum of the five institutions is an important factor to consider. While HCI is core in both IITG and DMU programs, the Indian students seemed more intrinsically motivated and proactive to engage in the tasks than Chinese students, who were mainly reactive and followed the instructions of their tutors. While we cannot establish or isolate the main reasons for this difference, the fact that IITG students were in a design school and DMU students were in an engineering school could be a contributing factor. For the UK (UWL) students, HCI is a core module shared in most of the information technology degree courses, with the students from different nationalities ranging from those with a business specialism to those on more programming focused programs, which may explain the more even spread of the CSI profiles and workshop performance. ITAM students in Mexico took HCI as an option in the later stages of their business educational program, and the value of the HCI subject in their education was not always immediately clear as expressed in comment during the workshops. In London, UWL students in the more technical programs made similar comments about not seeing how HCI can help them 'build software programs'. This is an important observation where institutions with a techno-centric culture will present bigger challenges to the adoption of HCI in their programs, which coincides with findings from a recent case study of HCI education in Egypt [56].

6.5 Implications for HCI Education Curriculum Development and Delivery

Our findings suggest that HCI education face two major challenges. One is supporting the cognitive styles necessary for learning and doing the creative tasks in HCI. The other is supporting the steadily increasing diversity in delivery, location, and face value of HCI education curriculum.

First, our findings show that HCI students are less analytical than CS but more than art students, and that there is a clear advantage of being adaptive-analytical in the current HCI curricula. This suggests that we should perhaps promote tolerance towards both analytical and creative styles within class and within the individual HCI students. We should think of HCI students as creative designers who should be encouraged to be intuitive and thinking like the programmers studies by Capretz and others, e.g. [6, 39, 40]. It is less clear, however, how to support intuitive thinking in HCI students, or how to make students become more adaptive rather than pure analytical.

One way we observed this could be done is by recruitment. In India the national admission system and technological universities favour and recruit clearly analytical thinkers and then put them into a clearly design oriented study program that requires intuitive thinking [4]. This could also be done the other way around, recruiting mainly intuitive thinkers to more analytical HCI study programs, e.g. more evaluation oriented study programs. However, while we as teachers of HCI perhaps tend to teach the analytical curriculum, or we do it with an analytical approach, there is a clear need to develop a dedicated curriculum for intuitive-adaptive students, and to support the student-as-designer's cognitive style in HCI education.

Second, we found many differences in the delivery of HCI education between institutions, disciplines, and countries that we found in this study. Such results imply that we should support diversity in delivery, location, and value of HCI curricula. HCI literature already has good awareness and acceptance of such diversity, e.g. pointing to the challenges faced by HCI in Brazil of lacking good HCI books in Portuguese to teach [15], or focusing on emic perspectives in the global south [57]. As pointed out by other authors, e.g. [13], the promotion of HCI communities is really important to the growth of the field. We will add that the promotion of the HCI community should be sensitive to and support diversity in the development of HCI communities, while at the same time keeping the international outlook in the HCI curricula.

Overall, this study helps to increase awareness of diversity in cognitive style and institutions and countries. Such awareness can be used not necessarily to align with students' cognitive styles, but rather to support and inform student study strategies, making the teacher aware of typical student outcome in HCI courses, and in general support of more metacommunication within and around HCI education.

7   Conclusions

The overall aim of this study is to explore the interactions of the HCI curriculum with students in different types of institutions and disciplines internationally. In doing this, we promote and contribute to an understanding of diversity in HCI education, which is crucial given the main mission of this discipline is to support human interactions from diverse backgrounds with technology. We have focused on the relation between cognitive styles as a cultural and learning construct [28], and how undergraduate students of HCI engage with analytical and creative tasks. Our findings have implications not only for HCI education but also for wider professional field. The findings also contribute to the field of cognitive styles by providing normative data for a hundred students of HCI.

We were able to empirically confirm our expectation that HCI students tend to display adaptive cognitive styles. Compared with normative data for cognitive styles in other disciplines and professions, HCI can be seen as an adaptive field between those of psychologists, and engineers and computer scientists, and above the more intuitive field of art and design. There is also an observed correlation between cognitive styles and performance in heuristic evaluation. Statistically significant differences were also encountered in how groups performed the evaluation and creative tasks.

At a higher level, there are also interesting observations about how student engagement with the workshops was shaped by institutional, disciplinary and national factors. While these factors cannot be empirically isolated in this exploratory study, there are interesting convergences between CSI profiles, cultural behaviors and task performance. For example, we have seen how the group with the highest concentration of adaptive students, delivered the richest set of evaluations; or how the group with the highest concentration of intuitive and quasi-intuitive students produced personas with lowest number of features, fulfilling a cultural high-context expectation for Namibia. We can also see how the relative position and value of HCI in the curricula of the studied universities corresponded with the level of student participation at the workshop stage.

7.1   Key Insights for the Nature of HCI Tasks and Education

What can this mean in practice for teaching HCI in the Global South, and/or introducing HCI as a new subject in strongly technical, design or business driven institutions? The key insights for the nature of HCI tasks and education have already been discussed above, but in short form the takeaways are that we as HCI educators should:

- Develop a dedicated curriculum for intuitive-adaptive students, and which supports the student-as-designer's cognitive style in HCI education;
- Support diversity in delivery, location, and value of HCI curricula, including HCI in different types of school around the world, e.g. business, design, or computer science;
- Promote the HCI communities with a focus on local institutions, disciplines, and students' needs, while at the same time keeping the international outlook of HCI;
- Increase our awareness of diversity in students' cognitive style in various institutions and countries; and
- Support more metacommunication within and around HCI education.

This study is one small contribution to enable metacommunication about HCI education.

7.2   Limitations and Further Work

The limitations of this study are plenty since HCI education hardly is a stable easily studied topic. However, we feel that by focusing on well-defined constructs of cognitive styles and measuring these, and then placing the findings in rich and detailed descriptions of the educational, disciplinary and country contexts, we provided a contribution to the HCI community's knowledge about HCI education. Despite this, and given the value of what we found, we acknowledge that a more balanced and systematic approach combining qualitative and quantitative methods is needed for to the study of culture and context in HCI education. The time and resource constraints under which this project was conducted made it challenging to follow such an approach.

In this study we have highlighted the need for, on one hand, more controlled and extensive studies to establish relation between cognitive styles (and other constructs such as cultural attitudes) and student performance and experience; and, on the other hand, studies aimed at sharing of practice and experiences across different institutional and disciplinary context to understand the opportunities and constraints to develop a more diverse HCI curriculum as suggested by Churchill et al. [9]. An obvious next step is study progression in HCI curricula – some courses should be basic and some advanced – to see how progression and diversity in HCI education can get together across institutions, disciplines and countries. We are also currently engaged in ongoing research focusing on the cognitive styles and preferences of HCI professionals, including practitioners and educators to have a better understanding of the gaps between education and practice [50].

References

1. Gross, T.: Human-Computer Interaction Education and Diversity. In: Kurosu, M. (ed.) HCI 2014. LNCS, vol. 8510, pp. 187–198. Springer, Cham (2014). doi:10.1007/978-3-319-07233-3_18

2. Clemmensen, T., Nørbjerg, J.: Separation in theory, coordination in practice – teaching HCI and SE. Softw. Process Improv. Pract. **8**, 99–110 (2003)

3. Gasparini, I., Salgado, Luciana C.de C., Pereira, R.: The Brazilian HCI Community Perspectives in Cultural Aspects in HCI. In: Rau, P.-L.P. (ed.) CCD 2016. LNCS, vol. 9741, pp. 53–62. Springer, Cham (2016). doi:10.1007/978-3-319-40093-8_6

4. Yammiyavar, P.: Status of HCI and Usability Research in Indian Educational Institutions. In: Katre, D., Orngreen, R., Yammiyavar, P., Clemmensen, T. (eds.) HWID 2009. IAICT, vol. 316, pp. 21–27. Springer, Heidelberg (2010). doi:10.1007/978-3-642-11762-6_2

5. Zhang, L.-F.: Revisiting the predictive power of thinking styles for academic performance. J. Psychol. **138**, 351–370 (2004)

6. Cruz, S., da Silva, F.Q., Capretz, L.F.: Forty years of research on personality in software engineering: A mapping study. Comput. Hum. Behav. **46**, 94–113 (2015)

7. Moore, S., O'Maidin, D., McElligott, A.: Cognitive styles among computer systems students: Preliminary findings. J. Comput. High. Educ. **14**, 45–67 (2003)

8. Carter, L., Jernejcic, L., Lim, N.: Success in CS: Is culture a factor? In: 2007 37th Annual Frontiers in Education Conference - Global Engineering: Knowledge Without Borders, Opportunities Without Passports, pp. T3A–16–T3A–21 (2007)

9. Churchill, E.F., Bowser, A., Preece, J.: The Future of HCI Education: A Flexible, Global, Living Curriculum. Interactions, vol. 23, pp. 70–73 (2016)

10. Collazos, C.A., Granollers, T., Gil, R., Guerrero, L.A., Ochoa, S.F.: Multicultural aspects in HCI-curricula. Innov. Creat. Educ. **2**, 1584–1587 (2010)

11. Abdelnour-Nocera, J., Michaelides, M., Austin, A., Modi, S.: A Cross-national Study of HCI Education Experience and Representation. In: HCI International 2013 (2013)

12. Douglas, I., Liu, Z. (eds.): Global Usability. Springer, London (2011)

13. Sari, E., Wadhwa, B.: Understanding HCI education across Asia-Pacific. In: Proceedings of the ASEAN CHI Symposium 2015, pp. 36–41. ACM, New York (2015)

14. Boscarioli, C., Silveira, Milene S., Prates, R.O., Bim, S.A., Barbosa, S.D.J.: Charting the Landscape of HCI Education in Brazil. In: Kurosu, M. (ed.) HCI 2014. LNCS, vol. 8510, pp. 177–186. Springer, Cham (2014). doi:10.1007/978-3-319-07233-3_17

15. de Souza, C.S., Baranauskas, M.C.C., Prates, R.O., Pimenta, M.S.: HCI in Brazil: lessons learned and new perspectives. In: Proceedings of the VIII Brazilian Symposium on Human Factors in Computing Systems, pp. 358–359. Sociedade Brasileira de Computação, Porto Alegre, Brazil (2008)

16. Prates, R.O., Filgueiras, L.V.L.: Usability in Brazil. In: Douglas, I., Liu, Z. (eds.) Global Usability, pp. 91–109. Springer, London (2011)

17. Liu, Z., Zhang, J., Zhang, H., Chen, J.: Usability in China. In: Douglas, I., Liu, Z. (eds.) Global usability, pp. 111–135. Springer, London (2011)
18. Calderon, M.: Teaching human computer interaction: First experiences. CLEI Electron. J. **12**, 1–9 (2009)
19. Joshi, A., Gupta, S.: Usability in India. In: Douglas, I., Liu, Z. (eds.) Global Usability, pp. 153–168. Springer, London (2011)
20. Rocha, M.A.M.: Usability in Mexico. In: Douglas, I., Liu, Z. (eds.) Global Usability, pp. 223–236. Springer, London, London (2011)
21. Winschiers, H.: The challenges of participatory design in a intercultural context: designing for usability in namibia. In: PDC, pp. 73–76 (2006)
22. Sharkey, E., Paynter, J.: CHI education in New Zealand. Bull. Appl. Comput. Inf. Technol. **2**(3) (2004). http://www.naccq.ac.nz/bacit/0203/2004Sharkey_CHINZ.htm
23. Pribeanu, C., Chisăliță, C.: A historical perspective of HCI development in Romania. In: CHI 2004 Extended Abstracts on Human Factors in Computing Systems, pp. 1023–1024. ACM, New York (2004)
24. Kotzé, P.: Directions in HCI education, research, and practice in southern Africa. In: CHI 2002 Extended Abstracts on Human Factors in Computing Systems, pp. 524–525. ACM, New York (2002)
25. Oestreicher, L., Gulliksen, J.: HCI education in Sweden. SIGCHI Bull. **31**, 4–7 (1999)
26. Day, J., Foley, J.: Evaluating web lectures: a case study from HCI. In: CHI 2006 Extended Abstracts on Human Factors in Computing Systems, pp. 195–200. ACM, New York (2006)
27. Nisbett, R.E., Miyamoto, Y.: The influence of culture: holistic versus analytic perception. Trends Cogn. Sci. **9**, 467–473 (2005)
28. Hayes, J., Allinson, C.W.: Cultural differences in the learning styles of managers. Manag. Int. Rev. **28**, 75–80 (1988)
29. Hofstede, G.: Cultures and Organizations: Software of the Mind. Mc Graw-Hill, Berkshire (1991)
30. Honey, P., Mumford, A.: 7 Styles of learning. Gower Handb. Manag. Dev. **101**, 101–111 (1994)
31. Allinson, C.W., Hayes, J.: The cognitive style index: A measure of intuition-analysis for organizational research. J. Manag. Stud. **33**, 119–135 (1996)
32. Hodgkinson, G.P., Sadler-Smith, E.: complex or unitary? a critique and empirical re-assessment of the allinson-hayes cognitive style index. J. Occup. Organ. Psychol. **76**, 243–268 (2003)
33. McElroy, J.C., Hendrickson, A.R., Townsend, A.M., DeMarie, S.M.: Dispositional factors in internet use: personality versus cognitive style. MIS Q. **31**, 809–820 (2007)
34. Evans, C., Cools, E., Charlesworth, Z.M.: Learning in higher education–how cognitive and learning styles matter. Teach. High. Educ. **15**, 467–478 (2010)
35. Cools, E., Armstrong, S.J., Verbrigghe, J.: Methodological practices in cognitive style research: Insights and recommendations from the field of business and psychology. Eur. J. Work Organ. Psychol. **23**, 627–641 (2014)
36. Allinson, C., Hayes, J.: The cognitive style index: Technical manual and user guide. (2012). Accessed 13 Jan 2014
37. Park, Y., Black, J.B.: Identifying the impact of domain knowledge and cognitive style on web-based information search behavior. J. Educ. Comput. Res. **36**, 15–37 (2007)
38. Armstrong, S., Allinson, C.W., Hayes, J.: The implications of cognitive style for the management of student-supervisor relationships. Educ. Psychol. **17**, 209–217 (1997)
39. Bishop-Clark, C.: Cognitive style, personality, and computer programming. Comput. Hum. Behav. **11**, 241–260 (1995)

40. Capretz, L.F.: Personality types in software engineering. Int. J. Hum.-Comput. Stud. **58**, 207–214 (2003)
41. Capretz, L.F., Ahmed, F.: Why do we need personality diversity in software engineering? ACM SIGSOFT Softw. Eng. Notes. **35**, 1–11 (2010)
42. Clemmensen, T., Hertzum, M., Hornbæk, K., Shi, Q., Yammiyavar, P.: Cultural cognition in usability evaluation. Interact. Comput. **21**, 212–220 (2009)
43. Nisbett, R.E., Peng, K., Choi, I., Norenzayan, A.: Culture and systems of thought: holistic versus analytic cognition. Psychol. Rev. **108**, 291 (2001)
44. Bennett, S.: Creative Thinking: Do Creative People have Distinctive Cognitive Styles? (2010)
45. Papavero, E.: Software engineers in China and the US: A comparison of cognitive styles. Presented at the American Psychological Association Convention (2005)
46. Frampton, K., Thom, J.A., Carroll, J., Crossman, B.: Information technology architects: approaching the longer view. In: Proceedings of the 2006 ACM SIGMIS CPR Conference on Computer Personnel Research: Forty Four Years of Computer Personnel Research: Achievements, Challenges & the Future, pp. 221–229. ACM, New York (2006)
47. Corbett, A.C.: Learning asymmetries and the discovery of entrepreneurial opportunities. J. Bus. Ventur. **22**, 97–118 (2007)
48. Castro, L.A., Gonzalez, V.M.: Hometown websites: continuous maintenance of cross-border connections. In: Proceedings of the Fourth International Conference on Communities and Technologies, pp. 145–154. ACM, New York (2009)
49. Cooper, A.: The Inmates are Running the Asylum–Why High-Tech Products Drive Us Crazy and How 2 to Restore the Sanity (1999)
50. Austin, A., Abdelnour Nocera, J.: So, Who exactly IS the HCI professional? In: Proceedings of the 33rd Annual ACM Conference Extended Abstracts on Human Factors in Computing Systems, pp. 1037–1042. ACM, New York (2015)
51. Vermunt, J.D., Vermetten, Y.J.: Patterns in student learning: relationships between learning strategies, conceptions of learning, and learning orientations. Educ. Psychol. Rev. **16**, 359–384 (2004)
52. Copeland, L., Griggs, L.: Getting the best from foreign employees. Manage. Rev. **75**, 19–26 (1986)
53. Winschiers-Theophilus, H.: Cultural appropriation of software design and evaluation. In: Handbook of Research on Socio-technical Design and Social Networking Systems, pp. 699–710. IGI Global, Pennsylvania (2009)
54. Oyugi, C., Abdelnour-Nocera, J., Clemmensen, T.: Harambee: a novel usability evaluation method for low-end users in Kenya. In: Proceedings of the 8th Nordic Conference on Human-Computer Interaction: Fun, Fast, Foundational, pp. 179–188. ACM, New York (2014)
55. Winschiers-Theophilus, H., Bidwell, N.J.: Toward an Afro-Centric indigenous HCI paradigm. Int. J. Hum.-Comput. Interact. **29**, 243–255 (2013)
56. Lazem, S.: A case study for sensitising egyptian engineering students to user-experience in technology design. In: Proceedings of the 7th Annual Symposium on Computing for Development, pp. 12:1–12:10. ACM, New York (2016)
57. Jordan, Z., Nocera, J.A., Peters, A., Dray, S., Kimani, S.: A living HCI curriculum. In: Proceedings of the First African Conference on Human Computer Interaction, pp. 229–232. ACM, New York (2016)

UX Professionals' Definitions of Usability and UX – A Comparison Between Turkey, Finland, Denmark, France and Malaysia

Dorina Rajanen[1([⊠])], Torkil Clemmensen[2], Netta Iivari[1], Yavuz Inal[3],
Kerem Rızvanoğlu[4], Ashok Sivaji[5], and Amélie Roche[6]

[1] University of Oulu, Oulu, Finland
{dorina.rajanen,netta.iivari}@oulu.fi
[2] Copenhagen Business School, Copenhagen, Denmark
tc.itm@cbs.dk
[3] Atilim University, Ankara, Turkey
yavuz.inal@atilim.edu.tr
[4] Galatasaray University, Istanbul, Turkey
krizvanoglu@gmail.com
[5] MIMOS Technology Solutions,
Federal Territory/WP, Kuala Lumpur, Malaysia
ashok.sivaji@mimos.my
[6] ENSC, Bordeaux, France
amelie.roche@ensc.fr

Abstract. This paper examines the views of user experience (UX) professionals on the definitions of usability and UX, and compares the findings between countries and within different socio-cultural groups. A mixed-method analysis was employed on data gathered on 422 professionals through a survey in Turkey, Finland, Denmark, France, and Malaysia. Usability appears to be an established concept, respondents across all countries agreeing on the importance of the ISO 9241-11 definition. There is also a tendency that UX professionals attach organizational perspective to usability. UX professionals diverge when defining UX, and there are systematic differences related to socio-cultural conditions. UX professionals in Finland and France incline more towards the definition highlighting the experiential qualities, when compared to Turkey and Malaysia that incline towards the definition reflecting the ease of use, utility, attractiveness, and degree of usage. Further research should address the implications of the diverse meanings and contexts of usability and UX.

Keywords: User experience · Usability · UX professional · Cross-cultural HCI

1 Introduction

As Human Computer Interaction (HCI) ~~communities emerge all over the world, user~~ experience (UX) professionals may find themselves as leaders in an emerging field, who have the opportunity to spread the word and to establish its meaning and value for many stakeholders. Currently, the UX field is not clearly defined and professionals' roles and competences are positioned along a continuum between the pure user-research for understanding and the applied design of objects, systems, or interactions[1].

Despite having established standards that define usability (ISO 9241-11; [1]) and UX (ISO 9241-210; [2]), HCI has so far failed to establish solid consensus about a scientific definition of usability and UX. The discipline of HCI appears to have accepted various loosely defined notions of usability, see e.g., [3]. For UX, the controversy about the scientific use of the concept is even more obvious. Sustained efforts over the years have aimed at defining UX (see e.g., [4–7]), connecting UX to existing HCI theory (e.g., [8–10]), or connecting UX to system development and design literature (e.g., [11–13]). However, it is fair to say that UX as a research area still can neither define the concept of UX, agree on how to capture the experiential qualities, or provide unified guidelines for experience design [7].

Our aim is to contribute to the clarification of the use of key concepts in the UX community. To this end, we focus on how UX professionals define usability and UX and on the socio-cultural factors that may influence the UX professionals' perspectives. By socio-cultural factors, we refer to certain demographic and professional background variables that have been shown to influence the way usability and UX professionals understand and apply usability and UX concepts in their work, such as gender, educational background, country of work, job titles, hierarchical positions in the organization. Based on a survey conducted in five countries, this paper shows that UX professionals agree on the ISO definition of usability, but diverge when defining UX, and that there are systematic differences related to socio-cultural conditions.

2   UX Communities in Turkey, Malaysia, France, Finland and Denmark

In this paper, we compare views of UX professionals from UX communities in Turkey, Malaysia, France, Finland, and Denmark as these together represent geographic and cultural diversity. We relied on convenience sampling, executing the study in countries of the researchers showing initial interest in this study. However, we also intentionally included diversity into the sample. The selection includes countries with an extensive background in HCI (Finland, Denmark) and in ergonomics (France), as well as countries with a relatively recently established UX community (Turkey, Malaysia). Moreover, we intentionally wished to include cultural diversity into the sample and tried to locate countries representing variety in terms of geographical position such as North-European, Central-European, South-East-European, and Asian.

In Turkey, the dominant UX community is UXPA Turkey Chapter, which was launched in 2014 in Istanbul as a non-profit local chapter of the global UXPA[2] to serve interaction designers, usability/UX professionals, HCI specialists, etc. In the email list of UXPA Turkey, there are more than 500 recipients, which present a variety in terms of professional practice.

---

[1] http://interactions.acm.org/blog/view/ux-research-vs.-ux-design.

[2] UXPA (The User Experience Professionals Association).

In Malaysia, there is a recently established Human Computer Interaction Special Interest Group (SIGHCI) under the Human Factors and Ergonomics Society of Malaysia. The SIG plans to work with other technical committees and institutions in the development of usable products and services. In addition, UX Malaysia is an active and the largest UX-related social media group in Malaysia, comprising of UX practitioners in Malaysia and around the world. Founded in 2012, the group consists of 1897 members on Facebook. Another Facebook group known as SIGHCI Malaysia comprising of 75 members promotes HCI activities among Malaysian universities.

In France, FLUPA (France-Luxembourg User Experience Professionals' Association) was founded in 2008 as the France-Luxembourg branch of UXPA. In the email list, there are more than 500 recipients. In addition, Ergo IHM is a mailing list available in French community that reaches more than 800 HCI professionals and students.

In Finland, there is an ACM SIGCHI[3] Chapter, namely SIGCHI Finland, founded in 2001. SIGCHI Finland is a scientific association that aims at gathering together researchers and practitioners in HCI, usability, and user experience in Finland. The email list includes around 450 recipients. In addition to SIGCHI Finland, there are several practitioner-oriented communities operating in Finland: IxDA Helsinki, IxDA Tampere, and KäytettävyysOSY, all having dedicated Facebook and LinkedIn groups that include several hundred members.

In Denmark, the dominant UX community is Sigchi.dk, which in 2015 changed its name to UX Denmark. Sigchi.dk (uxdanmark.dk) is associated with ACM SIGCHI and UXPA, but not a formal chapter of any of those. Sigchi.dk was launched in 1999 as a web site for interaction designers, usability professionals, HCI specialists, and so forth. The website uxdanmark.dk has about 1348 registered members from industry, government, and academia. The UX Denmark social media groups (LinkedIn UX Denmark and Facebook SIGCHI.dk page) have each about 491 members.

3 Related Work

3.1 HCI Definitions of Usability

Usability is a concept that stems from the research in ergonomics done in 80's on the interactive systems, and gradually evolved into a definition of quality in use [14]. The current standard definition of usability adopted by the HCI community (ISO 9241-Part 11; [1]) reflects quality in use[4] and stresses out the outcome the users gain by interacting with a system [14]. This definition states that usability is "the extent to which a product can be used by specified users to achieve specified goals with effectiveness, efficiency and satisfaction in a specified context of use" [1]. This definition and the definitions of each of its three aspects are supposed to be a common reference for HCI researchers and UX professionals alike. However, the meaning of the usability construct and its implications for how to measure usability appear to be undecided in HCI

---

[3] ACM SIGCHI (ACM Special Interest Group on Human-Computer Interaction).

[4] In this paper, quality in use has the same meaning as the broad view of usability expressed in ISO 9241-11 [1], in conformance also with [15–17].

discipline (see e.g., [18]). Accordingly, studies of correlations among usability aspects have been a standard way to try to define usability, see e.g., [19], though not with much success. A meta-analysis of usability studies indicated diversity in conclusions on if and how different aspects of usability were correlated [17]. Hertzum [3] describes six different perspectives on usability: universal usability, situational usability, perceived usability, hedonic usability, organizational usability, and cultural usability. While these six perspectives on usability have a shared essence, they differ in focus, scope, mindset, and the methods most appropriate for working with usability.

3.2   HCI Definitions of UX

The ISO 9241-210 [2] defines UX as "a person's perceptions and responses that result from the use or anticipated use of a product, system or service". UX focuses on the individual experience in relation to the use of a product, rather than on the effectiveness and efficiency of achieving a goal in a context of use of a product [14, 20, 21]. Bevan et al. [14], however, points out that satisfaction as an aspect of usability includes aspects of UX and this clarification is to be added to a future revision of ISO 9241-11. Early efforts in HCI to formulate a shared UX definition for academic research (see e.g., [4]) ended up formulating a gap between those UX professionals who view UX as related to design issues and those who view UX as something to measure or capture [6, 7]. Moreover, while some definitions of UX (e.g., the ISO standard for UX [2, 19]) explicitly mention the use of an interactive system, product, or service, other HCI researchers (and Don Norman[5]) focus on human experience with technology (see e.g., [23]). Moreover, while the original meaning of UX refers to momentary evaluation (see [20, 22]), Kujala et al. [22] explicitly aim at the evaluation of long-term experience with an interactive system, product, or service. Accordingly, there can be a difference in conceptualizing UX due to the scope; some definitions focus on (momentary) experiences of interaction with technology (e.g., [23]), while other focus on experience with long-term use and/or interaction with an interactive system, product, or service (see e.g., [22]). When referring to the long-term use of interactive systems, product, and services, Kujala et al. point out the following UX attributes: attractiveness of the system, ease of use, utility, and degree of usage [22]. This definition is referred to as system-oriented perspective of UX [24]. On the other hand, when referring to inter-action with technology, McCarthy and Wright define UX by four threads of experience: compositional, sensual, emotional, and spatio-temporal [23]; this view is referred to as human-oriented definition of UX [24].

3.3   How Usability and UX Are Construed by UX Professionals

Previous studies on how usability and UX are construed by UX professionals have examined system developers, users, and UX professionals' operational understanding of usability and UX [24–26]. The focus in these studies was on these stakeholders' understanding in use, which is different from giving definitions and explaining a

---

[5] https://www.nngroup.com/articles/definition-user-experience/.

concept such as usability and UX. In these studies [24–26], seventy-two participants across Europe (Denmark), India, and China elicited their personal constructs of quality in use in the context of using their computers in everyday life; e.g., how they thought about the use of their own email system. The studies employed the repertory-grid method (see [27]). The findings [24–26] showed differences in how UX professionals think about their own user experiences, compared to how developers and users think about theirs. The differences included that UX professionals in general focused more on describing the human user, and in particular more on the human subjective user experience, than the two other stakeholder groups who focused more on the systems and the context of use. Interestingly, UX professionals were not as concerned with the context of use as the users. Clemmensen et al. [24] also found that all four UX conceptual classifications that were used to do content analysis of the participants' answers (i.e., ISO 9241-210 user experience, objective vs. subjective UX, system-oriented UX, and human-experience of technology) could capture most of what participants said about their system use. In contrast, various views on usability definitions (i.e., ISO 9241-11 definition, utilitarian vs. experiential view, organizational usability, and user experience) turned out to be hard to fit to half of what the participants said about their use of their own systems (see [25]). Thus, it was found that the concept of usability as described in the literature appeared to be much narrower than UX when trying to fit it to the words that system developers, end users, and UX professionals use to construe quality in use in the context of their own use of computers in everyday life.

3.4 Socio-Cultural Factors Shaping UX Professionals' Understanding and Work Practices

HCI research has revealed that various socio-cultural factors affect perception and practice of usability and UX. Previous studies conducted on Danish, Chinese, and Indian UX professionals showed that nationality has an influence on the way UX professionals think about and perceive usability and UX [24–26]. A study on usability practices in game development in North-European countries (mostly Sweden, Finland, and UK) showed that more than 80% of Finnish game companies employ usability testing as compared to about 50% in the other surveyed countries [28]. A survey conducted in 2011 showed that while the UX practice has gained more attention in Malaysia, UX professionals are new to the terminologies of usability and UX [29]. Research with users also found that nationality affects the way usability is understood by users (e.g., Danish users emphasizing effectiveness and efficiency, while Chinese users, visual aspects [30]), and perceived (e.g., US users perceiving lower levels of user satisfaction, effectiveness and efficiency than Taiwanese users [31]).

Cross-cultural usability studies also indicate that cultural issues shape UX work practices. Cultural factors influence usability evaluations [32–34] and participatory design sessions [35, 36], as shown in studies carried out in different countries. Also organizational culture differences have been argued to shape UX work practices: usability is understood and practiced in different ways in organizations with cultural differences [37, 38]. Studies also show that very surprising and negative views may be attached to usability in organizations [39, 40].

Factors defined by the professional profile such as educational background and experience level have also been shown to influence the work practice. For example, the experience level of UX professionals may shape the outcomes of their work, such as in usability evaluation [41]. There is also a lot of diversity in the education of UX professionals – a multitude of disciplines contribute to and are relevant in UX work and this goes for the field of HCI overall (see e.g. [42–44]). Clemmensen [45] found that the UX community in Denmark mainly consisted of young people with less than five years of experience with usability work, and had an education in the social sciences or the humanities rather than a technical field. Most respondents in the survey had a keen interest in communication or participatory design.

Furthermore, the UX profession includes a variety of job titles emphasizing one or another aspect of work, and a variety of roles in the system development cycle. The label UX professional may refer to usability/UX designers, researchers, managers, engineers, and others (see e.g., [43, 46, 47]). Such a variety in job titles indicates that these professionals may be engaged with very different concerns in their work. A review [48] of ISO standards that address usability evaluation pointed out that ISO 9241-11 [1] targeting especially usability and UX professionals, provides guidelines on usability evaluation in various stages of system development such as the requirements, design, development, and use, but not in the post-implementation (maintenance) stage. On the other hand, ISO 13407 [49] (revised under ISO 9241-210 [2]) targeting designers of interactive systems, does not guide evaluation during the implementation stage. Standards targeting IT professionals, including software engineers, then again, refer also to evaluation at post-implementation stages such as support and maintenance [48].

Sivaji et al. [50] found that also gender has an effect on the effectiveness of a method used in usability evaluation, in particular when gender interacts with the social status of the users performing the evaluation.

3.5   This Study

Given the diversity of perspectives on usability and UX pointed out in our review, it is expected that different UX professionals may prefer different definitions of these concepts. Moreover, the diversity of socio-cultural conditions, which characterize and influence UX professionals' mindset and work practices, is expected to be also reflected in the diversity of ways UX professionals conceptualize usability and UX. In this study, we refer to socio-cultural conditions as being defined by the country of work, gender, educational background, experience level, hierarchical position in organization, job title, role in system development, and similar other variables that form the demographic and professional background of UX professionals. These variables represent social and cultural factors that influence people's mindset, attitude, and practices related to their profession.

Based on the related work, we maintain that if there are common understandings of usability and UX among professionals, it is not clear which are the shared understandings or how UX professionals define these concepts. There seems to be many aspects that may be shaping these understandings: there may be a difference in understanding related to the history of UX within a country, and to the profile (gender, educational background, job title, and design process participation, etc.) UX professionals have. In this study, we inquire these understandings and definitions and their relations to the socio-cultural factors. We are especially interested in examining whether there are differences that can be accounted by the local communities' different history in HCI and different cultural background as defined by the country of work. The overall aim is to clarify the use of key concepts in the UX community. Our research questions are:

- RQ1: How usability is defined by UX professionals?
- RQ2: How UX is defined by UX professionals?
- RQ3: Does country of work have an impact on the way UX professionals define usability and UX?
- RQ4: Do other socio-cultural factors than country of work (e.g., demographic and professional background) impact the way UX professionals define usability/UX?

4 Method

4.1 Research Design

An online survey was administered over a period of eight weeks from January to March, 2016. Data were collected from the UX professionals working in Turkey, Denmark, France, Finland, and Malaysia. The survey was distributed in local languages through the UX communities' mailing lists and social media of each country.

4.2 Variables

Dependent variables. To measure and capture UX professionals' definitions and understanding of usability and UX, we asked the respondents to choose their position on a scale between two polar versions of usability and UX, respectively (see Tables 1 and 2). For usability we chose the ISO 9241-11 definition [1] versus the Elliott and Kling's organizational perspective on usability [51] (see also [3, 52]). The idea was that though the ISO definition is widely known, UX professionals working in companies and large organizations may prefer the organizational usability definition. Moreover, Bevan et al. [14] pointed out that organizational perspective should be included in the next revision of ISO 9241-11.

For UX, we chose two definitions that have a different focus; the first is based on Kujala et al. [22], which is in line with ISO 9241-210 [2] and reflects a system-oriented definition of UX [21]. The second represents the McCarthy and Wright's view on UX and focuses on the experience of interaction with technology [23], and represents a human-oriented view of UX [24]. As McCarthy and Wright's view [23] is more on the human experience of using technology, we expected that as practitioners, UX professionals would clearly prefer the system-oriented definition of UX.

Regarding the capture of usability and UX understandings, respondents were also invited to provide their own definitions, which resulted in a relatively large amount of qualitative data to be coded and analyzed.

Table 1. Definitions of usability rated in the survey

Definitions of usability	Based on
1: Usability describes how a product can support its users to be effective, efficient and satisfied in its use	ISO 9241-11, 1998 [1]
2: Usability describes the match between the product and the organization adopting it	Elliot & Kling, 1996 [51]

Table 2. Definitions of UX rated in the survey

Definitions of UX	Based on
1: UX is the perceived attractiveness, ease of use, utility, and degree of usage of the product	Kujala et al., 2011 [22]
2: UX is the combined experience of the composition of the elements, sensory qualities, related emotions, and the context	McCarthy & Wright, 2004 [23]

Independent variables. To answer the research questions, the socio-cultural factors acting as independent variables were captured in terms of demographics (e.g., age, gender, education, occupation status, graduation field), and professional profile (HCI education, work experience, UX knowledge, and job characteristics such as job title, job position, stage in system development when involved).

4.3 Sample

The target participants were practitioners who would self-identify as usability/UX professionals; they had to be knowledgeable about usability and UX in order to be able to answer the questions about their background. We aimed to include both in-house UX professionals and external consultants, and we had a question where participants had to identify as one of these groups. At the same time, our participants should have a local association, a country of work, so people from e.g., Norman Nielsen and other similar groups should participate in the survey only if they had a presence in the countries we aimed to include. To ensure the best sampling, we used local UX groups' email lists, social media groups, and – to a wide extent – our own and our colleagues' personal networks, so we utilized theory-based convenience sampling.

4.4 Questionnaire

The questionnaire contained 62 questions that aimed to gather information related to the following seven categories: organization and work environment, usability/UX understanding, usability/UX activities and tools utilized in work, integration of usability/UX work, usability/UX communities, usability/UX in the country of work, and background including demographics and professional information. In this paper, in order to answer the research questions, we report data from 19 questions that focused on usability/UX understanding and on the background information.

4.5   Data Analysis

For the data analysis, we employed a mixed-method approach. The quantitative data were coded to allow statistical data analysis in SPSS. Variables were not normally distributed, thus we used the Mann-Whitney test to compare the importance ratings given by the respondents in different countries. Wilcoxon signed-rank test was employed to test whether the two definitions elicit significantly different importance scores within the same socio-cultural group (e.g., same hierarchical position).

The qualitative data – obtained from open-ended questions – were coded in Excel and Nvivo using the content analysis method. In both categories of definitions, usability and UX, we labeled different aspects (attributes, descriptions, and perspectives) that were pointed out in previous studies (e.g., [3, 14, 24–26]). Moreover, other aspects that emerged in a data driven manner during the qualitative analysis of the definitions were also extracted such as subjectivity and objectivity of the constructs, and the customer perspective of usability and UX.

5   Results

5.1   Demographic and Professional Profile of UX Professionals

A total of 422 valid participants were retained for analysis after cleaning the data. The professionals are relatively mature regarding age (*median* = 34; M = 35.2; SD = 8.3), and have in average 5 years of experience in UX field (*median* = 5; M = 6.7; SD = 5.6). The average experience in the current job title position is 3 years (*median* = 3; M = 4.3; SD = 4.6). The age ranges from 19 to 66 years, and the total work experience from 0 to 43 years (*median* = 10; M = 11.2; SD = 7.9), thus the sample represents a wide and heterogeneous population of UX professionals in terms of age and work experience. The sample distribution by country was as follows: 21.3% of participants were from Turkey, 11.6% from Denmark, 15.4% from France, 20.4% from Finland, and 29.1% from Malaysia (see Table 3). Ten (2.4%) were classified as "Other" because the respondents belonged to different countries than where the survey was conducted (e.g., Germany, Mexico). Among participants, 4.7% were of foreign nationality relative to the survey country and 90.3% were locals; the rest did not disclose their nationality.

Table 3 presents the demographics of the UX professionals participating in our survey; the first data column presents the figures for the entire sample, the second and third summarize the characteristics of the UX professionals who provided free-form definitions of usability and UX in the open-ended questions. The respondents who provided free-form definitions have similar profiles as the whole sample; however, regarding the country distribution, France is slightly more represented in the free-form definitions.

Table 4 presents the professional profile of the survey respondents. Most UX professionals are involved in early stages or all stages of system development. Early stages included kick-off or initialization, requirements, and design. Late stages included development, testing, and implementation phases. Post-implementation was coded as not really involved in the development. According to their self-evaluation, the participants have medium or higher level of knowledge on UX, and most of them keep up

Table 3. Demographic profile of UX professionals (*N* = 422)

		Entire sample (N = 422)		Provided usability definition (N = 120)		Provided UX definition (N = 104)	
		n	*%*	*n*	*%*	*n*	*%*
Country of work	Denmark	49	11.6	9	7.5	8	7.7
	Finland	86	20.4	20	16.7	22	21.2
	France	64	15.2	39	32.5	32	30.8
	Malaysia	123	29.1	30	25.0	23	22.1
	Turkey	90	21.3	18	15.0	16	15.4
	Other	10	2.4	4	3.3	3	2.9
Gender	Female	188	44.5	59	49.2	50	48.1
	Male	213	50.5	61	50.8	54	51.9
	Missing	21	5.0	0	0	0	0
Occupation status	Employed	352	83.4	97	80.8	83	79.8
	Freelance	16	3.8	7	5.8	5	4.8
	Entrepreneur	30	7.1	6	5.0	7	6.7
	Other	24	5.7	10	8.3	9	8.7
Education level	Basic or diploma	21	5.0	1	.8	2	1.9
	Bachelor degree	118	28.0	32	26.7	29	27.9
	Master degree	213	50.5	72	60.0	63	60.6
	PhD degree	49	11.6	15	12.5	10	9.6
	Missing	21	5.0	0	0	0	0
Graduation field	Computer/information[a]	136	32.2	34	28.3	28	26.9
	Media/communication[b]	56	13.3	19	15.8	20	19.2
	Psychology	29	6.9	15	12.5	8	7.7
	Arts	23	5.5	6	5.0	4	3.8
	Business/management[c]	22	5.2	3	2.5	2	1.9
	Electronic/automation[d]	18	4.3	2	1.7	2	1.9
	Other	115	27.3	40	33.3	40	38.5
	Missing	23	5.5	1	.8	0	0

Notes: [a] Computer and information sciences; [b] Media and Communication; [c] Business and management; [d] Electronic, automation and communication engineering, Electronics.

with the evolution of the field by using different information media such as conferences, courses, books, blogs, magazines, and scientific articles. Most UX professionals have one or two types of formal HCI education such as HCI courses, theses, and/or project experience. The most common hierarchical position are lower or middle management, and top management. Regarding the job titles, there is a balance between titles specifying usability and UX (such as usability or UX specialist) and those that do not (such as product manager or service designer). Similar distributions are found in the groups providing own usability and UX definitions; however, a larger proportion of usability/UX jobs are found among the providers of UX definitions.

Table 4. Professional profile of UX professionals ($N = 422$)

		Entire sample ($N = 422$)		Provided usability definition ($N = 120$)		Provided UX definition ($N = 104$)	
		n	%	n	%	n	%
HCI formal education	No formal HCI	16	3.8	5	4.2	4	3.8
	1 type	179	42.4	47	39.2	40	38.5
	2 types	57	13.5	22	18.3	18	17.3
	3 or more types	57	13.5	17	14.2	19	18.3
	Missing	113	26.8	29	24.2	23	22.1
UX vocational education	No vocational UX training	318	75.4	90	75.0	78	75.0
	Vocational UX training	82	19.4	30	25.0	26	25.0
	Missing	22	5.2	0	0	0	0
Job title	UX or usability in job title	192	45.5	58	48.3	60	57.7
	No UX or usability in title	199	47.2	61	50.8	43	41.3
	Missing	31	7.3	1	0.8	1	1.0
Job hierarchy	Entry level	34	8.1	8	6.7	6	5.8
	Specialist	16	3.8	7	5.8	6	5.8
	Lower/middle management	106	25.1	33	27.5	26	25.0
	Top management	66	15.6	16	13.3	14	13.5
	Outside hierarchy or other	26	6.2	13	10.8	8	7.7
	Missing	174	41.2	43	35.8	44	42.3
Keeping up with UX field	Keep up	355	84.1	112	93.3	98	94.2
	Do not keep up	46	10.9	8	6.7	6	5.8
	Missing	21	5.0	0	0	0	0
UX expertise level	Novice	36	8.5	8	6.7	7	6.7
	Little expertise	35	8.3	11	9.2	6	5.8
	Medium expertise	119	28.2	45	37.5	30	28.8
	Considerable expertise	149	35.3	38	31.7	38	36.5
	Expert	62	14.7	18	15.0	23	22.1
	Missing	21	5.0	0	0	0	0
Stage in system development (SD)	Not involved in SD	20	4.7	5	4.2	3	2.9
	Late stage	19	4.5	1	0.8	1	1.0
	Early stage	174	41.2	52	43.3	44	42.3
	All stages	206	48.8	61	50.8	55	52.9
	Missing	3	0.7	1	0.8	1	1.0

5.2 Usability Understanding

Answering RQ1, "How usability is understood/defined by UX professionals?", we found that most professionals (77.8% of 414 respondents who rated the definitions) preferred the ISO 9241-11 definition [1] rather than the organizational usability definition by Elliott and Kling [51] (see Table 5). However, a relatively large number of respondents (76; 18.4%) found both definitions important.

A substantial number of participants (120; 28%) have commented the existing definitions or entered their own definitions on usability. Content analysis of the free-form usability definitions showed that 108 (90%) of the answers described usability by different **attributes** of usability or of usable systems/products/services (e.g., "efficiency", "easy to use"), or **requirements** of usability or of usable systems/products/services (e.g., "you can use it without instructions"). These descriptions were expressed as standalone definitions, explanations, or additions to the definitions 1 and 2 provided in the questionnaire. The rest of free-form answers (10%) were comments on the survey definitions, reference to standards, or some other personal insights about usability that were not interesting from the research point of view.

Among the words used to describe usability, the most predominant were efficiency, effectiveness (also utility, usefulness, and helpfulness), functionality, ease of use (learnability, accessibility, cognitive load), accomplishing (user, business) goal, meeting needs, requirements and expectations of the user or business/organization. There were also references to attributes related to emotions and feelings (satisfaction, pleasantness, stress-free, emotional load, enjoyable). In the free-form answers, 13 respondents referred to the **concept of experience** (use experience, user experience, and service experience) when discussing the concept of usability. Respondents also stressed that usability is a **subjective and/or objective** quality. Moreover, respondents pointed out that usability should also take into account the **business/organization needs and goals** and that usability is not only about users, but also about **customers** highlighting that users' and customers' requirements "are not always the same thing".

Table 5. Which definition is the most important? (N = 414)

	Ratings for Usability		Ratings for UX	
	n	(%)	n	(%)
Definition 1 is the most important	231	(55.8)	70	(16.9)
Definition 1 is somewhat more important	91	(22.0)	44	(10.6)
Both definitions are equally important	76	(18.4)	131	(31.6)
Definition 2 is somewhat more important	12	(2.9)	92	(22.2)
Definition 2 is the most important	4	(1.0)	77	(18.6)

5.3   UX Understanding

Answering RQ2, "How UX is understood/defined by UX professionals?", we found that when contrasting the Kujala et al. [22] and McCarthy & Wright's [23] definitions, participants were not in a consensus on the importance of these two definitions (Table 5). Many participants found both definitions important (31.6%). A higher proportion of respondents (40.8%) inclined towards the second definition highlighting the sensorial and emotion-related qualities. Overall, according to Sign test, the second definition was rated as statistically significantly more important across all data ($Z = -3.14; p = 0.002$); however, according to Wilcoxon signed-rank test which takes into account also the magnitude of the differences between two paired scores, the preference towards the second definition failed to reach statistical significance at 0.05 ($Z = -1.69; p = 0.09$).

Participants provided 104 definitions and/or clarifications as free-form answers, representing about a quarter of the total respondents (see Tables 3 and 4). Content analysis of the free-form UX definitions showed that 83 (80%) of the answers were **descriptions of UX** that referred to or reflected **attributes or requirements** of UX and/or of systems/products/services. We grouped the attributes and/or requirements in the following categories: (1) formal and aesthetic; (2) performance/operation-related; (3) information related, (4) emotion, feelings and cognitive; (5) experience related; and (6) other. The most predominant characterizations were those invoking emotions, feelings, experiences, performance and usability attributes. It was observed that, when describing UX with own words, UX professionals still addressed the performance and operation qualities of the product such as ease of use and effectiveness. We found also that professionals considered usability as a quality of UX and as being part of UX. Moreover, it was pointed out that the product has to match the goals, needs, and expectations of the users. As anticipated, emotion- and experience-related qualities were frequently mentioned among the descriptions of UX. Interestingly, but not entirely unexpectedly, UX professionals pointed out descriptors such as fashion and branding, that we grouped in the category of formal and aesthetic qualities, and descriptors such as memory trace, sense making and meaning creation that we grouped with the emotional and cognitive attributes. Not the least, the references to business value, customers, and company's marketing strategy indicate the broad view on UX that transcends the boundaries of users' satisfaction and reaches out to the company's returns.

When **describing what UX is,** respondents utilized various terms and conceptualizations such as: UX is (about) emotions/feelings/perception/understanding of the user, UX is (about) (use/user) (overall/entire) experience, UX is a (user centered design) method/methodology. Other participants referred to UX as being attribute(s) (related to the systems) such as satisfaction, ease of use, suitability, etc. (see above), a process, all aspects/dimensions of use/interaction, and results/effects/reactions. Further, other characterizations were found in terms of business branch, memory trace, aesthetic elements, and adaptation of tool to user.

Regarding the **organizational and business perspective**, five respondents pointed out concepts such as business needs, company marketing's strategy, business outcomes, and three respondents brought up the **customer's perspective** by stating that the UX is defined by the customer, UX has to be designed in accordance with the customer requirements, and UX impacts customer's system use.

5.4   Country Specific Usability and UX

For answering RQ3, "Does country of work have an impact on the way UX professionals understand/define usability and UX?", we tested whether there were any significant differences in rating the importance of usability and UX definitions between countries. Table 6 shows the ratings of the usability definitions by country. There was a clear agreement among countries that the ISO definition of usability (Definition 1) is more important than the organizational definition; however, there were variations in the degree of importance and at those agreeing with both definitions. According to the Mann-Whitney test, there was a significant difference in the ratings between Finnish and French UX professionals, the former had stronger preferences towards the ISO definition compared to French respondents ($U = 2184$; $p = 0.017$).

Table 7 shows the ratings of UX definitions by country and the medians of each definition's ratings. There were statistically significant differences between France and Finland, on one hand, and Malaysia and Turkey, on the other hand (see Table 8). Turkey and Malaysia significantly preferred Definition 1 highlighting system-oriented UX, as compared to Finland and France who preferred the experiential definition. Slight differences, but not reaching statistical significance at 0.05 were observed between Denmark and France, and between Finland and France (Table 8).

Table 6. Rating of Usability definition (% by country)

	Denmark	Finland	France	Malaysia	Turkey
Definition 1 is the most important	63.4%	59.3%	46.9%	57.7%	54.4%
Definition 1 is somewhat more important	12.2%	31.4%	21.9%	13.0%	27.8%
Both definitions are equally important	22.0%	9.3%	26.6%	24.4%	11.1%
Definition 2 is somewhat more important	2.4%	0%	3.1%	4.9%	3.3%
Definition 2 is the most important	0%	0%	1.6%	0%	3.3%
Total %	100.0%	100.0%	100.0%	100.0%	100.0%

Table 7. Rating of UX definition (% by country)

	Denmark	Finland	France	Malaysia	Turkey
Definition 1 is the most important	17.1%	8.1%	6.3%	22.8%	25.6%
Definition 1 is somewhat more important	9.8%	17.4%	4.7%	6.5%	13.3%
Both definitions are equally important	29.3%	24.4%	31.3%	39.0%	31.1%
Definition 2 is somewhat more important	22.0%	26.7%	25.0%	22.0%	15.6%
Definition 2 is the most important	22.0%	23.3%	32.8%	9.8%	14.4%
Total %	100.0%	100.0%	100.0%	100.0%	100.0%

Table 8. Significant and near significant differences among countries

	Rating of UX definitions			
	Mann-Whitney U	*p*	Definition 1 more preferred by	Definition 2 more preferred by
Turkey vs. France	1773.500	**0.000**	Turkey	France
Turkey vs. Finland	2915.500	**0.004**	Turkey	Finland
France vs. Malaysia	2503.000	**0.000**	Malaysia	France
Finland vs. Malaysia	4157.500	**0.007**	Malaysia	Finland
Denmark vs. France	1036.500	0.061	Denmark	France
France vs. Finland	2328.500	0.097	Finland	France

5.5   Impact of Demographic and Professional Profile on Usability and UX Understanding

In answering RQ4, the Wilcoxon signed-rank test showed that, with regard to usability, there was a clear and significant consensus towards Definition 1 across all socio-cultural groups. However, with respect to UX, there was no clear consensus towards one definition across the social-cultural groups, thus different social-cultural profiles had different preferences towards the UX definitions as shown in Table 9. The upper part of Table 9 shows the profiles that rated Definition 2 as being more important. The lower part of table shows profiles that inclined towards Definition 1. UX professionals involved early in system development (SD) or not really involved in SD showed a preference towards Definition 2, while people involved in late stages had a preference towards Definition 1. Professionals in France and Finland had a significantly stronger preference for Definition 2 when compared to Definition 1. People self-evaluating themselves as having expert knowledge on UX had a stronger preference towards Definition 2, however the difference only approaching significance. Top management UX professionals tended to prefer Definition 2, while entry-level professionals inclined towards Definition 1. Similar pattern was observed between people keeping up with the evolution of the UX field and people not keeping up, and between professionals with Master degree and professionals with only Bachelor degree. There were stronger preferences for Definition 2 among those graduated in psychology, business and management, and fields classified as "others". Males, professionals with usability or UX in the job title, and with work experience in the UX positions between 7 and 12 years strongly preferred Definition 2 to Definition 1.

Table 9. Profiles that have a significant or near significant impact on UX definitions preference

Type of profile	n	Definition 2 preferred to Definition 1		Definition 1 preferred to Definition 2	
		Z	p	Z	p
Early SD stages involvement	166	–1.96	**0.050**		
Not involved in SD	20	–2.43	**0.015**		
Finland	86	–2.81	**0.005**		
France	64	–4.06	**0.000**		
Expert level of UX knowledge	62	–1.80	0.072		
Does keep up with UX field	355	–2.50	**0.013**		
Usability/UX in job title	192	–2.99	**0.003**		
Top management position	66	–1.81	0.070		
Psychology as graduation field	29	–2.22	**0.026**		
Business and management as graduation field	22	–1.72	0.085		
Other grad fields	101	–2.19	**0.029**		
Master degree	213	–3.19	**0.001**		
Male	213	–2.23	**0.026**		
UX work experience between 7 and 12 years	62	–2.86	**0.004**		
Bachelor degree	118			–1.88	0.061
Entry level position	34			–1.66	0.097
Does not keep up with UX field	46			–1.80	0.071
Late SD stages involvement	19			–2.02	**0.043**

6 Discussion

6.1 Consensus About Usability Definition Across Countries and Social-Cultural Groups

There was a clear consensus towards the importance of ISO 9241-11 definition [1] of usability among the UX professionals across all countries and socio-cultural profiles analyzed in this paper. This indicates that the ISO definition of usability, reflecting individual empowerment of end users, is widely accepted and adopted in the UX community as pointed out also in [14].

6.2 Organizational Usability and Other Perspectives on Usability

The definition addressing organizational usability [51] was rated clearly less important, however a relatively large number of UX professionals acknowledged the equal importance of both definitions. Moreover, the analysis of open answers showed that the UX professionals wished to extend the ISO usability definition with experience, business, and organization related aspects. This shows that, though the ISO 9241-11 usability [1] is an established concept among professionals, the concept is still evolving. The announced forthcoming changes to ISO 9241-11 by Bevan and colleagues [14] to include organizational perspective are in line with our findings. The references to business, organizational, and customer perspective in the open answers as well as the acknowledged importance of both definitions among some UX professionals show that defining usability by addressing the business benefits starts to become important. Thus, usability starts to be recognized as a success and strategic factor for companies, in line with research on usability cost-benefit analysis models [53–55]. Some practitioners have also already adopted the customer perspective, which is in line with the recent emphasis on service design as opposed to physical product design [56].

Moreover, our results indicate that besides organizational usability, situational usability, perceived usability, and hedonic usability [3] featured in the open answers. The variety of attributes in the free-form definitions shows that the diversity in HCI research [17] exists also among HCI practitioners. This has implications on how UX professionals actually operationalize the ISO 9241-11 definition [1] and measure the usability attributes in practice.

6.3   Diversity in UX Definitions

There was no clear consensus as regards the UX definition among the UX professionals; however, the preference towards the definition highlighting the experiential qualities during the use of a product [23] was approaching statistical significance when compared to the definition emphasizing system qualities in use [22]. Therefore, UX professionals generally preferred a human-oriented, experiential definition of UX, reflecting more consumer psychology than the work context. This result aligns with the original meaning of UX pointed out in [14, 20, 21] and with the new emphasis on service design (see e.g., [56]).

We anticipated a stronger preference for the definition reflecting system qualities in use given the fact that these are easier to capture and measure in practice; the results showed that, indeed, certain socio-cultural groups of UX professionals preferred this definition. The comparison between countries showed that Turkey and Malaysia, which represent relatively young UX communities have a stronger preference towards the system-oriented UX definition versus the human-oriented one when compared to Finland and France. However, the preference for the former definition was not statistically significant within the countries, showing quite heterogeneous ratings. On the other hand, both Finnish and French communities showed stronger preferences towards the latter definition.

Further analysis within each socio-cultural group showed that the system-oriented UX definition was preferred by profiles who reported late involvement in system development, and who might not yet have a firmly established foundation of UX knowledge and practice (they were graduates of Bachelor degree, worked in entry-level positions, and did not keep up with the UX field). On the other hand, the definition stressing the experiential qualities was strongly preferred by socio-cultural profiles that reported involvement in early stages of system development or were not really involved, and that had a stronger background in usability and UX studies and work.

These findings may also relate to the organizational culture and background in usability work. Research has reported that organizations tend to start usability and UX work with usability testing in the end (e.g., [57]), while organizations should move towards starting usability and UX work early and continuing it thorough the phases of system development (e.g., [38, 47]). Thus, the maturity of organizations in terms of UX work, combined with the professional profile of the UX practitioners, would be interesting to examine in relation to the UX understandings of the practitioners.

The free-form definitions of UX revealed an extensive list of attributes. Unlike it was recommended by Bevan et al. [14], UX is viewed by some UX professionals as sharing characteristics with usability by addressing effectiveness, efficiency, and goals. The diversity of attributes assigned to UX by professionals parallels with the divergent discourses on defining UX in HCI (e.g., [4, 6, 7]). This shows that research efforts of this kind are indeed necessary in order to clarify the true meaning of UX and ways to operationalize it and to measure it.

6.4   Implications for Practice and Research

This study has implications for the design and evaluation of interactive systems, products, and services, as it points out that practitioners should be aware that usability and UX concepts are diverse, while pivotal in achieving the objective of excellence in user interface, quality in use, and service design (see e.g., [15, 16, 56]). Diversity in the understandings of the UX professionals indicates that there likely is diversity in how UX professionals operationalize usability and UX in practice and in how they strive for high quality usability and UX in their design and evaluation practices. Concepts are still evolving as new dimensions and perspectives emerge; thus, practitioners should keep up with the evolution of the field, and with the practices and conceptualizations adopted by competitors.

Our findings showed that our approach of including diversity in the sample in terms of UX community maturity and geographic location was beneficial for understanding the perspectives and perceptions of both definitions of usability and UX. It is important for practitioners to observe and respond to the global trends across UX communities and countries. We reported also the near-significant results as they may indicate tendencies in the respective community, but also transitions from one perspective to another. Longitudinal studies observing the evolution of views on UX within different socio-cultural groups would confirm or disconfirm the trends. Thus, our research points out that one could trace the development and adoption of usability and UX definitions based on the UX community maturity and geographical location. Further research including other countries would then complete the picture of perspectives and perceptions of usability and UX. Thus, more countries with varying levels of usability and UX history should be included in further analyses to confirm the patterns observed in this study and to provide a mapping of how the field evolves.

Further research should also investigate the implications that adopting one definition or another has on the usability and UX work practices. We plan to extend the analysis to the activities, methods, and tools employed by UX professionals who provided different views on usability and UX. Further research should also examine whether there are differences in usability and UX understanding due to organizational characteristics such as size, type, and culture. This research has not addressed the comparison of views regarding usability and UX, and we plan further analyses to assess the extent to which these views overlap. We plan also to address the time dimension of usability and UX, and the views of UX professionals on this aspect.

7 Conclusion

This paper examined the views of UX professionals on the definitions of usability and UX, and compared the findings between five countries and within different socio-cultural groups. The paper contributes by showing that usability is now an established concept among UX professionals; the respondents across the five surveyed countries recognized the importance of the ISO 9241-11 definition. Moreover, the paper showed that UX professionals increasingly recognize usability as a construct important for the organization, business, and customers, not just for users. The views on UX diverge among different socio-cultural groups when contrasting the experiential qualities with the system qualities in use. Especially UX professionals with a stronger socio-cultural background in usability and UX work preferred the experiential definition.

The paper contributes also by pointing out that UX professionals refer to a variety of characteristics and attributes associated with usability and UX that parallels the struggles in HCI research on finding the best ways to capture the essence of these concepts, as they evolve in time. These findings show that research is still needed on capturing and clarifying the meanings of usability and UX, as well as the implications of this diversity on the UX professionals' design and evaluation practices. Practitioners should be aware of the diversity of usability and UX definitions and adapt their practices to the global trends. We suggest also that further revisions of ISO 9241-11 should make the distinction between usability and UX clearer and firmer, and provide guidelines on using the two concepts in design and evaluation within organizations.

References

1. ISO 9241-11: Ergonomic Requirements for Office Work with Visual Display Terminals (VDTs) - Part 11: Guidance on Usability. International Standard Organization, Geneva (1998)
2. ISO 9241-210: Ergonomics of Human-System Interaction - Part 210: Human-Centred Design for Interactive Systems. International Standard Organization, Geneva (2010)
3. Hertzum, M.: Images of usability. Int. J. Hum.-Comput. Interact. 26(6), 567–600 (2010)
4. Law, E., Roto, V., Vermeeren, A.P., Kort, J., Hassenzahl, M.: Towards a shared definition of user experience. In: CHI 2008 Extended Abstracts on Human Factors in Computing Systems (2008)
5. Law, E.L.-C.: The measurability and predictability of user experience. In: Proceedings of the 3rd ACM SIGCHI Symposium on Engineering Interactive Computing Systems (2011)
6. Law, E.L.-C., van Schaik, P.: Modelling user experience–an agenda for research and practice. Interact. Comput. 22(5), 313–322 (2010)
7. Law, E.L.-C., van Schaik, P., Roto, V.: Attitudes towards user experience (UX) measurement. Int. J. Hum.-Comput. Stud. 72(6), 526–541 (2014)

8. Obrist, M., Law, E., Väänänen-Vainio-Mattila, K., Roto, V., Vermeeren, A., Kuutti, K.: UX research: what theoretical roots do we build on–if any? In: CHI 2011 Extended Abstracts on Human Factors in Computing Systems (2011)
9. Obrist, M., Roto, V., Law, E.L.-C., Väänänen-Vainio-Mattila, K., Vermeeren, A., Buie, E.: Theories behind UX research and how they are used in practice. In: CHI 2012 Extended Abstracts on Human Factors in Computing Systems (2012)
10. Obrist, M., Roto, V., Vermeeren, A., Väänänen-Vainio-Mattila, K., Law, E.L.-C., Kuutti, K.: In search of theoretical foundations for UX research and practice. In: CHI 2012 Extended Abstracts on Human Factors in Computing Systems (2012)
11. Law, E.L.-C., Abrahão, S.: Interplay between user experience (UX) evaluation and system development. Int. J. Hum.-Comput. Stud. **72**(6), 523–525 (2014)
12. Law, E.L.-C., Hassenzahl, M., Karapanos, E., Obrist, M., Roto, V.: Tracing links between UX frameworks and design practices: dual carriageway. In: Proceedings of Human-Computer Interaction Korea (2014)
13. Roto, V., Väätäjä, H., Law, E., Powers, R.: Experience design for multiple customer touchpoints. In: Proceedings of the 9th Nordic Conference on Human-Computer Interaction (2016)
14. Bevan, N., Carter, J., Harker, S.: ISO 9241-11 revised: what have we learnt about usability since 1998? In: Kurosu, M. (ed.) HCI 2015. LNCS, vol. 9169, pp. 143–151. Springer, Cham (2015). doi:10.1007/978-3-319-20901-2_13
15. Bevan, N.: Quality in use: meeting user needs for quality. J. Sys. Softw. **49**(1), 89–96 (1999)
16. Bevan, N.: Measuring usability as quality of use. Softw. Qual. J. **4**(2), 115–130 (1995)
17. Hornbæk, K., Law, E.L.-C.: Meta-analysis of correlations among usability measures. In: Proceedings of the SIGCHI Conference on Human Factors in Computing Systems (2007)
18. Tractinsky, N.: The usability construct: a dead end? Human–Computer Interaction (2017, accepted)
19. Frøkjær, E., Hertzum, M., Hornbæk, K.: Measuring usability: are effectiveness, efficiency, and satisfaction really correlated? In: Proceedings of the SIGCHI Conference on Human Factors in Computing Systems (2000)
20. Hassenzahl, M.: User experience (UX): towards an experiential perspective on product quality. In: Proceedings of the 20th Conference on l'Interaction Homme-Machine, pp. 11–15. ACM (2008)
21. Bargas-Avila, J.A., Hornbæk, K.: Old wine in new bottles or novel challenges: a critical analysis of empirical studies of user experience. In: Proceedings of the SIGCHI Conference on Human Factors in Computing Systems, pp. 2689–2698. ACM (2011)
22. Kujala, S., Roto, V., Väänänen-Vainio-Mattila, K., Karapanos, E., Sinnelä, A.: UX curve: a method for evaluating long-term user experience. Interact. Comput. **23**(5), 473–483 (2011)
23. McCarthy, J., Wright, P.: Technology as experience. Interactions **11**(5), 42–43 (2004)
24. Clemmensen, T., Hertzum, M., Yang, J., Chen, Y.: Do usability professionals think about user experience in the same way as users and developers do? In: Kotzé, P., Marsden, G., Lindgaard, G., Wesson, J., Winckler, M. (eds.) INTERACT 2013. LNCS, vol. 8118, pp. 461–478. Springer, Heidelberg (2013). doi:10.1007/978-3-642-40480-1_31
25. Hertzum, M., Clemmensen, T.: How do usability professionals construe usability? Int. J. Hum.-Comput. Stud. **70**(1), 26–42 (2012)
26. Hertzum, M., Clemmensen, T., Hornbæk, K., Kumar, J., Shi, Q., Yammiyavar, P.: Usability constructs: a cross-cultural study of how users and developers experience their use of information systems. In: Aykin, N. (ed.) UI-HCII 2007. LNCS, vol. 4559, pp. 317–326. Springer, Heidelberg (2007). doi:10.1007/978-3-540-73287-7_39
27. Kelly, G.: The Psychology of Personal Constructs. Routledge, New York (2003)

28. Rajanen, M., Nissinen, J.: A survey of game usability practices in Northern European game companies. IRIS-Sel. Pap. Inf. Syst. Res. Semin. Scand. **2015**(6), 1–15 (2015). Paper 8

29. Hussein, I., Mahmud, M., Tap, A.O.M.: A survey of user experience practice: a point of meet between academic and industry. In: Proceedings of the 3rd International Conference on User Science and Engineering (i-USEr) (2014)

30. Frandsen-Thorlacius, O., Hornbæk, K., Hertzum, M., Clemmensen, T.: Non-universal usability?: a survey of how usability is understood by Chinese and Danish users. In: Proceedings of the SIGCHI Conference on Human Factors in Computing Systems, pp. 41–50. ACM (2009)

31. Wallace, S., Yu, H.C.: The effect of culture on usability: comparing the perceptions and performance of Taiwanese and North American MP3 player users. J. Usab. Stud. **4**(3), 136–146 (2009)

32. Clemmensen, T., Hertzum, M., Hornbæk, K., Shi, Q., Yammiyavar, P.: Cultural cognition in usability evaluation. Interact. Comput. **21**(3), 212–220 (2009)

33. Oyugi, C., Dunckley, L., Smith, A.: Evaluation methods and cultural differences: studies across three continents. In: Proceedings of the 5th Nordic Conference on Human-Computer Interaction: Building Bridges, pp. 318–325. ACM (2008)

34. Oyugi, C., Abdelnour-Nocera, J., Clemmensen, T.: Harambee: a novel usability evaluation method for low-end users in Kenya. In: Proceedings of the 8th Nordic Conference on Human-Computer Interaction: Fun, Fast, Foundational, pp. 179–188. ACM (2014)

35. Yasuoka, M., Nakatani, M., Ohno, T.: Towards a culturally independent participatory design method: fusing game elements into the design process. In: 2013 International Conference on Culture and Computing, pp. 92–97. IEEE (2013)

36. Yasuoka, M., Sakurai, R.: Out of Scandinavia to Asia: adaptability of participatory design in culturally distant society. In: Proceedings of the 12th Participatory Design Conference: Exploratory Papers, Workshop Descriptions, Industry Cases, vol. 2, pp. 21–24. ACM (2012)

37. Iivari, N.: Representing the user'in software development—a cultural analysis of usability work in the product development context. Interact. Comput. **18**(4), 635–664 (2006)

38. Iivari, N.: Culturally compatible usability work - an interpretive case study on the relationship between usability work and its cultural context in software product development organizations. J. Organ. End User Comput. **22**(3), 40–65 (2010)

39. Cajander, Å.: Usability–who cares?: the introduction of user-centred systems design in organisations. Doctoral Dissertation, Acta Universitatis Upsaliensis. (2010)

40. Rajanen, M., Iivari, N.: Usability cost-benefit analysis: how usability became a curse word? In: Baranauskas, C., Palanque, P., Abascal, J., Barbosa, S.D.J. (eds.) INTERACT 2007. LNCS, vol. 4663, pp. 511–524. Springer, Heidelberg (2007). doi:10.1007/978-3-540-74800-7_47

41. Hertzum, M., Jacobsen, N.E.: The evaluator effect: a chilling fact about usability evaluation methods. Int. J. Hum.-Comput. Interact. **13**(4), 421–443 (2001)

42. Blevis, E., Stolterman, E.: FEATURE transcending disciplinary boundaries in interaction design. Interactions **16**(5), 48–51 (2009)

43. Clemmensen, T.: Four approaches to user modelling—a qualitative research interview study of HCI professionals' practice. Interact. Comput. **16**(4), 799–829 (2004)

44. Sharp, H., Preece, J., Rogers, Y.: Interaction design - beyond human - computer interaction. Wiley, Chichester (2015)

45. Clemmensen, T.: Community knowledge in an emerging online professional community - The case of Sigchi.dk. Knowl. Process. Manag. **12**(1), 43–52 (2005)

46. Gulliksen, J., Boivie, I., Göransson, B.: Usability professionals—current practices and future development. Interact. Comput. **18**(4), 568–600 (2006)

47. Iivari, N.: Understanding the work of an HCI practitioner. In: Proceedings of the 4th Nordic Conference on Human-Computer Interaction: Changing Roles, pp. 185–194. ACM (2006)

48. Marghescu, D.: Usability evaluation of information systems: a review of five international standards. In: Wojtkowski, W., Wojtkowski, G., Lang, M., Conboy, K., Barry, C. (eds.) Information Systems Development, pp. 131–142. Springer, Boston (2009). doi:10.1007/978-0-387-68772-8_11

49. ISO 13407: Human-Centred Design Processes for Interactive Systems (1999)

50. Sivaji, A., Nielsen, S.F., Clemmensen, T.: A textual feedback tool for empowering participants in usability and UX evaluations. Int. J. Hum.-Comput. Interact. **33**(5), 1–14 (2016)

51. Elliott, N., Kling, R.: Organizational usability of digital libraries in the courts. In: Proceedings of the Twenty-Ninth Hawaii International Conference on System Sciences, vol. 5, pp. 62–71. IEEE (1996)

52. Sørensen, C., Al-Taitoon, A.: Organisational usability of mobile computing—volatility and control in mobile foreign exchange trading. Int. J. Hum.-Comput. Stud. **66**(12), 916–929 (2008)

53. Rajanen, M.: Usability cost-benefit models–different approaches to usability benefit analysis. In: Proceedings of the 26th Information Systems Research Seminar in Scandinavia (IRIS26), Haikko, Finland (2003)

54. Rajanen, M.: Applying Usability Cost - Benefit Analysis – Explorations in Commercial and Open Source Software Development Contexts. Acta Universitatis Ouluensis, Ser. A, Scient. rerum nat, 587 (2011)

55. Rajanen, M., Jokela, T.: Analysis of usability cost-benefit models. In: ECIS 2004 Proceedings, 115 (2004)

56. Lewis, J.R.: Usability: lessons learned… and yet to be learned. Int. J. Hum.-Comput. Interact. **30**(9), 663–684 (2014)

57. Karat, J.: Evolving the scope of user-centered design. CACM **40**(7), 33–38 (1997)

Virtual Reality and Feeling of Immersion

Estimating Visual Discomfort in Head-Mounted Displays Using Electroencephalography

Christian Mai[1(✉)], Mariam Hassib[1,2], and Rolf Königbauer[1]

[1] LMU Munich, Munich, Germany
{christian.mai,rolf.konigbauer}@ifi.lmu.de
[2] University of Stuttgart (VIS), Stuttgart, Germany
mariam.hassib@vis.uni-stuttgart.de

Abstract. Head-Mounted displays, while providing unprecedented immersiveness and engagement in interaction, can substantially add mental workload and visual strain on users. Being a novel technology, users often do not know what to expect and therefore accept visual stress as being state of the art. Assessing visual discomfort is currently possible through questionnaires and interviews that interrupt the interaction and provide only subjective feedback. Electroencephalography (EEG) can provide insights about the visual discomfort and workload of HMDs. We evaluate the use of a consumer-grade Brain Computer Interface for estimating visual discomfort in HMD usage in a study with 24 participants. Our results show that the usage of a BCI to detect uncomfortable viewing conditions is possible with a certainty of 83% in our study. Further the results give insights on the usage of BCIs in order to increase the detection certainty by reducing costs for the hardware. This can pave the way for designing adaptive virtual reality experiences that consider user visual fatigue without disrupting immersiveness.

Keywords: Virtual reality · Electroencephalography · Head-mounted displays · Visual fatigue · Brain-computer interface

1 Introduction

Visual stress, eye strain or other symptoms caused by the visual load in a head mounted display (HMD) are under research for decades (e.g. [1,15]). Reasons for the existing discomfort are the physical and optical properties of the HMD and its eyepieces or the mismatch to natural vision caused by the computer rendered picture [1,12,15]. Arising symptoms of asthenopia (eye strain) range from double vision, prismatic effects, blurry vision and more [1,15]. With the introduction of fully immersive HMDs like the Oculus Rift to the consumer market, new challenges arise for the usability of HMDs [11]. With the absence of professional guidance during private use, these symptoms can lead to a bad experience or might even cause health risks [1].

© IFIP International Federation for Information Processing 2017
Published by Springer International Publishing AG 2017. All Rights Reserved
R. Bernhaupt et al. (Eds.): INTERACT 2017, Part IV, LNCS 10516, pp. 243–252, 2017.
DOI: 10.1007/978-3-319-68059-0_15

During the usage of a HMD, stress caused by the visual channel is even worse then in traditional screen-based applications. The reason for this is that the HMD user can not simply look away from the screen to relax his eyes and further the HMD should not be taken off in order to keep the users' mental state of being present in the virtual environment (VE). A possible reason for uncomfortable vision are virtual objects appearing in very close position to the users eyes. In this case disparity between the left and the right eyes picture and very strong vergence-accommodation conflict are the reason for the discomfort [10]. To assess if a user experiences visual discomfort, the most common method is to use qualitative questionnaires as used by Shibata et al. [19], with the drawback of missinterpretations and missing real time ability [3]. Frey et al. [3] presented an objective method to assess visual discomfort using medical-grade Electroencephalography (EEG) device using a screen-based setup [3]. Their results show, that it is possible to detect the users brain reacting to the visual discomfort. In our work, we focus on the detection of visual discomfort using consumer EEG devices in a VE. We focus on a low number of electrodes and a consumer EEG device building on top of Frey et al.'s earlier work [4] to test the feasibilty of automatic detection of visual discomfort in a setup that is wearable and low-cost compared to medical-grade EEG. In a study with 24 participants in a VE we test the impact of close and far object locations in a VE on EEG data and prove the feasibility of detecting visual discomfort with a certainity of 83% with 2 electrodes.

2   Background and Related Work

The research on the effects of viewing stereoscopic pictures is ongoing for decades (e.g. [9,10,12,17]), in particular as visual discomfort is a central health issue when using a HMD [1]. The important outcome of this research regarding our study is that mistakes in the rendering of the left and right picture of the stereo image pair can trigger visual discomfort or even pain. For binocular pictures the zone of comfortable viewing [3] can be violated, for example when looking at an object that is very close to the user's eyes. This happens, as the computer generated picture for the left and the right eyes image need to be disparate to create the binocular perception of depth [10]. At one point the disparity gets too high and the user's brain is unable to fuse the two images into one.

There are several models which describe the emergence of this effect, but not to its full extent and without recognizing individual differences [10]. Visual discomfort describes this individual feeling of a user under certain visual conditions. Visual fatigue is the counterpart that can be objectively measured for example due to accommodation power or visual acuity [10]. These measurement methods need optometric instruments which cannot be used when wearing a HMD or for detecting visual stress in real time. Further they do not reflect the individual properties of the user, therefore questionnaires are used [10]. These include the user experience and expectations on the technology. However questionnaires have the risk of misinterpretation by the user. There are several different questionnaires as summarized by Lambooij et al. [10], which rate uncomfortable vision, burning or irritation of the eyes, to name but few. We will build upon a questionnaire suggested by Sheedy et al. [18].

With the onset of consumer EEG devices in the market, their use in interface and system evaluation is made more feasible. Monitoring brain activity using consumer EEG is a promising way of detecting visual stress, as it enables near real time reaction to the user's visual perception and does not interfere with the visual experience of the user in the HMD [4]. An medical EEG device can detect the brain wave signals introduced by a stereoscopic image on a screen and classify the results within the time window of one second as it could be shown by Frey et al. [4]. Our focus is on the objective detection of visual discomfort by measuring the brain activity in VR in order to take individual factors like individual predisposition or training into account.

3 Study

Our study is designed to evaluate the use of consumer EEG for detecting visual discomfort in VR. Similar to Frey et al. [3], we use Shibatas et al. [19] estimation of comfortable (C) and non-comfortable (NC) depths to show objects in the VE.

3.1 Apparatus

An Oculus Rift CV1, with a minimum of 90 frames per second rendered with Unity 5.4.1f1, was used during the study. The focal point of the Oculus is calculated to be about 1.3 m away from the users eyes [16]. EEG signals were acquired using the Emotiv EPOC with a sampling rate of 128 Hz[1] (Fig. 1, left). The EPOC has 14 felt electrodes that are positioned according to the 10–20 positioning system (e.g. [7]).

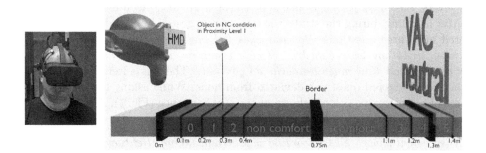

Fig. 1. Left: A participant wearing the HMD and the EPOC EEG. Right: The C and NC conditions as used in the study.

---

[1] www.emotiv.com.

3.2 Stimuli

To generate visual stress, we build upon the method suggested by Frey et al. [3]. They use the *vergence-accommodation conflict* (VAC) to stimulate the visual system. Our independent variable therefore is the spatial position of objects in front of the users eyes, which codes the visual disparity leading to visual discomfort. Objects in six different spatial levels are presented to the participant (Fig. 1, right). The presented objects are scaled in order to be perceived to be constant in size on all levels of depth. Three of these levels lie in a range of visual comfort (C) and three in a visual discomfort (NC). As calculated, only objects presented in the visual discomfort zone are supposed to create visual stress [19] and the calculated border matches the general advice from the Oculus Rift developer guide with 0.75 m [16]. In Fig. 1 the objects position changes in increments of 0.1 m with NC between 0.1 und 0.4 cm and C conditions between 1.1 m and 1.4 m in front of the users' eyes. The VAC neutral position at 1.3 m defines the spatial depth without difference in vergence and accommodation. The objects presented are ball, cylinder and cube in random depths levels, timespans, position in X and Y direction frontal to the user, rotation and time, between 2.7 s to 3.2 s.

3.3 Measures

We collected subjective measures during a questionnaire phase in order to confirm existing knowledge. EEG data measured by the EPOC EEG are recorded during the measurement phase. Questionnaire phase and measurement phase are conducted alternating, three times each. Both phases are described in detail below.

Questionnaire phase - subjetive rating of stimuli position: In this phase participants had to rate the stimulus on a 7 point likert scale from none, slight, medium to severe. Intermediate stages like none to slight are also taken into account. For better handling during the study, the items as suggested by Sheedy [18] are clustered into three questions: *Do your eyes feel impaired? For example: burning, aching, irritation, watery or dry?, Is your vision impaired? For example: blurred or double?* and *How much headache do you feel?*. The single items were ranked when the clustered questions deviated from none. While asking the questions a cube of a contrasting color is shown at the VAC distance (Fig. 1). All six comfort levels are rated three times by each participants.

Measurement phase - EEG recording with accompanying attention task: The pure EEG measures were recorded during the measurement phase, when the random object was presented. After that the participants had to conduct an attention task to prevent looking away from the object. The procedure was the same as in the questionnaire-phase, but instead of asking the participants for a subjective rating after the object presentation, a small green ball in the center of the view appears for 0.7 to 1 s at the VAC position after the random stimuli object disappeared. The users task was to move this ball to the X and Y position of the presented stimuli by a game pad. After that the next randomized object appears until all 6 comfort levels are presented. In total each level is presented 60 times.

3.4 Participants

We advertised the study through University mailing lists and social media. 24 participants took part in our study (8 female, Mage = 25 years, SD = 5). All participants had normal or corrected-to-normal vision. None of the participants suffered from neurological disorders. 59% participants had prior experience with HMDs. Participants were awarded 10 Euro for participation. A Titmus ring stereotest with a minimum detection of 100 arcseconds disparity was passed by all participants to check for missing binocular vision [20].

3.5 Procedure

Participants were first greeted and the study procedure and purpose was explained. They then signed informed consent forms, answered demographics questions and the Titmus stereo test was conducted. We then fitted participants with the Emotiv EPOC and the Oculus Rift devices. The EPOC was adjusted and the electrodes were wet using saline solution. The EPOC control panel software was used to ensure that all electrodes were achieving excellent connectivity. The interpupillar distance was set for the HMD as measured with a pupillometer [2]. Participants practiced the *measurement* phase until they felt comfortable with the gamepad. A simulator sickness questionnaire (SSQ) was asked before and after the study [8]. Then the study started with a *questionnaire* phase alternating followed by a *measurement* phase. Both phases are presented three times during the study. Between the phases users where allowed to rest and move their heads. The duration of the study was approximately 1 h with 30 min using the HMD. The study took part in a quiet room with dimmed light.

4 Results

4.1 Subjective Rating of the Comfort Zones

All ratings in the questionnaire phase (none, slight, medium and severe) are translated into points from 0 to 4 respectively. Using a Wilcoxon Signed Rank test, we found significantly higher score for the NC conditions than the C conditions, for the following items: *eye-discomfort*:MdnNC = 10.2, MdnC = 3.6 (T = 102.00, p <.02), *vision*: MdnNC = 12.5, MdnC = .01 (T = 300.00; p <.01). The *headache* item was insignificant (p >.125). The overall results for the short questionnaires show a significantly higher rating in NC condition (Mdn = 12.5), than in C condition (Mdn = .01, T = 300.00, p <.01). The comparison of the total SSQ score shows significant higher results after the experiment (Mdn = 13.64) then before the experiment (Mdn = 6.1), T = 245.5, p <.01).

4.2 EEG Analysis

EEG analysis was done using EEGLab V14 toolbox and Matlab 2017A. We first applied a band pass filter between 0.5 Hz and 25 Hz to remove DC drift and high frequency artifacts from muscle movements. Independent Component Analysis was applied to identify components with eye-movement. The identified muscle and eye-movement components were rejected and the rest of the analysis was done using the remaining components. The data was then divided into epochs starting 0.7 s before each stimulus and ending 2.7 s after each stimulus. This resulted in 198 epochs per participant and overall 4752 epochs. As suggest by Ghaderi [5] electrooculographic activity are identified with the ADJUST toolbox and removed. Epochs containing electrodes with a distance from positive to negative peaks of more than 150µV are regarded noisy and rejected [13]. Figure 2 shows the average EEG activity in microvolts for all participants between NC and C conditions and all 14 electrodes just before, during, and after the onset of the stimulus (at 0 ms). The red graph represents the event related potentials (ERP) of NC conditions and the green graph the ERP of C conditions. Both graphs develop quite similarly, but part in between 500 ms and 1400 ms. Close similarity can be found in the peak at 300 ms representing the P300 signals. Both graphs start to rise to this peak at the same time, the graph for NC condition drops down at a later time. Analysing the data shows, that the electrodes P7, P8, O1 and O2 show the strongest brain reaction.

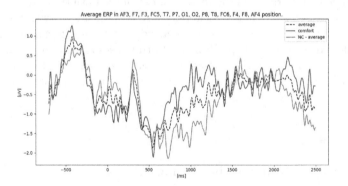

Fig. 2. Averaged ERP in NC and C condition for 14 electrodes.

Figure 3 shows the ERP for C and NC conditions using electrodes P7 and P8 on the parietal lobe of the brain, wich is responsible for perception [6]. A steep peak at 300 ms is followed by a more consistent rise with a climax at about 550 ms and a slow descent that reaches ground level at 1000 ms. The graph of NC condition shows minor peaks in the first 300 ms, where the graph representing C condition rather drops below ground level. Overall the graph of NC condition is at a higher level in between 0 ms and 1000 ms.

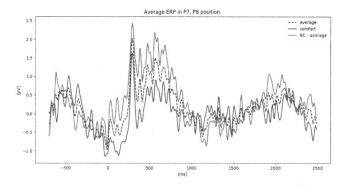

Fig. 3. ERP of perceptual related brain areas with electrodes P7 and P8 [6], visualized into NC and C conditions with stimuli appearance at 0 ms.

Figure 4 shows the ERPs for C and NC conditions from the two electrodes O1 and O2 on the occipital lobe related to vision [6]. In both graphs, a peak at 300 ms and around 500 ms appears. The first peak, at 300 ms, reaches a higher level in C condition than in NC. The second peak, around 500 ms is reached steeper in C than in NC condition. The graph in C condition drops faster to ground level than the graph from NC condition. Based on the anomalies in between the delay of the peak arising at 500 ms we build a binary classifier. The classifier compares the values of the interval between 547 ms to 570 ms with the values between 586 ms to 609 ms after the events stimulus. Based on the average values, it is decided whether a participants' ERP is created out of NC or C conditions. The classifiers' accuracy results in 71% correct classification for C condition and 83% for NC condition, by using the data from O1 and O2 electrodes.

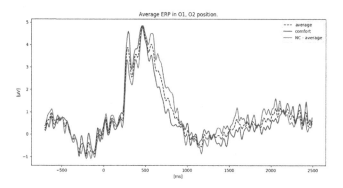

Fig. 4. ERP of visual related brain areas O1 and O2 [6] in NC and C conditions with stimuli appearance at 0 ms. The graphs part in between 300 ms and 900 ms.

5   Limitations

The SSQ showed a degradation of the user discomfort before and after the experiment. This might have a negative effect on the ratings in the later questionnaire phases and especially on the rating in the C zone. However, as discussed above, we are still able to detect a difference to a high certainty, which is important when using a BCI during development or usage of a HMD experience. That our results hold in a field environment, when movement and the content of the experience comes into play, needs to be examined in future work.

6   Discussion

Our study indicates the feasibility of using consumer BCIs to objectively detect visual stress when using a HMD and the ability to classify the level of discomfort experienced by the user. The used questionnaire confirmed the existing literature on calculating zones of comfort and discomfort for stereoscopic images [19]. Participants report more visual discomfort in NC condition than in C condition. The symptoms got worse from eye strain, to double vision without the ability to fuse the stereoscopic picture the closer the object appeared in the NC condition. This means our EEG measurements represent the users' actual experience. The EEG analysis gives promising insight on detecting visual stress either through monitoring the parietal or occipital lobes of the brain with 2 electrodes. The high classification rate of 71% for C and 83% for NC condition when using the O1 and O2 electrode [6] proves the applicability of using a BCI to detect visual stress within a HMD. Furthermore, the finding that only two electrodes are needed make it easy to wear as it might be integrated into the headstraps of an HMD. Also it makes it a relatively low-cost tool that does not interfere with the users experience at all. The signal monitored in the two brain regions react differently to the presented stimuli. The perceptual related areas react with a delay of about 500 to 700 ms later in the NC then in the C condition, which might be explained by the higher cognitive workload needed in the NC condition [14]. The visual related areas react to the stimuli between 300 and 500 ms with approximately $1 \mu V$ higher values for the C then for the NC condition. In combination this means, for faster detection the visual parts of the brain should be monitored and monitoring the perceptual related areas increase the certainty of the detection. The approach of cleaning the data and classifying the detected signal is simple and fast enough to be used in real time during the HMD usage. Therefore our system can be extended as a tool to detect and adapt virtual environments by scientist and practitioners during the runtime of a HMD experience.

7   Conclusion and Future Work

We could show that using consumer BCIs can be used to detect visual stress of a HMD user using two electrodes with up to 83% accuracy. In the future we will be testing the system in more natural virtual reality experiments as well as testing other factors causing visual stress such as blurred pictures. In addition, we will investigate increasing the classification accuracy by looking at combinations between the occipital and parietal lobe electrodes as well as more sophisticated machine learning classifiers.

References

1. Costello, P.J.: Health and safety issues associated with virtual reality - a review of current literature. Advisory Group Comput. Graph. **37**, 371–375 (1997)
2. Essilor Intruments USA: The corneal reflection pupillometer for precise pd measurements (2017). http://www.essilorinstrumentsusa.com/DispensingArea/MeasurementDispensingTools/Pages/Pupillometer.aspx
3. Frey, J., Appriou, A., Lotte, F., Hachet, M.: Estimating visual comfort in stereoscopic displays using electroencephalography: a proof-of-concept (2015). arXiv:1505.07783
4. Frey, J., Appriou, A., Lotte, F., Hachet, M.: Classifying EEG signals during stereoscopic visualization to estimate visual comfort. Comput. Intell. Neurosci. **2016**, 7:1–7:7 (2016)
5. Ghaderi, F., Kim, S.K., Kirchner, E.A.: Effects of eye artifact removal methods on single trial P300 detection, a comparative study. J. Neurosci. Methods **221**, 41–47 (2014)
6. Jasper, H.H.: The ten twenty electrode system of the international federation. Electroencephalogr. Clin. Neurophysiol. **10**, 371–375 (1958)
7. Jurcak, V., Tsuzuki, D., Dan, I.: 10/20, 10/10, and 10/5 systems revisited: their validity as relative head-surface-based positioning systems. NeuroImage **34**(4), 1600–1611 (2007)
8. Kennedy, R.S., Lane, N.E., Berbaum, K.S., Lilienthal, M.G.: Simulator sickness questionnaire: an enhanced method for quantifying simulator sickness. Int. J. Aviat. Psychol. **3**(3), 203–220 (1993)
9. Kooi, F.L., Toet, A.: Visual comfort of binocular and 3d displays. Displays **25**(2), 99–108 (2004)
10. Lambooij, M., Fortuin, M., Heynderickx, I.: Visual discomfort and visual fatigue of stereoscopic displays: a review. J. Imaging Sci. Technol. **53**(3), 030201–030214 (2009)
11. Lamkin, P.: The best VR headsets: the virtual reality race is on (2017). https://www.wareable.com/vr/best-vr-headsets-2017
12. Menozzi, M.: Visual ergonomics of head-mounted displays. Jpn. Psychol. Res. **42**(4), 213–221 (2000)
13. MNE Developers: Rejecting bad data (channels and segments) (2017). http://martinos.org/mne/dev/auto_tutorials/plot_artifacts_correction_rejection.html
14. Mun, S., Park, M.C., Yano, S.: Evaluation of viewing experiences induced by curved 3D display. In: Proceedings of SPIE, vol. 9495 (2015)
15. Nichols, S., Patel, H.: Health and safety implications of virtual reality: a review of empirical evidence. Appl. Ergon. **33**, 251–271 (2002)
16. Oculus VR Inc.: Binocular vision, stereoscopic imaging and depth cues (2017). https://developer3.oculus.com/documentation/intro-vr/latest/concepts/bp_app_imaging/

17. Patterson, R., Winterbottom, M.D., Pierce, B.J.: Perceptual issues in the use of head-mounted visual displays. Hum. Factors **48**(3), 555–573 (2006)
18. Sheedy, J.E., Hayes, J.N., Engle, J.: Is all asthenopia the same? Optom. Vis. Sci. **80**(11), 732–739 (2003). Official publication of the American Academy of Optometry
19. Shibata, T., Kim, J., Hoffman, D.M., Banks, M.S.: Visual discomfort with stereo displays: effects of viewing distance and direction of vergence-accommodation conflict. In: Proceedings of SPIE, vol. 7863, pp. 78630P–78630P-9 (2011)
20. Vision Assessment Corporation: Random Dot Stereopsis Test with LEA Symbols®(2016). http://www.visionassessment.com/1005.shtml

Experience Probes: Immersion and Reflection Between Reality and Virtuality

Max Willis[1,2(✉)], Antonella De Angeli[2,3], and Massimo Zancanaro[4]

[1] SKIL Joint Open Lab TIM, Povo, Trento, Italy
max.willis@unitn.it
[2] University of Trento, Trento, Italy
[3] University of Lincoln, Lincoln, UK
adeangeli@Lincoln.ac.uk
[4] Fondazione Bruno Kessler, Povo, Trento, Italy
zancana@fbk.eu

Abstract. This research addresses the issue of the memory-experience gap, the disconnect between momentary perceptions and post experience reporting as relates to HCI research methodologies and the study of immersive technology-mediated experiences in particular. The paper presents an overview of contemporary understanding of immersion and examines HCI methods that investigate participant experiences. We introduce Experience Probes, an integrated design and evaluation methodology that affords momentary reporting by blending states of reflection and immersion in a structured activity situated within the immersive experience. A pilot study is presented that examines an immersive soundscape installation and an Experience Probe enacted through participant-authored sound maps. The maps provide data for thematic analysis, and are coded for signs of *self-perception* and a *sense of place* to evaluate participants' sensations of presence and immersion. Preliminary results are discussed in relation to the reality-virtuality continuum and suggest that the reflective act of reporting, and the experience of immersion within the soundscape installation are not mutually exclusive. This research seeks to extend HCI methods by overcoming the memory-experience gap in the evaluation of technology-mediated experiences.

Keywords: HCI evaluation methods · Immersive experiences · Momentary assessment · Mixed reality environments

1 Introduction

Immersion and reflection are often considered as opposing [7] or alternating states [9] of experience, and while these aspects of perception in lived experiences have been investigated long before the emergence of digital media, the development of augmented- and virtual reality technologies has revitalized investigations into the inter-related concept of presence [30]. In a technology-mediated environment, there is often no escaping the existence of devices, equipment and interfaces, the technological materiality that drives and delivers digital content. Attention to these aspects of the experience can remind participants that they are engaging with a generated or

© IFIP International Federation for Information Processing 2017
Published by Springer International Publishing AG 2017. All Rights Reserved
R. Bernhaupt et al. (Eds.): INTERACT 2017, Part IV, LNCS 10516, pp. 253–262, 2017.
DOI: 10.1007/978-3-319-68059-0_16

semi-synthetic environment and hamper the sense of immersion. Likewise, in the evaluation of experiences that elicit immersion and flow, these states can potentially break when a participant is interrupted to answer questions or reflect. Study of these experiences relies heavily on post-experience questionnaires and qualitative debriefings. However, research in cognitive science has shown that post-experience reporting can be biased by a number of factors, leading to a condition known as the experience-memory gap [26]. In this paper we propose a new method of Experience Probes (EP) that integrates design, experience and evaluation, engaging participants in the virtual world through reflective, investigative activity. EP is demonstrated with a pilot study in an immersive soundscape installation to demonstrate the potential for examining participants' perceptions from within an immersive experience through the analysis of participant-authored mapping artifacts.

One key observation of this work is that visitors to the soundscape installation, when engaged in listening and sound mapping exercises (reflecting), overwhelmingly describe ambience and experience of the virtual place rather than that of the installation, often expressing a feeling of 'being there' (immersion). Another important finding from these preliminary results is that the sense of presence is proportionally represented in participant reporting even when specific attention is given to the technological materiality of the experience. Results are examined with reference to the reality-virtuality continuum [28] and portray participants' momentary experiences, untainted by the experience-memory gap. This work contributes to the investigation of technology-mediated environments with a method to bind the experience of immersion in a technology-mediated environment with the activities of evaluation.

2   Related Work

Definitions of immersion range from "the experience of being transported to an elaborately simulated place" [27] to "unreflective absorption in an activity" [23]. These two definitions mirror the shift in focus in two decades of HCI research, from usability to experience [3, 18]. Presence, initially examined as the perception of being 'in' a place, achievable by effectively masking the medium of experience [30] has similarly evolved in HCI literature to address perceptions of agency within that place, including social, cultural and material dimensions [33]. Contemporary study of technology-mediated environments questions what exactly constitutes immersion and experience and how to measure them [1, 2, 12, 16, 20, 29, 34]. Kristina Höök addresses the challenges in [16] decrying the mismatch between traditional HCI methods that are largely concerned with usability and the concept and aims of evaluation in interactive art. Her recognition that traditional HCI methods need expanding to encompass the lived experiences of technology are reinforced in [22, 24], specifically concerning interactive art installations and mixed reality environments in [35] experience design in [36] and prototyping interactions in [5].

Immersion in any form, be it narrative, theatrical or technology-driven is related to the 'willing suspension of disbelief', the idea that an observer consciously disregards the fact that a situation is beyond the ordinary reality in order to follow or participate, accepting the logic of the experience regardless that it may deviate from that of the real world [25].

This is essential to understanding technology-mediated experiences as virtual worlds, games and interactive installation involve hybrid situations that fluctuate along the reality-virtuality continuum [28]. The real and the virtual in this model are located at the extremes and the space between regarded as mixed reality. Augmented reality, the overlay of virtual elements on the real world is positioned towards the real environment. Augmented virtuality, the implementation of objects and elements from the real world within the virtual, is located towards virtuality.

Considering immersion as a complete captivation [27], reflective thought and contemplation of the immersive experience might seem to inhabit the opposite end of the continuum [15]. This is congruent with Schon's perspectives of reflection-in-action, the conscious renegotiation of knowledge and practice within an activity, and reflection-on-action, the post-experience review of knowledge gained through an activity [31]. However there remains considerable debate over design and evaluation of immersive experiences. Numerous studies [2, 6, 11, 17, 18] examine participation and collaboration in interactive art installations attempting to quantify emotional reactions and social engagements with techniques such as Positive and Negative Affect Schedule (PANAS), Collaborative Analysis Framework and the Repertory Grid. Other methods employ video-cued recall [2] to supplement questionnaires and multimodal investigations such as Gaver's design probes, cultural commentators [14] and polyphonic assessment [13] draw on various lines of qualitative analysis taking into account the subjective interpretations of participants. The Sensual Evaluation Instrument (SEI) [21] introduces nonverbal assessments of emotions and the affective properties of computational artifacts, another unique approach to addressing the methodological deficit. However the majority of HCI research into experience evaluation relies on post-experience reporting which fails to access the thoughts, feelings and emotions of participants from within the lived experience.

The importance of extracting participants' perspectives momentary impressions is related to the potential, and sometimes marked dissonance between the emotions, sensations and the perceptions of the moment and those recalled afterward [19]. This dissonance is referred to as the memory-experience gap [26] and it has driven the development of methods to address the immediate experience in cognitive science research [10] and behavioral medicine [32]. The discrepancy between momentary and retrospective data in reporting is attributed to a variety of experiential, environmental, memory and cognitive factors [26]. An excellent introduction to the topic in the framework of HCI and user experience evaluation can be found in [4].

3 The Technology-Mediated Environment: Soundscape

This pilot study of Experience Probes examines the immersive soundscape installation *Listening to the Walkable City* that was constructed in an underground car park as part of the COOP2016 conference in Trento, Italy (Fig. 1). Its material components were a circular array of six audio monitors on stands, a north arrow marked on the floor in the center and a bamboo street-sweeping broom. Several chairs and tables were located to the sides supporting computer, audio equipment, and a coffee machine. The car park was accessible by stairs leading down from a small courtyard at the conference venue.

The real environments portrayed in the soundscape were pedestrian stairs in Hong Kong that ascend relatively steep inclines in the city and are capped at each end by auto traffic. These are public spaces interspersed with small parks, public toilets and lined with trees, local small businesses and outdoor restaurants. The social and cultural activity of the stairs are the focus of the research project "Hong Kong Stair Archive: Documenting the Walkable City" [8] that grounded initial investigations into the stairs soundscapes.

Fig. 1. Installation environment in Trento, Italy and real environment, Hong Kong

The soundscape was composed of street recordings made on the stairs following several listening surveys of the area. Recordings were made mornings, afternoons and evenings on three separate stairs, and the final soundscape installation condensed a nearly 300 m transect of the city into an exhibition circle approximately eight meters in diameter. The soundscape installation loosely reflected the real world situation in Hong Kong, with an outdoor restaurant located at the bottom of the stairs on a small street with delivery trucks and pedestrian traffic. The stairs led 'up' through the installation area, with sounds of local businesses on each side, and footsteps tripping up and down slightly off-center. At the southern, top of the staircase could be heard the sounds of a heavily trafficked road, with further in the distance a jackhammer and school playground. The street sweeper could be heard in two locations on the stairs.

Sound recordings on site were made with a handheld audio recorder with background sound s of traffic, construction, birdsong, rain and the outdoor restaurants captured by a wide audio image. Isolated sounds were recorded using a very narrow audio image and included footsteps, the rattling of delivery carts and the street sweeper. Audio clips were filtered and assigned unique positions and animated trajectories within the soundscape installation to mimic the natural dynamics of the stairs' sonic environment. Additional sounds were contributed by the installation space, such as the operation of the coffee machine, voices of participants and researcher, the occasional opening of the car-park garage doors, and the action of a broom sweeping the concrete floor.

4   Experience Probe

A total of 34 participants undertook the experience probe. Demographic data was not collected, however participants were roughly balanced male and female, between 30 and 60 years of age, mostly self-selected from the conference attendees. The conference was not sound specific, though many of the participants had prior experience with qualitative data collection methods. Once in the installation space, participants were allowed a few minutes to explore before being offered a clipboard and pen and invited to take part in the evaluation. The probe activity was orientated on a printed form with basic instructions and a map circle with a 'North' arrow. This arrow was replicated on the floor of the installation and orientates between the virtual soundscape, the car park installation space and the evaluation map (Fig. 2).

Participants were asked to *"Describe (in any language) some of the sounds that you hear. Number them 1,2,3... and mark their position on the map."* Additionally they were asked to *"Describe the ambience that this installation presents."* and after, to *"Describe your experience, impressions, or comment on this installation."* Resulting evaluations were written in English, Italian, German, and one in Danish. Participation was largely individual with little discussion or collaboration during the mapping exercise. Several participants sat in one of the chairs to write in more detail, though most remained standing. Instructions were left deliberately simple, and participants took various approaches to completing the exercise.

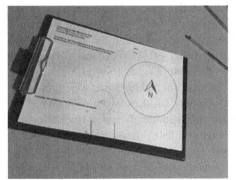

Fig. 2. EP mapping form and north marker on floor

The probe produced 34 participant-authored maps that were translated into English by native speakers. Transcripts were thematically analyzed using AtlasTi, first grouping descriptions of sound sources together, such as "broom" and "sweeping", "auto", "car" and "traffic" and then examining for inscriptions of senses of self and place. *Self-perception* was identified for example in *"I feel"*, *"feeling"* and *"I am"*, references to memories such as *"in some ways it remembers a bit Beijing or Hong Kong"* and creative or imaginative declarations, as in *"These sounds are really inspiring for writing poetry!"* and *"...crimescene"*. *Sense of place* was noted in comments such as *"It seems to be in a shop overlooking the street in a pedestrian district..."* and *"People passing by or exiting the workshop; happy because their work time has finished."* Frequencies were determined not by word occurrences, but by the number of participants reporting in each category, as many participants repeated words and phrases. Participants' maps were further sorted by the method used to map, for example numbering of sounds or speakers, showing motion, and text entered direct on the map (Fig. 3).

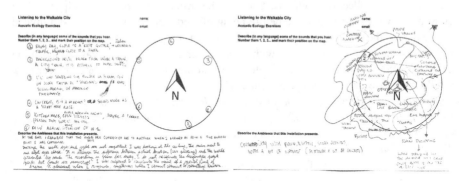

Fig. 3. Experience Probe sample results

5   Results and Discussion

The descriptions provided by participants reflected a true-to-life perception of the actual place in Hong Kong, highlighting the capacity of soundscape to accurately transmit ambience. The most frequently recognized sound within the installation was the street sweeper, reported by 31 of 34 participants (91%). This was followed by sounds of traffic (82%), water and rain (70%), nature sounds (67%), voices (61%), footsteps (52%) and noise (52%). Birdsong, construction and car horns were among the other frequently reported sounds. Participants' ability to identify the elements of the soundscape, however, was to be expected, as the installation was a straightforward arrangement of familiar urban sounds in an enclosed listening environment.

Our main interest is in participants' reporting of these sounds in relation to their awareness of self and presence in the environment. *Self-perception* (41%) was identified in statements such as *"If I close my eyes I have the impression of find myself elsewhere"* and *"Impression that around you is an oriental market in action"*. *Sense of place*, or first-hand experience of the ambience of the soundscape (38%) was marked in texts such as *"It seems to be in a shop overlooking the street in a pedestrian district [...]"* and more imaginatively, *"A gutter, a water loss slips unseen in a silent narrow street, on the margin of the big and noise metropolitan arteries [...]"* Nearly a third (29%) of participants expressed both self and place, clear signs of presence in the virtual that signal immersion. Several participants addressed the overlap of real and virtual presence directly, for example *"During the walk eyes and site are not important: I was looking at the ceiling the man next to me kept eyes closed. It is strange the difference between actual location (car parking) and the world presented by sounds."* and *"I felt I was walking a bit in circles; maybe moving back-and-forth; am I looking for an address?; The sounds move from one side to another; but I felt more like it was me that was moving."*

Examining how the participants enacted their mapping, we observe another important overlap between reality and virtuality on the continuum. Of the 34 participants, one group of 18 (52%) numbered their sounds and marked them on the map, while a second group of 10 participants numbered the six audio monitors on the map and described the sounds they perceived were emanating from each source. Many of this second group of participants stood in front of each audio monitor and listened intently, clearly orientating on the material element of the installation, towards the reality end of the continuum. Yet reporting of *self-perception* and *sense of place* in the virtual remained consistent across both groups, shown in Table 1.

Table 1. Number and % of participants, map style, reporting self and place

	Participants N.	Reporting self	Reporting place	Reporting self & place
Overall	34 (100%)	14 (41%)	13 (38%)	9 (26%)
Mapping sounds	18 (52%)	6 (33%)	6 (33%)	5 (27%)
Mapping speakers	10 (29%)	5 (50%)	7 (70%)	3 (30%)
other	6 (17%)	3 (50%)	0 (0%)	0 (0%)

The percentage of participants simultaneously reporting reflection and immersion remained constant, regardless if individuals were consciously attending to the installation environment or were focused on the virtual world of the soundscape. This supports the idea that a hybrid state of real-virtual, reflective-immersive experience is being initiated through the probe. That 38% of participants described movement within the soundscape, and 26% depicted motion on the map further suggests that participants were cognizant of their own position, as listeners, in relation to both the real and the virtual environments.

This preliminary investigation of the Experience Probes (EP) technique demonstrates the potential to engage participants in reflective practice and gather data from directly within the immersive experience. The probe's participant-authored maps provide sufficient detail to establish that nearly one third of participants experienced self reflection and sense of place, with some participants reporting from a state that clearly fluctuates along the reality-virtuality continuum. The proposition that one can reflect while immersed is borne out even among participants acting with acute awareness to the technological mediation of the installation. Though the use of pen and paper mapping worked well for the small-scale investigation of soundscape installation, it may not be suitable for examining all immersive experiences, particularly those with active visuals or tangible interactions. Yet the EP method is applicable to other domains with some adjustment to the form of data collection. Where a handheld device is appropriate for engaging participants, EP can be enacted through a digital interface to facilitate data collection, storage and filtered retrieval for analysis and visualization.

If collaboration or cooperation is fundamental to a particular experience, EP can be implemented as a game or playful engagement. In any form, central to implementing a successful probe is to ensure that the reflective practice that produces data is mediating and not disturbing the immersive experience.

6   Conclusion

With the increasing technological mediation of our everyday lives, we inhabit what has become a Mixed Reality Environment. HCI as a field has pressing needs to develop new practices to design for and evaluate experiences in this environment. This research presents Experience Probes, an approach to momentary assessment of participant experiences in transition zones between reality and virtuality. The case study presents a soundscape installation and describes the facilitation of a hybrid state among participants in which the experience of immersion is investigated through conscious real-time reflection on a mapping exercise. Expressions produced in this state have been examined for insights into participants' perceptions and we describe how participants express a sense of self-perception as well as a sense of place, intimating their presence and immersion in the virtual space. We surmise from this that with this method the reflective activity of reporting may not necessarily detract from immersion. Experience Probes thus represent an expansion of traditional HCI methodologies to include assessment of participants' momentary perceptions, bypassing the memory-experience gap to evaluate technology-mediated immersive experiences.

Acknowledgments.   Special thanks to the organizers of COOP2016 and to Melissa Cate Christ. This work was supported by a fellowship from TIM.

References

1. Al-Shamaileh, O., Sutcliffe, A.: Investigating a multi-faceted view of user experience. In: Proceedings of the 24th Australian Computer-Human Interaction Conference, Melbourne, Australia, pp. 9–18. ACM (2012)
2. Bilda, Z., Costello, B., Amitani, S.: Collaborative analysis framework for evaluating interactive art experience. CoDesign 2(4), 225–238 (2006)
3. Bødker, S.: Third-wave HCI, 10 years later—participation and sharing. Interactions 22(5), 24–31 (2015)
4. Bruun, A., Ahm, S.: Mind the gap! Comparing retrospective and concurrent ratings of emotion in user experience evaluation. In: Abascal, J., Barbosa, S., Fetter, M., Gross, T., Palanque, P., Winckler, M. (eds.) INTERACT 2015, Part I. LNCS, vol. 9296, pp. 237–254. Springer, Cham (2015). doi:10.1007/978-3-319-22701-6_17
5. Buchenau, M., Suri, J.F.: Experience prototyping. In: Proceedings of the 3rd Conference on Designing Interactive Systems: Processes, Practices, Methods, and Techniques, pp. 424–433. ACM, New York (2000)
6. Candy, L., Ferguson, S.: Interactive experience, art and evaluation. In: Candy, L., Ferguson, S. (eds.) Interactive Experience in the Digital Age: Evaluating New Art Practice. SSCC, pp. 1–10. Springer, Cham (2014). doi:10.1007/978-3-319-04510-8_1

7. Carlson, M.: Performance: A Critical Introduction, 2nd edn., 276 p. Routledge, New York (2004)
8. Christ, M.C.: Hong Kong Stair Archive. http://www.transversestudio.com/Hong-Kong-Stair-Archive. Cited 19 April 2017
9. Csikszentmihalyi, M.: Beyond Boredom and Anxiety. 25th Anniversary edn., xxx, 231 p. Jossey-Bass Publishers, San Francisco (2000)
10. Csikszentmihalyi, M.: Flow: The Psychology of Optimal Experience. Harper Collins, New York (1994)
11. Edmonds, E.A.: Human computer interaction, art and experience. In: Candy, L., Ferguson, S. (eds.) Interactive Experience in the Digital Age: Evaluating New Art Practice. SSCC, pp. 11–23. Springer, Cham (2014). doi:10.1007/978-3-319-04510-8_2
12. Forlizzi, J., Battarbee, K.: Understanding experience in interactive systems. In: Proceedings of the 5th Conference on Designing Interactive Systems: Processes, Practices, Methods, and Techniques, Cambridge, MA, USA, pp. 261–268. ACM (2004)
13. Gaver, W.: Cultural commentators: Non-native interpretations as resources for polyphonic assessment. Int. J. Hum. Comput. Stud. **65**(4), 292–305 (2007)
14. Gaver, W.W., et al.: Cultural probes and the value of uncertainty. Interactions **11**(5), 53–56 (2004)
15. Hansen, L.K.: Contemplative interaction: alternating between immersion and reflection. In: Proceedings of the 4th Decennial Conference on Critical Computing: Between Sense and Sensibility, Aarhus, Denmark, pp. 125–128. ACM (2005)
16. Höök, K., Sengers, P., Andersson, G.: Sense and sensibility: evaluation and interactive art. In: Proceedings of the SIGCHI Conference on Human Factors in Computing Systems, Ft. Lauderdale, Florida, USA, pp. 241–248. ACM (2003)
17. Jacucci, G., et al.: ParticipArt: exploring participation in interactive art installations. In: 2010 IEEE International Symposium on Mixed and Augmented Reality - Arts, Media, and Humanities (2010)
18. Waterworth, J., Fallman, D.: Dealing with user experience and affective evaluation in HCI design: a repertory grid approach. In: CHI 2005 Workshop on Evaluating Affective Interfaces - Innovative Approaches (2005)
19. Kahneman, D., Jason, R.: Living, and thinking about it: two perspectives on life. In: Huppert, F.A., Baylis, N., Keverne, B. (eds.) The Science of Well-Being. Oxford University Press (2005)
20. Väänänen-Vainio-Mattila, K., Roto, V., Hassenzahl, M.: Towards practical user experience evaluation methods. In: Meaningful Measures: International Workshop on Valid Useful User Experience Measurement (VUUM), Reykjavik, Iceland (2008)
21. Isbister, K., Höök, K., Sharp, M., Laaksolahti, J.: The sensual evaluation instrument: developing an affective evaluation tool. In: Proceedings of the SIGCHI Conference on Human Factors in Computing Systems, Montreal, Quebec, Canada, pp. 1163–1172. ACM (2006)
22. Kaye, J.J.: Evaluating experience-focused HCI. In: CHI 2007 Extended Abstracts on Human Factors in Computing Systems, San Jose, CA, USA, pp. 1661–1664. ACM (2007)
23. Kwastek, K.: Aesthetics of Interaction in Digital Art, xxii, 357 p. The MIT Press, Cambridge (2013)
24. MacDonald, C.M., Atwood, M.E.: Changing perspectives on evaluation in HCI: past, present, and future. In: CHI 2013 Extended Abstracts on Human Factors in Computing Systems, Paris, France, pp. 1969–1978. ACM (2013)
25. Mateas, M.: A neo-Aristotelian theory of interactive drama. In: AAAI Spring Symposium on Artificial Intelligence and Interactive Entertainment, Palo Alto, California (2000)

26. Miron-Shatz, T., Stone, A., Kahneman, D.: Memories of yesterday's emotions: does the valence of experience affect the memory-experience gap? Emotion 9(6), 885–891 (2009)
27. Murray, J.H.: Hamlet on the Holodeck: The Future of Narrative in Cyberspace, 324 p. The Free Press (1997)
28. Milgram, P., Kishino, F.: A taxonomy of mixed reality visual displays. IEICE Trans. Inf. Syst. E77-D(12), 1321–1329 (1994)
29. Peters, C., Castellano, G., de Freitas, S.: An exploration of user engagement in HCI. In: Proceedings of the International Workshop on Affective-Aware Virtual Agents and Social Robots, Boston, Massachusetts, pp. 1–3. ACM (2009)
30. Riva, G., Mantovani, F.: Extending the self through the tools and the others: a general framework for presence and social presence in mediated interactions. In: Riva, G., Waterworth, J., Murray, D. (eds.) Interacting with Presence: HCI and the Sense of Presence in Computer-mediated Environments, pp. 12–34. De Gruyter Open, Berlin
31. Schön, D.A.: The Reflective Practitioner: How Professionals Think in Action, x, 374 p. Basic Books, New York (1983)
32. Smyth, J.M., Stone, A.A.: Ecological momentary assessment research in behavioral medicine. J. Happiness Stud. 4(1), 35–52 (2003)
33. Spagnolli, A., Gamberini, L.: A place for presence. Understanding the human involvement in mediated interactive environments. PsychNology J. 3, 6–15 (2005)
34. Vermeeren, A.P.O.S., et al.: User experience evaluation methods: current state and development needs. In: Proceedings of the 6th Nordic Conference on Human-Computer Interaction: Extending Boundaries, Reykjavik, Iceland, pp. 521–530. ACM (2010)
35. Georgiou, Y., Kyza, E.A.: The development and validation of the ARI questionnaire: an instrument for measuring immersion in location-based augmented reality settings. Hum. Comput. Stud. 98, 24–37 (2017)
36. Obrenovic, Z., Martens, J.-B.: Sketching interactive systems with sketchify. ACM Trans. Comput. Hum. Interact. 18(1), 1–38 (2011)

Guidelines for Designing Interactive Omnidirectional Video Applications

Santeri Saarinen[✉], Ville Mäkelä, Pekka Kallioniemi,
Jaakko Hakulinen, and Markku Turunen

Tampere Unit for Computer-Human Interaction,
University of Tampere, Tampere, Finland
{santeri.saarinen, ville.mi.makela, pekka.kallioniemi,
jaakko.hakulinen, markku.turunen}@sis.uta.fi

Abstract. Interactive omnidirectional videos (iODV) can offer informative, entertaining, and immersive experiences, especially when combined with novel platforms such as head-mounted displays. However, omnidirectional videos, and interaction with them, present many unique challenges. In the absence of existing guidelines that accommodate for these challenges, we present dos and don'ts for designing and producing interactive omnidirectional videos. We base these guidelines on numerous interactive systems that we have produced in the recent years. Our work offers useful guidance for those working with omnidirectional videos, especially when designing interactivity and navigation within such systems.

Keywords: Omnidirectional videos · Virtual reality · Head-mounted displays

1 Introduction

Omnidirectional videos (ODV) have received a lot of attention lately due to new technologies for recording and producing such content. They are typically recorded with cameras that cover up to 360 degrees of the scene. Active research efforts have been taken in different domains of ODV ecosystem, including capturing, displaying and interaction technologies, and platforms such as YouTube and Facebook have provided their own content distribution channels for sharing ODV content. This study focuses on iODVs, which are ODV applications with additional interaction in addition to looking around the scene [8]. This interaction could be, for example, in the form of activating UI elements for more information on different objects in the scene, or transitioning from one ODV scene to another. We do not limit on which platform the iODVs should be viewed, although our research concentrates more on content displayed with a head-mounted display (HMD).

Albeit being a relatively new technology, omnidirectional videos have already been used in many domains and contexts. Some examples include use in remote operations and telepresence applications [4, 5], consumer products [9], museums [10], and theatre [6]. Many of these applications offer interactive content and have UI elements which are often crucial features for pleasant user experience [3, 14]. Different interaction techniques in iODV applications have also been researched in many studies.

R. Bernhaupt et al. (Eds.): INTERACT 2017, Part IV, LNCS 10516, pp. 263–272, 2017.
DOI: 10.1007/978-3-319-68059-0_17

Some examples of these include head-position, dwell-time based interaction [8], gesture-based interaction [2, 13, 16] and second screen interfaces [15].

Despite growing interest in interactive omnidirectional videos, most existing research has focused on applying iODVs in specific contexts, or on evaluating a specific design solution. However, the many unique challenges in the production and design of iODVs have gone largely unreported. Therefore, we believe reporting our extensive experiences with various iODV applications in varying environments are useful to other researchers and practitioners.

In this paper, we present guidelines to help in the design, recording, and production of interactive omnidirectional video applications. In particular, we focus on the design of omnidirectional videos with regards to interaction and navigation. With interaction, we primarily refer to embedded content, such as text and pictures that can be utilized to offer more information on important objects within a scene. With navigation, we refer to the ability to move between several videos, which can be used to e.g., move through an industrial hall, or view an object from several angles. Some of our guidelines are highlighted especially for certain platforms. Argyriou et al. [1] have presented similar guidelines for omnidirectional videos in their research. While their work was comprehensive in regards to immersion and some technical aspects of implementation, we offer new guidelines as well as alternative solutions to some problems.

We base our recommendations on several real-world projects we have developed over the recent years which have utilized iODV content in different ways. In the next chapter, we describe some of these projects, after which we present our guidelines. Finally, we conclude with a summary of our work.

2 Interactive Omnidirectional Video Applications

In this section, we present iODV applications based on which we present our guidelines later in this paper. The use cases vary from entertainment to navigation and industrial use, and were carried out in collaboration with several large industrial companies and cultural institutions.

Fig. 1. Interaction with hotpots. A: A hotspot is embedded on a building. B: The user focuses the hotspot at the center of the viewport, and the hotspot starts growing to visualize dwell time. C: The hotspot is triggered, and the content is shown.

In most presented cases, embedded content (*hotspots*) appear in the depicted scenes in the form of small icons (Fig. 1A). When using a head-mounted display, users generally trigger these hotspots through dwell time, i.e., they center the hotspot in the middle of the viewport and wait for a short period for it to activate. During this time, the hotspot grows larger to visualize that it is being triggered (Fig. 1B).

There are two types of hotspots. *Info hotspots* offer additional information on a corresponding object, usually in the form of text (Fig. 1C) or pictures. The appearing information dialog is closed by simply moving the viewport away from it. *Navigation hotspots* transfer the user to another ODV, allowing users to move within the depicted location.

2.1   Maintenance Procedures

We developed several systems in cooperation with industrial partners to aid with maintenance of different industrial machines and equipment, for example large-scale fuel engines or vehicle-mounted aerial work platforms (AWPs). These iODV applications provide the user with remote access to the worksite while preparing for maintenance visit or while learning to use different equipment. These industrial sites have the need for both general and in-depth views of the target vehicle/machine as well as the environment it is located in.

With our iODV solution we are able to offer the user the possibility to view the target equipment from different angles, move around it, take a closer look at important parts and to view how different operations are conducted. This is done by combining short, looping iODVs from different angles and distances from the target machine and longer, non-looping iODVs, which present different actions the machine in question can perform. Therefore, a large network of omnidirectional videos is created, in which the user can move freely, and access information about the machine as well as the location.

2.2   Simulator Installations

We created two recreational simulator installations that utilize iODV content. They utilize videos filmed inside or on top of a vehicle while the vehicle in question is moving. Both simulators are currently in active use in an automobile museum.

The first simulator presents a road grader (Fig. 2A). It includes a low-tech cabin, including the seat, steering wheel and pedals, and a three-display set surrounding the front side of the cabin. This display is used to present the video material, and the user can interact with it by using the steering wheel to rotate the view and by pressing the gas pedal to simulate speeding up.

The second simulator is a rally car installation that uses the Samsung Gear VR headset and headphones inside an actual, stationary rally car. ODV content is presented in a Gear VR application, which shows a video filmed during a test drive by a professional rally driver (Fig. 2B). This allows the user to experience the feeling of sitting inside a rally car, while actually sitting inside a rally car.

The use of iODVs in these simulators is relatively similar. Both utilize long, moving videos filmed inside (or in the case of the road grader, on top of) a vehicle. These films by themselves are not interactive, but the interactivity in the simulators is

Fig. 2. Simulators using ODV content. A: A road grader simulator where the video is projected on the wall using three projectors. B: Rally car simulator used with a VR headset.

done in other ways compared to the industry demos presented earlier. In the road grader simulator, the presentation of iODV content is changed based on user interaction, by rotation, or by adding effects to the video to simulate faster speed. In the rally simulator, the interactivity is limited to starting the rally session, as it is more concentrated on immersion and the experience of rally driving, which most people have no other chance of experiencing. In the next version, we will provide the user with more interactive content such as information on the route driven.

2.3 Virtual Tour Applications

We created several virtual tour applications that utilize iODV content, which concentrate on free-form navigation between videos. Tour applications can be utilized in various ways. Our city tour application was used for language learning, where two students needed to collaborate in a foreign language to find the correct location in a city.

Another use case was with a university campus tour project, which was especially intended as a novel way for new students to familiarize themselves with the campus and the buildings and services within. As a third use case, we created virtual industrial complex tours for our industrial partners. These were used, e.g., for promotional purposes in exhibitions.

3 Guidelines for Designing IODV Applications

In this section, we describe guidelines derived from our experiences with iODV applications. In these guidelines, we concentrate on issues related to interactivity and user experience of iODV applications, instead of issues arising from the context of filming ODV content.

3.1 Avoid Objects Very Close to the Camera

Objects very close to the camera can obstruct useful information and can be disturbing to the user, especially so if the video is viewed on a head-mounted display. In ODVs, the camera within the video is a point-like object in the world space. As such, the objects can exist as close to the camera as the developer/producer wishes. However, when using the iODV application, the user with HMD assumes his body takes up the same amount of space that it normally does. This causes an invading feeling, if some objects are too close. These objects can be anything from walls to tables to other people. The feeling of "in your face" can be off-putting and invasive, and should be accounted for in the production phase. This effect of invading the 'peripersonal space' has been studied extensively in both real world [11] and in virtual environments [12]. This was especially noticeable in our virtual city tour application where the videos were shot in the middle of a city. People passing by were interested in the camera, and often lingered around it or looked straight at it, sometimes at very close distance (Fig. 3A).

Another example is the rally simulator, as the space inside the car was very cramped, and offered limited options for attaching the camera. Moreover, rules and regulations applied for filming inside rally cars, for instance, the camera was not allowed to reach into the front seat area, and had to remain further back. To get a good view of the windshield and the road ahead, however, we put the camera roughly between the two front seats (Fig. 2B). While the primary goal was reached with a good view of the cockpit and the road, the front seats ended up being somewhat disturbing as they seemed to be unnaturally close to the viewport when users were looking around in the car with a HMD (Fig. 3B).

Fig. 3. Examples of disrupting objects. A: A man looking straight at the camera as he is passing by. B: The navigator's seat in the rally simulator.

3.2   Consider an Appropriate Viewpoint

It is important that the viewpoint, i.e., where the camera is placed, supports the context and the use case. For instance, it may be of importance that the camera is placed (a) on a platform that is accessible to people, and (b) at around the same height as the person's viewpoint would be if they really were in the location. This guideline also relates to the notion of making the navigation in the virtual environment natural, as mentioned in related work by Argyriou et al. [1]. In some of our industrial cases, iODVs were used as a way for technicians to familiarize themselves with the location before going on-site in person. Therefore, the view in the videos needed to represent what the technicians would actually see when arriving at the site. Moreover, some users reported feeling dizzy when viewing a video that was filmed from the top of a ladder. This was relatively surprising, as the camera was no more than around three meters above the floor. The ladder was used in an industrial setting to provide a full view of an industrial hall, but in this case the solution worsened the user experience.

3.3 Present Details with Embedded Content

Some low-level details and procedures are difficult to present with ODVs. For example, in industrial context, we aimed to record ODVs of maintenance procedures, to be used as reference material and documentation for future maintenance technicians. We found that capturing the fine details of the procedure, such as interacting with a complicated control panel in a correct way, was problematic. Primarily, it was difficult to place the camera close enough to show that much detail properly (Fig. 4A). Moreover, the technician conducting the procedure would often obstruct the object from the camera (Fig. 4B). In these situations, the role of embedded content, such as pictures, text, and 2D video, is emphasized, to better visualize the details. It is also worthwhile to note that with embedded content (hotspots), one can better guide the user's attention to meaningful objects and events, without the need to rely on the user to always know what to focus on. While Argyriou et al. [1] argued that the UI should be subtle and non-intrusive, in some cases, more disruptive elements could be utilized if it is important to direct the user's attention towards certain elements which she might not otherwise notice. This would be the case in scenarios with a more focused narrative, such as the aforementioned maintenance procedures.

Fig. 4. Situations where embedded content is needed. A: A technician operating a large control panel. B: A technician adjusting a small part of a crane, blocking the view with his hands.

3.4 Ensure the Visibility and Clarity of Interactive Objects and Pathways

When interactive hotspots are added to the scene, it should be clear to the user which objects these hotspots are referring to. Whether a hotspot can be overlaid directly on the object depends on a multitude of characteristics, such as the overall clarity of the scene as well as the density of interactive and important objects. In some cases, hotspots can occlude the object they are referring to, or otherwise make the scene difficult to make sense of. In our industrial applications, we noticed that placing hotspots right on top of certain objects made the application more difficult to use, as the users were not aware of which object was under the interactional element. This primarily applied to scenes that contained many fine details, for example, a control panel with a large number of buttons, switches, and screens. Another example is our city tour application: in Fig. 5A, the information hotspot on the right seemed confusing to users, as it was blocking the view forward and it was not clear what it was referring to. In another application, we successfully used transparent hotspots to more clearly highlight important objects without occluding them (Fig. 5B).

With regards to navigation, the user should be able to understand where a navigation hotspot will take them. For example, in a scene where a large skylift was shown, and a path to the other side of the skylift was offered, it turned out to be confusing as we placed the hotspot on the skylift itself as if traveling "through" it (Fig. 5C). Instead, the hotspot could be visualized to suggest that the user is going around the vehicle. Also, the pathway to the following scene should not be completely covered by the interactional elements. As found by Kallioniemi et al. [7], obscuring the visibility of such routes makes the navigation tasks in 360 degree environments more difficult.

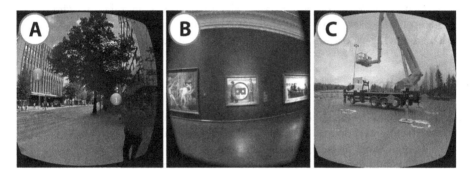

Fig. 5. Interactive objects embedded in omni-directional videos. A: The hotspot on the right is blocking the view forward, and it is unclear what the hotspot is referring to. B: An example of a clear, transparent hotspot, containing more information of a painting. C: Examples of unclear navigation hotspots.

3.5 Visualize Transitions When They are Not Obvious

Moving between several omnidirectional videos may quickly make the user lose sense of where they came from and where their current location is relative to other videos they have moved through. Maintaining navigational awareness is especially important for applications that aim to familiarize users with a remote location before moving on-site.

To support navigational awareness in our campus tour project, we included fast-forwarded non-interactive omnidirectional videos between transitions. These were useful when, e.g., transitioning from one building to another, to visualize which door and path to take to get to the next building. However, if the start point of the transition is visible from the end point, it is not necessary to display a transitional video, but simple fade-in technique is enough.

On a related note, the user should be correctly oriented after each transition. For instance, when transitioning to the next room through a door, the user should be oriented with their back against the door they came through. While this may seem obvious, it is worthwhile to note that in order to achieve this, the relative orientation between each link must be set. Therefore, if three paths lead to the same video, the orientation for each path is different.

3.6 Plan the Complete Pathways Ahead of Time

The complete pathways and transitions between videos should be planned ahead of time, by e.g., writing a script with the full experience in mind. This becomes especially important with more complex applications. For example, in one of our industrial applications, users could move around an industrial hall both indoors and outdoors, and e.g., travel high above the ground riding a skylift (Fig. 5C). Therefore, the application consisted of both looping and non-looping videos. Looping videos were those where users could spend as much time as they want, until they chose to move to a different scene through a hotspot. When users chose to ride up on the skylift, a non-looping crane video would start, at the end of which the users would automatically transition to a new looping video on top of the crane, which would play until the user chooses to take the pathway back down. Therefore, to seamlessly integrate transitions as well as static and moving videos, the full path needs to be carefully planned.

4 Conclusion

Interactive omnidirectional videos (iODVs) can offer a wide variety of useful, exciting, and entertaining experiences. As a relatively new platform, however, iODVs seem to lack basic guidelines to guide practitioners.

Our guidelines for interactive omnidirectional video application, are summarized as follows: (1) Avoid objects very close to the camera, as they obstruct large segments of the surroundings, and may be disturbing to the user. (2) Choose a viewpoint that supports the context and use case of the application. (3) Present details with embedded content, as omnidirectional videos alone cannot always present fine details clearly. (4) Ensure the visibility and clarity of interactive objects and pathways. Using different visual cues, make sure that the link between a hotspot and the related object is clear. In the case of navigational hotspots, communicate clearly where the hotspots will take the user. (5) Visualize transitions when they are not obvious. Navigational awareness is important, especially if the iODV application aims to familiarize users with the depicted location. An especially useful trick is to include fast-forwarded omnidirectional videos between transitions, to e.g. visualize a transition from one building to another. (6) Plan the complete pathways ahead of time. This is especially important when combining free-roaming multi-path videos with static videos – ensuring smooth transitions and avoiding "dead-ends" requires prior planning.

We based our guidelines on numerous projects we have worked on over the recent years. We focused especially on applications that offer interactivity through embedded content, and allow transitioning between multiple videos. With our work, we hope to guide those working with omnidirectional videos, especially when designing interactivity and navigation within such systems.

References

1. Argyriou, L., Economou, D., Bouki, V., Doumanis, I.: Engaging immersive video consumers: Challenges regarding 360-degree gamified video applications. In: IEEE International Conference on Ubiquitous Computing and Communications and 2016 International Symposium on Cyberspace and Security, IUCC-CSS 2016, pp. 145–152. IEEE (2016)
2. Benko, H., Wilson, A.D.: Multi-point interactions with immersive omnidirectional visualizations in a dome. In: ACM International Conference on Interactive Tabletops and Surfaces (ITS 2010), pp. 19–28. ACM, New York (2010)
3. Berning, M., Yonezawa, T., Riedel, T., Nakazawa, J., Beigl, M., Tokuda, H.: 360 degree interactive video for augmented reality prototyping. In: Proceedings of the 2013 ACM Conference on Pervasive and Ubiquitous Computing Adjunct Publication, UbiComp 2013, pp. 1471–1474. ACM, New York (2013)
4. Boult, T.E.: Remote reality via omnidirectional imaging. In: ACM SIGGRAPH 1998 Conference Abstracts and Applications (SIGGRAPH 1998). ACM, New York (1998)
5. De la Torre, F., Vallespi, C., Rybski, P.E., Veloso, M., Kanade, T.: Omnidirectional video capturing, multiple people tracking and identification for meeting monitoring. Technical report (2005). http://repository.cmu.edu/robotics/128/
6. Decock, J., Van Looy, J., Bleumers, L., Bekaert, P.: The pleasure of being (There?). An explorative study into the effects of presence and identification on the enjoyment of an interactive theatrical performance using omnidirectional video. In: Proceedings of the International Society for Presence Research Annual Conference (Edinburgh, Scotland, October 26–28, 2011), ISPR 2011, 12 p. Edinburgh Napier University, Edinburgh (2011)
7. Kallioniemi, P., Hakulinen, J., Keskinen, T., Turunen, M., Heimonen, T., Pihkala-Posti, L., Uusi-Mäkelä, M., Hietala, P., Okkonen, J., Raisamo, R.: Evaluating landmark attraction model in collaborative wayfinding in virtual learning environments. In: Proceedings of the 12th International Conference on Mobile and Ubiquitous Multimedia (MUM 2013). ACM, New York (2013)
8. [Redacted]. User Experience and Immersion of Interactive Omnidirectional Videos in CAVE Systems and Head-Mounted Displays (2017). in Press
9. Kasahara, S., Nagai, S., Rekimoto, J.: First person omnidirectional video: system design and implications for immersive experience. In: Proceedings of the ACM International Conference on Interactive Experiences for TV and Online Video, Brussels, Belgium, 3–5 June 2015
10. Kwiatek, K.: How to preserve inspirational environments that once surrounded a poet? Immersive 360° video and the cultural memory of Charles Causley's poetry. In: 2012 18th International Conference on Virtual Systems and Multimedia (VSMM), pp. 243–250 (2012)
11. Lourenco, S.F., Longo, M.R., Pathman, T.: Near space and its relation to claustrophobic fear. Cognition 119, 448–453 (2010)
12. Iachini, T., Coello, Y., Frassinetti, F., Ruggiero, G.: Body space in social interactions: a comparison of reaching and comfort distance in immersive virtual reality. PLoS ONE 9(11), e111511 (2014)
13. Petry, B., Huber, J.: Towards effective interaction with omnidirectional videos using immersive virtual reality headsets. In: Proceedings of the 6th Augmented Human International Conference (AH 2015). ACM, New York (2015)
14. Ramalho, J., Chambel, T.: Windy sight surfers: sensing and awareness of 360° immersive videos on the move. In: Proceedings of the 11th European Conference on Interactive TV and video, EuroITV 2013, pp. 107–116. ACM, New York (2013)

15. Zoric, G., Barkhuus, L., Engström, A., Önnevall, E.: Panoramic video: design challenges and implications for content interaction. In: Proceedings of the 11th European Conference on Interactive TV and Video, pp. 153–162. ACM (2013a)
16. Zoric, G., Engström, A., Barkhuus, L., Ruiz-Hidalgo, J., Kochale, A.: Gesture interaction with rich TV content in the social setting. In: Exploring and Enhancing the User Experience for Television, Workshop of ACM SIGCHI Conference on Human Factors in Computing Systems, CHI 2013, April 2013, Paris, France (2013b)

How Real Is Unreal?

Virtual Reality and the Impact of Visual Imagery on the Experience of Exercise-Induced Pain

Maria Matsangidou[1(✉)], Chee Siang Ang[1], Alexis R. Mauger[2], Boris Otkhmezuri[1], and Luma Tabbaa[1]

[1] Intelligent Interactions Research Group, Department of Engineering and Digital Arts, University of Kent, Canterbury, UK
{M.Matsangidou,C.S.Ang,bo201,
L.A.M.N.Tabbaa}@kent.ac.uk
[2] Endurance Research Group, School of Sport and Exercise Sciences, University of Kent, Chatham, UK
L.Mauger@kent.ac.uk

Abstract. As a consequence of prolonged muscle contraction, acute pain arises during exercise due to a build-up of noxious biochemicals in and around the muscle. Specific visual cues, e.g., the size of the object in weight lifting exercises, may reduce acute pain experienced during exercise. In this study, we examined how Virtual Reality (VR) can facilitate this "material-weight illusion", influencing perception of task difficulty, which may reduce perceived pain. We found that when vision understated the real weight, the time to exhaustion was 2 min longer. Furthermore, participants' heart rate was significantly lower by 5-7 bpm in the understated session. We concluded that visual-proprioceptive information modulated the individual's willingness to continue to exercise for longer, primarily by reducing the intensity of negative perceptions of pain and effort associated with exercise. This result could inform the design of VR aimed at increasing the level of physical activity and thus a healthier lifestyle.

Keywords: Pain · Exercise · Virtual reality · Material-Weight illusions · Body representation

1 Introduction

Exercise is essential in helping to maintain and improve a healthy way of living, but intense or prolonged exercise can cause a degree of discomfort and pain. The International Association for the Study of Pain (IASP) [1] defines pain as "an unpleasant sensory and emotional experience associated with actual or potential tissue damage", which suggests that pain has both a nociceptive and subjective element to its perception. Therefore, whilst the sensory signal of pain for a given exercise intensity/duration is unavoidable, the intensity of pain that someone consciously experiences may not always be the same.

© IFIP International Federation for Information Processing 2017
Published by Springer International Publishing AG 2017. All Rights Reserved
R. Bernhaupt et al. (Eds.): INTERACT 2017, Part IV, LNCS 10516, pp. 273–288, 2017.
DOI: 10.1007/978-3-319-68059-0_18

Pain has an important role in protecting the body from damaging stimuli through avoidance behavior, and so pain during exercise may influence decision making that either results in the individual reducing the exercise intensity (so that pain is reduced), or withdrawing from the exercise entirely [2]. In either scenario, this could have negative consequences for the individual's physical activity level and/or training stimulus. If pain perception could be offset during exercise, this could result in individuals having an increased willingness to either increase their exercise intensity or continue exercise for a longer period of time. This would potentially result in an increased level of physical activity and thus a healthier lifestyle.

A number of studies have used brain-imaging approaches to examine if pain expectations are associated with concomitant changes in nociceptive circuitry. Some studies have looked into the relationship between expectations and pain experience. Interestingly, it has been found that expectations about a painful stimulus can profoundly influence the brain and pain perception [3]. This suggests that pain expectations can influence neurobiological responses to noxious stimuli. Therefore, mental representations of an impending painful sensory event can shape neural processes that result in an actual painful sensory experience or moderate perception of the nociceptive stimulus [3–5].

It has been shown that individuals initially apply force to lift an object based on the visual material properties, e.g., the size [6, 7]. Consequently, the object size is important to shape material expectations, which are used to produce target force. The perception of object weight is usually based on memory-driven expectations [8] which are termed "material-weight illusions" (MWI) [9] and may be also responsible for providing expectations of task difficulty and consequently the expected pain perception arising from the subsequent muscle force requirement. Therefore, moderating the expectation (by deception of object size) of the difficulty of an exercise task may affect the subsequent pain perception caused by it.

1.1 Virtual Reality and Pain Management

VR is a technology that allows users to experience a computer-simulated reality based on visual cues, enhanced with auditory, tactile and olfactory interactions. The system provides the user with an overall illusion of different senses and creates an immersive experience [10]. Indeed, a range of studies have explored clinical uses of VR, including pain management, physical rehabilitation and psychotherapy [11–13]. In recent years, low cost consumer-facing immersive VR systems have become widely available (e.g., Google Cardboard, Gear VR, Oculus Rift[1]). These affordable immersive VR technologies provide us with feasible solutions, which could be used in a range of real world settings, including homes, sport centers, hospitals, etc. [14].

Whilst a variety of pharmacological analgesics and psychological methods have been used as medical treatments for pain among patients. Research in the past decades has suggested that VR technology could provide an alternative solution to pain

---

[1] https://store.google.com/product/google_carboard, www.samsung.com/global/galaxt/wearables/gear-vr, www.oculus.com.

management [10–13]. For instance, VR can allow a patient to concentrate on the virtual experience, thus distracting him/herself from the perception of nociceptive signals, and pain [15].

These studies suggest that distraction strategy using VR is a common and successful treatment of pain, with most predominantly focused on pain from burn injury (and thermal stimuli-induced pain) and the analgesic effect of distraction via VR [16–20]. However, more recent studies using an Altered Visual Feedback strategy (AVF) suggests an alternative approach to pain management, which may be more appropriate for pain caused by physical movement [21–23].

1.2   Virtual Reality and Altered Visual Feedback Strategy

Previous studies have used VR and AVF to treat kinesiophobia - a fear of movement. It more frequently occurs in patients with chronic pain and can lead to a reduction in physical activity. In a study by Bolete et al. [21], a virtual basketball arena was used to help people overcome kinesiophobia. The participants were located in the centre of the virtual arena and performed a virtual basketball catching task based on their body rotation. The participants stood still on the ground and small manipulations were applied to the visual feedback to alter the way the neck, back and hip contributed to the catching rotation. It was shown that VR enabled the participants to increase their range of motion.

In addition, altered visual cues were also used to examine pain caused by neck movement [23]. In this study, patients with chronic neck pain were asked to rotate their heads. However, the visual feedback of the rotation via VR was manipulated to overstate or understate the real rotation by 20% more or less of the actual movement. The results revealed that altered visual feedback might increase or decrease the pain perception based on the visual proprioceptive feedback. These results [21, 23] showed that AVF increased movement amplitudes in participants with chronic back/neck pain.

However, there were some limitations in these studies [21, 23]. First, the visual feedback manipulation of both studies was small (e.g., up to 20%). There is a need to conduct experiments which manipulate the visual feedback of the participant (e.g., 50%), in order to be able to identify clearly the effect of AVF strategy. In addition, both studies examined if the participants overcame kinesiophobia and rotated their neck, back and hip a bit more because of the visual manipulation. However, whilst an improved range of movement may benefit some patients in terms of engaging in physical activity, it does not necessarily mean they could exercise for longer and therefore acquire a greater training stimulus. As a result, there is a need to conduct an experiment to address the effect of AVF on how well a participant can tolerate a given level of exercise intensity. By asking participants to perform a static exercise task with and without employing AVF strategy, we are able to more accurately explore how AVF may moderate the naturally occurring pain during exercise. In pilot testing conducted in our laboratory, we established that the appearance of a 20% smaller/larger weight was difficult to distinguish, whereas a 50% difference in the visual appearance of a weight created a more obvious distinction between the conditions.

In conclusion, although positive results were found in using VR and AVF to manage kinesiophobia and chronic pain, little has been done to study the use of VR for reducing the naturally occurring pain experienced during strenuous exercise. In this study, we aim to investigate how VR and AVF strategy may affect the perception of exercise-induced pain (EIP) among healthy people. In particular, using a low-cost VR technology, we aim to examine how our material expectations influence our perception of task difficulty and our exercise performance. We also aim to investigate how visual cues may influence the level of pain and discomfort caused by an exhaustive muscle contraction. To examine this, we changed people's expectations of exercise by deceiving them about the size of a weight lifted using VR visual stimulation. In particular, we test the following hypotheses:

H1:   *Altered Visual Feedback strategy in Virtual Reality will influence perception of task difficulty during exercise.*

H2:   *Altered Visual Feedback strategy in Virtual Reality will influence endurance performance during exercise.*

H3:   *Altered Visual Feedback strategy in Virtual Reality will affect pain experienced during exercise.*

2   Materials and Methods

2.1   Participants

Thirty healthy participants (males = 16 and females = 14), aged between 24 to 45 years (M = 35.60, SD = 7.05) participated in this the study. Participants' 1RM (one repetition maximum, i.e. the heaviest weight they could lift) for 180 degrees of dominant arm elbow flexion ranged from 4 to 25 kg (M = 13.92, SD = 5.77). 56% of the participants did not do any resistance exercise training and 33% did not do any aerobic training during the week. Overall, they had a weakly mean workout time of 4 h. All participants had normal or corrected to normal vision and no disability in their hand, arm, shoulder, neck, back or another area that could affect their performance of the exercise task. All participants had no history of any cardiovascular, mental or brain disorders or were taking any chronic medications that affect the central nervous system.

2.2   Ethics

The study was approved by University of Kent SSES Research Ethics & Advisory Group (ref. Prop. 112_2015_2016). All participants signed a consent form prior to the study and the study was performed in accordance with the Declaration of Helsinki.

2.3   Procedure

The experiment required the participant to pay four separate visits to the laboratory. The first visit involved the calculation of the 1RM and the VR familiarization session, whilst the second, third and fourth visit involved a Control and two VR intervention sessions.

Phase 1. On the first day of the experiment, we calculated the 1RM of each participant. The participants stood with their back straight against a wall, with their elbow and wrist joint at a 180° angle. Participants were asked to bicep curl a dumbbell weight through a full range of motion (180°-full flexion-180°) (Fig. 1). Then, weights were added to the dumbbell until the participant could no longer perform a bicep curl through the full range of motion. The heaviest weight the participant was able to lift was set as their 1RM. From the 1RM, a weight of 20% was calculated and set as their baseline weight:

$$Baseline\,Weight\,(kg) = \frac{1RM * 20}{100}$$

The participants then rested for 10 min and moved on to the VR familiarization.

During VR familiarization, the participants sat on a chair with their elbow rested on a table in front of them. A yoga mat was placed under their elbow to ensure that the position was comfortable. With their elbow at an angle of 90° flexion, and their wrist joint 20 cm above the table surface, the participants were instructed to hold their Baseline Weight in an isometric contraction for as long as they could (Fig. 1). A Samsung Galaxy Gear (see footnote 1) head mounted VR was placed on the participants' head, where they saw their virtual body sitting on a virtual chair in a neutral room. In the virtual room, there was a virtual table with a yoga mat on it, imitating the real environment. The participant's hand held the weight in the 90° position in VR (Fig. 2). No other elements were added to the virtual room since different environmental factors may distract the participant. The VR was connected with a Microsoft band, so as to record the movement of the participant's hand. Once the participant were familiarized with the Virtual Environment (VE), we then placed the dumbbell in the participant's hand and asked him/her to lift it and keep his/her hand in the isometric position. The participants did not see the real weight before VR experience.

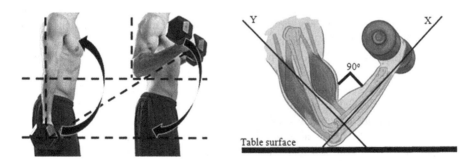

Fig. 1. To the left: Bicep curl 180°-full flexion-180°. To the right: Bicep curl Isometric Position.

Apparatus. The VR system was developed using Unity3D 5 to work with Samsung Gear VR and Samsung Galaxy S6 phone. The 3D models (human upper body, the virtual room and barbells) (Fig. 2) were created in Maya version 2016. The system we developed allows the researchers to customize the VR scenarios, including the gender of the human body, dominant hand, skin colors, colors of the t-shirt, and the weights of the barbells. In order to create a sense of embodiment, we used Microsoft Band's

Fig. 2. Human 3D model – user's perception.

gyroscope[2] to animate the virtual arm, reflecting the movement of participant's arm (rotation X and Y).

During the VR familiarization exercise, the following data were collected:

- Heart Rate (HR), was recorded continuously with a telemetric device (Polar Electro, N2965, Finland). Heart Rate is a continuous physiological signal, which allows us to record physiological changes and correlations between exercise intensity. It is an objective measurement, recommended to ensure an inclusive approach whilst conducting clinical pain experiments [24, 25].
- Time to Exhaustion (TTE), was measured based on the amount of time the participants spent holding the weight. Time to occurrence of pain has been previously assessed during a continuous induced pain task [26–28]. A time to exhaustion task, together with parallel measures of exercise-induced pain (EIP) has been previously used to assess the effect of EIP of exercise performance [29].
- Pain Intensity (PIR), was assessed during the exercise task using the 1-10 Cook Scale [30]. Participants' perceived pain was reported for every minute during the exercise task.
- Rating of Perceived Exertion (RPE), was assessed during the exercise task using the 6-20 Scale [31]. Participants' perception of effort (defined as the sensation of how hard they are driving their arm in order to maintain the muscle contraction) was recorded for every minute elapsed during the exercise task.

---

[2] http://www.dyadica.co.uk/controlling-virtual-experiences-using-biometrics/.

After the familiarization session, a questionnaire was given to the participants in order to rate their sense of Presence in the VR (e.g. in the computer generated world, I had the sense of "being there"), the sense of Hand Ownership (e.g. I had the feeling that the hand in the VR glasses is my hand; It felt like I was looking directly at my hand rather than at a fake hand; It felt like the hand I was looking at was my hand), their Comfort (e.g. how comfortable did you find the set up (lift the weight) through the VR glasses) and Motivation (e.g. could you imagine motivating yourself to use the VR glasses to exercise everyday for 10 min). Participants rated their statements on a 7-point Likert scale anchored "Not at all" and "Very much".

Phase 2. In the second, third and fourth day, the participant came to the lab believing that they would do the same exercise again in three separate sessions. There was a control session which was exactly the same as the familiarization session. However, in the two other sessions, we modified the VR visual feedback, unbeknownst to the participants. Specifically, the visual weight as presented in the VR, understated or overstated the real weight by 50% more or less than the control session (Fig. 3). The real weight that was actually lifted remained the same in all three sessions. The three sessions were carried out in a counterbalanced design, to reduce the changes of the order of the sessions adversely influencing the results. At the end of the experiment, we asked if the participant was able to identify a difference between the three sessions, and if they were what the difference was.

Fig. 3. The depicted images represent the three sessions in this order: Understated – Control – Overstated.

The same data (pain related and VR related measurements) were collected during all the sessions.

3   Results

3.1   Pain Measurements

Heart Rate (HR). To investigate whether there was a difference between the participants overall mean HR in the three sessions, an ANOVA with repeated measures followed by Bonferroni post hoc test was conducted. The analysis revealed a significant difference between HR during the three sessions ($F = 14.73$, $df = 2, 58$, $p < .001$). Post hoc tests using the Bonferroni correction revealed that there was a significant

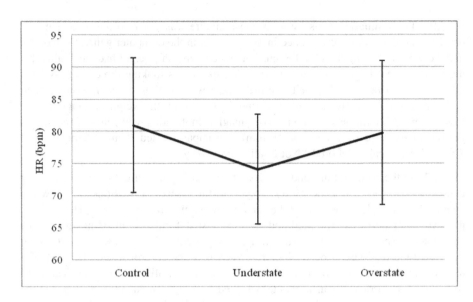

Fig. 4. Mean HR during the three sessions.

difference between the mean HR in the Understate session (M = 74.07, SD = 8.58), and the Control session (M = 80.93, SD = 10.50). There was also a significant difference between the Understate (M = 74.07, SD = 8.58) and the Overstate session (M = 79.73, SD = 11.21) (Fig. 4).

Additional analysis was conducted to investigate whether there was a difference between the participants HR in the three sessions based on the ISO time (ISOtime = 3 min), which is the shortest time to exhaustion across all subjects in all conditions.

The analysis showed a significant difference for the HR during the three sessions at the first three minutes (ISO time) (F = 15.37, df = 2, 58, p < .001). Post-hoc paired comparisons with Bonferroni corrections indicated that the mean HR in the understate session (M = 72.29, SD = 3.04) was significantly lower in comparison to control (M = 79.34, SD = 2.00) and overstate (M = 77.97, SD = 2.22) sessions.

There was also a significant difference for the HR and the ISOtime (F = 15.89, df = 1.47, 42.70, p < .001 with Greenhouse-Geisser correction). Post hoc tests using the Bonferroni correction revealed that there was a significant difference between the first (M = 75.24, SD = 11.81), and the third (M = 77.84, SD = 10.61) minute. There was also a significant difference between the second (M = 76.51, SD = 10.87) and the third (M = 77.84, SD = 10.61) minute.

Time to Exhaustion (TTE). To investigate whether there was a difference between the participants Time to Exhaustion (TTE) in the three sessions, an ANOVA with repeated measures followed by Bonferroni post hoc test was conducted. The analysis revealed a significant difference for the TTE during the three sessions (F = 23.50, df = 1.60, 46.33, p = .000 with Greenhouse-Geisser correction). Post-hoc paired comparisons with Bonferroni corrections indicated that the mean TTE in the understate session (M = 7.45, SD = 3.15) was significantly longer than during the control (M = 5.46, SD = 2.25) and the overstated (M = 5.47, SD = 2.46) sessions.

During the understate session, the minimum time to exhaustion a participant lasted was 3.29 min and the maximum was 13.21 min. The minimum time to exhaustion for the control session was 2.59 min and the maximum was 8.11 min, similarly, during the overstate session the minimum time to exhaustion was 3.03 min and the maximum was 7.50 min.

Pain Intensity (PIR). To investigate whether there was a difference between the Pain Intensity reported by the participants in the three sessions for the ISO time (ISO time = 3), an ANOVA with repeated measures followed by Bonferroni post hoc test was conducted. The analysis revealed a significant difference for the Pain Intensity during the three sessions for the first three minutes (F = 9.45, df = 2.65, 76.73, p = .000 with Greenhouse-Geisser correction). Post-hoc paired comparisons with Bonferroni corrections indicated that the mean Pain Intensity in the understate session at each minute (Mmin1 = .65, SD = .93), (Mmin2 = 1.78, SD = 1.84), (Mmin3 = 3.30, SD = 2.18) was significantly lower than the control (Mmin1 = 1.23, SD = .88), (Mmin2 = 2.93, SD = 1.70), (Mmin3 = 4.92, SD = 2.30) and the overstate conditions (Mmin1 = 1.48, SD = 0.98), (Mmin2 = 3.40, SD = 1.49), (Mmin3 = 5.48, SD = 2.17) sessions (Fig. 5).

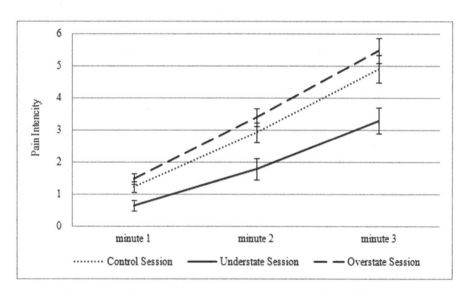

Fig. 5. Mean Pain Intensity rates for three sessions, for each ISO minute.

Rating of Perceived Exertion (RPE). To investigate whether there was a difference between the Rating of Perceived Exertion (RPE) reported by the participants in the three sessions for ISO time (ISOtime = 3), an ANOVA with repeated measures followed by Bonferroni post hoc test was conducted. The analysis revealed a significant difference for the RPE during the three sessions in the first three minutes (F = 4.56,

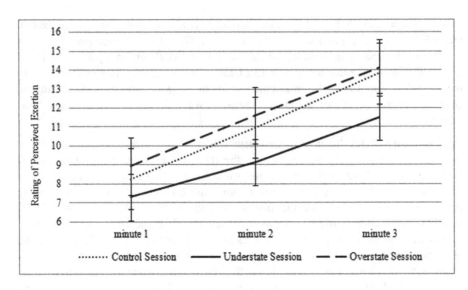

Fig. 6. Mean number of Rating of Perceived Exertion for three sessions, for each ISO minute.

df = 4, 116, p < .005). Post-hoc paired comparisons with Bonferroni corrections indicated that the mean RPE in the understate session at each minute point was (Mmin1 = 7.30, SD = 1.70), (Mmin2 = 9.13, SD = 2.66), (Mmin3 = 11.53, SD = 2.76) significantly lower than the control (Mmin1 = 8.27, SD = 1.66), (Mmin2 = 10.97, SD = 2.40), (Mmin3 = 13.83, SD = 2.63) and the overstated (Mmin1 = 8.93, SD = 1.93), (Mmin2 = 11.60, SD = 2.51), (Mmin3 = 14.13, SD = 2.66) session (Fig. 6).

3.2 Virtual Reality (VR)

Overall, our participants reported high rates of Immersion (> 3.5). Based on their rating, our VR application produced a high degree of Presence, Hand Ownership and Comfort. In addition, most participants reported that the VR application motivated them positively.

Presence. In both phases, participants reported high levels of presence. However, participants reported slightly higher levels of presence during phase 1 (M = 5.27, SD = 1.57) than phase 2 (M = 5.20, SD = 1.67).

Hand Ownership. In both phases, participants reported moderate to high levels of hand ownership. However, participants reported slightly higher levels of hand ownership during phase 2 (M = 4.22, SD = 1.61) than during phase 1 (M = 4.13, SD = 1.12).

Ratings of Comfort. In both phases, participants reported high levels of comfort. However, participants reported slightly higher levels of comfort during phase 2 (M = 6.13, SD = 1.96) than during phase 1 (M = 5.80, SD = 1.58).

Ratings on Motivation. Finally, in both phases, participants reported high levels of motivation. However, participants reported slightly higher levels of motivation during phase 2 (M = 5.30, SD = 1.93) than during phase 1 (M = 5.13, SD = 2.11).

Awareness of Visual Feedback Modification. Six out of 30 participants reported that they were aware of the visual feedback modification (e.g. they knew the physical weight was the same in all three conditions in phase 2), which was a significant part of our sample (t (29) = 24.23, p < 0.001). A paired sample t test was used to compare the difference between TTE of individuals who identified the modification and individuals who failed to identified it. Our results showed significant differences on TTE between the individuals who identified the visual feedback modification and the one who didn't. Specifically, significant results were reported during understate (t (28) = 1.39, p < 0.05), control (t (28) = 1.39, p < 0.005) and overstate (t (28) = 1.35, p < 0.005) sessions (Table 1).

Table 1. Mean RPE for the three sessions, based on the identification of the visual feedback modification.

	Mean time (min): Control session	Mean time (min): Understate session	Mean time (min): Overstate session
Identified the visual feedback modification	06:59	09:23	07:07
Didn't identified the visual feedback modification	05:28	07:21	05:27

4 Discussion and Future Research

4.1 Discussion

The use of VR technology to influence individual perception is a relatively new approach to acute pain management. In our study, we found that VR through Altered Visual Feedback strategy (AVF) interventions appeared to be very effective for this sample of 24 to 45 year old adults of both genders.

H2 is accepted since the results demonstrated a significant increase in Time to Exhaustion (TTE) during the VR understate session in contrast to the control and overstate sessions. Overall our participants lasted approximately two minutes longer during the understate session in contrast to the control and overstate sessions. Interestingly, during the understate session the maximum time to exhaustion was 13.21 min which is in great contrast to the control and the overstate sessions, with an approximately five minute difference. Previous research found that mental and material representations could shape the neural processes that result in an actual painful sensory experience [3–5]. Therefore, in our study, we moderated the expectation of the participant by understating the visual feedback by 50%. This moderation might have affected the subsequent pain perception caused by the exercise task. As a result, the participant perceived less pain and therefore exercised for longer.

The effectiveness of VR and AVF was further highlighted by the lower HR during the understate session. Our findings suggested that there was a significant difference, which indicates that during the whole understate session the participants' heart rate was significantly lower by 5-7 bpm, than during the control and overstate session. As explained above, HR is an objective measurement of a continuous physiological signal, which has been used in the assessment of clinical pain experiments [2, 25]. HR allows us to record physiological changes and correlations between exercise intensity. With this in mind and based on evidence that individuals initially apply force to lift an object based on the visual material properties [6, 7], we believe that the perception of exercise difficulty during the understate session was modulated by the visual material properties. Therefore, the mental representation of Pain Intensity might shape the physiological response, by decreasing the participant's HR, likely in an anticipatory manner.

H3 is accepted since the findings are further supported by the fact that VR AVF led to a significant decrease in participant rates of Pain Intensity. Interestingly, during the understate session, the mean Pain Intensity reported by our in the first minute was approximately 50% lower than the mean Pain Intensity during the control and overstate sessions. Even though during the following minutes, there was a modest decrease between the differences of Pain Intensity rates in the three sessions, there were still significant differences. In addition to previous studies [23], our findings suggest that the participant not only lasted longer during the understate session but also felt and reported lower rates of pain during the understate session.

Similarly, *H1* is accepted since there was a significant decrease in participants' rating of perceived exertion (RPE) during the understate session in regards to the control and overstate sessions. Participants' sensation of how hard they were driving their arm in order to maintain the muscle contraction was considerably lower during the understate session.

A particularly promising result was that even though some of our participants were able to identify feedback modification, there was still a positive effect of the VR AVF on the participants. During the understate sessions, the participants who knew that the visual feedback modified still lasted approximately two minutes longer than the control and the overstate sessions. This result highlights the effectiveness of VR AVF and the potential applications it has for use in home based training sessions.

These results support the assumption made in [14] that low-cost VR HMD with AVF strategy has the potential to be used in exercises to reduce pain. Although the current study was carried out with healthy participants, a fruitful future research direction will be to explore its use in pain management in healthcare settings. Due to the low cost nature, it is practical to carry out this type of intervention at home. We therefore further hypothesize that this will lead to the improvement of health care and pain management, since individuals will be able to manage pain and improve their physical activity on a daily basis.

The overall findings of this study are consistent with other studies in the literature [21, 23], which suggest that VR AVF is an effective tool for pain management and rehabilitation. However, the magnitude of effects in the current study exceeds those of other studies. To the best of our knowledge, this study is the only one of its kind to find significant improvements due to VR AVF in all of the aforementioned indices of the pain experience within a single sample.

The results of this study provide further evidence that AVF technique with VR technology can play a significant role in the improvement of pain management. In particular, our findings show the positive consequences of being able to offset pain perception during exercise. Overall, our results suggest that VR AVF can increase TTE and decrease HR, Pain Intensity and RPE. This results in individuals having an increased willingness to continue exercise for a longer period of time. Therefore, VR has to potential to reduce EIP, and thus presents opportunities to use VR to increase physical activity. In addition, our participants reported high rates of motivation and willingness to carry on with more exercise sessions with the VR headset.

4.2 Future Research and Conclusions

A key motivation for the current study is the potential use of the VR application in home based training sessions in order to improve frequency of physical activity and minimize the perceived pain and/or exertion. Therefore, there is need for future research of home VR training in order to examine the long-term effectiveness, user experience and motivation of the VR AVF. In addition, there is a need to examine its effectiveness in an uncontrolled home based environment.

Overall, our study showed that our VR application supports VR's analgesic effectiveness, even when the participant was aware of the visual feedback modification. However, there is a need for further research to ensure that the effect can still be observed in home based training sessions. Our study also revealed high rates of motivation for using the VR application, although further research is needed to investigate the sustainability of user's motivation over a longer period of time.

In addition, the present results support the notion that minimizing the virtual weight presented through the VR systems will help maximize the duration of the training sessions and minimize the pain. Additional work in the field should examine how changes in the actual weight when the visual feedback is kept constant will affect participants performance and pain perception. Also, more work is needed to explore other elements and features that might enhance and maximize the VR AVF pain management effect in medium to long-term use. We believe that future research could focus on the following areas:

Natural Environments: A pleasant nature scene may decrease pain perception and stress by causing positive emotional responses. There is some evidence to suggest that viewing nature can aid recovery from stress and that blood pressure tends to decline within a few minutes of viewing unspectacular nature [32–36]. Therefore, we suggest enhancing the positive effect of AVF with elements that contain natural environments and pleasant natural sounds (e.g., birds singing).

Single Game Distraction: The effectiveness of VR distraction as a strategy is well established in the literature [16–20, 26–28]. Therefore, we suggest enhancing the AVF with a simple game distraction task. For example, in the existing neutral virtual room with the understate weight condition, a jumping ball can be added and the participant will be required to count the number of jumps. Based on distraction mechanism and selective attention theory [37], we hypothesize that this might enhance the induced analgesia.

Advance Ice-features Distraction: Several studies that went beyond the line of single distraction strategy incorporated ice-features in the Virtual Environment (VE) (e.g., Icy 3D Canyon, SnowWorld) [17–19, 38, 39]. As a result, these VRs with Snow-VE provided an illusion of a "cooling" effect by having the participants look at the snowy environment. This VE provides the user with a complimentary useful feature on distraction strategy, as it is creating a "virtual cooling sensation". Functional magnetic resonance imaging (fMRI) demonstrated a great reduction in participants' pain-related brain activity, while they were using SnowWorld game during thermal experiment [40, 41]. We believe that ice-features could be useful prior to exercise in the heat, as pre-cooling in advance of the exercise would be of benefit to the exercise performance and capacity.

Social interaction: As aforementioned, the VR has the potential to produce applications for clinical populations at home. In many cases, due to their conditions, patients become homebound for a long period of time and hence lack social interactions. Therefore, we believe that it may be beneficial to have a VR that will allow the patient to carry out daily exercises along with other people and interact with them virtually.

In conclusion, our study provided promising results in the use of a low cost VR system as an effective solution for reducing perceived pain in resistance exercise among a healthy population. This opens up research possibilities to investigate other VR design strategies, which will ultimately allow people to use the technology reliably at home. Crucially, we would like to extend this work to include patient groups who could benefit from engaging in an effective VR-based rehabilitation in the home environment.

References

1. Merskey, H., Bogduk, N.: Classification of Chronic Pain, IASP Task Force on Taxonomy. International Association for the Study of Pain Press, Seattle (1994), www.iasp-painorg
2. Mauger, A.R.: Factors affecting the regulation of pacing: current perspectives. Open Access J. Sports Med. **5**, 209–214 (2014)
3. Atlas, L.Y., Wager, T.D.: How expectations shape pain. Neurosci. Lett. **520**(2), 140–148 (2012)
4. Atlas, L.Y., Bolger, N., Lindquist, M.A., Wager, T.D.: Brain mediators of predictive cue effects on perceived pain. J. Neurosci. **30**(39), 12964–12977 (2010)
5. Koyama, T., McHaffie, J.G., Laurienti, P.J., Coghill, R.C.: The subjective experience of pain: where expectations become reality. Proc. Natl. Acad. Sci. U.S.A. **102**(36), 12950–12955 (2005)
6. Adelson, E.H.: On seeing stuff: the perception of materials by humans and machines. In: Photonics West 2001-Electronic Imaging, pp. 1–12. International Society for Optics and Photonics, June 2001
7. Johansson, R.S., Westling, G.: Coordinated isometric muscle commands adequately and erroneously programmed for the weight during lifting task with precision grip. Exp. Brain Res. **71**(1), 59–71 (1988)
8. Gordon, A.M., Westling, G., Cole, K.J., Johansson, R.S.: Memory representations underlying motor commands used during manipulation of common and novel objects. J. Neurophysiol. **69**(6), 1789–1796 (1993)

9. Seashore, C.E.: Some psychological statistics. 2. The material-weight illusion. Univ. Iowa Stud. Psychol. **2**, 36–46 (1899)
10. Li, A., Montaño, Z., Chen, V.J., Gold, J.I.: Virtual reality and pain management: current trends and future directions. Pain Manage. **1**(2), 147–157 (2011)
11. Morris, L.D., Louw, Q.A., Grimmer-Somers, K.: The effectiveness of virtual reality on reducing pain and anxiety in burn injury patients: a systematic review. Clin. J. Pain **25**(9), 815–826 (2009)
12. Riva, G.: Virtual reality in psychotherapy: review. Cyberpsychology & Behav. **8**(3), 220–230 (2005)
13. Rothbaum, B.O., Hodges, L., Kooper, R.: Virtual reality exposure therapy. J. Psychother. Pract. Res. (1997)
14. Matsangidou, M., Ang, C.S., Sakel, M.: Clinical utility of virtual reality in pain management: a comprehensive research review from 2009 to 2016. Br. J. Neurosci. Nurs. (2017)
15. Hoffman, H.G., Seibel, E.J., Richards, T.L., Furness, T.A., Patterson, D.R., Sharar, S.R.: Virtual reality helmet display quality influences the magnitude of virtual reality analgesia. J. Pain **7**(11), 843–850 (2006)
16. Czub, M., Piskorz, J.: How body movement influences virtual reality analgesia? In: 2014 International Conference on Interactive Technologies and Games (iTAG), pp. 13–19 (2014). ieeexplore.ieee.org
17. Hoffman, H.G., Meyer III, W.J., Ramirez, M., Roberts, L., Seibel, E.J., Atzori, B., Patterson, D.R.: Feasibility of articulated arm mounted oculus rift virtual reality goggles for adjunctive pain control during occupational therapy in pediatric burn patients. Cyberpsychology Behav. Soc. Networking **17**(6), 397–401 (2014)
18. Maani, C.V., Hoffman, H.G., Morrow, M., Maiers, A., Gaylord, K., McGhee, L.L., DeSocio, P.A.: Virtual reality pain control during burn wound debridement of combat-related burn injuries using robot-like arm mounted VR goggles. J. Trauma **71**(1), 125–130 (2011)
19. Markus, L.A., Willems, K.E., Maruna, C.C., Schmitz, C.L., Pellino, T.A., Wish, J.R., Schurr, M.J.: Virtual reality: feasibility of implementation in a regional burn center. Burns: J. Int. Soc. Burn Injuries **35**(7), 967–969 (2009)
20. Wender, R., Hoffman, H.G., Hunner, H.H., Seibel, E.J., Patterson, D.R., Sharar, S.R.: Interactivity influences the magnitude of virtual reality analgesia. J. Cyber Ther. Rehabil. **2**(1), 27–33 (2009)
21. Bolte, B., de Lussanet, M., Lappe, M.: Virtual reality system for the enhancement of mobility in patients with chronic back pain. In: Proceedings of the 10th International Conference Disability, Virtual Reality & Associated Technologies (2014)
22. Chen, K.B., Ponto, K., Sesto, M.E., Radwin, R.G.: Influence of altered visual feedback on neck movement for a virtual reality rehabilitative system. In: Proceedings of the Human Factors and Ergonomics Society Annual Meeting, vol. 58(1), pp. 693–697. SAGE Publications, September 2014
23. Harvie, D.S., Broecker, M., Smith, R.T., Meulders, A., Madden, V.J., Moseley, G.L.: Bogus visual feedback alters onset of movement-evoked pain in people with neck pain. Psychol. Sci. **26**(4), 385–392 (2015)
24. McGrath, P.J., Walco, G.A., Turk, D.C., Dworkin, R.H., Brown, M.T., Davidson, K., Hertz, S.H.: Core outcome domains and measures for pediatric acute and chronic/recurrent pain clinical trials: PedIMMPACT recommendations. J. Pain **9**(9), 771–783 (2008)
25. von Baeyer, C.L., Spagrud, L.J.: Systematic review of observational (behavioral) measures of pain for children and adolescents aged 3 to 18 years. Pain **127**(1), 140–150 (2007)

26. Dahlquist, L.M., Herbert, L.J., Weiss, K.E., Jimeno, M.: Virtual-reality distraction and cold-pressor pain tolerance: does avatar point of view matter? Cyberpsychology Behav. Soc. Networking 13(5), 587–591 (2010)
27. Dahlquist, L.M., Weiss, K.E., Clendaniel, L.D., Law, E.F., Ackerman, C.S., McKenna, K. D.: Effects of videogame distraction using a virtual reality type head-mounted display helmet on cold pressor pain in children. J. Pediatr. Psychol. 34(5), 574–584 (2009)
28. Sil, S., Dahlquist, L.M., Thompson, C., Hahn, A., Herbert, L., Wohlheiter, K., Horn, S.: The effects of coping style on virtual reality enhanced videogame distraction in children undergoing cold pressor pain. J. Behav. Med. 37(1), 156–165 (2014)
29. Astokorki, A.H., Mauger, A.R.: Tolerance of exercise-induced pain at a fixed rating of perceived exertion predicts time trial cycling performance. Scand. J. Med. Sci. Sports (2016), doi:10.1111/sms.12659
30. Cook, D.B., O'Connor, P.J., Eubanks, S.A., Smith, J.C., Lee, M.I.N.G.: Naturally occurring muscle pain during exercise: assessment and experimental evidence. Med. Sci. Sports Exerc. 29(8), 999–1012 (1997)
31. Borg, G.: Borg's perceived exertion and pain scales. Hum. Kinet. (1998)
32. Altman, I., Wohlwill, J.F. (eds.): Behavior and the Natural Environment, vol. 6. Springer Science & Business Media (2012)
33. Maller, C., Townsend, M., Pryor, A., Brown, P., St Leger, L.: Healthy nature healthy people: 'contact with nature' as an upstream health promotion intervention for populations. Health Promot. Int. 21(1), 45–54 (2006)
34. Pretty, J., Peacock, J., Sellens, M., Griffin, M.: The mental and physical health outcomes of green exercise. Int. J. Environ. Health Res. 15(5), 319–337 (2005)
35. Ulrich, R.S.: Effects of interior design on wellness: theory and recent scientific research. J. Health Care Inter. Des. 3(1), 97–109 (1991)
36. Ulrich, R.S., Simons, R.F., Losito, B.D., Fiorito, E., Miles, M.A., Zelson, M.: Stress recovery during exposure to natural and urban environments. J. Environ. Psychol. 11(3), 201–230 (1991)
37. Chabris, C.F., Simons, D.J.: The Invisible Gorilla: Thinking Clearly in a World of Illusions. HarperCollinsPublishers (2010)
38. Carrougher, G.J., Hoffman, H.G., Nakamura, D., Lezotte, D., Soltani, M., Leahy, L., Patterson, D.R.: The effect of virtual reality on pain and range of motion in adults with burn injuries. J. Burn Care Res. Official Publ. Am. Burn Assoc. 30(5), 785–791 (2009)
39. Schmitt, Y.S., Hoffman, H.G., Blough, D.K., Patterson, D.R., Jensen, M.P., Soltani, M., Sharar, S.R.: A randomized, controlled trial of immersive virtual reality analgesia, during physical therapy for pediatric burns. Burns: J. Int. Soc. Burn Injuries 37(1), 61–68 (2011)
40. Hoffman, H.G., Richards, T.L., Coda, B., Bills, A.R., Blough, D., Richards, A.L., Sharar, S. R.: Modulation of thermal pain-related brain activity with virtual reality: evidence from fMRI. NeuroReport 15(8), 1245–1248 (2004)
41. Hoffman, H.G., Richards, T.L., Van Oostrom, T., Coda, B.A., Jensen, M.P., Blough, D.K., Sharar, S.R.: The analgesic effects of opioids and immersive virtual reality distraction: evidence from subjective and functional brain imaging assessments. Anesth. Analg. 105(6), 1776–1783 (2007)

Increasing Presence in Virtual Reality with a Vibrotactile Grid Around the Head

Oliver Beren Kaul[✉], Kevin Meier, and Michael Rohs

University of Hannover, Hannover, Germany
{kaul,rohs}@hci.uni-hannover.de, kevin.meier@netzdenke.de
http://hci.uni-hannover.de/

Abstract. A high level of presence is an important aspect of immersive virtual reality applications. However, presence is difficult to achieve as it depends on the individual user, immersion capabilities of the system (visual, auditory, and tactile) and the concrete application. We use a vibrotactile grid around the head in order to further increase the level of presence users feel in virtual reality scenes. In a between-groups comparison study the vibrotactile group scored significantly higher in a standardized presence questionnaire compared to the baseline of no tactile feedback. This suggests the proposed prototype as an additional tool to increase the level of presence users feel in virtual reality scenes.

Keywords: Vibrotactile feedback · Virtual reality · Immersion · Presence

1 Introduction

Current generation virtual reality (VR) head-mounted displays (HMDs) use high-quality visual displays in order to stimulate the user's visual sense for a variety of applications. Along the visuals, common VR applications also use spatial sound to increase the level of presence in certain situations such as in horror games. However, the tactile channel is largely neglected due to difficulties in finding a suitable solution that is acceptable in terms of aesthetics, price, and implementation complexity.

In a previous work we presented *HapticHead* [20,22], a vibrotactile display around the head consisting of a bathing cap with a chin strap and a total of 20 vibrotactile actuators (see Fig. 1). We showed that our prototype can be used in 3D guidance and localization scenarios in both VR and augmented reality (AR) with relatively high precision and low task completion time. It has already been shown that different kinds of tactile feedback increase the level of presence in a VR scene or game [4,5,9]. The purpose of this work is to investigate the effect of a vibrotactile around-the-head HMD on the level of presence that users experience in a VR environment. In order to do this, we implemented two VR scenarios enhanced by vibrotactile feedback and compared them to no vibrotactile feedback in a between-groups comparison study.

© IFIP International Federation for Information Processing 2017
Published by Springer International Publishing AG 2017. All Rights Reserved
R. Bernhaupt et al. (Eds.): INTERACT 2017, Part IV, LNCS 10516, pp. 289–298, 2017.
DOI: 10.1007/978-3-319-68059-0_19

2   Related Work

2.1   Tactile Displays

In the research area of tactile displays Paneels et al. [16] investigate tactile patterns on a bracelet for indicating directions and find that static patterns are not well recognized due to the actuators being too close and being recognized as one impulse instead of multiple impulses (funneling illusion) while dynamic patterns are recognized with higher accuracy.

ActiveBelt [8] is the first vibrotactile belt for directional navigation. Vibrotactile belts have also been used to increase the situational awareness of gamers [13] and for guiding visually impaired people [17].

Haptic Radar [10] is a ring around the head, consisting of multiple infrared sensors and vibrotactile actuators in order to give users a "spider sense" of approaching objects. A similar concept is Proximity Hat [19], which uses pressure instead of vibrotactile actuators and stimulates other receptors (*Merkel disks*). Kerdegari et al. [21] developed a firefighter helmet with seven vibrotactile actuators on the forehead. Their experiment shows lower route deviation times in a navigation task for vibrotactile compared to auditory feedback.

Israr et al. [15] present *Tactile Brush*, an interpolation concept for multiple tactile actuators arranged in a grid in order to purposefully generate a moving tactile funneling illusion, which simulates the feeling of a continuous motion with a single localization point even though multiple actuators are active at a time. Further work on the funneling illusion [18] shows that the spacing of actuators should be 2.5 cm or less on the forehead for the funneling illusion to occur for most users. HapticHead uses a spacing of at least 8 cm, so we do not expect the funneling illusion to arise. Myles et al. [12] investigate the vibrotactile sensitivity of different head regions and use a headband with 4 actuators to provide navigational cues to soldiers. They found that soldiers preferred a tactile to a visual or auditory display for directional cueing and that the forehead, frontal, parietal, and temple regions were most sensitive to tactile stimuli.

2.2   Immersion and Presence in Virtual Reality

In this paper we use the terms immersion and presence following the definition by Slater [6]. *Immersion* refers to the objective level of sensor fidelity a VR system provides, while *presence* refers to a user's subjective psychological response to a VR system. Of course, the level of presence is somewhat correlated to the level of immersion a system can provide but also highly dependent on the concrete VR scene.

Pausch et al. [2] investigated the performance difference of a system with and without increased visual immersion in a search task scenario and found that users were faster in the immersive condition because they had a better spatial understanding of their virtual surroundings. Dinh et al. [4] evaluated the effect of haptic feedback (wind and heat) on user presence in VR. The effect of a vibrotactile vest and pants on user presence and collision detection in VR was explored by Ryu et al. in [7]. They found that their prototype did enhance the user's sense of presence, especially when combined with spatial sound. Just like the system by Ryu et al., our system aims to increase the level of presence in VR. However, we decided to give vibrotactile feedback around the head as such feedback could easily be integrated into existing VR HMDs instead of requiring additional garments.

3   Prototype

Myles and Kalb [12] recommend actuators on the head to operate at frequencies between 32 and 150 Hz because of discomfort above that threshold. We decided to use actuators operating at 150 Hz at maximum because actuator size increases for equally strong impulses at lower frequencies.

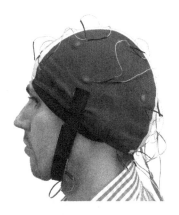

Our prototype consists of a bathing cap with 17 vibration motors (Parallax, 12 mm coin type, 3.3 V, 90 mA, 9000 rpm) attached on the inside and distributed on the whole surface (Fig. 1). The non-stretchable chinstrap hosts another three vibration motors and can be adjusted to different head sizes using a Velcro fastener. The vibration motors are controlled by PWM signals of four Arduino Nanos on a

Fig. 1. HapticHead prototype, to be combined with an HMD.

switchboard, which are connected to a stationary PC through USB and are updated at 90 Hz. This prototype was first presented in [20], in which its performance for 3D guidance was evaluated.

On the software side, vibration motors are modeled at their corresponding position in a Unity scene [23]. This allows for easy spatial activation of selected motors, depending on the VR scene and task. The user's head is tracked by the internal sensors of the HMD that is used in conjunction with HapticHead. In the experiment reported below we use an Oculus Rift CV1.

4   Experiment

We designed an experiment to measure possible effects of vibrotactile feedback in VR scenes on presence. Our initial hypothesis was that appropriate tactile feedback increases the level of presence in VR scenes. We chose a between-subjects study design where the experiment group experienced the VR scenes with tactile feedback and sound, while the control group experienced the same VR scenes with sound but without tactile feedback.

A total of 20 participants (6 female, mean age 24.1, SD 2.5 years) were invited and split up in equally sized experiment and control groups. 11 participants had previous experience with VR HMDs and applications. All participants filled out a mandatory informed consent form and optionally a photographic release form.

4.1   Measuring Presence

In a measurement of psycho-physiological parameters for presence (e.g., electromyography or galvanic skin response) Nacke and Lindley showed significant differences for different experiment conditions [11]. However, these significant differences could not be clearly correlated to participants' responses in accompanying questionnaires, which means that the real causes and effects of those differences still need to be researched.

Instead of trying to measure presence in a quantitative psycho-physiological way, we decided to use a widely used qualitative method presented by Witmer et al. [3]. Their "Immersion Tendency Questionnaire" (ITQ) measures how likely a person is immersed by a movie or game in general and the "Presence Questionnaire" (PQ) measures the level of presence a person was experiencing in a previous experimental condition. This method requires a between-subjects study design for comparable results as all other effects need to be canceled out.

Witmer et al. evaluated their original ITQ and PQ questionnaires, identified and removed irrelevant questions which did not correlate with the overall result and the participants' own assessment of the level of presence [3]. We used these reduced questionnaires and translated the remaining questions to German (the native language of the participants). We further rephrased all of them as statements in order to measure agreement with 7-point Likert scales instead of the proposed 7-point semantic differential scales. We used Likert scales because they are easier to answer (always strongly disagree to strongly agree as options) and often less vague depending on the adjectives used in semantic differential scales which can cause reliability issues [1]. We also added one statement to the PQ, letting participants state how well they were able to survey their environment due to haptic clues. Witmer et al. did not use any haptic stimulations in their experiments.

4.2   Virtual Reality Environments

Two VR environments were implemented as exemplary cases. These were augmented by tactile feedback.

Header Simulation. In our soccer header simulation (HS) four catapults and occasionally a plane above the user throw balls in the direction of the user's head. The user's position is right in the center between four goals.

In the beginning of the 20-minute header simulation scene, only a few balls are thrown towards the user one by one. The task of the user is to head the ball into any of the goals. As time progresses the frequency of balls being thrown increases and it may also happen that multiple balls arrive at the same time. In the last third of the simulation planes appear occasionally and drop balls on top of the user in order to increase the challenge. Users can see a goal score indicator for further motivation (Fig. 2).

Participants can locate the balls visually and through spatial sound from the catapults when a new ball is being launched. In the vibrotactile feedback group

(a) From the outside   (b) Participant's view

Fig. 2. Soccer header simulation in VR.

participants also experience vibrotactile stimuli interpolated between the three closest motors in the direction of the ball. One stimulus is played when the ball is launched (100 ms) and another stimulus is played when the ball impacts on the participant's head (200 ms).

Viking Village. In the viking village simulation (VV) we took one of Unity's standard environments called "Viking Village" from the Unity asset store and enhanced it with visual, auditory, and vibrotactile rain and snow effects (Fig. 3).

(a) Rain effects   (b) Snow effects

Fig. 3. Enhanced viking village VR scene with different weather effects.

The user experiences a 15-minute camera tour on a wooden wagon, hears effects such as rain (5 min), snow (5 min), and cracking flames. Participants of the experiment group also feel rain or snow as single droplets hit their head causing small vibrotactile stimuli at the nearest actuator position. A slightly less intense effect for snowflakes (100 ms, 75% of the maximum intensity) than for rain droplets (200 ms, 100% of the maximum intensity) is played. It is possible to play "catch the particle" by moving the head towards nearby rain droplets or snowflakes and then feel their impact at the corresponding position. Obviously, feeling impacts on facial areas is not correctly modeled as there are no actuators between forehead and chin.

4.3   Procedure

After arriving in our lab, participants were introduced to the Oculus Rift CV1. If they were part of the experiment group, they were also introduced to the HapticHead prototype. In addition, they were informed about the experimental procedure and filled out consent forms as mentioned above. Furthermore, they filled out the modified "Immersion Tendency Questionnaire" before starting with the first experimental condition.

Depending on whether the participants were in the experiment or control group, they experienced the soccer header VR scene, as explained above, with or without tactile feedback generated by the HapticHead prototype. After finishing the first VR scene there was a pause and participants were asked to fill out the modified PQ.

In the second part of the experiment, participants experienced the viking village VR scene, again with or without tactile feedback depending on whether they were in the experiment or control group and filled out another modified PQ. We further asked the participants to estimate how much time had passed after each VR scene because an increased level of presence can alter time perception [14]. Participants of the experiment group finally filled out another questionnaire on the usefulness and appropriateness of the tactile feedback.

5   Results

Results from the Likert scales in both, the ITQ and PQs were summed up per participant, resulting in the total ITQ and PQ scores per participant as intended by Witmer et al. [3]. Even though Likert scales are usually ordinal scales we chose to also report the mean and standard deviation due to large variances between participants and for comparability (Witmer et al. also chose to report mean and standard deviation in their work [3]).

The modified ITQ yielded a median total score of 79.5 (mean 78.6, SD $= 12.6$) for the control group and 91.5 (mean 87.7, SD $= 12.9$) for the experiment group. A Mann-Whitney U test reveals a slight tendency, but no statistically significant differences between the groups ($p = 0.08 > 0.05$).

After the first VR scenario (soccer header simulation), the modified PQ yielded a median total score of 71.5 (mean 69.7, SD $= 14.1$) for the control group and 91.0 (mean 87.7, SD $= 14.3$) for the experiment group. A Mann-Whitney U test reveals a statistically significant difference between the two groups ($p < 0.01$).

When asked about the total time they thought the 20-minute soccer header simulation took, the participants of the control group (mean 26.5 min) estimated almost the same time as the participants of the experiment group (mean 26.0 min).

The modified PQ after the second VR scenario (viking village simulation) yielded median total scores of 60.0 (mean 57.2, SD $= 17.5$) for the control group and 77.5 (mean 74.7, SD $= 22.3$) for the experiment group. A Mann-Whitney U test reveals a statistically significant difference between the two groups (p = 0.027 < 0.05).

When asked about the total time they thought the 15-minute viking village simulation took, again the participants of the control group (mean 18.8 min) estimated almost the same time as the participants of the experiment group (mean 19.0 min).

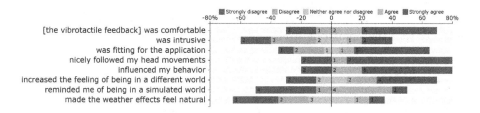

Fig. 4. Appropriateness of vibrotactile feedback

The participants of the experiment group filled out a questionnaire on vibrotactile appropriateness and usefulness at the end of the experiment. Results are shown in Fig. 4. Interestingly, there are some statements with very mixed opinions between participants. As a common pattern, some participants rated the vibrotactile feedback negatively in most of the statements while others rated it positively in most statements which comes down to whether they liked it overall or not. Some participants who disliked the feedback also stated that they disliked the humming sounds of the vibration motors which were close to the ears. Eight of 10 participants of the experiment group agreed that such vibrotactile technology should be incorporated into other applications.

6   Discussion

The difference between the immersion tendency scores of the experiment and control groups is unfortunately close to being statistically significant. This indicates that the two groups were not perfectly balanced. Ideally, the ITQ-scores of both groups should be equal and the p-value should be larger. We suspect that the number of 10 participants per group was too small to cancel out outliers effectively. However, as the difference in ITQ-scores between the groups is not statistically significant, we can compare the results of the presence questionnaires directly.

Both presence questionnaires yielded a statistically significant difference between the two groups. This means that the vibrotactile feedback definitely had an effect on the level of presence users were experiencing in the VR scenes. The participants' duration estimates of the scenes were not significantly different between groups, but both longer than the actual time the scenes took. We suppose that this is due to the scenes being rather long, which may have resulted in boredom and exhaustion.

Estimated duration values for the viking village scene were generally lower in both groups than for the soccer header scene. We suppose that this is caused by the much lower degree of interactivity of the viking village scene compared to the soccer header scene. The former was essentially just a camera tour through the scene and the participant could only move sideways a little and turn the head on the camera wagon. The scene was also quite long at 15 min, which led some participants to complain about being bored as to the low degree of interactivity. Furthermore, the vibrotactile augmentation did not make the weather effects feel more natural to the majority of the members of the experiment group. This indicates that the simulation itself could be improved.

7   Limitations

The relatively low number of 10 participants per group led to a tendency of the groups being almost statistically different in the ITQ results. More balanced groups would have been preferable.

The vibrotactile augmentation of the weather effects in the viking village scene did not lead to more a natural experience for the majority of the participants. Our concrete implementation lacked and could probably be improved using an iterative design approach for the weather effects.

8   Conclusion

The presented study shows that adding vibrotactile feedback around the head can significantly increase the level of presence a user experiences in certain VR scenes. This can be applied in immersive games as well as certain VR training simulations where the level of presence or spatial awareness (including collision prevention) is important such as in complex maintenance jobs, anxiety therapy, or flight training.

HapticHead is a relatively complex prototype with questionable aesthetics, but it could be integrated with future VR HMDs to enable 3D tactile feedback in VR environments. A greater vision of this vibrotactile prototype is to combine it with other tactile garments and produce a fully tactile and very immersive VR experience. This paper is also a first step in finding implications for the design of vibrotactile feedback in VR scenes such as what kind of vibrotactile feedback works best for the simulation of virtual rain. We will investigate these implications in future work.

References

1. Tucker, R.K.: Reliability of semantic differential scales: the role of factor analysis. West. Speech **35**(3), 185–190 (1971). doi:10.1080/10570317109373702. ISSN: 0043-4205

2. Pausch, R., Proffitt, D., Williams, G.: Quantifying immersion in virtual reality. In: Proceedings of the 24th Annual Conference on Computer Graphics and Interactive Techniques - SIGGRAPH 1997, pp. 13–18. ACM Press, New York (1997). doi:10.1145/258734.258744. ISBN: 0897918967

3. Witmer, B.G., Singer, M.J.: Measuring presence in virtual environments: a presence questionnaire. Presence Teleoperators Virtual Environ. **7**(3), 225–240 (1998). doi:10.1162/105474698565686

4. Dinh, H.Q., et al.: Evaluating the importance of multi-sensory input on memory and the sense of presence in virtual environments. In: Proceedings IEEE Virtual Reality (Cat. No. 99CB36316), pp. 222–228. IEEE Computer Society (1999). doi:10.1109/VR.1999.756955. ISBN: 0-7695-0093-5

5. Sallnäs, E.-L., Rassmus-Gröhn, K., Sjöström, C.: Supporting presence in collaborative environments by haptic force feedback. ACM Trans. Comput. Hum. Interact. **7**(4), 461–476 (2000). doi:10.1145/365058.365086. ISSN: 10730516

6. Slater, M.: A note on presence terminology. Presence Connect **3**(3), 1–5 (2003)

7. Ryu, J., Kim, G.J.: Using a vibro-tactile display for enhanced collision perception and presence. In: Proceedings of the ACM Symposium on Virtual Reality Software and Technology - VRST 2004, p. 89. ACM Press, New York (2004). doi:10.1145/1077534.1077551. ISBN: 1581139071

8. Tsukada, K., Yasumura, M.: ActiveBelt: belt-type wearable tactile display for directional navigation. In: Davies, N., Mynatt, E.D., Siio, I. (eds.) UbiComp 2004. LNCS, vol. 3205, pp. 384–399. Springer, Heidelberg (2004). doi:10.1007/978-3-540-30119-6_23

9. Sanchez-Vives, M.V., Slater, M.: Opinion: from presence to consciousness through virtual reality. Nat. Rev. Neurosci. **6**(4), 332–339 (2005). doi:10.1038/nrn1651. ISSN: 1471-003X

10. Cassinelli, A., Reynolds, C., Ishikawa, M.: Augmenting spatial awareness with haptic radar. In: Proceedings - International Symposium on Wearable Computers, ISWC, pp. 61–64 (2007). doi:10.1109/ISWC.2006.286344. ISSN: 15504816

11. Nacke, L., Lindley, C.A.: Flow and immersion in first-person shooters. In: Proceedings of the 2008 Conference on Future Play Research, Play, Share - Future Play 2008, p. 81. ACM Press, New York (2008). doi:10.1145/1496984.1496998. ISBN: 9781605582184

12. Myles, K., Kalb, J.T.: Guidelines for Head Tactile Communication (2010)

13. Pielot, M., Krull, O., Boll, S.: Where is my team? Supporting situation awareness with tactile displays. In: Proceedings of the 28th International Conference on Human Factors in Computing Systems - CHI 2010, p. 1705. ACM Press, New York, April 2010. doi:10.1145/1753326.1753581. ISBN: 9781605589299

14. Sanders, T., Cairns, P.: Time perception, immersion and music in videogames, pp. 160–167. British Informatics Society (2010). ISBN: 9781780171302

15. Israr, A., Poupyrev, I.: Tactile brush. In: Proceedings of the 2011 Annual Conference on Human Factors in Computing Systems - CHI 2011, p. 2019. ACM Press, New York, May 2011. doi:10.1145/1978942.1979235. ISBN: 9781450302289

16. Paneels, S., et al.: What's around me multi-actuator haptic feedback on the wrist. In: 2013 World Haptics Conference, WHC 2013, pp. 407–412 (2013)

17. Cosgun, A., Akin Sisbot, E., Christensen, H.I.: Evaluation of rotational and directional vibration patterns on a tactile belt for guiding visually impaired people. In: IEEE Haptics Symposium, HAPTICS, pp. 367–370. IEEE Computer Society (2014)

18. Kerdegari, H., Kim, Y., Stafford, T., Prescott, T.J.: Centralizing bias and the vibrotactile funneling illusion on the forehead. In: Auvray, M., Duriez, C. (eds.) EUROHAPTICS 2014. LNCS, vol. 8619, pp. 55–62. Springer, Heidelberg (2014). doi:10.1007/978-3-662-44196-1_8

19. Berning, M., et al.: ProximityHat. In: Proceedings of the 2015 ACM International Symposium on Wearable Computers - ISWC 2015, pp. 31–38. ACM Press, New York (2015). doi:10.1145/2802083.2802088. ISBN: 9781450335782

20. Kaul, O.B., Rohs, M.: HapticHead: 3D guidance and target acquisition through a vibrotactile grid. In: Proceedings of the 2016 CHI Conference Extended Abstracts on Human Factors in Computing Systems - CHI EA 2016, pp. 2533–2539. ACM Press, New York, May 2016. doi:10.1145/2851581.2892355. ISBN: 9781450340823

21. Kerdegari, H., Kim, Y., Prescott, T.J.: Head-mounted sensory augmentation device: comparing haptic and audio modality. In: Lepora, N.F., Mura, A., Mangan, M., Verschure, P.F.M.J., Desmulliez, M., Prescott, T.J. (eds.) Living Machines 2016. LNCS, vol. 9793, pp. 107–118. Springer, Cham (2016). doi:10.1007/978-3-319-42417-0_11

22. Kaul, O.B., Rohs, M.: HapticHead: a spherical vibrotactile grid around the head for 3D guidance in virtual and augmented reality. In: Proceedings of the 2017 CHI Conference on Human Factors in Computing Systems - CHI 2017, pp. 3729–3740. ACM Press, New York (2017). doi:10.1145/3025453.3025684. ISBN: 9781450346559

23. Unity Technologies. Unity - Game Engine. https://unity3d.com/. Accessed 9 Dec 2016

User Experience and Immersion of Interactive Omnidirectional Videos in CAVE Systems and Head-Mounted Displays

Pekka Kallioniemi[1(✉)], Ville Mäkelä[1], Santeri Saarinen[1],
Markku Turunen[1], York Winter[2], and Andrei Istudor[2]

[1] Tampere Unit for Computer-Human Interaction, University of Tampere,
Tampere, Finland
{pekka.kallioniemi,ville.makela,santeri.saarinen,
markku.turunen}@uta.fi
[2] Department of Neurobiology, Humboldt-University Berlin, Berlin, Germany
{york.winter,andrei.istudor}@charite.de

Abstract. Omnidirectional video (ODV) is a medium that offers the viewer a 360-degree panoramic video view of the recorded setting. In recent years, various novel platforms for presenting such content have emerged. Many of these applications aim to offer an immersive and interactive experience for the user, but there has been little research on how immersive these solutions actually are. For this study, two interactive ODV (iODV) applications were evaluated: a CAVE system and a head-mounted display (HMD) application. We compared the users' expectations and experience and the level of immersion between these systems. Both indoor and outdoor recorded environments were included. First, the results indicate that the user's experiences with these applications exceed their expectations greatly. Second, the HMD application was found to be more immersive than the CAVE system. Based on the findings of this study, both systems seem to have a great potential for presenting ODV content, thus offering the user an immersive experience for both indoor and outdoor content.

Keywords: Immersion · User experience · Omnidirectional video · CAVE · Head-Mounted displays

1 Introduction

Omnidirectional videos (ODV) have been making their way into the mainstream in the last years. These videos are typically recorded with a set of cameras that cover 360 degrees of the recorded scenery. ODV content has been utilized in several interactive applications, including capturing events such as mountain climbing[1] and musical concerts[2]. As the full contents of these videos cannot be viewed as-is due to the

---

[1] Mammut #project360. Home page: https://play.google.com/store/apps/details?id=ch.mammut. project360&hl=en (Retrieved on 29.7.2015).
[2] Concert - 360-degree video from ZuZuVideo. https://www.youtube.com/watch?v=1Kp1_icG328 (Retrieved on 29.7.2015).

© IFIP International Federation for Information Processing 2017
Published by Springer International Publishing AG 2017. All Rights Reserved
R. Bernhaupt et al. (Eds.): INTERACT 2017, Part IV, LNCS 10516, pp. 299–318, 2017.
DOI: 10.1007/978-3-319-68059-0_20

limitations in the human field of view, they pose two main design challenges: presentation of the content and interacting with it.

There are several different methods for ODV playback. Often these mediums are some kind of Virtual Reality (VR) applications, ranging from CAVEs (Cave Automatic Virtual Environment) [24] to HMDs [18], but ODV content can also be played with web-based applications (Youtube and Facebook 360 video support) and tablets [33]. In addition to the growing consumer markets, VR applications are used in many domains. For example, they have been found to be a promising tool for treating different kind of phobias, such as acrophobia [6] and agoraphobia [21]. ODV's also have potential in industry use, where they could replace for example 3-dimensional models or content recorded with a single camera, which are often used for demonstrating or training purposes. While numerous interesting solutions and applications exist, thorough understanding of omnidirectional video as a medium and its possibilities in different application domains is yet to be achieved. Our study focuses on iODVs, application that utilize ODV with additional interaction in addition to looking around the scene. This interaction could be, for example, in the form of activating UI elements for more information on different objects in the scene, or transitioning from one ODV scene to another.

One of the most important features of virtual reality applications, also the one's that utilize ODVs, is immersion. For example, in a study by Slater, Alberto and Usoh [27] results indicated that those individuals with a higher sense of immersion achieved better performance overall. The term itself has many definitions in the scientific community, but it is commonly referred to as the feeling of "being there". Our study looked into the differences in the feeling of immersion in two different interactive applications displaying omnidirectional video content – a CAVE system and a HMD application. Both mediums have been studied thoroughly in different contexts but in our study, we wanted to explore these applications further in the context of user experience and immersion. As they are both used extensively, e.g. in industrial use, the results from our study can help in designing future applications. Comparing two different methods of displaying interactive content can be very useful for future designs in this domain. In the two applications we implemented, the user could interact with the environment by activating either exits that took the user to another video or hotspots that offered the user contextual information about the environment. In addition to measuring the sense of immersion, we evaluated the user experience on both applications in order to validate them and to measure the differences in both expectations and experiences between the two systems. The user experience metrics measured the participant's opinion for example on usefulness, pleasantness and clarity of the application. In addition, we compared the different video content types to see if there are any differences between them in the user experience or in the feeling of immersion.

Our main research questions for this study were:

- What are the differences in the user experience between CAVE and HMD applications?
- How immersive are interactive CAVE and HMD applications utilizing omnidirectional videos and are there differences in the level of immersion between these two mediums?

Our findings suggest that the users' experiences exceeded their expectations greatly, especially with the HMD application. The user experience results were very positive in general, and both applications received high scores on the 7-point Likert scale on pleasantness, clearness and performance. One explanation for the contrast between expectations and experiences with the HMD application can be in its "black box" nature, which offers barely any cues on the method of interaction or the overall experience to the user. In the case of CAVE systems, their large size and futuristic look might increase the users' expectations. The positive feedback the HMD application received is also interesting when considering its technical limitations in the presentation of the content: our HMD application offered relatively limited field of view of 60 degrees, which is much more limited than that of the human eye, whereas the CAVE system had no physical limitations on its field of view. Interestingly, none of the users reported this as a limitation.

Regarding immersion, our results indicate that ODV is a very immersive medium. Overall, the HMD application was considered more immersive than the CAVE system with both indoor and outdoor video content. For this difference, we have three explanations: (a) HMD obscures the outside world completely from the user, thus allowing them to better focus on the content, (b) the sense of depth created by the stereoscopic effect (separate viewports for both eyes), and (c) the viewport on the display is based on head orientation, allowing the user to naturally look around.

The motivation for this study stems from the extensive use of CAVE systems in various fields, e.g. in the industry. We argue that HMD systems offer many unique and new application areas requiring immersion, and our results seem to support this argument. The benefits of HMDs come from their portability, as they are often small and mobile, and scalability, as they are less dependent on specific equipment or physical setup. Omnidirectional content could prove useful for example in situations where several people manipulate large objects (such as skylifts) at the same time, as they can show relevant information in multiple directions. CAVE systems also have their uses, for example in situations where the information needs to be presented to multiple persons at the same time.

In the following, we first analyze and summarize the related work in this field of research, which is then followed by a comprehensive description of both applications and their differences. Next, we introduce the methodology used in this study and then report the results of the evaluation along with the discussion on the main findings. We conclude the paper by discussing how these results could be used in designing more immersive interactive ODV applications that offer a better user experience.

2 Related Work

2.1 Immersion in Virtual Environments

The term immersion has many definitions in the scientific community, and there is clearly some discrepancy on what the term actually means. There are no prior evaluations on immersion in interactive ODV applications, and therefore the related work presented below is based on studies on immersion in VR applications. Immersion is an important aspect of virtual reality applications, as it is believed to affect user's behavior with and in these applications [31]. Based on Slater [26], the level of immersion is dependent only on the system's rendering software and display technology. By this definition, immersion is objective and measurable. What some researchers refer to as immersion, Slater defines as presence. According to them, presence is "an individual and context-dependent user response" [26], as in the experience of 'being there'. In short, *immersion* is defined as objective level of sensory fidelity the system provides, whereas *presence* refers to the user's subjective experience and response to the system. Using Slater's definitions, the level of immersion easier to measure, but restricts the evaluation so that it can made only on the technological level. This includes only the technical aspects such as field of view (FOV), field of regard (FOR), display size and resolution and the use of stereoscopy. There are several evaluation methods for measuring immersion/presence (based on the definition used), for example the ones by Witmer & Singer [32], Schubert, Friedmann & Regenbrecht [25] and Usoh et al. [30].

Immersion has also been studied extensively in the context of video games, and Brown and Cairns [5] attempted to resolve the disparity with the term. They conducted a qualitative study amongst gamers and talked to them about their experience on playing video games. The study resulted a grounded theory where immersion was used to describe a person's "degree of involvement with the game". This finding supported the idea that immersion is a cognitive phenomenon. The theory also identified restrictions that could limit the degree of user's involvement, including engagement, engrossment and total immersion.

As the related work shows, immersion can be defined in several ways, depending on many factors such as the emphasis on technology, the research domain and the method of evaluation. With VR related studies, Slater's [26] division of immersion and presence is more prevalent, whereas in video game related studies the term immersion is used more often. In this paper, immersion is referred as perceptual phenomenon that is dependent on the individual and the context.

2.2 Omnidirectional Videos

Lot of scientific research has been done to enable the use of omnidirectional video. There exists a large variety of algorithms and devices to capture, construct, project, compress, display and automatically analyze omnidirectional video content.

Application domains, where omnidirectional video has received wider interest include remote operation and telepresence applications [4] [20] [8], some of which include automatic situation tracking based on the omnidirectional imagery and directional audio. Another application field identifiable in literature is remote operation of unmanned machines and vehicles, for example drones by using omnidirectional video. Applications where omnidirectional video is used by consumers [17] [13] [3] provide immersive experiences to cultural contents, e.g., in museums [15] [14] [19] and theatre [9]. Other application domains include education, e.g., teaching sign language [12], and health care, e.g., relieving stress during medical care [10], and therapy [23]. There has been little research on using ODV in industrial use, for example in demonstrating or training purposes.

From the human-computer interaction perspective, augmenting omnidirectional video with interactive content [2] and UI elements [22] are crucial features in many applications. Another field is multisensory augmentations of video content, e.g., simulated wind [22], to further immerse the viewer and improve sense of presence. Interaction studies have also looked at gesture-based interaction [34] [24] and second screen interfaces [33] to interact with omnidirectional video content. For example, Benko and Wilson [1] present the Pinch-the-Sky Dome, which projects a full 360 view of omnidirectional data onto an inner side of a dome-shaped structure. The view is controlled using mid-air gestures from anywhere inside the space, and it supports several simultaneous users. They found that mid-air gestures could enhance immersion in an omnidirectional context.

3   iODV Applications

In this section, we introduce the iODV applications that were built for this study. Both applications used the same ODV content with length of 60 s. When the content is finished, it starts again from the beginning. Both applications have two types of user interface elements: exits and hotspots. When activated, an exit takes the user to another video that is linked to that particular exit element, and hotspots provide contextual information about the environment. First, we introduce the video production procedure used for content creation, and then explain the basic features and interaction techniques for both applications. Finally, we compare the main differences between these two applications.

3.1   Video Production

The videos used in this study were recorded with six GoPro 4 cameras attached to a Freedom360 mount on top of a tripod. The resulting six videos from each shot were converted into 4 k omnidirectional videos by using AutoPano Video Pro 2 and AutoPano Giga 4 software. Panoramic images and videos are usually divided into either cylindrical (limited vertical field of view – VFOV) or spherical (360° × 180°) views.

For this study, we produced a total of six videos, three of which were shot indoors, and three in an outdoor environment. Each video was roughly one minute long. Indoor videos were recorded in an industrial hall used for repairing and maintenance of skylifts. Each video contains some movement, such as people walking around and working, and a forklift riding around the hall. Two of the indoor videos were recorded from a top of a ladder to offer a better view of the surroundings. The outdoor videos were recorded in downtown Tampere, Finland. These videos were recorded during quiet hours, but nonetheless contained a relatively large amount of movement, i.e., people walking on the streets.

3.2   cCAVE

For our first experiment, we implemented a multimodal CAVE application, circular CAVE (cCAVE), where the user can explore omnidirectional videos via eight displays set in the form of an octagon. A cylindrical view where the horizontal FOV is 360 degrees and vertical 150 degrees was used in the application. In this system, the user is located at the center of the octagon, sitting on a rotating chair (see Fig. 1). The chair has a rotating sensor that sends the rotational axis to the computer. This sensor data is used to update user interface elements on one of the displays, e.g. when the chair is pointing at specific coordinates. The application was developed with Vizard virtual reality software. The omnidirectional video content is then displayed on a 3-dimensional cylinder that is divided between the displays so that each monitor covers 45 degrees of the content.

Each interface element (exits and hotspots mentioned earlier) has a coordinate range (i.e. when the rotating chair is pointed at this range) in which they are shown on the screen. The interface elements are triggered by dwelling, i.e. by focusing an element in the center of the view (by turning the chair towards it) and waiting for five seconds. Dwelling is a relatively common technique for selecting targets with e.g. gaze and mid-air gestures, which is utilized by a number of applications (e.g. [16]). Before the hotspots are activated, they are presented on the screen as blue circles with an exclamation mark inside. Exits are presented as green arrows. During the activation period, the element is scaled up in order to visualize that it is being selected. Users can cancel the activation process by turning away from the element. Similarly, a hotspot dialog is closed by turning away from it.

Fig. 1. The cCAVE system. The rotating chair used for interaction is at the center of the system. Eight monitors (only 6 shown in the image) each show 45 degrees of the omnidirectional video content. The two monitors in front are attached to the doors that are opened for entrance and closed during use.

We used a set of eight Eyevis Eye-LCD 4000 M/W monitors. Each monitor has a screen diagonal of 40 inches with full HD resolution and they were raised 77 cm from the ground. They were 91 cm high, 53 cm wide and 13 cm thick. The bezel between two monitors was 28 mm (14 mm in one monitor). These monitors were set up so that they covered an area of 360 degrees around the user. The rotating chair's seat height was adjusted to 50 cm and the distance from the user's head to the monitors was approximately 60 cm. The outer walls of the cCAVE installation were 175 cm wide and 192 cm high. The total resolution for the application was 4320×3840 pixels. The monitors were connected to AMD HD 7870 display adapter with 1 GHz processor and 2 gigabytes of GDDR5 memory.

3.3 Amaze360

Amaze360 is an iODV application for HMDs that allows the user to freely observe omnidirectional videos by simply turning one's head in the desired direction. The screen is divided into two separate viewports in order to create a stereoscopic effect, thus creating a sense of depth. This effect is done with the spherical presentation of the video content, as the video content itself is not stereoscopic. The video content used by the application has 360-degree horizontal and 180-degree vertical field of view and the video is projected on a virtual sphere. The viewport's field of view is 60 degrees.

Interface elements (exits and hotspots) in Amaze360 are also triggered by dwelling, but with slight differences. These elements are activated by focusing on an element in the center of the view (by turning the head towards it) and waiting for two seconds. The hotspot and exit icons in Amaze360 are similar to the ones used in cCAVE (blue circle with an exclamation mark inside for the hotspots, and green arrows for the exits). The entire set up and a screenshot of the Amaze360 application with hotspot activation can be seen in Fig. 2.

Amaze360 is C# application built on the Unity platform, and it utilizes the Oculus Mobile SDK 1.0.0.0 for iODV features. The application also uses the Easy Movie Texture plugin to enable smooth video playback on mobile devices. It is run on Samsung Note 4 and utilizes the Samsung GEAR headset.

3.4 Differences Between the Applications

Even though the two applications are intended for the same purpose, there are obvious differences ranging from physical setup and display devices to interaction mechanics. These differences further affected some design choices for both applications. A general overview of the features and differences can be seen in Table 1.

The primary difference between the two applications is in how content is presented – cCAVE shows the ODV in multiple monitors whereas the Amaze360 uses a stereoscopic presentation on a mobile device. In other words, cCAVE always physically displays the full 360-degree view of the content. Therefore, the user sees the content with the full field of view of the human eye. Amaze360, on the other hand, is limited to a 60-degree sector of the content at any given time.

Another major difference is in how the applications are interacted with, i.e. how hotspots and exits are activated. The cCAVE system utilizes the rotation of the chair,

Fig. 2. Top: Amaze360 physical setup. **Bottom:** Amaze360 application view. The video is shown as a stereoscopic presentation. Activated hotspot is shown at the center of screen.

Table 1. Differences between the two applications

	CAVE	Amaze360
Application Field of View (Horizontal*Vertical, in degrees)	180*150	60*60
Interaction Method	Rotational chair (sensor)	Head/device orientation based activation
Contextual information activation range	X-axis	X- and Y-axis
Contextual information location on the screen	Bottom center	Center
UI Element Activation Time (seconds)	5	2

and therefore only uses the X axis (chair's rotation relative to the screens) for activating UI elements. Amaze360 relies on head orientation, and hence uses both X and Y axes. For illustration on these differences, see Fig. 3.

Due to the difference in how UI elements are activated, both applications vary in how contextual information is presented. In cCAVE, textual content is shown (when a hotspot is activated) at the bottom of the screen. This design choice was made so that the textual content would not obscure the object it is referring to. In Amaze360, textual information was presented on top of the corresponding hotspot (see Fig. 4).

Fig. 3. The hotspot activation sectors illustrated in both applications. The gray coordinate area represents the coordinate rate of hotspots in cCAVE, and the circular area represents the X- and Y- coordinate range used in Amaze360.

Fig. 4. Hotspot locations in the two applications. HMD hotspot location is presented in white dotted line and CAVE system hotspot location in black dotted line.

This was due to the interaction method: as the user activates hotspots by turning their head towards them, it makes sense that the displayed information is displayed in the same position so that the user does not need to adjust the head once more. Furthermore, this allows closing activated hotspots by turning the head away from them, similar to closing hotspots in cCAVE by rotating the chair to another position.

Finally, the activation time for UI elements was also different between the applications because of the conclusions made during pilot testing: a short activation time sometimes caused accidental activations in the CAVE system, whereas with Amaze360 these were not as prevalent. This was caused by the slower interaction with the chair – turning one's head is much faster and more precise than turning on a chair. The pilot tests verified that the Amaze360 application could have a significantly shorter activation time (2 s) for the UI elements than the CAVE system (5 s).

4 Experiment of CAVE and HMD

For this study, we conducted two separate experiments which evaluated the user experience, level of immersion and spatial abilities in immersive virtual environments that utilize omnidirectional videos. Experiment 1 was conducted with the CAVE system and Experiment 2 was conducted with a HMD and the Amaze360 application.

4.1 Participants

A total of 34 participants took part in the study, both experiments having 17 participants. The cCAVE was evaluated by 8 females and 9 males aged 30.9 on average (SD = 5.46) and the Amaze360 system also by 8 females and 9 males with an average age of 30.7 (SD = 5.43). They were recruited from around a university campus and were compensated with a movie ticket for their participation. All participants were naïve with respect to interacting with omnidirectional videos, as in they had not use CAVE, HMD or other type of applications that utilize these type of videos.

4.2 Procedure

In the evaluation scenario the participants were asked to explore the virtual environments that consist of omnidirectional videos. Both indoor and outdoor environments were presented to the user as separate scenarios (one could not move from inside locations to the outside locations, and vice versa). They could move from one location to another after they had spent thirty seconds in one location. The time limitation was set in order to encourage exploration and looking around the scenery instead of just moving quickly from one scenery to another. Each location also contained two hotspots which, when activated, offered contextual information about the object they were referring to. Both indoor and outdoor video content consisted of three different locations and the last location led the user back to the first one, which made it possible for the participant to explore the locations indefinitely.

No specific tasks were given to the participants because we wanted to emphasize the explorative nature of the experiment. This way the participants could concentrate solely on experiencing the virtual environment. The users could use the system under evaluation as long as they wanted to. They informed the researcher when they were finished with each scenario (indoor and outdoor). Participants used each system (both indoor and outdoor scenarios combined) for approximately 10 min on average.

In Experiment 1 the participants used the cCAVE system in a laboratory setting while sitting on the rotating chair. In Experiment 2 they used the Amaze360 application also in a laboratory setting while standing and wearing the HMD. Both locations were approximately the same size. For both experiments, conditions were balanced so that half of the users started using the system in indoor locations and the remaining half in outdoor locations. A researcher was present during the procedure for support in case of a technical fault or other disturbance, but did not otherwise intervene with the evaluation.

4.3   Data Collection and Analysis

We gathered general information from all participants, including age, gender, and experience level with the iODV applications. For the user experience evaluation, we used the SUXES [29] method. It is an evaluation method for collecting subjective user feedback of multimodal systems. In this method, the participants fill out a subjective feedback form about their expectations and experiences on using the system. The form consisted of 9 user experience related claims to which the participants responded on a 7-point Likert scale, where 1 = "Totally disagree", 4 = "Neither agree nor disagree" and 7 = "Totally agree".

Participants filled the expectations form after the user had been informed of the procedure and had been shown to the basics of the system, but before the user personally experienced the system. Then, after they had used the application, users filled out their experiences on a similar form. In addition, after the experiment, participants answered to question regarding their level of immersion during the use of the system ("While using the system, I felt like I was actually standing on the streets/industrial hall"). The same 7-point Likert scale was used for the questions regarding immersion. We decided to disregard the existing evaluation methods for measuring immersion for practical reasons – our custom-made questionnaire allows us to compare the results with the UX results for different modalities using the SUXES method [29]. Finally, we logged basic interactions with timestamps in both systems, such as start and end times of the application, activations of hotspots, and movements from one video to another. We also considered adding the Santa Barbara Sense-of-Direction questionnaire [11] to the evaluation, but decided against it as the evaluation itself was not about measuring spatial ability.

5   Results

The main research interests in this study were the feeling of immersion and the user experience with the two applications. In addition, we report the results from logged interaction data. For all results, a Bonferroni-corrected independent t-test was conducted to compare the results between the two systems. Here, we treat the disagree-agree-like scale to be equidistant, which is why the t-test for analyzing the results was used. For the statistical analysis, an average UX score of both indoor and outdoor video content was used.

5.1 Expectations Versus Experiences

When comparing the UX results of the two experiments, statistically significant differences were discovered between the expectations and the actual user experience on both applications, especially with the HMD. For average UX ratings on all statements in both systems, see Fig. 5.

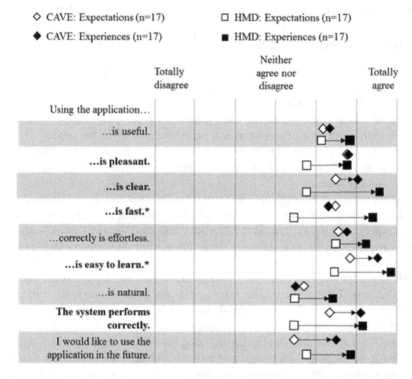

Fig. 5. Average UX ratings for expectations and experiences on both systems. Arrows indicate the direction of the change between expectations and experiences. The statements in bold had statistically significant differences between the applications regarding expectations, and those marked with asterisk in experience.

In almost all metrics the actual use experience exceeded the expectations, especially so with the HMD. Using both systems were considered to be very easy to learn by the participants. All participants except for two in the first experiment and one in the second one agreed (scored either 5, 6 or 7 on the Likert scale) with the statement that the system is useful (Experiment 1, M = 5.29, SD = 1.047 and Experiment 2, M = 5.82, SD = .883).

Participants had higher expectations on the cCAVE system used in the first experiment. Statistically significant effects were detected in expectations on pleasantness (Experiment 1, M = 5.71, SD = .920 and Experiment 2, M = 4.76, SD = 1.251); t (32) = 2.499, p < 0.05, and clarity (Experiment 1, M = 5.53, SD = 1.125 and Experiment 2, M = 4.71, SD = .849); t(32) = 2.410, p < 0.05, where the users anticipated more from the CAVE system. cCAVE users were also more optimistic on how fast the system is (Experiment 1, M = 5.47, SD = 1.179 and Experiment 2, M = 4.41, SD = .939); t(32) = 2.896, p < 0.05, and if it performs correctly (Experiment 1, M = 5.29, SD = 1.263 and Experiment 2, M = 4.47, SD = .874) was found; t (32) = 2.210, p < 0.05.

Regarding the user experience, the questionnaire results on both applications were generally positive. With cCAVE, 88% of the users gave positive feedback (scored either 5, 6 or 7 on the Likert scale) on the system's usefulness. 82% of the users thought that the system was pleasant to use, and 100% of the users felt that the use of the system is easy to learn (where 2.9% ranked it at 5, 29.5% ranked it 6 and 67.6% ranked it at 7 on the Likert scale). The HMD application received even more positive results, where 94% of the users thought that the system is useful and pleasant to use. Like with cCAVE, all of the HMD users felt that the system is easy to learn.

Comparing the results from the two experiments, some statistically significant findings were discovered. The HMD application (M = 6.35, SD = .862) was considered to be faster than the cCAVE system (M = 5.29, SD = 1.532); t(32) = −2.484, p < 0.05. Participants also felt that the HMD application (M = 6.88, SD = .332) is easier to learn than cCAVE (M = 6.53, SD = .514); t(32) = −2.376, p < 0.05.

5.2   Immersion and System Interaction

The main interest in addition to the user experience was the feeling of immersion experienced during the use. Between the two applications, statistically significant differences were observed with both indoor video content (Experiment 1, M = 5.18, SD = 1.629 and Experiment 2, M = 6.18, SD = .883); t(32) = −2.225, p < 0.05, and outdoor video content (Experiment 1, M = 5.18, SD = 1.510 and Experiment 2, M = 6.29, SD = .686); t(32) = −2.779, p < 0.05. The immersion level of participants for both applications with indoor and outdoor videos can be seen in Fig. 6.

Based on interaction log data, some statistically significant differences in the application use times were observed. cCAVE was used for longer periods of time (in seconds) in total (both outdoor and indoor scenarios combined) than the HMD application (Experiment 1, M = 884.47, SD = 357.91 and Experiment 2, M = 561.41, SD = 214.52); t(32) = 3.193, p < 0.05. Participants also used the CAVE system for longer periods with the indoor video content (Experiment 1, M = 502.82, SD = 303.77 and Experiment 2, M = 260.76, SD = 92.96); t(32) = 3.142, p < 0.05. There was no observed effect with outdoor video content. The total times spent with both indoor and outdoor video content can be seen in Fig. 7.

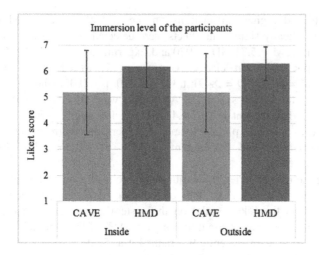

Fig. 6. Average immersion level of the participants in both applications with indoor and outdoor video content

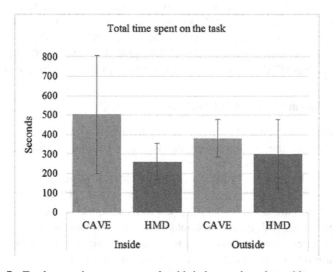

Fig. 7. Total mean time spent on task with indoor and outdoor video content

6 Discussion

6.1 Expectations Versus Experiences

The most interesting finding regarding the user experience was that in almost all metrics the actual use experience exceeded the expectations, especially so in the second experiment with the HMD. The interaction method in the cCAVE experiment can be the reason for the difference in expectations on pleasantness – sitting and interacting with a chair can be expected to be more comfortable for users than standing up while wearing the HMD. In addition, it might be difficult to make any estimates on the pleasantness and clarity on the sort of a "black box" HMD device, which offers no cues on the method of interaction to the user. The cCAVE set up might be more impressive and futuristic looking than HMD devices in general. Another factor to consider is the physical set up of the two applications: cCAVE is a large installation built on a metallic rig with eight monitors, whereas the headset is using the smaller Samsung Gear headset and basic Samsung Note 4 mobile device. The system size difference itself might indicate that the cCAVE is more powerful than the compact HMD device. In addition, a desktop computer can be presumed to have better performance than a smaller mobile device, which might implicate to some participants that the system itself is also better graphics and performance-wise.

The HMD application was considered to be faster than cCAVE, which can be at least partly explained by the interaction method: head turning used with the HMD is much faster to perform than rotating the on cCAVE. As mentioned earlier, both systems were regarded as easy to learn, but for the HMD this metric was significantly higher. The intuitive method where the viewport is rotated based on the user's head orientation offers the user an efficient way to start interacting with the virtual world immediately after they wear the device. The UI elements draw the user's attention and when they concentrate on these elements, they are activated and animated which again hints the user that something is happening.

The implications of these results are that both CAVE systems and HMD applications utilizing ODVs are regarded as both useful and easy to learn. Both of the applications had very simple interaction methods which were based on dwell-time. This seems to be a meaningful way of interacting with these types of systems, especially when the interaction is kept simple. Nevertheless, more research is required in order to understand the relationship between complex UI elements and different interaction methods.

Overall, the positive feedback on both applications validates their use on this study. The applications were also very robust and had no technical faults during evaluations, which might have also affected the participant's feedback on the user experience. The actual user experience was much more positive than the user's expectations with both systems, but especially so with the HMD application.

6.2   Immersion and User Interaction

Our evaluation suggests that the Amaze360 application is more immersive than the cCAVE with both video content types. There are many possible explanations for this result. First, the headset obscures any other visual stimuli from the view, only showing the contents of the application to the user, whereas in the cCAVE the user can still observe objects outside the screens, including the bezels of the monitors. Second, the HMD provides a stereoscopic effect (coming from the spherical projection, not the video itself) which creates an illusion of depth. This is not provided in cCAVE. Third, since interaction with the Amaze360 is based on head orientation, it does not require any external devices which might enhance the feeling of immersion even further. In the first experiment the aim was to make the interaction as simple as possible with the use of the rotational chair, but it is still not as natural as interaction with the headset.

In future implementations a combination of body tracking and gaze tracking could be combined to produce a similar interaction solution as in the HMD application.

Despite the unique advantages of the HMD application, the positive feedback for this application is interesting when considering the current limitations of the technology. For instance, Amaze360 offers a relatively limited 60-degree field of view, which is much smaller than that of the human eye, whereas cCAVE had no such physical limitations. However, none of the users reported this as an issue.

Some cCAVE users had trouble finding the textual content from the bottom of screen even when they were informed about the location beforehand, during the introduction. Participants had no trouble finding or activating the hotspots with the Amaze360 application, but three participants noted that the hotspot text box obscures the visibility of the actual object behind it. One solution for this could be an opaque text box that does not hide the content. These findings indicate that the optimal location for the contextual information is somewhere around the center of the screen where the user is most often looking at, but that it also should not dominate the viewport. It should also be located close to the actual UI element activating it, so that the user quickly finds it.

One participant using cCAVE remarked that the reflection on the monitors broke the feeling of immersion, as the participant could see the monitors behind him reflected in the monitors in front of him. Four Amaze360 users reported that they felt dizzy during the indoor scenes, which were filmed on a ladder. This interesting finding and its connection to acrophobia could be an interesting topic of research, and has also been looked into by Coelho et al. [6]. None of the participants did not report any motion sickness effects in either applications. Three participants using cCAVE and one user using the Amaze360 stated that the resetting of the omnidirectional video content back to the beginning (due to looping videos) broke the immersion somewhat. In addition, some video production errors that caused distortions were breaking the feeling of immersion for one cCAVE user. These distortions can be eliminated with careful planning of the recording and editing phase of the ODV content. The biggest hurdles in the post-production phase are the color level differences between the cameras, stitching errors where the content between the cameras are not overlapping properly or displaying of the camera equipment in the recording. Also, if the content needs to loop, some attention should be paid to how smoothly the end of the content loops back to the beginning. These problems will likely dissipate once the ODV recording and production technologies advance. When comparing the results between outdoor and indoor video content, there was no significant difference in the feeling of immersion.

The difference in use times with the indoor video content is also an interesting finding. As this same effect was not observed in outdoor environments, one explanation for the difference between the systems could be in the claustrophobic nature of the indoor environment and the limited field of view used in the HMD application. Another explanation could be the filming location of the indoor video content. Two out of three of these videos were recorded from a higher ground, i.e., from a ladder. Four HMD users said that they felt dizzy during these scenes, which might affect the total time used with the indoor videos.

We also note that CAVE systems are diverse and may significantly vary between setups. The cCAVE system was unique but also relatively limited in regards to the rotating chair. It would be interesting to research immersion further with CAVE systems, in particular with larger installations inside which users could walk freely. Also, there are factors that should be taken into account in the future evaluations. For example, evaluating the participant's spatial abilities with Santa Barbara sense-of-direction scale [11] before they use the application.

6.3   Implications for iODV Applications

In the past, CAVE systems have been used extensively in many areas such as the industry [28] [7]. However, we argue that HMD systems offer many unique, new application areas because of two reasons. First, due to their small size and easy physical setups, HMDs are easily portable. Second, they are more scalable and adjustable, i.e. less dependent on specific equipment and a specific physical setup. These features could make HMDs a valuable asset in many situations. For instance, we recorded the indoor video content used in our experiments in a skylift maintenance hall. However, maintenance on skylifts is often conducted in the field. Field technicians could carry HMDs with them and access informative content on-the-spot, in case they needed additional guidance on e.g. how to conduct some specific maintenance procedure on a skylift model unfamiliar to them. We believe omnidirectional video content could prove useful in such situations, as a potentially complicated procedure may be difficult to fully document (and view) on a regular camera, especially if the procedure involves large objects.

7   Conclusion

In this paper, we investigated the user experience and level of immersion in iODV applications that utilize omnidirectional videos. We conducted a comparative study between two applications: a CAVE system, cCAVE, and a head-mounted display application, Amaze360. We collected and analyzed interaction logs and questionnaire data to gain insight on similarities and differences between these two systems and on the feeling of immersion and user experience in iODV applications in general.

Our main findings suggest that in regards to user experience in interactive ODV applications, the experiences exceed the user's expectations. These differences were especially evident with the HMD system, as the users' expectations were exceeded in many aspects such as pleasantness, clarity and performance of the system. Both the CAVE and the HMD applications were considered very easy to learn. Some of the differences in user experience between these two iODV applications can be explained by the different user interaction methods. Head orientation-based interaction used with theHMD is much faster to use than the rotating chair of the CAVE system.

Another interesting take away from our study is that ODV is a very immersive medium. Overall, the HMD application was considered to be more immersive than the CAVE system. This effect was observed with both indoor and outdoor video content. We primarily attribute the immersiveness of the HMD application to a) the head-mount that effectively blocks outside visual stimuli and allows concentration on the content, b) the stereoscopic view creating a sense of depth and c) the viewport on the display is based on head orientation, allowing the user to naturally look around.

As interactive ODV applications are becoming more available in the consumer market, further research on the possibilities of this medium is necessary. For future work, it would be meaningful to study the feeling of immersion on a video content with different heights (skyscraper versus a cave) and different types of background movement (crowded street versus peaceful forest), as these properties were not within the scope of this study. Also, the effect of a moving camera (e.g. a roller coaster or a racing car) and its effects on immersion should be evaluated. This could provide more insight on what kind of ODV content offers the most immersive experience to the user.

References

1. Benko, H., Wilson, A.D.: Multi-point interactions with immersive omnidirectional visualizations in a dome. In: ACM International Conference on Interactive Tabletops and Surfaces (ITS 2010), pp. 19–28. ACM, New York (2010)
2. Berning, M., Yonezawa, T., Riedel, T., Nakazawa, J., Beigl, M., Tokuda, H.: 360 degree interactive video for augmented reality prototyping. In: Proceedings of the 2013 ACM Conference on Pervasive and Ubiquitous Computing Adjunct Publication, UbiComp 2013, pp. 1471–1474. ACM, New York (2013)
3. Bleumers, L., Van den Broeck, W., Lievens, B., Pierson, J.: Seeing the bigger picture: a user perspective on 360° TV. In: Proceedings of the 10th European Conference on Interactive TV and Video (EuroiTV 2012), pp. 115–124. ACM, New York (2012)
4. Boult, T.E.: Remote reality via omnidirectional imaging. In: ACM SIGGRAPH 98 Conference abstracts and applications (SIGGRAPH 1998). ACM, New York (1998)
5. Brown, E., Cairns, P.: A grounded investigation of game immersion. In: CHI 2004, pp. 1279–1300. ACM Press, New York (2004)
6. Coelho, C.M., Waters, A.M., Hine, T.J., Wallis, G.: The use of virtual reality in acrophobia research and treatment. J. Anxiety Disord. **23**(5), 563–574 (2009)
7. Cruz-Neira, C.: Virtual reality based on multiple projection screens: the cave and its applications to computational science and engineering. Doctoral Dissertation, University of Illinois, Chicago, United States (1995)
8. De la Torre, F., Vallespi, C., Rybski, P.E., Veloso, M., Kanade, T.: Omnidirectional video capturing, multiple people tracking and identification for meeting monitoring. Technical report. (2005). http://repository.cmu.edu/robotics/128/
9. Decock, J., Van Looy, J., Bleumers, L., Bekaert, P.: The pleasure of being (there?). an explorative study into the effects of presence and identification on the enjoyment of an interactive theatrical performance using omnidirectional video. In: Proceedings of the International Society for Presence Research Annual Conference ISPR 2011. Edinburgh Napier University, Edinburgh (2011)
10. Fassbender, E., Heiden, W.: Atmosphaeres – 360° Video Environments for Stress and Pain Management. In: Ma, M., Oliveira, M.F., Baalsrud Hauge, J. (eds.) SGDA 2014. LNCS, vol. 8778, pp. 48–58. Springer, Cham (2014). doi:10.1007/978-3-319-11623-5_5
11. Hegarty, M., Richardson, A.E., Montello, D.R., Lovelace, K., Subbiah, I.: Development of a self-report measure of environmental spatial ability. Intelligence **30**, 425–448 (2002)
12. Järvinen, A., Ekola, L.: Turning point – A practical assessment of using 360 video in sign language interpreting studies. Diaconia University of Applied Sciences. Degree Programme in Sign Language Interpretation. Bachelor Thesis (2014)

13. Kasahara, S., Nagai, S., Rekimoto, J.: First person omnidirectional video: system design and implications for immersive experience. In: Proceedings of the ACM International Conference on Interactive Experiences for TV and Online Video, 03–05 June 2015, Brussels, Belgium (2015)

14. Kwiatek, K.: How to preserve inspirational environments that once surrounded a poet? Immersive 360° video and the cultural memory of Charles Causley's poetry. In: Virtual Systems and Multimedia (VSMM), 2012 18th International Conference, pp. 243–250 (2012)

15. Kwiatek, K., Woolner, M.: Transporting the viewer into a 360° heritage story: panoramic interactive narrative presented on a wrap-around screen. In: Virtual Systems and Multimedia (VSMM), 2010 16th International Conference, pp. 234–241 (2010)

16. Mäkelä, V., Heimonen, T., Luhtala, M., Turunen, M.: Information wall: evaluation of a gesture-controlled public display. In: Proceedings of the 13th International Conference on Mobile and Ubiquitous Multimedia (MUM 2014), pp. 228–231. ACM, New York (2014)

17. Neng, L.A.R., Chambel, T.: Get around 360° hypervideo. In: Proceedings of the 14th International Academic MindTrek Conference: Envisioning Future Media Environments (MindTrek 2010), pp. 119–122. ACM, New York (2010)

18. Neumann, U., Pintaric, T., Rizzo, A.: Immersive panoramic video. In: Proceedings of the Eighth ACM, pp. 493–494 (2000)

19. Okura, F., Kanbara, M., Yokoya, N.: Fly-through Heijo palace site: augmented telepresence using aerial omnidirectional videos. In: ACM SIGGRAPH 2011 Posters (SIGGRAPH 2011). ACM, New York (2011). Article 78

20. Onoe, Y., Yamazawa, K., Takemura, H., Yokoya, N.: Telepresence by real-time view-dependent image generation from omnidirectional video streams. Comput. Vis. Image Underst. **71**(2), 154–165 (1998)

21. Peñate, W., Pitti, C.T., Bethencourt, J.M., de la Fuente, J., Gracia, R.: The effects of a treatment based on the use of virtual reality exposure and cognitive-behavioral therapy applied to patients with agoraphobia. Int. J. Clin. Health Psychol. **8**(1), 5–22 (2007)

22. Ramalho, J., Chambel, T.: Windy sight surfers: sensing and awareness of 360° immersive videos on the move. In: Proceedings of the 11th European Conference on Interactive TV and Video, EuroITV 2013, pp. 107–116. ACM, New York (2013)

23. Rizzo, A.A., Ghahremani, K., Pryor, L., Gardner, S.: Immersive 360-degree panoramic video environments: research on creating useful and usable applications. In: Jacko, J., Stephanidis, C. (eds.) Human-computer interaction: theory and practice, vol. 1, pp. 1233–1237. Lawrence Erlbaum Associates, Mahwah (2003)

24. Rovelo Ruiz, G.A., Vanacken, D., Luyten, K., Abad, F., Camahort, E.: Multi-viewer gesture-based interaction for omnidirectional video. In: Proceedings of the 32nd Annual ACM Conference on Human Factors in Computing Systems, CHI 2014, pp. 4077–4086. ACM, New York (2014)

25. Schubert, T., Friedmann, F., Regenbrecht, H.: The experience of presence: Factor analytic insights. Presence Teleoper. Virtual Environ. **10**, 266–281 (2001)

26. Slater, M.: A note on presence terminology. Presence Connect **3**(3) (2003)

27. Slater, M., Alberto, C., Usoh, M.: In the Building or Through the Window? An Experimental Comparison of Immersive and Non-Immersive Walkthroughs, Virtual Reality Environments in Architecture, Leeds 2–3rd November 1994, Computer Graphics Society (1995)

28. Talaba, D., Amditis, A.: Product Engineering: Tools and Methods based on Virtual Reality, pp. 75–77. Springer, Netherlands (2008)

29. Turunen, M., Hakulinen, J., Melto, A., Heimonen, T., Laivo, T., Hella, J.: SUXES – user experience evaluation method for spoken and multimodal interaction. In: Proceedings of Interspeech 2009, pp. 109–112. ACM, New York (2009)

30. Usoh, M., Catena, E., Arman, S., Slater, M.: Using presence questionnaires in reality. Presence: Teleoper. Virtual Environ. **9**(5), 497–503 (2000)
31. Welch, R.B.: How can we determine if the sense of presence affects task performance? Presence: Teleoper. Virtual Environ. **8**(5), 574–577 (1999)
32. Witmer, B.G., Singer, M.J.: Measuring immersion in virtual environments. (ARI Technical Report 1014). Alexandria, VA: U. S. Army Research Institute for the Behavioral and Social Sciences (1994)
33. Zoric, G., Barkhuus, L., Engström, A., Önnevall, E.: Panoramic video: design challenges and implications for content interaction. In: Proceedings of the 11th European Conference on Interactive TV and Video, pp. 153–162. ACM, New York (2013)
34. Zoric, G., Engström, A., Barkhuus, L., Ruiz-Hidalgo, J., Kochale, A.: Gesture interaction with rich TV content in the social setting. In: Exploring and Enhancing the User Experience for Television, Workshop of ACM SIGCHI Conference on Human Factors in Computing Systems, CHI 2013 (Paris, France, April 2013, 2013) (2013)

Case Studies

A Digital Employability Marketplace

Ojas Vyas[✉] and Karan Rai Bahadur

Mindtree ltd, Bangalore, India
{ojas.vyas, karan.raibahadur}@mindtree.com

Abstract. The ecosystem of skilling & placement in India is faced with unique set of challenges. On one hand there are millions of unemployed youth looking for suitable opportunities in an apparently low demand market. While on the other, employers believe that there is a dearth of skilled talent. This problem persists despite numerous skill development programs being conducted by the government across the country. The prime reason for the lacuna is the absence of a scalable platform adopting a holistic approach towards solving these eco-system challenges, thereby unable to provide the right opportunity to all stakeholders. In order to address this employment paradox the social inclusion team at Mindtree, in collaboration with UNDP India, decided to develop a Digital Employability Marketplace based on the principle of platform economics. The idea was to develop a multi-sided cloud based platform leveraging information technology to enable meaningful interactions between stakeholders and processes.

Keywords: ICT in social development - interaction design for developing regions · User experience based approaches · User interfaces for web applications · e-Government

1 Introduction

The problem of accessibility to employment in India is multifold. The International Labour Organization's (ILO) 2017 World Employment and Social Outlook report projects unemployment in India to increase in the coming years. While the numbers stood at 17.7 million in 2016, it is projected to increase to 17.8 million in 2017 and 18 million next year. There is an urgent need to foster the right innovations in the sector to boost both the economy by reducing the social inequality gap and meet the aspirations of millions of youth joining the working class each year.

The Department of Skill Development, Entrepreneurship & Livelihood in the state of Karnataka wanted to tackle the challenge of unemployment at scale. To begin with, the objective was to meaningfully engage with more than 6, 00,000 youth registered on its official portal for employment and skilling. To analyze the situation on ground Mindtree's division for Social Inclusion collaborated with UNDP India to study the eco-system and understand the root cause. The team primarily identified 4 key issues:-

1. There is a mismatch between the skills that young people acquire and what the market needs
2. Currently there are multiple skill development programs but most of the interventions are on the supply side rather than demand driven

© IFIP International Federation for Information Processing 2017
Published by Springer International Publishing AG 2017. All Rights Reserved
R. Bernhaupt et al. (Eds.): INTERACT 2017, Part IV, LNCS 10516, pp. 321–325, 2017.
DOI: 10.1007/978-3-319-68059-0_21

3. The employers today lack access to quantitative information on how to convert nearly-employable candidate to employable. Nor do they have the ability to influence training courses at micro-level/job-skill-gap level
4. There is no single eco-system where different stakeholders from the skilling and placement sector can co-create opportunities for the unemployed

2 Key Interventions

In the study, UNDP contributed with its experience and network of partners on field, and Mindtree through its experience in technology enabled grassroots livelihood interventions. And after several rounds of stakeholder discussion and field engagements the teams at Mindtree and UNDP proposed a series of intervention. The proposed solution was to set-up a digital marketplace for skilling & employment in Karnataka. The digital market place would enable intelligent match-making and codify the principals of skilling, apprenticeships and entrepreneurship on to a single platform, made accessible through various mediums.

2.1 System Level Interventions

From the skilling & placement perspective the solution calls for creating a digital platform which constitutes of multiple smaller systems freely interacting to find logical value through mutual interactions. This is a basic principal codified in Mindtree's technology platform. The platform enables interaction through "Phygital" interventions; i.e. interventions involving both physical as well as digital aspects. And all the different stakeholders in the eco-system are brought together onto a single platform. This provided with the seamless capability for different stakeholders to interact and find value makes platforms unique.

Keeping in mind the various challenges and opportunities, the team proposed a 4-Fold Approach:

1. Enable candidates and Micro-entrepreneurs to upskill, and teach/enable access to job/self-employment market on the basis of their exact skills, gaps and strengths.
2. Enable employer to reach-out to candidates with the exact and specific needs in real time
3. Connect candidates/Micro-entrepreneurs, employers and supporting agencies like trainers, content creators, local skilling talent, hyper- local businesses onto a common digital marketplace
4. Create multiple channels of access so that youth from different sections and demography are able to find access to relevant opportunities with minimum or no-barriers.

2.2   Service Level Interventions

There solution makes three service level interventions. These are namely;

1. Counselling & Personalized handholding with unemployed candidates in order to help them make informed decisions
2. Facilitate collaboration and interaction between key market demand side players (employers, vocational training centers, apprenticeship centers)
3. Establish a process of continued engagement for candidates to access employment opportunities

Counselling and Personalized Engagement with Candidates: This would aim at providing a personalized handholding session for the candidate to help understand the various opportunities and future avenues she might have via counselling, skilling, upskilling (to cover a gap) and relevant job opportunities in the market. This would be carried out by the Candidate Engagement Unit which would be setup as a part of the program (Fig. 1).

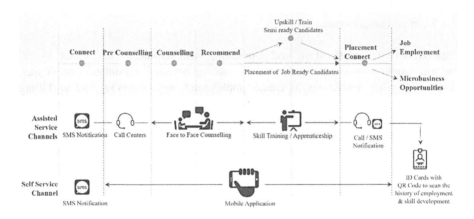

Fig. 1. Flow representing a candidate's engagement for skilling and employment opportunities

Engagement channels: The candidate engagement would carry personalized engagement with prospective job candidates and micro-entrepreneurs through various mediums.

- The primary one being face to face counselling via tablets in counselling centers where youth can walk in and discuss various avenues pertaining to their skilling and job opportunities.
- The counselling sessions will be sequenced after a pre-counselling phone call or self-service web/app connect with registered candidates.

Apart from Counselling at Taluka level, state sponsored employment exchange offices will be used to provide counselling to a larger set of candidate audience in order to increase the outreach leading to a wider solution adoption. The idea is to ensure inclusivity and greater coverage amongst those who might not have access to personal digital mediums.

These engagements will result in one of 4 specific recommendations for the candidate:

1. Upskilling
2. Apprenticeship
3. Candidate-Employer linking leading to employment
4. Micro-entrepreneurship

Employer Engagement: The primary role of this intervention team would be to gather skilling based insights from all stakeholders in the eco-system and incorporate these into the platform solution. The unit would look after job role curation, build assessment parameters based on the actual market requirements and develop insights for intelligent match making. These insights would be coded into the platform

The stakeholders on-boarded to the marketplace would include:

(1) Job Candidates
(2) Micro-Entrepreneurs
(3) Employers (large industries, SMEs, Hyperlocal)
(4) Field & Virtual Trainers
(5) Training content creators

Employment, Apprenticeship, and Upskilling Marketplace: The "I Got Skills" Platform would enable intelligent match making between candidates, employers, trainers and other institutions to create employment, apprenticeship and upskilling opportunities. All of these would get integrated over the digital platform to become a market place of opportunities. The Market Linkage Unit would create avenues to promote Short-term Internship and Micro-Entrepreneurship. A four member team of career coaches, would be stationed at the Model Career Center supported by Gov. of India. These coaches will receive incoming calls for assistance from candidates who have gone past the counselling stage (Fig. 2).

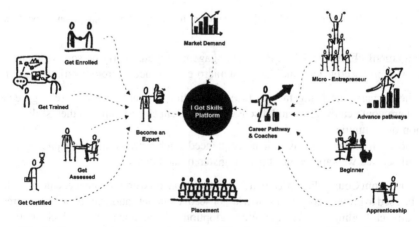

Fig. 2. Representation of a registered candidate's touch points with the platform

3 Conclusion

The proposed interventions aims to enable **"Acute Personalization"** for both the unemployed and the employer. The scope of the project is to cover more than 7, 00,000 unemployed in a structured manner over the course of the next 12 months. At the end of the program the following objectives would be achieved:

- Candidates connected to a market place
- Employers connected to a market place
- State level skill repository
- Demand data on a real time basis
- Demand-supply gap analysis by role & micro-skills

The platform approach has been adopted with the objective to build a digital eco-system which would be scalable with time. The objective in the long term is to make the platform accessible to a larger groups of stakeholders ensuring inclusivity. This would be achieved by reducing the barriers in technology adoption and making self-services option easily accessible.

Ability-Based Optimization: Designing Smartphone Text Entry Interface for Older Adults

Sayan Sarcar[1]([⊠]), Jussi Jokinen[2], Antti Oulasvirta[2], Xiangshi Ren[1], Chaklam Silpasuwanchai[1], and Zhenxin Wang[1]

[1] Center for Human-Engaged Computing,
Kochi University of Technology, Kami, Japan
{sayan.sarcar,ren.xiangshi,chaklam,wang.zhenxin}@kochi-tech.ac.jp
[2] Aalto University, Espoo, Finland
{jussi.jokinen,antti.oulasvirta}@aalto.fi

Abstract. Beside decreasing the abilities, individual difference prevails among older adults, as some individuals are completely healthy at the age 90 while some are not at even 60. In context of touchscreen interface design, it is critical to understand the design space as a function of abilities. In this work, we articulate a better understanding of the effects of ageing and examine their HCI task performing capabilities in terms of interfaces design. We design a text-entry interface in particular, as ageing users often achieve slow text entry performance, thus proving to be a bottleneck for technology use. Our developed text entry interface is tuned based on the parameter values for Elderly having finger tremor. We present initial study results showing the improvement of the accuracy of touch typing in smartphone over the baseline Qwerty keyboard. By carefully considering other sensorimotor abilities, we believe that the current smartphone text-entry interface designs will become more usable to the ageing populations.

Keywords: Ability-based design · Aging users · Text entry interface · Tremor

1 Introduction

By the year 2050, ageing populations are expected to cover 27% and 15% of developed and developing nations, respectively [1]. This paper is motivated by the need to design user interfaces (UIs) that better capture age-related changes in motor (dexterity such as tremor, Parkinson's) [8], perceptual (e.g., visual acuity, oculomotor performance) [3], and cognitive abilities (e.g., task-switching). The most striking factor about age-related change is its variability.

When it comes to interface design, the "one design fits all" approach does not work well. For example, the smartphones ($DORO^{TM}, Fujitsu, Softbank$),

© IFIP International Federation for Information Processing 2017
Published by Springer International Publishing AG 2017. All Rights Reserved
R. Bernhaupt et al. (Eds.): INTERACT 2017, Part IV, LNCS 10516, pp. 326–331, 2017.
DOI: 10.1007/978-3-319-68059-0_22

designed specifically for older adults, got failed to gain popularity within the target community. Are those provided best suitable user interfaces for somebody with, say, issues with tremor but with perfect vision? Thus, there is a clear need to complement interface design with a better understanding of effects of ageing. Although recent works have explored *Ability-Based Design* concept [2,4] to develop interfaces personalized to the abilities, little has been done to connect the psychological phenomena of ageing to design.

This paper aims to articulate a better understanding of the effects of ageing and examine their HCI significance in interface design. As a case study, we look at text-entry interfaces, given that ageing users were able to only achieve 7–8 WPM text typing speed with onscreen Qwerty keyboard [7] and thus prove to be real bottleneck when using technologies. The major takeaways of this paper: (1) development of a design space for text-entry interfaces and (2) design and initial evaluation of the keyboard interface suitable for older adults having tremor. In a broader sense, our work serve as initial attempt to build a psychological foundation that could guide text-entry design and interface design in general.

2   Approach to Design Text Entry Interface

This paper extends model-based UI optimization to ability-based design [9]. Figure 1 provides an overview of the approach. Application to ability-based design critically builds upon formulation of objective functions in such a way that individual differences can be expressed as part of the objective function. We here explore the idea to express individual differences as parameters (θ) of a predictive model. We call this the parametric approach.

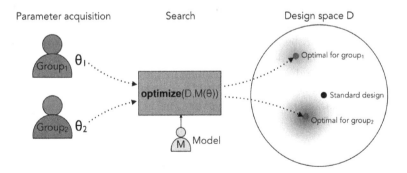

Fig. 1. Overview of parametric optimization of UI in ability-based design

This work extends ability-based optimization (first implemented the idea were shown by Gajos et al. (e.g., [2]) from the consideration of motor performance difference. However, they were limited to models of motor performance combined with simple heuristics to describe visual impairments. The problem with heuristics (such as "users with poor vision need a larger font") is that they are not able to resolve trade-offs in design.

Another advancement examined here is the use of *rational analysis* to predict how a user with given characteristic might start using a UI. We assume that interaction with a UI is associated with a space of possible strategies. One well-known strategy is speed–accuracy trade off in pointing: a person's decision to be faster at the expense of accuracy, or vice versa, be more accurate but at the expense of speed. The identification of relevant strategy spaces is outside the scope of this paper.

Procedurally, parametric model-based interface optimization has the five steps: (1) defining design space and objective function, (2) building a parametrizable predictive model of user behavior, including strategy adaptation, (3) acquiring parameters to describe abilities of a user group, (4) constructing an efficient combinatorial approach to solve the task and (5) testing the robustness of the design to differing assumptions (e.g., change in parameters or task).

Table 1 describes the design parameters, their value ranges, and their related abilities. Figure 2a depicts the design parameters. We selected this design parameters for its potential effects for ageing users and settled their value ranges through rigorous empirical and calibration studies.

In this work, we only focused on designing optimized text entry interface suitable for older people having finger tremor (essential tremor and parkinson's). Thus, we chose the keyboard UI from design space, through model-based optimization (details are in [6]), to support the users having tremor. The grouped keyboard layout (3×3 button grid) with multiple letter arranged into each button has been selected by optimizer following the situation that bigger sized keys are easier to be tapped by users having finger tremor (see Fig. 2b). We considered four design parameters for observing to the model: number of rows in the word prediction list (WPL), row height, number of words to be provided in each row of the list, and number of rows in text display area. It is to be noted that some parameters, which can be derived from the parameters list (e.g., area occupied with the keyboard can be defined, for a specified smartphone size, from key size, space between keys and number of columns in the keyboard; area occupied by the text display from keyboard size, WPL key size and number of rows in WPL list; number of characters to map at one key can be calculated by the grid type, whether 3×3 or 5×2).

3   Experiment and Initial Results

To judge the efficacy of the grouped layout, we conducted text typing experiment (comparison study) with two older adults (a 69 year aged male (P1) and a 67 year aged female (P2)). Participants performed a calibration study on the Samsung Galaxy S6 smartphone where they were asked to tap as quickly and accurately as possible. Next, we conducted text transcription tasks with two keyboards: baseline Qwerty (Fig. 2a) and grouped keyboard (Fig. 2b). Keyboards were selected in random order and were counterbalanced across participants. In the transcription task, participants were instructed to type a sentence repeatedly for 10 min

Table 1. Design space and value ranges. (* = have been studied in previous work [6], V = vision, A = Attention, M1 = Motor, M2 = Memory)

Area of interest	Parameter	Range/Possible values	Related abilities
Keyboard	K1: Key size	[26.5dp, 177.5dp]	V, M1
	K2: No. of keys in each row	2, 3, 4, 5, 7, 9, 10	V
	K3: Number of rows	[1,3]	V
	K4: Space between keys	[0dp, 10dp]	V, M1
	K5: Grid type	QWERTY, 2 × 2, 3 × 3, 5 × 2, 10 × 1	V, M1, M2
	K6: Visual feedback-keypress	0,1	V, M1, A
Word Prediction	W1: Key size	72.5dp, 96.6dp, 145dp	V, M1, A
	W2: No. of keys in each row*	[2, 4]	V
	W3: Number of rows*	[1, 5]	V
Text Display	D1: Text font size	25sp	V, A
	D2: Deleting strategies	no, letter, word	V, M1, A
	D3: Number of rows*	[2, 7]	V

for each keyboard. This repetition ensures the familiarity with both the layouts as our target was to analyze the natural text typing speed and accuracy, not the learnability. Also, we did not envision typing both upper and lower case letters with two layouts, as are interested in investigating atomic level typing speed and accuracy of users. We scheduled a 5-minute breaks after calibration and first transcription task.

First results showed that the average typing speed (in WPM, calculated as [5] was slightly higher for the Qwerty (7.35 WPM) compared to the grouped layout (5.28 WPM). In contrast, the average total error rate was much higher Qwerty (14.20%) than the grouped keyboard (6.71%). The reason of error occurrence in the Qwerty layout is improper aiming of tapping the button. The grouped layout supports less typing errors (mainly with inaccurate touch down activity), which suits the behavior of the older adults having essential tremors.

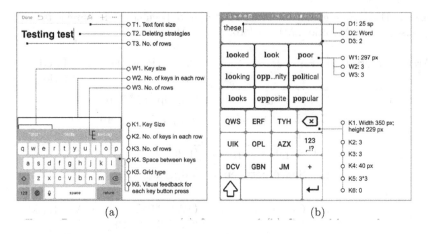

Fig. 2. Design parameters in (a) Qwerty and (b) Grouped layout design

4   Conclusion

This work is based on *Ability-Based Optimization* concept [6], which refers to the use of computational models to better address *individual differences* brought about by ageing. By formulating individual differences parametrically and also take into account how users adapt their behavioral strategies as a function of their abilities in a model, this method allows practitioners to investigate optimal designs and to examine trade-offs among several design factors. We believe that combining a scientifically-grounded design space with modeling and optimization can help bridge the gap. One possible next step is to design text entry interfaces considering other sensorimotor abilities and their combinations for older adults.

References

1. Fisk, A.D., Rogers, W.A., Charness, N., Czaja, S.J., Sharit, J.: Designing for Older Adults: Principles and Creative Human Factors Approaches. CRC Press, Boca Raton (2009)
2. Gajos, K.Z., Wobbrock, J.O., Weld, D.S.: Improving the performance of motor-impaired users with automatically-generated, ability-based interfaces. In: Proceedings of the SIGCHI conference on Human Factors in Computing Systems, pp. 1257–1266. ACM (2008)
3. Haegerstrom-Portnoy, G., Schneck, M.E., Brabyn, J.A.: Seeing into old age: vision function beyond acuity. Optom. Vis. Sci. Official Publ. Am. Acad. Optom. **76**(3), 141–158 (1999)
4. Hurst, A., Hudson, S.E., Mankoff, J., Trewin, S.: Automatically detecting pointing performance. In: Proceedings of the 13th International Conference on Intelligent User Interfaces, pp. 11–19. ACM (2008)
5. Nicolau, H., Jorge, J.: Elderly text-entry performance on touchscreens. In: Proceedings of the 14th International ACM SIGACCESS Conference on Computers and Accessibility, pp. 127–134. ACM (2012)

6. Sarcar, S., Joklnen, J., Oulasvirta, A., Silpasuwanchai, C., Wang, Z., Ren, X.: Towards ability-based optimization for aging users. In: Proceedings of IxAP 2016, pp. 77–86. ACM (2016)
7. Smith, A.L., Chaparro, B.S.: Smartphone text input method performance, usability, and preference with younger and older adults. Hum. Factors **57**(6), 1015–1028 (2015)
8. Sturman, M.M., Vaillancourt, D.E., Corcos, D.M.: Effects of aging on the regularity of physiological tremor. J. Neurophysiol. **93**(6), 3064–3074 (2005)
9. Wobbrock, J.O., Kane, S.K., Gajos, K.Z., Harada, S., Froehlich, J.: Ability-based design: concept, principles and examples. ACM Trans. Accessible Comput. (TACCESS) **3**(3), 9 (2011)

Adoption of Structural Analysis Capabilities in an IOT Based Scenario for Connected Assets

Sparshad Kasote[⊠], Suvodeep Das, and Santhosh Rao

Sap Labs India Pvt. Ltd., #138, EPIP Zone,
Whitefield, Bengaluru 560066, Karnataka, India
sparshad501@gmail.com

Abstract. This case study showcases the exploration and integration of structural analytical methods into an IOT based scenario which comprises of assets that have structural significance. The work showcased in this study was pursued at Sap Labs, Bengaluru as a part of the Digital Assets and IOT team. It would mainly revolve around the various stages and scenarios that the project underwent. The scenarios considered for the explorations were chosen based on their ability to portray what structural analysis is, and to portray how structural analysis would be critical when integrated in an IOT scenario.

Keywords: User experience · IOT · Structural analysis · Lifetime analysis · Interaction design · Industrial internet · Industry 4.0

1 Introduction

With the rise of Industry 4.0, the ability of Industrial IOT to impact lines of businesses in their fundamentals is growing. We all know that the adoption of Industrial internet is beginning to impact the optimum utilization of an asset and reduce operational cost in respective contexts. This in turn affects the sustainability ecosystem of the industrial scenario [1]. This case study elaborates the intent of the adoption of certain structural simulation technologies in an Industrial scenario. The broad goal of the adoption is to showcase the capability of structural analysis within two scenarios that comprise of connected assets. The structural integrity of these assets plays a critical role for that industry to operate within its digital economy. This capability is expected to enhance the optimum maintenance and operation of assets in their predictive life cycle, under the influence of external factors or natural wear and tear.

The assets that have structural significance in an industrial scenario could be from a large spectrum of sizes. From wind turbines and aircrafts, to oil well heads and railway switches, these assets are largely dependent on their structural integrity to efficiently operate in their respective industry. The adoption of this capability commenced when SAP acquired a dynamic structural simulation technology called 'FEDEM' (Finite element dynamics in elastic mechanisms).

© IFIP International Federation for Information Processing 2017
Published by Springer International Publishing AG 2017. All Rights Reserved
R. Bernhaupt et al. (Eds.): INTERACT 2017, Part IV, LNCS 10516, pp. 332–335, 2017.
DOI: 10.1007/978-3-319-68059-0_23

1.1   Structural Analysis Process

The approach used for structural analysis in the capability is the 'FEA' (Finite element analysis) approach. FEA is widely used in the field of mechanical systems to predict and visualize the stress and strain related parameters of a structure [2]. These parameters are then used to predict the useful lifetime of an asset. This method provides real time visualization of the physical state of the structure, which comprises of the fatigue and registered stress cycles. The historic analysis of these cycles estimates the lifetime consumption of the asset.

   This is visualized to the user by creating a digital twin of the structure which is actually a digital model of the asset. The stress and strain related data is overlaid on this model based on the information received from the sensors that are mounted on the asset (Fig. 1).

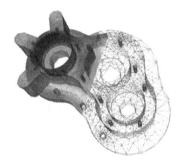

Fig. 1.   Finite element model with overlaid stress data.

1.2   Scenarios

The two scenarios considered for showcasing the adoption of this capability were that of a windfarm and a network of railway switches. Both these scenarios were considered for adoption, as they comprised of assets that have their structural integrity as a key performance indicator for that business. The maintenance costs, output efficiencies, safety measures and equipment investment of these scenarios were largely dependent on the structural integrity of their respective assets.

Windfarm Scenario
This scenario consists of a windfarm operator as a persona who is responsible for maintaining a set of windfarms that comprise of wind turbines as assets. With all the assets (wind turbines) being connected, the user is able to monitor the health of an asset and generate optimum maintenance requests, that reduce the total downtime. The stresses and loads experienced by each asset can be analyzed to a component level that in turn drives the maintenance schedules for required instances.

   In Fig. 2 we see a map view of a windfarm and a side panel on the right which shows relevant structural alerts of asset components. The user story revolves around the selection and inspection of an asset that needs attention, after which the user generates appropriate maintenance requests that ultimately optimize the lifetime of the asset. We shall see more about lifetime analysis in the following sections.

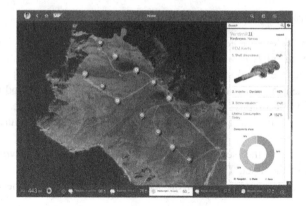

Fig. 2. Map view of a windfarm

Railway Switches Scenario

The scenario catered here is that of a railway network, where the user needs to monitor the railway switches in the respective railway cluster. The lifetime consumption of these switches is monitored and maintenance requests are scheduled efficiently. Figure 3 shows the railway switch cluster map that is shown to the user who is a railway switch operator.

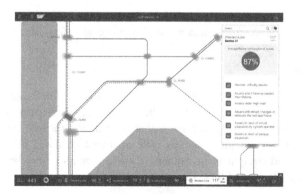

Fig. 3. Railway switch cluster map

2 Framework Approach and Discussion

To cater both the scenarios, a common framework was devised. Figure 4 shows the activity flow diagram of one of the use cases in the framework (windfarm).

Fig. 4. Activity flow

In the flow, the "digital inspection" and the "lifetime observation" steps showcase the structural capability of the adoption. Digital inspection is done with the alerts being played as a structural visualization on the 3D model of the asset. Figure 5 shows the lifetime consumption time series of the asset or component, where the expected life can be optimized by scheduling appropriate maintenances.

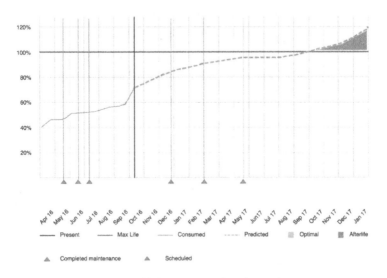

Fig. 5. Lifetime consumption time series

The framework devised in this adoption could be integrated in various industrial 4.0 scenarios in the future. With this framework, constructive measures could be taken to possibly reduce the maintenance cost and equipment investment and increase the operating efficiency of a large gamut of Industrial IOT scenarios. There also lies a vast opportunity in exploring this adoption for not only industrial but also consumer scenarios in which products or assets have structural significance.

References

1. Stock, T., Seliger, G.: Opportunities of sustainable manufacturing in Industry 4.0
2. Barath, P.: Applications of finite element analysis in mechanical system design (ma 12007)

Augmenting the Textbook for Enaction: Designing Media for Participatory Learning in Classrooms

Priyanka Borar[(✉)], Durgaprasad Karnam, Harshit Agrawal, and Sanjay Chandrasekharan

Homi Bhabha Centre for Science Education, TIFR, Mumbai, India
priyankaborar@gmail.com, karnamdpdurga@gmail.com,
harshitagrawal.iitr@gmail.com,
sanjay@hbcse.tifr.res.in

Abstract. This work discusses the affordances of the textbook in current classroom scenarios, and identifies the need to design learning media that support dynamism and enaction, specifically in science education. We illustrate this by a learning tool we've developed - Vector canvas, an AR based application linked with the textbook and the curricula. This is a work in progress attempting to observe and articulate changes in learning practice brought by introducing mixed media.

Keywords: AR · Mixed media · Dynamic systems · Enaction · Science education

1 Introduction

The current classroom environment relies heavily on print and paper media for teaching and learning practices. Through this case study we discuss the affordances of these media, its implications on science learning from a cognitive point of view, and limitations in supporting dynamic nature of concepts and imagination. We present a case for the need to integrate enactable formal systems into the classroom practice that allow the learners to be 'immersed' in the formal systems, and help them enact, and thus become part of the dynamics embedded in formal notations.

The resulting participatory experience is intended to help the students move from the current algorithmic/procedural understanding of formal systems to a modelling perspective. We illustrate this by a learning tool - Vector canvas, designed to augment the physics class XI NCERT[1] textbook to integrate the enactable nature of vectors through tasks designed based on the curricula.

---

[1] The National Council of Educational Research and Training (NCERT) is an autonomous organisation set up in 1961 by the Government of India to assist and advise the Central and State Governments on policies and programmes for qualitative improvement in school education.

© IFIP International Federation for Information Processing 2017
Published by Springer International Publishing AG 2017. All Rights Reserved
R. Bernhaupt et al. (Eds.): INTERACT 2017, Part IV, LNCS 10516, pp. 336–339, 2017.
DOI: 10.1007/978-3-319-68059-0_24

1.1   Agency in the Classroom

Given the affordances of the print and written media, the classroom practice is designed in a manner that the teacher enacts out concepts for the students explaining various physical phenomena by reading out laws, writing equations, sketching graphs and other diagrams on the board and, hold their attention. Students have at their disposal the pen and paper for note-taking and problem-solving. The classroom discourse is completely guided by the teacher and, the students are modelled as viewers. Experienced teachers are able to distribute agency and make the students participate in the classroom discourse.

The teacher uses language, diagramming and bodily gestures & movement for enactment. As the complexity of the concepts increases, it becomes difficult for the teacher to draw multiple representations and suggest dynamics embedded in the concepts and, hence it becomes difficult for the students to hold the concepts in their imagination & integrate these representations to make sense of the concepts. Once the teacher has enacted the concept, the only take-away for the student is the formula. Thus the student develops a tendency to have the formula as the starting point to engage with a problem, and the starting point for most teachers to initiate classroom discourse remains the textbook.

1.2   Affordances of the Textbook

The textbook as an artefact that involves the process of print and production, requires the design of the curricula to be modular, and the integration of modules is expected to be facilitated by the teacher in the classroom. This modularity could lead to some gaps in the concept flow. In our study, we started out by an extensive textbook analysis of the Class XII and XI physics and mathematics NCERT textbooks to map concept building on vectors and identifying gaps. To cite an example from our findings: vectors is first introduced in class XI as a part of the physics chapter on motion in a plane and then introduced only in class XII in mathematics.

A heavy dependency on the static media also leads to emphasising one method of working over another. For example, to quote the Physics class XII NCERT Chap. 4, p. 71, "Although the graphical method of adding vectors helps us in visualising the vectors and the resultant vector, it is sometimes tedious and has limited accuracy". This is a valid case of emphasising equation over geometry owing to the limitations of the medium, but we know that it's possible to work with accuracy in geometry, and integrate it with the equation, given the power of simulations and dynamic displays.

1.3   Emergence of Digital Learning Media

Digital learning media have started appearing in educational landscape in the form of online platforms for learning & educational games and, use of interactive boards and smart TVs in the classroom. We are interested in understanding what these media do to the teaching and learning practice, and what are the design considerations for shaping the learning behaviour through their use. For example, while online platforms like Khan Academy address the enaction of concepts by the teacher, digital apps like Touch Counts, GeoGebra and Graspable Math address the student enaction component.

While these platforms can be incorporated by the teacher or the students as part of the classroom practice, most of them are not designed with a specific intention to be integrated as learning tools to support the classroom and the curricula, which leaves practitioners with the integration & curation problem.

We propose a platform as an attempt to address these problems by use of mixed media in the classroom practice and a design approach that takes into consideration the flow & interactions in the classroom environment while hoping to leverage the agency of both the teacher and the learner.

2 Vector Canvas: A Case in Augmenting the Textbook

Vector canvas is a learning tool modelled as a digital slate to become part of the learning process. The objective of the tool is to make explicit the enactable nature of vectors through exploratory processes & support imagination for dynamic behaviour (Fig. 1).

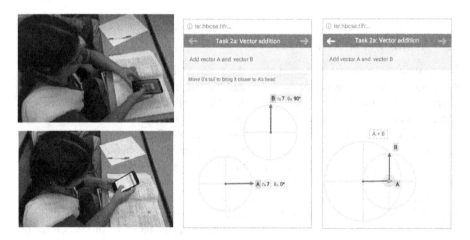

Fig. 1. A student performing the vector addition tasks and, task screens.

2.1 Design

The starting point for the design of the platform was a simulation developed at the Learning Sciences research lab, HBCSE, that models vectors as dynamic and manipulable concepts and integrates them with equations. The simulation allows to touch and hold the vector on a digital display and manipulate it to change its length and angle. Operations like resolution and addition are also supported, while making explicit the dynamics involved in them. The challenge was to design learning experience for the classroom by developing media that integrates the power of the simulation to the existing practice.

An early prototype was inspired by a parallel work at the lab experimenting with augmented reality to tackle the problem of 3D representation in vectors in the textbook. Building from that platform and looking at available technologies that can be made accessible to masses, a new platform was proposed to use a mobile device in context of the lesson plan in the textbook by placing QR codes as markers within the lesson to trigger specific tasks designed from the simulation. Major design considerations and decisions are summarised below:

- Specific visual elements have been introduced to scaffold imagination such as axes for reference, a boundary circle to suggest the span of the vector and animations to emphasise the mechanism of vector operations such as addition and resolution.
- Manipulation is supported both by geometry and algebra i.e., by manipulating the vector as well as editing the equation. Both modes are synchronised, change through one immediately reflect in the other.
- Gestures for manipulation have been inspired by the use of geometry tools that emphasise intent in action vs. use of one-click commands to perform actions, for example using holding and tapping to add vectors instead of using merge. While this increases learner's work, it also immerses her into the details of the concept.
- Tasks have been developed from the lesson plan and new exploratory tasks have been designed, for example, exploring all combinations of two vectors that give the same resultant by manipulating and adjusting given vectors.

2.2 Future Work

This is a work in progress with some initial field testing and validation. While we develop it further, we are interested in learning and contributing to the design approach for learning media while focusing on how it changes the practice.

Acknowledgments. The above work is being realised at the Learning Sciences research lab at the HBCSE, Mumbai. We would like to thank all the teachers & students participating in the research for their contributions.

Connected by Design - Our Learnings from Designing Digital Profiler Journeys

IDFC Bank Digital Experience

Debasish Biswas[(⊠)], Nihal Pimpale, and Konark Ashara

Moonraft Innovation Labs, Seattle, USA
{debasish,nihal,Konark}@moonraft.com

Abstract. This case study presents the key learnings derived from the twenty-user profiler journeys designed by Moonraft Innovation Labs for IDFC Bank. These profiler journeys were created to tackle challenges faced by banks in improving user engagement and simplifying data collection processes through digital experiences. These insights can be applied to create similar experiences for other sectors. The learnings are presented with examples.

Keywords: Banking · Profilers · Fintech · Digitization · Finance

1 Introduction

IDFC Bank is the 83rd Bank to enter a highly competitive and cluttered financial services landscape in India. Customers generally perceive banking as complex, frustrating and slow. Most private banks have adopted digitisation as a way forward to try and mitigate these issues. IDFC Bank's business model is based on a low physical footprint and a larger digital footprint. Traditionally banks have been using physical branches or relationship managers as the primary touch point for customer engagement. Going digital required these interactions to be seamlessly translated on to the digital medium. There were three major observations based on research conducted by an external consultant for IDFC Bank.

- Financial know-how is relatively new for masses in India. This creates a perception that financial planning is complex.
- Banks tend to aggressively push all their products without understanding the needs of the customer. This creates a general sense of mistrust among user towards the Bank.
- Banking involves a lot of form filling and documentation in the product purchase process. Customers need assistance during these processes.

We created a series of experiences addressing these observations. Leveraging digital to impart financial education to customers was imperative so that they could make an informed purchase decision. First, understanding the user's needs and aspirations and then recommending the most relevant solutions for them. We also helped in redesigning to enhance the form filling and documentation experience. We call these experiences profiler journeys.

© IFIP International Federation for Information Processing 2017
Published by Springer International Publishing AG 2017. All Rights Reserved
R. Bernhaupt et al. (Eds.): INTERACT 2017, Part IV, LNCS 10516, pp. 340–343, 2017.
DOI: 10.1007/978-3-319-68059-0_25

2   Learnings from the Profiler Journeys

An individual's life revolves around his lifestyle & needs. An individual spends a lot of time browsing through services and products on a banking website and trying to understand them. We created profilers journeys to address this. These are short digital experiences created to understand the user's need and provide relevant recommendations and financial education through story-telling. We created over 20 journeys for various solutions from IDFC Bank. Following are some of the key learnings from designing these journeys.

2.1   Input Driven Persuasion

Profiling requires form filling which involves several inputs and multiple steps. In order to persuade and motivate the user to keep providing information, we needed to bring out the value in their actions. We did this by showing the user relevant information for each step. This information was persuasive and insightful in nature. For example: In the insurance journey, a user gets a quote for his life cover in the first step itself. For the next steps, if the user chooses to secure his family and their health, the cover amount increases with each step. This creates reasoning to why that extra cover is required and user is persuaded to finish all the steps. As shown in example in Fig. 1.

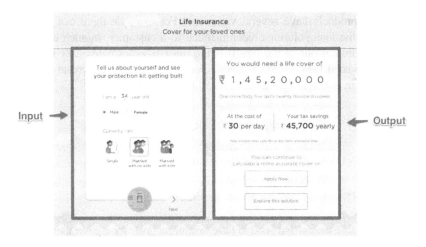

Fig. 1.   Input and output in personal insurance journey for desktop web

2.2   Metaphoric Interactive Graphs

For banking solutions like wealth management, that needed educating the user about the investment market behaviours, risk capacity, etc. it was necessary to use stock market based statistical graphs. For each personality of investor the predicted investment growth graph will be different. These graphs can be difficult to understand for a new user. New users don't understand which personality type they belong to.

We used real life metaphors to simplify the understanding of these personalities and the graphs. The actual meaning of the graphs is revealed to the user as they start interacting with he graph and explore how different personality types affect investment graphs. As shown in example in Fig. 2.

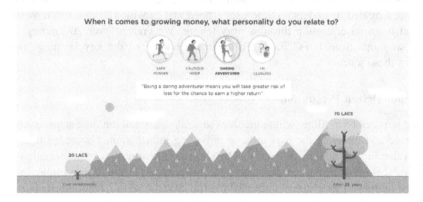

Fig. 2. Interactive graph with daring adventurer as personality type

2.3 Highlighted Recommendations

Most financial products have several variations. For example there can be multiple variations of home loan solutions recommended to a customer. In such cases clearly stating which solution out of the bunch is the most relevant helps user in making a selection. We created tags of "must haves" and "good to have" to create this distinction. As shown in example in Fig. 3.

Fig. 3. Essential and good to have investment goals for a given user

2.4 Story Based Form Filling

Forms are usually straight forward with more focus on keeping content scan-able and crisp. But users see banking solutions as a way to fulfill their life needs and aspirations. Therefore, the form filling should reflect these emotional connects between the product and user's need. Using story based content for form filling with a definite beginning, middle and conclusive end would help users connect with the solution through out the journey. Users would be able to associate with input flows and would be interested till the end of the journey to see the conclusion.

2.5   Visual Language that Connects

We focused on creating a visual language to resonate with the sentiments of the users. We wanted to breakaway from the traditional image of a bank. From serious and transactional to more playful and familiar. We created over 500+ icons and illustrations for the IDFC bank. These were based on being quietly Indian, with the essential Indian ness but not being loud about it. These were inspired by our rich folk art and diverse culture. As shown in example in Fig. 4.

Security   Home   Travel

Car   Fine Dining

Fig. 4. Few examples of icons from the quietly Indian set

3   Impact on User Engagement

Although most of the journeys have gone live recently, the initial bunch of data metrics show a marked improvement in user engagement compared to industry benchmarks. In this short span of time, IDFC Bank has one of the lowest drop-off rates as per industry benchmarks. Of the total user registrations, majority were through these profiler journeys offline.

Design and Development of a Location-Based Social Networking Mobile Application

Aditi Nettar, Nishita Chowdhari, Roxan Karanjia,
Pallavi Rao Gadahad[✉], and Sneha Deshmukh

Mukesh Patel School of Technology Management and Engineering,
NMIMS University, Mumbai, India
aditi8546@gmail.com, nishita c123@gmail.com,
roxankaranjia@gmail.com,
{pallavi.rao,sneha.deshmukh}@nmims.edu

Abstract. Location based services in social networking mobile applications are on the rise. Considering the benefits of incorporating location for collaboration amongst users, we were approached by a client to develop a location based social networking mobile application for a specific requirement. The mobile application thus developed was evaluated with users. Findings from the user study are summarized and recommendations for implementation and adoption of location based mobile social networking applications are discussed.

Keywords: Location based design · Social networking · Mobile application

1 Introduction

With the advent and growing ubiquity of mobile devices, there has been an increased use of such devices for social interactions. A significant value addition to such mobile social networking platforms can be in the form of location based services. Considering the benefits of incorporating location in mobile social networking platform, we were approached by a client to develop a location based mobile application for parents to collaborate. Our client, being a single working parent who had newly shifted to an area, faced problems because she did not know many other parents in the vicinity. As she did not have time to go and network with other parents in the vicinity, she realised the need of having a location based social networking mobile platform for parents to collaborate and requested us to build such an application (app).

Before proceeding with the app development, we delved into the challenges of incorporating location based services in mobile apps. One of the main technical challenges was excessive bandwidth consumption due to rendering of maps. Several mobile apps, particularly those developed for the tourism and travel domain, make use of maps to optimise user experience. Maps are one of the important visual cues in the case of location as they aid the user to view his or her position with respect to other elements in the app. However, the difficulty of rendering maps due to excessive bandwidth consumption must be considered, as well as privacy aspects of displaying location [1]. In this regard, studies [1–3] emphasise the importance of giving users the

R. Bernhaupt et al. (Eds.): INTERACT 2017, Part IV, LNCS 10516, pp. 344–347, 2017.
DOI: 10.1007/978-3-319-68059-0_26

control and choice to specify the situations where they want to reveal their location and also allow them the flexibility of choosing how it is displayed to other users.

Apart from the above technical challenge, users' privacy is also considered as one of the critical challenges in designing location based services [4]. However, past studies conducted in investigating users' perception towards sharing their location in a mobile platform, have contradicting viewpoints. For example, Tan et al. [1] highlights that users are reluctant to share their location with unknown users and discuss privacy controls to limit display of such information. On the contrary, Barkuus and Dey [5] state that the willingness of a user to share their location is directly correlated to the usefulness of the app to the user. While distinguishing between position aware apps (which simply displays users' location, automatically retrieved by the app or device) and location tracking apps (which actively use users' location to perform a task, typically mapping or tracking the users' route), the researchers [5] claim that location tracking apps are more intrusive than position aware apps. Thus, users were comfortable using and sharing location in position aware apps, particularly for socialising. In line with these findings, in a study on understanding the impact of location sharing on users' privacy, Fusco et al. [6], say that users' comfort with sharing their location increases over a period of time and with increased use.

After exploring the literature, we understood the technical challenges involved in developing location based services in mobile apps and incorporated a few suggestions to our design as suggested in the literature. It is also observed that, past studies have differing views on users' perceptions towards sharing location with unknown users. For investigating this further, we conducted user studies with real users. In sum, the purpose of this case study is to design, develop and evaluate location based services in a mobile social networking application for parents to collaborate.

2 Design and Development

For the time being, our client is interested only in the basic aspects in the app. She has plans to commercialize this later with added features. The beta version of the app we developed mainly consists of a location specific discussion forum for parents to collaborate. Along with this, there are other features such as book swap to facilitate creation of a virtual library, a message feature enabling one to one communication between parents and calendar synchronisation to keep track of scheduled events.

The app was developed using Android Studio. Considering that the primary focus of our users is to get to know other parents who live in areas near to them and not their exact location, we realised that we do not need to make extensive use of maps. This gives our users the privacy of not sharing their exact location as well as the benefit of interaction driven by location. Minimising the use of maps also enables faster rendering of screens and processing of location information, thus improving the overall user experience. Further, location filtering is done internally by the system and the area of filtering is visible to the user as text. However, the user must be aware of his own location so that he can make effective use of the app. To ensure this, we have provided the user a map as well as a text display of his location on his home screen.

Filtering threads by location is done by comparing the location value for the threads from the database to the current location. Threads are displayed if the area value in the address matches the user location area value. Filtering is done in a similar manner for other features of the app such as the book swap feature, which shows users, the books available in their vicinity.

3   User Study

After implementing the beta version of the app, we evaluated it with nine parents (ages 43 to 46; six female and three male). These parents mainly use location tracking apps (Google maps, Ola/Uber services) and find them very useful though some of them raised privacy concerns.

We gave a few tasks (such as opening and participating in a discussion thread, lending and borrowing books and creating an event to meet a parent) to the participants and observed them while they performed these tasks. All the participants were able to complete the tasks quickly (10 to 15 min). After the participants completed the tasks given to them, we interviewed them to probe further about their opinion on our app. The observation and interview sessions were audio recorded and transcribed individually and analyzed qualitatively. The analysis showed that all the study participants found that adding "location" to the discussion forum is very useful, making it a great source of finding help nearby and bringing parents together. Many of them specifically mentioned that "location filtering" is a very useful feature.

When asked about any concerns using these apps, two of the participants raised concerns on the topic of discussions in the forum and that there should be a mature communication. About future usage of this app, all the participants were ready to download and use it if launched on the Google Playstore. They felt that incorporating location in such discussion forums is an interesting concept and it will be of great help for parents to collaborate. One of the participants said that the app is a great beta version as the idea behind it is very good and upon refining it further, it can be an extremely useful app. Few participants suggested adding a nearby events feature to the app for sharing information of upcoming events in the vicinity.

4   Challenges

One of main concerns in incorporating location is users' privacy. In order to handle this, we did not make extensive use of maps in our app (unlike location tracking apps, our users simply need to know other parents in the vicinity, not their exact location). This gives our users the privacy of not sharing their exact location. Minimising the use of maps also enabled faster rendering of screens. However, a few participants in our user study still raised privacy concerns but found our app useful and did not mind sharing their location. The idea of collaborating with other parents might have made the participants feel more secure. Also, as highlighted by Barkuus and Dey [5], people are comfortable sharing location in position aware apps (like ours) rather than location tracking apps.

Another concern by the study participants was having mature content in the discussion forum as it is about parents discussing about their children and their activities. We have incorporated a moderator facility in the forum, ensuring that content can be moderated by the moderators, depending on how appropriate it is.

All the study participants were ready to use this app in future when it is refined and launched on Google Playstore as they found location based social networking apps an interesting and useful concept. Perhaps people are becoming comfortable with sharing location as the benefits they offer outweigh any concerns. Also, when the requirement is specific, they prefer such apps over social media groups. As highlighted by one of the study participants, these apps present information in an organized manner unlike any social media groups.

5 Recommendations

The study conducted showed that filtering threads by location is a very useful feature in the app. Also, there were suggestions for adding a "nearby events" feature for sharing information about upcoming events in the vicinity. Adding events such as book sale in the vicinity is not only useful for parents but can be commercially beneficial. We plan to incorporate this feature as well some other features (as requested by our client) before releasing the app to the market.

Implementation of location based services helps to build communities of support in the vicinity by facilitating communication and collaboration among users. The beta version of the app is an initial step in understanding the challenges of developing location based services in mobile social networking platform. The small scale user study may not be an actual indication of users' adoption intentions. Large scale investigation is preferred in this regard. However, designers and developers can use the recommendations summarized in this study for considering viable approaches to taking location based technology ahead.

References

1. Tan, C., et al.: A glimpse into the research space of location based services. J. Adv. Inf. Technol. 3(2), 91–106 (2012)
2. Zipf, A.: User-adaptive maps for Location-Based Services (LBS) for tourism, information and communication technologies in tourism 2002. In: Proceedings of the International Conference in Innsbruck, Austria, pp. 329–338 (2002)
3. Li, N., Chen, G.: Analysis of a location-based social network. In: CSE 2009 Proceedings of the 2009 International Conference on Computational Science and Engineering, pp. 263–270 (2009)
4. Wang, Y., Ma, J.: Mobile Social Networking and Computing: A Multidisciplinary Integrated Perspective. CRC Press, Boca Raton (2015)
5. Barkuus, L., Dey, A.: Location-based services for mobile telephony: a study of users' privacy concerns. In: Proceedings of Human-Computer Interaction INTERACT 2003: IFIP TC13 International Conference on Human-Computer Interaction (2003)
6. Fusco, S., et al.: Location-Based social networking: impact on trust in relationships. IEEE Technol. Soc. Mag. 31(2), 39–50 (2012)

Design Guidelines for Exploring Relationships in a Connected Big Data Environment

Jaison Jacob[(⊠)] and Santhosh Rao[(⊠)]

SAP Labs India, 138 EPIP, Whitefield Bangalore 560066, India
{jaison.jacob01,santhosh.rao}@sap.com

Abstract. Reimagining the 'SAP Investigative Case Management' frame-work from a log-based register of events to a direct interaction environment with the possibility to search, explore relationships between multiple entities in one or more cases/incidents. This case study is about our approach in conceptualizing a generic network visualization method by deconstructing the existing data models. We devised a set of guidelines that can be employed to represent a large number of entities with the intention of examining their relationships.

Keywords: Big-data · Network visualization framework · Visualizing connected data

1 Introduction

SAP Investigative Case Management is a SAP CRM[1] solution used by an investigator, detective, or user from law enforcement agencies to report a crime or offence or to investigate or probe a crime or offence. There are two types of incident reporting tools, viz. (1) systems for cases where there is a dispute between two people (2) systems for cases that require exploration of a network that has over 5000 entities. This type of data is dynamic in nature and grows over time. All of it can be thought of as "big data". Our secondary research [1] says that there are 23 types of incident reporter tools that an investigator can use to report an incident, and there exists a common task pattern amongst them: (1) **Users detect an incident.** On the event of an incident, the user travels to the incident location to gather artefacts. (2) **They create an incident report.** The incident report contains a description, location, date and time of incident occurrence, and user identification. (3) **Users follow up the incident to share information with other users.** Depending on the condition of the report, there may be organizational restrictions on sharing the outcome of the report once it is registered.

---

[1] SAP CRM is an integrated customer relationship management (CRM) software manufactured by SAP SE that targets business software requirements of midsize and large organizations in all industries and sectors.

© IFIP International Federation for Information Processing 2017
Published by Springer International Publishing AG 2017. All Rights Reserved
R. Bernhaupt et al. (Eds.): INTERACT 2017, Part IV, LNCS 10516, pp. 348–351, 2017.
DOI: 10.1007/978-3-319-68059-0_27

1.1 State of Art

There are several disadvantages in existing systems[2]: (1) **Limited parameters to describe/report an incident.** More parameters or entities = more detailed data. (2) **Report keeping and lack of categorization.** Storing a summary of incidents with no possibility to cross reference is of little or no use. (3) **Not configurable based on context.** If the reporter wants to add a new field called "sexual assault" with "men" as victims w.r.t the case details, it's not possible, because according to the existing system, sexual assault victims can only be female.

SAP Investigative Case Management or ICM improved this existing system by providing a configurable entity model with more entity 'fields', to empower the reporter to enter detailed data about the incident. It has a search feature that revolutionizes "incident probing". Now the case worker can go through historical records, based on very specific entity type search. With this the system moved from a 'incident reporting system' to a 'probing system'

The improved list of entity types is as follows: case, lead, geo-location, objects associated with the incident, person and organizations, incidents and activity. Above all, ICM focused on relationships between cases. A reporter can now create associations between data entities using relationships and then rate the reliability of the linked data using a reliability matrix. Here the reliability of the information and source of the information are evaluated. This information can pertain to a relationship, or to a description, or to the profile of a person. For e.g., if a relationship exists between a suspect and a victim based on a witness account, you would be able to set a reliability level for the witness, and another for the relationship between suspect and victim.

2 Approach

But ICM had their own problems. It was difficult to define a new relationship in the system as the user had to search and find cases that are similar in nature, go through them and deduce who is related to what and then define relationships based on this knowledge.

Reduce the ICM framework to 'atoms'. The core principle is to connect an incident with people; both are always related by a time stamp and a geolocation. The incident can later be drilled further into an object and a location associated with an incident. To detail the above classification, we came up with a 'non-hierarchical' classification of all the entities, (a "node"). A 'node' can be a person, a location, an event or an object involved in the incident.

---

[2] **Existing incident reporting systems**. Incident information is reported, more or less, by employing the following entities: (1) Incident Description. Textual description of the incident or by choosing a description from a list of predefined incident types. In some cases, description is accompanied by a picture of the incident. (2) Time of incident occurrence. (3) Incident location. This includes a "geo location pin", where the user can pinpoint the incident or an address of the location supported by landmarks. [1]

Deconstruct the ICM framework by creating a network of atoms. A 'node' can have a 'relationship' with 'another node'. It is a representation of how different types of entities are related to each other from the perspective of an incident.

The network visualization framework. A network diagram is a set of entities exhibiting linear as well as non-linear relationships, graphically represented as nodes (entities) connected with lines (relationships). A network of nodes can exhibit a non-hierarchical distribution, to help the user simplify a complex relationship network and vice versa. A node can be related to one or more nodes. A node can contain sub-nodes and these sub-nodes can contain more nodes and so on.

3   Design Guidelines

Tell a story using data. Every selected node in the UI should answer three questions: 'When'(time), 'Where'(geolocation) and 'How' (relation with other nodes in network). To perform this task, the user should have the right set of actions at the right time - "contextual menu". The menu should accommodate the following actions: expand nodes, collapse nodes, show information about the node in focus, select multiple nodes (for comparison), delete (non-related) nodes.

Power of choice and importance of probing path. Often, multiple nodes surround the node in focus. Now the user has to make a decision on which node to select to explore further. Each choice made, can lead to more nodes and eventually builds a path. This path can tell how the investigation progressed over a period of time.

Direction of the probing path matters. The network exploration path is important to understand how nodes are related. Relationships change with user's perspective.

Flexibility to zoom-in and out. UI should scale to accommodate details of a growing network. The user should be able to simplify the view so that he can see only the necessary information: Natural Zoom: Zoom in and Zoom out, Semantic Zoom: When a user zooms out of a canvas with a number of selected nodes, only these selected nodes and the relationships should be highlighted. The rest can be hidden. Clustering for nodes in geolocation: when user zooms out in a map view, the nodes on the map should exhibit clustering. All similar nodes should be replaced with a single representative node.

Divide and rule across data layers. Allow the user to choose visual filters: people, object, location and events. Possibility to view nodes on the canvas in an appropriate environment. Based on the context, show the nodes on a map, or as a network, or on a timeline.

Non-biased UI and the proof for taking 'informed' decision. The system should capture the probing path since big data is dynamic in nature. Since it's an informed decision, the decision changes with the UI. The system should not bias the user while making his decisions. It should only aid him in deducing results.

4   Conclusions and Future Work

The network visualization framework can be applied on any set of data that exhibits linear as well as nonlinear relationships. E.g., Healthcare domain. A doctor can view the patient's medical history by way of a network, use a timeline to organize a series of medical incidents. The doctor can see how these incidents are related with each other with respect to time, the doctors involved, diagnosis and medical reports. Similarly, we can also employ such a network in a scenario to help a recruiter look for candidates to fill a specific role.

Reference

1. Bach, C., Bernhaupt, R., D'Agostini, C.S., Winckler, M.: Mobile applications for incident reporting systems in urban contexts: lessons learned from an empirical study. In: ECCE 2013 Proceedings of the 31st European Conference on Cognitive Ergonomics, Article no. 29. ACM (2013)

Designing Interactive Spatiotemporal Visualizations to Enhance Movie Browsing

Ana Jorge[1,2(✉)], Nuno Correia[1], and Teresa Chambel[2]

[1] NOVA LINCS, Faculdade de Ciências e Tecnologia,
Universidade Nova de Lisboa, Lisbon, Portugal
ananunesjorge@gmail.com, nmc@fct.unl.pt
[2] LASIGE, Faculdade de Ciências, Universidade de Lisboa, Lisbon, Portugal
tc@di.fc.ul.pt

Abstract. This paper presents a case study on the design of spatiotemporal interactive visualizations of movies, both collections and contents, to provide enhanced support for conveying meaning and for browsing, targeting casual and professional users, with encouraging results for future research and adoption.

Keywords: Design · Interactive · Visualization · Movie · Time · Space · Evaluation

1 Introduction

Movies, with their rich contents conveyed in images, text, music and narration, along time, tell us stories of different places and have great emotional impact on us. Moreover, technological advances are making available huge amounts of movies over the years, on the Internet and interactive TV. However, the richness that makes these movies so interesting and accessible, comes with a challenging complexity, highlighting the need for new and powerful ways to access, browse, and view them, and interactive visualization can play an important role. In spite of the several contributions to this field, reviewed in previous publications [1, 2], most approaches and services for movies and video access do not fully support this richness, and the approaches to visualization in time and space [3] do not usually address video and movies. In this paper, we present a case study on the spatiotemporal interactive visualizations that we designed to help fulfill this need, both for movie collections and contents, as an extension to our previous work on: MovieClouds [4], an interactive web application that allows to browse movies based on their content, mainly audio and subtitles, with an emotional perspective; and Sight Surfers [5], an interactive web application for sharing and browsing georeferenced 360° interactive videos, in the context of the VIRUS and ImTV projects. The proposed visualizations contribute with visual, temporal and spatial dimensions, allowing to access movies released over time, and enriching the representations and access based on different aspects of their contents, along time and space. This approach [1, 2] has been refined with the ultimate goal of providing effective overviews and browsing mechanisms that may provide insights in analytical or more ludic uses, and its recent evaluation had very encouraging results towards their development and inclusion in real uses.

© IFIP International Federation for Information Processing 2017
Published by Springer International Publishing AG 2017. All Rights Reserved
R. Bernhaupt et al. (Eds.): INTERACT 2017, Part IV, LNCS 10516, pp. 352–355, 2017.
DOI: 10.1007/978-3-319-68059-0_28

2 Goals

In the design of the interactive visualizations we aimed at their effectiveness in showing meaning; their ability in providing good usability and user experience; and their usefulness and adequacy to be adopted by casual users and professionals in real scenarios. The evaluation assessed this, following the order of these research questions:

RQ1. Representations: are they intuitive and clear in reflecting meaning?

RQ2. Visualizations from collection to contents: are they able to effectively show the first level of information in a glance while guiding the user in the interaction towards a goal (learnability)?

RQ3. Navigation: are visualizations an added value to explore and access movies?

RQ4. Target: which target users take the most of visualizations?

3 Spatiotemporal Visualizations: Design and Evaluation

This section presents an overview of the main visualizations designed (Fig. 1) and some highlights about their recent evaluation, in order to provide insights and lessons to inform future research and developments. It was a Task-oriented evaluation focusing on the Observation of users performing the tasks, their hesitations and errors, and semi-structured Interviews focusing on perceived usefulness, ease of use and satisfaction (USE) with 1–5 scales, and ergonomic, hedonic and appeal Quality aspects [6], while providing comments as qualitative feedback, in sessions lasting on average one hour per participant. 20 participants aged 22–64, both from general public and professionals (e.g. movie directors and editors, film critics, and sound technicians).

Visualizations go from movie collections (Fig. 1 top) overviews (b-f, 2abc) or trajectories (3abc), to individual movie contents details (bottom) (4 and 5):

Time: the user can observe quantities of movies released over a year by genre (1a-b), and ask for details through titles by List (1c), where the most rated movies are highlighted; or by Spots (1d), each spot corresponding to one genre of the selected movie (half dimension, e.g., corresponds to a movie with two genres). These visualizations proved effective with almost all the participants accomplishing tasks such as locating the month with more movies released. The lower frequencies are the most difficult to perceive, but this issue is easily solved by zooming in. In (1e) users can compare movies in order to know about their images, speech, audio amplitude and genre, represented in circles that reflect the duration, being possible to disclose the title, plot, images of a requested moment of the movie (by hover), or the scene playing (by click). Many people would like to have this visualization available (M:3.8; Std:1.2) and most of them considered it more suited for exploration. A movie director called it an "Evocation of the film" due to its ability to reflect emotions. In general, the participants considered the visualization a good way to find a movie to watch, and used Supporting, Interesting, Pleasant and Comprehensible [7] to characterize it. When compared with Netflix, this visualization was considered more emotional and ludic although the traditional cover image was referred to complement information. Visualization in figure

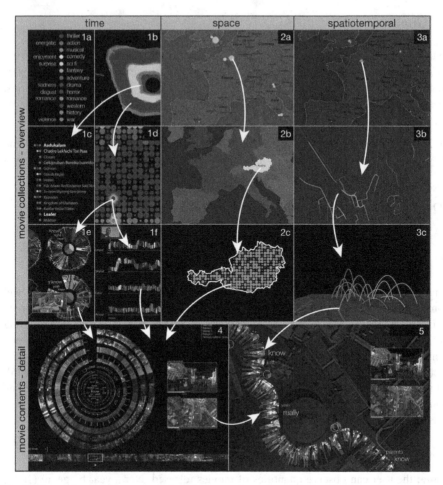

Fig. 1. Interactive spatiotemporal visualizations of movies. All visualizations allow to access more information; and to navigate, as shown by the arrows.

(1f) seemed clear since almost all the participants could identify the most dynamic movie. It was considered less innovative than the previous visualization for its resemblance to a bar chart and more suited for movie professionals due to its perceived accuracy, reflecting the "mood" of the movie and its structure.

Space: the amounts of genres released through location are represented (2a), being exemplified the detail of the romantic movies (2b) and choosing one to watch (2b-c). These visualizations were highly rated since genre and maps are commonly used.

Spatiotemporal: after being aware of the country with more movies shot (3a), one area can be zoomed in towards the more shot (3b), and detailed to the more dated (brownish) and slower (higher) (3c) trajectories. The latter visualization caused some strangeness due to its novelty, but the results were still encouraging (M: 3.8).

Movie contents: show the properties of a whole movie (4) through circular elements that represent properties over time/duration (motion, colors, scene length, audio, speech, expressed and felt emotions) with the selected property highlighted as a tag cloud in the center. The user drags the circular elements that rotate in synchrony with the timeline. On the right, current scene is playing, synchronized with corresponding trajectory in a map, that can be zoomed. This visualization revealed very good results with professional users more determined to use it. The possibilities both to hide and turn visible the tracks of information, and to change properties were strongly appreciated. Visualization (5) represents one trajectory through image, audio amplitude, speech and other videos shot in that area allowing to play video at the clicked position in the trajectory. In the e.g. Before Sunrise movie in Vienna. It was very appreciated and understood by the participants. The preferred visualizations were 1e, followed by 4, and 5, reflecting interest in visualizing and exploring content in richer ways.

4   Lessons Learned

The results were very encouraging since all visualizations were appreciated and most proposed tasks were readily accomplished. Regarding the 4 research questions: RQ1. Representations were easy to understand, e.g. users are able to relate and compare properties among scenes. RQ2. Visualizations show in a glance what they represent; and allow RQ3. Navigation to access rich information to be explored at different levels of detail, in time and space, e.g. enter one scene and explore the location where the movie happens. They were considered an added value by all the participants, being highlighted the aesthetics and ludic way of interacting. RQ4. Casual uses were the most referred, although professionals have mentioned their interest in this kind of visualizations.

Acknowledgments. This work is supported by an FCT fellowship under the UT Austin|Portugal Program (SFRH/-BD/51798/2011); LASIGE, Faculdade de Ciências (UL); and NOVA LINCS, Faculdade de Ciências e Tecnologia (UNL).

References

1. Jorge, A., Chambel, T.: Exploring movies through interactive visualizations. In: Proceedings of British HCI, 6 p. (2013)
2. Jorge, A., Serra, S., Chambel, T.: Interactive visualizations of video tours in space and time. In: Proceedings of British HCI, pp. 329–334 (2014)
3. Andrienko, G., Andrienko, N., Demsar, U., Dransch, D., Dykes, J., Fabricant, S., Jern, M., Kraak, M.-J., Schumann, H., Tominski, C.: Space, Time and Visual Analytics, vol. 24(10). Taylor & Francis, October 2010
4. Martins, P., Langlois, T., Chambel, T.: MovieClouds: content-based overviews and exploratory browsing of movies. In: Proceedings of Academic MindTrek, pp. 133–140. ACM (2011)
5. Noronha, G., Álvares, C., Chambel, T.: Sight surfers: 360° videos and maps navigation. In: Proceedings of the ACM Multimedia Workshop GeoMM 2012, pp. 19–22. ACM (2012)
6. Hassenzahl, M., Platz, A., Burmester, M., Lehner, K.: Hedonic and ergonomic quality aspects determine a software's appeal. In: Proceedings of CHI, pp. 201–208 (2000)

Enterprise Software Experience Design: Journey and Lessons

Bhuvana Sekar[(✉)]

Cisco Systems, Bangalore, India
bhsekar@cisco.com

Abstract. This paper is a case study of a user experience based project in an enterprise setting at Cisco systems, Bangalore to improve an agent desktop experience through HCD methodologies in an Agile software development setting. The core experience revolved around agents' interactions with customers to solve their queries and resolve them. The product, already existing in the market was dated and needed a user experience refresh. The product, already existing in the market was facing a crisis because customers were not using them actively. The design team was brought in to help design the upcoming features in a User-centered way. Intensive user-driven research using the principles of systems-oriented and interaction-design were applied and the team identified core personas, made task flows, collected customer feedback, conducted user interviews, customer validations and made design concepts, recommendations and approaches. Pursuing this path, the methodologies led to some changes - design, technical and operational. This case study explores the journey and underlying issues of what challenges were faced and lessons learned by the user experience design team in an enterprise setting.

Keywords: Usability and software · Enterprise user experience · Agile · Case study · User centered design · Enterprise software

1 Introduction

As a part of a company wide initiative to introduce design thinking, a deployment based software product was decided to be developed in a user centered design fashion, but within the existing legacy back end and system constraints. The design team created personas, investigated usage scenarios and established user pain-points. In conjunction with the stakeholders, task-flows were carved out, design requirements were groomed and several design concepts were iterated to align with the users' goals and customer demands. The task-flows and personas had a humongous impact, being used not just in design discussions to understand the user flows but also to raise questions about the current system constraints and envision a future experience, thereby creating further technical and design requirements. Personas print-outs were put up in various scrum rooms in the workplace to drive conversations keeping the end users in mind.

The product customers majorly relied upon the partner community and 3rd party developers to configure the product solution for their contact centers. They were intimately aware of the customer needs and were familiar with the competitive offerings by

© IFIP International Federation for Information Processing 2017
Published by Springer International Publishing AG 2017. All Rights Reserved
R. Bernhaupt et al. (Eds.): INTERACT 2017, Part IV, LNCS 10516, pp. 356–359, 2017.
DOI: 10.1007/978-3-319-68059-0_29

rivals as well and could configure gadgets and tweak them exactly as per customer goals, needs and demands. Therefore, both these stakeholders were a critical piece of the business and often had a huge say in how the products were designed – although they were not the end-users for the same who were agents and supervisors in contact centers.

2 Background and Context

The agent desktop framework housed multiple gadgets/widgets catering to various customer requirements that could be added/modified by partners/3rd party developers. The product, an in-house gadget within the framework, enabled agents to solve consumer issues through web chats and emails. The User-Interface (UI) had an extremely busy and dense interface, with multiple ongoing simultaneous interactions. Since the UI was also designed in an incremental approach, the feature designs contributed to a design debt resulting in a complicated and confusing UI and an overused phrase – "… Our users are used to this…". Secondly, the product catered to email and chat based query resolutions in contact centers and just had primitive features to do so but, there was a tendency to look at popular email and chat clients and simply emulate features from them. With this mindset, comparisons were drawn to look and behave like Gmail, Outlook etc. which just added to an increasing 'design debt' as the product had an extremely different Information Architecture.

The Project was done in a recursive cycle of 2 sprints over 11 months. We set off by identifying all pain-points observed for different personas, their goals, created task flows and identified areas of opportunity. We observed quite a few low-hanging fruits (such as excessive or poor labelling, too many simultaneous actions, improper hierarchal order of UI elements and usability) but decided to go the route of user feedback to create the awareness and need for bigger changes not just limited to just refreshing the UI but also the backend technological changes, to support user goals and in turn, positive customer benefits.

3 Methodologies

3.1 Mind-Mapping of the Gadget System and IA

The approach for this project began with a mind-map of system understanding and Information Architecture interdependencies. Personas and task flow paths were also identified and marked. Certain overlapping items and tasks emerged that were critical points of interactions that needed to be consistent across different personas.

This exercise led to certain insights – One, the IA for the gadget was driven by various stages of evolution of product, complicating the UI and leaning away from 'goal/task' based experiences. Second, due to the same reason, contextual actions that occur during a specific task became a necessity. For example: An Agent will need the most recent customer interactions and journey history next to the active chat/email interaction. But all customer history was on another tab, thereby - forcing the agent to switch views during the interaction, missing the context and completely breaking the experience.

3.2   User Interview Sessions

Post requirement grooming, concept visioning was done for a required feature. Later a qualitative-research plan was developed to understand the usage context, goals, pain-points, and any other peripherals/tools used to accomplish tasks. We conducted 1.5-hour interviews with 7 agent desktop users (agents and supervisors) - 5 remote and 2 in person. We used a semi-structured script and conducted the interviews via WebEx screen-sharing sessions. Participants were asked to walkthrough the screens to perform a given task and were encouraged to think-aloud during the entire process. They were given a mouse/keyboard and were asked to perform a task using 'In-vision' based mockups to understand interaction modalities and validate the flow and designs. We invited the product owners, managers, and team members to observe the session. Briefing sessions took place before the interviews to illustrate the importance of observation, not leading the users, noting down observations and insights etc. At the end of the sessions, a debriefing would take place where the stakeholders were invited to discuss their learning, feedback and interview highlights.

3.3   Artifacts and Types

Design awareness artifacts such as Oral storytelling, 'Vision design-discussions' and 'Stakeholder Readouts', were facilitated along with artifacts like flows, maps, and mockups. Backlog tracking experiments were visualized using Kanban boards and 'Rally' was used to manage, track and plan the design work ahead of sprints.

3.4   Design Delivery, Customer Demos, Guerilla Testing

The final signed-off designs were supplied to scrum teams ahead of at least one sprint. The teams often would participate in the earlier stages during the 50% and 80% scrum ceremonies where the design is discussed and critiqued. The design specifications and style guides were delivered via 'Berlinux' in HTML format. At the end of every sprint upon implementation, the designs were demoed to customers. Different product teams role-played various personas and conducted Guerilla testing to identify bugs and defects.

3.5   Problems and Solutions

Without any formal design pattern in place, it took a lot of time to make designs and often led to inconsistencies. This was solved by identifying and making a local design library. Another problem being the changing requirements and ad-hoc requests that came up to feed the scrum teams, was more or less tamed by tracking the design work and artefacts. Third, for validating proposed design decisions, user interviews and IA-gadget mind-mapping helped clear and drive this fact home. A big achievement here was, that a need for a better overall experience and visual design was deemed necessary and is being worked upon for the next upcoming product release.

4 Insights, Challenges and Learnings

1. **Customer goals are not the same as user goals:** It became another imperative goal for us to differentiate that our customers' goals might not be the same as our user goals, and therefore the requirements given did not provide the information to improve the user experience. Therefore, we often had discussions to reach a middle ground, where we would recommend designs but give the option of modifying it at discretion, to not kill the business model.

2. **Agile design debt:** In an incremental agile approach, products were built in terms of feature additions and their experiences designed in slices. Therefore things were force-fitted in the UI instead of being looked at holistically, which led to less than optimal end-user experiences.

3. **Designer to developer ratio:** Since the design work ranged from doing design visioning to designing, iterating, implementation support and doing demos, a 1:16 designer to developer ratio led to stress and a myriad of chocked deadlines.

4. **Fragmented end experiences:** Due to a top-down approach for delivering features, organizational and product boundaries start emerging and kill the experience and the overall level macro-level view was muddled and experience fragmented.

5. **Relevant hierarchical awareness:** From their point of view, for e.g.: to engineers – the importance of UI consistency across not just 'their' component but the entire solution by thinking in terms of an agent. To the Customer Representatives about asking the right questions and uncovering the hidden need rather than taking a customer demand at face-value. To the Executives- why a user-centered and consistent experience might be better to stay ahead of the competition pack by comparing with similar organizations who had also made positive changes to their products using design.

References

1. Pandey, S., Swati, S.: Data Driven enterprise UX: a case study of enterprise management systems. In: HCI (2014)
2. Gajendar, U.: Why I Design Enterprise UX, and You Should Too!: Medium, June 2015. https://medium.com/@udanium/why-i-design-enterprise-ux-fa74e9f12671
3. Cleveland, B.: Call Center Management on Fast Forward: Succeeding in the New Era of Customer Relationships. ICMI Press (2012)

Expectation and Experience: Passenger Acceptance of Autonomous Public Transportation Vehicles

Grace Eden[1(✉)], Benjamin Nanchen[1], Randolf Ramseyer[1],
and Florian Evéquoz[1,2]

[1] University of Applied Sciences of Western Switzerland, HES-SO,
3960 Sierre, Switzerland
{grace.eden, benjamin.nanchen, randolf.ramseyer,
florian.evequoz}@hevs.ch
[2] University of Fribourg, 1700 Fribourg, Switzerland
florian.evequoz@unifr.ch

Abstract. Passenger acceptance is a key factor for the successful integration, uptake and use of autonomous vehicles (AVs) in the domain of public transportation. Especially knowing opinions and attitudes around safety, comfort and convenience. We discuss a pilot study conducted as part of a larger research project where AVs are being tested to transport members of the general public on a specified route with designated stops. We present preliminary findings of fieldwork conducted where people were asked their opinions and attitudes both before and after riding on an AV shuttle as a passenger for the first time. This allows us to compare user expectation beforehand with actual experience afterwards.

Keywords: Autonomous vehicles · Public transportation · Human-machine interaction · Passenger acceptance · Fieldwork

1 Introduction and Background

Autonomous passenger vehicles are being piloted across the globe to assess their technically and operationally feasibility. In June 2016, PostBus, the primary public bus transportation provider in Switzerland and the Mobility Lab Sion-Valais joined together for a pilot study, the Sion Smart Shuttle. The project began in a cordoned-off private area from December 2015 to Spring 2016. However, once government approval was granted in June 2016, the testing was moved on to public roadways and dual use vehicle/pedestrian areas. This phase of the pilot will run until October 2017.

In this project commercial and academic partners collaborate to develop novel mobility services. In parallel with technical development, understanding customer behaviour and acceptance of the AVs and in particular passenger reactions to riding on the shuttle is also being investigated. This paper presents preliminary findings of a pilot case study as part of a larger project where we also investigate how other road users interpret AV behaviour [1]. For this pilot study we conducted interviews with

R. Bernhaupt et al. (Eds.): INTERACT 2017, Part IV, LNCS 10516, pp. 360–363, 2017.
DOI: 10.1007/978-3-319-68059-0_30

passengers both before and after riding on the shuttle to provide us with an opportunity to compare user expectation beforehand with actual experience afterwards.

2   Passenger Opinions of AV Public Transport

The Smart Shuttle is the first pilot project of AVs on public roads in Switzerland and operates on a route of 1.5 km in the Old Town district of Sion. After months of refining and stabilizing the technical aspects of the AVs mapping and sensor operations to ensure safety, the first passenger acceptance pilot study commenced over a one-month period from November-December 2016 with an aim to understand passenger opinions of AV public transportation.

The AV Shuttle can hold up to 11 people with an attendant on board monitoring, and at times taking over, its operation. We conducted nine fieldwork sessions with participants who agreed to be interviewed and to take a ride on the AV shuttle. The study included 17 passengers: 3 individuals, 4 couples, and 2 groups of three. In addition, the sessions were also video-recorded using two mounted action cameras: one with an interior view of passengers and the other with an exterior view of the road ahead (Fig. 1).

Fig. 1. Two mounted action cameras record passenger and road activity simultaneously.

The fieldwork had three components. First, participants were briefly interviewed before riding the shuttle and asked to describe their initial expectations including perceptions of safety, comfort and any other feelings and opinions. Second, we conducted video-based observation [2] of participants' actual journey on the shuttle. Third, after riding on the shuttle we conducted a post-ride interview with the same questions to compare if and how their opinions may have changed. The interview data was analyzed using qualitative methods informed by thematic analysis [3]. The preliminary findings discussed here are taken from the pre and post ride interviews with a focus on passengers' opinions related to the AV's safety, comfort and convenience.

2.1 Opinions About Safety

Before riding on the AV shuttle 4 participants expressed safety concerns because of news reports of an accident in September 2016 [4]. The shuttle hit the fender of a stationary van while in autonomous mode. Fortunately, there were no injuries as a result of the collision although the fact that it happened made some people uneasy. Others expressed concerns related to the reliability of braking and turning. Finally, the technology in general was brought into question as one participant noted: *"I don't trust it much because something could go wrong with the IT system. You go on it but you don't trust it 100%"*. Even so, the 13 remaining participants said they had no concerns before riding on the shuttle primarily because of its very slow speed (maximum of 20 km). Also, many had experience with other types of driverless transportation such as driverless metro trains at airports. Even though these are on guided tracks some people still felt that this experience was in some way similar.

After riding the shuttle all participants who had safety concerns beforehand no longer had them afterwards. These overall positive opinions were encouraging. Although, many passengers commented that seatbelts are necessary especially because the AV lurches forward when it makes sudden hard stops. It frequently does this when it detects an 'obstacle' such as a pedestrian, car or bicycle passing close by. Many participants said they were impressed with the automated navigation, including its steering ability through narrow spaces. Although participants responses were positive, there is an important caveat: most agreed that their perception of safety might change (safety concerns would increase) if it was a large-sized bus with no attendants on board travelling on an actual route at regular speed.

2.2 Satisfaction with Comfort and Convenience

Another key factor to passenger acceptance is comfort and convenience. The shuttle's large panoramic windows were received positively because of the wide view it provides to the outside world. However, most participants said that the comfort of the seats could be improved because they were too hard and that seatbelts are needed to prevent people from lurching forward during sudden hard stops. Additionally, 4 participants commented that the noise from the hydraulic compressor was too loud. Many participants commented on its small size saying that people are sitting too close together and that it would need to be larger to accommodate luggage and shopping bags.

Regarding convenience, all participants said that the current route was not practical because it is in a largely pedestrian area of the old town that people prefer to walk through. Rather, many said that they would like to use it for more practical journeys such as from the train station, the local airport, or the park and ride. This feedback indicates that there is acceptance of the AVs as a potentially useful addition to the public transportation network for smaller routes that may not be served by large buses. However, many participants felt that the hours of operation would need to be extended (it currently operates from 1–6 pm). Others wanted to become more involved in the project. For instance, by adding a social media component that would allow them to share their experience online with their friends and family. Also, some suggest that an information sheet be available explaining the technology and how the AV operates.

3 Discussion and Further Work

This pilot study provides valuable insights of passenger opinions related to safety, comfort and convenience (Table 1) with each of these dimensions having implications for scalability. For instance, many participants said that the speed is slow enough to feel safe but too slow for going to work in the morning.

Table 1. Dimension of safety, comfort, and convenience for AV shuttle passengers.

Safety	Comfort	Convenience
Braking	Windows	Route availability
Turning	Seats	Hours of operation
Speed	Hydraulic compressor noise	Speed
Human co-driver	Interior size	Luggage space

In further work we will conduct participatory design workshops with passengers to investigate possible future interactions with AV public transportation. These will examine designs for maintaining passenger trust. For instance, providing greater transparency of the AV decision-making process including the choices it makes around obstacle detection, braking and steering. In these workshops we will co-design and prototype a dedicated interface to monitor these activities. Lessons learned include the value of conducting fieldwork in three phases: pre and post ride interviews (for comparisons before and after) and video (for investigating communication between the AVs and other road users). In each of these areas, our aim is to inform the design of new communication and interaction mechanisms between AVs and humans.

References

1. Eden, G., Nanchen, B., Ramseyer, R., Evéquoz, F.: On the road with an autonomous passenger shuttle: integration in public spaces. In: Proceedings of CHI 2017, pp. 1569–1576. ACM Press, Denver CO, New York (2017)
2. Heath, C., Hindmarsh, J., Luff, P.: Video in Qualitative Research: Analysing social interaction in everyday life. Sage, London (2010)
3. Guest, G., MacQueen, K.M., Namey, E.E.: Applied Thematic Analysis. SAGE Publications, Thousand Oaks, CA (2012)
4. https://www.postauto.ch/en/news/smartshuttle-testing-sion-resumes

From Minutes of Meeting to 'Memories of Meeting'

How We Designed Impactful and Engaging Visual MoM for Client Visit

Lakshmi Deshpande[(✉)]

Tata Consultancy Services, Kensington-B,
Hiranandani SEZ, Powai, Mumbai 400076, India
lakshmi.deshpande@tcs.com

Abstract. Meetings in a business context are organized for a wide range of purposes and with varying contexts. Minutes of Meeting, are a good tool for capturing the formal discussions, but fail to capture finer details. Recognizing this limitation, Tata Consultancy Services (TCS) decided to use an innovative visual note-taking approach to capture a client visit. The objective was to have a single graphic encapsulate the events across all days of the visit, to ensure a good client recall and create a lasting impact.

Keywords: New work methodology · Design thinking · Visual meetings · Sketch notes · Doodling · Graphic recording · Visual listening · Collaboration tool · Client engagement · Customer relationship · Visualization technique

1 Introduction

Tata Consultancy Services (TCS) is a leading IT Services company based out of India providing IT and business solutions to global clients. Client engagement is an extremely important part of the business for TCS. An international client's top management was visiting India for four days to discuss TCS's capabilities in the space of Digital Re-imagination. From TCS's perspective, the visit was an opportunity to demonstrate capabilities to strengthen and grow the client-TCS relationship. Given the importance of the client, the business unit was keen on innovative approaches for creating greater impact. The User Experience (UX) team was thus approached. It was decided that a Visual MoM would greatly complement the standard Minutes of Meeting.

This approach to visual note-taking would entail a Graphic Recorder (GR), observe the events from the entire client visit. The idea was to switch from the conventional who-said-what, towards an event-capturing approach.

The intent of the graphic was to seize not only what happens in the meeting room, but also the experiences and memories of the client during their trip to the country. 'Memories of Meeting' would add a sense of personal touch as opposed to pure data capturing associated with Minutes of Meeting. The final output would be a printed Graphic- presented as a souvenir. This would remain with the clients as memories of their visit, and serve well for continued customer engagement.

© IFIP International Federation for Information Processing 2017
Published by Springer International Publishing AG 2017. All Rights Reserved
R. Bernhaupt et al. (Eds.): INTERACT 2017, Part IV, LNCS 10516, pp. 364–367, 2017.
DOI: 10.1007/978-3-319-68059-0_31

2 Preparation Prior to the Meeting

The meeting was spread across four days at various TCS offices across the country. A week before this, following preparation was done-

2.1 Preparatory Work

Even though most of the information for the graphic was to be gathered real-time, the GR did considerable prior preparation.

1. GR connected with the cross-located TCS teams to understand the purpose of the visit, client's background and also TCS capability to be showcased.
2. GR got an understanding of the key interest areas for the client. The client had operations in 100+ countries and the business focus was on continuous, reliable and sustainable performance.
3. Cultural aspects- GR tried to ensure that the graphic was sensitive to the cultural nuances of the client.
4. The method finalized for creating the visual- Sketch during the meeting, validate the visuals with stakeholders and finally print the digitized output.

2.2 Key Decisions for the GR

Mood: The GR decided to limit dry facts and numbers in the graphic. That information was to be reserved for accompanying business documents. The Visual MoM had to look lively yet corporate; personalized yet professional.

Layout and Illustrations: All four days had to be captured in one visual. Since a four-column layout would have been linear and somewhat rigid, the layout was divided into four quadrants, placing agenda center stage. A cyclic structure also emphasized the clients' round trip to India. All illustrations were hand-drawn on paper then digitized, set against a white canvas, for a good contrast.

Color Palette: Brand Identity colors of TCS (Blue) and its Client (Red), with Yellow accents for highlights were used. The interaction between the two organizations is depicted using these colors. The GR was aware that color semantics can greatly impact viewer's expectations, hence mindful while using the same.

Tools: For quick and efficient capturing of moments, GR had to use basic pen, paper and markers for creating the first draft of the Visual MoMs. Final graphic was created using HP inkjet scanner and printer, Adobe Photoshop, Wacom Pen tablet.

3 The Meetings

Day 1-Gandhinagar: This was an orientation session, showcasing overall TCS capabilities to the Client. The Client met the offshore team for the first time in person. This was the beginning of recording the key events of the client trip.

Day 2-Mumbai: TCS showcased its round the clock support to the onsite tech team. The GR sketched throughout- even during the meals and break times. This enabled GR to capture casual moments of the meeting as well. Indian food was frequently discussed. Including the same in the illustration, provided the necessary personal touch and increased recall at a later date for the client.

Day 3-Chennai: Technological capabilities were showcased in TCS labs. Capturing this was important for future client reference. Many casual topics were interspersed to increase the recall. For e.g. dramatic weather differences across India, an active topic of discussion, was included to make the graphic more detailed and personal.

Day 4-Mumbai: The closing discussion focused on the roadmap of the visit. At this point the client expected a recap of the points to take home. Again, keeping the formal and casual mix of the illustration, the GR captured the technical projects that were discussed along with the casual conversation like beverage preferences.

Wrap-Up: Post completion of the client visit, the GR set about collating the illustrations created during the course of the four days. Post collation and review by the business team, the illustrations were digitized. A high quality A3 sized print out of the Visual MoM was presented to each client, on their return to home country.

4   Challenges and Learnings

- **Groundwork:** Advance preparation ensured that during the actual meeting, focus was on understanding the happenings and translating them to visuals. Time spent prior on learning the basics of technical and business aspects was crucial.
- **Data Validation**: As a designer, the GR was not well versed with the technical aspects and the Client's business. Teaming up with stakeholders who understood the topics at hand well thus became very important.
- **Time Constraint**: GR had to work very fast to keep pace with the meeting schedule. There was limited time to experiment. Hence, an iterative approach with regular feedback had to be adopted. This saved significant rework in case of changes.
- **Voluminous Data**: There was a lot of collated data from the four day visit. Data refinement is a time consuming yet important activity, so as to have a crisp meaningful output. The advance preparation was helpful in identifying the important business aspects that were key to the Visual MoM. For informal and personal things, the GR went with her insights to ensure the Visual MoM has the desired feel.
- **Design Style:** The graphic stood out and was memorable because of its distinct illustrative style with touches of humor, which added the desired personality.
- **Discreteness:** The GR took visual notes discretely, so as to not impede the flow of discussions in any manner.

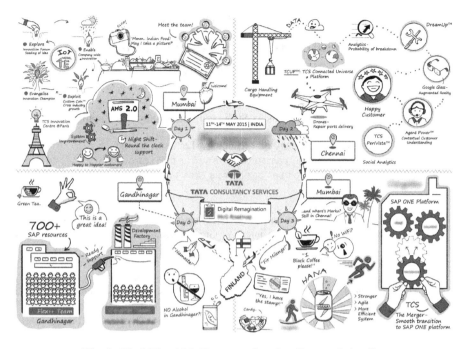

Fig. 1. Final Visual MoM presented to the client, at their office

5 Conclusion

Feedback from stakeholders: "*It was received extremely well by the customers! Already print outs have been made and displayed at their workstations! They appreciated the memory part, the fun part & the highlights of the visit -all mixed in a very balanced manner. They just loved it.*"

Such feedback demonstrated that the approach was effective in ensuring the key points of the meeting were highlighted and remained in Clients' memory.

The Visual MoM would go a long way in strengthening the Client-TCS relationship. Post the success of this engagement, this approach has been adopted for several important client engagements in TCS (Fig. 1).

Leveraging Virtual Trips in Google Expeditions to Elevate Students' Social Exploration

Antigoni Parmaxi[✉], Kostas Stylianou, and Panayiotis Zaphiris

Cyprus University of Technology, Lemesos, Cyprus
{antigoni.parmaxi,kostas.stylianou,
panayiotis.zaphiris}@cut.ac.cy

Abstract. This paper reports on an exploratory case study on the use of Google Expeditions in the context of an intensive Greek language course for specific academic purposes. Google Expeditions are collections of linked virtual reality content that can enable teachers to bring students on virtual trips to places like museums, human anatomy, surgical processes etc. Thematic analysis of instructors' field notes, students' reflections, interviews and focus group was employed aiming at identifying the potential of Google Expeditions for extending the language classroom through virtual trips. The use of Google Expeditions enabled students to extend the borders of the classroom by making virtual walkthroughs in places that would normally be unreachable and trigger social exploration through inter- and extra-VR communication, sharing of ideas, concepts and experiences. This study acts as a pilot with an eye to inform larger-scale investigation of Google Expeditions in the future.

Keywords: Computer-assisted language learning · Wearables · Constructionism · Social constructionism

1 Introduction

The onset of Virtual Reality (VR) technology can be traced to the 1960s in the entertainment industry. Since then, VR has been leveraged to meet the needs of curricula in subjects such as mechanics, art, medicine, science and language learning. Several studies indicate that these technologies provide fertile ground for visualizing abstract concepts, but also give opportunities to visit and interact with places or object that time or spatial restrictions might limit, engaging learners in authentic situations and interactive communication [1–3]. Despite the positive impact of VR, evidence also shows instructors' reluctance to engage in their use, as it requires a high level of advanced technology knowledge (e.g. in the case of Oculus VR, Google Glass and Samsung Gear; Yap [4]).

This study incorporated VR cardboard as a low-cost 3D viewer in conjunction with a smartphone in an intensive Greek language course. VR Cardboard is a low-cost technology product compared to other VR devices. On 2016, via Google Expeditions, Google has launched a number of virtual environments aiming at giving teachers and

R. Bernhaupt et al. (Eds.): INTERACT 2017, Part IV, LNCS 10516, pp. 368–371, 2017.
DOI: 10.1007/978-3-319-68059-0_32

students the opportunity to visit places or environment that are not able to visit ordinarily. Considering that nowadays most of the students own a smartphone, and also knowing that a VR cardboard can be purchased for less than 20 dollars, VR cardboard along with Google Expeditions is the cheapest solution in the market for creating VR environments.

Incorporating VR in the curricula of health-related professionals, such as perspective nurses, we explored their exposure to virtual environments with an eye to foster social exploration within small groups of language learners. This study confronts with the theoretical framework of social constructionism, giving students opportunities to explore a specific topic as an initial step for knowledge construction [5–7]. The uniqueness of this case study is that it explores the potential of a novel tool, such as Google Expeditions, for enhancing understanding of abstract concepts related to Nursing. The following research question guides this study:

– **How a low-cost VR kit in conjunction with Google Expeditions can facilitate social exploration within a small group of language learners?**

2   Setting

All data related to this study were collected at a public, Greek-speaking university in the Republic of Cyprus. The study took place in a Greek as a second language course, (October 2016–June 2017). The class met face-to-face every day for five hours, for a total of 650 h. The course was particularly designed to meet the needs of university students who planned to study Nursing. The participants were three male students from Kenya aged from 19–27 years.

3   Tools and Materials

Students used a virtual reality viewer and Android mobile phones in which they downloaded Google Expeditions application. Expeditions are group experiences with the instructor acting as a guide leading and the students following along (see Fig. 1).

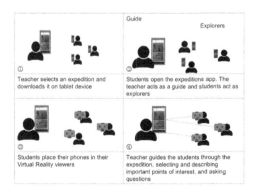

Fig. 1. Setting up google expeditions

The instructors controlled and guided students through Google Expeditions from an Android tablet. Google expeditions was incorporated in the existing curriculum of the course and explored both general topics (e.g. house description), as well as specific topics related to their profession (such as clinic admissions, surgical preparation etc.).

4   Methodology

Data was collected through a questionnaire, interviews, a focus group, daily field notes kept throughout the course by the instructor, instructors' and learners' reflective diary. To triangulate the findings, the study also collected data by observing students' behavior during the virtual field-trips. We analyzed the data set using the Qualitative Research Software Nvivo 11. The content of the utterances was read for meaning to define segment boundaries, thus, consecutive sentences that constructed the same meaning were taken as one text unit and coded into a single code [8]. The coding focused on the actions that took place in order for learners to socially navigate in a virtual field-trip.

5   Findings and Discussion

The study identified that a low-cost VR kit in conjunction with Google Expeditions can facilitate social exploration of authentic nursing-related contexts, providing opportunities for communication, sharing of ideas, concepts, experiences and artifacts.

5.1   Intra- and Extra- VR Communication

Google expeditions can facilitate intra and extra- VR communication and foster students' speaking and listening skills. Through virtual trips, (a) the instructor guided students and posed questions for specific important teaching moments given within the application; and (b) students listened to their instructors' guidance and describe what they could see during and after the exploration.

5.2   From Abstract to Tangible Concepts

Virtual trips act as a common experience for instructor and students making abstract concepts and ideas tangible and vivid. As noted by one student: *I was finding it hard to describe something [that I have not seen].* (S3, Interview)

5.3   Affordable Visit to Authentic Environments

Google expeditions provided a gateway for visiting places that students would not be able to visit and consequently practice language related to the specific context like *'being in the hospital'* (S2, focus group). Moreover, the use of virtual trips raised students' curiosity and interest for a specific topic. As noted by one student: *"by describing the pictures [...] makes learning interesting and sticks in the memory"* (S3, Reflections).

5.4   Vivid Exploration Leading to Artifact Construction

Having completed their exploration, students were then tasked to construct an artifact related to the specific environment, i.e. concretize what they had experienced in a report or a presentation related to the specific virtual trip. To facilitate the completion of the task, students were instructed to switch their Expedition from explorers to guiders.

6   Conclusion and Future Work

This case study reported on how the use of a low-cost VR kit in conjunction with Google Expeditions enabled students and instructors to extend the borders of the classroom by making virtual walkthroughs in places that would normally be unreachable. Virtual field trips triggered social exploration through inter- and extra-VR communication, sharing of ideas, concepts and experiences. We suggest that development emphasis should initially be on enriching the library of Google Expeditions, involving its users in making process. Future research should focus on further implementation of the specific technology in different settings (e.g. for healthcare and HCI education). Finally, longitudinal studies should also be conducted to assess the impact of the specific tool.

References

1. Merchant, Z., Goetz, E.T., Cifuentes, L., Keeney-Kennicutt, W., Davis, T.J.: Effectiveness of virtual reality-based instruction on students' learning outcomes in K-12 and higher education: a meta-analysis. Comput. Educ. **70**, 29–40 (2014)
2. Seo, J.H., Smith, B., Cook, M., Pine, M., Malone, E., Leal, S., Suh, J.: Anatomy builder VR: applying a constructive learning method in the virtual reality canine skeletal system. In: 2017 IEEE Virtual Reality (VR), pp. 399–400. IEEE, March 2017
3. Chen, Y.L.: The effects of virtual reality learning environment on student cognitive and linguistic development. Asia-Pac. Educ. Res. **25**(4), 637–646 (2016)
4. Yap, M.: Google Cardboard for a K12 Social Studies Module (2016). http://hdl.handle.net/10125/40604
5. Parmaxi, A., Zaphiris, P., Michailidou, E., Papadima-Sophocleous, S., Ioannou, A.: Introducing new perspectives in the use of social technologies in learning: social constructionism. In: Kotzé, P., Marsden, G., Lindgaard, G., Wesson, J., Winckler, M. (eds.) INTERACT 2013. LNCS, vol. 8118, pp. 554–570. Springer, Heidelberg (2013). doi:10.1007/978-3-642-40480-1_39
6. Parmaxi, A., Zaphiris, P.: Developing a framework for social technologies in learning via design-based research. Educ. Media Int. **52**(1), 33–46 (2015). doi:10.1080/09523987.2015.1005424
7. Parmaxi, A., Zaphiris, P., Ioannou, A.: Enacting artifact-based activities for social technologies in language learning using a design-based research approach. Comput. Hum. Behav. **63**, 556–567 (2016)
8. Chi, M.T.H.: Quantifying qualitative analyses of verbal data: a practical guide. J. Learn. Sci. **6**(3), 271–315 (1997)

On the Design and Evaluation of Nippon Paint Color Visualizer Application – A Case Study

Kuldeep Kulshreshtha[1(✉)], Andreea I. Niculescu[2(✉)],
and Bimlesh Wadhwa[3(✉)]

[1] UX Army, Singapore, Singapore
kuldeepk@uxarmy.com
[2] Institute for Infocomm Research (I2R), Singapore, Singapore
andreea-n@i2r.a-star.edu.sg
[3] National University of Singapore (NUS), Singapore, Singapore
bimlesh@nus.edu.sg

Abstract. In this paper, we present a case study focusing on the design challenges and evaluation process of *Color Visualizer,* a mobile phone application
developed for Nippon Paint Singapore. The application enables users to visualize paint color on home interiors and decide on the best color match. *Color
Visualizer* was incrementally built upon iterative design & successive development sessions, all based on extensive hours of user research. Design decisions, evaluation results, lessons learned and future work are presented.

Keywords: Coloring technology app · User research · Interaction design

1 Introduction

Color has always played a vital role in our lives as powerful tool of communication.
Also, it's a well-known fact, that colors can have a profound effect on our emotional
well-being. Thus, choosing the right color when painting our home is of crucial
importance. However, the selecting process can be daunting not only because of the
paradox of choice or conflict of preferences, but also because of the inability to
visualize several color effects on real walls. Paint companies are increasingly investing
in digital tools to help consumers overcome this challenge. *Color Visualizer* is one such
mobile application recently launched by Nippon Paint Singapore [1].

Designing a good color visualizer is a challenging process. Firstly, because digital
painting, in contrast to physical painting poses several technical hardships, such as
identify edges and corners in a room image, separate objects from walls, and handle
diversity in image attributes caused by different camera types and room illumination.
Especially, in cases where walls have irregular edges, rooms vary in style and illumination or pictures have low resolution the challenge is by far not trivial.

Secondly, there are obvious discrepancies in image processing performance
between humans and computers that tend to generate disappointment for first time
users: humans have excellent skills of understanding space semantics, i.e. distinguishing between walls, ceiling, objects placed in a room and as they often expect
computers to see the reality similarly to themselves (see Fig. 1).

© IFIP International Federation for Information Processing 2017
Published by Springer International Publishing AG 2017. All Rights Reserved
R. Bernhaupt et al. (Eds.): INTERACT 2017, Part IV, LNCS 10516, pp. 372–376, 2017.
DOI: 10.1007/978-3-319-68059-0_33

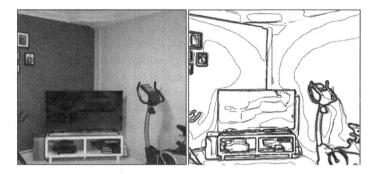

Fig. 1. View of a room: humans (LEFT) vs. computers (RIGHT)

Thirdly, differences in users' proficiency with image processing software, such as MS paint or Photoshop make hard to decide on the most appropriate interaction style: keeping operation tools similar to those found in such programs would beneficiate experts but exclude novice users; on the other side, designing new interaction ways would probably confuse MS paint and Photoshop experts.

Fourthly, budget and strict time limitation are adding up to existing challenges. Thus, the goal of our user studies was to determine what real painting elements are crucial for the app's user experience (UX), how users would 'paint' their walls using the app and whether there are any important user needs left unrecognized.

2 Iterative Design & Evaluation Studies

The first coloring app developed in this project enabled users to use different color schemes to color the walls by using finger tapping and selecting a color using the color bar. Deleting the color could be accomplished by dragging from an unfilled space into the colored area. Functions, such as saving projects for late re-use or for sharing with friends, as well as identifying paint store locations on a map were included in the app. Figure 2 shows the application's original design: the small size of the phone screen caused the color to spill over requiring several corrective touches.

Fig. 2. Screen shot first design

A first user study with 18 participants (11 female & 7 male) age 24-35yrs was performed in our lab. Our interest at this stage was to determine whether basic users' expectations toward the app were generally met. Participants were selected to fulfill the following criteria: own a house in Singapore, own an iPhone 5 and above, had significant involvement in painting their own house in the past 12 months or had plans to engage in painting activities within the following 12 month.

Participants were asked to perform the following tasks with the app: (1) 'paint' walls and ceilings using pictures taken from their own home or from the test lab[1] (2) save the 'painting' projects for later use; (3) buy paint using the app; (4) share the 'painting' screenshots with friends and relatives. Additionally, they were presented with two alternative features adopted from Photoshop: layering and masking, i.e. using a 'virtual' tape to cover furniture when 'painting' the walls. The features were part of other coloring applications from a competitor brand and we were interested to find out whether such functions could be useful for our app as well.

The sessions were conducted by a moderator accompanied by an observer. After completing each task, participants were interviewed using unstructured in-depth interview techniques. The questions were based on their immediate experience with the app. When discrepancies were found (between what was done vs. what was reported), laddering techniques were used to explore unconscious motivations behind users' actions. Each session lasted for 1 h and 15 min. Both interviews, as well as users' interactions with the app were recorded to facilitate further analysis.

The results uncovered several app deficiencies, such as confusing menus, unclear color recommendations, as well as lack of control when painting or deleting colors. The coloring screen was found to be complicated and hard to use while exported pictures were missing color codes making hard to identify the same color nuance in the shop. Users seemed uncomfortable sharing the pictures in social media, however saving and emailing pictures was found to be a useful feature. Masking and layering functionalities seemed to create problems to those unaccustomed to Photoshop who were unable to complete this task without facilitator's help. In general, participants found the app to be difficult to control, "unpredictable" in action and "inefficient" in execution. Overall, the impression was of a poor UX. The results obtained from the first user study made clear the app wasn't ready to launch yet.

Based on participants' feedback and careful analysis of video recordings, the team decided to re-design the coloring screen and simplify the coloring process. Confusing elements, such as 'delete color' was replaced with an eraser brush. An undo functionality was added to allow for more flexibility. The color bar was replaced with a color picker: users could select a color from a thumbnails palette and apply the color to any desired picture area. For coloring, re-coloring or erasing, simple tapping could be used. A gallery of pre-masked pictures was added in response to requests from several (mostly males) participants: such pictures would enable users to visualize on the spot how painted walls would look like in a fully furnished environment – see Fig. 3.

Another evaluation session was run with 30 participants (14 female & 16 male, aged 24–35yrs) to validate the improvements. Selection criteria, interviews techniques

---

[1] Pictures could be taken using the camera phone or chosen from the photo gallery.

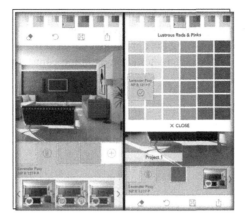

Fig. 3. App improved design

and scenario tasks remained identical to the first user study. Results confirmed improvements: the app was considered easy to use and allowing for a finer control during coloring and erasing. The colored walls shown on the user interface had a natural look with a better color effects visualization on shadows, sunlight and lighting.

Further, participants requested to use single taps to cover most of the wall/ceiling and tap rub to color the leftover area. Users also expressed the desire to see the color variation on the walls in picture thumbnails for comparison, as well as to have gallery pictures displaying typical Singapore home environments, i.e. the current app used mostly images from Western homes.

The design and development time between the user evaluations took almost 3 months. With another two months of fine tuning, the app was launched in December 2016 in iOS and android version. Currently, the app usage has grown in the past few months up to 30k downloads.

3   Conclusions and Future Work

While painting is a simple task in real life, translating it into the digital world turned out to be a challenge. In-depth interviews and user behavior analysis were of fundamental importance for understanding the user journey's utmost details. Such details sum up the ultimate user experience. Along the way, we learned a few lessons worth sharing: 1. design for simplicity; 2. focus on people's natural tendencies – for example, it was observed that users usually accomplish a task by single tapping at an interactive element; 3. wrongly assumed background knowledge in graphic tools, such as Photoshop and MS paint could be counterproductive. Particularly relevant to our application, we learned that the colour picker was indeed a useful feature for inspecting selected colours while the 3D model of a real room (with painted walls and furniture as in Fig. 3) helped users to decide more easily on the best colour match.

In the future, we plan to incorporate single toggle button for coloring/erasing, enable rubbing to add paint in left out areas, replacing colors using the palette with just one finger tap, keeping a history of colored room pictures for comparison, manage user expectation by recoloring uploaded pictures with the last used paint color. We also plan to persuade users to continue using the app by making coloring a fun experience so that Nippon can increase its sales and creates stronger brand connection with its customers.

Reference

1. Nippon Paint Mobile App - Color Visualizer. http://www.nipponpaint.com.sg/colours/nippon-paint-mobile-app/

Courses

Design of Location-Based Mobile Games: Introduction

Christos Sintoris[(⊠)], Nikoleta Yiannoutsou, and Nikolaos Avouris

HCI Group, University of Patras, 26504 Patras, Greece
{sintoris,nyiannoutsou,avouris}@upatras.gr

Abstract. The objective of this course, is to introduce the participants to location-based games and to the challenges relating to designing them. Key characteristics of this new genre are introduced first, followed by a design framework and a set of design guidelines. Examples of location-based games will be presented and typical design patterns as extracted from previous workshops will be discussed. This course has already been run in the frame of several conferences and summer schools (Sintoris 2015). Typical course participants include interaction designers, game designers and developers, practitioners and researchers interested in location-based games. The course is presented by researchers who have been involved in designing and studying human interaction with location-based games for many years. Examples of games developed by the course organizers include MuseumScrabble, RebelsVsSpies, Taggling, etc.

Keywords: Location-based games · Ideation · Game design · Card-based design methods

1 Introduction

This course introduces key concepts of location-based mobile games and their design. Location-based games are playful activities situated in specific real world locations. They involve human activity, as they necessitate moving in physical space, while it has been shown that they are conducive to learning, leading to acquisition of skills like critical thinking, curiosity, creativity, collaboration, consideration of multiple perspectives, social awareness, responsibility and media fluency (Schrier 2006). In addition, their content may relate to rich information about the game location.

Various terms have been used to describe location-based mobile games. They have been called pervasive games, hybrid reality games, augmented reality games, GPS games, emphasizing different aspects of them.

The course is 80' long and is made of four parts. (a) Introduction to key notions of location-based games, (b) A design framework for these games including design patterns from previous games, (c) Examples of games and (d) Hands on experience with ideation of a location based game for a specific location.

The course handouts include the set of slides that will be used, and background papers discussing key concepts, the design framework and typical game examples, as well as material for the hands-on part of the course.

© IFIP International Federation for Information Processing 2017
Published by Springer International Publishing AG 2017. All Rights Reserved
R. Bernhaupt et al. (Eds.): INTERACT 2017, Part IV, LNCS 10516, pp. 379–382, 2017.
DOI: 10.1007/978-3-319-68059-0_34

2 Principles of Location-Based Games

A recurring view of what constitutes the game-space of location-based games involves the consideration of their dual character of overlapping physical and digital dimensions. Some of the activity takes place in the physical domain and involves actions such as moving to a location, observing a physical object, taking pictures or recording sounds. At the same time, a part of the activity takes place in the digital domain where the players interact with simulated characters and events, where they generate information in digital form and consume information or engage in problem-solving activities like solving puzzles. The two spheres are not clearly separated though and involve deep interconnections between the social, physical and virtual spheres.

To describe and understand location-based games one needs to consider their main constituting dimensions: the *ludic*, the *learning*, the *spatial*, the *social*, and the *interaction* (Sintoris et al. 2010).

In the course, each one of them will be covered, with examples and design principles.

Any time we are engaged in playful activity we cross a "magical circle" and enter a new space: that of game play. New rules, new characters, new stories evolve in this new space. In location-based games the game activity takes place in a space where places may carry a meaning and participate in the game activity. In this case, we observe the co-existence of three interrelated spaces: the game space, as defined by the "magic circle" notion, the digital space and the physical space (see Fig. 1). Technology and mobility interrelate the three spaces, by augmenting the physical space and supporting the game mechanics.

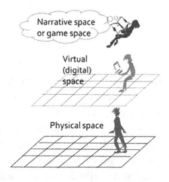

Fig. 1. Technology links different spaces: game, digital and physical (Avouris et al. 2013)

3 Course Structure

The course introduces the key characteristics of location-based mobile games. The underlying idea is that with these games the players interact with the real world, perform physical activities situated in the real world and relate knowledge with places rich in historic value. As noted in a survey of location-based games (Avouris and Yiannoutsou 2012), these games are conceived as tools that employ the fun of a game and engagement with a specific location. They may be played indoors (e.g. in a museum) or outdoors (e.g. in a city center). In this course examples of such games will be given, with special emphasis to games relating to cultural heritage.

In the second part of the course, the challenge of designing location based mobile games will be discussed. A design framework is presented and a set of guidelines that may inform design of such games. This includes a set of design patterns, which were extracted from game design workshops. Several workshops for designing location-based games were organized and the designers were asked to generate game concepts for a hypothetical location-based mobile game, where the players should engage simultaneously with the real-world but also with its game-world counterparts.

Designing a location-based mobile game is a complex undertaking. Besides considerations about game mechanics and fun, which are complex in themselves, other aspects such as interaction between the players, the physical location and objects, expected learning outcome, etc. make this endeavor even more difficult. Several design patterns to be used in the conceptualization of location-based mobile games are presented. These are building blocks or partial solutions that can support the generation of game concepts. As to be useful design tools, the design patterns aim to strike a balance between the aim to give designers enough options and to avoid prescribing static solutions.

Next, in the third part of the course examples from location-based games developed by the course organizers will be briefly presented and discussed, in terms of concepts, design and implementation decisions, including MuseumScrabble, RebelsVsSpies, Taggling, etc.

In the final part of the game the participants are asked to answer the following question: What are the components of a game? A good way to address this question is through an example. This question aims at grounding the design process in the deconstruction of existing games and to start thinking about a game in terms of its main components.

The participants of the hands-on activity follow a 'scenario' where they become game designers. In this scenario: The aim is the design of a game where the players move in specific site, use smartphones to interact with objects, buildings, locations in it, interact with each other forming teams, collaborating, competing or antagonizing, have fun and enjoy the game, learn about the site.

The participants form groups of 3–5 and receive the relevant material (http://hci. ece.upatras.gr/pompeiigame/).

The activity is structured in two symmetrical phases. Each phase is followed by a presentation. The aim of the first phase is to familiarize the team members with the material. The actual design work is expected to happen in phase two.

Phase one (10 min) A rapporteur is chosen from each team. Each team formulates an idea about a location based mobile game using the Worksheet 1 to describe it

Presentation (10 min) The rapporteur explains and pitches the idea in a very short presentation (1 min per team) Very fast!

Phase two (10 min) The teams get back and improve, detail and modify their games. They can use any of the other teams' ideas

Final presentation and discussion. The rapporteur explains and pitches the final idea in a short presentation. Discussion is encouraged.

References

Schrier, K.: Using augmented reality games to teach 21st century skills. In: ACM SIGGRAPH 2006 Educators Program, p. 15 (2006)

Sintoris, C., Yiannoutsou, N.: Learning in the city through pervasive games. The Hybrid City II: Subtle Revolutions, pp. 192–195 (2013)

Sintoris, C.: Extracting game design patterns from game design workshops. Int. J. Intell. Eng. Inf. 3(2–3), 166–185 (2015)

Sintoris, C., Yiannoutsou, N., Avouris, N.: Exploring cultural spaces through location-based mobile games. In: ACM CHI 2016 Pervasive Play Workshop, May 17, 2016, San Jose, USA (2016). http://hci.ece.upatras.gr/publications

Manoli, V., Sintoris, C., Yiannoutsou, N., Avouris, N.: Taggling game: learning about contemporary art through game play. In: Proceedings EDULEARN 2015, pp. 7684–7690, Barcelona, July 2015

Avouris, N., Yiannoutsou, N.: A review of mobile location-based games for learning across physical and virtual spaces. J. Univ. Comput. Sci. 18(15), 2120–2142 (2012)

Sintoris, C., Stoica, A., Papadimitriou, I., Yiannoutsou, N., Komis, V., Avouris, N.: MuseumScrabble: design of a mobile game for children's interaction with a digitally augmented cultural space. Int. J. Mob. Hum. Comput. Interact. 2(2), 53–71 (2010)

http://www.invisiblecity.gr/

http://hci.ece.upatras.gr/museumscrabble/

http://www.cityscrabble.gr

http://hci.ece.upatras.gr/pompeiigame/

Designing and Assessing Interactive Systems Using Task Models

Philippe Palanque[1], Célia Martinie[1], and Marco Winckler[1,2(✉)]

[1] IRIT – Université Paul Sabatier Toulouse 3, Toulouse, France
{palanque,martinie,winckler}@irit.fr
[2] Université Nice Sophia Antipolis (Polytech), Nice, France

Abstract. This two-part course takes a practical approach to introduce the principles, methods and tools in task modelling. Part 1: A non-technical introduction demonstrates that task models support successful design of interactive systems. Part 2: A more technical interactive hands-on exercise of how to "do it right", such as: How to go from task analysis to task models? How to assess (through analysis and simulation) that a task model is correct? How to identify complexity of user tasks.

Keywords: User interaction design · Task description and modelling

1 Introduction

Task analysis is meant to identify user goals and tasks when using an interactive system. In the case of users performing real life work, task analysis can be a cumbersome process gathering a huge amount of unorganized information. Task Models (TM) provide a mean for the analyst to store information gathered in an abstract way that can be further detailed and analyzed if needed. A task model allows HCI researchers and practionners to record in a systematic, complete and unambiguous way the set of user goals and the way those user goals can be performed on an interactive system. Reasoning about the Task Models produced supports the assessment of effectiveness of an interactive system (which is one of the most difficult dimension of usability to assess). Task models have also proven being of great help for structuring user documentation, designing and assessing a training program, assessing the complexity of the users' work. If used for analysis, they can also provide support for identifying types, location and likelihood of human errors. When used for design they also provide precious support for identification of good candidates for task migration towards automation.

2 Contribution and Benefit

This course intends to provide newcomers with background in task modeling. It provides an overview on how the recent advances in task description techniques can be exploited to design and assess interactive systems. As task models can be large, it is important to provide the analyst with computer-based tools for editing task models and

R. Bernhaupt et al. (Eds.): INTERACT 2017, Part IV, LNCS 10516, pp. 383–386, 2017.
DOI: 10.1007/978-3-319-68059-0_35

for analyzing them. To this end, this course provides attendees with the HAMSTERS task modeling tool that can be directly applied in practice.

3   Objectives

On completion of this tutorial, attendees will:

- Know the benefits of using task modeling techniques to design, structure and assess UIs,
- Be able to describe users' activities in a systematic and structured way,
- Have experience in analyzing an interactive systems focusing on the tasks users have to perform with it,
- Know how to use the HAMSTERS tool suite for editing, analyzing and simulating task models.

4   Description and Content

This course is intended to be taught in two consecutive parts, one focusing on basic principles and notations, the other focusing on interactive hands-on exercises, case studies and HAMSTERS tool practice:

Part 1: the basic principles for design and assessment of interactive systems using task models

- What task models are good for (recording the output of task analysis, performance evaluation of users, tasks complexity assessment [1, 5, 6] ...)
- Basic principles of task models (hierarchical view on human activities, abstraction and refinement, temporal ordering, objects, information and knowledge ... [8])

Part 2: the advanced techniques and case studies

- Automation design (identification of users' activities that could be good candidates for task migration towards automation, authority sharing, impact of automation degradation on tasks performance) [4, 9]
- Benefits of using task models in various stage of the interactive system development (structuring user documentation, designing and assessing a training program [7], assessing the complexity of the users' work)
- Taking into account human errors at design time using task models (identification of types, location and likelihood of human errors [2])
- Dealing with large-scale application using structuring mechanisms in task models [3, 10].

In addition, this course will provide attendees with:

- A state of the art on task modelling techniques
- A set of case studies (and their related task models) from various domains

5 Presentation

Lecture with slides, demonstrations and practical exercises. The course is approximately 60% tutorial and 40% activities with the HAMSTERS graphical editor and simulator.

6 Audience and Prerequisite

This course is open to researchers, practitioners, educators and students of all experience levels. No specific skills or knowledge are required beyond a background in User Centered Design.

7 Instructors' Background

The instructors have applied task modeling techniques to several industrial projects such as the design of collaborative environments to manage collision risks between satellite and space objects (more information can be found at: http://www.irit.fr/recherches/ICS/projectsummary/projects.html).

Philippe Palanque is Professor in Computer Science at University of Toulouse 3. He has been teaching HCI and task engineering classes for 20 years and is head of the Interactive Critical Systems group at the Institut de Recherche en Informatique de Toulouse (IRIT) in France. Since the late 80 s he has been working on the development and application of formal description techniques for interactive system. He has worked on research projects to improve interactive Ground Segment Systems at the Centre National d'Études Spatiales (CNES) for more than 10 years and is also involved in the development of software architectures and user interface modeling for interactive cockpits in large civil aircraft (funded by Airbus). He is also involved in the research network HALA! (Higher Automation Levels in Aviation) funded by SESAR program which targets at building the future European air traffic management system. The main driver of Philippe's research over the last 20 years has been to address in an even way Usability, Safety and Dependability in order to build trustable safety critical interactive systems. As for conferences he is a member of the program committee of conferences in these domains such as SAFECOMP 2013 (32nd conference on Computer Safety, Reliability and Security), DSN 2014 (44th conference on Dependable Systems and Networks), EICS 2014 (21st annual conference on Engineering Interactive Computing Systems) and was co-chair of CHI 2014 (32nd conference on Human Factors in Computing Systems) and research papers co-chair of INTERACT 2015.

Célia Martinie is Assistant Professor in Computer Science at University of Toulouse 3. She has been working on task modeling techniques for the design and development of interactive systems since the beginning of her PhD in 2009. Prior to that, she worked in the mobile industry (Motorola) during 8 years, and has contributed to the design and development of user interfaces for mobile devices. She is the principal investigator of the projects related to the design and development of the HAMSTERS notation and tools. She applied the task modeling approaches to a variety of systems including satellite ground segments, interactive cockpits of large civil aircrafts and air traffic control workstations.

Marco Winckler is full professor in Computer Sciences at Université Nice Sophia Antipolis (Polytech), Sophia Antipolis, France. He investigates models, methods, techniques and tools to support the development of reliable, usable and effective interactive systems. He obtained a PhD degree in Informatics (2004) from Université of Toulouse 1 Capitole (Toulouse, France), a Master's degree in Computer Science (1999) from the Universidade Federal do Rio Grande do Sul (Porto Alegre, Brazil) and a Post-doc degree from the Université catholique de Louvain (Louvain-la-Neuve, Belgium). His research combines topics of Engineering Interactive Systems, Human-Computer Interaction and Web Engineering. He also serves as chair for the IFIP working group 13.2 on Methodologies for User-Centered Systems Design and secretary of the IFIP TC 13 on Human-Computer Interaction.

References

1. Anett, J.: Hierarchical task analysis. In: Dan, D., Neville, S. (eds.) The Handbook of Task Analysis for Human-Computer Interaction, pp. 67–82. Lawence Erlbaum Associates (2004)
2. Fahssi, R., Martinie, C., Palanque, P.: Enhanced task modelling for systematic identification and explicit representation of human errors. In: Abascal, J., Barbosa, S., Fetter, M., Gross, T., Palanque, P., Winckler, M. (eds.) INTERACT 2015. LNCS, vol. 9299, pp. 192–212. Springer, Cham (2015). doi:10.1007/978-3-319-22723-8_16
3. Forbrig, P., Martinie, C., Palanque, P., Winckler, M., Fahssi, R.: Rapid task-models development using sub-models, sub-routines and generic components. In: Sauer, S., Bogdan, C., Forbrig, P., Bernhaupt, R., Winckler, M. (eds.) HCSE 2014. LNCS, vol. 8742, pp. 144–163. Springer, Heidelberg (2014). doi:10.1007/978-3-662-44811-3_9
4. Bernhaupt, R., Cronel, M., Manciet, F., Martinie, C., Palanque, P.: Transparent automation for assessing and designing better interactions between operators and partly-autonomous interactive systems. In: ATACCS 2015. ACM DL (2015)
5. Fayollas, C., Martinie, C., Palanque, P., Deleris, Y., Fabre, J.-C., Navarre, D.: An approach for assessing the impact of dependability on usability: application to interactive cockpits. In: IEEE European Dependable Computing Conference, pp. 198–209 (2014)
6. Greenberg, S.: Working through task-centered system design. In: Diaper, D., Stanton, N. (eds.) The Handbook of Task Analysis for Human-Computer Interaction. Lawrence Erlbaum Associates (2002)
7. Martinie, C., Palanque, P., Navarre, D., Winckler, M., Poupart, R.: Model-based training: an approach supporting operability of critical interactive systems. In: ACM SIGCHI EICS 2011, pp. 53–62 (2011)
8. Martinie, C., Palanque, P., Ragosta, M., Fahssi, R.: Extending procedural task models by systematic explicit integration of objects, knowledge and information. In: European Conference on Cognitive Ergonomics, pp. 23–34. ACM DL (2013)
9. Martinie, C., Palanque, P., Barboni, E., Ragosta, M.: Task-model based assessment of automation levels: application to space ground segments. In: IEEE SMC, pp. 3267–3273 (2011)
10. Martinie, C., Palanque, P., Winckler, M.: Designing and assessing interactive systems using task models. In: Book of Tutorials of the 14th Brazilian Symposium on Human Factors in Computing Systems, pp. 29–58. Springer

Designing for Accessibility

Helen Petrie[1], Gerhard Weber[2(✉)], and Jenny Darzentas[1]

[1] Department of Computer Science, University of York, York YO10 5GH, UK
{helen.petrie, jenny.darzentas}@cs.york.ac.uk
[2] Department of Computer Science,
Technische Universität Dresden, Dresden, Germany
gerhard.weber@tu-dresden.de

Abstract. Involving a wide variety of end users and in particular those with a disability or who are older when designing web pages and apps requires a good understanding of how to involve those end users, assistive technology, and evaluation methods. This course will introduce the basics of assistive technologies built into using mobile phones and describe major barriers in web pages, and how to analyze them with end users. It will also outline a range of appropriate tools to use in this work.

Keywords: Accessibility · Users with disabilities · Older users · Tools for accessibility

1 Introduction

Accessibility has been identified a sibling category to Human-Computer Interaction in the ACM 2012 classification, but many HCI people do not know about user needs and preferences if these users have a sensory, physical or mental disability, nor do they know specific evaluation methods suitable for these target groups. Often this is because specific forms of communication are needed such as a Sign Language, BLISS symbols or Braille. As current assistive technologies bridge the gap between developers and users, the main effort is to understand how to include these users and their assistive technologies in the development of interactive systems.

Learning Objectives

Participants will understand the difference between principles of universal design on the one hand and assistive technology on the other hand.

Given a particular technology, participants will be able explore and understand how the widest possible range of users can use it and what barriers they will experience in using it.

Participants will explore the assistive technology built into smartphones and its use for completing tasks specific to a particular disability by adding specific apps.

Participants will understand the accessibility issues most commonly found in static web pages and forms.

Participants will understand the importance of evaluation with disabled users as well as the use of web accessibility testing tools.

© IFIP International Federation for Information Processing 2017
Published by Springer International Publishing AG 2017. All Rights Reserved
R. Bernhaupt et al. (Eds.): INTERACT 2017, Part IV, LNCS 10516, pp. 387–390, 2017.
DOI: 10.1007/978-3-319-68059-0_36

2 Contents of the Course

Principles of universal design have been established to guide the design of environments, products and communications in a broad sense. These principles focus on designers as the matchmakers between technologies and the needs and preferences of users. In contrast, assistive technology focuses primarily on products and services solving information and communication problems.

This course covers some of the main assistive technologies addressing sensory disabilities such as magnification, false color presentation, Braille displays, screen readers, hearing aids and captioning. People with motor impairments benefit from scanning keyboards, trackballs, eye tracking or speech input to name a few common technologies. These are designed to replace keyboard and mouse input, while reducing the manual effort in general and use of hands more specifically. Participants will discuss how these technologies can be interfaced with existing off-the shelf computers.

Many consumer devices apart from off-the shelf computers also contain a user interface, but are less easily adapted to take assistive technology into account. Some of these can be designed for use by sensory disabled people such as the television, which now can provide captions for people who are Deaf or hard of hearing and audio description for people who are visually disabled. Participants will discuss tools for preparing captions and approaches to enhance time-based contents by audio descriptions, transcripts or a summary. Other devices such as the electronic whiteboard serve as an example for the need for collaboration by people with and without a disability in education and meetings and allow a more general discussion of the appropriateness of efforts to overcome barriers in the education system. Figure 1 shows a non-standard keyboard as it is typically used for speech-to-text transcription during live oral presentations for people with a hearing impairment.

Fig. 1. Keyboard for speech-to-text transcription

Smartphones are commonplace nowadays but only a few people are aware of the accessibility features built into Android and iOS versions of these devices. Smartphones address sensory and physical disabilities in various ways. Moreover, they can provide access to services needed by people with mental impairments, if caregivers become involved appropriately. Participants will become familiar with the screenreader in their mobile phone in the language as it is configured by the manufacturer and learn about the design of a gestural user interface for both the non-visual and visual use of the phone.

Several apps extend the basic assistive technology of a smartphone and thereby add more functionalities addressing other user needs in addition to making voice calls, texting or keeping one's diary. Apps may receive audio descriptions or captions in a public space such as in the cinema. Someone with low vision or with a hearing impairment will not be stigmatized for using an off-the-shelf smartphone or headset while still being able to contribute to the discussion of the movie with their friends.

Participants will understand the need for many different specific functions such as an app for identifying colors by blind mobile phone users and during the discussion they will encounter the need for elicitation of such requirements from end users systematically.

Colour identification serves as an example to learn more about the ability of a blind person to capture an image by a smartphone and will allow participants to discuss the design of a capturing device for reading important documents such as bills or even performing OCR on a menu or on a door label. Participants will be requested to ask their neighbor to become involved in a quick Wizard of Oz study on how they would focus on an object they cannot see and what the feedback should be like. An example for app developers interested in specific software technologies is navigation apps aimed at pedestrians with other needs than finding the shortest route but the best one to become able to avoid noisy, unsecure, or disorienting places. Participants will be pointed at further work on algorithms specifically needed for computing non-standard route calculations.

Smartphones and tablet computers are also suitable for browsing the web. This course coves some of the main barriers encountered in static web pages such as lack of headings, insufficient color contrast, too many links, or unusable forms. Sample web pages help to demonstrate what effort is needed to improve such HTML code. These web pages will become available to participants for their use during the course for exploring them with their mobile phone with or without a screen reader of screen magnifier enabled.

Participants will learn about appropriate guidelines allowing for the detection of such specific barriers and will discuss their ability to perform an assessment of barriers without using assistive technology. Tools for manual inspection as well as automatic analysis of web sites will be mentioned as well as the need for test cases to understand the quality of such tools.

Evaluation with disabled users as well as the use of web accessibility testing tools is much discussed in the community in order to develop services for professional assessments at a high quality. Participant will discuss some of the common approaches to support user tests with above mentioned heuristic approaches. The number of assessors, selection of appropriate web pages through identification of tasks will be contrasted and enable participants to collaborate with an existing professional service or continue their professional education to perform their own assessments.

References

1. Power, C., Freire, A.P., Petrie, H., Swallow, D.: Guidelines are only half of the story: accessibility problems encountered by blind users on the web. In: CHI 2012, pp. 433–442 (2012)
2. Miao, M., Pham, H.A., Friebe, J., Weber, G.: Contrasting usability evaluation methods with blind users. Univ. Access Inf. Soc. **15**(1), 63–76 (2016)
3. Accessibility gestures for Android 4.1 and later. https://support.google.com/accessibility/android
4. Involving users in accessibility testing. https://www.youtube.com/watch?v=QJaLbQyu3ak
5. Horton, S., Quesenbery, W.: A Web For Everyone: Designing Accessible User Experiences. Rosenfeld Media (2014)

Designing Valuable Products with Design Sprint

Eunice Sari[✉] and Adi Tedjasaputra

UX INDONESIA, Plaza Marein Level 23,
Jl Jendral Sudirman, Kav 76-78, Jakarta 12910, Indonesia
{eunice.sari,adit}@acm.org

Abstract. The shift of creating valuable products, from only aesthetically pleasing, usable, or loveable products, has required adjustment of skills to create value as well as a mindset change. Instead of spending weeks and months to design a product, a rapid validation process takes place to explore how a product should be transformed into a valuable one. This course will teach the participants several key Design Sprint techniques in a nutshell (80 min). Google Ventures initially introduced Design Sprint to tackle critical business problems and come up with viable solutions within five days. Open to anyone who is involved in product and service design, the course aims to teach Design Sprint key techniques to create meaningful insights and hands-on experience for the participants. At the conclusion of the course, the participants are expected to envision how the lessons learned from the course can be applied in either academia or industry.

Keywords: Product · Design · Sprint · Designsprint · Designthinking · Business · Teamwork · Agile · UX · Process

1 Introduction

Many organizations are getting better in designing aesthetically pleasing, usable, or loveable products. At the same time, in many product design processes, great physical forms, appearances and features are still often considered as the main factors that determine the success of a product. Spending a significant amount of resources, i.e. time, financial and human resources to design a product does not always create value to stakeholders, i.e. investors, companies, organizations or intended users. Thus, there has been a shift in paradigm to design valuable products with minimum resources.

In Human-Computer Interaction (HCI), user satisfaction can be increased by improving usability and accessibility of the product. Through User Experience (UX), user motivation and interaction are closely examined during a design process to plan for a successful adoption and acquisition.

To make this process more systematic, Google Ventures (GV) have created a framework to tackle the issues of designing value in the product using Design Sprint technique (Knapp, Zeratsky and Kowitz, 2016). This technique has been applied internally for Google products, as well as extensively across the world to design and

R. Bernhaupt et al. (Eds.): INTERACT 2017, Part IV, LNCS 10516, pp. 391–394, 2017.
DOI: 10.1007/978-3-319-68059-0_37

develop many award-winning products. The agility and effectiveness of Design Sprint has allowed for innovations that transform many companies and organizations.

2 Google Design Sprint

Design Sprint has been considered as an effective framework to validate ideas through rapid prototyping and user testing, and contains five stages: Understand, Diverge, Decide, Prototype, and Validate.

(a) **Step 1 - Understand:** Participants evaluate the problem they are trying to solve, the personas they are designing for, and the form factor they are going to use.
(b) **Step 2 - Diverge:** Participants are encouraged to let go of all their presumptions and engage in different activities to generate as many ideas as they can, regardless of how feasible or far-fetched they are.
(c) **Step 3 - Decide:** Through different activities, participants decide which ideas to pursue further.
(d) **Step 4 - Prototype:** Participants rapidly sketch, design and prototype their ideas, concentrating on User Interface (UI) flow.
(e) **Step 5 - Validate:** Participants put their product in front of users, test and are encouraged to show and tell when possible.

3 The Course

At INTERACT 2017, we deliver the introductory course on Designing Valuable Products with Design Sprint to showcase how UX professionals apply Design Sprint techniques to design and develop valuable products and services. During the course, we will introduce the 5-day techniques in a nutshell to give insights for the participants to experience the Design Sprint.

The course participants will be guided to develop solutions for a problem using step-by-step Design Sprint techniques. The participants will engage in a group of 4–5 people in various hands-on activities. The maximum number of participants who can take part in this course is 40 people, preferably a good mixed of academia and industries. There is no specific requirement for potential participants to participate in this 80 min hands-on activity. Anyone who are involved in the design and development of products or services, decision makers, business people, developers, researchers are encouraged to participate in this course.

By the end of the course, it is expected that the participants get meaningful insight about Design Sprint techniques and to be able to envision how the Design Sprint techniques can be applied to their own contexts at either academia or industries.

4 The Instructors

4.1 Dr Eunice Sari

Eunice is the CEO and Co-Founder of UX Indonesia, the first and premier UX Consulting, Training and Research company based in Indonesia. She is a leading UX/CX and ICT in Education Expert with more than 15+ years of experience working in both academia and industries. She has pioneered a number of forward-thinking and innovative projects, such as user experience for digital products and services, mobile learning, Internet of Things (IoT), service design and online community in order to effect changes in life and improve the bottom line of business in various vertical industries in USA, Europe, Australia and Asia.

She co-founded and chaired the Indonesia ACM SIGCHI Chapter (Association Computing Machinery Special Interest Group on Computer-Human Interaction a.k.a CHI UX Indonesia), and later the Association of Digital Interaction Indonesia – Perkumpulan Interaksi Digital Indonesia (PIDI). She is also the co-founder of ACM SIGCHI Southeast Asia community, the South East Asia Liaison for ACM SIGCHI Asia Development Committee, the Expert Member of the International Federation for Information Processing (IFIP) TC 13 – Human Computer Interaction (HCI) for Indonesia, and the Western Australia Representative for the Human Factors Ergonomic Association Computer Human Interaction Special Interest Group (HFESA CHISIG). With her roles, she facilitates the collaboration between academia and industry in the fields of Education, Technology, HCI and UX.

At Google, Eunice is the first female Google Expert in UX/UI from Indonesia who has helped hundreds of international startups from Indonesia, USA, Australia, Ireland, Brazil, India and Southeast Asian countries through Google Launchpad and Accelerator Programs to improve a range of complex product and service portfolios, evaluate them with users, as well as facilitating design and business workshops with key stakeholders. In addition to that, she is also a Google Certified Design Sprint Instructor who has run a number of public and private design sprint activities with startups and established organizations in many countries.

With her seasoned international experience from industry and academic, Eunice is passionately interested to help international business clients design experience strategy and roadmap that exceed customer expectations.

4.2 Josh (Adi Tedjasaputra, M.Sc)

Josh is the Director and Co-Founder of UX Indonesia, who has been working in both academia and industries for more than 15 years. Josh has a passion for the design, development, and use of Information and Communication Technology (ICT) for a better life. He has helped many companies, educational and non-profit organisations in Europe and Asia Pacific to achieve their business goals and make the best investment in ICT.

With his engineering and computer science background, he has introduced forward-thinking and innovative projects that improve the bottom line of businesses in different vertical industries through Human-centred design, computing and engineering.

Josh is currently leading the Indonesia ACM SIGCHI Chapter in Indonesia and running annual international HCI and UX conference mainly for Southeast Asian practitioners and academics in the region. At Google, Josh has been a global mentor for international startups in addition to his contribution to the development startup ecosystem in Indonesia. Josh has also been running a number of public and private Design Sprint activities

His current interests include the Internet of Things, Human-centred Computing, Computational Thinking, e-Learning, Moodle, WordPress and Agile and Lean UX.

References

1. Courtney, J.: It's no longer enough to build a great product you have to build the right product. https://blog.ajsmart.com/its-no-longer-enough-to-build-a-great-product-you-have-to-build-the-right-product-c798bb0cf52a
2. Google Venture: The Design Sprint. http://www.gv.com/sprint/
3. Knapp, J., Zeratsky, J., Kowitz, B.: Sprint: How to Solve Big Problems and Solve New Ideas in Just Five Days. Simon and Schuster, New York (2016)
4. Loose Coupling: Agile No Longer Addresses the Fundamental Bottleneck. http://www.loosecouplings.com/2016/05/agile-and-bottlenecks.html

Introduction to Service Design
for Digital Health

Ashley Colley[(✉)] and Henna Marttila

University of Lapland, Rovaniemi, Finland
{ashley.colley,henna.marttila}@ulapland.fi

Abstract. This course addresses the service design of wellness and health services which include digital components. The course will cover methodological and practical aspects of service design, focusing on three key methods – stakeholder maps, consumer journey and blueprint. The service design methods are tried out with interactive exercises, where participants in groups apply the methods to a digital health design case. Service design is an emerging field, which applies a holistic design approach to understand and design for human experience. With an increasing number of digital wellness and health services, both in commercial and public frontiers, it is important to develop services that are easy to use, and where the consumer's journey through the service pathways is fluent and consistent.

Keywords: Service design · User centric design · Participatory design · Wellness · Health · Digital health

1 Introduction

Service design is a design field which addresses design challenges in a holistic way, taking into account the different stakeholders involved with the product, and utilizing human centric design and co-design methods throughout the design process [5]. Digital wellness services and products utilize more and more versatile connected gadgets and sensor systems, and pervasive technologies are becoming an essential part of the digital health and wellness service ecosystems. Currently, we are lacking methods that address the challenges and opportunities of having combinations of non-digital and digital service components in the same holistic service pathway, working together to achieve a seamless service experience. Also, there is a need to consider how digital health technologies integrate with public sector healthcare services. With this growing and increasingly complex world of digital services and products, it is important that their design takes a holistic approach to ensure a good usability and user experience (UX).

1.1 Focus and Target of the Course

This course provides an introduction to service design as a field and selected key methods used in service design process. These methods are then applied to the problem area of digital health services, which are approached through practical exercises. In this course, researchers and practitioners from different fields – e.g. design, technology,

© IFIP International Federation for Information Processing 2017
Published by Springer International Publishing AG 2017. All Rights Reserved
R. Bernhaupt et al. (Eds.): INTERACT 2017, Part IV, LNCS 10516, pp. 395–398, 2017.
DOI: 10.1007/978-3-319-68059-0_38

and HCI - gather together to explore digital health and wellness research from the service design point of view. As the learning goal, the course seeks to provide an introductory overview to service design and its key methods. The target of the course is to foster a network of researchers and practitioners interested in service design for digital health, provide insight of service design approach to pervasive health domain, and to develop further service design methods applied in the area of health and wellness.

The target is to attract participants who wish to expand their work towards service design. The preferred number of participants for the course is approximately 20.

1.2   Topics of the Course

Service Design. The main focus is on the development of service experiences where the service responds to both the service user's needs and the service provider's goals. Service design develops and solves this service problems together with various stakeholders, especially the service's users and providers. The design process is based on user-centered and co-creative design, where everyone is encouraged to be creative and share their ideas [5].

Service design contains a variety of methods and tools. For example, the stakeholder map, consumer journey and blueprints are common tools that provide a good basic knowledge of the service situation [7]. These three tools provide visualized information from different parts of the service.

- **Stakeholder map** - shows visually who is involved in a particular service and how they are connected to each other.
- **Consumer journey** - visualizes the path of how the user experiences the service. It contains the user's interactions and feelings. With the help of the customer journey it is easier to identify problems and understand why actions happened as they did.
- **Blueprint** - specifies the service and gives more detailed information of an individual part of the service. It is a visualized map showing the various elements that are contained in different parts of the service.

The service design process typically emphasizes visualizations as a tool to support thinking and comprehending how different parts of the service link together [5]. The design process is based on testing, and is not linear but iterative. Together with the users, service providers and other stakeholders, service design seeks to develop new kinds of solutions that will better meet different stakeholders' needs. The aim of service design is to make services more user-friendly, efficient and desirable.

Digital Health. Digital technology has become an integral part of life in different sectors of society, including health and wellness. We have vast amounts of smart phone wellness applications with different types of UI solutions [2] and use different activity tracking technologies [8]. We have various forms of telemedicine applications [3], and can use social media for self-reflection on our lifestyle [4], gamified applications for rehabilitation [4], and make more healthy choices for our work routines. Digital health technology is researched from various viewpoints, including e.g. behavior change [1], or user's design preferences [6]. The list of available digital health technologies is getting longer, and they are increasingly much applied for preventive healthcare, in self-care, and in the institutional healthcare sector.

1.3 Course Structure

The course is organized as one 80 min session, consisting of short lectures, group exercises and discussions. Each participant will contribute to the group exercises. The schedule is as follows:

- Lecture: Introduction to service design
- Lecture: Stakeholder maps
- Exercise 1
- Lecture: Consumer journey
- Exercise 2
- Lecture: Blueprint
- Discussion and reflection

The first exercise focuses on drawing stakeholder maps for selected digital health scenarios. The second interactive exercise examines selected digital health service scenarios, around which the customer journey and service touch points are explored from the viewpoint of seamless integration of digital and non-digital elements.

1.4 Organizers

Ashley Colley (M) is a researcher at the University of Lapland, completing his doctor of arts in summer 2017. Colley has more than 25 years' professional industry experience, and has co-authored more than 50 peer-reviewed research papers. Additionally, Colley is an active entrepreneur, being a co-founder of OuraHealth Ltd. (www.ouraring.com) and a board member at QuietOn Ltd. (www.quieton.com). He is a multi-skilled creative technologist with hands-on capabilities on user centric design methods, interaction design, graphic design and software development.

Henna Marttila MA (F) is working as a research assistant specializing in service design at the University of Lapland, currently in the project Critical Communication, Safety and Human-centered Services of the Future (CRICS). One of her research focuses has been to improve people's wellbeing and safety. She sees communication one of the main things in designing these two issue. She is currently developing her skills in service design but also in the fields of graphic design and game design.

1.5 Reading for the Course

As background material, we recommend the following reading for the participants:

- Häkkilä, J., Alhonsuo, M., Virtanen, L., Rantakari, J., Colley, A., Koivumäki, T. (2016). MyData Approach for Personal Health – A Service Design Case for Young Athletes. In Proc. of HICSS 2016.
- Miettinen, S., Rontti, S., Jeminen, J. (2014). Co-prototyping emotional value. In Proc. of the 19th DMI: Academic Design Management Conference, 1228–1246.

As future reading, we recommend:

- Marc Stickdorn, Jakob Schneider. 2010. This is Service Design Thinking. Amsterdam: Bis Publisher.

References

1. Consolvo, S., McDonald, D.D., Landay, J.A.: Theory-driven design strategies for technologies that support behavior change in everyday life. In: Proceedings of CHI 2009, pp. 405–414. ACM (2009)
2. Häkkilä, J., Colley, A., Inget, V., Alhonsuo, M., Rantakari, J.: Exploring digital service concepts for healthy lifestyles. In: Marcus, A. (ed.) DUXU 2015, Part I. LNCS, vol. 9186, pp. 470–480. Springer, Cham (2015). doi:10.1007/978-3-319-20886-2_44
3. Hersh, W.R., Hickam, D.H., Severance, S.M., Dana, T.L., Krages, K.P., Helfand, M.: Diagnosis, access and outcomes: update of a systematic review of telemedicine services. J. Telemed. Telecare 12(Suppl. 2), 3–31 (2006)
4. Li, I., Dey, A., Forlizzi, J.: Grafitter: leveraging social media for self reflection. Crossroads 16(2), 12–13 (2009)
5. Miettinen, S., Valtonen, A.: Service Design with Theory. Lapland University Press, Rovaniemi (2012)
6. Rantakari, J., Inget, V., Colley, A., Häkkilä, J.: Charting design preferences on wellness wearables. In: Proceedings of AH 2016. ACM (2016). doi:10.1145/2875194.2875231
7. Stickdorn, M., Schneider, J.: This is Service Design Thinking. Bis Publisher, Amsterdam (2010)
8. Tholander, J., Nylander, S.: Snot, sweat, pain, mud, and snow: performance and experience in the use of sports watches. In: Proceedings of CHI 2015. ACM (2015)

The Science Behind User Experience Design

Asad Ali Junaid[(⊠)]

Bangalore, India
asadjunaid@gmail.com

Abstract. Planning and conducting User Experience (UX) activities in a structured and scientific manner has many advantages. It is important that UX Professionals understand the scientific basis of UX methods and leverage them to enhance the UX of the application being designed. It would also be easier for the UX designer to get a buy-in from the stakeholders if his design recommendations are based in scientific logic and whetted by supporting data. In this course, UX relevant social sciences based scientific concepts and methods will be presented to the audience in a way which is simple to understand and easily to assimilate.

Keywords: User Experience · Empirical research · Scientific methods · UX · Experimental design · Logic · Data collection and analysis · Data representation · Measuring user performance · Biases in research

1 Introduction

The underlying purpose of employing a scientific method in the User Experience profession is to make sure we, as User Experience (UX) Practitioners, have not been misled into thinking we have deduced something which is far from correct while making a design/process recommendation which in turn would adversely impact the application being built. In such situations, the credibility of the UX designer in an organization would be affected while the confidence of the stakeholders in the UX profession itself would erode.

Planning and conducting UX activities in a structured and scientific manner has many advantages. The primary end user would be the direct beneficiary – the application being built would be the designed and built for the user's ease-of-use while the stakeholders would also see the maximum returns on their investment in UX. The cost of development would also decrease drastically due to reduced rework when the primary end user has been thoroughly understood; screens have been logically designed and have been empirically tested by a UX designer.

2 Learning Objectives

It is important that UX Professionals understand the scientific basis of UX methods enough and leverage them for improving the UX of the application being designed. When the UX process and design recommendations are based on empirical evidence and irrefutable data, then they will be received well.

© IFIP International Federation for Information Processing 2017
Published by Springer International Publishing AG 2017. All Rights Reserved
R. Bernhaupt et al. (Eds.): INTERACT 2017, Part IV, LNCS 10516, pp. 399–401, 2017.
DOI: 10.1007/978-3-319-68059-0_39

By learning how to scientifically conduct UX studies, methodically analyzing data collected during such studies and subsequently providing sound design recommendations, the UX Professional will not just increase his own credibility within the organization but he will be easily able to evangelize and implement UX processes with a fair degree of ease across the organization.

Based on a deeper understanding of UX relevant scientific concepts and processes, the UX Designer would be able to better plan and conduct UX activities such as strategizing UX approach for solving the specific design problem, planning for and setting timelines of UX deliverables, planning and conducting User Research, creating and validating Personas, Heuristic Analysis of existing applications, planning and conducting Usability Tests, analyzing data obtained from User Research and Usability Tests and subsequently designing or proposing re-designs of applications/products.

3   Course Content and Schedule

My intent is to present some UX relevant social science based scientific concepts and process to the audience in a way which is simple to understand and easily to assimilate. With the knowledge and expertise gained from this course, the UX Professional would be able to take their UX practice a notch higher and by making recommendations which are scientific and data driven – in other words, recommendations which are credible and irrefutable. I will cover the essential fundamentals of the course in two 80 min sessions. The course content is detailed below:

- Origins and background of User Experience Design (20 min)
  - Introduce the audience to the principles of Human Factors and Human Computer Interaction which were precursors of the field of User Experience Design. This would enable the user to understand the origins and the scientific rationale behind some of the methods employed in UX Design
- Principles of Applied psychology in relevance to UX Design (80 min)
  - Introduce the audience to concepts of Cognitive Psychology, the Information Processing model, Memory, Sensation, Perception, Affordance and Attention in the contexts of Human Computer Interaction with specific examples.
- The concept of Empirical Research and takeaways for UX Design (40 min)
  - Introduce the concepts of Empirical Research, Hypothesis, Theory, Law, Experimental Design, Measuring Human Performance and Empirical Methods of Data collection & analysis [1].
- Data Science in the context of UX (20 min)
  - One of the goals Data Science is to communicate insights obtained from data gathering and analysis in the form of simple stories/visualizations that a layman can understand and come to conclusions on. Conducting UX activities in a structured and scientific manner yields plenty of data with invaluable insights hidden within it. When this data is cleaned up and visualized in a way which makes sense, deep awareness of end-user preferences and behaviors come to light. The last module focuses on Data Visualization Methods where insights

obtained from analysis of data can be represented in a way which the stake-holders can easily derive meaning out of.

4 Background of Attendees

The course would be interest to

i. UX Practitioners who want to understand the scientific basis behind the profession and to also understand how to logically and scientifically base their arguments for the designs or design process they will be proposing to stakeholders coming from varied backgrounds.
ii. Project Managers who want to get insights on the decision making process of UX practitioners and also to understand the importance of the scientific methodology behind some of the UX processes.
iii. Designers who are from a graphic design or content writing background and are not familiar with the core fundamentals and the empirical origins of the User Experience Profession
iv. The course would not be useful for someone who is well versed with the methodologies of social science research

5 Presentation Format

A set of presentation decks will be used to deliver the course contents to the audience. I am envisioning a workshop model with mini assignments and experiments within the course content to enable the audience to grasp the core takeaways from the course.

6 Audience Size

Anything around or above 20 participants would be a good audience size.

References

1. Kantowitz, B.H., Elmes, D.G., Roediger III, H.L.: Research Methods in Psychology (2011)

Demonstrations

Coaching Compliance: A Tool for Personalized e-Coaching in Cardiac Rehabilitation

Supraja Sankaran[1(✉)], Mieke Haesen[1], Paul Dendale[2,3], Kris Luyten[1], and Karin Coninx[1]

[1] Expertise Centre for Digital Media,
Hasselt University-tUL-imec, Diepenbeek, Belgium
{supraja.sankaran,mieke.haesen,kris.luyten,
karin.coninx}@uhasselt.be
[2] Faculty of Medicine and Life Sciences,
Hasselt University, Diepenbeek, Belgium
paul.dendale@uhasselt.be
[3] Department of Cardiology, Jessa Hospital, Hasselt, Belgium

Abstract. Patient coaching is integral to cardiac rehabilitation programs to help patients understand, cope better with their condition and become active participants in their care. The introduction of remote patient monitoring technologies and tele-monitoring solutions have proven to be effective and paved way for novel remote rehabilitation approaches. Nonetheless, these solutions focus largely on *monitoring* patients without a specific focus on *coaching* patients. Additionally, these systems lack personalization and a deeper understanding of individual patient needs. In our demonstration, we present a tool to personalize e-coaching based on individual patient risk factors, adherence rates and personal preferences of patients using a tele-rehabilitation solution. We developed the tool after conducting a workshop and multiple brainstorms with various caregivers involved in coaching cardiac patients to connect their perspectives with patient needs. It was integrated into a comprehensive tele-rehabilitation application.

Keywords: Technology in healthcare (primary keyword) · HCI · Remote rehabilitation · Information recommendation · Personalized coaching

1 Introduction

A rehabilitation program is typically composed of various elements such as monitoring and managing physiological parameters, physical exercise, medication intake, adherence, diet and coaching. Technology- assisted remote rehabilitation programs eliminate the need to visit rehabilitation centers by monitoring performed rehabilitation activities in a home environment [1]. While these have been proven to be effective [2], most programs focus exclusively on activity and progress monitoring with no focus on coaching.

Patients suffering from chronic illness such as cardiovascular diseases often lack awareness and knowledge of their condition, resulting in low adherence and increased drop-out rates over time. This reaffirms the law of attrition [3] of e-health technologies. Given the evolution towards patient-centered care systems [4], especially in remote

R. Bernhaupt et al. (Eds.): INTERACT 2017, Part IV, LNCS 10516, pp. 405–409, 2017.
DOI: 10.1007/978-3-319-68059-0_40

rehabilitation programs, there is a pressing need to enable patients to play an active role in understanding and managing their own disease. Patient coaching potentially facilitates in creating this awareness and goes beyond educating patients by 'coaching' them towards healthier behavior and lifestyle changes. To bridge this gap between tele-monitoring, patient education and coaching, e-coaching approaches also need to go beyond merely educating patients by being integrated into comprehensive tele-monitoring solutions and by personalizing coaching based on patient needs.

In our demonstration, we present an approach and corresponding tools, for personalized e-coaching. The approach focuses on awareness and tailored information provisioning for rehabilitation in cardiac patients.

2 Design Process

We followed a systematic approach to define a process to optimally generate personalized coaching trajectories for different patients. The approach we followed comprised of four phases; grounding the tool based on expert opinions of a multidisciplinary medical team.

The first phase focused on *generating coaching content*. In our context, the e-coaching content essentially refers to a collection of video fragments that have been developed specifically to coach rehabilitating cardiac patients. Unlike other e-coaching approaches that use text messages or emails [5], videos are a closer replacement for face-to-face coaching to educate patients and equip them to cope better with their condition. For generating the most appropriate content to address patient-specific needs, we conducted a workshop with experts from different medical domains specialized in guiding rehabilitation and coaching patients.

The focus of the second phase was to analyze the content and *identify all the dependencies*. 'Dependencies' in this context refers to which risk factors relate to which content categories and what specific topics fit into a certain category. 'Content categories' refers to broad themes targeting rehabilitation such as importance of compliance, understanding disease, medication and side effects, returning to work and so on. 'Risk factor tags' are related to modifiable risk factors [6] associated with cardiac diseases such as managing cholesterol and blood pressure, regulating weight and sugar etc. This enabled us to classify content into clusters, map dependencies and connect associated risk factors to the right coaching context.

A default prioritization of the fragments was also made based on importance of certain video content for rehabilitation with support for further personalization based on patient-specific needs. Based on the categorization made by domain experts, we prioritized the topics when filtered using the 'I♥Coaching' tool. For example, if four experts mapped a topic T1 to a category C1 and only 2 of them mapped topic T2 to the same category, T1 is displayed before (i.e. higher) T2 in the filtered list. The fact that I♥Coaching uses a default prioritization derived from inputs of different domain experts and provides for further personalization, is one of the core strengths of our approach.

The next phase involved *translating analyzed content clusters and dependencies into an algorithm* that can autonomously filter the most appropriate content to be shown to patients upon making specific selections. The selections were based on generic content themes, or more precisely, on patient-specific risk factors.

The final phase concerned the use of the developed algorithm to *generate a tailored patient-specific coaching trajectory* for each patient.

3   System Components

The overall system we demonstrate includes a dashboard application for caregivers, a mobile application for patients (HeartHab) [7] and an e-coaching recommendation tool (I♥Coaching) that is integrated in the dashboard application (Fig. 1a). While the dashboard and the HeartHab app include other components relevant to remote reha-bilitation of cardiac patients, the primary focus of this work is on how the I♥Coaching tool facilitates caregivers in generating personalized coaching trajectories for patients to consume using their mobile application in a remote setting.

Fig. 1. (a) Components in the tele-monitoring solution with the 'I♥Coaching tool' as a part of the caregiver's application. (b) Tailored list of coaching content presented in the HeartHab app. (c) Dynamically triggered content based on a monitored parameter. (d) Screenshot of the caregiver dashboard application used for monitoring patients' progress.

By means of the caregiver dashboard (Fig. 1d), the caregivers initially configure a patient-specific trajectory using the I♥Coaching tool along with prescribing other rehabilitation goals, such as weekly exercise targets, daily medication prescriptions etc. These recommendations are translated into rehabilitation goals in the HeartHab app that records patient's progress and activities. Based on the recommended personalized trajectory, the coaching video fragments are presented to the patient in that specific sequence via the application (Fig. 1b). Additionally, videos can also be triggered based on a parameter that is monitored by the application (for example, when medication compliance is low as shown in Fig. 1c).

3.1   I♥Coaching Tool Walkthrough

I♥Coaching includes the core coaching data that is required for generation of personal recommendations: (1) a set of topics covered by the video fragments used for e-coaching, (2) a classification of the video fragments in health-related categories, and (3) an exhaustive set of tags based on various coronary risk factors and content categories. First, an extensive list of coaching fragment topics (Fig. 2a) can be selected by caregivers by filtering on content categories or specific risk factor tags based on the personal profile of the patient and the importance of specific risk factors. Figure 2b shows an example of applying a filter based on the category 'disease specific information'. Using the individual risk factors of a patient, the set can be filtered further to identify most relevant fragments for that specific patient (e.g. reduce sugar and control cholesterol). The caregiver can then modify the default prioritization if needed, as shown in Fig. 2c.

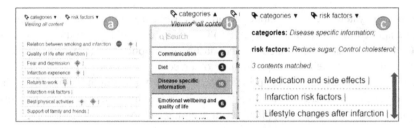

Fig. 2. (a) Screenshot of the I♥Coaching tool showing the list of video fragment topics. The tool enables caregivers to (b) filter topics based on categories or risk factors, and (c) modify prioritization by directly dragging and moving the topics in the list.

4 Conclusion

In the demonstration we present an approach and supporting tools that were designed and developed to personalize e-coaching with an aim to increase adherence of cardiac patients. The design of this approach was based on a series of brainstorms, interviews and a workshop with domain experts and caregivers involved in coaching patients. The tools and approach we demonstrate support a way to provide individually tailored coaching content to patients instead of hardcoding a pre-defined algorithm in a tele-monitoring application. Since the approach integrates the perspectives of multiple specialists, it supports caregivers to reason on a conceptual level and strive for a uniform coaching practices.

References

1. Jolly, K., Taylor, R., Lip, G., Stevens, A.: Home-based cardiac rehabilitation compared with centre-based rehabilitation and usual care: a systematic review and meta-analysis. Int. J. Cardiol. **111** (2005)
2. Hansen, D., Dendale, P., Raskin, A., et al.: Long-term effect of rehabilitation in coronary artery disease patients: randomized clinical trial of the impact of exercise volume. Clin. Rehabil. **24**, 319–327 (2010)
3. Eysenbach, G.: The law of attrition. J. Med. Internet Res. **7** (2005)
4. Krist, A.H., Woolf, S.H.: A Vision for Patient-Centered Health Information Systems
5. Vale, M.J., Jelinek, M.V., Best, J.D., et al.: Coaching patients On Achieving Cardiovascular Health (COACH). Arch. Intern. Med. **163**, 2775 (2003)

6. Cardiovascular disease risk factors | World Heart Federation, http://www.world-heart-federation.org/press/fact-sheets/cardiovascular-disease-risk-factors/
7. Sankaran, S., Frederix, I., Haesen, M., Dendale, P., Luyten, K., Coninx, K.: A grounded approach for applying behavior change techniques in mobile cardiac tele-rehabilitation. In: Proceedings of PETRA 2016, pp. 1–8 (2016). doi:10.1145/2910674.2910680

Inclusive Side-Scrolling Action Game Securing Accessibility for Visually Impaired People

Masaki Matsuo[1], Takahiro Miura[2(✉)], Masatsugu Sakajiri[1],
Junji Onishi[1], and Tsukasa Ono[1]

[1] Tsukuba University of Technology,
4-12-7 Kasuga, Tsukuba, Ibaraki 305-8521, Japan
mm163204@g.tsukuba-tech.ac.jp,
{sakajiri,ohnishi,ono}@cs.k.tsukuba-tech.ac.jp
[2] Institute of Gerontology, the University of Tokyo,
7-3-1 Hongo, Bunkyo-ku, Tokyo 113-8656, Japan
miu@iog.u-tokyo.ac.jp

Abstract. Though many computer games have recently become accessible for gamers with visual impairments, these players still face difficulty in manipulating game characters and acquiring visual information. It is true that although an increasing number of games for visually impaired people called audio games are being developed, many of these games cannot satisfy their basic needs because of the shortage of contents and are difficult for sighted people because of no visual information. Based on this situation, we have been developing accessible games for visually impaired people that feature enriched materials and multimodal information presentation. However, the needs of real-time action on accessible games remain unsolved. In this article, our objective is to develop an inclusive side scroller game with high real-time performance and accessibility functions for visually impaired people, and be available to play with more than one person including sighted persons.

Keywords: Visually impaired people · Inclusive game · Side scroller games · Game accessibility · Auditory display · Tactile display

1 Introduction

Computer games have become increasingly diversified. These games have been made in various formats, including commercial arcade games, consumer games, and personal computer games. The most recent games feature high-pixel density and high-definition displays, which have increased the amount of visual information that gamers receive. As a result, visually impaired and blind people frequently find it difficult to enjoy most of these games, regardless of the vast majority of research on game accessibility [1–4]. A sighted person can visually receive maps, text, and other game information. But for the visually impaired, the level of difficulty increases because of their reliance on sound information

© IFIP International Federation for Information Processing 2017
Published by Springer International Publishing AG 2017. All Rights Reserved
R. Bernhaupt et al. (Eds.): INTERACT 2017, Part IV, LNCS 10516, pp. 410–414, 2017.
DOI: 10.1007/978-3-319-68059-0_41

to play a game. For blind people to play independently, they need to memo-rize associations between the scenes and sound effects in the game. Also, they must remember everything from the menus and categories, and many other item orders, required to play the game. It takes extra effort on the part of visually impaired gamers to play regular games compared to the effort required of a sighted person.

In recent times, there has been progress in developing games intended for blind people. A report covering games that can be played by blind persons, on their own or with an assistance of others, was featured on the website *Audio-Games.net* [5]. This site is a collection of information on games for the visually impaired. These games are called *audio games*, which the visually impaired can play using a screen reader. However, many of these games cannot satisfy the basic needs of visually impaired people because of the shortage of content and are difficult for sighted people because of no visual information.

Based on this shortage, we have been developing accessible games for visually impaired people that feature enriched materials and multimodal information presentation. We developed an action RPG (role-playing game) that visually impaired, and sighted person can play together [6,7]. This RPG is able to present game information acoustically, tactually, and visually. The game was released on the web and is being played by users around the world. It has undergone several upgrades to implement improvements based on user feedback which has modified the game to be more enjoyable and easier to play. However, the needs of real-time action for accessible games remains unsolved. Of course, there are some exergames that the visually impaired can play, but these exergames usually require a large space and special sensors [9–11]. Thus, it is necessary to develop an accessible real-time action game that can run without any exceptional detectors.

In this article, our objective is to develop an inclusive side-scrolling action game with a high real-time performance for not only visually impaired but also sighted computer users. This game will also allow play by more than one person without peculiar input devices.

2 Inclusive Side Scroller Game

2.1 Overview

The screenshot of the game is shown in Fig. 1. The game we developed is a side-scrolling action game that sighted and visually impaired Windows users can play together with ordinary input devices. As is the case in the manipulations of our previous games, sighted persons control a game character with viewing infor-mation on the screen, while visually impaired persons handle a game character based on auditory information and/or tactile information. The game requires the users to recognize and judge the current game situation and to operate the alter ego in the game more quickly and precisely. In addition, this side-scroller can have multiple players including not only sighted but also visually impaired gamers cooperatively.

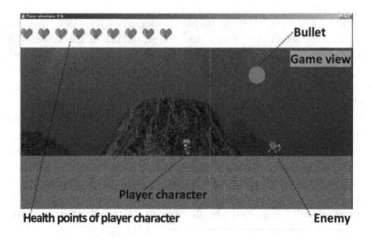

Fig. 1. A screenshot of the view of our side-scrolling action game with annotations of game elements.

2.2 Game Development Environment

We firstly prepared the game development environment for the computer user with total blindness, who is one of the authors. The programming language selected for game development using a screen reader was the Hot Soup Processor (HSP). This programming language was used to develop the game's basic algorithm. Additionally, the text and the screen displayed by the game was prepared using *Otonove* and *AudibleMapper*, which one of the authors had developed previously.

These tools were developed using the HSP and can be used even by individuals with visual impairments. *Otonove* makes it possible to prepare sound novel games (sound-based adventure games played primarily based on text information) by combining text information with available options as well as sound effects. *AudibleMapper* is a tool for creating 2D fields that support accessibility for totally blind people. It can create 2D bird's-eye fields with sound and without visual information. An example of the edited field and the corresponding game field is shown in Fig. 2.

Sound effects, background music, and graphic elements were selected from materials available on the Internet, either free or for a fee. We selected the processing methods and the allocation of background music and sound effects using free software that operates on the Windows operating system.

2.3 Game Flow

The primary control of this game is similar to other side-scrolling games: moving the player character left or right while using jump actions and utilizing weapons to beat down enemies. The field has obstacles including walls, valleys, and enemy characters. When the character falls into a valley, the player must

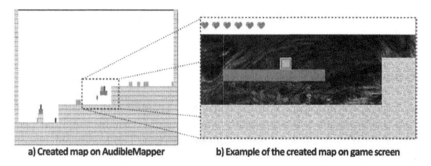

a) Created map on AudibleMapper   b) Example of the created map on game screen

Fig. 2. An example of edited maps created with *AudibleMapper* (Left) and correspond-ing game field (Right)

restart from the valley. Furthermore, we prepared a variety of gimmicks that our previous games did not contain, including movable scaffolds that the charac-ter can carry, footholds that move regularly, and rocks that decrease the health points of the character riding on them.

The player controls the character to avoid gimmicks with the jump control. The player battles against enemies and aims at the goal with the basic actions mentioned above. When two persons cooperatively play the game, one player mainly leads the game, while the other can freely move around and support his or her counterpart.

2.4   Auditory and Tactile Information Presentation

Information on the screen is presented using various sounds and other effects, which are heard by connecting stereo speakers or headphones to the computer. All the objects, including enemy characters and bullets on the field, have at least four sound effects corresponding to their movement, action, attack, and annihila-tion. Static objects also have sound effects that indicate their existence. Gaining an understanding of the positional relationship between these objects and the player's character is possible using the interaural difference of acoustic volume between the left and right to indicate horizontal distance, as well as differences in sound pressure level to indicate vertical distance. Furthermore, dedicated sound effects were incorporated to prompt the user about the character's situation such as approach walls, scaffoldings, or a valley. We also implemented the aural "birds-eye" view function. This function enables the player to pause the game and aurally overview the positional relationship of the nearby scaffold or object using cursor keys.

Besides, connecting a dot matrix display (e.g., KGS Corporation DV-2) to the computer makes it possible for the users to recognize the game screen by touching the tactile display. All screen information, including positions of the objects and the player character, are provided by a binary means that varies depending on whether the location is up or down in relation to the pin. Such information is indicated in real time, enabling the player to easily and immediately discern the status of the screen.

3 Conclusion

In this article, we introduced an inclusive side-scrolling action game with high real-time performance and accessibility functions for visually impaired people, and it is available to play with more than one person. The significant feature of this game is the accessibility functions for blind gamers, such as scanning the current view by audio feedback and compatibility to tactile display. Our future work includes the improvement of game usability and the development of an integrated game development tool for the visually impaired.

References

1. Yuan, B., Folmer, E., Harris Jr., F.C.: Game accessibility: a survey. Univ. Access Inf. Soc. **10**, 81–100 (2011)
2. Miesenberger, K., Ossmann, R., Archambault, D., Searle, G., Holzinger, A.: More Than Just a Game: Accessibility in Computer Games. In: Holzinger, A. (ed.) USAB 2008. LNCS, vol. 5298, pp. 247–260. Springer, Heidelberg (2008). doi:10.1007/978-3-540-89350-9_18
3. Porter, J.R., Kientz, J.A.: An empirical study of issues, barriers to mainstream video game accessibility. In: Proceedings ACM ASSETS 2013, pp. 3:1–3:8 (2013)
4. Zahand, B.: Making video games accessible: business justifications and design considerations. https://msdn.microsoft.com/en-us/library/windows/desktop/ee415219 (v=vs.85).aspx, (Accessed: 17 Apr 2017)
5. AudioGames.net http://www.audiogames.net/, (Accessed: 17 Apr 2017)
6. Matsuo, M., Miura, T., Sakajiri, M., Onishi, J., Ono, T.: Audible Mapper and ShadowRine: Development of Map Editor Using Only Sound in Accessible Game forBlind Users, and Accessible Action RPG for Visually Impaired Gamers. In: Miesenberger, K., Bühler, C., Penaz, P. (eds.) Computers Helping People with Special Needs. ICCHP 2016. Lecture Note in Computer Science, vol. 9759, pp. 537-544 (2016)
7. Matsuo, M., Miura, T., Sakajiri, M., Onishi J., Ono, T.: Experience Report of a Blind Gamer to Develop and Improve the Accessible Action RPG ShadowRine for Visually Impaired Gamers, J. Tech. Persons with Disabil. 5, 2017. (to Appear)
8. HSPTV!, http://hsp.tv/ (cited: 17 Apr 2017)
9. Morelli, T., Foley, J., Folmer, E.: VI-Tennis: a vibrotactile/audio exergame for players who are visually impaired. In: Proceedings FDG 2010, pp. 147–154 (2010)
10. Rector, K., Bennett, C. L., Kientz, J. A., "Eyes-free yoga: an exergame using depth cameras for blind & low vision exercise", In: Proceedings ASSETS '13, Article No. 12 (8 pages) (2013)
11. Morelli, T., Foley, J., Folmer, E.: Vi-bowling: a tactile spatial exergame for individuals with visual impairments. In: Proceedings ASSETS 2010, pp. 179–186 (2010)

Little Bear – A Gaze Aware Learning Companion for Early Childhood Learners

Deepak Akkil[1](✉), Prasenjit Dey[2], and Nitendra Rajput[3]

[1] University of Tampere, Tampere, Finland
deepak.akkil@uta.fi
[2] IBM Research, Bangalore, India
prasenjit.dey@in.ibm.com
[3] InfoEdge India Limited, Noida, India
nitendra@acm.org

Abstract. Computing devices such as mobile phones and tablet computers are increasingly used to support early childhood learning. Currently, touching the screen is the most common interaction technique on such devices. To augment the current interaction experience, overcome posture-related issues with tablet usage and promote novel ways of engagement, we propose gaze as an input modality in educational applications for early learners. In this demonstration, we present the Little Bear, a gaze aware pedagogical agent that tailors its verbal and non-verbal behaviour based on the visual attention of the child. We built an application using the Little Bear, to teach the names of everyday fruits and vegetables to young children. Our demonstration system shows the potential of gaze-based learning applications and the novel engagement possibility provided by gaze-aware pedagogical agents.

Keywords: Gaze · Touch · Pedagogical agent · Early-childhood learning · Vocabulary building · Games · Mobile devices · Engagement

1 Introduction

Touchscreen devices such as Apple iPad and Microsoft Surface tablets are increasingly applied in early childhood pedagogical environments, such as preschools and kindergartens. Growing popularity and access to mobile devices provide exciting opportunities to design innovative, ubiquitous, and constructive learning experiences for young children. While the immense potential of such devices for early childhood learning is well accepted, there are also many concerns regarding touch-based interaction on such devices in an early childhood learning environment.

There are several challenges in designing engaging and intuitive touch-based applications for young children. Plowman and Mcpake [12] note that if children do not understand what they need to do, the interactivity offered by such devices may be counter-productive to learning. This requires careful design of the stimuli and prompts,

---

This work was done when Nitendra Rajput was working for IBM Research.

R. Bernhaupt et al. (Eds.): INTERACT 2017, Part IV, LNCS 10516, pp. 415–419, 2017.
DOI: 10.1007/978-3-319-68059-0_42

to make the interaction intuitive [5]. In addition, the underdeveloped fine motor skills and finger dexterity in children [6] lead to difficulty performing certain touch gestures [11], lead to slower and error-prone interactions [15] and cause accidental or unintended touch [10], affecting the overall interaction.

Another concern regarding the use of a mobile device is to balance the placement of the device for optimal touch interaction and considerations of neutral posture of the child. Straker et al. [14] studied posture and muscle activity of children while using desktop computers and tablets and found that touch-based interaction on a tablet is linked with asymmetric spinal and strained neck postures. Similar concerns regarding posture and prolonged tablet use are also raised by teachers and parents [4]. Researchers have proposed several recommendations to overcome the problem, by promoting task variations [14] and encouraging elevated placement of the device which promote neutral viewing postures [16]. In turn, elevated placement of the device may make the touch interaction difficult.

A third challenge in designing learning applications for children is that children have very limited attention spans and easily get distracted by environmental factors (e.g. noise from the hallway, or a colourful object in the tablet screen of a peer) [2]. Luna [9] note that the younger the children, the more easily they get distracted. It is hence important that educational applications designed for early learners are aware of children's attention and that they employ ways to reorient the attention when the child is distracted, to facilitate learning.

We propose gaze as a viable and potentially beneficial input modality in learning applications for children. Unlike explicit touch-based interaction that inherently requires the device to be placed close to the child, by using gaze, the child can interact with the device at a distance, enabling the device to be optimally placed to promote better posture.

Applications that are aware of the visual attention of the child could implicitly adapt themselves, by integrating learning with their curious visual exploration providing a rich and embodied experience. In addition, gaze has a strong association with attention and gaze-aware learning applications can also keep track of the attention of the child and employ means to reorient the attention when the child is distracted.

There are two distinct ways of using gaze information in learning applications. First, by using gaze as the only interaction modality, which could be useful in simple interaction tasks. Second, by using gaze in combination with conventional touch-based interaction, which could be suitable when more complex interactions are required. In this demonstration, we will focus on applications that use gaze as the only input modality. To showcase the interaction and engagement possibility offered by the modality, we designed Little Bear, an animated pedagogical agent capable of oral communication that is also aware of the visual attention of the learner.

Animated pedagogical agents or virtual characters designed to teach or guide users, provide engagement and motivational benefits in learning applications. However, Kramer and Bente [7] note that current generation of agents do not exhibit sophisticated non-verbal communication nor do they exert a social influence. They envision that agents that are more aware of the emotional and cognitive state of the user and show capacities for non-verbal communication, may have more pedagogical value. Gaze-aware agents have been studied in previous research for children with special needs [8, 13] and for adult users [3]. The novelty of our system is that the Little Bear, uses the gaze information to adapt its verbal as well as non-verbal behavior and exhibit emotional states as a mean to reorient attention of the child, when distracted from the learning activity.

2 Demonstration Application

We designed an application with the "little-bear", a bear-like animated pedagogical agent. The application was set in a garden-like 3D environment, where the agent would take the child for a walk, and the application was designed to teach children the names of some everyday fruits and vegetables. Different fruits and vegetables would appear on screen at pre-defined locations during the walk, which the child could interact with by using gaze (Fig. 1). When the child glanced at a specific fruit, the bear spoke an interesting detail about the fruit. The speech was powered by IBM Watson text to speech service, and further customized by choosing the parameters for the speed of speech, pitch and pauses between words, to make the speech feel natural, fitting to the character and easy to understand. The agent also exhibited realistic lip movement and blink behavior to complement the speech.

Fig. 1. Agent based learning application. The application can be interacted using gaze. The red boxes indicate the gaze reactive area. (Color figure online)

For accurate gaze tracking, we used Tobii EyeX, an off-the-shelf video-based gaze tracker. The agent used the gaze information to adapt its verbal and non-verbal behaviour. For example, when the child is distracted and does not look at the screen, the character becomes sad (see Fig. 2a) and uses speech to attract attention by saying, "*I become sad when you do not look at me.*"

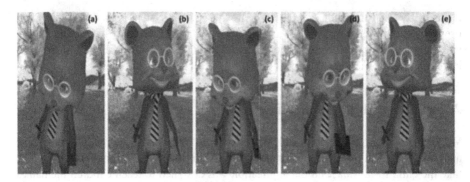

Fig. 2. Agent non-verbal behaviour in response to visual attention of the child. (a) A frame from the sad animation. (b)–(e) head orientation of the bear changes based on the visual attention of the child (agent looks where the child is looking).

A fixation of more than 500 ms on a fruit resulted in its activation and the agent spoke an interesting detail about the fruit (e.g. *you are looking at apple* or *apple is red in color*). The fixation duration was selected, based on previous works that suggest that the normal median gaze fixation duration for children in an image viewing task is 300 ms and that children have difficulty fixating at a target for longer durations. The speech after the activation of a fruit lasted for roughly 3–6 s, during which the application did not respond to any other gaze fixations. Choosing a relatively short fixation duration for activation allowed our application to be implicitly reactive to the interest/visual attention of the child, without requiring an explicit gaze action. When the character was not speaking, the head of the character would orient towards the direction the user was looking at, giving an implicit feedback of gaze tracking and helping establish joint attention. When the character was speaking, the head of the character was oriented directly ahead, abiding by the established social conventions of eye contact during face-to-face conversation.

3   Summary

In this paper, we described the challenges of using touch-based interaction on mobile devices for children and how gaze input could be used as a beneficial input modality in educational applications for children. We further presented the little-bear, a gaze aware pedagogical agent that tailors its verbal and non-verbal behavior in response to visual attention of the user. Our demonstration system will allow others to experience the potential of gaze-based interaction. The demonstration and the related user study [1] shows the novel engagement possibilities of a gaze aware pedagogical agent.

4   Requirements for the Demonstration Setup

The requirements for the demonstration setup are a desk, access to power sockets for the tablet, and preferably a demonstration area with no direct sunlight, or other intense sources of infrared light, immediately in front of, or behind, the user.

References

1. Akkil, D., Dey, P., Salian, D., Rajput, N.: Gaze awareness in agent-based early-childhood learning application. In: Proceedings of Human-Computer Interaction (2017)
2. Bruckman, A., Bandlow, A., Forte, A.: HCI for kids. In: Jacko, J., Sears, A. (ed.) Handbook of Human-Computer Interaction, pp. 793–809. Lawrence Erlbaum Associates (2008)
3. D'Mello, S., Olney, A., Williams, C., Hays, P.: Gaze tutor: a gaze-reactive intelligent tutoring system. Int. J. Hum. Comput. Stud. **70**(5), 377–398 (2012)
4. Fawcett, L.: Tablets in Schools : How Useful Are They ? (2016)
5. Hiniker, A., Sobel, K., Hong, S.R., Suh, H., Kim, D., Kientz, J.A.: Touchscreen prompts for preschoolers: designing developmentally appropriate techniques for teaching young children to perform gestures. In: Proceedings Interaction Design and Children, pp. 109–118 (2015)
6. Hourcade, J.P.: Interaction design and children. Found. Trends Hum.-Comput. Interact. **1**(4), 277–392 (2008)
7. Krämer, N.C., Bente, G.: Personalizing e-learning. The social effects of pedagogical agents. Educ. Psychol. Rev. **22**(1), 71–87 (2010)
8. Lahiri, U., Warren, Z., Sarkar, N.: Design of a gaze-sensitive virtual social interactive system for children with autism. IEEE Trans. Neural Syst. Rehabil. Eng. **19**(4), 443–452 (2011)
9. Luna, B.: Developmental changes in cognitive control through adolescence. Adv. Child Dev. Behav. **37**, 233–278 (2009)
10. McKnight, L., Fitton, D.: Touch-screen technology for children: giving the right instructions and getting the right responses. In: Proceedings of Interaction Design and Children, pp. 238–241 (2010)
11. Nacher, V., Jaen, J., Navarro, E., Catala, A., González, P.: Multi-touch gestures for pre-kindergarten children. Int. J. Hum. Comput. Stud. **73**, 37–51 (2015)
12. Plowman, L., McPake, J.: Seven myths about young children and technology. Child. Educ. **89**(1), 27–33 (2013)
13. Ramloll, R., Trepagnier, C., Sebrechts, M., Finkelmeyer, A.: A gaze contingent environment for fostering social attention in autistic children. In: Proceedings of Eye Tracking Research and Applications, pp. 19–26 (2004)
14. Straker, L.M., Coleman, J., Skoss, R., Maslen, B.A., Burgess-Limerick, R., Pollock, C.M.: A comparison of posture and muscle activity during tablet computer, desktop computer and paper use by young children. Ergonomics **51**(4), 540–555 (2008)
15. Vatavu, R.D., Cramariuc, G., Schipor, D.M.: Touch interaction for children aged 3 to 6 years: experimental findings and relationship to motor skills. Int. J. Hum. Comput. Stud. **74**, 54–76 (2015)
16. Young, J.G., Trudeau, M., Odell, D., Marinelli, K., Dennerlein, J.T.: Touch-screen tablet user configurations and case-supported tilt affect head and neck flexion angles. Work **41**(1), 81–91 (2012)

ReRide

A Platform to Explore Interaction with Personal Data Before, During, and After Motorcycle Commuting

Naveen Bagalkot[1(✉)], Tomas Sokoler[2], Riyaj Shaikh[1],
Gaurav Singh[1], Anders Edelbo Lillie[2], Pratiksha Dixit[1], Aditi Rai[1],
Chakravarthy Vignesh[1], and Ashwin Senthil[1]

[1] Srishti Institute of Art, Design, and Technology, Bangalore, India
{naveen, riyaj.shaikh}@srishti.ac.in
[2] Digital Design Department, IT University of Copenhagen,
Copenhagen, Denmark
sokoler@itu.dk

Abstract. The motorcycle could soon be the new frontier for the exploration of human interaction with advanced digital technology. In this paper we present a demo of a system designed and implemented to explore the design of personal informatics tools for motorbike commuting and help us conduct in-situ evaluation of such tools. We present the system architecture and demonstrate the capabilities of the system by presenting a case instantiation in the form of an interactive soft-and-hardware prototype that collects rider's posture data, visualizes the data on the motorbike dashboard in real-time, and pushes the data to the cloud server for later retrieval.

Keywords: Motorbike riding · Personal informatics · Cloud-based platform · Interactive prototype

1 Introduction

The motorcycle could soon be a new frontier for the exploration of human-computer interaction[1], particularly personal informatics. Personal informatics is a set of pervasive and mobile tools that are aimed at supporting people to collect, parse, and present personal information towards self-monitoring and self-reflection [3]. Currently, riders engage with multiple forms of digital information about the motorbike through the 'glanceable' dashboard. They also engage with non-digital 'cues' while riding such as traffic movement, road and weather conditions, etc., which constantly keep changing. What if information about the rider's condition such as body posture, lean angles, and heartrate, were also made available as part of the ride experience? This is an open research question inviting exploration. The enabling technology components seem to be mature but focused design efforts work is needed to put the components together and explore and define the multifaceted space of opportunities.

---

[1] Emerging works in HCI research has focused on exploring the means to display digital information to the rider [1, 2, 4, 5].

© IFIP International Federation for Information Processing 2017
Published by Springer International Publishing AG 2017. All Rights Reserved
R. Bernhaupt et al. (Eds.): INTERACT 2017, Part IV, LNCS 10516, pp. 420–423, 2017.
DOI: 10.1007/978-3-319-68059-0_43

In this paper we present a demo of a system designed and implemented to explore the design of personal informatics tools for motorbike commuting and help us conduct in-situ evaluation of such tools. We present the system architecture of our cloud based platform enabling wireless real-time data capture, storage and presentation across multiple devices. We demonstrate the capabilities of the system by presenting a case instantiation in the form of an interactive soft-and-hardware prototype that collects rider's posture data, visualizes the data on the motorbike dashboard in real-time, and pushes the data to the cloud server for later retrieval. We speculate this demonstration opens up the space for further designing, prototyping, and evaluation of personal informatics tools for motorbike commuting along multiple directions. For example, one direction is to explore presenting the information not only during the ride, but also before and after the ride. Another is to explore the design of Personal Informatics tools not only for a single rider but a group of riders sharing their data synchronously and asynchronously across devices and experiences.

2 System Architecture

The system architecture for the platform is made up of several individual components and programming modules (see Fig. 1). An input sensor, such as a Force Sensitive Resistor (FSR) is attached to a Genuino microcontroller with embedded Bluetooth capability, and an Internet connected smart phone make up the environmental sensing device. Data collected during the ride is pushed to the Amazon Web Services (AWS) IoT Cloud Platform, which does all the message relaying and cloud computing. This Platform-as-a-Service (PaaS) has much different functionality required to store, process and evaluate the data sent to it. Any Internet-connected client device can connect to the PaaS and subscribe to or pull information from a custom generated API, which can be visualized over either a browser or a native application.

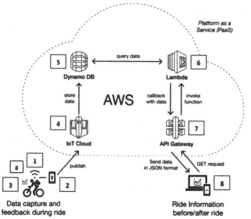

Program Modules in the System

1. Genuino with Curie BLE interfaces with the input sensors.
2. ReRide.js is a GATT server, establishes the pairing between the display device and the processing unit to get the sensor readings.
3. Data visualization (HTML + P5.js) module runs on the display device and along with the GATT server, visualizes the sensor data.
4. AWS IoT Cloud Platform. The sensor data is sent to the Dynamo DB stored in AWS, and can be retrieved later through Web/Mobile interface across devices
5. Dynamo DB. Database service in AWS; will receive sensor data from IOT Cloud and store for future retrieval.
6. Lambda. Computing Service in AWS; responsible for storing various queries for data retrieval.
7. API Gateway. API Service in AWS; will receive GET request from the Web/mobile devices.
8. Web/mobile Interface. The rider will use this to review real-time and historical data about the ride.

Fig. 1. System architecture and programming modules

3 Watching Your Back While Riding: An Instantiation

To demonstrate the system, we present one example instantiation, in the context of tracking and displaying data about the rider's lower-back posture during the ride[2]. Consider the following scenario: *Diva commutes to her work on her motorbike daily. She has been doing so for the past 5 years, and now is in the danger of developing repetitive strain injury of her lower back. To prevent the injury she has to perform stretching exercises, but she does not have the time or the energy at the end of day to do so. She then starts using ReRide. ReRide consists of two parts: (a) A sensing part that is part of the seat cushion and (b) a display unit that displays this information real-time, next to the motorbike's dashboard. As Diva rides her bike through the traffic she gets continuous feedback of her lower-back posture. During the ride she keeps changing adjusting her posture and stretching her back, thereby performing a part of her prescribed preventive exercises.*

4 Components of the Prototype

The interactive hard-and-software prototype comprises of (see Fig. 2):

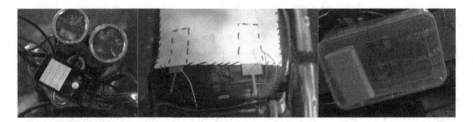

Fig. 2. The display, sensing unit, and the processing unit.

(1) A sensor patch placed right beneath the rider's seat consisting of two FSRs, which measure pressure to derive and inform variations in the posture while riding a motorbike. The sensor has a resolution of 1024 levels, with 0 being lowest and 1023 being the highest pressure. We segment this range into four equal parts. Pressure sensor reading are captured and colour coded into these four segments.

(2) Two square shaped force sensitive resistors (FSR) are sandwiched between the seat cushion and seat cover. To increase the pressure sensitivity, an additional layer of foam sheets has been applied on top of these sensors. The sensors are connected to Genuino analog input with a 10 KΩ fixed resistor in between. Wires connecting sensors with the breadboard are encapsulated inside a rubber tube.

(3) A processing unit with the Genuino board (with inbuilt Bluetooth Low Energy module), 9 V battery and circuit that reads the FSR value, timestamps it, and transmits it to the display device through bluetooth.

---

[2] The motivation behind the design is explained in [1], and is beyond the scope of this paper.

(4) A Display device positioned alongside the dashboard, which is bluetooth enabled touchscreen unit capable of running google chrome mobile browser[3]. It communicates with the processing unit via bluetooth, and to communicate with the AWS it uses a 3G/4G mobile internet connection. The Display is divided into two panels (see Fig. 2). The left panel displays live posture data in the form of a continuous horizontal scroll, displaying information for the past three minutes of the ride. We use color shade of the same tint to indicate how much the rider's back is under stress. The darker the shade, more the stress. The right panel displays rider's posture variation for the entire ride along with the ride duration.

5 Concluding Remarks

In this paper we presented a demo of a system designed and implemented as platform exploring the design of personal informatics tools for motorbike commuting and help us conduct in-situ evaluation of such tools. Currently we are working with industrial designers to shape the sensing and display units as integral parts of a motorbike. We are also working on building the prototype to cover other possible scenarios of engagement with lower-back posture data before and after the ride. We envision how a rider may check information about their last ride displayed on the motorbike just before they begin a new ride. Or dig deeper into their historic data, possibly in combination with other relevant data such as traffic patterns, on their personal smartphones while sitting in a lounge.

In this sense, one can see how the demonstration opens up the space for researchers to further explore the design of Personal Informatics tools for motorbike commuting across devices, experiences, and situations. As such, we present the demo as an invitation to Personal Informatics and HCI community to further explore the challenging, yet underexplored frontier of interacting with computation as part of motorbike commuting.

References

1. Bagalkot, N., Sokoler, T., Baadkar, S.: ReRide: performing lower back rehabilitation while riding your motorbike in traffic. In: PervasiveHealth 2016. ICST (2016)
2. Bial, D., Kern, D., Alt, F., Schmidt, A.: Enhancing outdoor navigation systems through vibrotactile feedback. In: CHI 2011, pp. 1273–1278. ACM (2011)
3. Li, I., Dey, A., Forlizzi, J.: A stage-based model of personal informatics systems. In: CHI 2010. ACM (2010)
4. Ogi, T.: Design and evaluation of HUD for motorcycle using immersive simulator. In: SIGGRAPH Asia 2015. ACM (2015)
5. Spelta, C., Manzoni, V., Corti, A., Goggi, A., Savaresi, S.M.: Smartphone-based vehicle-to-driver/environment interaction system for motorcycles. IEEE Embed. Syst. Lett. **2**(2), 39–42 (2010)

---

[3] For the purpose of demonstration we have used the Nexus 5X.

SoPhy: Smart Socks for Video Consultations of Physiotherapy

Deepti Aggarwal[1(✉)], Thuong Hoang[1], Weiyi Zhang[1],
Bernd Ploderer[1,2], Frank Vetere[1], and Mark Bradford[3]

[1] Microsoft Research Center for SocialNUI,
University of Melbourne, Melbourne, Australia
daggarwal@student.unimelb.edu.au
[2] Electrical Engineering and Computer Science,
Queensland University of Technology, Brisbane, Australia
[3] Department of Anaesthesia and Pain Management,
Royal Children's Hospital, Melbourne, Australia

Abstract. While physiotherapists are increasingly organizing video consultations, assessment of lower body movements over video remains a challenge. We present a wearable technology, *SoPhy* that captures and presents information related to three key aspects of lower limb movements - range of foot movement, weight distribution and foot orientation. *SoPhy* consists of a pair of socks embedded with sensors for the patients to wear, and a web-interface that displays the captured information to physiotherapists in real-time. The objective of this demonstration is to offer first-hand experience of *SoPhy* and to create conversations around designing technologies for supporting bodily communication in video consultations.

1 Introduction

Over the last decade, physiotherapists have started using video conferencing tools to offer diagnostic and therapeutic advice to patients living in remote or rural areas [2, 3]. While video consultations offer several benefits to patients and clinicians, our recent study [2] highlights the limitations of video technology in communicating the essential bodily information that physiotherapists need to formulate their assessment. The study showed that the physiotherapists found it difficult to understand the subtle differences in exercises such as depth of squats, and range of movements over video, particularly, for lower limb movements. The absence of the essential bodily information reduced clinician's confidence in assessing their patients and consequently, they offered less specific treatment over video than face-to-face consultations.

The importance of communicating rich information to clinicians is always emphasized [5], as it helps clinicians in making informed decisions and thereby, making the overall consultation effective. However, lesser attention has been paid to understand how new technologies could enhance clinician's ability to assess and treat patients during video consultations. We are interested in lower limb movements as they are more challenging to communicate over video. Video conferencing tools are typically configured to support talking heads conversations, and have little consideration

R. Bernhaupt et al. (Eds.): INTERACT 2017, Part IV, LNCS 10516, pp. 424–428, 2017.
DOI: 10.1007/978-3-319-68059-0_44

Fig. 1. Setup of *SoPhy* during a video consultation: (a) In left, a physiotherapist is using *SoPhy* web-interface to understand patient's movements. (b) In right, a patient is performing lower body movements by wearing *SoPhy* socks.

for the observation of full body movements [4]. Moreover, video technology possess limited visual acuity that further reduces clinician's ability to discern subtle changes in exercises e.g., point of balance and depth of squats [2].

This is the first attempt that extends video consultations beyond audio-video medium and explores the potential of a wearable technology to support the tasks of physiotherapists. We designed *SoPhy* that provides information of key aspects of lower limb movements during video consultations (refer Fig. 1). We conducted a laboratory study to investigate how *SoPhy* helps physiotherapists in assessing patients over video [1]. The findings showed that *SoPhy* increased their confidence in assessing low limb exercises like squats, and they required fewer repetitions of exercises to assess patients with *SoPhy*. Next we illustrate the design of *SoPhy*.

2 SoPhy: Our Proposed System

SoPhy stands for 'socks for physiotherapy'. *SoPhy* is a novel wearable technology consisting of (1) a pair of socks embedded with three pressure sensors and one Inertial Measurement Unit (IMU) that patients wear while performing lower body movements (Fig. 2a); and (2) a web-interface that visualizes information about weight distribution, range of foot movement and foot orientation to physiotherapists in real-time (Fig. 2b).

We have followed user-centered approach to iteratively design *SoPhy*, and collaborated with a senior physiotherapist (last author) at a leading hospital in Australia. To this end, the selection of different sensors and visualisation of the data are the results of multiple lab trials and feedback from the collaborating physiotherapist. Below we describe the bodily information supported by *SoPhy*.

Weight Distribution: Weight distribution describes the amount of weight a person bears in different areas of the foot e.g., on toes, balls and heel. While a healthy person distributes equal weight on each foot (leg), the pattern changes in case of an injured. For instance, if a person has injured his big toe, he may bear more weight on the outside of the foot. *SoPhy* captures the pattern of weight distribution on the balls and heel of the foot, through pressure sensors stitched on the *SoPhy* socks.

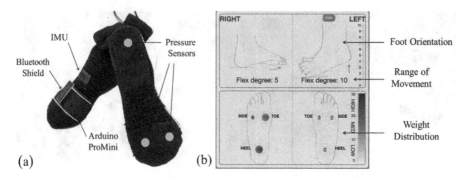

Fig. 2. *SoPhy* consists of two parts: (a) a pair of socks with sensors embedded, and (b) a web-interface that visualizes the information related to foot orientation, range of movement and weight distribution. (Color figure online)

The web-interface displays weight distribution on the feet sketches showing the feet from underneath (refer Fig. 2b). For each sensor, the pressure values are presented with a number on a scale of 0–30 and on a color spectrum of yellow to red.

Foot Orientation: Foot orientation refers to the alignment of foot in four directions. First is the dorsiflexion, which occurs when the person bears weight on the heel of the foot with toes lifted up in the air. Second is the plantarflexion where the weight is on the balls and toes of the foot with heel lifted up in the air. Third is the medial orientation where the weight is on the inside of the foot and the person lifts the outside of the foot up in the air. And final orientation is lateral orientation where the person bears weight on the outside of the foot and lifts the inside of the foot up in the air. In *SoPhy*, foot orientation is captured by the IMU sensor sewed on the socks on the bridge of the foot. We have used multiple foot sketches to present this information on the web-interface: three each for dorsiflexion and plantarflexion, and two each for medial and lateral orientation (refer Fig. 2b).

Range of Movement: Range of movement refers to the magnitude of the foot orientation across four directions described above. The range is defined on a scale of 1 to 10 and is calculated from the IMU data. On the web-interface, this value is represented as a 'Flex degree' under each foot (refer Fig. 2b).

3 Engaging with SoPhy

Figure 1 shows the setup of *SoPhy* during a video consultation. The patient wears the *SoPhy* socks before starting the video consultation with physiotherapist. During a video consultation, physiotherapist will ask the patient to perform different lower body exercises, e.g., dorsiflexion and plantarflexion, squats, and heel raises (refer Fig. 3). As the patient performs these exercises, the socks capture data about foot movements. This data is then sent to the web interface, where the physiotherapist can see the movement data in real-time. We designed a mobile app to support data communication between the socks and web interface via a Bluetooth shield attached on the *SoPhy* socks.

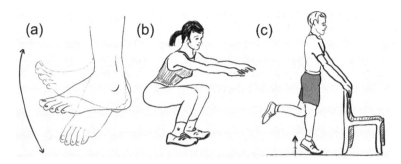

Fig. 3. Examples of lower limb exercises: (a) Dorsiflexion and Plantarflexion, (b) Squats (c) Single leg heel raises.

At the venue, visitors will be able to try out *SoPhy* in solo or in pairs. They can wear the *SoPhy* socks and check the visual feedback on the web-interface for different lower body movements. Alternatively, they can role-play as a physiotherapist and patient, to mimic a clinical consultation related to lower limb assessment. We anticipate that audience will get the following insights by interacting with *SoPhy*:

1. They will get an awareness of the role of different bodily cues related to lower body exercises.
2. They will become familiar with the emerging practice of video consultations and the challenges of video technology in communicating lower limb movements.
3. They will gain insights on the challenges faced by physiotherapists in assessing patients during video consultations, and how *SoPhy* can help them in their decision-making process.
4. They will get a first-hand experience of *SoPhy*, which will particularly, be of interest to DIY med-tech community.
5. Finally, it will potentially seed new interests and conversations around the development of future video consultation systems that provide essential bodily information to clinicians.

References

1. Aggarwal, D., Zhang, W., Hoang, T., Ploderer, B., Vetere, F., Bradford, M.: SoPhy: a wearable technology for lower limb assessment in video consultations of physiotherapy. In: Proceedings of the 2017 CHI Conference on Human Factors in Computing Systems (CHI 2017), pp. 3916–3928. ACM (2017)
2. Aggarwal, D., Ploderer, B., Vetere, F., Bradford, M., Hoang, T.: Doctor, can you see my squats? Understanding bodily communication in video consultations for physiotherapy. In: Proceedings of the 2016 ACM Conference on Designing Interactive Systems (DIS 2016), pp. 1197–1208. ACM (2016)

3. Ekeland, A.G., Bowes, A., Flottorp, S.: Effectiveness of telemedicine: a systematic review of reviews. Int. J. Med. Inf. **79**(11), 736–771 (2010)
4. Licoppe, C., Morel, J.: Video-in-interaction: "Talking heads" and the multimodal organization of mobile and Skype video calls. Res. Lang. Soc. Interact. **45**(4), 399–429 (2012)
5. Stewart, M.A.: Effective physician-patient communication and health outcomes: a review. J. Can. Med. Assoc. **15**(9), 1423–1433 (1995)

Interactive Posters

BendSwipe: One Handed Target Zooming for Flexible Handheld Display

Keyur Sorathia, Aditi Singh, and Mayank Chhabra[✉]

Indian Institute of Technology, Guwahati, India
mayankk.2109@gmail.com

Abstract. One-hand usage of handheld devices results in poor reachability, re-gripping, occlusion and reduced accuracy. This results in poor user experiences, especially with user interactions that require multi-finger usage. Use of deformation gestures can augment touch gestures to extend the limited functionalities experienced in one-handed usage. We present BendSwipe - a combined bend and touch enabled input interaction to perform target zooming on a flexible handheld device. It uses the bend gestures to augment a swipe interaction performed anywhere at the back of the device to perform target zoom-in and out on any area of the display content. This paper presents the details of proposed input interactions, prototype and future directions to evaluate the designs.

Keywords: Deformation based interactions · One-Handed usage · Bend & touch interactions

1 Introduction

Prior research findings show 74% users prefer to use mobile phones with one hand [13]. One handed usage of handheld devices is commonly observed in situational impairments, e.g. walking, sitting and standing where the other hand is busy doing real-world tasks [2]. Hence, the design of suitable input interactions for one-handed usage becomes critical in common scenarios of situational impairment.

The standard handheld devices pose several challenges during one-handed usage including limited reachability [9], re-gripping of the device [3], reduced accuracy [3], and increased occlusion [3]. These problems are primarily attributed to factors like the constantly increasing size of the device, hand-thumb morphology and interactions that demand the attention of both hands to perform certain tasks [7]. This leads to difficult user interactions with handheld devices, especially for the tasks that demand multi-finger and/or multi-step interactions such as target zooming [3, 5]. Target zooming is defined as zoom-in and zoom-out to a specific location of an interface (e.g. top-right & top-left corner, bottom-left & bottom-right corner etc.). These locations often demand multi-step interactions by enabling (a) access to unreachable areas and (b) further panning through diagonal, horizontal and vertical finger movements to achieve a user-defined target in an interface. These tasks are commonly performed in applications such as navigational maps and image gallery.

The problems with one-handed usage are not limited to standard handheld devices, but will also be experienced in future flexible handheld devices [13].

Published by Springer International Publishing AG 2017. All Rights Reserved
R. Bernhaupt et al. (Eds.): INTERACT 2017, Part IV, LNCS 10516, pp. 431–435, 2017.
DOI: 10.1007/978-3-319-68059-0_45

Although extensive research is conducted in improving one-handed interactions on standard handheld devices [1, 3, 9, 10], investigations targeting one-handed interactions for flexible handheld devices is insufficiently explored. These investigations are important as flexible devices offer opportunities of deformations that may result in intuitive and efficient one-handed user interactions. The potential of deformation is further amplified by bringing in touch capabilities as it is useful to offset against the inability to perform bimanual interactions in one-handed usage [14].

In this paper, we propose new input interactions – a combination of central bend based deformation gestures and touch supported swipe on back side of flexible handheld device to perform target zooming of an image.

2   Design of Proposed Input-Interactions

To illustrate the use case of target zooming using the BendSwipe interaction technique, we use an infographic image and divide it into a 3 × 3 grid (Fig. 1). BendSwipe uses bend and swipe gesture to manipulate the direction of zooming - directing towards specific location of 3 × 3 grid. The gesture involves central bending the flexible device in order to perform a center squeeze and performing a swipe action at the back of the device simultaneously.

Fig. 1. Division of grid of the infographic image

2.1   Design Rationale

To reduce occlusion and re-gripping events and enable easy target zooming, we chose a combination of bend gesture and touch supported swipe gesture on backside of flexible handheld device. We chose bend gestures due to its strong preference in current literature [1, 11, 13] which are less time consuming, easy to use, and intuitive; hence aiding in performing zooming tasks easily and quickly. We also chose touch based swipe gesture as common holding position in one-handed usage freed the index finger on the backside of the device [12]. Swiping the index finger in specific direction aides in identifying the zooming direction; hence enabling target zooming. We believe that combination of bend and swipe gesture on backside of flexible handhelds can effectively reduce the current challenges of occlusion, reachability and re-gripping and enable target zooming easily and quickly.

2.2 BendSwipe Walkthrough

Zoom-in and out is triggered by performing a bend and swipe gesture simultaneously. Performing a center squeeze which bends the central vertical axis (X-X' in Fig. 2) towards the user is called bend-in. A bend-in displays the navigation wheel as displayed in Fig. 2(a). Performing a linear swipe gesture in any direction on the back of the device triggers the zoom-in which triggers in the exact direction of the swipe gesture; hence performing a target zoom-in. The zoom-in is performed as long as a touch is detected at the end coordinate of the swipe gesture. For example, to zoom-in towards the area in grid 8 (Fig. 1) the user needs to perform a bend-in, followed by a swipe gesture in the South-East (SE) direction anywhere on the back of the device.

Performing a center squeeze which bends the central vertical axis (X-X' in Fig. 2) away from the user is called bend-out. A bend-out displays the navigation wheel as displayed in Fig. 2 (b). Performing a linear swipe gesture in any direction on the back of the device triggers the zoom-out which triggers in the exact direction of the swipe gesture; hence performing a target zoom-out. Similar to zoom-in, zoom-out is performed as long as a touch is detected at the end coordinate of the swipe gesture. For example, to zoom-out towards the area in grid 8 (Fig. 1) the user needs to perform a bend-out, followed by a swipe gesture in the SE direction anywhere on the back of the device.

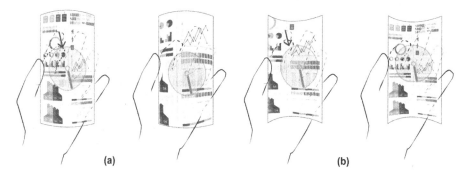

Fig. 2. (a) Bend-in and swiping in the SE direction for Zoom-In in the same direction, (b) Bend-out and swiping in the SE direction for Zoom Out in the same direction

3 Prototype

The flexible prototype is made out of a thin sheet of paper (5.5 size) laminated with plastic sheets on both sides. The plastic coating gives the device the ability to bend and twist easily along with elasticity. A bend sensor is located diagonally (on the backside) to detect bend-in and bend-out of the flexible device (Fig. 3). To detect and track the finger swipe gesture at the back of the device, a deformable and conductive transparent sensor material [8] is used that is placed on the backside of flexible device.

The movement as well as the location of a finger can be followed across the cross-grid sensor array that results in the tracking of finger swipe direction. The bend sensor and the conductive sensor material sends the data to the Arduino microcontroller to control the image size using Processing software. Moreover, the display content is integrated with the device by means of a top projection.

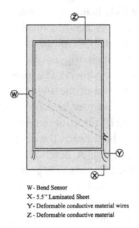

W- Bend Sensor
X- 5.5" Laminated Sheet
Y- Deformable conductive material wires
Z - Deformable conductive material

Fig. 3. Placement of sensors for BendSwipe prototype

4 Conclusion and Future Work

In this paper, we explored the capabilities of deformation gestures to augment touch gestures in order to extend their functionality for one-handed hand-held usage. We designed a method of target zooming using the central bend gesture and the swipe gesture at the back of the device to overcome the challenges experienced in one-handed usage. These challenges are yet to be explored sufficiently for flexible handheld devices. We presented an input method to zoom-in or out towards any area in a continuous and controlled manner. To evaluate the effectiveness of this interaction technique, we will conduct a comparative evaluation with the standard smartphone. The comparative study will investigate variables (a) task completion time to zoom to several specific target areas and (b) number of re-gripping events while performing the target zooming during the task. We will also measure 4 usability constructs (i) ease of use, (ii) intuitiveness, (iii) ease of learning and (iv) behavioral intention. In addition to the effectiveness of the proposed input interactions, the study can potentially bring some insights on the effectiveness of swipe as a back interaction used along with deformation gesture in one-handed scenario.

References

1. Holman, D., Hollatz, A., Banerjee, A., Vertegaal, R.: Unifone: designing for auxiliary finger input in one-handed mobile interactions. In: Proceedings of the 7th International Conference on Tangible, Embedded and Embodied Interaction (TEI 2013), pp. 177–184. ACM, New York (2013). doi:10.1145/2460625.2460653

2. Pascoe, J., Ryan, N., Morse, D.: Using while moving: HCI issues in fieldwork environments. ACM Trans. Comput.-Hum. Interact. **7**(3), 417–437 (2000). doi:10.1145/355324.355329

3. Lai, J., Zhang, D.: ExtendedThumb: a target acquisition approach for one-handed interaction with touch-screen mobile phones. Proc. IEEE Trans. Hum.-Mach. Syst.

4. Ti, J., Tjondronegoro, D.: TiltZoom: tilt-based zooming control for easy (2012)

5. Karlson, A.K., Bederson, B.B., Contreras-Vidal, J.L.: Studies in one-handed mobile design: Habit, desire and agility. In: Proceedings of the 4th ERCIM Workshop User Interfaces All (UI4ALL) (2006)

6. Karlson, A.K., Bederson, B.B., Contreras-Vidal, J.L.: Understanding one-handed use of mobile devices. In: Proceedings of the Handbook of Research on User Interface Design and Evaluation for Mobile Technology (2008)

7. Karlson, A.K., Bederson, B.B.: ThumbSpace: generalized one-handed input for touchscreen-based mobile devices. In: Baranauskas, C., Palanque, P., Abascal, J., Barbosa, S.D.J. (eds.) INTERACT 2007. LNCS, vol. 4662, pp. 324–338. Springer, Heidelberg (2007). doi:10.1007/978-3-540-74796-3_30

8. Sarwar, M.S., et al.: Bend, stretch, and touch: locating a finger on an actively deformed transparent sensor array. Sci. Adv. **3**(3), e1602200 (2017)

9. Yu, N.-H., Huang, D.-Y., Hsu, J.-J., Hung, Y.-P.: Rapid selection of hard-to-access targets by thumb on mobile touch-screens. In: Proceedings of the 15th International Conference on Human-Computer Interaction with Mobile Devices and Services (MobileHCI 2013), pp. 400–403. ACM, New York (2013). doi:10.1145/2493190.2493202

10. One-handed mobile interactions. In: Proceedings of the Internet of Things Workshop, OZCHI 2012: Integration, Interaction, Innovation, Immersion, Inclusion, Melbourne, Victoria, Australia, pp. 1–5 (2012)

11. Ahmaniemi, T.T., Kildal, J., Haveri, M.: What is a device bend gesture really good for? In: Proceedings of the SIGCHI Conference on Human Factors in Computing Systems (CHI 2014), pp. 3503–3512. ACM, New York (2014). doi:10.1145/2556288.2557306

12. Wobbrock, J.O., Myers, B.A., Aung, H.H.: The performance of hand postures in front-and back-of-device interaction for mobile computing. Int. J. Human-Comput. Stud. **66**(12), 857–875 (2008)

13. Girouard, A., Lo, J., Riyadh, M., Daliri, F., Eady, A.K., Pasquero, J.: One-handed bend interactions with deformable smartphones. In: Proceedings of the 33rd Annual ACM Conference on Human Factors in Computing Systems, pp. 1509–1518. ACM, April 2015

14. Riyadh, Md.: Exploring tapping with thumb input for flexible tablets. In: CHI 2014 Extended Abstracts on Human Factors in Computing Systems. ACM (2014)

Crowdsourcing of Accessibility Attributes on Sidewalk-Based Geodatabase

Michaela Riganova, Jan Balata[✉], and Zdenek Mikovec

Faculty of Electrical Engineering, Czech Technical University in Prague,
Prague, Czech Republic
balatjan@fel.cvut.cz

Abstract. Although the issue of limited mobility affects a large portion of the population, current navigation systems working with roadway-based geodatabases are designed primarily for cars and therefore cannot efficiently help. Usage of the professionally created sidewalk-based geodatabase is a solution. However, the professional geographical "on-site reconnaissance" is labor demanding. In this poster, we report on results of preliminary research focused on a design of the gamified collection of accessibility attributes by non-expert crowd, which will reduce the data collection cost. Preliminary results suggest the feasibility of the approach supported by a proper guidance of non-experts and creativity of achieving precise measurements.

1 Introduction

According to Sammer et al. [9], almost 16% of the population is limited in mobility, namely visually impaired, hearing impaired, wheelchair users, and people with impaired ability to walk. Appropriate navigation system considering sidewalks and their accessibility attributes can help significantly. However, current navigation systems are created for cars, thus ignoring sidewalks, crosswalks, landmark information and important accessibility attributes.

To address this issue, we designed a sidewalk-based geodatabase[1] (Geographical Information System – GIS) with the following features: line features tied to large part of the pedestrian segment (a sidewalk, a crosswalk, an underpass) with attributes (sidewalk slope, material, light signalization, traffic noise); point features tied to short part of the pedestrian segment that acts as a barrier (a staircase, obstacle) or a landmark (corner, recess) with attributes (corner shape, number of steps, unobstructed width).

The GIS is created in two phases: (1) Pedestrian segments with line and point features are drawn into the GIS by a professional using resources such as satellite imaging, a "map of town utilities," creating a template for the second phase. (2) The template is filled in with attributes assigned to the features via professional "on-site reconnaissance," which is highly labor demanding. The features

---

[1] Route4All – http://www.route4all.eu/en/.

© IFIP International Federation for Information Processing 2017
Published by Springer International Publishing AG 2017. All Rights Reserved
R. Bernhaupt et al. (Eds.): INTERACT 2017, Part IV, LNCS 10516, pp. 436–440, 2017.
DOI: 10.1007/978-3-319-68059-0_46

and their attributes were carefully designed and selected in cooperation with orientation and mobility specialists. The GIS enabled us, for example, to generate landmark-enhanced itineraries for blind pedestrians [1].

Our aim is to design a mobile application for collection of pedestrian attributes of segment features in the field using crowdsourcing. The non-experts will fill the data in the professionally created template of the GIS for a fraction of the effort of professional "on-site reconnaissance." The research questions are: How to accommodate the expert language to be well understood by non-experts? What methods will non-experts use for measurements? How to efficiently visualize pedestrian segments on a map? What is the quality of non-expert collected geodata? What is the efficiency of introduced gamification elements?

2   Related Work

Recently, there were attempts to improve sidewalk accessibility using Google Street View: a collection of crossroads data [3] and public transport stations locations [5] to be described to visually impaired people, or barriers on sidewalks and crosswalks [6] to hint wheelchair users about accessibility. However, neither used the data in sidewalk-based GIS to enable efficient routing and route description.

Comparing the quality of crowdsourced geodata from experts and non-experts, See et al. [10] conclude that it do not differ significantly and non-experts can improve using training or examples (especially concerning accessibility where they are not as proficient [11]). Moreover, the crowd can not only provide the data, but also provide their validation [2]. Regarding motivation of the crowd, Mooney and Corcoran [8] conclude that majority of geodata is often contributed by the minority of users. On the other hand, crowdsourcing geodata that brings benefit to the community of contributors can be used as a motivation [7]. The gamification proved to be a good motivation for crowdsourcing, using concepts like points, leaderboards, etc. [4].

3   Crowdsourcing of Accessibility Attributes

In our research, we consider following scenarios of crowdsourcing: (1) collecting new attributes for the features like sidewalk slope and material, corner shape, crosswalk curbs, ramps and signalization, (2) reporting temporary obstacles like potholes or construction works, (3) crowd validation of the crowdsourced geodata.

3.1   Design Process and Preliminary Results

The expert language is often complex and not well understood by non-experts. To observe relevant non-expert language conventions for attributes description and their skills when collecting accessibility geodata without any special equipment,

Fig. 1. (a) A map representing template of the GIS – shapes depict features for which the attributes were collected; (b) examples of measuring methods used.

we organized three focus group sessions with 11 participants of various age (22–26, 27–35, 35–51).

Each group received a simplified hand-drawn map of pedestrian segments with line and point features of our interest (see Fig. 1a). The tasks were to name depicted features and collect data about their accessibility attributes. We were interested mainly in the shapes of corners, properties of crosswalks (such as a presence of tactile pavement, audio signalization, a presence of ramp or curb), positions of obstacles, passable widths, slopes and materials of pedestrian segments and properties of tram stops.

All participants were able to agree on a single term for given features. On the other hand, the participants struggled to name some of their attributes (e.g., the shape of a corner, different kinds of a slope, type of tactile paving surfaces). Regarding the slope, in the end, participants agreed on "direct slope" for longitudinal slope and "side slope" for cross slope.

The participants were not provided with any special tools for measuring required attributes. For measuring length, width, and depth, the most common technique was stepping or using their feet. They also used credit cards and squared paper as compensation for a meter (see Fig. 1b). However, the participants struggled to measure an exact slope of pedestrian segments; they even tried using a mobile app. However, it was not sensitive enough. Instead, they used terms as "gentle," "small," "smooth" or "slightly" uphill/downhill.

Based on the results from focus groups, we designed pictograms in combination with easy-to-understand language for the description of pedestrian segment features and their attributes. We conducted 4 design probe sessions based on paper mock-ups concluding that most participants do not want to spend too much time collecting the geodata and they proposed faster methods of input such as sliders, drop-down menus, or drag&drop instead of text fields for precise values. Further, they doubted clarity of pictograms for complicated attributes such as a presence of guiding lines for visually impaired on crosswalks and they mentioned that they would prefer additional photo example.

3.2 Gamification Elements

Further, we elaborated on suitable gamification elements to engage crowdsourcing activities. Based on [4], we selected weekly and overall leaderboards, badges,

Fig. 2. From the left: a pedestrian segment visualization with features; gamification elements; obstacle reporting; crosswalk ramps; recapitulation of collected data.

weekly missions – where the task is to collect accessibility attributes for a particular combination of features, and credibility – based on validation of user's crowdsourced data by other users. Moreover, we introduced personalizations such as profile photo and nickname. These gamification elements were later included in a further design process.

3.3   Next Steps

Currently, we are creating a hi-fi prototype using HTML and JavaScript. The main challenges are a visualization of the pedestrian segments, features and attributes over Google Maps on a mobile device; and how to support the identification of the desired features or reported obstacles by non-expert users (see Fig. 2). After the usability inspection of the hi-fi prototype, we plan to conduct a long-term experiment evaluating the quality of collected accessibility attributes and efficiency of gamification elements.

4   Conclusion

We present first design steps of the application for crowdsourced collection of pedestrian accessibility attributes in the urban environment. Focus group sessions were directed at accommodation of the expert language to non-expert users and the methods they can use for attributes measurement. Created paper mockup was evaluated in design probes. In the future, we aim to compare the quality of the collected data by non-experts and efficiency of gamification elements.

Acknowledgements. The research has been supported by the project Navigation of handicapped people funded by grant no. SGS16/236/OHK3/3T/13 (FIS 161 – 1611663C000) and by Czech Radio Foundation project "Světluška".

References

1. Balata, J., Mikovec, Z., Bures, P., Mulickova, E.: Automatically generated landmark-enhanced navigation instructions for blind pedestrians. In: 2016 Federated Conference on Computer Science and Information Systems (FedCSIS), pp. 1605–1612. IEEE (2016)
2. Goodchild, M.F., Li, L.: Assuring the quality of volunteered geographic information. Spat. Stat. 1, 110–120 (2012)
3. Guy, R., Truong, K.: Crossingguard: exploring information content in navigation aids for visually impaired pedestrians. In: Proceedings of the SIGCHI Conference on Human Factors in Computing Systems, pp. 405–414. ACM (2012)
4. Hamari, J., Koivisto, J., Sarsa, H.: Does gamification work?-a literature review of empirical studies on gamification. In: 2014 47th Hawaii International Conference on System Sciences (HICSS), pp. 3025–3034. IEEE (2014)
5. Hara, K., Azenkot, S., Campbell, M., Bennett, C.L., Le, V., Pannella, S., Moore, R., Minckler, K., Ng, R.H., Froehlich, J.E.: Improving public transit accessibility for blind riders by crowdsourcing bus stop landmark locations with google street view: an extended analysis. ACM Trans. Access. Comput. (TACCESS) 6(2), 5 (2015)
6. Hara, K., Le, V., Froehlich, J.: Combining crowdsourcing and google street view to identify street-level accessibility problems. In: Proceedings of the SIGCHI Conference on Human Factors in Computing Systems, pp. 631–640. ACM (2013)
7. Klettner, S., Huang, H., Schmidt, M., Gartner, G., Buchroithner, M., Prechtel, N., Burghardt, D.: Acquisition and cartographic applications of subjective geodata. In: Cartography from Pole to Pole: Selected Contributions to the XXVIth International Conference of the ICA, Dresden 2013 (2014)
8. Mooney, P., Corcoran, P.: Characteristics of heavily edited objects in openstreetmap. Future Internet 4(1), 285–305 (2012)
9. Sammer, G., Uhlmann, T., Unbehaun, W., Millonig, A., Mandl, B., Dangschat, J., Mayr, R.: Identification of mobility-impaired persons and analysis of their travel behavior and needs. Transp. Res. Rec.: J. Transp. Res. Board 2320, 46–54 (2012)
10. See, L., Comber, A., Salk, C., Fritz, S., van der Velde, M., Perger, C., Schill, C., McCallum, I., Kraxner, F., Obersteiner, M.: Comparing the quality of crowdsourced data contributed by expert and non-experts. PLoS ONE 8(7), e69958 (2013)
11. Zeng, L., Kühn, R., Weber, G.: Improvement in environmental accessibility via volunteered geographic information: a case study. Universal Access in the Information Society, pp. 1–11 (2016)

Dual-Mode User Interfaces for Web Based Interactive 3D Virtual Environments Using Three.js

Matthew Stanton[1], Thomas Hartley[2(✉)], Fernando Loizides[2],
and Adam Worrallo[2]

[1] Maths and Computer Science Department,
University of Wolverhampton, Wolverhampton, UK
macast.web@gmail.com
[2] Emerging Interactive Technologies Lab & Maths and Computer
Science Department, University of Wolverhampton, Wolverhampton, UK
{t.hartley2,fernando.loizides,A.Worrallo}@wlv.ac.uk

Abstract. 3D objects are now being embedded within HTML pages without the
need for additional software, such as browser plug-ins. However, 2D and 3D web
content are still typically treated as separate entities with limited interaction. Our
research presents a working prototype implementation of a dual-mode user
interface for interactive 3D environments. The developed interface allows the user
to instantly switch between a traditional hypertext interface and an immersive 3D
environment that incorporates 2D HTML elements. The results from an initial
user study show that 2D and dual-mode interfaces allow for quicker retrieval of
information than 3D websites alone and result in higher user satisfaction.

Keywords: Dual-Mode user interfaces · 3D web · Three.js

1 Introduction

Innovations in web technology (e.g. HTML5 and WebGL) are allowing for advanced
3D graphics to be integrated and rendered directly in a web page without the need for
additional software, such as browser plug-ins. However, there are currently no standard
approaches to effectively combining traditional 2D web content, such as text and
images with interactive 3D environments. Furthermore, while 3D graphics provide a
more immersive and richer user experience; they also have the potential to inhibit the
user because they add additional user interface interactions. For example, 3D environments require a user to interact with content via a viewport and typically require a
user to navigate to a location to retrieve information. This slows down a user's ability
to complete common web tasks, such as retrieval of textual information. In this paper,
we present a prototype implementation of a dual-mode approach to interface design for
information dissemination in interactive 3D environments using Three.js, a WebGL 3D

---

https://threejs.org/

© IFIP International Federation for Information Processing 2017
Published by Springer International Publishing AG 2017. All Rights Reserved
R. Bernhaupt et al. (Eds.): INTERACT 2017, Part IV, LNCS 10516, pp. 441–444, 2017.
DOI: 10.1007/978-3-319-68059-0_47

graphics JavaScript library. A web-based interactive digital heritage application is created that allows a user to switch instantaneously between 2D and 3D user interfaces. We also present a user study to identify the initial effectiveness of the prototype.

2 Background and Related Work

Advanced 3D graphics are increasingly being used in web applications in a variety of areas [1], such as digital heritage [2, 3], surgical training and museum exhibitions. However, the use of interactive 3D web environments for web content is still limited, despite the availability of modern graphics hardware. A key reason for this limited use is the lack of integration between traditional 2D content and 3D environments [2]. Often 3D applications, such as virtual museums focus on graphics, immersion, and interactivity rather than traditional web tasks such as the locating and viewing of information. Interactive 3D web environments need a more integrated approach to 3D and 2D content if they are to see greater adoption.

Seo, Yoo and Ko [1, 4] explore how 3D objects and 2D HTML elements can be more tightly integrated by having HTML elements exist within 3D space and associating them with the 3D objects they are referencing. Jankowski and Decker [5] propose a dual-mode user interface where a user can switch between a hypertext mode and a 3D mode at any time. The hypertext mode incorporates 3D objects alongside hypertext based interactions. The 3D mode adds hypertext annotations to a 3D scene. Their results show that the dual-mode user interface had the "best overall task performance" when compared to hypertext and 3D alone. However, while the dual-mode was rated the highest overall, the hypertext UI was rated "easier to learn" than the 3D UI and dual-mode UI. Participants also found that presentation and readability of text in the 3D UI was worse when compared to the dual-mode and hypertext UI. There were also improvements suggested by the testers, which included a preference towards a keyboard control system in addition to the mouse control system that was already in place. Searching for content was not available in the dual-mode UI, meaning that searching for content on a webpage, commonly performed by pressing Ctrl+F on a Windows PC, could not be performed and therefore slowed down the retrieval of data. Despite these limitations, the dual-mode user interface was the clear winner, both practically, aesthetically, and preferably [5].

3 System Description

The prototype system implements a digital heritage application in the form of a 1960s diner. The application allows a user to explore a recreation of a 1960s diner and objects that might be found in a diner of this era, such as a juke box and pinball machine. The prototype system was implemented using HTML5, CSS3, JavaScript and WebGL via the Three.js JavaScript library. Three applications were created, a "2D Website", which is a 'flat' web page, that contains 3D renders of the objects in the diner, as shown in Fig. 1 left. The second application, shown in Fig. 1 right, is a "3D Website" implemented using Three.js. It contains a 3D diner that the user can explore and interact with specific objects. When the user is within the vicinity of an object 2D textual information is presented. Finally, a "Dual-Mode Website" was implemented which combines both the "2D Website" and "3D Website" together, enabling users to switch between the two websites by pressing the "2" and "3" keys on the keyboard, respectively. The dual-mode website has the added functionality of seamless transitions between modes.

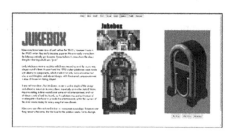

Fig. 1. Left - "2D Website", which allows a user to select a tab at the top, and then learn about each component of the diner, complete with 3D rendered images. Right - "3D Website" which allows the user to interact with objects to display information.

4   Testing

The prototype testing focused on measuring the speed at which information could be retrieved using the three applications to assess the effectiveness of the user interface. In the 2D mode participants were required to retrieve the answer using standard hypertext and mouse click interactions. In the 3D interface participants had to navigate the 3D environment to retrieve information from information boards. In the dual-mode the user could switch between user interfaces at any point; however, the questions in the "Dual-Mode" encouraged the user to return to 3D mode to avoid them simply staying in the 2D mode. Each question was timed from the moment the user made interaction with the application after reading the question and the timer was stopped the moment the participant finished writing their answer. Once the speed tests were complete, participants were asked to fill out a questionnaire which would measure their satisfaction with each application and how much they agreed with a series of statements on a Likert Scale that targeted the user interface, the aesthetics, the performance, the ease at which information could be retrieved and the simplicity of switching modes. To test the prototype, we recruited 11 participants. Each participant was given a brief description of the experiment, a consent form, and a short pre-study questionnaire before the testing to establish the participants' profile. Following the testing participants were given a post-study questionnaire. The questionnaire asked each participant to state how much they agreed with statements relating to the user interface, the ease at which information could be obtained, how aesthetically pleasing the applications were and the website's performance. The ratings are calculated by scoring a 1 for "Strongly Disagree", 2 for "Disagree", 3 for "Neutral, 4 for "Agree" and 5 for "Strongly Disagree".

The results from the prototype testing indicate that the 2D website achieved the highest rating for the user interface, with the dual-mode website only one point lower.

The ease at which information could be found was rated the highest on the dual-mode website, with the 2D website close behind. The 3D website was regarded as the most aesthetically pleasing and the 2D Website was considered to have the best performance. These results will inform the progression of the research and development process. It was clear that both the 2D and dual-mode websites were close in every test, as well as the feedback that was given about them, and it was made apparent that the 3D website lacked in all but one area, obtaining lower satisfaction ratings, as well as lower speed test times. These findings are comparable to the research by Jankowski and Decker [5], who identified that their dual-mode applications are easier and more efficient than 2D or 3D interfaces alone [5].

5   Conclusions and Future Work

We have presented a dual-mode user interface to enhance user interaction with web content when presented in conjunction with 3D virtual environments. This pilot study has shown the promise of dual-mode interfaces for 3D virtual environments. Future work will improve the dual-mode interface by integrating the 3D view more closely with the 2D view and expand the 2D annotations within the 3D content. We will also expand the scope of the study to fully assess the merits of dual-mode interfaces.

References

1. Seo, D., Yoo, B., Ko, H.: Web3D 2015 Proceedings of the 20th International Conference on 3D Web Technology. ACM, New York (2015)
2. Kukka, H., Ojala, T.: mobileDOK: culture in your pocket. In: Mobility 2006 Proceedings of the 3rd International Conference on Mobile Technology, Applications & Systems. ACM, New York (2006)
3. Barreau, J.B., Gaugne, R., Bernard, Y., Cloirec, G.L., Gouranton, V.: Virtual reality tools for the west digital conservatory of archaeological heritage. In: VRIC 2014 Proceedings of the 2014 Virtual Reality International Conference. ACM, New York (2014)
4. Seo, D., Yoo, B., Choi, J., Ko, H.: Webizing 3D contents for super multiview autostereoscopic displays with varying display profiles. In: Web3D 2016 Proceedings of the 21st International Conference on Web3D Technology, pp. 155–163 (2016)
5. Jankowski, J., Decker, S.: On the design of a Dual-Mode User Interface for accessing 3D content on the World Wide Web. Int. J. Hum Comput Stud. **71**, 838–857 (2013)

Fine-Grained Privacy Setting Prediction Using a Privacy Attitude Questionnaire and Machine Learning

Frederic Raber, Felix Kosmalla[(✉)], and Antonio Krueger

DFKI, Saarland Informatics Campus, Saarbrücken, Germany
{frederic.raber,felix.kosmalla,krueger}@dfki.de

Abstract. This paper proposes to recommend privacy settings to users of social networks (SNs) depending on the topic of the post. Based on the answers to a specifically designed questionnaire, machine learning is utilized to inform a user privacy model. The model then provides, for each post, an individual recommendation to which groups of other SN users the post in question should be disclosed. We conducted a pre-study to find out which friend groups typically exist and which topics are discussed. We explain the concept of the machine learning approach, and demonstrate in a validation study that the generated privacy recommendations are precise and perceived as highly plausible by SN users.

1 Introduction

The tradeoff between privacy and utility in a social network (SN) has been a research problem from the beginning, since SNs are largely used in public. Still, there is no acceptable solution that provides an optimal tradeoff between privacy and utility while keeping the user burden at a minimum. Social network providers tried to tackle this problem by introducing *friend* lists or *circles*. Users create one or more lists containing a subset of their online friends, and publish a new post exactly to the people inside these lists. Still, the SN users have the burden of manually setting the appropriate privacy setting for each of these groups in order to achieve a perfect privacy setting. Recent studies have shown that only 17% of all posted content is shared using friend lists [5].

We argue that every single post needs its own privacy setting, and should only be disclosed to a specific list of users, depending on the *topic* of the post. To decrease the user burden, the privacy settings should be derived automatically, for example by using a machine learning approach. Although most social networks like Facebook or Google+ only allow a binary decision on the privacy settings (e.g. to disclose or not), we think that a user decision on privacy is a decision that is not ultimately binary. A SN user does not only think "I do not at all want my drinking buddies to know that I am a ballet dancer as a hobby" or "I would really like my co-dancers to see the pictures of that ballet contest". There are also some groups of people, like university friends, where a user would

© IFIP International Federation for Information Processing 2017
Published by Springer International Publishing AG 2017. All Rights Reserved
R. Bernhaupt et al. (Eds.): INTERACT 2017, Part IV, LNCS 10516, pp. 445–449, 2017.
DOI: 10.1007/978-3-319-68059-0_48

say "It is OK if they see it. I do not want to completely cut them off from that information, but I also do not want to draw too much attention to it". In this case, the user would take some middle road, for example by sharing the post and the pictures with the university friends, but hiding them from their timelines.

2 Related Work

Several publications in the past have offered questionnaires to capture privacy attitudes. Starting with Westin scales [3] as a very general form of questionnaire, newer questionnaires like the IUIPC [4] provide a very specific privacy attitude regarding privacy towards online companies. Wisniewski et al. [10] created a privacy scale to observe how social connectedness corresponds with a user's privacy desires on a social network, which we also included in our questionnaire.

There are also other systems that use machine learning for the prediction of privacy settings, for example by labeling some of the friends with privacy permissions and using a supervised learning approach [2,6,7]. Other approaches additionally take the post content into account, by using latent Dirichlet allocation (LDA) and maximum entropy to predict settings for a new post based on the privacy settings chosen in earlier posts [8]. Although the idea seems promising, research has shown that privacy behavior in online social networks does not correspond to actual privacy desires; this is known as the privacy paradox [1]. We therefore decided to capture the privacy attitude using a distinct privacy questionnaire rather than trying to extract it from the user's SN behavior. Furthermore, all approaches so far rely on a binary decision (disclose/undisclose) for a privacy setting, whereas our approach offers five distinct privacy levels.

3 Approach

In a final implementation of our approach, the post topic is extracted and shown on the left side in Fig. 1, while the proposed privacy settings for a selection of friend groups are displayed on the right side. As stated in the introduction, the proposed privacy settings are not only disclose/undisclose, but five different privacy levels as follows: On level 1, everything is disclosed and shown on the wall. Level 2 means the content does not appear on the recipients' news wall, whereas level 3 completely hides comments and graphical content. Level 4 hides the entire post, and level 5 also hides it from the recipient's direct friends, so it cannot be propagated to him by word of mouth. What exactly is hidden, is denoted by the small pictograms next to each friend group.

For suggesting the permissions, we use a machine learning technique called ridge regression. As input features, we use the measures calculated from the answers to the aforementioned two questionnaires [4,10] and the topic of the post, or only the questionnaire answers (called "generic" in Table 1). As an output, we receive for every friend group a privacy level between 1 and 5.

We performed three user studies to first find out which topics are most frequently discussed in people's social activities (online and offline) and which friend

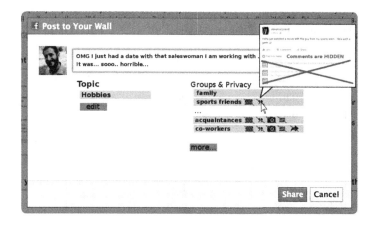

Fig. 1. Envisioned user interface concept of a privacy setting prediction system.

groups exist; second, to gather training data for the machine learning algorithm and to validate its precision; and third, to validate the approach in a scenario as realistic as possible, introducing the proposed settings of our machine learning prediction to Facebook users. All studies were performed using online questionnaires; participants were recruited using *prolific academic*, an online recruiting portal similar to Amazon Mechanical Turk.

For the first, we asked 15 participants to list their friend groups and most frequently discussed topics in their social life in a free-text form. We merged the answers using an axial coding approach [9]. The most frequent topics were (in descending order) family affairs, events, movies, politics, food, work, hobbies, travel, music and sports. The friend groups that were mentioned most frequently were extended and immediate family, work friends, close friends, acquaintances and school/university as well as online and sports friends.

In the second study ("main study"), we let 100 participants first answer the two aforementioned questionnaires, followed by a matrix where they had to enter a privacy level for each topic/friend group pair. We trained and validated the regression with a ten-fold cross validation. The mean squared error (MSE) between the prediction and the actual result can be found in Table 1.

For the third study, called the "validation study", we again let 31 persons fill out the two privacy questionnaires in the first part. But this time, we let them copy and paste ten of their own Facebook posts that match our list of topics, and enter the topic of the post into the questionnaire. The website then proposed a privacy setting, using the ridge regression trained with the data of the former study. The participants were asked to adapt the settings if needed, and answer on a five-point Likert scale whether they would use the system on Facebook. Again we calculated the mean squared error between the adapted and the proposed settings. 67% of the participants stated that they would likely or very likely use our system, supporting the design of our approach. The results in Table 1 show that the trends are similar for both studies: For almost all topics,

Table 1. Amount of posts and mean squared error for the selected topics with machine learning in the main and the validation study.

Topic	Main study	Validation study	
	Mean squared error	*Mean squared error*	*# posts*
Family	0.87	0.93	38
Events	0.91	0.85	24
Movies	0.91	0.26	23
Politics	1.05	0.91	14
Food	0.88	0.46	28
Work	1.00	1.17	18
Hobbies	0.83	0.86	29
Travel	0.88	0.64	17
Sports	1.31	0.6	22
Generic	0.96	0.78	230

we can achieve a mean squared error less than one. Hobbies, travel and family are predicted best, whereas sports and politics are hardest to predict; maybe because of the diverse nature of sports, where the exact sport affects whether it is likely to be shared or not. Posts about football are more common and socially accepted than posts about ballet, for example. Politics and work are also hard to predict by privacy attitude; this could be caused by the fact that here, the political interest or the job itself affects whether you want to share your thoughts, rather than a pure privacy attitude. A professor is more likely to share his work with a community than a cleaner would be.

4   Lessons Learned and Future Work

We did background research to find friend groups and topics that are present in people's online and offline social life, and conducted two studies to find out whether it is possible to propose fine-grained privacy settings based on privacy attitude and the topic of the post. We tested and evaluated in two different scenarios: In the main study, users had no proposed setting, and had to enter their desired setting without support. In contrast to this, they had a proposed setting they had to adapt in the validation study. In both cases, we achieved an acceptable precision for most of the topics. Nevertheless, there are some topics like work and politics that seem not to depend on the privacy attitude, but rather on the actual occupation or political interest of the person.

Instead of a binary decision, our approach supports five privacy levels of disclosure, which offer to show only parts of the post to some friend groups, such as only the textual content without images or comments. For this study, we used an example implementation of the privacy levels. In future work, we would like to conduct further studies to determine which parts of the post users would hide depending on the post's sensitivity, and how an optimal implementation of the levels looks. Finally, we would like to offer a prototype of the proposed interface as a Facebook plugin, to be able to check whether the achieved prediction precision is sufficient for everyday use, and whether the tool is accepted by users.

References

1. Barnes, S.B.: A privacy paradox: social networking in the united states. First Monday **11**(9) (2006). http://firstmonday.org/ojs/index.php/fm/article/view/1394
2. Fang, L., LeFevre, K.: Privacy wizards for social networking sites. In: Proceedings of the 19th International Conference on World Wide Web, WWW 2010, NY, USA, pp. 351–360 (2010). doi:10.1145/1772690.1772727
3. Kumaraguru, P., Cranor, L.F.: Privacy Indexes: A Survey of Westin's Studies. Technical report CMU-ISRI-5-138, Institute for Software Research International, School of Computer Science, Carnegie Mellon University, Pittsburgh, PA, December 2005
4. Malhotra, N.K., Kim, S.S., Agarwal, J.: Internet users' information privacy concerns (iuipc): the construct, the scale, and a causal model. Info. Sys. Res. **15**(4), 336–355 (2004). doi:10.1287/isre.1040.0032
5. Mondal, M., Liu, Y., Viswanath, B., Gummadi, K.P., Mislove, A.: Understanding and specifying social access control lists. In: Symposium On Usable Privacy and Security (SOUPS 2014), pp. 271–283. USENIX Association, Menlo Park, (July 2014). https://www.usenix.org/conference/soups2014/proceedings/presentation/mondal
6. Shehab, M., Cheek, G., Touati, H., Squicciarini, A., Cheng, P.C.: User centric policy management in online social networks. In: 2010 IEEE International Symposium on Policies for Distributed Systems and Networks (POLICY), pp. 9–13, (July 2010)
7. Shehab, M., Touati, H.: Semi-supervised policy recommendation for online social networks. In: Proceedings of the 2012 International Conference on Advances in Social Networks Analysis and Mining (ASONAM 2012), ASONAM 2012, pp. 360–36 (2012). doi:10.1109/ASONAM.2012.66
8. Sinha, A., Li, Y., Bauer, L.: What you want is not what you get: predicting sharing policies for text-based content on facebook. In: Proceedings of the 2013 ACM Workshop on Artificial Intelligence and Security, AISec 2013, NY, USA, pp. 13–24 (2013). doi:10.1145/2517312.2517317
9. Strauss, A., Corbin, J.M.: Basics of Qualitative Research : Techniques and Procedures for Developing Grounded Theory. SAGE Publications, Thousand Oaks (1998). http://www.amazon.co.uk/exec/obidos/ASIN/0803959400/citeulike-21
10. Wisniewski, P., Islam, A.N., Knijnenburg, B.P., Patil, S.: Give social network users the privacy they want. In: Proceedings of the 18th ACM Conference on Computer Supported Cooperative Work #38; Social Computing, CSCW 2015, NY, USA, pp. 1427–1441 (2015). doi:10.1145/2675133.2675256

Interactive Reading Using Low Cost Brain Computer Interfaces

Fernando Loizides[1(✉)], Liam Naughton[1,2], Paul Wilson[1],
Michael Loizou[1], Shufan Yang[1], Thomas Hartley[1], Adam Worrallo[1],
and Panayiotis Zaphiris[2]

[1] Emerging Interactive Technologies Lab and Maths and Computer
Science Department, University of Wolverhampton, Wolverhampton, UK
{fernando.loizides, L.Naughton,
PaulJWilson, Michael.Loizou2, S.Yang, T.Hartley2,
a.worrallo}@wlv.ac.uk
[2] Cyprus Interaction Lab Department of Multimedia and Graphic Arts,
Cyprus University of Technology, Limassol, Cyprus
panayiotis.zaphiris@cut.ac.cy

Abstract. This work shows the feasibility for document reader user applications using a consumer grade non-invasive BCI headset. Although Brain Computer Interface (BCI) type devices are beginning to aim at the consumer level, the level at which they can actually detect brain activity is limited. There is however progress achieved in allowing for interaction between a human and a computer when this interaction is limited to around 2 actions. We employed the Emotiv Epoc, a low-priced BCI headset, to design and build a proof-of-concept document reader system that allows users to navigate the document using this low cast BCI device. Our prototype has been implemented and evaluated with 12 participants who were trained to navigate documents using signals acquired by Emotive Epoc.

Keywords: Document reader · Brain computer interface · Document navigation

1 Introduction

Brain Computer Interfaces (BCIs) offer a way of communicating electrical activity produced by a user's thoughts and intents to a machine. Different actions (and specifically action intents – which is the intention or desire to stimulate an action) are associated with different patterns of electrical activity. Affordable brain-computer interface type technology has only recently become accessible to users with limited and experimental software. The effect of a brain computer interface is primarily to introduce another level of multimodality to a user. In this work, we utilize an affordable, non-intrusive BCI type device to investigate the efficacy of allowing motion restricted elementary control over a document reader. By detecting signals from the Emotiv Epoc and mapping the cognitive functions to physical actions, users are able to navigate through a document without any movement from their limbs. We situate the reader

© IFIP International Federation for Information Processing 2017
Published by Springer International Publishing AG 2017. All Rights Reserved
R. Bernhaupt et al. (Eds.): INTERACT 2017, Part IV, LNCS 10516, pp. 450–454, 2017.
DOI: 10.1007/978-3-319-68059-0_49

with background and related work. We then present the prototype and the user study description followed by the results and discussion.

2 Background and Related Work

A brain computer interface (BCI) device provides a new channel for communication and control [1, 2]. Traditionally BCI related research is based on expensive and complex prototypes such as the Graz Brain-Computer Interface II [3, 4]. The cost for conducting research using EEG based BCI devices has generally been high and using such equipment often requires the assistance of specially trained experts [5, 6]. During the last decade, more affordable/consumer BCI devices have become available and they have begun to be used for academic research purposes. These include for example the Neurosky Mindset Headset, used to enhance cognitive functions and increase satisfaction within a game called 'Neuro Wander' [7]; the Myndplay Brainband, used to elicit different mind states of participants viewing emotional videos [8]; and the OpenBCI system, used for investigating optimal electrode placement for motor imagery applications [9]. The Emotiv Epoc device is inexpensive, commercially available and has been used extensively in the past for similar types of research with good results [10]. Stytsenko et al. reported that Epoc was "able to acquire real EEG data which is comparable to the one acquired by using conservative EEG devices" [11]. It is noted that Emotiv measures EEG signal and ambiguous EMG at the same time [11]. However, in this work we aim to illustrate the use of the Emotive Epoc to operate the document navigation software and therefore focus on the interactivity capability rather than the clarity of the signal.

3 System Description

The prototype system architecture consists of four key components (See Fig. 1: Left). These are: (a) Emotiv Epoc Headset (b) EmoKey Software (c) Epoc Control Panel (d) MindReader Software. The Emotiv Epoc Headset is used to receive raw data from the individual and send the signal to the Epoc Control Panel. The BCI contains 14 channels. It uses a sequential sampling rate of 2048 Hz, a bandwidth of 0.2–43 Hz, digital notch filters (at 50 Hz and 60 Hz) and a dynamic range of 8400 μV(pp). The P300 evoked potential causes a 300 ms delay after a relevant sensory stimulus. The **Control Panel** then clears the noise and separates distinct and recognizable pattern actions such as "think push", "think pull", "think lift", "smile" and "Clench". Upon detecting one of the selected patterns that constitute a specific action, the control panel then triggers the (customized) Emokey Software. **Emokey Software** translates the user actions to physical keyboard keystrokes. In turn, keystrokes are detected by the MindReader Software which instigates navigational actions on the document reader.

Our prototype software **MindReader** is written in C# through WinForms under the .NET framework. The specific release (Beta V.01) presented in the paper and used for the user testing comprises of a document reader that loads a series of documents that have been translated to images from PDFs. In this work, the MindReader software

Fig. 1. (left) Key components to operate MindReader system (centre) MindReader beta version (right) User interacting with MindReader

produces a two page reading format (See Fig. 1: Centre) for the user but can also be adapted to a single page view. The software in its current beta form allows for user testing controls; namely, the investigator can imitate a "start task" trigger which will take readings such as location, navigation speed and user intent (actions performed). The software is also able to use simple key strokes or buttons to move between the pages but these are only visible as an addition for future work involving the integration of eye-tracking equipment with BCI devices. Users are able to navigate forward and backward one page at a time, controlled by the Emotiv Epoc.

4   Testing

To test the prototype we recruited 14 participants; 2 of which acted as pilot subjects. The 12 main participants (5 female, 7 male) were given a bill of rights and consent form before the testing. The participants were then given a short description of the experiment and each was given a choice of actions that they could choose from in order to calibrate the forward and backward actions. Specifically, participants could choose from "Think Push", "Think Pull", "Lift", "Clench" and "Smile". Once the participant had chosen a set of actions, they would then be calibrated to the specific individual, a process that took no more than 5 min per participant (See Fig. 1: Right). Once the BCI connection was established and calibrated, our prototype software, MindReader was loaded with a document containing 16 pages in a two page view (book style view) and the participants were then given a set of tasks to complete. Usually interfaces are tested with the participants using think-aloud comments as to what they are thinking and what is happening. For the specific evaluation, no think–aloud comments were permitted so as to not influence and skew the results. After the tasks a semi-structured interview was conducted for qualitative feedback. The tasks were (1) Navigate to the Contents Page – this was page 1 (2) Navigate back to the beginning – page 0 - (3) Navigate to Page 6 (4) Navigate back to the beginning (5) Navigate to Page 12 (6) Navigate back to the beginning (7) Navigate to the last Page (8) Navigate back to the beginning (9) Answer the question:

Table 1. Data overview (including time and errors)

Task	Number error free	Number errors	Minimum time (seconds)	Maximum time (seconds)
1	9	1	2	8
2	7	5	2	7
5	8	9	8	29
6	8	4	7	41
7	8	18	8	40
8	11	1	8	50

How many babies do female goats give birth to? - the answer is on page- (10) Feel free to browse the magazine (for qualitative feedback). Table 1 presents an overview of the tasks and the time taken, as well as the errors that were made in taking the tasks.

5 Conclusions and Future Work

We present a prototype of a document reader using affordable BCI to control elementary functions. A pilot test with 14 participants provided feedback of the efficacy of using this affordable BCI to control the elementary navigation of a document reader and acted as a cycle in our user centered design process. Our experiment results demonstrate that participants can navigate through the pages of a document reader in order, although minimal calibration is needed and errors were present (such as overshooting pages). We were able to also identify some potential limitations, for example, increased number of pages in a document increases the navigational effort and fatigue and increases the error rate (a limitation that needs to be addressed using improved interaction). Specifically, the future work will aim to (a) reduce errors through improving the software algorithms and by testing further hardware variations; (b) answer behavioral and interactivity questions such as "Is getting further in the document of proportional effort to getting to an earlier page?" We also plan to include further compliments to the setup that will give richer interaction to the users, such as pairing the BCI with an eye-tracker for gaze fixation recognition.

References

1. Guger, C., et al.: How many people are able to operate an EEG-based brain-computer interface (BCI)? IEEE Trans. Neural Syst. Rehabil. Eng. **11**(2), 145–147 (2003)
2. Mühl, C., et al.: Which factors drive successful BCI skill learning? In: 6th International BCI Conference (2014)
3. Maynard, E.M., Nordhausen, C.T., Normann, R.A.: The utah intracortical electrode array: a recording structure for potential brain-computer interfaces. Electroencephalogr. Clin. Neurophysiol. **102**(3), 228–239 (1997)
4. Kalcher, J., et al.: Graz brain-computer interface II: towards communication between humans and computers based on online classification of three different EEG patterns. Med. Biol. Eng. Compu. **34**(5), 382–388 (1996)

5. Blankertz, B., et al.: The Berlin brain-computer interface: EEG-based communication without subject training. IEEE Trans. Neural Syst. Rehabil. Eng. **14**(2), 147–152 (2006)

6. McFarland, D.J., Todd Lefkowicz, A., Wolpaw, J.R.: Design and operation of an EEG-based brain-computer interface with digital signal processing technology. Behav. Res. Methods Instrum. Comput. **29**(3), 337–345 (1997)

7. Yoh, M.-S., Kwon, J., Kim, S.: NeuroWander: a BCI game in the form of interactive fairy tale. In: Proceedings of the 12th ACM International Conference Adjunct Papers on Ubiquitous Computing-Adjunct. ACM (2010)

8. Man, J.: Analysing emotional video using consumer EEG hardware. In: Kurosu, M. (ed.) HCI 2014. LNCS, vol. 8511, pp. 729–738. Springer, Cham (2014). doi:10.1007/978-3-319-07230-2_69

9. Suryotrisongko, H., Samopa, F.: Evaluating OpenBCI Spiderclaw V1 headwear's electrodes placements for brain-computer interface (BCI) motor imagery application. Proc. Comput. Sci. **72**, 398–405 (2015)

10. Andujar, M., Gilbert, J.E.: Let's learn!: enhancing user's engagement levels through passive brain-computer interfaces. In: CHI 2013 Extended Abstracts on Human Factors in Computing Systems. ACM (2013)

11. Taylor, G.S., Schmidt, C.: Empirical evaluation of the Emotiv EPOC BCI headset for the detection of mental actions. Proc. Hum. Factors Ergon. Soc. Ann. Meeting **56**(1), 193–197 (2012). SAGE Publications

Investigating Control of Virtual Reality Snowboarding Simulator Using a Wii FiT Board

Rhiannon Wood[1], Fernando Loizides[2(✉)], Thomas Hartley[2],
and Adam Worrallo[2]

[1] Maths and Computer Science Department,
University of Wolverhampton, Wolverhampton, UK
rtylaw@outlook.com
[2] Emerging Interactive Technologies Lab & Maths and Computer
Science Department, University of Wolverhampton, Wolverhampton, UK
{Fernando.loizides,t.hartley2,A.Worrallo}@wlv.ac.uk

Abstract. This work presents a virtual reality snowboarding application which uses a Nintendo Wii balance board for richer interaction modalities. We present the application and test the prototype with 7 participants to investigate immersion, enjoyability and to an extent performance. The outcomes from the study will be used to start forming research directions and questions to indicate likely research and development directions for future research.

Keywords: Virtual reality · Snowboarding · HMD · Wii FiT board

1 Introduction and Motivation

Modern gaming is a competitive and continuously evolving area with companies constantly looking for innovations. With technology in the gaming industry moving more and more towards multimodal interaction, it is unsurprising that virtual reality head mounted displays are being revisited despite previous failings in the gaming industry during the 1980s and 1990s (for example one of the earliest virtual reality headsets in the domestic gaming market was the Virtual Boy, released by Nintendo in 1995). Technology advancements allow for both simulations and more interactive and immersive games to be created in a virtual reality setting, with better graphics and realism. Furthermore, the advancement of multimodal interaction techniques becoming more ubiquitous permits the integration of novel interaction within the experience.

With this principle and momentum in mind, we developed and present the initial stages of a prototype snowboarding system using virtual reality. By extending control to more than a standard game controller, we begin to experiment with improving the realism within a game. In order to make an environment to be experienced as 'real' two conditions must be met: immersion and presence [1]. Witmer and Singer [2] describe presence as the feeling of being in a particular environment or location when you're physically in another. Essentially, higher levels of presence means the player feel more a part of the game they're playing; something game developers continue to strive for as

R. Bernhaupt et al. (Eds.): INTERACT 2017, Part IV, LNCS 10516, pp. 455–458, 2017.
DOI: 10.1007/978-3-319-68059-0_50

they develop games. Many factors can affect presence, such as human and technological. A talk about virtual reality at Steam Dev Days [3] highlighted several standards that virtual reality headsets need to meet in order to achieve a high level of presence. The first is field of view, a high field of view is necessary for headsets to be able to mimic a real scene with a high level of presence. The second is high resolution. This is where head mounted displays face some issues. Due to having a wider field of view the pixels are magnified, the per-degree pixel density of a device like the Oculus Rift is serious set-back. Technological progress has been rapidly developing and so work advocating for the slow improvement in this area may not be as accurate as previously though [4].

To simulate a snowboarding task and enhance the user experience we developed a prototype that allows the user to control input via a Wii Fit board. Beyond presenting the prototype, we present findings from a pilot test involving 7 participants which give insights into different experience factors and supply us with material to reflect on from the first test in a user centered design approach. We also recognize other limitations when interacting in virtual reality; namely, that users also experience side effects such as nausea and headaches, overall making for a very poor experience, both as a virtual reality device and in general [5]. We are sensitive to the fact that adding another dimension such as the balance board to control the interaction may also add to these effects.

2 Prototype

The developed prototype is a simple snowboarding game where the player snowboards downhill toward a goal and repeats this process over three laps with their performance being timed in the top right corner. We implemented control by a Nintendo Wii Balance Board as a controller in an attempt to mimic a snowboard. The player is constantly being propelled forward both by gravity and extra momentum being programmed into the game. By transferring their weight the player can move themselves left and right in the game and jumping on the board will also jump in the game.

The user's virtual self materializes on the top of a snowy slope and is propelled forward, having obstacles such as rocks and trees to overcome by sliding left and right. Movement is also encouraged by curves in the track. A pitfall jump is also present in the level which makes the user have to produce a jump action successfully to overcome (See Fig. 1).

3 User Testing

A pilot test was carried out to progress the prototype as per our user-centred design methodology. The experiment was run on an Oculus Rift DK2 headset. The DK2 has an OLED display which contains 3 different sensors, a magnetometer, gyroscope and accelerometer. The native resolution is 1920×1080 or 960×1080 for each eye. The display has an overall field of vision of $100°$ and a max refresh rate of 75 Hz. The HMD weighs 0.95 lb. The test involved 12 individuals that use the prototype and HMD in one condition as well as a screen and keyboard for a second condition. None of the participants had experience using an HMD. To reduce bias, 6 participants were

Fig. 1. Different scenes from the snowboarding experience

introduced to the HMD version first while the other 6 participants the screen and keyboard version. We then interviewed for qualitative feedback while recording some qualitative measures, not to make a statistical relevance calculation but to receive preliminary information to guide further research and development direction.

Time Performance. The times for each play through were recorded and the results indicated towards player performance to be improved with the HMD. The average time with the HMD was 6:07 min and the average time without the HMD is 7:50 min there is a notable difference.

The participants commented on increased **enjoyability and 'fun'** using the HMD as opposed to the screen and keyboard. The HMD scored an average of 8.2/10 while 6.8 without. One note is there's the possibility of the higher rate of enjoyment with the HMD to be due to the novelty of using a virtual reality headset. The balance board was also given mention and appeared to be fairly popular with people stating they enjoyed how it controls similar to a real snowboard.

In terms of **perceived difficulty** in control there did not seem to be a noticeable difference between the comments received between the HMD condition and the keyboard scenario. We direct the reader to Lugrin et al. [6] whose research found that even in the situations where players performed worse with the HMD due to difficulty, they still enjoyed it more. The main comments from the interviews which related to difficulty in the HMD condition was the Wii Fit board, with participants reporting difficulty balancing on the board. There was also mention of the HMD making the balance problems worse due to participants being unable to see their feet.

Immersion was rated higher on the HMD, both in the comments as well as scoring, 6.4/10 for the HMD scenario and 4.4/10 for the screen and keyboard. Positive HMD comments included being "able to look around the scene", "having the screen covering the eyes" and "blocking external distractions".

Lastly, players were asked about any **negative side effects** they experienced from the HMD and balance board combination. Whilst there were no issues with most participants, one player experienced disorientation, balance issues and slight nausea.

Feedback for improvements was limited, with the only suggestion made to be able to adjust your speed, (i.e. going faster or slower) at will rather than a constant speed.

4   Conclusions and Future Work

The work presents the initial stages of research into creating an affordable virtual reality snowboarding simulation using feet control. A prototype level was created and tested with 12 participants which produced positive qualitative feedback to progress the development. Future work is aiming to create a much larger scope of levels and challenges, improve the realistic tracks of the environment and also allow for body tracking using a Kinect sensor to produce a within simulation body movement for the user, thus increasing the feel of immersion.

References

1. Eichenberg, C.: Application of virtual realities in psychotherapy: possibilities, limitations and effectiveness. In: Virtual reality, pp. 481–496. InTech, Rijeka (2011)
2. Witmer, B., Singer, M.: Measuring Presence in Virtual Environments: A Presence Questionnaire, 1st edn. U.S. Army Research Institute for the Behavioral and Social Sciences, Orlando (2016). http://webstaff.itn.liu.se/~matco/TNM053/Papers/presence.pdf. Accessed 9 May 2016
3. Abrash, M.: What VR could, should, and almost certainly will be within two years (2016). http://media.steampowered.com/apps/abrashblog/Abrash%20Dev%20Days%202014.pdf. Accessed 9 May 2016
4. Fenlon, W.: The Promise and Challenges of Head-Mounted Virtual Reality Displays. Tested (2013) http://www.tested.com/tech/gaming/454559-valves-michael-abrash-promise-and-chall enges-vr/. Accessed 10 May 2016
5. King, G., Krzywinska, T.: Tomb Raiders and Space Invaders. I.B. Tauris, London (2006)
6. Lugrin, J.-L., et al.: Immersive FPS games: user experience and performance. In: Proceedings of the 2013 ACM International Workshop on Immersive Media Experiences. ACM (2013)

Pragati - A Mobile Based Virtual Reality (VR) Platform to Train and Educate Community Health Workers

Keyur Sorathia, Kshipra Sharma$^{(\boxtimes)}$, Shimmila Bhowmick,
and Preetham Kamidi

Indian Institute of Technology, Guwahati, India
kshipra.22sharma@gmail.com

Abstract. Accredited Social Health Activists (ASHAs) are essential link to healthy communities in resource-constrained environments. However, they are insufficiently trained to solve community health challenges. In this paper, we present *Pragati* - a mobile-based Virtual Reality (VR) platform to train and educate ASHAs in rural Assam, India. Mobile based VR platform was chosen due to its ability to increase focus, attention and learnability among users. We developed 3 modules on maternal and child healthcare. Modules were presented via audio-visual interface in local Assamesse language. This paper presents the design of *Pragati*, user interactions, technology implementations and future directions of our study.

Keywords: ICT in social development - interaction design for developing regions · Technology in healthcare · Virtual reality · Medical training · Community health workers

1 Introduction

ASHAs act as a primary tool against the menace of child malnourishment, infant mortality and aide in curbing preventable diseases in rural communities in India specially in rural areas [6, 7]. Despite being an essential link to quality healthcare, they are often ignored. Their health education and skillsets are often limited due to delayed due to insufficient training, the use of non-engaging methods, outdated health information and little or no feedback on their training and education [6, 8]. This presents an opportunity to design solutions that timely train ASHAs through engaging methods in order to improve community healthcare in developing regions.

Penetration of Information Communication Technology (ICT) tools, especially mobile phones have increased accessibility in remote regions and provided with better opportunities for digital services [1]. They possess benefits of easy outreach and information access, repetitive learning [4], cost-effective information sharing [3] and communicating sensitive health information effectively [2]. Moreover, mobile phone interventions supported through VR interfaces provide rich, immersive, and engaging educational context supporting experential learning [5], which results in increased learnability, attention and memorability among targeted users [9]. In this paper,

© IFIP International Federation for Information Processing 2017
Published by Springer International Publishing AG 2017. All Rights Reserved
R. Bernhaupt et al. (Eds.): INTERACT 2017, Part IV, LNCS 10516, pp. 459–463, 2017.
DOI: 10.1007/978-3-319-68059-0_51

we present the design of *Pragati*- a mobile based VR interface targeted towards training ASHAs in the state of Assam in India. This is followed by details of technology implementation and future directions of our study.

2 Design of VR Interface

Pragati is a mobile phone based VR interface aimed at training and educating ASHAs in Assam, India. We created a 360 degree virtual environment of a traditional Assamese home where the modules are demonstrated. Audio-visual animations related to maternal and child healthcare were created in local Assamese language. We designed two personas 'ASHA baidew (sister)' - who moderated and guided users through each module and 'Meera' - who enacts as the woman going through pregnancy to increase familiarity and acceptance among users. Figure 1(a), (b) and (c) showcases virtual environment, ASHA baidew and Meera respectively. Information was presented in a mobile phone mounted on a Google cardboard. This is due to its lower cost and potential scalability among targeted user group.

Fig. 1. (a) Virtual (360°) environment of Assamese home (b) persona of ASHA baidew and (c) persona of Meera

Each information module is narrated in 5 main sections - (i) introduction of the module by ASHA baidew (ii) narration of healthcare content (iii) intermediate interactive task/questions (iv) summary of the module and (v) questions relevant to the module. Figure 2 showcases the module framework for *Pragati*.

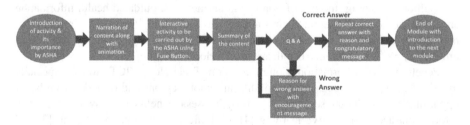

Fig. 2. Framework structure of information modules of *Pragati*

We designed following 3 modules on the maternal and child health. We chose the modules based on high priority training subjects in the ASHA training curriculum.

Module 1: Safe delivery

The module presents the methods of healthy delivery of a pregnant women in a home setting. The role of ASHAs is to assist in performing the delivery activities through recommended steps. It presents 3 stages of delivery and relevant precautions undertaken for safe and healthy delivery.

Module 2: Newborn examination

The newborn needs to be examined at birth for stillbirth or any other health related precautions by immediate examination after birth. This is performed by observing breathing, limb movement and crying of a newborn. It also recommends carious activities in case of a potential stillbirth.

Module 3: Normal care provision to newborn

This module presents steps for immediate post-partum care for the newborn. Appropriate methods of drying the baby and mantaining the baby's temperature are recommended during this module.

We explain the design of *Pragati* in 3 sections - (i) design of virtual environment and personas (ii) interactive tasks and activities and (iii) input interactions

2.1   Design of Virtual Environment and Persona

We created virtual simulation of traditional Assamese home environment, a persona of 'ASHA baidew', and a young mother 'Meera' and to increase familiarity of the context among users. Persona of 'ASHA baidew (sister)' imitates a 45 year old Assamese lady with over 10 years of experience as ASHA. The role of ASHA baidew is to introduce each module, indicate the significance, provide tasks and activities and guide the users through each module. Meera imitates a young and first time pregnant woman who enacts various stages of pregnancy and problems that occure during pregnancy.

2.2   Interactive Tasks, Activities and Questions

We presented activities and tasks in between each module to increase focus and attention among users. We scripted activities, tasks and intermediate questions into the dialogue during the training sessions. For example, module 3 demands drying and cleaning of a newborn immediately after delivery. An activity of drying the newborn is proposed during the module. The module resumes when the drying and cleaning activity is completed by users. Similarly, a series of questions are asked to users post module description. For example, module 1 demonstrates Meera's womb activity which releases colored fluid during break down of amniotic sac. The color of fuild determines its infectuous stage. A question is asked to users post completion to module - "Which fluid color indicates infection?" The user can choose the answer from choices provided on the interface. Correct answers are appreciated through congratulatory messages where as incorrect answers are supplemented by reasons and given another chance to answer questions.

2.3 User Interactions

We designed *Pragati* for mobile based VR mounted on a Google cardboard (or similar cheap cardboards) to increase scalability. Hence, our proposed interactions are limited to fuse button mounted on Google cardbaord. Users select the given options by pressing the fuse button multiple times i.e. tap once to choose option one, tap twice to choose option two and tap thrice to choose third option. We presented audio instructions to aide in choosing relevant options. A horizontal menu selection user interface was presented to choose relevant options. The menu selection options were tracked and presented to user irrespective of head position. Figure 3 showcases the horizontal menu user interface proposed in *Pragati*.

Fig. 3. Proposed horizontal menu user interface for *Pragati*

3 Technology Implementation

Andriod, Unity 3D and Google's VR Software Development ToolKit (SDK) was used to develop *Pragati*. We used 2D graphics as objects instead of 3D objects based virtual environment using unity skybox in order to make it compatible low end smartphones. This also enabled quick modifications as per our requirements. Each module was further animated using Adobe After effects with specified user interactions at regular intervals. We develop 2.5D environment using parallax-style animation to reduce rendering intensity and memory requirements. Figure 4 shows the schematic diagram of technology implementation of *Pragati*.

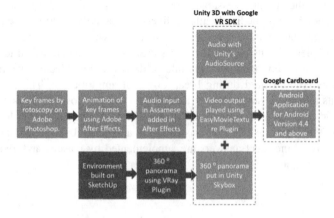

Fig. 4. Schematic diagram of technology implementation of *Pragati*

4 Conclusion and Future Work

In this paper, we presented *Pragati* –a mobile phone based VR platform to train and educate ASHAs in Assam, India. *Pragati* used audio-visual information modules communicated through familiar virtual environment and personas. Interactive tasks, activities and questions were used during and post module sessions to increase attention and focus among users. We developed 3 modules on maternal and child healthcare on home delivery, newborn examination, and newborn care. These modules were interacted through fuse button based input interactions and horizontal menu based user interfaces. We have developed the protoype and field trails are in process to study overall acceptance, engagement and learnability as compared to traditional training methods. We aim at conducting longitudnal studies by incorporating *Pragati* with traditional training sessions to study the retention rates and learnability and present empirical findings in future. Moreover, we will be using Pragati to conduct a camparative evaluation study to investigate self-efficacy, learnability, engagement and presence across three common information dissimenation platform (a) traditional 2D audio-video module (b) modules presented on mobile phones based VR without head mounted display and (c) module presented on mobile phone based VR with head mounted display.

References

1. Telecom Regulatory Authority of India, Annual Report on Penetration of Mobile phone (2009)
2. Fiore-Silfvast, B., Hartung, C., Iyengar, K., Iyengar, S., Israel-Ballard, K., Perin, N., Anderson, R.: Mobile video for patient education: the midwives' perspective. In: Proceedings of the 3rd ACM Symposium on Computing for Development, p. 2. ACM, January 2013
3. Kallander, K., Tibenderana, J.K., Akpogheneta, O.J., Strachan, D.L., Hill, Z., ten Asbroek, A. H., Meek, S.R.: Mobile health (mHealth) approaches and lessons for increased performance and retention of community health workers in low-and middle-income countries: a review. J. Med. Internet Res. **15**(1), e17 (2013)
4. Li, J., Alem, L.: Supporting distributed collaborations between mobile health workers and expert clinicians in home care. In: Extended Abstracts on Human Factors in Computing Systems, CHI 2013, pp. 493–498. ACM, April 2013
5. Mantovani, F.: VR learning: Potential and challenges for the use of 3D environments in education and training. In: Riva, G., Galimberti, C. (eds.) Towards Cyber Psychology: Mind, Cognitions and Society in the Internet Age, pp. 207–226. IOS Press, Amsterdam, The Netherlands (2001)
6. Molapo, M., Marsden, G.: Software support for creating digital health training materials in the held. In: Proceedings of the Sixth International Conference on Information and Communication Technologies and Development: Full Papers, vol. 1, pp. 205–214. ACM, December 2013
7. Molapo, M., Marsden, G.: Health education in rural communities with locally produced and locally relevant multimedia content. In: Proceedings of the 3rd ACM Symposium on Computing for Development, p. 25. ACM, January 2013
8. Pakenham-Walsh, N., Priestley, C., Smith, R.: Meeting the information needs of health workers in developing countries. Br. Med. J. **314**, 90 (1997)
9. Youngblut, C.: Educational uses of virtual reality technology. Institute for Defense Analyses, Alexandria (1998). http://papers.cumincad.org/data/works/att/94ea.content.pdf

Shifting from the Children to the Teens' Usability: Adapting a Gamified Experience of a Museum Tour

Vanessa Cesário[1,2(✉)], Marko Radeta[1], António Coelho[2],
and Valentina Nisi[1]

[1] Madeira Interactive Technologies Institute, 9020-105 Funchal, Portugal
{vanessa.cesario,marko.radeta,
valentina.nisi}@m-iti.org
[2] Faculty of Engineering, University of Porto, 4200-465 Porto, Portugal
acoelho@fe.up.pt

Abstract. In this poster, we are addressing the topic of "system's evaluation" from the point of view of assessing the usability of a gamified experience with 20 teenagers aged 15–17 years. The currently tested experience was ideally designed for children 9–10 years. In order to adapt the application to teenagers, we tested it with 20 targeted users. In this poster, we share the results and encourage a discussion among the researchers about how to adapt the gamified experience designed for children to a teenage audience.

Keywords: Usability · Evaluation · Interface · Teenagers · Children · Gamified experience · Selfies

1 Introduction

Measuring and evaluating usability of interactive systems and interfaces is an ongoing challenge for teams that are concerned with improving the user experience [1]. The success of any software depends on several factors and usability is one of the most significant ones [2]. Numerous usability evaluation methods can be used to estimate the usability problems at the earlier stage of a software design in order to overcome the severity level and withdraw the rework of design [1–4]. Nowadays, usability is the core cause of the success of any technical product [2] which if it is hard to use, will most possibly fail at the market level [2].

As we currently are in the era of interfaces and user experiences, it is quintessential to understand whether how we could adapt an interface to several demographics. Is the concept *one size fits all* suited for children and teens? The museum specific mobile application, *Ocean Game*, was designed for the Natural History Museum of Funchal (NHMF), Portugal, in order to engage 9–10 years old children with the museum exhibits, and it was first tested with these target users. After discovering the difficulties of the NHMF in attracting teenagers there, we were given a chance to rethink the same concept for teens aged 15–17. In this context, the following questions arose: How does an application for children fit the world of today's teenagers? What usability issues are relevant to these young people? The adaptation was initiated through the usability tests below.

© IFIP International Federation for Information Processing 2017
Published by Springer International Publishing AG 2017. All Rights Reserved
R. Bernhaupt et al. (Eds.): INTERACT 2017, Part IV, LNCS 10516, pp. 464–468, 2017.
DOI: 10.1007/978-3-319-68059-0_52

2   *Ocean Game*: The Product to Be Tested

The *Ocean Game* is a children's gamified experience to guide a visit throughout the Natural History Museum of Funchal, Madeira Island, Portugal (Fig. 1). The experience aims to explore the museum content and collect information about its 13 main creatures using a smartphone. This information is presented in a textual form, describing several scientific curiosities about each animal. The *Ocean Game* uses proximity beacons and visual cues in the form of stickers in order to signal the presence of digital content. The process is as follows: (i) when children approach the sticker, a short animation appears on the smartphone screen suggesting some key information regarding that animal; (ii) children can explore more information by scrolling through tweet-sized texts; (iii) after reading them, children are prompted to take a picture of themselves together with the current animal; (iv) this allows them to collect an icon specifically created for each individual animal which will be found in their inventory inside the mobile application; (v) the more creatures the children collect, the higher the level they can reach; (vi) each level awards a star as an achievement and a catalyst in order to push their motivation forward; (vii) at the end of the experience, users take inside of the application a quiz consisting of 13 questions about the animals (these questions are tailored to the information that they just learned during the experience); and (vii) after completing the quiz, the children are presented with a digital postcard containing their self-portrait and ranking.

Fig. 1. Print screens of the *Ocean Game*: curiosity about the animal explained in text and taken selfie above it (left); inventory of collected species (middle); and digital postcard with results of the gamified experience (right)

3   Method: Usability Procedure

In this section, we describe the *Ocean Game*'s usability individual sessions with 20 students, aged 15 to 17, from a local secondary school in Funchal, Island of Madeira, Portugal. In overall, our sample included 13-male students and 7-female students. Their average age was 16,7. Students were enrolled in multimedia and informatics courses. Each participant participated in the usability test in the school premises where we run the gamified experience in a specially fitted classroom, where the beacons with images had been displaced. At the room entrance, users were given a smartphone and a list of tasks. The tasks were the following: (1) open the app; (2) go over the tutorial; (3) input name, email, age and gender; (4) start playing; (5) collect the 13 species; (6) answer the quiz; (7) check your award; (8) go out the app. During the user test, the researcher was *observing* and taking notes regarding participants' behaviors. At the end, they were required to answer a *survey* on a computer as well as to verbally explain their thoughts of what they *liked* and *disliked* more and about their views regarding the *selfies*.

The surveys delivered were using the System Usability Scale (SUS) [5], translated and validated for the Portuguese language [6], and the Net Promoter Score (NPS) [7]. Our rationale for using these surveys is that they were used also with new mobile technologies [8–10]. The SUS and the NPS make it possible to gather personal feedback on system's quality, and in order to use that feedback for comprehending how the system compares to other alternatives and to identify areas of improvement.

4 Main Findings

In this section, we describe the findings regarding the *observations* taken by the researcher, the results of the *surveys* that participants were required to answer, their answers about what they *liked* and *disliked* more, and also their thoughts about the *selfies*.

Observations. Besides having a list of tasks, we noticed 7 users who were thinking out loud, being confused at the beginning without knowing what to do in the test. In addition, we also noticed that some of the participants did not know when to catch the species or how to take a photo. Others asked if it was necessary to take a properly formed selfie. In overall, they were excited with the user testing when they saw a smartphone to interact with, and we registered the following expression. *This is too much technology together, and it is absorbing,* which expresses their excitement during the test. We also noticed that almost all people tend to click on the species' animation and also on the species' icons placed in their digital inventory. This suggests that students tend to explore more the circular icons with animals and are expecting to see more interactions after tapping the icons.

Surveys. The overall System Usability Scale had the average score of 83.125 out of 100, which is considered as a "good user experience". The Net Promoter Score had an average of 8 out of 10 which considers the users to be "passively satisfied".

Like. Participants were asked to express themselves what they liked more in the application. In total, 52 insights were obtained which we grouped into 7 categories. The categories were: (1) Learning (12 insights): they enjoy *reading information about the species* which prompted them to learn; (2) Selfies (10 insights): they enjoy taking *selfies with the discovered species*; (3) Interaction (10 insights): they like the *interaction of approaching the species* through the beacon; (4) Usage (8 insights): they value the *easy utilization* of the application such as the system's easy and fast answers; (5) Quiz (6 insights): they liked to be prompted with a *quiz to test* their knowledge capacities; (6) Design (3 insights): 3 participants found the application's *design appealing*; (7) Gamified experience (2 insights): 2 participants enjoyed the challenge of *going further in the gamified experience* by achieving stars.

Dislike. Participants, when asked about what they disliked in the application, came up with 11 insights, which we grouped into 4 categories. Namely: (1) Selfies (4 insights): participants felt *embarrassed while taking self-portraits*, they would rather take pictures of the species than of themselves; (2) Quantity (3 insights): it was reported that the gamified experience had *too few animals*; (3) Quiz (2 insights): at least 2 participants didn't like the fact of being *mandatory to answer* the 13 questions; (4) Images (2 insights): also 2 people didn't like *the design* of our icons arguing that *they could be real rather than a vector image*.

Selfies. Regarding the selfies, all the participants were verbally asked about their opinion. We had 16 positive answers and 4 negative answers. Those who answered positively argued that they would *take selfies even without the application*. They would also value more if the application could add *Augmented Reality icons to the selfies and social component as Snapchat does*. However, those who did not enjoy the selfies specified that *it would be better to take a photo of the species, not a selfie*; and at least one argued that it would be *boring to take selfies to all* the animals and they would rather take to the animals that they liked, not all of them.

5   Concluding Remarks

These findings contribute to the broader literature on gamified experiences for teenagers in the field of HCI, arguing that it is possible to adapt a gamified experience designed for children into one for teenagers, when the first contains elements that are considered as novel approaches by the "new generation" [11] such as mobile applications, taking pictures and interaction through proximity. Our findings highlight that the selfie element catches teens' attention, although some of them would rather take a picture of the species than taking self-portraits. In fact, our results resonate with the broader literature which indicates that young people today are born into the world flooded by novel technologies [11, 12] because they were comfortable and excited with the user tests. On this view, [12] reports that the "Generation Z" (teenagers in particular) is more and more engaged with open platforms for information sharing, seeing technology as a vital part of their lives. Besides, more studies argue that when working with this age group, emphasis should be placed on producing combined communication policies that connect the use of interactive technologies with the more conventional media channels [11]. In essence, our study highlights how much children and teens value the technology in their museum experiences and would appreciate the integration of playful approaches with the learning goals of museums to have more enjoyable experiences. For the future work, we will iterate the *Ocean Game* application based on the usability problems that were verified, such as allowing users to tap on the species' icons, and to give them freedom either to take a self-portrait or simply to take a picture of the species. Although we have not asked them directly about whether the design of the gamified experience was appealing (which is a limitation of this work), only two people stated they would prefer real images rather than our images (Fig. 1). This insight will be taken into consideration when iterating the *Ocean Game* application. After these improvements, we will commence the user tests inside the premises of the museum, not only using the SUS [5] and the NPS [7], but also using the MUX scale [3] with the aim to address mobility issues which were not addressed in-situ during the above user tests. Furthermore, testing inside the premises of the museum will enable us to address the engagement and visitor experience of the users regarding the gamified experience and the exhibition (repeat play value, relatability with the exhibits) during the museum tour.

Acknowledgments. The research leading to this work has received funding from ARDITI (Agência Regional para o Desenvolvimento da Investigação, Tecnologia e Inovação), under the project number M14-20-09-5369-FSE-000001. Our gratitude also goes to Prof. Sónia Matos for her support gathering the curiosities of each of the 13 species, and to the students and teachers of the Multimedia and Informatics class at Francisco Franco's Secondary School. We would also like to thank the Museum of Natural History of Funchal for their timely support and feedback.

References

1. Finstad, K.: The usability metric for user experience. Interact. Comput. **22**, 323–327 (2010)
2. Sauro, J.: SUPR-Q: a comprehensive measure of the quality of the website user experience. J Usability Stud. **10**, 68–86 (2015)
3. Djamasbi, S., Wilson, V.: MUX: development of a holistic mobile user experience instrument. In: Proceedings of the 50th Hawaii International Conference on System Sciences (2017)
4. Lund, A.: Measuring Usability with the USE Questionnaire.pdf | Usability | Questionnaire. Scribd. 3–6 (2001)
5. Brooke, J.: SUS: a quick and dirty usability scale. Usability Eval. Ind. **189**(194), 4–7 (1996)
6. Martins, A.I., Rosa, A.F., Queirós, A., Silva, A., Rocha, N.P.: European portuguese validation of the system usability scale (SUS). Procedia Comput. Sci. **67**, 293–300 (2015)
7. Reichheld, F.F.: The One Number You Need to Grow. https://hbr.org/2003/12/the-one-number-you-need-to-grow
8. Djamasbi, S., Gomez, W., Kardzhaliyski, G., Liu, T., Oglesby, F.: App-like mobile optimization and user experience. In: SIGHCI 2013 Proceedings (2013)
9. Chomutare, T., Tatara, N., Årsand, E., Hartvigsen, G.: Designing a diabetes mobile application with social network support. Stud. Health Technol. Inform. **188**, 58–64 (2013)
10. Brade, J., Lorenz, M., Busch, M., Hammer, N., Tscheligi, M., Klimant, P.: Being there again – presence in real and virtual environments and its relation to usability and user experience using a mobile navigation task. Int. J. Hum.-Comput. Stud. **101**, 76–87 (2017)
11. Napoli, J., Ewing, M.T.: The Net Generation. J. Int. Consum. Mark. **13**, 21–34 (2000)
12. Wikia: Generation Z: a Look at the Technology and Media Habits of Today's Teens. http://www.prnewswire.com/news-releases/generation-z-a-look-at-the-technology-and-media-habits-of-todays-teens-198958011.html

TTracker: Using Finger Detection to Improve Touch Typing Training

Elvin Kollie[1]([⊠]), Fernando Loizides[2]([⊠]), Thomas Hartley[2],
and Adam Worrallo[2]

[1] Maths and Computer Science Department,
University of Wolverhampton, Wolverhampton, UK
koyanwollie@hotmail.co.uk
[2] Emerging Interactive Technologies Lab & Maths and Computer
Science Department, University of Wolverhampton, Wolverhampton, UK
{fernando.loizides,t.hartley2,a.worrallo}@wlv.ac.uk

Abstract. Touch typing software teaches a user to use the correct finger combinations with the correct keyboard buttons. The ultimate goal is to teach the typist to type faster, more accurately and ergonomically correct. Our research presents the working prototype of a software and hardware setup that tracks not only the speed and accuracy of the correct buttons being pressed but also which fingers are used to press them; a dimension of training that has previously not been integrated into touch typing tutorials. We use novel technology (leap motion) to detect the accurate interaction between the user and the keyboard, giving precise feedback to the user in order for him or her to improve.

Keywords: Finger detection · Leap motion · Touch typing

1 Introduction and Motivation

Touch-typing is a psychomotor skill involving combining a users' cognitive functions with physical movement. Touch-typing involves more than simply increasing typing speed, in that it enables typists to split the cognitive processing by offloading information from the visual channel. This means typists can designate more focus to interacting with the screen and therefore inadvertently increasing their typing speed in the process [5]. This makes touch typing beneficial in note taking, programming, live communication and many other aspects of computer use. Touch-typing is conventionally learned via websites that teach touch-typing concepts and finger mappings [1]. The websites or stand-alone software identify which keys are pressed and the time taken to do so; thus giving feedback to the users in order to improve their performance. The positive influence that feedback has on typing proficiency has been proven multiple times on multiple devices [2–4]. What the current feedback does not provide the user is the fingers used to press the keys, one of the areas in which the most mistakes may be made. In order to provide this type of feedback on touch-typing a method to track finger key associations needs to be in place. It would be impossible for a human to consistently detect finger-key associations over long periods of time.

R. Bernhaupt et al. (Eds.): INTERACT 2017, Part IV, LNCS 10516, pp. 469–472, 2017.
DOI: 10.1007/978-3-319-68059-0_53

Leveraging hand tracking technology, it is possible to identify if a user is touch-typing or not, providing a method to give feedback to people learning how to touch-type. The feedback provided could prove to be a more effective method of teaching people how to touch-type. In order to prove the concept of the new technology, a system is developed using the Leap Motion controller[1] to track hands actively typing on a keyboard. In this paper we present the working prototype system and setup created to facilitate finger detection and feedback. We also present a pilot user test to identify initial interaction effectiveness of the prototype and to feed back in the development according to a user centered design approach. The next section presents the technology (software and hardware) while the subsequent section presents the pilot test with some of the main findings.

2   System Description

The prototype system consists of two parts, the software called TTracker and the hardware setup. The hardware part consists of a laptop or PC with a Leap Motion mounted on top of the keyboard area (See Fig. 1). The Leap Motion controller is a USB peripheral device capable of tracking hands with a submillimeter accuracy. The leap motion uses infrared cameras to collect information at up to 200 frames per second. The effective range of the Leap Motion controller extends from approximately 25 to 600 mm above the device (1 inch to 2 feet). The field of view is 150° with roughly 8 cubic feet of interactive 3D space. If for some reason a finger were to be obstructed from the view of the Leap Motion it would use its predictive model to infer the location [6]. The Leap Motion then filters all of the unneeded information within the snapshot and expresses the results as a series of frames. These frames hold data such as fingertip location, palm location and finger direction.

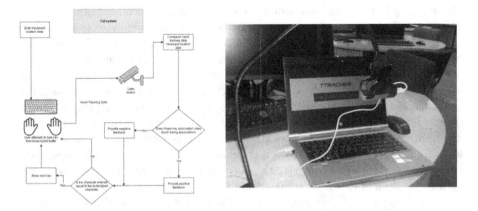

Fig. 1. (left) the prototype architecture (right) the physical setup

---

[1] https://www.leapmotion.com/ (accessed December 2016).

The TTracker software was written in Unity[2] and, although not open source, can be provided to researchers upon request (See Fig. 2). The software has two modules working together. The first module is the finger-key tracking module, which gathers information from the Leap Motions. The second module is the learning environment, which was put together with the first module to create the complete system.

Fig. 2. (left) the development process of TTracker (right) the prototype software showing the left index finger as the suitable finger for the next button press. (Color figure online)

Specialized sentences and letters appear on the screen for the user to type. There are different levels depending on the skill level of the user. In order to teach touch mapping without breaking the user's focus from the screen, the application was set up so that the next finger to use on the to-be-typed screen flashes blue. After a key is pushed, the application checks if touch-typing was used, the finger used glows red for incorrect finger to key touch or green if the correct finger to key is used. The user gains 5 points for typing the correct letter but if they used touch-typing, they gain 10 points thereby incentivizing the use of touch-typing. If the user types the wrong letter, he /she loses 1 point. Sound was added to the application; a different audio file is played depending on touch-typing implementation.

3 Pilot User Testing

We wanted to test the prototype to improve the usability before releasing a beta version to the general public. To this end a pilot study took place with 10 participants aged 20–60 for qualitative and quantitative feedback. The test involved a pre-study interview in order to record the participants' profiles, a hands-on test with the prototype which lasted no more than 20 min and a semi-structured post-test interview.

The pre-study interview revealed some demographics about the participants and the level of touch typing experience that the participants had. 6 of the participants had knowledge of what touch typing was. 3 of the participants had previously tried (limited) to learn touch typing using an online resource. None of the participants were able to touch type in any formal way. All participants would use a computer at least 5 days a week and 7 would use it daily.

---

[2] https://unity3d.com/.

We want to find out how many errors users make while touch-typing and attempt to discover new ways to prevent these errors. Identifying how long it takes users to learn the touch-typing mapping is also imperative. During the prototype testing we were able to successfully record errors in using the correct finger to press specific keys (see Fig. 3). With this method we can give individual feedback to each user on the areas they need to be improve specifically and also be able to feedback from all the users on the most common problematic keys and adjust the software training to cater for those.

Fig. 3. Errors in matching the correct finger to the correct key press for an individual user

In the post-study interview, the main questions revolved around the usability of the system. All participants agreed that the software' learnability was easy to grasp. The participants were unanimous in agreeing that highlighting the finger that is needed to press the next key on the screen was sometimes confusing. Visual attention is focused on the letters appearing on the screen and is therefore difficult to be shared with the image of the fingers. Longitudinal testing we hypothesize will gradually help the users learn the finger positions at which point they will not rely on the on screen finger animation. The general outcome was that the software would be better for registering and giving feedback after, rather than at, real time training. Only one participant reported the accuracy of the setup (finger to key detection) as less than 'extremely accurate' and we attribute this as an outlier due to calibration issues. The next version of the software was also suggested to include different auditory feedback for different types of presses.

References

1. Poole, D., Preciado, M.: Touch typing instruction: elementary teachers' beliefs and practices. Comput. Educ. **102**, 1–14 (2016)
2. Tittelbach, D., Fields, L., Alvero, A.: Effects of performance feedback on typing speed and accuracy. J. Organ. Behav. Manag. **27**(4), 29–52 (2008)
3. Kim, J., Tan, H.: A study of touch typing performance with Keyclick feedback. In: Haptics Symposium, pp. 227–233. IEEE, New York (2014)
4. Kim, J., Tan, H.: Effect of information content in sensory feedback on typing performance using a flat keyboard. In: World Haptics Conference, pp. 228–234. IEEE, New York (2015)
5. Feit, A., Weir, D., Oulasvirta, A.: How we type: movement strategies and performance in everyday typing. In: #Chi4good, pp. 4262–4273 (2016)
6. Colgan, A.: How does the leap motion controller work? leap motion blog (2014). http://blog.leapmotion.com/hardware-tosoftware-how-does-the-leap-motion-controller-work/. Accessed 14 Sep 2016

URetail: Privacy User Interfaces for Intelligent Retail Stores

Frederic Raber[(✉)] and Nils Vossebein[(✉)]

DFKI, Saarland Informatics Campus, Saarbrücken, Germany
`frederic.raber@dfki.de, Nils.Vossebein@gmx.de`

Abstract. Amazon recently opened its first intelligent retail store, which captures shopper movements, picked-up products and much more sensitive data. In this paper we present a privacy UI, called *URetail*, that returns to the customer control over his own data, by offering an interface to select which of his private data items should be disclosed. We use a radar metaphor to arrange the permissions with ascending sensitivity into different clusters, and introduce a new multi-dimensional form of a radar interface called the privacy pyramid. We conducted an expert interview and a pilot study to determine which types of data are recorded in an intelligent retail store, and grouped them with ascending sensitivity into clusters. A preliminary evaluation study shows that radar interfaces have their own strengths and weaknesses compared to a conventional UI.

1 Introduction

Retail stores like Amazon Go collect a massive amount of deanonymized private data on each of their customers in order to offer their services. Amazon uses "sensor fusion" to follow the customer from the entrance gate throughout the shop, registering products being picked up, placed back and/or viewed, stopping points and most likely also the exact route throughout the store. Although the Amazon Go service saves time and is very convenient, not all the shoppers are happy with the new store concept: The whereabouts of the data and what else it is used for remains as unclear as the description of technologies used and what data is recorded by them.

2 Related Work

There is plenty of work regarding data privacy in social networks [6,9], location sharing [5] and mobile app permission setting [7], but so far, to the best of our knowledge, nobody has explored how these interfaces work for retail data, or how they could be improved. Privacy setting interfaces are mostly realized as list-based interfaces, as for example on Facebook: All data types (photos, videos, comments etc.) are listed one after the other, with a button or slider next to

R. Bernhaupt et al. (Eds.): INTERACT 2017, Part IV, LNCS 10516, pp. 473–477, 2017.
DOI: 10.1007/978-3-319-68059-0_54

each item, to switch the privacy policy to disclose/undisclose for that type of data. Although such interfaces can be efficient for the setting task alone, it is hard to have a clear overview on the current state of the settings as a whole, and which settings might be unusual and need some tuning [1]. Furthermore, it is obvious that they are not perceived as attractive and fun to use: Research in the past has shown that tuning the privacy settings is mostly perceived as a burdensome and boring task [3,8], which leads the users to almost never adjust the standard settings, resulting in suboptimal privacy settings.

A different UI concept that is used in research is the *radar metaphor*: The different data items are first clustered into different groups of data types. In the second step, the items of each cluster are sorted by ascending privacy rating, for example. Christin et al. provided such an interface, called *privacy radar* [1], to visualize the privacy threats in participatory sensing applications. Their evaluation has shown that the radar interface provided a clearer overview on the privacy threats, and significnatly raised user awareness and interest in adjusting privacy settings. The radar metaphor is also highly appropriate [2] for space-constrained devices like smartphones. The concept of radar interfaces has also been used to select post recipients in social networks: Privacy Wedges [9] aligns the friends of a Facebook user, clustered into friend groups and ordered by ascending tie strength.

In this paper we want to examine whether a radar metaphor can be applied to the domain of intelligent retail data. We did some background research to investigate what data is typically collected inside an intelligent retail store, and checked whether the typical constraints of a radar interface (clustering data and sorting the clusters) can be met. We implemented a prototype of both a conventional list-based and extended radar interface, that allows the simultaneous view of several radar layers at once in a three-dimensional privacy pyramid. We compared the performance and user experience of both approaches in a preliminary evaluation.

3   Background Research

We interviewed an employee of the Innovative Retail Laboratory [10], an intelligent retail store concept similar to Amazon Go, regarding the data that is gathered inside an intelligent retail store, to create a list of privacy-sensitive data, later called *permissions* or *items*. We went through the assistance systems of the IRL and the Amazon Go store, and collected data that is recorded to make the services work. In addition to the services and data types, we also recorded the stakeholders that are interested in this type of data or that offer the service. In a second step, we asked five participants (employees of our university) to cluster and sort the data types.

Table 1 contains a list of observed private retail data items together with the service where the data is used and the interested stakeholders. The participants stated a similar order for all clusters, except for the *personal data* cluster. This cluster was therefore realized as a list in URetail. The items in the other clusters are sorted with ascending privacy rating in the table.

Table 1. Data recorded in an intelligent retail store and services where it is used, assigned to groups and sorted with ascending sensitivity.

		Services	Stakeholders
Personal data	*Address*	Invisible checkout	Retailer, friends, family
	Birthday		
	Name		
	Gender		
	Income	Product recommender	Retailers, 3rd parties
Location data	*Recent visits:*	Invisible checkout	Retailer, friends, family
	- Province		
	- City		
	- Address		
	Movement	Customer heatmap	Retailer
Shopping receipt	*Loyalty points*	Invisible checkout	Retailer, friends, family
	Items bought:		
	- Amount		
	- Category		
	- Price		
Interests	*Wishlist*	Digital shopping list	Retailer, friends, family
	Recently viewed	Product recommender	Retailers, 3rd parties

4   URetail: A Radar Interface for Intelligent Retail Store Data

Inside URetail, the data clusters are visualized by wedges in the radar; the layers inside each wedge represent the different data types, ordered in ascending sensitivity from the center to the rim. To set the disclosure settings for a data group, the user clicks on a wedge layer or drags from the center of the radar to a wedge layer (1). All data types inside the group from the lowest sensitivity (center) up to the selected layer are then set to disclose. If the severity order is not correct, the user can modify the order by drag & drop in the list view beneath each wedge (2). Alternatively, to adjust the disclosure settings using the radar interface, the user can also disclose/undisclose a data type by clicking on the data items inside the list view (2). The four different *stakeholders* are again realized by four different webpages, accessible by a navigation bar on the left-hand side just like in the list interface.

The radar interface also supports an overview of the settings of all stakeholders at one glance, using a 3D pyramid below the wedges of the radar (3), later called the *privacy pyramid*. The pyramid consists of four different layers, representing the four different *stakeholders*. Each layer has four edges, representing the four different *data groups*. The more data is disclosed inside a data group, the larger is the corresponding edge in the pyramid. To get an impression

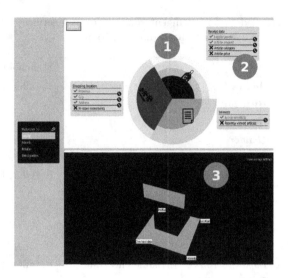

Fig. 1. Radar interface: data types are arranged in groups, sorted by sensitivity.

of where the settings are unusual and probably misconfigured, it is possible to display the privacy pyramid of an average user as a transparent overlay. (Fig. 1)

5 Evaluation and Discussion

For evaluation purposes, we implemented a list-based interface, as described in the "Work done so far" section, and let 21 participants (students and university employees) test both interfaces on a desktop pc, followed by an interview where they also had to rate on a scale from 1 (best) to 5 (worst) which interface was better to spot *whether* there are differences from an average privacy profile, *where* they are and how an average profile looks, followed by the attrakdiff [4] usability questionnaire. The participants stated that they first had to get used to the radar interface, but after a short trial phase, it feels faster to use, which is also reflected in a higher pragmatic score in attrakdiff ($M_{radar} = 1.99$, $M_{list} = 0.69$, $Z = -3.785$, $p < 0.001$). The privacy pyramid makes it easier to spot *whether* there are differences ($M_{radar} = 1.62$, $M_{list} = 2.14$, $T = 2.75$, $p = 0.012$), whereas it easier to see *which* items are different ($M_{radar} = 2.19$, $M_{list} = 1.67$, $T = 2.95$, $p = 0.008$) and *how an average setting* looks ($M_{radar} = 2.62$, $M_{list} = 1.81$, $T = 3.07$, $p = 0.012$) with the list-based UI. According to the attrakdiff results, the radar interface had a significantly better user experience and was more fun to use ($M_{radar} = -0.745$, $M_{list} = 2.28$, $Z = -4.02$, $p < 0.001$). To conclude, both radar and list interface have their own strengths and would have to be combined to achieve an optimal performance. The radar is perceived as more interesting and fun to use, which allows better motivation of users to do the boring task of privacy setting. Furthermore, it is perceived as faster after a training phase. In future work, we would like to conduct a lab study to explore whether the concept is applicable for mobile devices, how both interfaces can be combined and how the time needed for interaction changes over time, once the subjects get used to the interface.

References

1. Christin, D., Michalak, M., Hollick, M.: Raising user awareness about privacy threats in participatory sensing applications through graphical warnings. In: Proceedings of International Conference on Advances in Mobile Computing #38; Multimedia, MoMM 2013, NY, USA, pp. 445:445–445:454 (2013). http://doi.acm.org/10.1145/2536853.2536861

2. Christin, D., Reinhardt, A., Hollick, M., Trumpold, K.: Exploring user preferences for privacy interfaces in mobile sensing applications. In: Proceedings of the 11th International Conference on Mobile and Ubiquitous Multimedia, MUM 2012, NY, USA, pp. 14:1–14:10 (2012). http://doi.acm.org/10.1145/2406367.2406385

3. Ghazinour, K., Matwin, S., Sokolova, M.: Monitoring and recommending privacy settings in social networks. In: Proceedings of the Joint EDBT/ICDT 2013 Workshops, EDBT 2013, NY, USA, pp. 164–168 (2013). http://doi.acm.org/10.1145/2457317.2457344

4. Hassenzahl, M., Burmester, M., Koller, F.: Attrakdiff: ein fragebogen zur messung wahrgenommener hedonischer und pragmatischer qualitaet. In: Szwillus, G., Ziegler, J. (eds.) Mensch & Computer 2003: Interaktion in Bewegung, pp. 187–196. B. G. Teubner, Stuttgart (2003)

5. Jedrzejczyk, L., Price, B.A., Bandara, A., Nuseibeh, B.: "privacy-shake": a haptic interface for managing privacy settings in mobile location sharing applications. In: Proceedings of the 12th International Conference on Human Computer Interaction with Mobile Devices and Services, MobileHCI 2010, NY, USA, pp. 411–412 (2010). http://doi.acm.org/10.1145/1851600.1851690

6. Kauer, M., Franz, B., Pfeiffer, T., Heine, M., Christin, D.: Improving privacy settings for facebook by using interpersonal distance as criterion. In: CHI 2013 Extended Abstracts on Human Factors in Computing Systems, New York, NY, USA, pp. 793–798 (2013). http://tuprints.ulb.tu-darmstadt.de/3490/

7. Lin, J., Liu, B., Sadeh, N., Hong, J.I.: Modeling users' mobile app privacy preferences: restoring usability in a sea of permission settings. In: Symposium On Usable Privacy and Security (SOUPS 2014), pp. 199–212. USENIX Association, Menlo Park. https://www.usenix.org/conference/soups2014/proceedings/presentation/lin

8. Majeski, M., Johnson, M., Bellovin, S.M.: The failure of online social network privacy settings. Technical report CUCS-010-11, Department of Computer Science, Columbia University, February 2011

9. Raber, F., Luca, A.D., Graus, M.: Privacy wedges: area-based audience selection for social network posts. In: Twelfth Symposium on Usable Privacy and Security (SOUPS 2016). USENIX Association, Denver (2016). https://www.usenix.org/conference/soups2016/workshop-program/wpi/presentation/raber

10. Spassova, L., Schoening, J., Kahl, G., Krueger, A.: Innovative retail laboratory. In: Roots for the Future of Ambient Intelligence, European Conference on Ambient Intelligence (Am I-09), 3rd November, Salzburg, Austria, pp. 18–21 (2009). https://www.dfki.de/web/forschung/publikationen/renameFileForDownload?filename=AmI-Landscape-InnovativeRetailLab.pdf&file_id=uploads_338

Versatile Classroom Management Solution for Teachers in Developing Countries

Muhammad Zahid Iqbal[(⊠)]

Information Technology University, Lahore, Pakistan
Hello.Zahid@outlook.com

Abstract. Bringing interactivity and effectiveness of teaching in the classroom is always challenging especially in the developing countries. Previous studies show best practices of smart technologies in the classroom.

This research was conducted to develop an efficient and low-cost solution for teachers in managing the higher number of students, assessing progress and increasing student engagement in the classroom. We developed *My Class Manager*; a Smartphone application for quiz and paper marking, audio quiz for native language learning and performance management throughout the semester. We conducted a series of five evaluations of three classes of sizes 30, 35 and 40. Results of the evaluations show an increasing interest of students in the classroom, improved class engagement & attentions. It creates a time-efficient learning environment.

Keywords: ICT in education · m-learning · Smart education · Smartphone interactions · Teaching methodologies · e-learning · Interaction methodologies · Human centered design

1 Introduction

Education in the developing countries and rural areas is always a problem due to lack of resources and teachers. Due to large classes' size, teachers enable to provide attentions to students which lead to poor performance.

Smart phones are integrating rapidly in the lives there is a big move towards the implementing these applications in the education. Distance learning has been totally changed with these applications [1]. Lots of students' engagement strategies are being adopted in the different countries which definitely bring results to a great extent [2, 12]. Singapore & Australia have brilliant experience of ICT based solution in the early classes' school education and really get appreciated results [6, 10].

Wankel & Charles worked for students' engagement in the classroom by using the latest technology. They worked with the social media, communication mediums and web 2.0 to bring an innovation in the classroom environment [3].

Tondeur, Jo, and et al have worked out to find how ICT interact with the policy of the schools. They have shown their finding as it is hard to implement any new technology in the classroom in the public sector because of policy restrictions [4]. Sutherland and Rosamund have worked out to find the efficiency of use of ICT in the classroom and outside the classroom [5].

R. Bernhaupt et al. (Eds.): INTERACT 2017, Part IV, LNCS 10516, pp. 478–481, 2017.
DOI: 10.1007/978-3-319-68059-0_55

Choy and Doris Wong have briefly explained what is happening in the classroom in Singapore. They have explored the smart classroom of the Singapore which delivers best results in the World [6].

Jung, and Insung worked with ICT-Pedagogy integration in the teachers training workshop to deliver the best practices and providing ICT experience for teachers [7]. Kennewell and Steve worked on learning outcomes from a technology rich classroom environment for teachers. They have explored the benefits of technology on learning and teaching with ICT-based pedagogy [8].

Markett, and Carina have introduced an SMS based system to create interactivity in the classroom where students get involved with SMS with instructors [9]. Meurant, and Robert have also used SMS teaching methodology which provides quite successful results [11]. This method also adopted in Pakistan which is SMS based quiz system.

Mertler, Craig A., and Cynthia Campbell developed Assessment Literacy Inventory (ALI) and evaluated with 152 teachers to find the performance of traditional teaching methods and new interventions of technology in teaching pedagogy [10].

We conducted survey and interviews to find and explore the local challenges. Despite all of the above mentioned great inventions. In the public sector schools, Classes size is too big and teachers vs. students ratios highly low. It creates a gap between delivery of knowledge and time efficiency. There is a need of a comprehensive solution for the classroom which can help teachers to conduct quiz and make assessment easily.

2 Proposed Solution

We developed a smart phone application for teachers named My Class Manager for Android OS devices. Android is one of the most popular OS used in smart phones in Pakistan as more than 90% Smart phones are Android OS based.

Basic interface has been shown in Fig. 1. A server is linked with the Android application where teachers can create their quiz/papers and conduct in the classroom. Teachers provide the answer sheets to the students and play the audio quiz in the classroom.

Fig. 1. Right to Left, Splash Screen, Login Screen Dashboard and audio quiz of application

In the concept of the audio quiz teacher enables to manage a large class size by creating attention and delivering the quiz with native English language accent. Teachers can make their digital quiz anytime in the class and conduct for students.

After finishing the quiz time, teacher will scan the answer sheets of all the students through application. Application sends scanned answer sheets to server & provides the results on the base of correct answers. Application provides text to speak, English to Urdu and Urdu to English dictionary to help teachers in the native English accent which is lack in the Pakistan.

3   Evaluations

Application tested in three different classes. These tests conducted in 6th, 7th and 8th class with 40 students each. A Smartphone given to every teacher with application installed inside and guided about the testing procedure of the application. There were Eight (3) teachers who participated in the testing. Students participated in the research are 12–16 years old. Teachers participated in the research have 3–7 years experience in teaching English and science subjects.

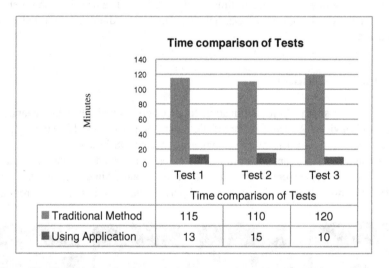

	Time comparison of Tests		
	Test 1	Test 2	Test 3
Traditional Method	115	110	120
Using Application	13	15	10

Fig. 2. This graphs shows evaluations conducted in the three classes

As checking a manual papers/quiz manually takes 80–120 min for 20 one page MCQs papers. Using the *My Class Manager* teachers checked 40 papers within Ten 10–15 min, show in Fig. 2. It saved about two hours just for simple paper which test the students' performance easily and provided whole class average results without any effort. As explained by teacher who has about seven years experience in teaching English says, *"I am teaching 55 students and it is not possible for me to provide individual attentions and conducting students' assessment by paper work due to large class size."*

4   Conclusion

Teachers show a great attraction towards using ICT in classroom for making their life easier and using modern teaching pedagogy. Teachers show a great attraction towards using ICT in classrooms for making their life easier and using modern teaching pedagogy. Paper & Quiz checking speed and getting full assessment of the large class size is highly improved which is one of the basic need for teachers. As for generating progress reports for parents and management of students' data for the whole years need lots of time with manual working, *My Class Manager* can do this work without any effort.

In the further investigation, we are working to approve the application by adding new features which can create more interactive classroom environment.

References

1. Paris, S.G., Paris, A.H.: Classroom applications of research on self-regulated learning. Educ. Psychol. **36**(2), 89–101 (2001)
2. Christenson, S.L., Amy, L., Reschly, A.L., Wylie, C. (eds). Handbook of Research on Student Engagement. Springer, New York (2012)
3. Wankel, C., Blessinger, P.: Increasing Student Engagement and Retention in e-Learning Environments: Web 2.0 and Blended Learning Technologies. Emerald Group Publishing, Somerville (2013)
4. Tondeur, J., et al.: ICT integration in the classroom: challenging the potential of a school policy. Comput. Educ. **51**(1), 212–223 (2008)
5. Sutherland, R., et al.: Transforming teaching and learning: embedding ICT into everyday classroom practices. J. Comput. Assist. Learn. **20**(6), 413–425 (2004)
6. Choy, D., Wong, A.F.L, Ping, G.: Singapore's preservice teachers' perspectives in integrating information and communication technology (ICT) during practicum
7. Jung, I.: ICT-pedagogy integration in teacher training: application cases worldwide. Educ. Technol. Soc. **8**(2), 94–101 (2005)
8. Kennewell, S., Gary, B.: The influence of a technology-rich classroom environment on elementary teachers' pedagogy and children's learning. In: Proceedings of the International Federation for Information Processing Working Group 3.5 Open Conference on Young Children and Learning Technologies, vol. 34. Australian Computer Society, Inc. (2003)
9. Markett, C., et al.: Using short message service to encourage interactivity in the classroom. Comput. Educ. **46**(3), 280–293 (2006)
10. Mertler, C.A., Campbell, C.: Measuring Teachers' Knowledge and Application of Classroom Assessment Concepts: Development of the Assessment (2005). Online Submission
11. Meurant, R.C.: Cell phones in the L2 classroom: thumbs up to SMS. In: 2006 International Conference on Hybrid Information Technology, vol. 1. IEEE (2006)
12. Lindquist, D., et al.: Exploring the potential of mobile phones for active learning in the classroom. ACM SIGCSE Bull. **39**(1), 384–388 (2007)

Field Trips

ICT Based Interventions for Anganwadi Healthcare Workers in Mumbai

Biju Thankachan[1(✉)], Sumita Sharma[1], Markku Turunen[1],
Juhani Linna[1], Heli Väätäjä[2], Reinier Kortekaas[3], and Tom Gross[4]

[1] TAUCHI, University of Tampere, Tampere, Finland
Biju.Thankachan@uta.fi
[2] Tampere University of Technology, Tampere, Finland
[3] Siemens Healthineers, Erlangen, Germany
[4] University of Bamberg, Bamberg, Germany

Abstract. Anganwadi workers [1] form the core of healthcare system for a large section of rural and semi-urban population in India. They provide care for newborn babies and play an important role in immunization programs, besides providing health related information to pregnant women. Traditionally these Anganwadi workers use paper based information leaflets as a part of their job to spread awareness among the people. Although mobile phones have made their inroads into the day to day life of these workers for basic communication (making a call), however it is yet to be seen how a mobile device is being used as a technological aid for their work. There are enormous challenges in addressing these issues especially in developing regions owing to numerous reasons such as illiteracy, cognitive difficulties, cultural norms, collaborations, experience and exposure, motivation, power relations, and social standing [2]. The purpose of this field visit would be to enquire the role of mobile devices in their day-to-day work; and if being used as a technological intervention, then in what manner and form is it being used? The methodology used to conduct the study would involve contextual enquiry, open-ended interviews and observing the Anganwadi workers using ICT solutions and other informational artefacts.

Keywords: Low-literate users · Emergent users · Healthcare workers · ICT4D · HCI4D · Anganwadi · Mitanins

1 Project Description

Anganwadi worker are involved in spreading healthcare information, contraceptive counselling and nutrition education in rural and urban areas across India. We have been conducting a similar study with Mitanins [3] (Community Healthcare Volunteers in Chhattisgarh State), who can be considered as counterpart of Anganwadi workers in the state. As both Mitanins and Anganwadi workers have a similar job profile (like door-to-door household visits to spread health and nutrition related information), it would be interesting to study what and how technological interventions are being used by the Anganwadi workers in their work life; for example, to observe how a mobile phone is used to spread information and educating people. As many of these volunteers

© IFIP International Federation for Information Processing 2017
Published by Springer International Publishing AG 2017. All Rights Reserved
R. Bernhaupt et al. (Eds.): INTERACT 2017, Part IV, LNCS 10516, pp. 485–487, 2017.
DOI: 10.1007/978-3-319-68059-0_56

are low literate (both Anganwadi workers and Mitanins), heavily text based ICT solution for them would be futile. This study would provide us with valuable information as to how they use mobile devices, what applications are being used, how they make sense of the written material/information. Interactive videos, animations (instead of paper leaflets) and simple games related to health and nutrition could be used to educate the mothers of new-born babies and children. This in turn would help us in developing text free user interfaces for low literate users. Novel and innovative adaptation of technology by one user groups could be easily adapted by the other groups, and would provide insight on developing newer solutions.

1.1 Methodology

One-day field visit to interact with the Anganwadi workers of Mumbai.

- Contextual Enquiry, Semi-structured Interviews (open ended), Observations.
- Data would be collected as field notes, and audio recorders with permission, as well as photos and video-clips are shot in case the participants agree to capture their device use and relevant other informational or other artifacts used.
- Quick comparison and juxtaposing the profiles of Mitanins and Anganwadi workers.
- Observing the ICT interventions being used.
- Probably, a rapid prototyping, or at least paper/sketch solution.

1.2 Expected Outcomes

Based on the above study, we will analyze and gain insight on the differences and similarities between Anganwadi workers and Mitanins, and what ICT interventions are being used by them? We would analyze, what approach and solutions used by one group could be successfully used/adapted by the other and what opportunities arise for novel solutions to be developed? Although currently, mobile devices are seldom used for spreading health related information by Anganwadi workers/Mitanins, yet in the days to come, it is expected that these devices will be adopted for educating people. Our focus is on using mobile devices is to understand how these devices can act as a tool in educating and spreading information to the general population. We are also in the process of collaborating with the stakeholders in the government, so that new interventions developed through this research.

2 Team

The team consists of *Prof. Markku Turunen*, Head of the Masters Programme in Human-Technology Interaction, the Speech-Based and Pervasive Interaction Research Group and the India Network at the University of Tampere. He is also the principal research investigator for the INCEPT India project.

Prof. Heli Väätäjä who is involved in the INCEPT India project from the Tampere University of Technology.

Doctoral Student Biju Thankachan whose focus is on developing text-free user interfaces for low-literate users, for societal impact.

Researcher Juhani Linna who focuses on the in varying industry and societal contexts, from a sustainable business perspective.

Researcher Sumita Sharma, whose doctoral thesis work on designing novel interactive educational application for under-served Indian children aligns with the study.

Reinier Kortekaas is involved with user interface designer at Siemens Healthineers, Germany.

Tom Gross is professor and chair of Human-Computer Interaction at University of Bamberg, Germany. He is the official representative of Germany in the TC.13 on Human-Computer Interaction of IFIP.

References

1. Ministry of Women and Child Development, Government of India. http://icds-wcd.nic.in/issnip/home.htm
2. Medhi, I., Cutrell, E., Toyama, K.: It's not just illiteracy. In: Proceedings of the 2010 International Conference on Interaction Design & International Development, pp. 1–10. British Computer Society, Swinton (2010). http://dl.acm.org/citation.cfm?id=2227347.2227348
3. Mitanin Programme. Department of Health and Family Welfare, Government of Chhattisgarh

Investigating Perceptions of Personalization and Privacy in India

Hanna Schneider[✉], Ceenu George, Malin Eiband, and Florian Lachner

LMU Munich, Munich, Germany
hanna.schneider@ifi.lmu.de

Abstract. Technological products are increasingly equipped with data collection and personalization mechanisms that allow them to adapt to an individual user's needs [4]. However, the value and perception of these practices for users is still unclear. This field trip proposal investigates users' mental models of personalization as well as perceived benefits and drawbacks using semi-structured interviews. The interviews make use of the critical incident technique and drawing tasks. We expect that findings from the field trip will result in rich understanding of the prospective of a collectivist society on personalization and privacy. Results of the field trip can, hence, be contrasted to the results of an equivalent study conducted in Germany, an individualistic society. The overall goal of our studies is to highlight differences in user needs of collectivist and individualistic societies for researchers and practitioners who develop highly personalized systems.

Keywords: Privacy · Personalization · Value-driven design

1 Introduction

As data collection and processing techniques improve, technological products are increasingly equipped with personalization mechanisms that allow them to adapt to an individual user's needs [4]. One of the main purposes of personalization and customization is to evoke or foster a feeling of individuality or "me-ness", which is especially important in individualistic and particularly Western societies [4,8]. However, the notions of individuality and privacy are perceived very differently, and often in a negative light, in societies with a collectivist world view [7], e.g. in the Arab Gulf [1], in Africa [3], or in India [2]. The goal of this fieldtrip is to investigate users' perceptions of benefits and drawbacks of personalization in India. Currently, we are conducting an equivalent study in Germany. The pre-study in Germany indicated differing mental models of personalization and varying privacy sensibility when using personalized products or services. We, therefore, want to further investigate this relation. However, to objectively address this research question, we want to understand privacy concerns of personalization in both individualistic and collectivist countries.

© IFIP International Federation for Information Processing 2017
Published by Springer International Publishing AG 2017. All Rights Reserved
R. Bernhaupt et al. (Eds.): INTERACT 2017, Part IV, LNCS 10516, pp. 488–491, 2017.
DOI: 10.1007/978-3-319-68059-0_57

Both studies will be conducted in similar settings hence we expect that findings from the field trip in India (a more collectivist country in contrast to Germany, an individualistic country [7]) will enrich our study with an alternative perspective to personalization and privacy and enable us to critically reflect on values and assumptions that underlie the design of personalized technologies. We hope that our findings will inform researchers and practitioners who develop personalized systems of similarities and differences in user needs between these two societies.

2   Project Plan

2.1   Goals

- Defining the necessity of personalization in a collectivist country
- Understanding needs for personalization and privacy in different contexts
- Analyzing culturally sensitive aspects of personalization and privacy

2.2   Locations

For this study, we propose two different contexts, namely (1) urban and (2) rural areas. We believe that this would provide an interesting setting to study the perception of personalization and privacy, as we believe that the perception will vary based on distance to the city. Participants should also be from a broad age group and gender should be equally distributed. We will split up into teams, each team targeting a different context. However, to select specific locations around Mumbai, we would appreciate advice from the organisational team of the conference or local universities. We are flexible on the exact locations as long as we can target the proposed geographical group of people.

2.3   Method

Our study plan is focused on qualitative data collection techniques. We combine semi-structured interviews, based on the critical incident technique [5], and drawing tasks to elicit users' mental models of personalization [9]. The interview script consists of questions about demographic data as well as users' technology use, their mental model of personalization and their perception of benefits and drawbacks. The ten main questions of the semi-structured interviews are:

1. Which specific websites did you visit last week?
2. What was your goal when you visited the websites?
3. Did you use different devices?
4. Did you notice that either the content or the interface of the webpage were tailored to you in any way?
5. Did you find this tailoring to you good/bad/helpful/useful? How did you like it?
6. Do you have any concerns about this tailoring?

7. Can you give us an example of a website you visited and you were concerned about the tailored website?
8. Do you think the page knows something about you, and if so, what?
9. How do you think this tailoring was done? Could you please draw and explain your thoughts?
10. Is there anything that you would have (not) liked to be tailored to you?

To better understand the context of use, interviewers may ask additional questions and note down observational data as needed. Moreover, as we assume that individual attitudes towards individualism and collectivism will be of importance for the analysis of the qualitative data, we will use standardized quantitative scales such as INDCOL [10] or the Culture Orientation Scale [6] to better understand our participant sample.

2.4 Participants, Recruiting and Ethical Considerations

All interview questions were designed according to ethical guidelines and all data will be stored and analysed anonymously. Participants will be informed about the goals of our study and asked for their consent before the interview. They will be paid Rs.200 as a token of compensation.

2.5 Schedule

Day 1

– 9:00–10:00: Team meeting, briefing, splitting up in smaller groups
– 10:00–17:00: Groups go out to their locations and conduct interviews and observations

Day 2

– 9:00–11:00: Groups share their findings + insights
– 9:30–12:00: Clustering of insights + definition of focus group topics
– 12:00–13:00: Lunch
– 13:00–14:00: Focus groups and scenario sketching
– 14:00–15:00: Summary of results + extracting of recommendations
– 15:00–15:30: Wrap-up + definition of next steps

3 Expected Outcome

Findings will help to contrast the views of personalization and privacy as prevalent in Western societies. The findings will further be used to create recommendations and guidelines for personalization and privacy for technological products targeting the Indian market.

4   Field Trip Participants

The field trip will be carried out by researchers from various disciplines and both academia and industry:

Hanna Schneider (Organizer, LMU Munich)
Florian Lachner (Organizer, CDTM Munich)
Elaine Brechin Montgomery (Facebook)
Alfred Kobsa (University of California, Irvine)
Panayiotis Zaphiris (Cyprus University of Technology)
Corinne Longman (Google)
Beth Bergen (Google)
Anjali Kukreja (HealthKart Gurgaon, India)
Pratiksha Dixit (Srishti Institute of Art, Design and Technology)

References

1. Abokhodair, N., Vieweg, S.: Privacy & social media in the context of the arab gulf. In: Proceedings of the 2016 ACM Conference on Designing Interactive Systems, DIS 2016, NY, USA, pp. 672–683 (2016). http://doi.acm.org/10.1145/2901790.2901873
2. Asokan, A.: The space between mine and ours: exploring the subtle spaces between the private and the shared in india. In: Ethnographic Praxis in Industry Conference Proceedings, vol. 2008, pp. 175–191. Wiley Online Library (2008)
3. Bidwell, N.: Ubuntu in the network: humanness in social capital in rural africa. Interactions **17**(2), 68–71 (2010)
4. Blom, J.: Personalization: a taxonomy. In: CHI 2000 Extended Abstracts on Human Factors in Computing Systems, pp. 313–314. ACM (2000)
5. Flanagan, J.C.: The critical incident technique. Psychol. Bull. **51**(4), 327 (1954)
6. Gudykunst, B., Singelis, T., Trafimow, D., Realo, A., Triandis, C., Street, E.D.: Converging measurement of horizontal and vertical individualism and collectivism. J. Pers. Social Psychol. **74**(1), 118–128 (1998)
7. Hofstede, G., Hofstede, G.J., Minkov, M.: Cultures and Organizations. Software of the Mind. McGraw-Hill, Maidenhead (2010)
8. Kalyanaraman, S., Sundar, S.S.: The psychological appeal of personalized content in web portals: does customization affect attitudes and behavior? J. Commun. **56**(1), 110–132 (2006)
9. Kang, R., Dabbish, L., Fruchter, N., Kiesler, S.: "my data just goes everywhere:" user mental models of the internet and implications for privacy and security. In: Eleventh Symposium on Usable Privacy and Security (SOUPS 2015), pp. 39–52. https://www.usenix.org/conference/soups2015/proceedings/presentation/kang
10. Singelis, T.M., Triandis, H.C., Bhawuk, D.P., Gelfand, M.J.: Horizontal and vertical dimensions of individualism and collectivism: a theoretical and measurement refinement. Cross Cult. Res. **29**(3), 240–275 (1995)

IVR Wizard of OZ Field Experiment
with Less-Literate Telecom Customers

Deepak Ranjan Padhi$^{(\boxtimes)}$ and Rohit Gupta

Indian Institute of Technology Bombay, Mumbai, India
{deepak.padhi,rohit7gupta}@iitb.ac.in

Abstract. Interactive Voice Response (IVR) is a popular and one of the most deployed technology interventions in the developing countries. One of the primary business drivers is that it does not mandate the user to use any technologically advanced device. On the other hand, IVR has been studied for its usability issues. Even for the service providers, IVR costs are higher than services on data channels. However, given the sunk costs and low-technology investments, they are an attractive business proposition and continue to garner support. In this field trip, we propose to have an "experiential" trip of manning and experiencing the system when in use by a less-literate user. Our field trip would allow the participants to "listen" onto and experience first-hand the roller coaster experiential ride when using an IVR system. This will help us to reveal a lot of contextual data such as performance of a low-literate user with IVR, turn taking behaviour, machine and user relationship building, ambiguities etc. This will lead to interventions in the development of dialog structure personification, emotional value association, interaction design and user experience design. The methodology used to conduct the study would be wizard of context, and field observations followed by an affinity analysis.

Keywords: IVR · Low literate · Affinity diagram · Wizard of OZ

1 Project Description

This project is mainly focused on experiencing the different challenges of IVR while interacting with low-literate users. With a virtual set up of a call centre, participants can understand how an IVR works? what are the different issues? What are the opportunities? How to make an IVR better? Through this project a wizard will be built to facilitate interactions between the user and the participant (Behaving as a machine with an IVR script). Our report will include the social aspects of IVR along with the technological aspects. We will highlight the established relationship between a man and a machine. We will also propose the opportunities to support IVRs and making it better in future.

2 Theoretical Framework

Interactive Voice Response Systems (IVRs) are used to deliver different services of public interest in developing regions such as banking, healthcare, e-governance, agriculture etc. [1–4]. IVRs are assumed to be easier systems to deploy and sustain.

© IFIP International Federation for Information Processing 2017
Published by Springer International Publishing AG 2017. All Rights Reserved
R. Bernhaupt et al. (Eds.): INTERACT 2017, Part IV, LNCS 10516, pp. 492–495, 2017.
DOI: 10.1007/978-3-319-68059-0_58

They do not seem to need high-end dedicated resources at the user end but, in fact, can capitalize on fast growing mobile phone networks in the developing regions. In fact, there are more than 7 billion mobile phones around the world as per the report of ICT data and statistics division, May 2015 [5] and 60% of the subscribers live in developing countries. However, the non-literate and low literate people face great difficulties in using these ICTs having complex information architecture, interactions, navigation and textual interfaces. This brings the question of how to make these ICTs accessible by these users who contribute to more than 15% population of the world. Researchers have conducted several empirical studies using non-textual UIs, GUIs, IVRs, IVRs with visual augmentations for different types of menu structures, menu positions etc. One of the prime intervention of designing user interfaces targeting these emergent users is IVRs. Interactive voice response (IVR) is a technology that allows a computer to interact with humans through the use of voice. IVRs dialog prompts are usually directed in nature and can engage users with minimal or no training. For example, press 1 for doing an action. However, users in the developing regions are still challenged by the usability issues of such IVRs [6–8]. Users report getting frustrated out of their poor interaction with IVRs. The ephemeral nature of audio prompts brings poor 'referability' in users' interaction with the IVRs. Tatchell [9] observes that the services activated using IVRs are difficult to learn, easy to forget and confusing. Users must win over a sequential and hierarchical menu structure using key presses and/or commands to distil the required information. Our main motivation is to find out these challenges within the scope of our experiment and propose solutions for IVR applications.

3   Method: Wizard of Oz

We propose a field trip of two days. We intend to setup a virtual call centre which would be manned by volunteers who can speak either of the 3 languages, namely, the local state language (Marathi), the national language (Hindi) and English. Each volunteer would be provided a cell phone and a IVR voice prompt script. We would also print a low-cost A5 sheet pamphlet advertising the availability of free talk time to callers of the published number in a particular time window. We would then circulate this pamphlet amongst the mess workers and house-keeping staff of IIT Bombay. We would also publicize this on WhatsApp messaging platform, as well as directed WhatsApp messages to the target audience. Their participation will be voluntary in nature. They will have to perform a navigation task of mobile recharge using our IVR service.

On the other side, within the Industrial Design Centre, we would setup the Conference Room-1 as our call centre. There will be 5 volunteers with the cell phones and script. Each volunteer would also be trained on these scrips. During the call, they are required to voice record, using the phone's built-in feature, each IVR interaction. Each phone would also be provided with a split stereo connector so that other field trip participants can also be able to listen to the conversation along with the volunteers. They will also interpret the conversation.

We believe this "listening-in" experiential aspects would be appreciated by the International Researchers, at the emotive and voice modulation level even though the language is foreign. After each call, the volunteers would then switch the phone to

"Airplane Mode" and explain the conversation to the participants. We would also provide a speaker phone so that the community could live-listen to the experiment.

We hope to highlight the challenges experienced by our users in using the system and connect with those challenges at the personal level using this setup.

The recorded voice conversations would then be subjected to note-taking and the notes created would be analysed using "Affinity Diagrams". The findings from the affinity diagrams would constitute the report.

4 Outcome/Deliverable

Presentation and report will constitute the following:

1. Challenges in IVR
2. Experiential aspects of IVR

5 Team

Team Size: 10

Group Facilitators (2) - Deepak Ranjan Padhi – PhD scholar at IDC School of Design, IIT Bombay, with focused interest in designing user interfaces with IVRs.

- Rohit Gupta – M.Des student at IDC School of Design, IIT Bombay, to help in designing the wizard and call centre set up.

We are expecting participation from a diverse group of people who would be interested to work in similar area.

Researchers (2) - Preferably, candidates belonging to an advanced digitalized country, who can contribute for experiment design and analysis.

Field representatives (5) - To help in recruiting users, conducting primary user studies and running a virtual call centre. This position seeks knowledge of Hindi and Marathi and a combination of male and female candidates.

Designers (1) - To help in affinity analysis, creating quick mock-ups of ideas and simulations, sketches and illustrations.

References

1. Barnard, E., Plauché, M., Davel, M.: The utility of spoken dialog systems. In: Spoken Language Technology Workshop, SLT 2008. IEEE, pp. 13–16 (2008)
2. Kumar, A., Rajput, N., Chakraborty, D., Agarwal, S. K., Nanavati, A.A.: WWTW: the world wide telecom web. In: Proceedings of the 2007 Workshop on Networked Systems for Developing Regions, p. 7. ACM (2007)
3. Plauche, M., Nallasamy, U., Pal, J., Wooters, C., Ramachandran, D.: Speech recognition for illiterate access to information and technology. In: International Conference on Information and Communication Technologies and Development, ICTD 2006, pp. 83–92. IEEE (2006)

4. Shrivastava, A., Joshi, A.: Effects of visuals, menu depths, and menu positions on IVR usage by non-tech savvy users. In: Proceedings of the India HCI 2014 Conference on Human Computer Interaction, p. 35. ACM (2014)
5. ICT Facts and Figures. https://www.itu.int/en/ITUD/Statistics/Documents/facts/ICTFacts Figures2015.pdf
6. Marics, M.A., Engelbeck, G.: Designing voice menu applications for telephones. In: Handbook of human-computer interaction, pp. 1085–1102 (1997)
7. Resnick, P., Virzi, R.A.: Skip and scan: cleaning up telephone interface. In: Proceedings of the SIGCHI Conference on Human Factors in Computing Systems, pp. 419–426. ACM (1992)
8. Yin, M., Zhai, S.: Dial and see: tackling the voice menu navigation problem with cross-device user experience integration. In: Proceedings of the 18th Annual ACM Symposium on User Interface Software and Technology, pp. 187–190. ACM (2005)
9. Tatchell, G.R.: Problems with the existing telephony customer interface: the pending eclipse of touch-tone and dial-tone. In: Conference Companion on Human Factors in Computing Systems, pp. 242–243. ACM (1996)

Modeling Less-Literate User's Choices of Smartphone Authentication Modes

Pankaj Doke, Sylvan Lobo$^{(\boxtimes)}$, V.S. Shyama, Ulemba Hirom,
and Mridul Basumotari

Tata Consultancy Services Ltd., Mumbai, India
{pankaj.doke,sylvan.lobo,shyamav.s,ulemba.h,
mridul.basumotari}@tcs.com

Abstract. Smartphones are increasingly becoming a device of choice or are imperative in the discourse of Digitization of services such as banking within a developing country like India. At the same time, a large population within India is less-literate [1, 4, 5] who are also the primary beneficiaries of our research. We believe that Emergent Users [2] are the next set of users who are likely to adopt smartphones and technology in a larger context. Amongst these emergent users we expect that a large class of users are less-literate, more comfortable with native languages and have never directly consumed any digital technology based information system. For this fieldtrip study, we would be considering only users who fall under such criteria. Specifically those within an age limit of 40 years, prior exposure to a smartphone for a duration of at least 6 months, education not more than class 10, and no prior (non-mediated) use of desktop computer information systems.

Within the ecosystem of the smartphone, namely, the phone itself comprising of an operating system and mobile applications on the phone, as well as those on the Internet cloud, a mandatory creation of a Digital Identity in the form of a Google Account is required.

Currently, the notion of digital identity Authorization in most smartphone-based applications is implemented using a variety of choices, such as, password, PIN, patterns, biometrics such as fingerprint, voice. In the context of our users, namely emergent users [2], each of these authentication modes has a Usability aspect to it, which has a strong influence on the user and their adoption. For example, issues such as literacy levels are expected to play a role in the composition of passwords or use of local languages in usability of passwords.

In this Field Study, we wish to explore the Migration Model of the users amongst all these authentication modes. For example, how do users trade off PIN to Passwords to Biometrics; what triggers in their context of use, bring about these migrations when potentially the user may have chosen an alternative authentication mode.

Keywords: Less-literate users · Usable security · Smartphone · Demonetization · Digitization · Migration model · User modeling

© IFIP International Federation for Information Processing 2017
Published by Springer International Publishing AG 2017. All Rights Reserved
R. Bernhaupt et al. (Eds.): INTERACT 2017, Part IV, LNCS 10516, pp. 496–500, 2017.
DOI: 10.1007/978-3-319-68059-0_59

1 Introduction

Smart phone adoption in India is increasing across the society and there is a significant push towards Digitization at various levels within the country. At the same time, a large population within India is less-literate [1, 4, 5] and have technology adoption challenges. We also observe rapid adoption of smartphones in the country by less-literate users [2] with no prior familiarity with computers and Internet ecosystem. Digitization, for example of services like Banking, DigiDhan [6], could leave the user vulnerable to a variety of cyber-security attacks. The theoretical security measures available against such attacks are lowered by user behavior, which stems from poor Usability [3]. The available digital identity authorization modes in smartphones are subject to adoption by emergent users [2] based on various aspects of usability. In this study, we are trying to understand the influence of "Context of Use" on the adoption of authentication mechanisms. We are trying to model how context dictates adoption of security modes, rather than security or strength as a decider or a user preference in isolation from the context.

In this study, we are modeling the intersection of smartphone, security and specifically authentication modes, by exploring what forces are at play and how they affect each other. This investigation may help in design interventions based on the model for making security contextually usable.

2 Plan

2.1 User Group and Recruitment Criteria

The field trip would be for one day and comprise of either 9 or 15 participants. Each team would have 3 participants of which one would be a local language or national language speaking person. Each team would interact with either 3 or 5 users, totaling 9 or 15 users. Effectively each participant would get an opportunity to interact with 1 user. Users would be chosen through stratified convenient sampling. 6–8 female users and 6–8 male users would be chosen from the mess and housekeeping staff at Indian Institute of Technology Bombay as well as the residential areas around the Campus with the help of NGOs like Vidya.

An alternative location could be APMC (Agricultural Produce Market Committee) in Navi Mumbai – which is Asia's largest market. Here we could interact with the users who are loader-unloaders of gunny bags – called Mathadi. For female users, we could interact with those who work in the shops/establishments at APMC.

We may identify users with the following criteria: An age limit of 40; Prior exposure to a smartphone for duration of at least 6 months; Education not more than class10; No prior (non-mediated) use of desktop computer information systems.

One pilot test would be conducted and all the users would be recruited prior to the field trip.

2.2 Method and Agenda

The team briefing would start at around 1000 h and be limited to 1100 h. We would followed two methods (1) retrospective data elicitation and (2) speculative data elicitation.

Retrospective data elicitation. Expecting the migration of authentication have happened in the past, one can only recall the account through retrospection and the data elicitation could be via Contextual Inquiry. At some point the Trigger could take longer time frame for instance, a recently married mother may have a pattern password, but after having the child she may have migrated to PIN or Password, this could be due to propensity of the child to play with phone and draw patterns on it. We could also investigate the lack of child-profile which could be tailored for the child. Similarly, for the case of an auto-driver, they may have chosen a password due to the demands of their profession. In these contexts, we cannot trigger a natural occurrence of a scenario and context and hence have no recourse but to rely and use data from retrospective accounts. Since the Field trip is limited to 1 day and we desire to interact with either 9 or 15 users within a span of half a day, retrospective accounts seems the only recourse at the moment for data acquisition.

Speculative data elicitation. Users are requested to visit to the lab and speculate with a given scenarios which trigger their past/retrospective accounts of password change, e.g. rainy season, taking a child to hospital or shop. By stitching the field interaction and lab conversations, we would be able to gather a data point on how adoption and migration of authentication modes happen on the smartphone. We believe that not in all circumstances would it be possible to recreate natural scenarios for example, Mother–child case. Hence we would have imaginary scenarios which possibly act as triggers for decision making with users in a lab environment. And believe that their reasoning and thoughts would reflect in action or course of action in future they are likely to reason and follow in the future, if faced with such a situation.

The data could be possibly triangulated by cross positioning the question. e.g. an unmarried person would be asked what he/she would do after marriage and child or observed a married person on what they do with authentication or asking an non-auto drivers on what if they were auto driver. Later the data could be collated and validate through data triangulation with the users in the context and in lab environment.

In the lab environment, the user would be shown a paper prototype of an android phone and briefed that she could assume this to be their personal phone and have valuable data such as their Aadhaar card photo, PAN card photo, PayTM, WhatsApp and personal family photographs. The user would then have to participate in three scenarios as described below. The 3 scenarios would be conducted using paper prototypes of various authentication modes.

- **Scenario 1.** The user is provided with paper prototypes of multiple authentication modes and has to choose one out of them for safeguarding their phone.
- **Scenario 2.** In this scenario, user would be provided with the same choices of authentication modes, but in addition the user would also receive another set of cards which depict the scenarios from his context of use. User then has to make associations between the authentication modes provided and the context scenarios mentioned in

the cards. Examples of context could be: Parent trying to make a mobile based payment in a dispensary while accompanied by a child who needs treatment; Paying school fees for child while parent stands in a queue in the rainy season; Paying the local vegetable vendor on the way back from school; etc. – i.e. scenarios where the users could be at risk while using their phone (data or monetary loss, privacy).

- **Scenario 3.** In this scenario, user has already chosen a preferred authentication mode based on the context provided in Scenario 2. For that particular authentication mode within the context, user is provided with a preset of password options. The password options are based on researcher assessed usable complexity. For example an L or Rangoli pattern for a pattern lock. The user is then asked to choose a password they prefer from the choices provided.

At the end of the tasks, we will also do a qualitative open-ended interview with the users to capture summative information or any formative data points we may have missed. After coming back from field trip around 5 pm, all the participants would submit the field finding in the form of field note capture in excel file including the photos and videos in shared folder. Then everyone attempt to do the migration model with the team whosoever come first.

3 Participants

We would have 9 or15 participants which comprises of:

- **Facilitator and Research Team:** Researchers would help in recruitment of the users, training and project management.
- **Mediators and Design Team:** Local Language speakers, who would help in translation. Designers for making deriving design insights.
- **Senior Researchers:** At least one researcher (desirable not mandatory) who has similar experience in a developed country and at least one researcher who has a mobile security awareness.

The participants in this field trip will get first hand user study exposure on practices and adoptions of security practices by emergent users in a developing country. They would do the actual user study and scenario triggering with the user. At the end for user, as a take-away, they would be informed on how to set better password using textual passwords and gain knowledge on what comprise a good password.

4 Requirements

We would be considering the location on the basis of lesser commute timing (not more than 30 min) either at IIT Bombay and surrounding areas or APMC. We need some assistance in recruitment process and also travel expenses (in case the location is APMC, our suggestion would be IITB bus rented for a half-day trip). We also need some budget on gifts which would be given as a gesture of appreciation to users, refreshments (lunch), internet connection, stationery and room space in conference venue.

5 Expected Outcomes

We expect to have a report on the observations and insights of the usability issues of the various authentication schemes in a context when used by an emergent user. We also hope to model the user-technology-migration as indicated by the data.

References

1. Chandramouli, C.: Rural Urban Distribution of Population (Provisional Population Totals). http://censusindia.gov.in/2011-prov-results/paper2/data_files/india/Rural_Urban_2011.pdf. Accessed 31 Jan 2017
2. Devanuj, J.A.: Technology adoption by "emergent" users: the user-usage model, pp. 28–38. ACM (2013)
3. Dourish, P., Redmiles, D.: An approach to usable security based on event monitoring and visualization, pp 75–81. ACM (2002)
4. State-wise Literacy Rates. In: Open Gov. Data OGD Platf. India (2013). https://data.gov.in/catalog/state-wise-literacy-rates. Accessed 31 Jan 2017
5. Performance of States of India (Rural) - ACER 2009. http://planningcommission.nic.in/data/datatable/data_2312/DatabookDec2014%20231.pdf. Accessed 31 Jan 2017
6. DigiDhan Mela. https://digidhan.mygov.in/. Accessed 31 Jan 2017

Parental Perspectives Towards Education Technology in Low-Income Urban Households

Sumita Sharma[1]([⊠]), Juhani Linna[1], Biju Thankachan[1],
Markku Turunen[1], Heli Väätäjä[2], Pekka Kallioniemi[1],
Janet C. Read[3], and Gavin Sim[3]

[1] TAUCHI, University of Tampere, Tampere, Finland
sumita.s.sharma@sis.uta.fi
[2] Tampere University of Technology, Tampere, Finland
[3] ChiCI Group, University of Central Lancashire, Preston, UK

Abstract. Government and NGO schools catering to children from low-income urban environments are increasingly introducing technology in the Indian classroom. However, one of the challenges is convincing low-literate parents the potential benefits of technology in education. In this study, we aim to uncover the concerns and expectations of low-income low-literate parents towards educational technology for their children, through semi-structured interviews. This is an extension of our ongoing work in designing sustainable educational technology models for low-literate urban populations.

Keywords: Sustainable EdTech · Low-income urban population

1 Research Agenda

The aim of the INCEPT project at the University of Tampere is to define a sustainable model for educational technology acceptance and adoption in low-income urban households. As a first step in this process we focused on the micro-level context of a child's learning environment, namely, the people they interact with every day as defined by Bronfenbrenner's Ecological Systems Model [1]. This includes parents, children, teachers, and volunteers (especially in the case of NGO schools). These different stakeholders have individualistic motivations towards technology acceptance and adoption. For instance, most schools charge extra tuition for computer courses, or additional 'maintenance' charges for purchasing smart boards, which parents should feel worthwhile to pay for. Moreover, there is fear of technology influencing children negatively, and making them easy prey for people with malicious intent.

Studies with rural Indian parents shed light on the challenges in technology adoption and acceptance in low-literate communities [2]. However, we have found that the challenges faced by low-income low-literate *rural* parents are different from those faced by low-income low-literate *urban* parents. This is because parents in urban areas are more exposed to technology (smart phones, tablets, computers) in their environment. Thus, what works for one group, may not work for the other. Currently (low-income low-literate urban) parental perspectives towards educational technology is largely under studied. To bridge this research gap, we conducted semi-structured

© IFIP International Federation for Information Processing 2017
Published by Springer International Publishing AG 2017. All Rights Reserved
R. Bernhaupt et al. (Eds.): INTERACT 2017, Part IV, LNCS 10516, pp. 501–503, 2017.
DOI: 10.1007/978-3-319-68059-0_60

interviews with several (low and middle income) parents in Delhi, and now extend our work to Mumbai.

The one-day field work will consist of semi-structured interviews with the parents of children in grades 5–8th studying in the local schools. About 5–10 parents will be inter-viewed. The interview questions are based on parental perspectives and insights towards educational technology – including **economic** (disposable assets, monthly budgets), **socio-cultural** (social practices, technology aspirations, positive aspects and expectations, and inhibitions), **organizational/political** (regulations and organizational practices e.g. syllabus, chain of commands) and **environmental** (e.g. current state of technology usage in the school, infrastructure) **perspectives**. Children, if present during the interviews, will be asked their ambitions in life, their favorite games (computer/mobile), about technology in their school and technology they wish their school/home had. Additionally, background information of the participants will be collected, along with short videos and pictures of the interview environment, and if possible, one of the schools. Parents will not be asked to try any technology or artifact. With this work, we aim to understand how these perspective can potentially influence the use and adoption of educational technology. Furthermore, we draw parallels between low income low literate parents living in two of India's largest cities: Delhi and Mumbai.

2   Team

The team consists of *Prof. Markku Turunen*, Head of the Masters Programme in Human-Technology Interaction, the Pervasive Interaction research group and the India Network at the University of Tampere. He is also the principal research investigator for the INCEPT India project.

Postdoctoral Researcher Heli Väätäjä, who is participating in the INCEPT India project from the Tampere University of Technology, with a strong research experience in mobile system use and field studies, and has published on mobile mathematics learning in South Africa.

Researcher Juhani Linna, who focuses on novel interaction methods in varying industry and societal contexts, from a sustainable business perspective.

Doctoral Candidate Biju Thankachan, whose focus is on developing text-free user interfaces for low-literate users, for societal impact.

Researcher Sumita Sharma, whose doctoral thesis work on designing novel interactive educational application for under-served Indian children aligns with the study.

Researcher Pekka Kallioniemi, whose doctoral thesis work is concentrating on wayfinding on virtual environments. He has also been involved in several ICT4D related projects, including Rural Voice where mobile applications for farmers in rural Karnataka were developed.

Prof Janet C Read, whose research group (ChiCi) has been looking at the design of serious games for children with an emphasis being on the design of serious games for children in developing countries.

Dr. Gavin Sim, who is an expert in usability and user experience evaluation with children, and is working with the ChiCI Group, at the University of Central Lancashire, UK. His research interests include the design and evaluation of technology for children, with a focus on the evaluation of educational games and technology.

References

1. Bronfenbrenner, U.: Ecological models of human development. In: Gauvain, M., Cole, M. (eds.) Readings on the Development of Children, 2nd edn, pp. 37–43. Freeman, New York (1994)
2. Pal, J., Lakshmanan, M., Toyama, K.: My child will be respected: Parental perspectives on computers and education in Rural India. Inf. Syst. Front. **11**(2), 129–144 (2009)

Understanding Early Technology Adoption by the Emergent Older Adults in Dharavi

Shaon Sengupta[1,2(✉)], Sayan Sarcar[1,2], and Anirudha Joshi[1,2]

[1] Indian Institute of Technology, Bombay, India
shaon.sengupta@gmail.com, mailtosayan@gmail.com
[2] Kochi University of Technology, Kami, Japan

Abstract. This field trip proposes a two-day program to understand and evaluate technology adoption of digital wallets among the elderly population in one of the urban slums of Mumbai, through training, probes and shadowing. The aim of the study is to analyse perceived challenges, influences & motivations, barriers to adoption and issues faced during wallet transactions. The findings from this study will be interpreted to formulate design recommendations and guidelines, useful to deploy meaningful propositions suitable for the elderly population, especially to facilitate a smooth transition to the digital vision of India.

Keywords: Emergent users · Elderly · Digital wallets · Demonetization · India

1 Introduction

On the evening of Nov. 08, the Prime Minister of India announced demonetization of the Rs.500 and Rs.1,000 notes, the two big currency denominations that account for 86% of the money in circulation [1]. The move was an effort to stop counterfeiting of the current banknotes allegedly used for funding terrorism, as well as a devise to crackdown on black money in the country [2]. In the long-term, India aimed to become a cashless society and embrace the transparency of currency digitization.

However, in the days following the announcement, the country witnessed severe cash shortages that caused great inconveniences to its people. A large mass of the Indian population, who are disadvantaged by the 'digital divide' - the gap that stops people from benefiting from ICTs [3], could not quite comprehend the cashless vision and lined-up to withdraw their money, standing in serpentine queues. The poor, the disabled and elderly citizens were most inconvenienced, as they had to wait for long hours to withdraw money. This led to several unfortunate deaths due to anxiety, panic and exhaustion.

This disadvantaged population that India hosts, are the emergent users - those who are less educated, economically disadvantaged, geographically dispersed, and culturally heterogeneous [3]. The user-usage model for the emergent user reports that age and educational levels are the highest significant predictors of technology usage for the emergent users. It also states that the emergent users are likely to be Basic Users and Navigators. We can extrapolate this model to state that young people are more likely to be more tech-savvy. Conversely, older people are expectedly less tech-savvy.

© IFIP International Federation for Information Processing 2017
Published by Springer International Publishing AG 2017. All Rights Reserved
R. Bernhaupt et al. (Eds.): INTERACT 2017, Part IV, LNCS 10516, pp. 504–508, 2017.
DOI: 10.1007/978-3-319-68059-0_61

The study also states that for such users, the task typologies of 'Text Inputter', 'Transactor' and 'Account Holder' should be avoided [3].

Clearly, in the context of how the elderly population is coping at this time of currency distress is understandable. The download rates of such mobile wallets and other digital mechanisms have been rather sparse. This digital barrier and eventual conversion to be able to be a 'Transactor' requires a combination of several facets. It includes understanding of the concept of a virtual personal wallet, a digital identity of an account holder, and trust in the virtual banking system to carry out the transactions, which are barriers for the senior population who perhaps do not have the requisite mental model for the same [3]. The confluence of this necessary conversion (Being a 'Transactor' of a mobile wallet) vis-a-vis the seemingly constant stage of use ('Unexposed', and no prior intention to progress) of the elderly, brings us to an opportunity for an interesting research space, which defines the motivation of this study. Hence, this study will particularly focus on issues and concerns that arise in the early phase of technology adoption by this particular population group.

2 Background

With the expansion of digital age, it is imperative that as a society, we need to brace for a future that takes care of its elderly. There are known challenges that they face, including impairment of special sensory functions like vision and hearing, decline in overall immunity, age related physiologic changes (motor skills, frailty), morbidities due to ageing of the brain, socio-economic factors such as breakdown of the family support systems and decrease in economic independence and decreasing funds. Socio-economic factors such as breakdown of the family support systems also lead to a host of psychological illnesses. Topped to this, is the risk and genetic predisposition to acquire chronic diseases, such as anemia, hypertension, dementia, Alzheimer's, chronic obstructive airway disease (COAD), cataract etc. the senior population are becoming vulnerable more rapidly than we would imagine.

Naturally, older adults find adoptions to new technologies difficult. There are unique barriers to this adoption like physical challenges, skeptical attitudes and difficulty in learning new things [6]. Combined to this is the physical aspect of the mobile phones where size of the screen, sound quality or voice inputs are often not compatible to the needs of the elderly [5]. Elderly also use only a limited set of functions in their mobiles phones and have a lack of understanding of hierarchical menus [5].

It will be worthwhile to investigate in the context of these known challenges to understand how such models might help to design solutions that help manoeuvre the difficulties around the imminent era of cashless society.

3   Plan

3.1   User Group, Recruitment and Facilitation

Owing to the unique limitations of emergent users and the specific challenges of old age that adds to this situation, the study focuses on the elderly fraction of the emergent user group. The study proposes Emergent Older Adults between age 60–75.

The study recommends the following recruitment criteria for the users:

– Are in possession of a smart phone
– Have no prior exposure to any digital payments (e.g. mobile wallets etc.)
– Are physically fit and mobile

The recruited users will be paid Rs. 500 as a token compensation that will be loaded in their digital wallets. The decision of the goods purchased with this amount will be a prerogative of the users. Through this exercise, the participants will be educated/trained to use an online wallet application. The outcomes of this study will also aim to work as design inputs for designers of such wallets, as they will be conscious about the specific needs of the elderly population, which in turn will be suitable for participants and users of similar profile.

3.2   Location: Dharavi

The study is proposed to be conducted at Dharavi, owing to its potential in translating its business acumen and eventually surviving the cashless journey. Dharavi was founded in 1882 during the British colonial era. The slum grew in part because of an expulsion of factories and residents from the peninsular city-centre by the colonial government, and from rural poor migrating into urban Mumbai. It is currently a multi-religious, multi-ethnic, diverse settlement. Estimates of Dharavi's total population vary between 700,000 to about 1 million. With recent digitalization programs in several pockets of Dharavi, it becomes important to see how this acceleration aids in empowering its elderly. How digitalization of the immediate context might have the potential to promote knowledge, openness and adoption of its elderly. To recruit appropriate users in this location, we will need to work with local organisations.

3.3   Method: Technology Probe

A technology probe will be used in this study to understand and map user behaviour. A suitable example is Paytm, the most popular mobile wallet in India, today. The method will consist of the following steps:

Day 1

• 9 am–11 am Introduction to wallets, training, loading, mutual exchange
• 11 am–1 pm First shopping experience along with the participant
• 2 pm–4 pm Shadowing the users to understand tasks & behaviour

Day 2

- 10 am–12 pm Focus group and discussion with the users
- 1 pm–3 pm Wrap up, summarising and recommendations

Training will include helping users understand the concept of digital wallets, downloading the relevant wallet app in their phones, explaining basic features and key use cases and setting expectation of the study. The study will also seek approval from the users owing to their age, possible health threats and their consent to use their experiences to draw inferences. Notes on planning - Field trip is suggested for 2 days where we will be testing PayTM mobile app. Place for research is Dharavi as it is technologically advanced while being a slum. However, any other comparable location is acceptable.

3.4   Participants

Group Facilitator (1) - Shaon Sengupta – PhD Candidate at IDC, IIT Bombay, with focused interest in the elderly population. Role to help with training, time keeping and consolidation of activities.

Senior Researcher (1) - Sayan Sarcar- Post Doc researcher from KUT, Japan. The researcher brings thorough understanding and expertise of research techniques to trigger and provoke users during focus groups and the project team during the brain-storming session.

Field representatives (3) - Andreea Ioana Niculescu, Lou-Ann Castelino, Anjali Kukreja. To help lead in observation and shadowing activities. This position seeks knowledge of Hindi and Marathi and a combination of male and female candidates.

Designer (1) - Pratiksha Dixit - To help in creating quick mock-ups of ideas and simulations to connect recommendations to visualized sketches.

4   Expected Outcomes

The outcome of the two-day trip will include a highly engaging report and presentation consolidating top findings and insights drawn from observations, artefacts, verbatims etc. The findings will further be used to create design recommendations and guidelines for design payment mechanism that are suitable to our target population. The design recommendations will finally lead to quick prototypes demonstrating the translation of issues and relevant design visualisations.

References

1. Quartz India, Timeline: 20 days of demonetisation, Narendra Modi's biggest gamble with the Indian economy. http://qz.com/846454/timeline-20-days-of-demonetisation-narendra-modis-biggest-gamble-with-the-indian-economy/
2. Indian 500 and 1000 rupee note demonetisation. https://en.wikipedia.org/wiki/Indian_500_and_1000_rupee_note_demonetisation/

3. Devanuj, J.: Technology Adoption by 'Emergent' Users – The User-Usage Model. In: APCHI, Bangalore (2013)
4. Dharavi. https://en.wikipedia.org/wiki/Dharavi
5. Renaud, B.: Predicting technology acceptance and adoption by the elderly: a qualitative study. In: SAICSIT, South Africa (2008)
6. Older Adults and Technology Use. http://www.pewinternet.org/2014/04/03/older-adults-and-technology-use/
7. Liu, J., Yang, C.: Using the Technology Acceptance Model to Examine Seniors' Attitudes toward Facebook. International Scholarly and Scientific Research & Innovation (2014)

Understanding the Informal Support Networks of Older Adults in India

Arne Berger[✉]

Chemnitz University of Technology, Media Informatics,
09107 Chemnitz, Germany
arne.berger@informatik.tu-chemnitz.de

Abstract. We proposes a field trip to understand how older adults in India construct and maintain informal support networks. The aim of the study is to get a nuanced view on older adults' practices of receiving from and providing support to peers, family, friends, and neighbors. Group discussions and collaborative photography will be applied to investigate. Findings will be interpreted to understand implications for how to design for support.

Keywords: Older adults · Cultural comparison · Informal support · Home

1 Project Description

There exists a plethora of research on smart objects and services, their implementation and evaluation. In contrast relatively little is collectively known about how older adults perceive, construct and maintain communication and support structures for help, security and comfort, within their home and the artifact ecologies at their disposal. Our goal is to understand how older adults socially shape, perceive and use informal support networks. How do they cope with the growing need for support? How do they reciprocate? To investigate we are conducting a comparative cultural study in Germany, Australia, China and Mumbai, India (this proposal).

2 Method: Group Discussion and Collaborative Photography

This field trip is building upon a study that we conducted in Germany. There, we utilized two methods. We conducted narrative interviews, and asked the helping person (the supporter) and the person being helped (the supported) to collaboratively take and discuss photographs of places and objects that are important for their support relation. This is a combination of "reflexive photography" and "collaborative photography". The first aims on *"participants' interactions with their environment through their personal reflections on images"* [1] and arguably shares similarities with aspects of probes [2]. With reflexive photography people are asked to take photographs of objects, places and topics within their daily life, followed by a discussing with the researchers. With collaborative photography informants and researcher take the photographs together. Still, participants remain the leading creative force in this endeavor: *"Collaborating*

© IFIP International Federation for Information Processing 2017
Published by Springer International Publishing AG 2017. All Rights Reserved
R. Bernhaupt et al. (Eds.): INTERACT 2017, Part IV, LNCS 10516, pp. 509–512, 2017.
DOI: 10.1007/978-3-319-68059-0_62

with informants to produce images need not involve the ethnographer taking the lead as photographer" [3]. A combination of both methods has proven to be insightful to understand the cooperation and communication between supporter and supported. Most importantly, to observe the cooperation and communication between the supporter and the supported while taking the photographs is prerequisite to get a nuanced view on the bond between them. In addition, older adults may not be acquainted with digital photography which makes the presence of the researchers helpful.

3   Plan

Our field trip is focusing on two local areas with different social geography. We look for people with at least two different socioeconomic backgrounds. We are aware that those different areas will call for different methodological approaches. With this proposal we can only give an estimate for the field trip plan. In the *first phase* we will explore general issues. We will conduct interviews with people reflecting on situations where they help older adults. In the *second phase* we aim to interact with individual pairs of supporter and supported. We will explore the neighborhood of the supporter and supported and shadow them. When possible we will interact directly with both supporter and supported and hold narrative interviews with both parties in order to gain insight into their support relations. *Further*, we will encourage the supporter and supported to take photographs of objects and places that are meaningful for their support relation and to comment on them. Also, we will document those objects and places via field photographs and field sketches. We plan to do this routine on both days of this field trip.

3.1   User Group

We look for various pairs of supporter and supported. Within these pairs, one person is occasionally or habitually helping the other. Preferably both are older adults, but at least one of them should be 60 years or older. It is important that we can visit the supported person in or near their home together with the supporter.

3.2   Location

We aim at two neighborhoods where people do not have servants to run their household. We rather look for neighborhoods where people are engaging in neighborhood help. As we are not acquainted with the local areas we trust the expertise of the local researchers to lead us to a suitable area for the field trip. We are open to all suggestions from the local researcher regarding a suitable location as well as socioeconomic background. And we need help from the local researchers in contacting people in these locations.

3.3   Schedule for Day 1 and Day 2

09 am–10 pm demographic profiling of the neighborhood, participant sampling
11 pm–12 pm group discussion/shadowing/exploring

01 pm–03 pm individual pairs of supporter and supported
03 pm–04 pm debriefing of the researchers

3.4 Participating Researchers

Arne Berger
Faculty for Computer Science, Chemnitz University of Technology
    Chemnitz, Germany

Julia Weller
Artist, Leipzig, Germany

Dhaval Vyas
Queensland University of Technology (QUT)
    Brisbane (QLD) Australia

Alessandro Soro
Queensland University of Technology (QUT)
    Brisbane (QLD) Australia

Andreea Ioana Niculescu
Human Language Technologies, Institute for Infocomm Research, Singapore

Pascal Weidenmüller
Designer, Plauen, Germany

3.5 Ethical Considerations and Financial Aid

To engage the interviewees in the aim of our study, we trust that the interviewees in India can relate to the pictures we show and stories we tell from home. These vignettes will illustrate, how this study was done in cultural comparison. We trust that the local researchers will help us to organize financial compensation for the interviewees. We have funds available for gifts or a small honorarium to the interviewees or a donation for the benefit of the local area.

3.6 Material

We will bring cameras, dictaphones, notebooks. We trust the local researchers to help with travel arrangements.

4 Expected Outcomes

The field trip is part of a comparative cultural study. Overall it will result in a description of how older adults design communication and support for help, security and comfort within the infrastructure of their domestic environment. Through the comparison we aim to understand these networks in areas that are shaped differently regarding their social geography and cultural background. This is an ethnographical study meant to inform the future design for support. The aim of this study is to help designers to align their work more closely with the needs and demands of older adults who are already engaged in informal network structures.

In reflection of previous studies we adopted a mixed method of interview and reflexive photography. We found it helpful to augment the interviews of supporter and supported with opportunities for them to directly reflect moments and places through collaborative photography. In observing and analyzing these acts of collaborate meaning making, issues of trust, values, and relevance structures will surface that may not emerge in interviews only. These issues, values, and relevance structure will in turn inform designers to better design for support.

References

1. Amerson, R., Livingston, W.G.: Reflexive photography: an alternative method for documenting the learning process of cultural competence. J. Transcult. Nurs. **25**(2), 202–210 (2014)
2. Gaver, B., Dunne, T., Pacenti, E.: Design: cultural probes. Interactions **6**(1), 21–29 (1999). doi:10.1145/291224.291235
3. Pink, S.: Doing Visual Ethnography. Images, Media and Representation in Research. SAGE, London (2001)

Workshops

Beyond Computers: Wearables, Humans, And Things - WHAT!

Nahum Gershon[1], Achim Ebert[2], Gerrit van der Veer[3],
and Peter Dannenmann[4(✉)]

[1] The MITRE Corporation, Bedford, USA
schmooz@mac.com
[2] Computer Graphics and HCI Group, University of Kaiserslautern,
Kaiserslautern, Germany
ebert@cs.uni-kl.de
[3] Department of Computer Science, Vrije Universiteit Amsterdam,
Amsterdam, The Netherlands
gerrit@acm.org
[4] Department of Engineering, RheinMain University of Applied Sciences,
Wiesbaden, Germany
peter.dannenmann@hs-rm.de

Abstract. This workshop aims at developing and discussing ideas how Human-Machine-Interaction can develop beyond the interaction mechanisms that are available today. Especially this workshop will focus on discussing interaction mechanisms with wearable and implantable devices as well as integrating Internet-of-Things technology with new interaction paradigms.

Keywords: Wearable devices · Implantable devices · Internet of things

1 Introduction

Considerable attention has been paid for years to the relationships between humans and computers. But, over the years, the computer chip migrated from the computer internal organs to many other devices - to things, wearables, and even onto the skin (skinnables) and into the human body (implantables). This workshop will focus on how this revolution may affect the way we look at the relationships between humans and among humans, human elements and computing devices and what should be done to improve these interactions and "entanglements" and to understand them better.

2 Objectives

In this workshop, we provide a platform for discussions about the relationships among humans, technology embedded in the environment (networked or not), and humans whose physical, physiological or/and mental capabilities are extended and/or modified by technology. Given these extended realities, the interface as we have known it and even the practical meaning of the word "interaction" have changed. This workshop is

© IFIP International Federation for Information Processing 2017
Published by Springer International Publishing AG 2017. All Rights Reserved
R. Bernhaupt et al. (Eds.): INTERACT 2017, Part IV, LNCS 10516, pp. 515–517, 2017.
DOI: 10.1007/978-3-319-68059-0

intended to provide a platform for scholars, practitioners, and students to think together about how to frame the new interaction, engagement, and relationship between technology, humans, "modified" humans and the new reality.

We encourage researchers and practitioners to share their ideas and experience for these new realities of interaction, engagement, and interface mechanisms with the community. Researchers and practitioners from the areas of the Internet of things (IoT), wearables, implantables, skinnables, and embedded computing are in particular encouraged to participate.

3 Topics

Some of the issues to be discussed by the participants are:

- Commercial things, wearables, skinnables and implantables vs. medical grade devices. What is the value to non-medical grade devices?
- Possibilities of relationships among WHATs - e.g., interaction and symbiosis. Could we define a scale from minimal interaction to full symbiosis?
- Holistic views: When does a group of WHATs become a team, group of organisms, or agents?
- What makes a device smart? Are all smarts the same or are there varying degrees of smartness (e.g., a scale)?
- Could we develop a theory for SMART relationships?
- When does a wearable, an implantable, or a thing become part of the human?
- The interplay among various degrees of digital and analog.
- What is the role of system thinking and practice in dealing and managing arrays of WHATs?
- A broader view on experience: WHAT and the integration of senses (e.g., touch and smell).

4 Target Audience

The workshop aims at scholars and students from the domains of:

- Interaction Design
- Cognitive Science
- Visualization and Multimedia
- Artificial Intelligence and Robotics
- Developers and practitioners of wearables, implantables, skinnables and the Internet of Things
- Common sense practitioners

5   Expected Outcomes

Participants in the workshop will present their ideas in position papers and workshop talks. Position papers and talks are grouped according to specific topics like "wearables", "skinnables", or "implantables". For every topic we expect about four position papers or talks. After the presentations related to one topic there will be a specific block where all workshop participants openly discuss the position papers and talks. Thus we will have a view on multiple aspects of WHATs in several blocks consisting of papers/talks and subsequent discussion sessions. First discussions will even start previous to the workshop in the Facebook page: Wearables, Humans And Things - WHAT (https://www.facebook.com/WHAT2016/).

During the workshop, in each discussion block we want to summarize the discussions and present this summary to the main conference.

After the Workshop, we will continue the discussions in the Facebook page and will encourage the participants to send papers to the organizers for publishing e.g. in a Springer LNCS book or in a special issue of a suitable journal/magazine.

Cross Cultural Differences in Designing for Accessibility and Universal Design

Helen Petrie[1(✉)], Gerhard Weber[2], Jennifer S. Darzentas[1,3],
Charudatta Jadhav[4], and Zhengjie Liu[5]

[1] Department of Computer Science, University of York, York, UK
{helen.petrie, jenny.darzentas}@york.ac.uk
[2] Department of Computer Science, Technische Universität Dresden,
Dresden, Germany
gerhard.weber@tu-dresden.de
[3] Department of Product and Systems Design Engineering,
University of the Aegean, Ermoupoli, Greece
[4] Accessibility and Inclusive Design Group, Tata Consultancy Services,
Mumbai, India
charudatta.jadhav@tcs.com
[5] Sino-European Usability Center, Dalian Maritime University,
Dalian, People's Republic of China
liuzhj@dlmu.edu.cn

Abstract. This workshop brings together researchers and practitioners interested in cross cultural differences and cultural sensitivities in accessibility, assistive technologies, inclusive design and methods for working with disabled and older users. It will provide an opportunity to discuss and debate the opportunities and challenges for developing accessible and usable technologies for people with disabilities and older people in different cultural contexts.

Keywords: Cross cultural differences · Cultural sensitivities · Accessibility · Universal design · Assistive technology · Users with disabilities · Older users

1 Overview

The population of older people and people with disabilities is growing rapidly throughout the world, due to many complex changes in societies from decreasing birth rates to increasing survival rates from accidents and chronic health conditions. There are currently between 110 and 190 million people with substantial disabilities [1] and approximately 901 million older adults (meaning people aged 60 or older), worldwide [2]. The United Nations (UN) predicts that the population of older adults will increase to more than 2 billion by 2050. The UN also predicts that the number of older people will exceed the number of the young people, aged 15 or younger, for the first time in 2047. This change in the balance of older to younger people (known as the age dependency ratio) has many consequences, one of them being that older adults and people with disabilities will need to live more independently, without as many of the younger generations to care for them. Many analysts and researchers [e.g. 3] believe

R. Bernhaupt et al. (Eds.): INTERACT 2017, Part IV, LNCS 10516, pp. 518–520, 2017.
DOI: 10.1007/978-3-319-68059-0

that technology will provide at least a partial solution to this problem, allowing older adults to live in their own homes safely and independently for as long as possible.

These demographic changes are worldwide phenomena, although different countries are experiencing them at different rates and in different ways. In addition, there are many cultural sensitivities and differences in attitudes to disability and old age, which have important implications for designing interactive systems for disabled and older people. However, designing for cultural diversity is an aspect of universal design can increase the overall number of users and the usability of interactive systems for those users [4]. Therefore we believe that bringing together researchers and practitioners from different cultures with an interest in accessibility, assistive technologies, Universal Design and methods for working with disabled and older users will be beneficial to exchange ideas and good practice and develop greater understanding and synergies across cultures.

People with disabilities and older people have needs and wishes for technology that HCI designers and developers are often unaware of or fail to understand fully. In European countries we have observed that designers and developers of interactive systems also often have difficulty establishing contact with disabled and older people and lack a good range of techniques to work with them in the development process, in spite of being eager to develop technologies to support these user groups.

There are also many cultural and societal differences between countries which affect needs and attitudes towards technologies for disabled and older people. For example, the effects of demographic changes in China are comparable to European countries, but attitudes to family are typically somewhat different from European attitudes (although there is much variety across Europe), as is the acceptability of older people taking physical exercise in public. These and many similar factors can have a substantial effect on what kind of interactive systems might be developed to support older people, how they are developed and how they are used. In relation to disability, there are also very different attitudes and policies in different countries there as to whether people with disabilities should be integrated into mainstream society or cared for separately. These attitudes and policies have a great effect on the development of interactive systems.

The workshop will address a wide range of topics in this area, depending on the interests of participants. We will work towards producing a jointly authored paper for publication on the challenges in cultural differences and sensitivities in accessibility assistive technologies and Universal Design.

2 About the Organizers

Professor **Helen Petrie** who holds the Chair in HCI at the University of York (UK), current chair of IFIP WG 13.3. Her research focuses on the design and evaluation of technology for disabled and older people.

Professor **Gerhard Weber** who holds the Chair in HCI at Technische Universität Dresden (Germany), past chair of IFIP WG 13.3. His research focuses on personalization of multimodal systems for the benefit of people with a disability.

Dr **Jenny Darzentas** who is a Marie Sklodowska Experienced Researcher at the University of York (UK), and Adjunct Lecturer at the University of the Aegean (Greece), working on supporting designers and developers to design for older people.

Charudatta Jadhav who is Head of the Accessibility Centre of Excellence at Tata Consultancy Services (Mumbai, India), working in research areas such as automation in accessibility assessment, inclusive interaction and service design, accessible security.

Professor **Zhengjie Liu** who is Founder and Director of the Sino European Usability Center (SEUC), Professor at School of Information Science & Technology of Dalian Maritime University (DMU), Director of NCR-DMU HCI Research Center, Co-founder and Co-chair of ACM SIGCHI China.

References

1. http://www.who.int/mediacentre/factsheets/fs352/en/
2. United Nations, World Population Ageing (2015)
3. Mynatt, E., Melenhorst, A.-S., Fisk, A.D, Rogers, W.A.: Aware technologies for aging in place: understanding user needs and attitudes. Pervasive Comput. **3**(2) (2004). ISSN 1536-1268
4. Marcus, A., Aykin, N.M., Chavan, A.L., Prabhu, G.V., Kurosu, M.: SIG on one size fits all? Cultural diversity in user interface design. In: CHI Extended Abstracts, p. 342 (1999)

Dealing with Conflicting User Interface Properties in User-Centered Development Processes

IFIP WG 13.2 + 13.5 Workshop at INTERACT 2017

Marco Winckler[1,2(✉)], Marta Larusdottir[3], Kati Kuusinen[4],
Cristian Bogdan[5], and Philippe Palanque[1]

[1] ICS-IRIT, Université Toulouse 3, Toulouse, France
{winckler,palanque}@irit.fr
[2] Université Nice Sophia Antipolis (Polytech), Sophia Antipolis, France
[3] Reykjavik University, Reykjavik, Iceland
Marta@ru.is
[4] University of Southern Denmark, Odense, Denmark
kaku@mmmi.sdu.dk
[5] KTH Royal Institute of Technology, Stockholm, Sweden
cristi@csc.kth.se

Abstract. Whilst usability has been the most prominent user interface property in early Human-Computer Interaction (HCI) research other properties such as accessibility, inclusive design, user experience and, more recently security, trust and resilience (among many others) might also be important for the development of interactive system. It is interesting to notice that user interface properties might overlap and sometimes create conflicting recommendations. A good example is security which, by recommending users to deal with passwords reduces system usability by placing a burden on users. The ultimate goal of this workshop is to promote the investigation of multiple user interface properties in a user-centered design process. We are concerned by theories, methods and approaches for dealing with multiple user interface properties when developing interactive system. This workshop is organized by the IFIP WG 13.2 on Human-Centered Software Methodologies and the WG 13.5 on Resilience, Reliability, Safety and Human Error in System Development.

Keywords: User-centered design process · User interfaces properties · Usability · UX · Resilience · Reliability · Multiple perspectives in user interface design

1 Overview and Goals

Whilst *usability*, *accessibility* and, more recently, *user experience* have been prominent in the HCI research other properties such as *privacy*, *trust*, *security*, and *reliability* (among others) might also affect the development process of interactive systems. In some cases, a property might complement or enlarge the scope of another. For example,

R. Bernhaupt et al. (Eds.): INTERACT 2017, Part IV, LNCS 10516, pp. 521–523, 2017.
DOI: 10.1007/978-3-319-68059-0

whilst accessibility addresses the needs of impaired users to accomplish their tasks with the system [1], UX goes beyond the pragmatic aspect of usability by taking into account dimensions such as emotion, aesthetics or visual appearance, identification, stimulation, meaning/value or even fun, enjoyment, pleasure or flow state experience [2]. In some situations, a property might be tributary to another one such is the case of *reliability* and *usability* when non *reliability* of interactive software can jeopardize usability evaluation by showing unexpected or undesired behaviors [5]. Moreover, there are some evidence that properties can trade off against each other as it is the case of *usability* and *security* [3]. For example, requiring users to change their passwords periodically may improve security but reduce usability as it represents a burden for users to frequently create and remember passwords. As a consequence, users might be keen to workarounds, such as when users take hard notes of hard-to-remember passwords.

Conflicting user interface properties often appear in recommendations for user interface design [4]. The resolution of conflicts between user interface properties is a daunting and demanding task that might require taking into account the trade-offs associated with alternative design choices. It is interesting to notice that when the conflict between properties is understood, the effects of conflicts can be mitigated/reduced by appropriate design. Examples of conflict resolution between *usability, privacy* and *security* can be found at the SOUPS (https://cups.cs.cmu.edu/soups/) community. In this workshop we aimed at enlarge the scope of the research and promote the study of the interplay of multiple user interface properties in a user-centered design process. Our aim is to cover a large set of user interface properties and try to revel their inner dependencies. We are also interested in understand how different stakeholders value user interface properties. In a long run, this workshop aims at helping the development of theories, methods, tools and approaches for dealing with multiple properties that should be taken into account when developing interactive system.

2   Target Audience and Expected Outcomes

This workshop is open to everyone who is interested in multiple user interface properties while building their systems and how different these are valued by different stakeholders. We expect a high participation of the members of IFIP WG 13.2 and IFIP WG 13.5. We invite participants to present position papers describing real-life case studies that illustrate the tradeoffs between two or more user interface properties. Any property related to user interface design is welcome but two or more properties should be addressed in the same contribution. We are also interested in methods, theories and tools for managing multiple user interface properties. Position papers will be published in adjunct conference proceedings of INTERACT 2017. During the workshop we also expect to discuss how to disseminate individual contributions to the community in the form of a special issue in a HCI journal.

3 Organizers

Marco Winckler is Assistant Professor at University Toulouse 3, Toulouse, France. His research interests focus on model-based approaches for the design and evaluation of interactive systems. He currently serves as chairperson of the IFIP working group 13.2.

Marta Larusdottir is an associate professor at Reykjavik University. Iceland. Her main research topic is the collaboration with users during design and evaluations of user interfaces. Lately Marta has focused on studying agile processes, especially Scrum, and how the usage of agile processes affect IT professionals in involving users in the development. She is in the board for IFIP working group 13.2 and the national member for Iceland in the IFIP TC13 committee.

Kati Kuusinen is an Assistant Professor at the University of Southern Denmark. Her research focuses on the social aspects of modern software engineering. She currently serves as secretary of the IFIP working group 13.2.

Cristian Bogdan is Associated Professor at KTH Royal Institute of Technology, Stockholm, Sweden. His research interests include support for rapid interactive system prototyping and development, model-based UI development and improving user understanding and sustainability through UI design in advanced areas like robotics, electric vehicles, smart grid and modern heating systems. He is vice-chair of the IFIP working group 13.2

Philippe Palanque is Professor in Computer Science at the University Toulouse 3 – Paul Sabatier and is head of the Interactive Critical Systems group at the Institut de Recherche en Informatique de Toulouse (IRIT) in France. The main driver of Philippe's research over the last 20 years has been to address in an even way Usability, Safety and Dependability in order to build trustable safety critical interactive systems. He currently serves as secretary of the IFIP working group 13.5 on Resilience, Reliability, Safety and Human Error in System Development.

References

1. W3C Accessibility, Usability, and Inclusion: Related Aspects of a Web for All. Available online at: https://www.w3.org/WAI/intro/usable (2016)
2. Hassenzahl, M.: The interplay of beauty, goodness, and usability in interactive products. Hum Comp. Interact. **19**(4), 319–349 (2004)
3. Sasse, M.A., Smith, M., Herley, C., Lipford, H., Vaniea, K.: Debunking Security-Usability Tradeoff Myths. IEEE Security & Privacy **14**(5), 33–39 (2016)
4. Masip, M., Martinie, C., Winckler, M., Palanque, P., Granollers, T., Oliva, M.: A Design Process for Exhibiting Design Choices and Trade-Offs in (Potentially) Conflicting User Interface Guidelines. In: Winckler, M., Forbrig, P., Bernhaupt, R. (eds.) HCSE 2012, LNCS, vol. 7623, pp. 53–71, Springer, Heidelberg (2012)
5. Palanque, P., Basnyat, S., Bernhaupt, R., Boring, R., Johnson, C., Johnson, C.: Beyond usability for safety critical systems: how to be sure (safe, usable, reliable, and evolvable)? CHI, pp. 2133–2136, Extended Abstracts (2007)

Designing Gestures for Interactive Systems: Towards Multicultural Perspectives

Anne Dubos[2], Frédéric Bevilacqua[1(✉)], Joseph Larralde[1],
Joël Chevrier[3], and Jean-François Jégo[4]

[1] STMS Lab IRCAM-CNRS-UPMC, Paris, France
frederic.bevilacqua@ircam.fr
[2] Institut d'Etudes Avancées and Little Heart Movement, Nantes, France
[3] CRI-Paris Université Paris Descartes, Paris, France
[4] INReV, Université Paris 8, Saint-Denis, France

Abstract. This practice-based workshop aims at exploring various methodologies and tools to design gestures that could be used in interactive systems. We argue that *gesture design*, which can be seen as being a smaller part of the interaction design process, is generally overlooked. Our goals are to develop various methods, some being inspired by performing arts practices, and to discuss the multicultural aspects of gesture design.

Keywords: Gesture · Design · Multi-Modal interfaces · International and cultural aspects of HCI · Interactive systems

1 Context and Objectives

We address in this workshop the problem of designing gestures in interactive systems. Current multi-touch and motion sensing technologies allow for capturing a large scope of gestures and movements that can be used to interact expressively with various media. Yet, the common use of gestures remains limited to few well-known strokes such as wipes and pinches. The use of hand or body movements is even more rare, with the exception of some video-game systems using the Wii or the Kinect.

Several issues can be invoked to explain the difficulties to include rich and expressive gestural input in interactive systems. First, the choice of possible gestures is generally imposed by manufacturers that focus on easiness of use (and even patent them). Only few systems let users to propose their own movement vocabularies. Second, we argue that shared methodologies for *designing and learning* gestures and movement are generally lacking in the engineering fields.

Our aim is precisely to explore the questions of *gesture and movement design* in a participatory workshop. In particular, we wish to guide the discussion on differences in cultures and contexts, and how these elements might affect either positively or adversely the appropriation of shared gestural interaction paradigms.

© IFIP International Federation for Information Processing 2017
Published by Springer International Publishing AG 2017. All Rights Reserved
R. Bernhaupt et al. (Eds.): INTERACT 2017, Part IV, LNCS 10516, pp. 524–526, 2017.
DOI: 10.1007/978-3-319-68059-0

2 Workshop Program

This one-day workshop is practice-based. After a short presentation of the different methods, the participants will be asked to collectively participate to the elaboration of gesture/movement vocabularies. The creation of the gestures will be guided using different methods and technologies, from the use of game-like scenarios to technological tools such as interactive machine learning [1, 2]. Tools and methods are to be submitted by the participants before the workshop, documented by an extended abstract and video materials that will be made available.

3 Target Audience

The workshop is open to participants of diverse backgrounds, including engineering, human and social sciences, design and the performing arts. We will particularly encourage culture diversity and gender balance.

4 Expected Outcomes

The outcome of the collective experiments will be documented by video recording and collecting material such as sketching. The different artefacts produced will be made available on the website (http://gesturedesign.ircam.fr), and possibly displayed during the whole conference (with the consent of the participants). We believe that this workshop will trigger stimulating discussions and provide for the participants new design methods and tools. The gather material could be used for subsequent collective publications. Moreover, we ambition that this workshop will initiate a series of international events and multicultural collaborations on this topic (including India).

5 Key Organisers

The organizers have recently led participatory design workshops, hackathons and gamejam. Anne Dubos is an anthropologist and a transmedia artist, with expertise on the gesture transmission in contemporary theatre in Kerala (South India). Frédéric Bevilacqua and Joseph Larralde are researchers on the development of gesture-based interactive systems and movement-sound interaction. Joël Chevrier is a physics professor currently developing new methodologies to introduce science and technology to broad audiences. Jean-François Jégo is an artist-researcher, expert on virtual reality & augmented reality.

Acknowledgements. We acknowledge from the Rapid-Mix project (H2020-ICT-2014-1 Project ID 644862).

References

1. Bevilacqua, F., Zamborlin, B.,Sypniewski, A., Schnell, N., Guédy, F., Rasamimanana, N.: Continuous realtime gesture following and recognition. In: Kopp, S., Wachsmuth, I. (Eds.) GW 2009. LNAI, Vol. 5934, pp. 73–84. Springer, Heidelberg (2010)
2. http://rapidmix.goldsmithsdigital.com/rapid-api/. Accessed 31 Jan 2017

Designing Humour in Human Computer Interaction (HUMIC 2017)

Anton Nijholt[1], Andreea I. Niculescu[2(⊠)], Alessandro Valitutti[3],
and Rafael E. Banchs[2]

[1] University of Twente, HMI, Enschede, The Netherlands
anijholt@cs.utwente.nl
[2] Institute for Infocomm Research (I2R), Singapore, Singapore
{andreea-n, rembanchs}@i2r.a-star.edu.sg
[3] University College Dublin (USD), Dublin, Ireland
alessandro.valitutti@gmail.com

Abstract. Humor is a social phenomenon pervasive in all human societies. Due to its importance in interpersonal relations, in this workshop we are focusing on the integration of humor in HCI exploring its benefits and downsides, as well as design and evaluation approaches for humorous machines. The workshop will provide a forum for discussions to all researchers and practitioners interested in this topic covering both verbal and non-verbal aspects of humor in HCI.

Keywords: Humor · Human computer interaction · Artificial intelligence · Verbal and nonverbal interactions

1 Introduction and Motivation

Humour is pervasive in human social relationships and one of the most common ways to produce a positive affect in others. Research studies have shown that innocent humour increases likeability and interpersonal relations, boosts friendship and trust, fosters social cohesion, alleviate stress, reduce tensions, encourage creativity and improve teamwork [1]. Humour can be spontaneous or be deliberately used not only in conversations with friends, but also in more formal environments [2]. Large corporations such as IBM, Kodak and AT&T hire humour experts to help improve teamwork, stimulate creativity and motivate employees [3].

While humour is a well-established branch in artificial intelligence and natural language processing communities, in the HCI field humour appears to be rather a marginal research topic, despite its positive effects scientifically proven by decades of research [4]. One reason is that HCI traditionally focus on interfaces meant to increase task performance on one side, and minimize task duration, learning time and error rate, on the other side. Since the use of humour would distract the users from their tasks increasing the total completion time, it would contradict HCI policies of maximizing efficiency in interaction [1]. However, researchers in the field showed that such assumptions are not true task competition time and amount of effort to be mainly unaffected by incorporating humour in interaction [9].

© IFIP International Federation for Information Processing 2017
Published by Springer International Publishing AG 2017. All Rights Reserved
R. Bernhaupt et al. (Eds.): INTERACT 2017, Part IV, LNCS 10516, pp. 527–530, 2017.
DOI: 10.1007/978-3-319-68059-0

In the future we can expect HCI to become less goal directed, not only in entrainment computing, but also in our ordinary daily life. Technology moves slowly from our working environments to our living rooms where computers and artificial entities become social actors [8]. In a such context, it is important for designers to take into account the social aspect of interaction between humans and computers as humour might become an influential ingredient towards technology acceptance and overall satisfaction.

2 Topics of Interest and Goals

Humour embraces various types of expression - both verbal (puns, jokes, irony, incongruity etc.) and non-verbal (situational humour, mimic, gestures etc.) and can be used to enhance the interaction outcome [7] while being socially and culturally appropriate. In this context, HUMIC (**HUM**or in Intera**C**tion) workshop aims to explore challenges in designing [5] and evaluating [6] humourful interactions, as well as benefits and downsides of using humour in interactive tasks with artificial entities. The workshop will provide a platform for discussions on how humour can help designing better user experiences in HCI by responding to questions, such as:

- How knowledge from different disciplines, e.g. linguistics, psychology, sociology, literature, art, comedy etc. can help designing funnier interaction with technology?
- What methods and approaches are appropriate for creating humour in HCI?
- What cultural and social constrains apply when designing humorous interactions?
- What situations can benefit/suffer from using humour in interaction with machines, e.g. where humorous interaction should/shouldn't be used?
- What characteristics poses an interactive humours system in order to be called funny, e.g. how to evaluate humorousness?
- Can humour in HCI be useful beyond its intended purpose, e.g. can comedians use interactive technologies to create humorous situations?

The discussions are however, not limited to the above questions as the ultimate goal of the workshop is to deepen and broaden the understanding towards the appropriate design of humours interactions with technology.

3 Target Audience and Expected Outcome

The audience targeted are researchers and practitioners from a wide range of disciplines, including human-computer interaction, computational linguistics, artificial intelligence, psychology, media and arts interested in the topic of humour. The accepted workshop position papers will be published in the official adjunct conference proceedings. Extended versions of selected papers will be invited for a special issue in a journal (currently being organized). More information is available on the workshop website: http://workshop.colips.org/humic/.

4 Workshop Plan

HUMIC will include a keynote talk, short presentations of accepted papers, discussion sessions, as well as a hands-on design exercise session, during which workshop participants - divided into small groups - will design an interactive humours application in a given context; the groups will present their work at the end of the workshop.

5 Organizers

- **Prof. dr. ir. Anton Nijholt -** *University of Twente, HMI, The Netherlands*
  Anton Nijholt has a background in human-computer interaction and entertainment computing. He is part of the Human Media Interaction group of the University of Twente, and is also involved with the Imagineering Institute in Johor Bahru, Malasia. He has been program chair of the main international conferences on intelligent agents, multimodal interaction, affective computing, faces & gestures and entertainment computing. His recent (edited) books are on playful user interfaces, entertainment computing, and playable cities. In recent years he published many papers on humour and digital technology, in particular humour in smart environments
- **Dr. Andreea I. Niculescu -** *Institute for Infocomm Research (I^2R), Singapore*
  Andreea I. Niculescu works as a scientist at Institute for Infocomm Research, in the Human Language Technology department, Dialogue Technology Group. Her main interests are UX and interaction design focusing on user interface for speech and multimodal interactions. Her current research work is concerned with the use of humour for enhancing interactions with dialogue systems and social robot.
- **Dr. Alessandro Valitutti -** *Università di Bari, Italy*
  Alessandro Valitutti is currently working as a senior researcher at the Dept. of Computer Science, University of Bari, Italy. He is involved in the SentiQuest Project, whose primary goal is to automatically detect irony and sarcasm in online Q&A websites and social networks. His past research activity was mainly on the computational treatment of emotions, creativity, and humour. Specifically, he developed ideas and resources for sentiment analysis and affect detection from texts, kinetic typography, humour generation, computational poetry, and fictional ideation. More recently, his interest is focusing on interactive humour.
- **Dr. Rafael E. Banchs -** Institute for Infocomm Research (I^2R), Singapore
  Rafael E. Banchs is currently the Head of the Dialogue Technology Group in the Human Language Technology department within the Institute for Infocomm Research in Singapore. His recent areas of research include Machine Translation, Information Retrieval, Cross-language Information Retrieval, Sentiment Analysis and Dialogue Systems. More specifically, he has been working on the application of vector space models along with linear and non-linear projection techniques to improve the quality of statistical machine translation and cross-language information retrieval systems, as well as on chatbots using humour as a mechanism to support error recovery.

References

1. Niculescu, A., van Dijk, B., Nijholt, A., Li, H., See, S.L.: Making social robots more attractive: the effects of voice pitch, humor and empathy. Int. J. Social Robot. **5**(2), 171–191 (2013)
2. Nijholt, A.: Conversational agents and the construction of humorous acts. In: Conversational informatics: an engineering approach. Wiley, Chichester, pp. 21–47 (2007)
3. Gibson, D.E.: Humor consulting: laughs for power and profit in organizations. Humor **7**(4), 403–428 (1994)
4. Nijholt, A.: The Humor Continuum: From Text to Smart Environments. In: Proceedings of International Conference on Informatics, Electronics & Vision (ICIEV). IEEE Xplore, Kitakyushu, Fukuoka, Japan (2015)
5. Valitutti, A.: How many jokes are really funny? Towards a new approach to the evaluation. In: Human-Machine Interaction in Translation: Proceedings of the 8th International NLPCS Workshop, vol. 41, p. 189 (2011). Samfundsliteratur
6. Valitutti, A., Veale, T.: Infusing humor in unexpected events. In: International Conference on Distributed, Ambient, and Pervasive Interactions, pp. 370–379. Springer International Publishing (2016)
7. Niculescu, A.I., Banchs, R.E.: Strategies to cope with errors in human-machine spoken interactions: using chatbots as back-off mechanism for task-oriented dialogues. In: Proceedings of ERRARE, Sinaia, Romania (2015)
8. Nijholt, A.., Stock, O., Dix, A., Morkes, J.: Humour modeling in the interface. In: CHI'03 Extended Abstracts on Human Factors in Computing Systems, pp 1050–1051. ACM (2003)
9. Morkes, J., Kernal, H.K., Nass, C.: Effects of humour in task-oriented human computer interaction and computer- mediated communication: a direct test of SRCT theory. Human-Comput. Interac. **14**(4), 395–435 (1999)

Human Work Interaction Design Meets International Development

Pedro Campos[1(✉)], Torkil Clemmensen[2], Barbara Rita Barricelli[3],
Jose Abdelnour-Nocera[4], Arminda Lopes[1], and Frederica Gonçalves[1]

[1] Madeira-ITI, University of Madeira, Funchal, Portugal
{pedro.campos,arminda.lopes,
frederica.goncalves}@m-iti.org
[2] Copenhagen Business School, Frederiksberg, Denmark
tc.itm@cbs.dk
[3] Università Degli Studi Di Milano, Milan, Italy
barricelli@di.unimi.it
[4] University of West London, London, UK
Jose.Abdelnour-Nocera@uwl.ac.uk

Abstract. Over the last decade, empirical relationships between work domain analysis and HCI design have been identified by much research in the field of Human Work Interaction Design (HWID) across five continents. Since this workshop takes place at the Interact Conference in Mumbai, there is a unique opportunity to observe technology-mediated innovative work practices in informal settings that may be related to the notion of International Development. In this unique context, this workshop proposes to analyze findings related to opportunities for design research in this type of work domains: a) human-centered design approaches for specific work domains (workplaces, smart workplaces); b) visions of new roles for workplaces that enhance both work practice and interaction design. In order to do this, participants engage with field trips, gather data and discuss their experience at the workshop on the following day.

Keywords: Human work interaction design · International development · User experience · Smart workplaces

1 Overview

Today, it is a true challenge to design applications that support users of technology in complex and emergent organizational and work contexts. To meet this challenge, the Working Group 13.6 (WG13.6) on Human Work Interaction Design (HWID) was established in September 2005 as the sixth working group under the International Federation for Information Processing specifically the Technical Committee 13 on Human Computer Interaction (HCI). A main objective of the WG13.6 as defined in 2012 is the analysis of this complexity and its relationships between extensive empirical work domains studies and HCI designs [1].

© IFIP International Federation for Information Processing 2017
Published by Springer International Publishing AG 2017. All Rights Reserved
R. Bernhaupt et al. (Eds.): INTERACT 2017, Part IV, LNCS 10516, pp. 531–532, 2017.
DOI: 10.1007/978-3-319-68059-0

This workshop follows along the – already long – series of HWID discussions, focusing on identifying HCI patterns and its relations to the HWID field and related fields. On this occasion and since this workshop takes place at the Interact Conference in Mumbai, there is a unique opportunity to observe technology-mediated innovative work practices in informal settings, in a social development context. This is why WG 13.6 has decided to offer this workshop jointly with WG. 13.8 on Interaction Design in International Development, whose main interest since its creation in 2006 is to promote the application of interaction design to address the needs, desires and aspirations of people across the developing world.

Today's technologies change the way we work with pervasive interfaces and smart places, often shifting our physical boundaries and our operational modes. From health care, to traffic control, interaction with new technologies, researchers have raised challenging issues for HCI researchers and experts. This is even more challenging when one is away from the mainstream industrial sites of the global north.

In line with recent suggestions that HCI should "turn to practice" [2] and do practice based research [3], the utility and merit of defining a field from its published works stems from providing a conceptual frame to organize a variety of issues emerging in recent HCI research [4]. In this workshop, we take a practice oriented, bottom up approach where a group of HCI researchers will analyze and synthesize relevant field work in an around Mumbai completed on the previous day.

Stephanidis [4] states that interactive technologies are entering all aspects of everyday life, in communication, work and collaboration, health and well-being, home control and automation, public services, learning and education, culture, travel, tourism and leisure, and many others. An extensive variety of technologies are already available, and new ones tend to appear frequently, and on a regular basis. Because of this we have to be attentive towards the development of studies that will help the growth of new technologies itself.

To fully exploit the opportunity mentioned above, we define a liaison between field trips and workshop, which is conducted in three major stages: (i) pre-field trip, (ii) the field trip (day one) and the workshop itself (day two), and (iii) a post-workshop reflection.

References

1. Campos, P., Clemmensen, T., Abdelnour-Nocera, J., Katre, D., Lopes, A., Ørngreen e, R. (eds.) Human work interaction design – work analysis in HCI. IFIP AICT, vol. 407, Springer (2012)
2. Kuuttie, K., Bannon, L.J.: The turn to practice in HCI: towards a research agenda. In: Proceedings of the 32nd annual ACM conference on Human Factors in computing systems, pp. 3543–3552. ACM (2014)
3. Wulf, V., Müller, C., Pipek, V., Randall, D. Rohde, M., Stevens, G.: Practice-based computing: empirically grounded conceptualizations derived from design case studies designing socially embedded technologies in the real-world, In: Wulf, V., Schmidt, K., Randall D. (eds.), pp. 111–150, Springer (2015)
4. Stephanidis, C.: Design for all, The encyclopedia of Human Computer Interaction 2nd edition. Interaction Design Foundation, pp. 2453–2550 (2015)

Multimodality in Embodied Experience Design
Workshop at INTERACT 2017, Mumbai, INDIA

Mehul Bhatt[1,2(✉)] and Clayton Lewis[3]

[1] Örebro University, Orebro, Sweden
http://www.mehulbhatt.org
[2] University of Bremen, Bremen, Germany
[3] University of Colorado, Boulder, USA
http://spot.colorado.edu/clayton/

Abstract. The workshop on Multimodality in Embodied Experience Design addresses the role of multimodality and mediated interaction for the analysis and design of human-centred, embodied, cognitive user experiences. Research topics being addressed encompass formal, computational, cognitive, design, engineering, empirical, and philosophical perspectives at the interface of artificial intelligence, cognitive science, and interaction design.

Keywords: Multimodality · Embodiment · Cognitive science · Artificial intelligence · Design · Media

1 About the Workshop

This workshop addresses the role of **multimodality and mediated interaction** for the analysis and design of human-centred, embodied, cognitive user experiences.

The workshop focusses on multimodality studies aimed at the semantic interpretation of human behaviour, and the empirically-driven synthesis of embodied interactive experiences in real world settings. In focus are narrative media design, architecture & built environment design, product design, cognitive media studies (film, animation, VR, sound & music), and user interaction studies. In these and other design contexts, the workshop emphasises evidence-based multimodality studies from the viewpoints of visual (e.g., attention and recipient effects), visuo-locomotive (e.g., movement, wayfinding), and visuo-auditory (e.g., narrative media) cognitive experiences. Modalities being investigated include, but are not limited to:

1. Visual attention (e.g., by eye-tracking), gesture, speech, language, facial expressions, tactile interactions, olfaction

© IFIP International Federation for Information Processing 2017
Published by Springer International Publishing AG 2017. All Rights Reserved
R. Bernhaupt et al. (Eds.): INTERACT 2017, Part IV, LNCS 10516, pp. 533–534, 2017.
DOI: 10.1007/978-3-319-68059-0

2. Human expert guided event segmentation (e.g. coming from behavioural or environmental psychologists, designers, annotators, crowd-sensing)
3. Deep analysis based on dialogic components, think-aloud protocols

The **scientific agenda** of the workshop focusses on the multi-modality of the embodied visuo-spatial thinking involved in "problem-solving" for the design of objects, artefacts, and interactive people-experiences emanating therefrom. **Universality and inclusion** in design are of overarching focus in all design contexts relevant to this workshop; here, the implications of multimodality studies for inclusive design, e.g., creation of presentations of the same content in different modalities, are also of interest.

The workshop brings together experts in:

- Human-Computer Interaction
- Spatial Cognition and Computation
- Cognitive Science and Psychology
- Artificial intelligence
- Neuroscience
- Communications and Media
- Design Studies

The workshop provides a platform to discuss the development of next-generation embodied interaction design systems, practices, and (human-centered) assistive frameworks & technologies encompassing the multi-faceted nature of embodied interaction design conception and synthesis. Contributions addressing the workshop themes from formal, computational, cognitive, design, engineering, empirical, and philosophical perspectives are most welcome.

2   Workshop Chairs

Mehul Bhatt is Professor at Örebro University (Sweden), and Professor at the University of Bremen, Germany. He leads the Human-Centred Cognitive Assistance Lab at the University of Bremen, Germany (http://hcc.uni-bremen.de/), and is co-founder of the research and consulting group DesignSpace (www.design-space.org). Mehul's research encompasses the areas of artificial intelligence, cognitive science, and human-computer interaction.

Clayton Lewis is Professor of Computer Science and Fellow of the Institute of Cognitive Science at the University of Colorado, Boulder (United States). He is well known for his research on evaluation methods in user interface design, and contributions in the thinking aloud method and cognitive walkthrough methods. He was elected to the ACM CHI Academy in 2009, recognizing his contributions to the field of human-computer interaction. In 2011 he was further recognized by the ACM CHI Social Impact Award, for his work on technology for people with cognitive, language, and learning disabilities.

Service Design Meets Design for Behaviour Change: Opportunities and Challenges

Ravi Mahamuni[1(✉)], Pramod Khambete[2],
and Ravi Mokashi-Punekar[3]

[1] Tata Research Development and Design Center, Tata Consultancy Services,
Hadapsar Industrial Estate, Pune, Maharashtra, India
Ravi.mahamuni@tcs.com
[2] Independent Consultant, Pune, Maharashtra, India
pramod@pramodkhambete.com
[3] Indian Institute of Technology Guwahati, Guwahati, India
mokashi@iitg.ernet.in

Abstract. There is a growing recognition about a need to influence and change user behaviours in their own interest to meet several social challenges, be it at the level of an individual or society. Designers intentionally or unintentionally end up shaping the user behaviour. Service Design and Design for Behaviour Change have significant congruence in terms of concern for value creation over long duration, dynamic usage contexts and accounting for diversity of users, among others. However, despite the affinity of these two fields, we do not come across works that demonstrate practice that blends both the fields or synthesised design knowledge base. Practitioners might be tacitly blending these two disciplines. This workshop aims to understand these practices currently, the challenges designers are facing and how they are addressing those. We hope to uncover this tacit knowledge, provide preliminary knowledge from the disciplines and synthesise through hands on work followed by collective reflection.

Keywords: Design · Service design · Behaviour change · Participatory design · Multidisciplinary team · Organizational design practices

1 Introduction

User activities and behaviours are "scripted" by the products they use. Therefore, designers intentionally or unintentionally end up shaping the user behaviour. There is a growing recognition that "designers are in the behaviour (change) business" [1]. This idea is not only relevant to products, but equally, if not more for services. Service design, which factors in longer span of user engagement has arguably great potential to influence user behaviour through the appropriately designed product-service systems. The need to influence and change user behaviours in their own interest while balancing the concerns of user freedom and privacy is coming to fore to meet several social challenges, be it at the level of an individual (e.g. health and well-being) or society (e.g. global warming). The overlaps and relationship between these two fields Service Design and Design for Behaviour Change is presented in Table 1:

© IFIP International Federation for Information Processing 2017
Published by Springer International Publishing AG 2017. All Rights Reserved
R. Bernhaupt et al. (Eds.): INTERACT 2017, Part IV, LNCS 10516, pp. 535–537, 2017.
DOI: 10.1007/978-3-319-68059-0

Table 1. The overlaps between Service Design and Design for Behaviour Change.

	Service Design	Design for Behaviour Change
Complexity	Yes	Yes
Long temporal span (initiation to embeddedness in life)	For maximising the value	For stabilising the changed behaviour
Changing user goals and contexts from initiation to embeddedness in life	Yes	Yes
Effective design dependent on multiple fields of knowledge	Yes	Yes
Cumulative effect of individual experience "episodes"	Cumulative effect of encounters over time	Cumulative effect of instances of changed behaviour
Relevance for addressing individual well-being	Yes	Yes
Relevance for addressing social issues	Yes	Yes

Clearly, the two disciplines have significant congruence. There are several models [2, 3] and high level guidance for design for behavioural change [4–7]. Similarly, there is ample guidance in service design (e.g.[8, 9]). However, despite the affinity of these two fields, we do not come across works that demonstrate practice that blends both the fields or synthesised design knowledge base. This is one of the triggers behind the workshop.

Secondly, we find several instances where the merger of Service Design and Design for Behaviour Change would be critical to fruitful interventions for individual and societal well-being. The recent "demonetisation" in India, which invalidated over 80% of cash in circulation, followed by the intense drive towards less-cash economy is a case in point. The effective interventions in behaviour change in a wide variety of citizens in terms of demographics, literacy, and technology readiness would pose challenges in all sectors of the economy. These cannot be addressed by mere redesign of existing products – physical or digital. Thoughtful service design blended with design for behaviour change would be necessary. Challenges in individual and societal behaviour changes (e.g. sustainability, wellness …) too calls for a similar approach.

2 Objective and Expected Outcome

It is likely that practitioners would be tacitly using design knowledge from behavioural change domain in service design, and vice versa. Intention of this workshop is to understand how it is practiced currently, the challenges designers are facing and how they are addressing those. It would be helpful if the practices are reflected upon in a group to make explicit that knowledge and design principles underlying the practice.

As well, it is hoped that applying the uncovered knowledge, albeit limited in scope due to the constraint of the workshop format, would nevertheless allow a degree of internalisation.

3   Intended Audience

This workshop is focused on service design practitioners (as well as aspiring service design practitioners) and researchers who are associated with designing and implementing services in any domain. Those involved in healthcare, social impact ventures and citizen services might be particularly interested. Since both service design and design for behaviour change require multidisciplinary participation, interested designers and practitioners from any discipline are welcome.

References

1. Stanton, N., Baber, C.: Designing for consumers: editorial. Applied Ergonomics **29**(1), 1–3 (1998)
2. Fogg, B.: A behavior model for persuasive design. In : Proceedings of the 4th international Conference on Persuasive Technology, p. 40 (2009)
3. Mohr, D., Schueller, S., Montague, E., Burns, M., Rashidi, P.: The behavioral intervention technology model: an integrated conceptual and technological framework for eHealth and mHealth interventions. Journal of medical Internet research **16**(6), e146 (2014)
4. Michie, S., Stralen, M., West, R.: The behaviour change wheel: a new method for characterising and designing behaviour change interventions. Implementation science **6**(1), 42 (2011)
5. Oinas-Kukkonen, H., Harjumaa., M.: A systematic framework for designing and evaluating persuasive systems. In : Proceedings of International Conference on Persuasive Technology, pp. 16–176 (2008)
6. Lockton, D.: Design with intent: a design pattern toolkit for environmental and social behaviour change. Doctoral dissertation, Brunel University School of Engineering and Design (2013)
7. Thaler Richard, H., Sunstein, C.: Nudge: Improving decisions about health, wealth, and happiness. Yale University Press (2008)
8. Stickdorn, M., Schneider, J., Andrews, K., Lawrence, A.: This is service design thinking: Basics, tools, cases. Wiley, Hoboken, NJ (2011)
9. Zomerdijk, L., Voss, C.: Service Design for Experience-centric Services. Journal of Service Research **13**(1), 67–82 (2010)

Symposium on Asian HCI Research

Yoshifumi Kitamura[1(✉)], Zhengjie Liu[2], Eunice Sari[3],
and Anshuman Sharma[4]

[1] Tohoku University, Sendai, Japan
`kitamura@riec.tohoku.ac.jp`
[2] Dalian Maritime University, Dalian, China
`liuzhj@dlmu.edu.cn`
[3] Edith Cowan University, Joondalup, Australia
`eunice.sari@gmail.com`
[4] LnT Infotech, Mumbai, India
`anshuman.sharma@lntinfotech.com`

Abstract. In this one-day symposium in which we propose to bring together 10 to 12 researchers from Asia to come together to share their work and to discuss collaboration opportunities. This would be followed by a session in which we would explore and brainstorm about joint work and possibilities of collaboration.

Keywords: Human-computer interaction · Asia · Research in HCI

1 Introduction

Asia is a complex continent filled with diversity. It comprises of both developing countries and developed countries. With a population of 4.4 billion, the continent houses about 2/3rds of the world's population. In many ways, the problems faced by Asia are no different from the problems faced by the rest of the world. In some other ways though, the issues and concerns are unique.

Asia currently boasts of significant research in human-computer interaction (HCI). In the last 10 years, several international HCI conferences have been organised in Asia, including HCI International 2007 in China, CHI 2015 in South Korea, UIST 2016 in Japan, and the forthcoming INTERACT 2017 conference in India. Asia has also been a host of several local HCI events such as Chinese HCI conference, India HCI, CHI IndoUX etc. Unfortunately, there have not been too many opportunities for people to discuss and exchange ideas across the Asian countries. The APCHI conference that used to target the Asia-Pacific population has not run for the past three years.

Similar is the case with movement of researchers. There are several outstanding universities and industrial labs in Asia where HCI research takes place. Many universities from Asia are often involved in exchange of visits with universities in Europe and North America. Many students from Asia travel to do their masters and doctoral research in Europe and North America. Unfortunately, there has been relatively less research visits and student exchange within Asia.

© IFIP International Federation for Information Processing 2017
Published by Springer International Publishing AG 2017. All Rights Reserved
R. Bernhaupt et al. (Eds.): INTERACT 2017, Part IV, LNCS 10516, pp. 538–542, 2017.
DOI: 10.1007/978-3-319-68059-0

We believe that Asian researchers have a lot to share among themselves. Given that the INTERACT 2017 conference will attract several Asian researchers to Mumbai, we propose to organise a one-day symposium.

2 The Proposal

We propose to organise a one-day symposium to celebrate the diversity of Asian HCI research. The organisers propose to invite about 10 of the following researchers to present their work. As many of these researchers come from developing countries, the organisers are looking for funding opportunities of partly supporting the travel costs of some of these researchers.

- Yoshifumi Kitamura, Japan
- Takahiro Miura, Japan
- Xiangshi Ren, Japan
- Zhengjie Liu, China
- Eunice Sari, Indonesia
- Shendong Zhao, Singapore
- Bimlesh Wadhwa, Singapore
- Ellen Do, Singapore
- Indika Perera, Sri Lanka
- Kaveh Bazargan, Iran
- Chui Yin Wang, Malaysia
- Nova Ahmed, Bangladesh

2.1 Need

Several students, teachers and industry professionals in Asian countries are aware of the research activities going on in Asia and their respective countries. One of the main difficulties for such people is to connect with like-minded people in order to start or augment their research interests. As discussed in Sect. 1, the availability of research opportunities in the developing countries of Asia are limited. Travelling is also an issue. People wait for events to be organized in their countries to build network with people to take their research interest ahead. There are challenges in having access to laboratory set-up as well.

This symposium will help people connect with researchers for funding, research opportunities and collaborations.

Given that we might be able to get some thought leading speakers from various countries, the symposium is likely to attract a large number of participants including current and prospective students, researchers and industry professionals.

2.2   The Programme

The symposium will consist of invited talks and a session for exchange of research areas, topics of interest, case studies, trends, and collaborations. We propose the following programme for the symposium:

- Session 1: 9 am to 11 am
  - Introductions, plans
  - Presentations by researcher 1, 2, 3, 4
- Session 2: 11:30 am to 1 pm
  - Presentations by researcher 5, 6, 7
  - Session 3: 2 pm to 3:30 pm
    - Presentations by researcher 8, 9, 10
    Session 4: 4 pm to 5 pm
  - 3 parallel sessions on possible research areas for collaboration across Asian countries
  - Conclusion

2.3   Topics

The probable topics of activities/events for this symposium would be:

1. Presentation by Asian researchers

   - Focus areas
   - Topics of interest
   - Discussion on Case Studies

2. Current trends
3. Upcoming research areas
4. Challenges in research and how to overcome them
5. Possible areas of collaboration
6. Possible funding and research opportunities
7. Student/researcher/faculty exchange programmes

   At the end of the day, we propose to have a session that will allow participants to discuss future collaborations and student and faculty exchange among universities.

3   The Organisers

3.1   About Yoshifumi Kitamura

Yoshifumi Kitamura is active researcher from Japan. He has been active in organising several conferences and events including UIST 2016 and SIGGRAPH Asia 2015 in recent times. He represents Japan on the IFIP TC13, and is a member of the ACM SIGCHI Asian Development Committee. He received the B.Sc., M.Sc. and PhD. degrees in Engineering from Osaka University in 1985, 1987 and 1996, respectively. From 1987 to 1992, he was at the Information Systems Research Center of Canon Inc., where he was involved in research on artificial intelligence, image processing, computer vision, and 3D data processing. From 1992 to 1996, he was a researcher at ATR Communication Systems Research Laboratories, where he worked on sophisticated user interface in virtual environments. From 1997 to 2002, he was an Associate Professor at Graduate School of Engineering, and from 2002 to 2010, he was an Associate Professor at Graduate School of Information Science and Technology, Osaka University. From April 2010, he is currently a Professor at Research Institute of Electrical Communication, Tohoku University. His research interests include interactive content design, human computer interactions, and 3D user interfaces.

3.2 About Zhengjie Liu

Zhengjie is Professor at Dalian Maritime University and founding director of Sino European Usability Center. He has been involved in human-computer interaction (HCI) since 1989 and has helped the germination and growth of this field especially user experience practice in China. He is experienced in consultancy and training to industry including many multinational companies. His area is human-computer interaction design focusing on issues related to user experience and user-centered design and innovation. He is a co-founder of SIGCHI China and has served on roles at ACM SIGCHI executive committee supporting HCI growth in developing worlds and at IFIP TC.13 Committee on HCI. He is on editorial board of several journals in HCI and ISO working groups on usability and human-centered design. He is awardee of IFIP TC13 Pioneers Award in 2013.

3.3 About Eunice Sari

Dr. Sari is the CEO and Co-Founder of UX Indonesia (uxindo.com) – the first HCI and UX business in Indonesia since 2002. She is also the first Indonesian Female Google Expert in UX/UI who have helped over a hundred of start-ups around the world. As a UX/CX Expert and ICT in Education Expert, she has more than 15 + years of experience working in both academia and industries. She has pioneered a number of forward-thinking and innovative projects in order to effect changes in life and improve the bottom line of business in various vertical industries in USA, Europe, Australia and Asia. Eunice is a leading UX/CX expert in Southeast Asia. She co-founded and chaired the Indonesia ACM SIGCHI Chapter (Association Computing Machinery Special Interest Group on Computer-Human Interaction a.k.a CHI UX Indonesia), and later the Association of Digital Interaction Indonesia - Perkumpulan Interaksi Digital Indonesia (PIDI). She is also the co-founder of ACM SIGCHI Southeast Asia community, the South East Asia Liaison for ACM SIGCHI Asia Development Committee, the Expert Member of the International Federation for Information Processing (IFIP) TC 13 – Human Computer Interaction (HCI) for Indonesia, and the Western Australia Representative for the Human Factors Ergonomic Association Computer Human Interaction Special Interest Group (HFESA CHISIG). With her roles, she facilitates the collaboration between academia and industry in the fields of Education, Technology, HCI and UX, particularly in Southeast Asia and Pacific.

3.4   About Anshuman Sharma

Anshuman Sharma has over 20 years of industry experience in the field of HCI - in areas of Interaction Design, Usability and User Research. He has held senior positions in organizations like Siemens, TCS and PlayTech. At present, he is Global Head of User-Experience Design (UXD) practice at LnT Infotech, Bangalore, India where he supports Application IP development and supports many Fortune 500 clients globally. His areas of work are Application Design & Transformation, Creativity & Innovation models in UX, User Research, Usability Analysis and Interaction Design. He has experience in domains like BFSI, eCommerce, Telecom, Product Lifecycle Management (PLM), Online Gaming and eLearning. He has published several research papers and has a patent to his name. He received his Master's Degree (M.Des.) in Industrial Design from Instrument Design & Development Center (IDDC) IIT Delhi and B.Tech. in City & Urban Planning from GRD School of Planning, Amritsar, India. He is on Scientific panel and International Programme committee of conferences on research on creativity and design like International Conference on Research into Design (ICoRD) and International Conference on Creativity and Cognition in Art and Design (ICCCAD).

Author Index

Printed in the United States
By Bookmasters